Stanley Gibbo

GREAT BRITAIN CONCISE STAMP CATALOGUE

1998 Edition

Stanley Gibbons Ltd
London and Ringwood

By Appointment to Her Majesty The Queen
Stanley Gibbons Ltd., London
Philatelists

Published by **Stanley Gibbons Publications**
Editorial, Sales Offices and Distribution Centre:
5 Parkside, Christchurch Road, Ringwood,
Hants BH24 3SH

First Edition — May 1986
Second Edition — May 1987
Third Edition — May 1988
Fourth Edition — May 1989
Fifth Edition — May 1990
Sixth Edition — May 1991
Seventh Edition — May 1992
Eighth Edition — April 1993
Ninth Edition — April 1994
Tenth Edition — April 1995
Eleventh Edition — April 1996
Twelfth Edition — April 1997
Thirteenth Edition — April 1998

ISBN: 0-85259-443-7

Item No. 2887 (98)

Origination by Stanley Gibbons Ltd., Ringwood, Hampshire.
Made and Printed in Great Britain by Black Bear Press Limited, Cambridge.

THE GREAT BRITAIN CONCISE CATALOGUE

1998 Edition

The *Concise Catalogue*, now in its thirteenth year of publication, has rapidly established itself as an essential guide for the "one-country" collector of Great Britain.

The popularity of Great Britain stamps continues to grow — the *Concise Catalogue* supplies the information to enhance your collection.

The *Concise* listings are based on the Great Britain section of our *Part 1 (British Commonwealth) Catalogue*, but there is much more additional material within its pages:

- All issues from the Penny Black of 1840 to 24 February 1998 including Regional, Postage Due, Official and Postal Fiscal stamps.
- All different stamp designs are illustrated.
- Every basic stamp listed, including those with different watermarks or perforations and those showing graphite lines or phosphor bands.
- Unmounted mint and mounted mint prices quoted for 1887 "Jubilee" series and all King Edward VII and King George V issues.
- Missing colours, missing embossing, watermark errors, imperforate errors and phosphor omitted varieties from those stamps normally issued with phosphor bands.
- Gutter Pairs and "Traffic light" Gutter Pairs listed in mint sets.
- First Day Covers for Special Issues from 1924 and for King Edward VIII and King George VI definitives. For the present reign the coverage also extends to Sponsored Booklet panes and Regionals. All British Post Office special First Day of Issue postmarks are illustrated and priced on cover.
- Post Office Picture Cards (PHQ cards) are priced as sets, both mint and used with First Day of Issue postmarks.
- Presentation, Collector and Gift Packs, including the scarce versions with foreign inscriptions.
- Quick-reference diagrams for listed Machin decimal booklet panes.
- Design Index for Commemorative and Special Stamps after the Philatelic Information Section.
- Machin and commemorative underprints given separate catalogue numbers.
- Post Office Yearbooks.
- Royal Mail Postage Labels priced in mint or used sets and on British Post Office First Day Covers.
- Wartime issues for the Channel Islands.
- Separate section for Post Office Stamp Booklets with dated editions of King George VI listed separately.
- Helpful introductory section providing definitions and guidance for the collector and including all watermark illustrations shown together to assist identification.
- Separate section for Postmaster and U.P.U. Specimen overprints.
- Addresses for specialist philatelic societies covering Great Britain stamps.
- Recently discovered errors and varieties listed. See Nos. 66bWi, 87c, 397a, 679pEb, 713pEb, 783c, 935Eab, 1095a, 1578Eb, 1620a, 1658a, Y1692a, Y1751Ey, Y1751lEy, Y1753Ey, 1965a, 1972a, 1978a, 1996a, 2006a, FH41a, FW9a, GJ1a, KX7a.

David J. Aggersberg

Stanley Gibbons Holdings Plc.

STANLEY GIBBONS LTD, STANLEY GIBBONS AUCTIONS

399 STRAND, LONDON WC2R 0LX

Auction Room and Specialist Departments. Open Monday–Friday, 9.30 a.m. to 5.00 p.m.
Shop: Open Monday–Friday 8.30 a.m. to 6.00 p.m. and Saturday 10.00 a.m. to 4.00 p.m.
Telephone 0171 836 8444 and **Fax 0171 836 7342 for all departments.**

STANLEY GIBBONS PUBLICATIONS

5 PARKSIDE, CHRISTCHURCH ROAD, RINGWOOD, HANTS BH24 3SH

Telephone 01425 472363 (24 hour answerphone service), **Fax 01425 470247** and **E-mail info@stangib.demon.co.uk**
Publications Showroom (at above address). Open Monday–Friday 9.00 a.m. to 3.00 p.m.
Publications Mail Order. FREEPHONE 0800 611622. Trade Desk, 01425 478776.
Monday–Friday 8.30 a.m. to 5.00 p.m.

URCH HARRIS & CO.,

1 DENMARK AVENUE, BRISTOL BS1 5HD

Open Monday–Friday 8.30 a.m. to 5.00 p.m.
Telephone 0117 9349333 and **Fax 0117 9273037**

FRASER'S

399 STRAND, LONDON WC2R 0LX

Autographs, photographs, letters and documents

Open Monday–Friday 9.00 a.m. to 5.30 p.m. and Saturday 10.00 a.m. to 4.00 p.m.
Telephone 0171 836 8444 and **Fax 0171 836 7342**

Great Britain Philatelic Societies

The Great Britain Philatelic Society. Hon. Membership Secretary: A. G. Lajer, The Old Post Office, Hurst, Berkshire, RG10 0TR.

The British Decimal Stamps Study Circle. The Secretary: S. van Kimmenade, 32 Beaufort Heights, Beaufort Road, St. George, Bristol, BS5 8JX.

The Great Britain Decimal Stamp Book Study Circle. Hon. Membership Secretary: A. J. Wilkins, 3 Buttermere Close, Brierley Hill, West Midlands, DY5 3SD.

The Great Britain Collectors Club. The Secretary: F. Koch, P.O. Box 309, Batavia, Ohio 45103–0309, U.S.A.

Contents

Queen Victoria Issue 1
Key to Line-engraved Issues 6
Key to Surface-printed Issues 1855–83 13
Key to Surface-printed Issues 1880–1900 18
King Edward VII Issues 23
King George V Issues 25
King Edward VIII Issues 34
King George VI Issues 34
Queen Elizabeth II Issues 39
Decimal Machin Index 78
Decimal Machin Multi-value Coil Index 83
Decimal Machin Booklet Pane Guide 84
Decimal Machin with Elliptical Perforations Index 186
Royal Mail Postage Labels 216
Regional Issues 216
Channel Islands: General Issue 1948 216
Northern Ireland 216
Scotland 219
Wales 222
Guernsey 225
Isle of Man 226
Jersey 226
Postage Due Stamps 227
Official Stamps 230
Postal Fiscal Stamps 233
Postmaster and U.P.U. Specimen Overprints 236
Post Office Stamp Booklets 238
King Edward VII 238
King George V 238
King Edward VIII 241
King George VI 241
Queen Elizabeth II 244
I. £.s.d. Booklets 1953–70 244
II. Decimal Booklets 1971 onwards 253
A. Stitched Booklets 253
B. Folded Booklets 260
Christmas Booklets 1978–86 276
Greetings Booklet 1989 277
III. Barcode Booklets 278
C. Machin Booklets 1987 onwards 278
D. Machin NVI Booklets 1989 onwards 282
E. Machin Penny Black Anniversary Booklet, 1990 288
F. Greetings Booklets 1990 onwards 288
G. Christmas Booklets 1990 onwards 290

STANLEY GIBBONS PUBLICATIONS

OVERSEAS REPRESENTATION

Stanley Gibbons Publications are represented overseas by the following sole distributors (*), distributors (**) or licensees (***)

Australia
Lighthouse Philatelic (Aust.) Pty Ltd*
PO Box 763
Strawberry Hills
New South Wales 2012
Australia

Stanley Gibbons (Australia) Pty Ltd***
Level 6
36 Clarence Street
Sydney
New South Wales 2000
Australia

Belgium and Luxembourg**
Davo
c/o Philac
Rue du Midi 48
Bruxelles 1000
Belgium

Canada*
Lighthouse Publications (Canada) Ltd
255 Duke Street
Montreal
Quebec
Canada H3C 2M2

Denmark**
Davo
c/o Lindner Falzlos
Gl Randersvej 28
8450 Hammel
Denmark

Finland**
Davo
c/o Suomen Postimerkkeily
Ludvingkatu 5
SF-00130 Helsinki
Finland

France*
Davo France (Casteilla)
10 Rue Leon Foucault
78184 St. Quentin Yvelines Cesex
France

Germany and Austria*
Leuchtturm Albenverlag Gmbh u. Co.
Am Spakenberg 45
Postfach 1340
D21495 Geesthacht
Germany

Hong Kong**
Po-on Stamp Service
GPO Box 2498
Hong Kong

Israel**
Capital Stamps
PO Box 3769
Jerusalem 91036
Israel

Italy*
Secrian Srl
Via Pantelleria 2
1-20156 Milano
Italy

Japan**
Japan Philatelic Co Ltd
PO Box 2
Suginami-Minami
Tokyo
Japan

Netherlands*
Davo Publications
PO Box 411
7400 AK Deventer
Netherlands

New Zealand***
Stanley Gibbons (New Zealand) Ltd
PO Box 80
Wellington
New Zealand

Norway**
Davo Norge A/S
PO Box 738 Sentrum
N-01 05 Oslo
Norway

Singapore***
Stanley Gibbons (Singapore)
Pte Ltd
Raffles City
PO Box 1689
Singapore 9117

South Africa**
Republic Coin and Stamp
Accessories (Pty) Ltd
PO Box 11199
Johannesburg
RSA 2000

Sweden*
Chr Winther Sorensen AB
Box 43
S-310 Knaered
Sweden

Switzerland**
Phila Service
Burgstrasse 160
CH4125 Riehen
Switzerland

West Indies/Caribbean**
Hugh Dunphy
PO Box 413
Kingston 10
Jamaica
West Indies

PRICES

> The prices quoted in this catalogue are the estimated selling prices of Stanley Gibbons Ltd at the time of publication. They are, *unless it is specifically stated otherwise*, for examples in fine condition for the issue concerned. Superb examples are worth more; those of a lower quality considerably less.

All prices are subject to change without prior notice and Stanley Gibbons Ltd may from time to time offer stamps below catalogue price. Individual low value stamps sold at 399, Strand are liable to an additional handling charge. Purchasers of new issues are asked to note that the prices charged for them contain an element for the service rendered and so may exceed the prices shown when the stamps are subsequently catalogued.

No guarantee is given to supply all stamps priced, since it is not possible to keep every catalogued item in stock.

Quotation of prices. The prices in the left-hand column are for unused stamps and those in the right-hand column are for used.

A dagger (†) denotes that the item listed does not exist in that condition and a blank, or dash, that it exists, or may exist, but no market price is known.

Prices are expressed in pounds and pence sterling. One pound comprises 100 pence (£1 = 100p).

The method of notation is as follows: pence in numerals (e.g. 5 denotes five pence); pounds and pence up to £100, in numerals (e.g. 4·25 denotes four pounds and twenty-five pence); prices above £100 expressed in whole pounds with the "£" sign shown.

Unused and Used stamps. The prices for unused stamps of Queen Victoria issued before 1887 are for lightly hinged examples. Unused stamps of the 1887 "Jubilee" issue and from the reigns of King Edward VII and King George V are priced in both unmounted and mounted condition. Unused prices for King Edward VIII to Queen Elizabeth II issues are for unmounted mint (though when not available, mounted mint stamps are often supplied at a lower price). Prices for used stamps are for postally used examples.

Prices quoted for bisects on cover or on large piece are for those dated during the period officially authorised.

Minimum price. The minimum price quoted is 10 pence. For individual stamps prices between 10 pence and 30 pence are provided as a guide for catalogue users. The lowest price *charged* for individual stamps purchased from Stanley Gibbons Ltd is 30p.

Set prices. Set prices are generally for one of each value, excluding shades and varieties, but including major colour changes. Where there are alternative shades, etc., the cheapest is usually included. The number of stamps in the set is always stated for clarity.

The mint prices for sets containing *se-tenant* pieces are based on the prices quoted for such combinations, and not on those for individual stamps. The used set price is for single stamps.

Gutter Pairs. These, and traffic light gutter pairs, are priced as complete sets.

Used on Cover prices. To assist collectors, cover prices are quoted in a third column for postage and Official stamps issued in the reign of Queen Victoria and in boxed notes for the 1887 "Jubilee" issue and for King Edward VII and King George V stamps.

The cover should be of non-philatelic origin, bearing the correct postal rate for the period and distance involved and cancelled with the markings normal to the offices concerned. Purely philatelic items have a cover value only slightly greater than the catalogue value for the corresponding used stamps. This applies generally to those high-value stamps used philatelically rather than in the normal course of commerce.

Oversized covers, difficult to accommodate on an album page, should be reckoned as worth little more than the corresponding value of the used stamps. The condition of a cover affects its value. Except for "wreck covers", serious damage or soiling reduce the value where the postal markings and stamps are ordinary ones. Conversely, visual appeal adds to the value and this can include freshness of appearance, important addresses, old-fashioned but legible handwriting, historic town-names, etc. The prices quoted are a base on which further value would be added to take account of the cover's postal historical importance in demonstrating such things as unusual, scarce or emergency cancels, interesting routes, significant postal markings, combination usage, the development of postal rates, and so on.

First Day Cover prices. Prices are quoted for commemorative first day covers from 1924 British Empire Exhibition pair onwards. These prices are for special covers (from 1937) franked with complete sets and cancelled by ordinary operational postmarks to the end of 1962 or the various standard "First Day of Issue" markings from 1963.

Prices are provided for King Edward VIII and King George VI definitives on plain covers with operational postmarks of the first day of issue. For some values special covers also exist and these are worth more than the prices quoted.

The Philatelic Bureau and other special "First Day of Issue" postmarks provided by the Post Office since 1963 are listed under each issue. Prices quoted are for these postmarks used on illustrated covers (from 1964 those produced by the Post Office), franked with complete sets.

The British Post Office did not introduce special First Day of Issue postmarks for definitive issues until the first instalment of the Machin £sd series, issued 5 June 1967, although "First Day" treatment had been provided for some Regional stamps from 8 June 1964 onwards. Prices for the First Day Covers from 1952 to 1966, showing definitive stamps are for the stamps indicated, used on illustrated envelopes and postmarked with operational cancellations.

From 1967 onwards the prices quoted are for stamps as indicated, used on illustrated envelopes and postmarked with special First Day of Issue handstamps. Other definitives issued during this period were not accepted for "First Day" treatment by the British Post Office.

Guarantee

All stamps are guaranteed genuine originals in the following terms:

If not as described, and returned by the purchaser, we undertake to refund the price paid to us in the original transaction. If any stamp is certified as genuine by the Expert Committee of the Royal Philatelic Society, London, or by B.P.A. Expertising Ltd, the purchaser shall not be entitled to make any claim against us for any error, omission or mistake in such certificate.

Consumers' statutory rights are not affected by the above guarantee.

The recognised Expert Committees in this country are those of the Royal Philatelic Society, 41 Devonshire Place, London W1N 1PE, and B.P.A. Expertising Ltd, P.O. Box 137, Leatherhead, Surrey KT22 0RG. They do not undertake valuations under any circumstances and fees are payable for their services.

CONTACTING THE CATALOGUE EDITOR

The Editor is always interested in hearing from people who have new information which will improve or correct the Catalogue. As a general rule he must see and examine the actual stamps before they can be considered for listing; photographs or photocopies are insufficent evidence.

Submissions should be made in writing to the Catalogue Editor, Stanley Gibbons Publications. The cost of return postage for items submitted is appreciated, and this should include the registration fee if required.

Where information is solicited purely for the benefit of the enquirer, the editor cannot undertake to reply if the answer is already contained in these published notes or if return postage is omitted. Written communications are greatly preferred to enquiries by telephone and the editor regrets that he or his staff cannot see personal callers without a prior appointment being made. Correspondence may be subject to delay during the production period of each new edition.

Please note that the following classes of material are outside the scope of this Catalogue:

(a) Non-postal revenue or fiscal stamps.
(b) Postage stamps used fiscally.
(c) Local carriage labels and private local issues.
(d) Punctured postage stamps (perfins).
(e) Telegraph stamps.
(f) Bogus or phantom stamps.
(g) Railway or airline letter fee stamps, bus or road transport company labels.
(h) Postal stationery cut-outs.
(i) All types of non-postal labels and souvenirs.
(j) Documentary labels for the postal service, e.g. registration, recorded delivery, airmail etiquettes, etc.
(k) Privately applied embellishments to official issues and privately commissioned items generally.
(l) Stamps for training postal staff.

We regret we do not give opinions as to the genuineness of stamps, nor do we identify stamps or number them by our Catalogue.

GENERAL ABBREVIATIONS

Alph	Alphabet
Anniv	Anniversary
Brt	Bright (colour)
C,c	Chalky paper
C.	Overprinted in carmine
Des	Designer; designed
Dp	Deep (colour)
Eng	Engraver; engraved
Horiz	Horizontal; horizontally
Imp, Imperf	Imperforate
Inscr	Inscribed
L	Left
Litho	Lithographed
Lt	Light (colour)
mm	Millimetres
MS	Miniature sheet
O,o	Ordinary paper
Opt(d)	Overprint(ed)
P, Perf	Perforated
Photo	Photogravure
Pl	Plate
Pr	Pair
Ptd	Printed
Ptg	Printing
PVA	Polyvinyl alcohol (gum)
R	Right
R.	Row
Recess	Recess-printed
T	Type
Typo	Typographed
Un	Unused
Us	Used
Vert	Vertical; vertically
W or wmk	Watermark
Wmk s	Watermark sideways

(†) = Does not exist.
(—) (or blank price column) = Exists, or may exist, but no market price is known.
/ between colours means "on" and the colour following is that of the paper on which the stamp is printed.

PRINTERS

B.W.	Bradbury Wilkinson & Co, Ltd.
D.L.R.	De La Rue & Co, Ltd, London, and (from 1961) Bogota, Colombia.
Enschedé	Joh. Enschedé en Zonen, Haarlem, Netherlands.
Harrison	Harrison & Sons, Ltd, High Wycombe.
J.W.	John Waddington Security Print, Ltd, Leeds.
P.B.	Perkins Bacon Ltd, London.
Questa	Questa Colour Security Printers, Ltd.
Waterlow	Waterlow & Sons, Ltd, London.
Walsall	Walsall Security Printers, Ltd.

PHILATELIC INFORMATION

Catalogue Numbers

The catalogue number appears in the extreme left column. The boldface Type numbers in the next column are merely cross-reference to illustrations. Catalogue numbers in the *Gibbons Stamp Monthly* Supplements are provisional only and may need to be altered when the lists are consolidated.

Our Catalogue numbers are universally recognised in specifying stamps and as a hallmark of status.

Inverted and other watermark varieties incorporate "Wi", etc., within the number. Other items which appear in this Catalogue but not *Part 1 (British Commonwealth) Catalogue*, incorporate "Ea", etc.

Catalogue Illustrations

Stamps and first day postmarks are illustrated at three-quarters linear size. Stamps not illustrated are the same size and format as the value shown, unless otherwise indicated. Overprints, surcharges and watermarks are normally actual size. Illustrations of varieties are often enlarged to show the detail. Illustrations of miniature sheets are half linear size and their dimensions, in millimetres, are stated with the width given first.

Designers

Designers' names are quoted where known, though space precludes naming every individual concerned in the production of a set. In particular, photographers supplying material are usually named only when they also make an active contribution in the design stage; posed photographs of reigning monarchs are, however, an exception to this rule.

Printing Errors

Errors in printing are of major interest to this Catalogue. Authenticated items meriting consideration would include: background, centre or frame inverted or omitted; centre or subject transposed; error of colour; error or omission of value; double prints and impressions; printed both sides; and so on. Designs *tête-bêche*, whether intentionally or by accident, are listable. Colours only partially omitted are not listed. However, stamps with embossing, phosphor or both omitted and stamps printed on the gummed side are included.

Printing technology has radically improved over the years, during which time photogravure and lithography have become predominant. Varieties nowadays are more in the nature of flaws which are almost always outside the scope of this book.

In no catalogue, however, do we list such items as: dry prints, kiss prints, doctor-blade flaws, colour shifts or registration flaws (unless they lead to the complete omission of a colour from an individual stamp), lithographic ring flaws, and so on. Neither do we recognise fortuitous happenings like paper creases or confetti flaws.

Paper Types

All stamps listed are deemed to be on "ordinary" paper of the wove type and white in colour; only departures from this are normally mentioned.

A coloured paper is one that is coloured right through (front and back of the stamp). In the Catalogue the colour of the paper is given in *italics*, thus:

purple/*yellow* = purple design on yellow paper.

Papers have been made specially white in recent years by, for example, a very heavy coating of chalk. We do not classify shades of whiteness of paper as distinct varieties.

The availability of many postage stamps for revenue purposes made necessary some safeguard against the illegitimate re-use of stamps with removable cancellations. This was at first secured by using fugitive inks and later by printing on chalky (chalk-surfaced) paper, both of which made it difficult to remove any form of obliteration without also damaging the stamp design. We have indicated the existence of the papers by the letters "**O**" (ordinary) and "**C**" (chalky) after the description of all stamps where the chalky paper may be found. Where no indication is given the paper is "ordinary".

Our chalky paper is specifically one which shows a black mark when touched with a silver wire. Stamps on chalk-surfaced paper can easily lose this coating through immersion in water.

Perforation Measurement

The gauge of a perforation is the number of holes in a length of 2 cm.

The Gibbons *Instanta* gauge is the standard for measuring perforations. The stamp is viewed against a dark background with the transparent gauge put on top of it. Though the gauge measures to decimal accuracy, perforations read from it are generally quoted in the Catalogue to the nearest half. For example:

Just over perf $12\frac{3}{4}$ to just under $13\frac{1}{4}$	= perf 13
Perf $13\frac{1}{4}$ exactly, rounded up	= perf $13\frac{1}{2}$
Just over perf $13\frac{1}{4}$ to just under $13\frac{3}{4}$	= perf $13\frac{1}{2}$
Perf $13\frac{3}{4}$ exactly, rounded up	= perf 14

However, where classification depends on it, actual quarter-perforations are quoted. Perforations are usually abbreviated (and spoken) as follows, though sometimes they may be spelt out for clarity.

P 14: perforated alike on all sides (read: "perf 14").

P 14 x 15: the first figure refers to top and bottom, the second to left and right sides (read: "perf 14 by 15"). This is a compound perforation.

Such headings as "*P* 13 x 14 (*vert*) and *P* 14 x 13 (*horiz*)" indicate which perforations apply to which stamp format—vertical or horizontal.

From 1992 onwards most definitive and greetings stamps from both sheets and booklets occur with a large elliptical (oval) hole inserted in each line of vertical perforations as a security measure. The £10 definitive, No. 1658, is unique in having two such holes in the horizontal perforations.

Elliptical Perforations

Perforation Errors

Authenticated errors, where a stamp normally perforated is accidentally issued imperforate, are listed provided no traces of perforations (blind holes or indentations) remain. They must be provided as pairs, both stamps wholly imperforate, and are only priced in that form.

Numerous part-perforated stamps have arisen from the introduction of the Jumelle Press. This has a rotary perforator with rows of pins on one drum engaging with holes on another. Engagement is only gradual when the perforating unit is started up or stopped, giving rise to perforations "fading out", a variety mentioned above as not listed.

Stamps from the Jumelle printings sometimes occur imperforate between stamp and sheet margin. Such errors are not listed in this catalogue, but are covered by the volumes of the *Great Britain Specialised Catalogue*.

Pairs described as "imperforate between" have the line of perforations between the two stamps omitted.

Imperf between (*horiz pair*): a horizontal pair of stamps with perfs all around the edges but none between the stamps.

Imperf between (*vert pair*): a vertical pair of stamps with perfs all around the edges but none between the stamps.

Imperf between
(vertical pair)

Imperf horizontally
(vertical pair)

Where several of the rows have escaped perforation the resulting varieties are listable. Thus:

Imperf vert (horiz pair): a horizontal pair of stamps perforated at top and bottom; all three vertical directions are imperf—the two outer edges and between the stamps.

Imperf horiz (vert pair): a vertical pair perforated at left and right edges; all three horizontal directions are imperf—the top, bottom and between the stamps.

Varieties of double, misplaced or partial perforation caused by error or machine malfunction are not listable, neither are freaks, such as perforations placed diagonally from paper folds, nor missing holes caused by broken pins.

Phosphor Issues

Machines which sort mail electronically have been introduced progressively and the British Post Office issued the first stamps specially marked for electronic sorting in 1957. This first issue had easily visible graphite lines printed on the back beneath the gum (see Nos. 561/6). They were issued in the Southampton area where the experiment was carried out.

The graphite lines were replaced by phosphor bands, activated by ultra-violet light. The bands are printed on the front of the stamps and show as a matt surface against the usual smooth or shiny appearance of the untreated surface of the paper. The bands show clearly in the top or bottom horizontal margins of the sheet.

The first phosphor issues appeared in 1959 (see Nos. 599/609) and these stamps also had graphite lines on the back. Further details will be found in the listings above No. 599 and 619. From 1962 onwards most commemoratives were issued in versions with or without bands. From 1967 all commemorative stamps had phosphor bands, but from 1972 they were replaced by "all-over" phosphor covering the entire area of the stamp.

After a considerable period of development a special paper was produced in which the phosphor had been incorporated into the coating. From 15 August 1979 phosphorised paper was accepted for use generally, this paper replacing phosphor bands on most issues for all values except the second class letter rate. Phosphorised paper can only be identified by ultra-violet light. The Stanley Gibbons Uvitec Micro ultra-violet lamp is firmly recommended for use in identifying the phosphor stamps listed in this Catalogue. *Warning*. Never stare at the lighted lamp but follow the manufacturer's instructions.

During the years 1967 to 1972, when all issues, except the high values, should have shown phosphor bands, a number of stamps appeared with them omitted in error. These varieties are listed in this Catalogue. Stamps with "all-over" phosphor omitted can only be detected by the use of an ultra-violet lamp and these varieties are listed in the Stanley Gibbons *Great Britain Specialised Catalogue*. Note that prices are for unmounted mint examples only. Varieties such as double bands, misplaced or printed on the back are not listed in this Catalogue.

Gum Description

All stamps listed are assumed to have gum of some kind and original gum (o.g.) means that which was present on the stamp as issued to the public. Deleterious climates and the presence of certain chemicals can cause gum to crack and, with early stamps, even make the paper deteriorate. Unscrupulous fakers are adept in removing it and regumming the stamp to meet the unreasoning demand often made for "full o.g." in cases where such a thing is virtually impossible.

The gum normally used on stamps has been gum arabic until the late 1960's when synthetic adhesives were introduced. Harrison and Sons Ltd for instance use *polyvinyl alcohol*, known to philatelists as PVA (see note above SG723).

Colour Identification

The 200 colours most used for stamp identification are given in the Stanley Gibbons Stamp Colour Key. The Catalogue has used the Colour Key as a standard for describing new issues for some years. The names are also introduced as lists are rewritten, though exceptions are made for those early issues where traditional names have become universally established.

In compound colour names the second is the predominant one, thus:

orange-red = a red tending towards orange.

red-orange = an orange containing more red than usual.

When comparing actual stamps with colour samples in the Colour Key, view in a good north daylight (or its best substitute: fluorescent "colour-matching" light). Sunshine is not recommended. Choose a solid portion of the stamp design; if available, marginal markings such as solid bars of colour or colour check dots are helpful. Shading lines in the design can be misleading as they appear lighter than solid colour. Furthermore, the listings refer to colours as issued: they may deteriorate into something different through the passage of time.

Shades are particularly significant when they can be linked to specific printings. In general, shades need to be quite marked to fall within the scope of this Catalogue.

Modern colour printing by lithography is prone to marked differences of shade, even within a single run, and variations can occur within the same sheet. Such shades are not listed.

Errors of Colour

Major colour errors in stamps or overprints which qualify for listing are: wrong colours; albinos (colourless impressions), where these have Expert Committee certificates; colours completely omitted, but only on unused stamps (if found on used stamps the information is usually footnoted) and with good credentials, missing colours being frequently faked.

Colours only partially omitted are not recognised. Colour shifts, however spectacular, are not listed.

Booklet Stamps

Single stamps from booklets are listed if they are distinguishable in some way (such as watermark or phosphor bands) from similar sheet stamps.

Booklet Pane with Printed Labels

Se-tenant Pane of Four

Booklet panes are listed where they contain stamps of different denominations *se-tenant*, where stamp-size printed labels are included, or where such panes are otherwise identifiable. Booklet panes are placed in the listing under the lowest denomination present.

In the listing of complete booklets the numbers and prefix letters are the same as used in the Stanley Gibbons *Great Britain Specialised Catalogue*.

Coil Stamps

Stamps only issued in coil form are given full listing. If stamps are issued in both sheets and coils, the coil stamps are listed separately only where there is some feature (e.g. watermark sideways or gum change) by which single stamps can be distinguished. Coil strips containing different values *se-tenant* are also listed.

Multi-value Coil Strip

Coil join pairs are generally too random and easily faked to permit listing; similarly ignored are coil stamps which have accidentally suffered an extra row of perforations from the claw mechanism in a malfunctioning vending machine.

Gutter Pairs

In 1988 the recess-printed Castle high value definitives were issued in sheets containing four panes separated by a gutter margin. All modern Great Britain commemoratives and special stamps are produced in sheets containing two panes separated by a blank horizontal or vertical margin known as a gutter. This feature first made its appearance on some supplies of the 1972 Royal Silver Wedding 3p and marked the introduction of Harrison & Sons' new "Jumelle" stamp-printing press. There are advantages for both the printer and the Post Office in such a layout which has been used for most commemorative issues since 1974.

The term "gutter pair" is used for a pair of stamps separated by part of the blank gutter margin as illustrated below.

Most printers include some form of colour check device on the sheet margins, in addition to the cylinder or plate numbers. Harrison & Sons use round "dabs", or spots of colour, resembling traffic lights. For the period from the 1972 Royal Silver Wedding until the end of 1979 these colour dabs appeared in the gutter margin. There was always one example to every double pane sheet of stamps. They can also be found in the high value Machin issue printed in photogravure. Gutter pairs showing these "traffic lights" are worth considerably more than the normal version.

Gutter Pair

Traffic Light Gutter Pair

Miniature Sheets

A miniature sheet contains a single stamp or set with wide inscribed or decorated margins. The stamps usually also exist in normal sheet format. This Catalogue lists, with **MS** prefix, complete miniature sheets which have been issued by the Post Office and which are valid for postal purposes.

Miniature Sheet containing a set of stamps

Se-tenant Combinations

Se-tenant means "joined together". Some sets include stamps of different design arranged *se-tenant* as blocks or strips and, in mint condition, these are usually collected unsevered as issued. Such *se-tenant* combinations are supplied in used condition at a premium over the used prices of the individual stamps. See also the note on Set Prices.

Specimen Stamps

Stamps of Great Britain overprinted "SPECIMEN" for circulation to postmasters and the Universal Postal Union are listed in a special section following the Postal Fiscal stamps. For other "SPECIMEN" overprints see Stanley Gibbons *Great Britain Specialised Catalogue*.

Presentation and Souvenir Packs

Special Packs comprising slip-in cards with printed commemorative inscriptions and notes on the back and with protective covering, were introduced in 1964 for the Shakespeare issue. Definitive issues first appeared in Presentation Packs in 1960. Notes will be found in the listings to describe souvenir books issued on special occasions.

Issues of 1968–1969 (British Paintings to the Prince of Wales Investiture) were also issued in packs with text in German for sale through the Post Office's German Agency and these are also included.

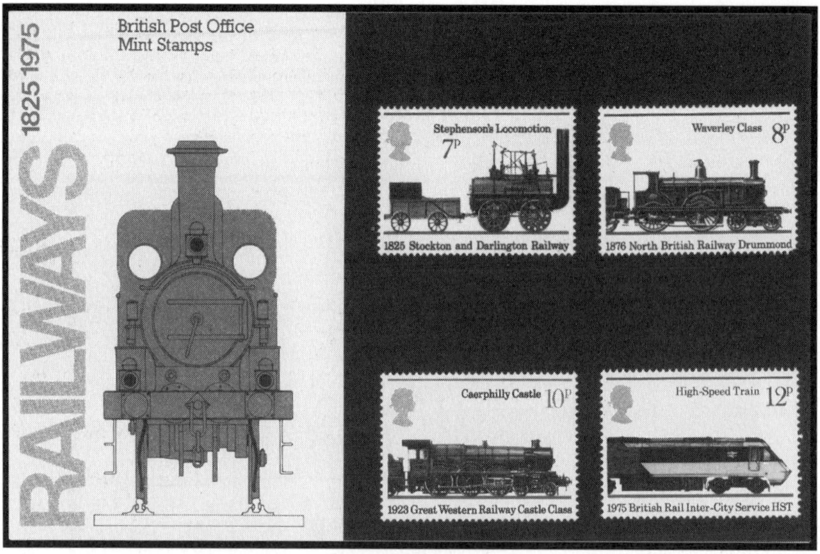

13 August 1975 Public Railways Presentation Pack

Collectors packs, first called gift packs, containing commemoratives issued in the preceding twelve months, first appeared in 1967. These are listed and priced.

Yearbooks

Special Post Office Yearbooks were first available in 1984. They contain all of the commemorative issues for one year in a hardbound book, illustrated in colour complete with slip case. These are listed and priced.

Commemorative First Day Covers

Until 1963 the Post Office did not provide any special first day of issue postmark facilities for collectors. Several philatelic organisations and stamp dealers did produce pictorial covers for the various commemorative issues and collectors serviced these to receive ordinary operational postmarks. Occasionally a special handstamp was produced which coincided with a new stamp issue, or relevant slogan postmarks, like the 1953 "Long Live the Queen" type, were in general use at the time.

On 21 March 1963 the Post Office installed special posting boxes at eleven main post offices so that collectors could obtain "uniformly high standard" impressions, from normal operational postmarks, for their first day covers. From 7 May 1963 special "First Day of Issue" slogans (Type A) were applied to mail posted in these special boxes, whose number had, by then, risen to thirty. The Philatelic Bureau accepted orders by post for such covers from the issue of 16 May 1963 onwards.

The slogan type was replaced on 23 April 1964 by "First Day of Issue" handstamps (Type B). These were, initially, of considerable size, but were later replaced by smaller versions (Type C) which remain in service today at nearly 200 principal offices. From 1970 the Bureau postmarks as Type C were inscribed "British Philatelic Bureau".

Since 1972 the Post Office has provided for virtually all issues an "alternative" pictorial "First Day of Issue" cancellation, additional to that of the Philatelic Bureau, at a town connected with the issue. Being available from the Bureau, these cancellations are illustrated and listed in this catalogue.

From time to time "First Day of Issue" postmarks, of standard or pictorial type, have been provided on a "one-off" basis for places linked to particular stamp issues, e.g. Weymouth for 1975 Sailing set. Such postmarks, which are not available from the Bureau, are footnoted.

Royal Mail established Special Handstamp Centres in 1990 where all sponsored special handstamps and many "First Day of Issue" postmarks are now applied.

Local pictorial "First Day of Issue" postmarks are provided for Durham (showing Cathedral), City of London, EC (coat of arms), and St. Albans (Cathedral), introduced in 1988, 1989, and 1995 respectively. (A similar postmark, showing the Tyne Bridge, was used at Newcastle upon Tyne, 1992-94.) The Scotland and Northern Ireland Special Handstamp Centre (Glasgow) uses two pictorial "First Day of Issue" handstamps. One, showing the Scottish Lion, is applied to all items posted in "First Day" boxes in Scotland. The second, used on request, has a design appropriate to both Scotland and Northern Ireland. Pictorial "First Day of Issue" postmarks for "London" (no postal district shown) and "Birmingham" were introduced in 1993 and 1997; the design changes for each issue. Such postmarks are available from the appropriate Special Handstamp Centre, not the Bureau, so are not included in this catalogue.

Type A. First Day of Issue Slogan

Type B. Large Handstamp

Type C. Small Handstamp

Type D. Maltese Cross

Type E

Type F. £ Sign

Type G. Three Lions

Type H. Four Castles

Type I. Windsor Keep

PHQ Cards

From 1973 the Post Office produced sets of picture cards to accompany commemorative issues which can be sent through the post as postcards. Each card shows an enlarged colour reproduction of one stamp, initially of a single value from one set and subsequently of all values. The Post Office gives each card a "PHQ" serial number, hence the term. The cards are usually on sale shortly before the date of issue of the stamps, but there is no officially designated "first day".

PHQ Card cancelled on First Day of Issue

Cards are priced in fine mint condition for complete sets as issued. Used prices are for cards franked with the stamp affixed, on the obverse, as illustrated above, or reverse; the stamp being cancelled with an official postmark for first day of issue.

Watermark Types

Stamps are on unwatermarked paper except where the heading to the set states otherwise.

Watermarks are detected for Catalogue description by one of four methods: (1) holding stamps to the light; (2) laying stamps face down on a dark background; (3) by use of the Morley-Bright Detector, which works by revealing the thinning of the paper at the watermark; or (4) by the more complex electric watermark detectors such as the Signoscope.

The diagram below shows how watermark position is described in the Catalogue. Watermarks are usually impressed so that they read normally when looked through from the printed side. However, since philatelists customarily detect watermarks by looking at the back of the stamp, the watermark diagram also makes clear what is actually seen. Note that "G v R" is only an example and illustrations of the different watermarks employed are shown in the listings. The illustrations are actual size and shown in normal positions (from the front of the stamps).

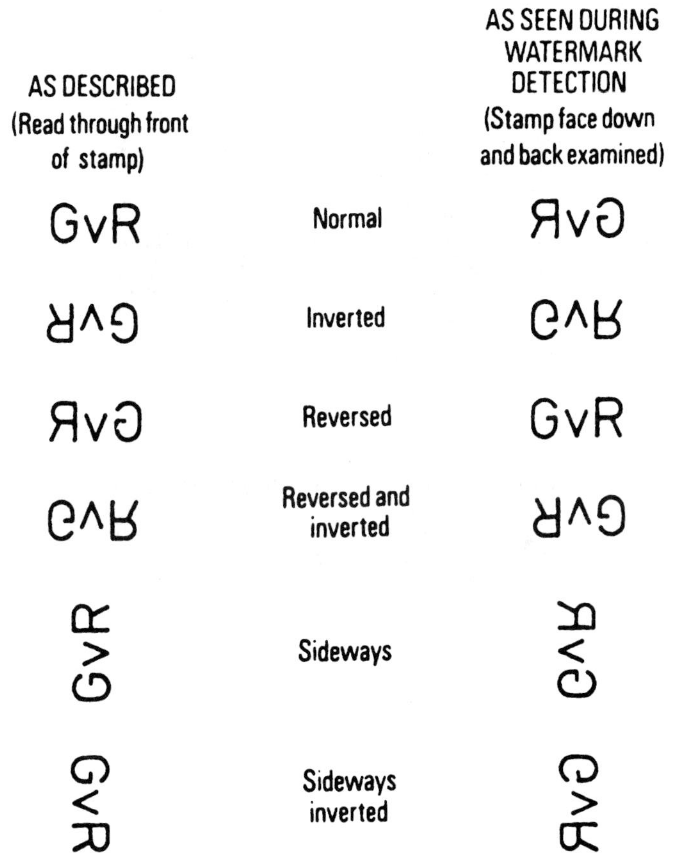

General Types of watermark as seen through the front side of the stamp.

2 Small Crown

4 Large Crown

9 (Extends over three stamps)

13 V R

15 Small Garter

16 Medium Garter

17 Large Garter

20 Emblems

33 Spray of Rose

39 Maltese Cross

40 Large Anchor

47 Small Anchor

48 Orb

49 Imperial Crown

100 Simple Cypher

103 Multiple Cypher

110 Single Cypher

111 Block Cypher

117 PUC £1

125 E8R

127

133

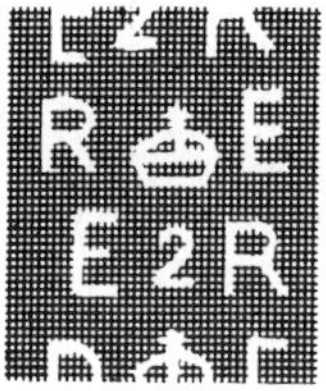

153 Tudor Crown

165 St. Edward's Crown

179 Multiple Crowns

Postal Fiscals

F5 Double-lined Anchor

F6 Single-lined Anchor

Watermark Errors and Varieties

Watermark errors are recognised as of major importance. They comprise stamps showing the wrong watermark devices or stamps printed on paper with the wrong watermark. Stamps printed on paper showing broken or deformed bits on the dandy roll, are not listable.

Underprints

From 1982 various values appeared with underprints, printed on the reverse, in blue, over the gum. These were usually from special stamp booklets, sold at a discount by the Post Office, but in 1985 surplus stocks of such underprinted paper were used for other purposes.

In this Catalogue stamps showing underprints are priced mint only. Used examples can be obtained, but care has to be taken in floating the stamps since the ink employed to print the device is solvent in water.

Underprint Types

1 Star with central dot

2 Double-lined Star

3 Double-lined "D"

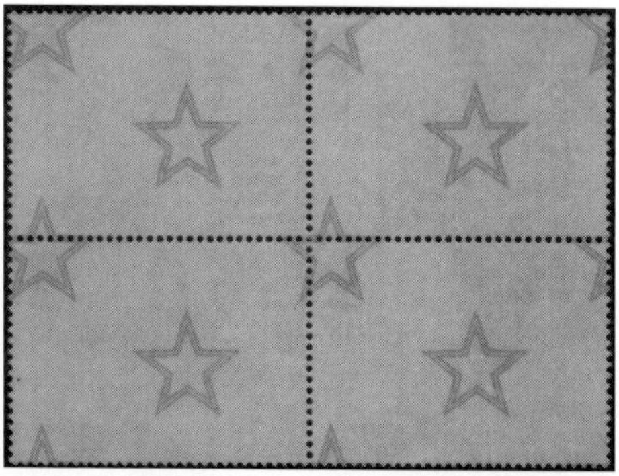

4 Multiple double-lined Stars

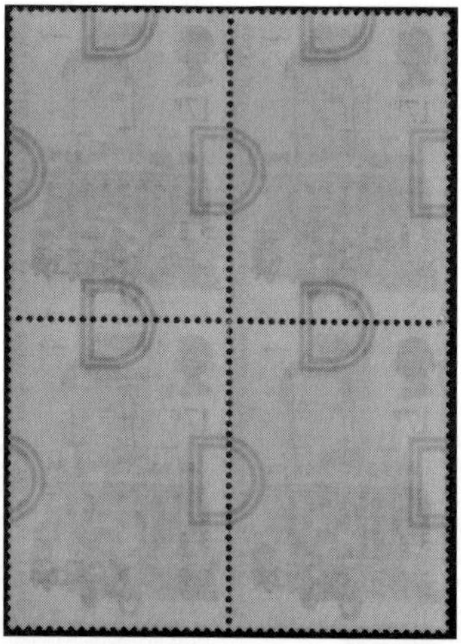

5 Multiple double-lined "D"

*(Types **4/5** are shown $\frac{3}{4}$ actual size)*

Note: Types **4/5** are arranged in a random pattern so that the stamps from the same sheet or booklet pane will show the underprint in a slightly different position to the above. Stamps, when inspected, should be placed the correct way up, face down, when comparing with the illustrations.

COMMEMORATIVE DESIGN INDEX

This index gives an easy reference to the inscriptions and designs of the Special Stamps 1953 to February 1998. Where a complete set shares an inscription or type of design, then only the catalogue number of the first stamp is given in addition to separate entries for stamps depicting popular thematic subjects. Paintings, inventions, etc., are indexed under the name of the artist or inventor, where this is shown on the stamp.

1. £.s.d. ISSUES 1953–70

Aberfeldy Bridge 764
Alcock, John (aviator).......... 791
Antrim 690
Arbroath Declaration, 650th Anniversary 819
Architecture: Cathedrals.......... 796
Rural.......... 815
Atlantic Flight, 50th Anniversary.......... 791
Automatic Sorting.......... 811

Battle of Britain, 25th Anniversary.......... 671
Battle of Hastings, 900th Anniversary.......... 705
Blackbird 699
Black Headed Gull.......... 696
Blue Tit.......... 697
Bridges 763
Brown, Arthur (aviator).......... 791
Burns, Robert 685

Cairngorms.......... 692
Canterbury Cathedral 799
C.E.P.T. 621, 626
Christmas 1966, Children's Paintings (3d., 1s. 6d.).......... 713
1967, Paintings (3d., 4d., 1s. 6d.) 756
1968, Children's Toys (4d., 9d., 1s. 6d.).......... 775
1969, Traditional Religious Themes (4d., 5d., 1s. 6d.) 812
1970, Lisle Psalter (4d., 5d., 1s. 6d.) 838
Churchill, Winston 661
Commonwealth Arts Festival.......... 669
Commonwealth Cable.......... 645
Commonwealth Games (1958).......... 567
Commonwealth Games (1970).......... 832
Commonwealth Parliamentary Conference 629
Concorde 784
Constable, John (artist).......... 774
Cook's First Voyage of Discovery, 200th Anniversary. 770
Co-operative Alliance, 75th Anniversary.......... 821
Coronation 532
Cotswold Limestone.......... 816
Cutty Sark 781

Dickens, Charles, Death Centenary 824
Durham Cathedral 796

East Indiaman.......... 780
E.F.T.A. 715
Elizabethan Galleon 779
"Elizabeth I" 771
England Winners World Cup Football Championships, 1966 700
Europa, C.E.P.T., 1st Anniversary 621
Europa, C.E.P.T., 10th Anniversary.......... 792

Fife Harling 815
First England-Australia Flight, 50th Anniversary.......... 795
Flowers.......... 717
Forth Road Bridge 659
Freedom from Hunger 634

Gandhi, Mahatma, Birth Centenary 807
General Letter Office, Tercentenary.......... 619
Gipsy Moth IV 751
Great Britain 782

Harlech Castle 691
Hovercraft.......... 703

International Botanical Congress.......... 655
International Geographical Congress 651
International Labour Organisation, 50th Anniversary. 793
International Lifeboat Conference.......... 639
International Telecommunications Union, Centenary. 683

Jet Engine.......... 754
Jubilee Jamboree (1957) 557

Landscapes 689
Lawrence, Thomas (artist) 748, 772
Le Nain, Louis (artist).......... 758
Lister, Joseph.......... 667
Liverpool Metropolitan Cathedral 801
Lowry, L.S. (artist).......... 750

Mauritania 783
Mayflower, 350th Anniversary of Voyage 822
Menai Bridge.......... 765
Montfort's Parliament, 700th Anniversary 663
Motor Cars 702
Murillo (artist) 757
M4 Viaduct.......... 766

National Giro.......... 808
National Nature Week 637
National Productivity Year.......... 631
Nightingale, Florence, 150th Birth Anniversary.......... 820
North Atlantic Treaty Organisation (NATO), 20th Anniversary.......... 794
Nuclear Power 704

Paris Postal Conference, Centenary 636
Parliamentary Conference.......... 560
Parliament, 700th Anniversary 663
Penicillin.......... 753
Philympia 1970.......... 835
Piper, John (artist).......... 773
Post Office Savings Bank, Centenary 623
Post Office Tower 679
Prince of Wales, Investiture.......... 802

Queen Elizabeth 2 778

Radar.......... 752
Radio Telescope.......... 701
Red Cross Centenary Congress 642
Robin.......... 698
Royal Air Force, 50th Anniversary.......... 769
Royal Astronomical Society, 150th Anniversary.......... 823

St. Giles' Edinburgh 798
St. Paul's Cathedral.......... 800
Salvation Army Centenary 665
Seville School 756
Shakespeare Festival.......... 646
Stubbs, George (artist).......... 749
Sussex.......... 689

Tarr Steps.......... 763
Telecommunications.......... 809
Television.......... 755
Trades Union Congress, Centenary.......... 767

Ulster Thatch 818
United Nations, 20th Anniversary 681

Votes for Women, 50th Anniversary 768

Welsh Stucco 817
Westminster Abbey, 900th Anniversary 687
World Cup Football Championships, 1966 693
Wordsworth, William, 200th Birth Anniversary 828

York Minster 797

2. DECIMAL CURRENCY 1971-98

Abbotsbury Swannery 1639
Aberystwyth University College 890
Accession, 40th Anniversary 1602
"Acid Rain Kills" 1629
Age of Steam 1795
Aircraft Designers 1984
Airmail, blue van and postbox 1930 956
Alexandra Palace 1493
Alice's Adventures in Wonderland 1094
American Independence Bicentennial 1005
Amser Haf/Summertime 1834
Animals, Species at Risk 1320
Anne of Cleves 1968
Architecture: Modern University Buildings 890
  Village Churches 904
  Historic Buildings 1054
Armada, 400th Anniversary 1400
Armagh Observatory 1522
Arthurian Legends 1294
Astronomy 1522
Athletics 1134, 1328
Austen, Jane, Birth Centenary 989
Austin (cars) 1198
Austin-Healey (cars) 1947
Australian Bicentenary 1396
Autumn 1779
Avocet (bird) 1420
Avro Lancaster Mk 1 1985

Babbage-Computer 1547
Badger 1043
Ballyroney, County Down 2000
Barbirolli, Sir John (conductor) 1133
Bawden, Edward 1768
BBC, 50th Anniversary 909
Beddgelert, Gwynedd 1999
Beecham, Sir Thomas (conductor) 1131
Beetle 1280
Bell, Alexander Graham, First Telephone Call Centenary 997
Ben Arkle 1811
Biddulph Grange 1224
"Bird of Hope" 1632
Birds 1109, 1915
Bishop, Ronald 1986
Black Prince 961
Blake, Admiral and *Triumph* 1188
Blanchflower, Danny 1929
Blenheim Palace 1225
Blues and Royals Drum Horse 1991
Blyton, Enid (authoress) 2001
Boleyn, Anne 1966
Boxing 1136
Braemar (highland games) 1833
British Architects in Europe 1355
British Army Uniforms 1218
British Composers 1282
British Council 1263
British Horse Society 1989
British Legion, 50th Anniversary 887
British Philatelic Bureau, Edinburgh 1495
British Rail Inter-City Service HST 987
British Textiles 1192
Brontë, Charlotte (authoress) 1125
Brontë, Emily (authoress) 1127
Brown Hare 1040
Buckingham Palace 1120
Bumble Bee 1277
Burns, Robert (poet) 1901
Bush-cricket 1279
Bush House, Bristol 1247
Butterflies 1151

Caernarvon Castle 1056
Caerphilly Castle (railway loco) 986
Camm, Sir Sidney 1988
Canals 1775
Carnoustie: "Luckyslap" (golf) 1831
Carriage Horse 1989
Carter, George 1987
Castell Y Waun 1810
Catherine of Aragon 1963
Cats 1848
Cattle 1240
Caxton, William 1014
Chadwick, Roy 1985
Channel Tunnel, Opening of 1820
Chaplin, Charlie 1300
Charity 970
Charlotte Square, Edinburgh 975
Chequered Skipper (butterfly) 1154
Children's Television, 50th Anniversary 1940
Children's Toys and Board Games 1436
Chillingham Wild Bull 1241
Chirk Castle 1810
Christmas:
  1971. Stained Glass Windows ($2\frac{1}{2}$p., 3p., $7\frac{1}{2}$p.) 894
  1972. Angels ($2\frac{1}{2}$p., 3p., $7\frac{1}{2}$p.) 913
  1973. Scenes depicting carol "Good King Wenceslas" (3p. × 5, $3\frac{1}{2}$p.) 943
  1974. Roof Bosses ($3\frac{1}{2}$p., $4\frac{1}{2}$p., 8p., 10p.) 966
  1975. Angels ($6\frac{1}{2}$p., $8\frac{1}{2}$p., 11p., 13p.) 993
  1976. Embroideries ($6\frac{1}{2}$p., $8\frac{1}{2}$p., 11p., 13p.) 1018
  1977. The Twelve Days of Christmas (7p. × 5, 9p.) 1044
  1978. Carol Singers (7p., 9p., 11p., 13p.) 1071
  1979. Scenes depicting the Nativity (8p., 10p., $11\frac{1}{2}$p., 13p., 15p.) 1104
  1980. Christmas Decorations (10p., 12p., $13\frac{1}{2}$p., 15p., $17\frac{1}{2}$p.) 1138
  1981. Children's Paintings ($11\frac{1}{2}$p., 14p., 18p., 22p., 25p.) 1170
  1982. Carols ($12\frac{1}{2}$p., $15\frac{1}{2}$p., $19\frac{1}{2}$p., 26p., 29p.) 1202
  1983. Birds ($12\frac{1}{2}$p., 16p., $20\frac{1}{2}$p., 28p., 31p.) 1231
  1984. Scenes depicting the Nativity (13p., 17p., 22p., 31p., 34p.) 1267
  1985. Pantomime (12p., 17p., 22p., 31p., 34p.) 1303
  1986. Christmas Legends (12p., 13p., 18p., 22p., 31p., 34p.) 1341
  1987. A Child's Christmas Day (13p., 18p., 26p., 31p., 34p.) 1375
  1988. Christmas Cards (14p., 19p., 27p., 32p., 35p.) 1414
  1989. 800th Anniversary of Ely Cathedral (15p., 15p. + 1p., 20p + 1p., 34p. + 1p., 37p. + 1p.) 1462
  1990. Christmas Scenes (17p., 22p., 26p., 31p., 37p.) 1526
  1991. Illuminated Manuscripts from the Bodleian Library, Oxford (18p., 24p., 28p., 33p., 39p.) 1582
  1992. Stained Glass Windows (18p., 24p., 28p., 33p., 39p.) 1634
  1993. 150th Anniv of *A Christmas Carol* by Charles Dickens (19p., 25p., 30p., 35p., 41p.,) 1790
  1994. Children's Nativity Plays (19p., 25p., 30p., 35p., 41p.,) 1843

1995. Christmas Robins (19p., 25p., 30p., 41p., 60p.) 1896
1996. Biblical Scenses (2nd, 1st, 31p., 43p., 63p.) . 1950
1997. 150th Anniv of the Christmas Cracker (2nd, 1st, 31p., 43p., 63p.) 2006
Churches 904
Churchill, Winston, Birth Centenary 962
Cinema Centenary 1920
Civil War, 350th Anniversary 1620
Classic Sports Cars 1945
Coal 1051
Coastguard, 150th Anniversary 902
Colchicum (flower) 1350
Columbus, 500th Anniversary of Discovery of America 1617
Commercial St. Development, Perth 1248
Common Dormouse 2015
Commonwealth Day 1211
Commonwealth Games, Edinburgh, 1986 1328
Commonwealth Heads of Government Meeting, 1977 1038
Commonwealth Parliamentary Conf. 939, 1335
Computed Tomography 1842
Computer 1547
Contemporary Art 1767
Coronation, 25th Anniversary 1059
County Cricket, Centenary 928
Court Masque Costumes 935
Court Masque Stage Scene 938
Cowes (sailing) 1836
Cricket 1137
Cultural Traditions 1010
Cunningham, Viscount and H.M.S. *Warspite* 1191
Cycling 1878-1978 1067

Dangermouse 1944
Darwin, Charles 1175
D-Day, 50th Anniversary 1824
Dean, Dixie 1925
Deer 1587
De Havilland Mosquito B Mk XVI 1986
Derby Bicentenary 1087
Dersingham 1813
Derwentwater, England 1156
Devil's Bolete 2020
Diana, Princess of Wales 2021
Dickens, Charles 1790
Dinosaurs 1573
Dipper 1110
Dogs 1075, 1531
Dolwyddelan 1814
Domesday Book 1324
Dowding, Lord and Hawker Hurricane 1336
Dracula 1980
Dragonfly 1281
Drake, Francis (explorer) 925
Dr. Jekyll and Mr. Hyde 1982
Duckling 1481
Duke of Edinburgh Award Scheme 1162
Duke of Edinburgh's Horse 1992
Du Maurier 1938

Earls Barton, Northants 905
Echeveria (flower) 1349
Echinops (flower) 1348
Edwards, Duncan 1927
Eisteddfod of Wales 1010
Electricity 1053, 1546
Eliot, George (authoress) 1126
"Elizabeth of Glamis" (rose) 1006
Endangered Species 2015
Energy 1050
Engineering Achievements 1215
Environment 1629

"Europa" 1984 1249
European Architectural Heritage Year 975
European Assembly Elections 1083
European Communities 919
European Football Championship 1925
European Parliament, Third Direct Elections 1433
Europe in Space 1560
Explorers 923
Expo '92, Seville 1619

Fairs 1227
Famous Five 2002
Famous Women 1935
Faraday-Electricity 1546
Faraway Tree 2004
Films 1227
Fire Engines 950
First official airmail Coronation 1911 955
Fisher, Lord and H.M.S. *Dreadnought* 1190
Fishes 1207
Fishing 1166
Flower Paintings 1955
Flowers 1347
Fonteyn, Margot 1936
Food and Farming Year 1989 1428
Football 1391
Ford (cars) 1199
Four Seasons:
Spring 1853
Summer 1834
Autumn 1779
Winter 1587
Fox 1587
Frankenstein 1981
Franklin, Benjamin 1005
Frink, Elizabeth 1937
Frobisher, Martin (explorer) 898
Fruits and Leaves 1779
Fry, Elizabeth 1004

Gaillardia (flowers) 1347
Gallantry Awards 1517
Gaskell, Mrs. (authoress) 1128
General Post, c. 1839 1096
Giant's Causeway, N. Ireland 1158
Gilbert and Sullivan Operas 1624
Glasgow, School of Art 1494
Glenfinnan, Scotland 1155
Globe Theatre 1882
Gloster Meteor F Mk 8 1987
Glyndwr, Owain 959
Golf, Scottish Courses 1829
"Grandpa Dickson" (rose) 1007
Gray, Thomas, Death Bicentenary 885
Great Britons 958
Great Western Railway Castle Class 986
"Greenhouse Effect" 1631
Greensted-juxta-Ongar, Essex 904
Greenwich Meridian 1254
Gymnastics 1388

Halley's Comet 1312
Hampton Court Palace 1057, 1123
Hardy, Thomas, 150th Birth Anniversary 1506
Hare 1587
Haroldswick, Shetland 1997
Harris, Sir Arthur and Avro Lancaster 1339
Harrison, John, 300th Birth Anniversary 1654
Hartman, Marea 1939
Hawker Hunter FGA Mk 9 1998
"Health and Handicap" Charities 970
Hedgehog 1039

Helpringham, Lincolnshire 907
Henry V 960
Henry VIII 1187, 1971
Henry VIII, 450th Death Anniversary 1965
Hepburn, Thomas 1001
Heraldry 1236, 1363, 2026
Hereford Bull 1242
Highland Cow 1240
Highland Gathering 1012
High-Speed Train 987
Hill, Rowland 1095, 1887
Hitchcock, Alfred 1302
Hockey Cup 1332
Hodgkin, Dorothy 1935
Holmes, Sherlock 1784
Holyroodhouse 1055
Horror 1980
Horse Chestnut 949
Horse racing paintings 1087
Horses 1063
Hound of the Baskervilles 1983
Howard, Catherine 1969
Hudson, Henry (explorer) 899
Huish Episcopi, Somerset 908
Humber Bridge 1215

Imperial Airways Flying Boat 1937 957
Industry Year 1986 1308
Information Technology 1196
Inland Waterways 1775
Insects 1277
International Stamp Exhibition 1118
International Year of Disabled People 1147
Inter-Parliamentary Union Conference 988, 1435
Iolair (oilfield support vessel) 1217
Irish Moiled Cow 1244
Irish Setter 1078
Ironbridge, Shropshire 1440

Jaguar (cars) 1200, 1948
Jet Engine-Whittle 1549
Jones, Inigo, 400th Birth Anniversary 935

Keats, John, 150th Death Anniversary 884
Kemp Experiment 1897 912
Kensington Palace 1124
Kew Gardens 1840-1990 1502
Kingfisher 1109
Kitten 1479

Ladybird 1278
Lady's Slipper Orchid 2016
Lammastide 1145
Lancaster House 1253
Large Blue (butterfly) 1152
Leaf Sculptures 1853
Lear, Edward 1405
Leigh, Vivien 1301, 1921
Letheringsett, Norfolk 906
Lifeguards' Horse 1990
Linnean Society 1788/1988 1380
Liverpool and Manchester Railway 1830 1113
Liverpool, Garden Festival Hall 1245
Livingstone, David (explorer) 923
Llanelwedd, Royal Welsh Show 1834
London 1980 1118
London Post, c. 1839 1097
Lord Mayor's Show, London 1457
Lord's (cricket) 1832

Magnetic Resonance Imaging 1841
Malory Towers 2005
Marconi Experiment 1897 912
Marconi First Wireless Message 1895 1889
Marine Timekeeper No.4 1654
Maritime Heritage 1187
Mary Rose 1187
Medals and Decorations 1517
Medical Discoveries 1839
Medieval Mummers 1146
MG (cars) 1946
Milburngate Centre, Durham 1246
Mills, New Lanark, Strathclyde 1442
Mitchell, Reginald 1984
Mole Cricket 2019
Moore, Bobby 1926
Moore, Henry 1767
Moorhen 1111
Morgan (cars) 1949
Morris Dancing 1011, 1144
Motor Car Industry 1198
Mourne Mountains 1812
Muffin the Mule 1940
Muirfield: 18th Hole (golf) 1830
Music 1282

National Theatre, London 979
National Trust 1155, 1868
Natural Gas 1052
Nature Conservation 1320
Nelson, Lord and H.M.S. *Victory* 1189
Newton, Sir Isaac 1351
Nicholson, Ben 1770
Niven, David 1299
Noddy 2001
North British Railway Drummond (railway loco) 985

Oak 922
Odeon, Harrogate 1920
Oil 1050
Old English Sheepdog 1075
Olivier, Laurence 1921
Olympic and Paralympic Games, Atlanta 1930
Olympic Games, Barcelona 1615
Operation Raleigh 1618
Orchids 1659
Ordnance Survey (maps) 1578
Otter 1042
Owen, Robert 1002
Oystercatcher (bird) 1421
"Ozone Layer" 1630

Painswick, Gloucestershire 1998
P & O packet steamer *Peninsular* 1888 954
Paralympics, Barcelona 1616
Parr, Catherine 1970
Pathé 1923
Peace and Freedom 1873
Peacock (butterfly) 1153
Penny Black, 150th Anniversary 1467, **MS**1501
Perch 1210
Philatelic Bureau, Edinburgh 1495
Pictorial Postcards 1894-1994 1815
Pike 1208
Pioneers of Communications 1887
Pitmedden, Scotland 1226
Polar Explorers 897
Police 1100
Pontcysyllte Aqueduct, Clwyd 1443
Portal, Lord and Mosquito 1340
Postal Telegraph & Telephone, Int. World Congress 1434
Pottery 1371
Prince of Wales Investiture Anniversary 1810
Prince's Lodging, Newmarket 937
Public Education. 150th Anniversary 1432

Puffin (bird) 1419
Puppy 1482

Queen Elizabeth II Accession 40th Anniversary 1602
Queen Elizabeth II 60th Birthday 1316
Queen Mother's 80th Birthday 1129
Queen Mother's 90th Birthday 1507
Queen's Award to Industry 1497

Rabbit 1480
Racket Sports 1022
Radar-Watson Watt 1548
Raeburn, Sir Henry, 150th Death Anniversary 932
Railway Locomotives 984, 1113, 1272, 1795
Raleigh, Walter (explorer) 926
Red Cross 1874
Red Squirrel 1041
Redwing 1587
Reynolds, Sir Joshua, 250th Birth Anniversary 931
Robert the Bruce 958
Robin 1896
Rolls-Royce (cars) 1201
Roman Britain 1771
"Rosa Mundi" (rose) 1008
Roses 1006, 1568
Ross, James Clark (explorer) 897
Rowing 1329
Royal Air Force 1336
Royal Institute of Chemistry 1029
Royal Mail Coach, 200th Anniversary 1258
Royal Mail, 350 Years Service 1290
Royal Microscopical Society, 150th Anniversary 1453
Royal Observatory, Greenwich 977, 1524
Royal Opera House 1122
Royal Troon: The Postage Stamp (golf) 1832
Royal Wedding 941, 1160, 1333
RSPB 1889-1989 (birds) 1419
RSPCA 1840-1990 (animals) 1479
Rugby Football Union, 100th Anniversary 889
Rugby League, Centenary 1891
Rugby Union 1135
Rugby World Cup 1991 1567

Safety at Sea 1286
Sailing 980
St. Andrews, The Old Course (golf) 1829
St. Augustine 1974
St. Columba 1972
St. George's Chapel, Windsor 978
St. John Ambulance 1887–1987 1359
St. Kilda, Scotland 1159
St. Paul's, Covent Garden 936
St. Valentine's Day 1143
Salmon 1207
Sargent, Sir Malcolm (conductor) 1132
Scanning Electron Microscopy 1840
Science Fiction 1878
Scientific Achievements 1546
Scott, Robert Falcon (explorer) 900
Scott, Sir Walter, Birth Bicentenary 886
Scottish Heraldry 1363
Secret Seven 2003
Sellers, Peter 1298
Seymour, Jane 1967
Shaftesbury, Lord 1003
Shakespeare's Globe Theatre 1882
Sheep 1587
Shetland Pony 1064
Shining Ram's-horn Snail 2018
Shire Horse 1063
Shooting 1331
Silver Jubilee 1033
Silver Wedding 916
Single European Market 1633
Sissinghurst, Kent 1223
Skiing 1389
Small Tortoiseshell (butterfly) 1151
Social Reformers 1001
Song Thrush 2017
Sooty 1941
Spencer, Stanley 1769
Spring Flowers 1079
Springtime 1853
Stackpole Head, Wales 1157
Stanley, Henry (explorer) 924
Stephenson's *Locomotion* 984
Stingray 1942
Stockton and Darlington Railway 984
Stonehenge 1525
Stubbs, George (artist) 1531
Sturt, Charles (explorer) 927
Sub Post Offices 1997
Summertime 1834
Supermarine Spitfire MkIIA 1984
Swans 1639
"Sweet Briar" (rose) 1009

Tedder, Lord and Hawker Typhoon 1337
Telephone, First call by Alexander Graham Bell, Centenary 997
Templeton Carpet Factory, Glasgow 1496
Tennis 1390
Tennyson 1607
Textiles 1192
Thames Flood Barrier 1216
The Albert Memorial 1121
Theatre 1183
The Clangers 1943
The Rows, Chester 976
The Tale of Peter Rabbit 1091
The Wind in the Willows 1092
Thoroughbred 1066
Tin Mine, St. Agnes, Cornwall 1441
Titanic (liner) 1890
Tower of London 1054
Toys and Games 1436
Trains 1272
Transport 1392
Trees 922, 949
Trenchard, Lord and De Havilland DH9A 1338
Triumph (cars) 1945
Trout 1209
Tunnicliffe 1915
Turberry, 9th Hole (golf) 1833
Turner, Joseph, Birth Bicentenary 971
Tutankhamun Discovery, 50th Anniversary 901

"Ulster '71" Paintings 881
Ultrasonic Imaging 1839
Uniform Postage, 1840 1098
United Nations 1876
Universal Postal Union Centenary 954
University of Essex 893
University of Leicester 892
University of Southampton 891
Urban Renewal 1245

Vaughan Williams, Ralph, Birth Centenary 903
VE Day 1873, 1875
Victoria 1367
Victorian Britain 1367

Waverley Class (railway loco) 985
Weightlifting 1330
Wells, H.G. 1878

Welsh Bible 1384
Welsh Black Bull 1243
Welsh Pony 1065
Welsh Springer Spaniel 1076
West Highland Terrier 1077
Westminster Palace 988
Wildfowl and Wetlands Trust 1915
Wimbledon (tennis) 1835
Winnie-the-Pooh 1093
Wintertime 1587
Wireless First Message 1895 1889
Wood, Sir Henry (conductor) 1130
World Student Games 1991 1564
Wright, Billy 1928

Yachts 980
Year of the Child 1091
Yellow Wagtail 1112
York, 1900th Anniversary 888
Youth Organisations 1179

GREAT BRITAIN CONCISE

BUYER'S GUIDE

The Great Britain Concise Suppliers Guide

The Great Britain Concise Suppliers guide is your comprehensive, ***at-a-glance*** guide to the philatelic industry. Broken down by classifications, the Suppliers guide is an invaluable information service covering many dealers.

Whatever you require, simply turn to the guide for a selection of names, addresses and telephone numbers covering your specialist area.

Compilation

The Great Britain Concise Suppliers guide is compiled and published by Stanley Gibbons Publications. Every effort has been made to ensure the accuracy of all the entries in the directory, however, Stanley Gibbons Publications cannot in any circumstances be responsible for or accept any liability for any loss or damage of any kind which may arise or result from any errors or omissions in any entry, whether relating to wording, space, position, artwork or telephone number.

✦ AUCTIONS

Stanley Gibbons Publications
5 Parkside, Christchurch Road, Ringwood, Hants,
BH24 3SH, England..Tel: 01425 472362
Fax: 01425 470247
e-mail: sales@stangib.demon.co.uk

✦ EDWARD VII

Malcolm Sprei - M&S Stamps
Stamp Centre, 79 Strand, London, WC2R 0DE, UK
....Tel: 0171 240 3778
Fax: 0171 240 5419

Richard Allan Postal Auction
Stamp Centre, 79 Strand, London, WC2R 0DE, UK
....Tel: 0171 379 5439
Fax: 0171 240 5419

Royale Stamp Company
110 St. Martins Lane, London, WC2N 4AZ, UK
....Tel: 0171 240 1963
Fax: 0171 240 5419

Stanley Gibbons Publications
5 Parkside, Christchurch Road, Ringwood, Hants,
BH24 3SH, England..Tel: 01425 472362
Fax: 01425 470247
e-mail: sales@stangib.demon.co.uk

Steven Scott
Stamp Centre, 79 Strand, London, WC2R 0DE, UK
....Tel: 0171 836 2341
Fax: 0171 240 5419

✦ EDWARD VIII

Malcolm Sprei - M&S Stamps
Stamp Centre, 79 Strand, London, WC2R 0DE, UK
....Tel: 0171 240 3778
Fax: 0171 240 5419

Richard Allan Postal Auction
Stamp Centre, 79 Strand, London, WC2R 0DE, UK
....Tel: 0171 379 5439
Fax: 0171 240 5419

Royale Stamp Company
110 St. Martins Lane, London, WC2N 4AZ, UK
....Tel: 0171 240 1963
Fax: 0171 240 5419

Stanley Gibbons Publications
5 Parkside, Christchurch Road, Ringwood, Hants,
BH24 3SH, England..Tel: 01425 472362
Fax: 01425 470247
e-mail: sales@stangib.demon.co.uk

Steven Scott
Stamp Centre, 79 Strand, London, WC2R 0DE, UK
....Tel: 0171 836 2341
Fax: 0171 240 5419

✦ GENERAL

Andrew Lajer
The Old Post Office, Hurst, Berks, RG10 0TR, UK
....Tel: 01189 344151
Fax: 01491 579148

Arthur Ryan & Co
2, The Square, The Quadrant, Richmond, Surrey, TW9 1DY
....Tel: 0181 940 7777
Fax: 0181 940 7755

See Main Advertisement - opposite page 1 in catalogue.

Avon Mixtures
P.O. Box 99, Market Harborough, Leicester, LE16 8ZR, UK

Bath Stamp & Coin Shop, The
12/13 Pulteney Bridge, Bath, Avon, BA2 4AJ UK
....Tel: 01225 463073
Fax: 01225 463073

Bushell & Wright
PO Box 3788, London, SE1 5NE, UK
....Tel: 0171 232 0944
Fax: 0171 232 0944

Cecil Court Stamp Shop
6 Cecil Court, London, WC2N 4HE, UK
....Tel: 0171 240 1051

David & Lori Spragg
P.O. Box 70, Marlow, Bucks, SL7 1EU, UK.....Tel: 01628 476041
Fax: 01628 476027

Embassy Philatelists
Marlborough House, P.O.Box 23, Winchester, Hants, SO22 4RE
....Tel: 01962 854307
Fax: 01962 841830

Epsom Stamp Company, John Marshall,
23 Waterloo Road, Epsom, Surrey, KT19 8EX, UK
....Tel: 01372 720051

Martin Townsend
PO Box 10, Hitchin, Herts., SG4 9PE, UK......Tel: 01462 420678
Fax: 01462 420678

Peter Mollett Philatelist
PO Box 1934, Ringwood, Hants, BH24 2YZ, UK
....Tel: 01425 476666

Philatelic Software
British Philatelic Burea, 20 Brandon Street, Edinburgh, EH3 5TT
....Tel: 0345 641641

Ringdale Philatelics
Dept. CBS, 242 Stroud Road, Gloucester, GL4 0AU, UK
....Tel: 01452 411942

Rowland Hill Stamps,
Early Wants Lists Welcome
193 Comberton Hill, Kidderminster, Worcs, DY10 1QG, UK
....Tel: 01562 851101
Fax: 01562 851824

Rushstamps
P.O. Box 1, Lyndhurst, SO43 7PP, UK ....Tel: 01703 282044
Fax: 01703 282982

Stanley Gibbons Publications
5 Parkside, Christchurch Road, Ringwood, Hants,
BH24 3SH, England..Tel: 01425 472362
Fax: 01425 470247
e-mail: sales@stangib.demon.co.uk

T Lester (Coventry Auctions)
29 Momus Boulevard, Binley Road, Coventry, CV2 5NA, UK
....Tel: 01203 454908
Fax: 01203 650109

Warwick & Warwick Ltd,
See Main Advert on Page 30
Pageant House, 2 Jury Street, Warwick, CV34 4EW, UK
....Tel: 01926 499031
Fax: 01926 491906

✦ GEORGE V

Malcolm Sprei - M&S Stamps
Stamp Centre, 79 Strand, London, WC2R 0DE, UK
....Tel: 0171 240 3778
Fax: 0171 240 5419

Richard Allan Postal Auction
Stamp Centre, 79 Strand, London, WC2R 0DE, UK
....Tel: 0171 379 5439
Fax: 0171 240 5419

Royale Stamp Company
110 St. Martins Lane, London, WC2N 4AZ, UK
....Tel: 0171 240 1963
Fax: 0171 240 5419

Stanley Gibbons Publications
5 Parkside, Christchurch Road, Ringwood, Hants,
BH24 3SH, England.......................................Tel: 01425 472362
Fax: 01425 470247
e-mail: sales@stangib.demon.co.uk

Steven Scott
Stamp Centre, 79 Strand, London,
WC2R 0DE, UK...Tel: 0171 836 2341
Fax: 0171 240 5419

✦ GEORGE VI

Richard Allan Postal Auction
Stamp Centre, 79 Strand, London, WC2R 0DE, UK
....Tel: 0171 379 5439
Fax: 0171 240 5419

Royale Stamp Company
110 St. Martins Lane, London, WC2N 4AZ, UK
....Tel: 0171 240 1963
Fax: 0171 240 5419

Stanley Gibbons Publications
5 Parkside, Christchurch Road, Ringwood, Hants,
BH24 3SH, England.......................................Tel: 01425 472362
Fax: 01425 470247
e-mail: sales@stangib.demon.co.uk

Steven Scott
Stamp Centre, 79 Strand, London,
WC2R 0DE, UK...Tel: 0171 836 2341
Fax: 0171 240 5419

✦ QUEEN ELIZABETH II

Richard Allan Postal Auction
Stamp Centre, 79 Strand, London,
WC2R 0DE, UK...Tel: 0171 379 5439
Fax: 0171 240 5419

Royale Stamp Company
110 St. Martins Lane, London, WC2N 4AZ, UK
....Tel: 0171 240 1963
Fax: 0171 240 5419

Stanley Gibbons Publications
5 Parkside, Christchurch Road, Ringwood, Hants,
BH24 3SH, England.......................................Tel: 01425 472362
Fax: 01425 470247
e-mail: sales@stangib.demon.co.uk

Steven Scott
Stamp Centre, 79 Strand, London, WC2R 0DE, UK
....Tel: 0171 836 2341
Fax: 0171 240 5419

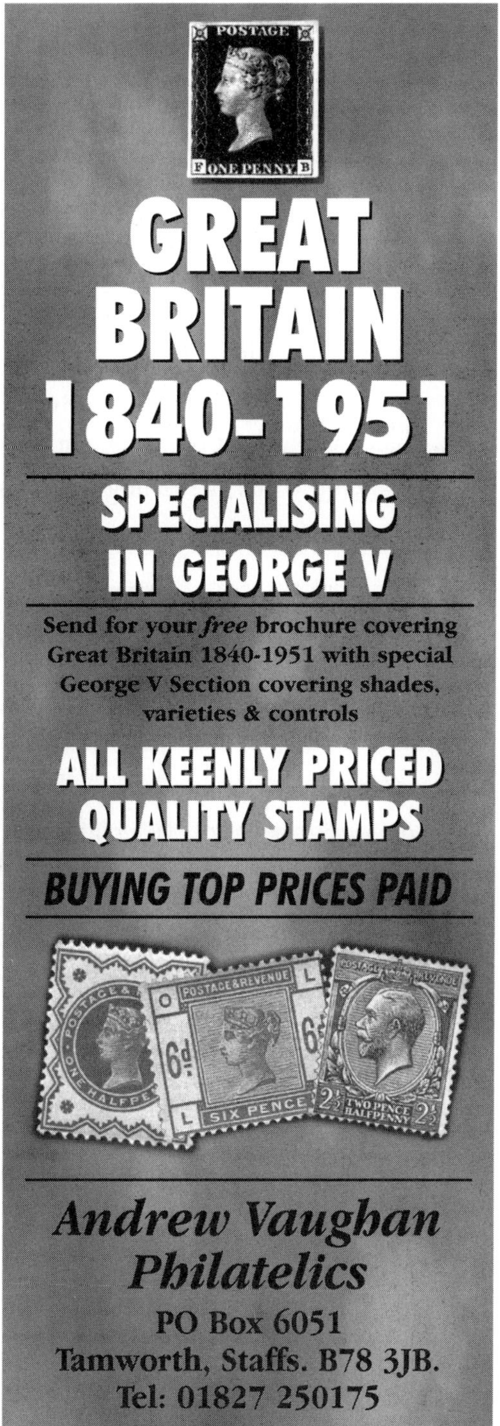

✦ POSTAL HISTORY

POSTAL HISTORY

GB Postal History, Counties/Subject, All periods to 1930s. Beginners/Advanced Collectors welcome. Established 1981.

David Shaw, 63 Millhey,
Haworth, Keighley, **Tel: 01535 645656**
Yorks., BD22 8NA **Fax:01535 645656**

Stanley Gibbons Publications
5 Parkside, Christchurch Road, Ringwood, Hants,
BH24 3SH, England..Tel: 01425 472362
Fax: 01425 470247
e-mail: sales@stangib.demon.co.uk

✦ POSTAL STATIONERY

ANDREW A WHITWORTH

Price List FREE for 9" x 6 1/2" SAE, stamped for 250g.
I BUY any quantity clean GB and overprints mint pre-1967 and used pre-1927.

1 Prizet House,
Kendal, Cumbria,
LA8 8AB **Tel: 015395 60848**

Stanley Gibbons Publications
5 Parkside, Christchurch Road, Ringwood, Hants,
BH24 3SH, England..Tel: 01425 472362
Fax: 01425 470247
e-mail: sales@stangib.demon.co.uk

✦ QUEEN VICTORIA

D. Forbes-Smith
12 Christmas Steps, Bristol, BS99 7LZ, UK...Tel: 0117 929 2677
Fax: 0117 922 1882

ERIC PAUL

Publishers of the Essential Guide to the Line Engraved 1840 to 1864 1d & 2d Stars by Kenneth Statham AND A Comprehensive GB Price list.

PO Box 44, Marple **Tel: 0161 427 2101**
SK6 7EE **Fax: 0161 427 6386**

Malcolm Sprei - M&S Stamps
Stamp Centre, 79 Strand, London,WC2R 0DE, UK
....Tel: 0171 240 3778
Fax: 0171 240 5419

MG STAMPS ***Members of the PTS***

For Victorian GB, send wants lists from basic to scarcer items including stamps/covers/illustrated envelopes etc.
We urgently need to buy the above. Please contact:

Guy Kent
PO Box 11602
London E11 2XE **Tel: 0181 989 1628**

Richard Allan Postal Auction
Stamp Centre, 79 Strand, London, WC2R 0DE, UK
....Tel: 0171 379 5439
Fax: 0171 240 5419

Royale Stamp Company
110 St. Martins Lane, London, WC2N 4AZ, UK
....Tel: 0171 240 1963
Fax: 0171 240 5419

Stanley Gibbons Publications
5 Parkside, Christchurch Road, Ringwood, Hants,
BH24 3SH, England..Tel: 01425 472362
Fax: 01425 470247
e-mail: sales@stangib.demon.co.uk

Steven Scott
Stamp Centre, 79 Strand, London, WC2R 0DE, UK
....Tel: 0171 836 2341
Fax: 0171 240 5419

UNITED KINGDOM OF GREAT BRITAIN AND IRELAND

QUEEN VICTORIA

20 June 1837-22 January 1901

MULREADY ENVELOPES AND LETTER SHEETS, so called from the name of the designer, William Mulready, were issued concurrently with the first British adhesive stamps.

1d. black

Envelopes: ...... £140 *unused*; £210 *used*.
Letter Sheets: ... £125 *unused*; £190 *used*.

2d. blue

Envelopes: ...... £210 *unused*; £625 *used*.
Letter Sheets: ... £200 *unused*; £600 *used*.

LINE-ENGRAVED ISSUES

GENERAL NOTES

Brief notes on some aspects of the line-engraved stamps follow, but for further information and a full specialist treatment of these issues collectors are recommended to consult Volume 1 of the Stanley Gibbons *Great Britain Specialised Catalogue*.

Alphabet I

Alphabet II

Alphabet III

Alphabet IV

Typical Corner Letters of the four Alphabets

Alphabets. Four different styles were used for the corner letters on stamps prior to the issue with letters in all four corners, these being known to collectors as:

Alphabet I. Used for all plates made from 1840 to the end of 1851. Letters small.

Alphabet II. Plates from 1852 to mid-1855. Letters larger, heavier and broader.

Alphabet III. Plates from mid-1855 to end of period. Letters tall and more slender.

Alphabet IV. 1861. 1d. Die II, Plates 50 and 51 only. Letters were hand-engraved instead of being punched on the plate. They are therefore inconsistent in shape and size but generally larger and outstanding.

While the general descriptions and the illustrations of typical letters given above may be of some assistance, only long experience and published aids can enable every stamp to be allocated to its particular Alphabet without hesitation, as certain letters in each are similar to those in one of the others.

Blued Paper. The blueing of the paper of the earlier issues is believed to be due to the presence of prussiate of potash in the printing ink, or in the paper, which, under certain conditions, tended to colour the paper when the sheets were damped for printing. An alternative term is bleuté paper.

Corner Letters. The corner letters on the early British stamps were intended as a safeguard against forgery, each stamp in the sheet having a different combination of letters. Taking the first 1d. stamp, printed in 20 horizontal rows of 12, as an example, the lettering is as follows:

Row 1. A A, A B, A C, etc. to A L.

Row 2. B A, B B, B C, etc. to B L.

and so on to

Row 20. T A, T B, T C, etc. to T L.

On the stamps with four corner letters, those in the upper corners are in the reverse positions to those in the lower corners. Thus in a sheet of 240 (12 × 20) the sequence is:

Row 1.	A A A A	B A A B	C A A C	etc. to	L A A L
Row 2.	A B B A	B B B B	C B B C	etc. to	L B B L
	and so on to				
Row 20.	A T T A	B T T B	C T T C	etc. to	L T T L

Placing letters in all four corners was not only an added precaution against forgery but was meant to deter unmarked parts of used stamps being pieced together and passed off as an unused whole.

Dies. The first die of the 1d. was used for making the original die of the 2d., both the No Lines and White Lines issues. In 1855 the 1d. Die I was amended by retouching the head and deepening the lines on a transferred impression of the original. This later version, known to collectors as Die II, was used for making the dies for the 1d. and 2d. with letters in all four corners and also for the $1\frac{1}{2}$d.

The two dies are illustrated above No. 17 in the catalogue.

Double letter

Guide line in corner

Guide line through value

Double Corner Letters. These are due to the workman placing his letter-punch in the wrong position at the first attempt, when lettering the plate, and then correcting the mistake; or to a slight shifting of the punch when struck. If a wrong letter was struck in the first instance, traces of a wrong letter may appear in a corner in addition to the correct one. A typical example is illustrated.

Guide Lines and Dots. When laying down the impressions of the design on the early plates, fine vertical and horizontal guide lines were marked on the plates to assist the operative. These were usually removed from the gutter margins, but could not be removed from the stamp impression without damage to the plate, so that in such cases they appear on the printed stamps, sometimes in the corners, sometimes through "POSTAGE" or the value. Typical examples are illustrated.

Guide dots or cuts were similarly made to indicate the spacing of the guide lines. These too sometimes appear on the stamps.

Ivory Head

"Ivory Head". The so-called "ivory head" variety is one in which the Queen's Head shows white on the back of the stamp. It arises from the comparative absence of ink in the head portion of the design, with consequent absence of blueing. (*See* "Blued Paper", on page 1).

Line-engraving. In this context "line-engraved" is synonymous with recess-printing, in which the engraver cuts recesses in a plate and printing (the coloured areas) is from these recesses. "Line-engraved" is the traditional philatelic description for these stamps; other equivalent terms found are "engraving in *taille-douce*" (French) or "in *intaglio*" (Italian).

Plates. Until the introduction of the stamps with letters in all four corners, the number of the plate was not indicated in the design of the stamp, but was printed on the sheet margin. By long study of identifiable blocks and the minor variation in the design, coupled with the position of the corner letters, philatelists are now able to allot many of these stamps to their respective plates. Specialist collectors often endeavour to obtain examples of a given stamp printed from its different plates and our catalogue accordingly reflects this depth of detail.

Maltese Cross

Type of Town postmark

Type of Penny Post cancellation

Example of 1844 type postmark

Postmarks. The so-called "Maltese Cross" design was the first employed for obliterating British postage stamps and was in use from 1840 to 1844. Being hand-cut, the obliterating stamps varied greatly in detail and some distinctive types can be allotted to particular towns or offices. Local types, such as those used at Manchester, Norwich, Leeds, etc., are keenly sought. A red ink was first employed, but was superseded by black, after some earlier experiments, in February 1841. Maltese Cross obliterations in other colours are rare.

Obliterations of this type, numbered 1 to 12 in the centre, were used at the London Chief Office in 1843 and 1844.

Some straight-line cancellations were in use in 1840 at the Penny Post receiving offices, normally applied on the envelope, the adhesives then being obliterated at the Head Office. They are nevertheless known, with or without Maltese Cross, on the early postage stamps.

In 1842 some offices in S.W. England used dated postmarks in place of the Maltese Cross, usually on the back of the letter since they were not originally intended as obliterators. These town postmarks have likewise been found on adhesives.

In 1844 the Maltese Cross design was superseded by numbered obliterators of varied type, one of which is illustrated. They are naturally comparatively scarce on the first 1d. and 2d. stamps. Like the Maltese Cross they are found in various colours, some of which are rare.

Re-entry

"Union Jack" re-entry

Re-entries. Re-entries on the plate show as a doubling of part of the design of the stamp generally at top or bottom. Many re-entries are very slight while others are most marked. A typical one is illustrated.

The *"Union Jack" re-entry*, so-called owing to the effect of the re-entry on the appearance of the corner stars (*see illustration*) occurs on stamp L K of Plate 75 of the 1d. red, Die I.

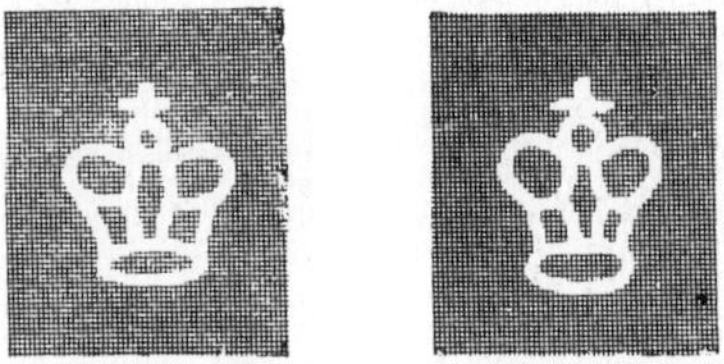

T A (T L) M A (M L)

Varieties of Large Crown Watermark

I Two states of Large Crown Watermark II

Watermarks. Two watermark varieties, as illustrated, consisting of crowns of entirely different shape, are found in sheets of the Large Crown paper and fall on stamps lettered M A and T A (or M L and T L when the paper is printed on the wrong side). Both varieties are found on the 1d. rose-red of 1857, while the M A (M L) variety comes also on some plates of the 1d. of 1864 (Nos. 43, 44) up to about Plate 96. On the 2d. the T A (T L) variety is known on plates 8 and 9, and the M A (M L) on later prints of plate 9. These varieties may exist inverted, or inverted reversed on stamps lettered A A and A L and H A and H L, and some are known.

In 1861 a minor alteration was made in the Large Crown watermark by the removal of the two vertical strokes, representing *fleurs-de-lis*, which projected upwards from the uppermost of the three horizontal curves at the base of the Crown. Hence two states are distinguishable, as illustrated.

CONDITION—IMPERFORATE LINE-ENGRAVED ISSUES

The prices quoted for the 1840 and 1841 imperforate Line-engraved issues are for "fine" examples. As condition is most important in assessing the value of a stamp, the following definitions will assist collectors in the evaluation of individual examples.

Four main factors are relevant when considering quality.

(a) **Impression.** This should be clean and the surface free of any rubbing or unnatural blurring which would detract from the appearance.

(b) **Margins.** This is perhaps the most difficult factor to evaluate. Stamps described as "fine", the standard adopted in this catalogue for pricing purposes, should have margins of the recognised width, defined as approximately one half of the distance between two adjoining unsevered stamps. Stamps described as "very fine" or "superb" should have margins which are proportionately larger than those of a "fine" stamp. Examples with close margins should not, generally, be classified as "fine".

(c) **Cancellation.** On a "fine" stamp this should be reasonably clear and not noticeably smudged. A stamp described as "superb" should have a neat cancellation, preferably centrally placed or to the right.

(d) **Appearance.** Stamps, at the prices quoted, should always be without any tears, creases, bends or thins and should not be toned on either the front or back. Stamps with such defects are worth only a proportion of the catalogue price.

Good

Fine

Very Fine

Superb

The actual size illustrations of 1840 1d. blacks show the various grades of quality. When comparing these illustrations it should be assumed that they are all from the same plate and that they are free of any hidden defects.

PRINTERS. Nos. 1/53*a* were recess-printed by Perkins, Bacon & Petch, known from 1852 as Perkins, Bacon & Co.

STAMPS ON COVER. Prices are quoted, for those Victorian and Edwardian issues usually found used on cover. In general these prices refer to the cheapest versions of each basic stamp with other shades, plates or varieties, together with unusual frankings and postmarks, being worth more.

1

1*a*

2 Small Crown

(Eng Charles and Frederick Heath)

1840 (6–8 May). *Letters in lower corners. Wmk Small Crown, W* **2**. *Imperf.*

				Un	Used	Used on cover
1	**1**	1d.	intense black	£3500	£225	
2		1d.	black	£3000	£160	£275
		Wi.	Watermark inverted	£3750	£450	
3		1d.	grey-black (worn plate)	£3000	£225	
4	**1***a*	2d.	dp full blue (8.5.40)	£7000	£400	
5		2d.	blue	£5500	£325	£750
		Wi.	Watermark inverted	£7000	£750	
6		2d.	pale blue	£7000	£375	

The 1d. stamp in black was printed from Plates 1 to 11. Plate 1 exists in two states (known to collectors as 1a and 1*b*), the latter being the result of extensive repairs.

Repairs were also made to plates 2, 5, 6, 8, 9, 10 and 11, and certain impressions exist in two or more states.

The so-called "Royal reprint" of the 1d. black was made in 1864, from Plate 66, Die II, on paper with Large Crown watermark, inverted. A printing was also made in carmine, on paper with the same watermark, normal.

For 1d. black with "VR" in upper corners *see* No. V1 under Official Stamps.

The 2d. stamps were printed from Plates 1 and 2.

Plates of 1d. black

Plate	*Un*	*Used*	*Used on cover*
1*a*	£4500	£180	£325
1*b*	£3000	£160	£275
2	£3000	£160	£275
3	£3500	£190	£350
4	£3000	£175	£300
5	£3000	£175	£300
6	£3000	£175	£300
7	£3250	£200	£350
8	£3500	£225	£375
9	£4000	£275	£425
10	£4500	£350	£650
11	£4500	£1600	£3250

Varieties of 1d. black

		Un	Used
a.	On *bleuté* paper (Plates 1 to 8) . . . *from*	—	£250
b.	Double letter in corner . . . *from*	£3000	£200
bb.	Re-entry . . . *from*	£3250	£225
bc.	"PB" re-entry (Plate 5, 3rd state)	—	£4000
c.	Guide line in corner	£3000	£200
cc.	Large letters in each corner (E J, I L, J C and P A) (Plate 1*b*) . . . *from*	£3500	£350
d.	Guide line through value	£3000	£200
g.	Obliterated by Maltese Cross		
	In red	—	£175
	In black	—	£160
	In blue	—	£2000
	In magenta	—	£700
	In yellow	—	—
h.	Obliterated by Maltese Cross with number in centre . . . *from*		
	No. 1	—	£2750
	No. 2	—	£1750
	No. 3	—	£1750
	No. 4	—	£1750
	No. 5	—	£1750
	No. 6	—	£1750
	No. 7	—	£1750
	No. 8	—	£1750
	No. 9	—	£1750
	No. 10	—	£1750
	No. 11	—	—
	No. 12	—	£1750
i.	Obliterated "Penny Post" in black . . . *from*	—	£1300
j.	Obliterated by town postmark (without Maltese Cross)		
	In black . . . *from*	—	£1300
	In yellow . . . *from*	—	£6000
	In red . . . *from*	—	£1400
k.	Obliterated by 1844 type postmark in black . . . *from*	—	£500

Plates of 2d. blue

Plate		Un	Used	Used on cover
1	*Shades from*	£5500	£325	£750
2	*Shades from*	£6500	£375	£750

Varieties of 2d. blue

		Un	Used
a.	Double letter in corner	—	£450
aa.	Re-entry	—	£500
b.	Guide line in corner	—	£400
c.	Guide line through value	—	£400
e.	Obliterated by Maltese Cross		
	In red	—	£350
	In black	—	£325
	In blue	—	£3000
	In magenta	—	£2500
f.	Obliterated by Maltese Cross with number in centre . . . *from*		
	No. 1	—	£2750
	No. 2	—	£2750
	No. 3	—	£2750
	No. 4	—	£2750
	No. 5	—	£2750
	No. 6	—	£3000
	No. 7	—	£2750
	No. 8	—	£2750
	No. 9	—	£3250
	No. 10	—	£3000
	No. 11	—	£3000
	No. 12	—	£2750
g.	Obliterated "Penny Post" in black . . . *from*	—	£1800
h.	Obliterated by town postmark (without Maltese Cross) in black . . . *from*	—	£1500
i.	Obliterated by 1844 type postmark		
	In black . . . *from*	—	£900
	In blue . . . *from*	—	£2500

1841 (10 Feb). *Printed from "black" plates. Wmk W* **2**. *Paper more or less blued. Imperf.*

			Un	Used	Used on cover
7	**1**	1d. red-brown (*shades*)	£500	50·00	90·00
		a. "PB" re-entry (Plate 5, 3rd state)	—	£1200	
		Wi. Watermark inverted (Plates 1b and 8)	—	£950	

The first printings of the 1d. in red-brown were made from Plates 1*b*, 2, 5 and 8 to 11 used for the 1d. black.

1d. red-brown from "black" plates

Plate	Un	Used	Used on cover
1*b*	£3000	£150	£275
2	£1750	£100	£175
5	£700	60·00	£110
8	£550	50·00	£100
9	£500	50·00	90·00
10	£525	50·00	£100
11	£550	50·00	90·00

1841 (late Feb). *Plate 12 onwards. Wmk W* **2**. *Paper more or less blued. Imperf.*

			Un	Used	Used on cover
8	**1**	1d. red-brown	£140	6·00	12·00
		Wi. Watermark inverted	£375	50·00	
8*a*		1d. red-brown on very blue paper	£160	6·00	
9		1d. pale red-brown (worn plates)	£225	15·00	
10		1d. deep red-brown	£160	8·00	
11		1d. lake-red	£650	£250	
12		1d. orange-brown	£300	50·00	

Error. No letter "A" in right lower corner (Stamp B (A), Plate 77)

			Un	Used
12a	**1**	1d. red-brown	—	£5000

The error "No letter A in right corner" was due to the omission to insert this letter on stamp B A of Plate 77. The error was discovered some months after the plate was registered and was then corrected.

There are innumerable variations in the colour shade of the 1d. "red" and those given in the above list represent colour groups each covering a wide range.

Varieties of 1d. red-brown, etc.

		Un	Used
b.	Re-entry . . . *from*	—	25·00
c.	Double letter in corner . . . *from*	—	16·00
d.	Double Star (Plate 75) "Union Jack" re-entry	—	£600
e.	Guide line in corner	—	9·00
f.	Guide line through value	—	15·00
g.	Thick outer frame to stamp	—	15·00
h.	Ivory head	£180	9·00
j.	Left corner letter "S" inverted (Plates 78, 105, 107) *from*	—	50·00
k.	P converted to R (Plates 30, 33, 83, 86) . . . *from*	—	40·00
l.	Obliterated by Maltese Cross		
	In red	—	£1100
	In black	—	15·00
	In blue	—	£160
m.	Obliterated by Maltese Cross with number in centre		
	No. 1	—	38·00
	No. 2	—	38·00
	No. 3	—	55·00
	No. 4	—	£130

	No. 5	—	38·00
	No. 6	—	32·00
	No. 7	—	30·00
	No. 8	—	28·00
	No. 9	—	35·00
	No. 10	—	55·00
	No. 11	—	65·00
	No. 12	—	80·00
n.	Obliterated "Penny Post" in black	—	£225
o.	Obliterated by town postmark (without Maltese Cross)		
	In black .... *from*	—	£150
	In blue .... *from*	—	£275
	In green .... *from*	—	£450
	In yellow .... *from*	—	—
	In red .... *from*	—	£2000
p.	Obliterated by 1844 type postmark		
	In blue .... *from*	—	40·00
	In red .... *from*	—	£950
	In green .... *from*	—	£250
	In violet .... *from*	—	£550
	In black .... *from*	—	6·00

Stamps with thick outer frame to the design are from plates on which the frame-lines have been straightened or recut, particularly Plates 76 and 90.

For "Union Jack" re-entry *see* General Notes to Line-engraved Issues.

In "P converted to R" the corner letter "R" is formed from the "P", the distinctive long tail having been hand-cut.

KEY TO LINE-ENGRAVED ISSUES

S.G. Nos.	*Description*	*Date*	*Wmk*	*Perf*	*Die*	*Alpha-bet*
	THE IMPERFORATE ISSUES					
1/3	1d. black	6.5.40	SC	Imp	I	I
4/6	2d. no lines	8.5.40	SC	Imp	I	I
	PAPER MORE OR LESS BLUED					
7	1d. red-brown	Feb 1841	SC	Imp	I	I
8/12	1d. red-brown	Feb 1841	SC	Imp	I	I
8/12	1d. red-brown	6.2.52	SC	Imp	I	II
13/15	2d. white lines	13.3.41	SC	Imp	I	I
	THE PERFORATED ISSUES					
	ONE PENNY VALUE					
16*a*	1d. red-brown	1848	SC	Roul	I	I
16*b*	1d. red-brown	1850	SC	16	I	I
16*c*	1d. red-brown	1853	SC	16	I	II
16*d*	1d. red-brown	1854	SC	14	I	I
17/18	1d. red-brown	Feb 1854	SC	16	I	II
22	1d. red-brown	Jan 1855	SC	14	I	II
24/5	1d. red-brown	28.2.55	SC	14	II	II
21	1d. red-brown	1.3.55	SC	16	II	II
26	1d. red-brown	15.5.55	LC	16	II	II
29/33	1d. red-brown	Aug 1855	LC	14	II	III
	NEW COLOURS ON WHITE PAPER					
37/41	1d. rose-red	Nov 1856	LC	14	II	III
36	1d. rose-red	26.12.57	LC	16	II	III
42	1d. rose-red	1861	LC	14	II	IV
	TWO PENCE VALUE					
19, 20	2d. blue	1.3.54	SC	16	I	I
23	2d. blue	22.2.55	SC	14	I	I
23a	2d. blue	5.7.55	SC	14	I	II
20a	2d. blue	18.8.55	SC	16	I	II
27	2d. blue	20.7.55	LC	16	I	II
34	2d. blue	20.7.55	LC	14	I	II
35	2d. blue	2.7.57	LC	14	I	III
36*a*	2d. blue	1.2.58	LC	16	I	III
	LETTERS IN ALL FOUR CORNERS					
48/9	½d. rose-red	1.10.70	W **9**	14		—
43/4	1d. rose-red	1.4.64	LC	14		II
53*a*	1½d. rosy mauve	1860	LC	14		II
51/3	1½d. rose-red	1.10.70	LC	14		II
45	2d. blue	July 1858	LC	14		II
46/7	2d. thinner lines	7.7.69	LC	14		II

Watermarks: SC = Small Crown, T **2**. LC = Large Crown, T **4**.
Dies: See notes above No. 17 in the catalogue.
Alphabets: See General Notes to this section.

3 White lines added

1841 (13 Mar)–**51**. *White lines added. Wmk W* **2**. *Paper more or less blued. Imperf.*

			Un	*Used*	*Used on cover*
13	**3**	2d. pale blue	£1500	60·00	
14		2d. blue	£1200	50·00	£200
		Wi. Watermark inverted	£2500	£300	
15		2d. dp full blue	£1600	65·00	
15*aa*		2d. violet-blue (1851)	£7500	£600	

The 2d. stamp with white lines was printed from Plates 3 and 4.

No. 15*aa* came from Plate 4 and the quoted price is for examples on thicker, lavender tinted paper.

Plates of 2d. blue

Plate		*Un*	*Used*
3	................*Shades from*	£1200	55·00
4	................*Shades from*	£1400	50·00

Varieties of 2d. blue

		Un	*Used*
a.	Guide line in corner	—	50·00
b.	Guide line through value	£1600	50·00
bb.	Double letter in corner	—	55·00
be.	Re-entry	£1900	70·00
c.	Ivory head	£1700	50·00
e.	Obliterated by Maltese Cross		
	In red	—	£5000
	In black	—	70·00
	In blue	—	£1200
f.	Obliterated by Maltese Cross with number in centre		
	No. 1	—	£200
	No. 2	—	£200
	No. 3	—	£200
	No. 4	—	£190
	No. 5	—	£275
	No. 6	—	£200
	No. 7	—	£375
	No. 8	—	£275
	No. 9	—	£375
	No. 10	—	£425
	No. 11	—	£275
	No. 12	—	£150
g.	Obliterated by town postmark (without Maltese Cross)		
	In black .... *from*	—	£450
	In blue .... *from*	—	£800

h. Obliterated by 1844 type postmark
In black .... *from* — 50·00
In blue .... *from* — £375
In red .... *from* — £4500
In green .... *from* — £700

1841 (Apr). *Trial printing (unissued) on Dickinson silk-thread paper without wmk. Imperf.*
16 **1** 1d. red-brown (Plate 11) £2000

Eight sheets were printed on this paper, six being gummed, two ungummed, but we have only seen examples without gum.

1848. *Wmk W* **2**. *Rouletted approx* $11\frac{1}{2}$ *by Henry Archer.*
16*a* **1** 1d. red-brown (Plates 70, 71) £4000

1850. *Wmk W* **2**. *P* 16 *by Henry Archer.*
16*b* **1** 1d. red-brown (Alph 1) (from Plates 90–101) *from* £600 £200
*b*Wi. Watermark inverted .... — £375

1853. *Wmk W* **2**. *Government Trial Perforations.*
16*c* **1** 1d. red-brown (*p* 16) (Alph II) (*on cover*) ...... † £5000
16*d* 1d. red-brown (*p* 14) (Alph I) £4000

SEPARATION TRIALS. Although the various trials of machines for rouletting and perforating were unofficial, Archer had the consent of the authorities in making his experiments, and sheets so experimented upon were afterwards used by the Post Office.

As Archer ended his experiments in 1850 and plates with corner letters of Alphabet II did not come into issue until 1852, perforated stamps with corner letters of Alphabet I may safely be assumed to be Archer productions, if genuine.

The Government trial perforations were done on Napier machines in 1853. As Alphabet II was by that time in use, the trials can be distinguished from the perforated stamps listed below by being dated prior to 28 January 1854, the date when the perforated stamps were officially issued.

Die I

Die II

4 Large Crown

Die I: The features of the portrait are lightly shaded and consequently lack emphasis.

Die II (Die I retouched): The lines of the features have been deepened and appear stronger.

The eye is deeply shaded and made more lifelike. The nostril and lips are more clearly defined, the latter appearing much thicker. A strong downward stroke of colour marks the corner of the mouth. There is a deep indentation of colour between lower lip and chin. The band running from the back of the ear to the chignon has a bolder horizontal line below it than in Die I.

1854–57. *Paper more or less blued. (a) Wmk Small Crown, W* **2**. *P* 16.

			Un	*Used*	★ *Used on cover*
17	**1**	1d. red-brown (Die I) (2.54)	£150	7·00	15·00
		a. Imperf three sides (horiz pair)	†	—	
		Wi. Watermark inverted	—	40·00	
18	**1**	1d. yellow-brown (Die I)	£240	18·00	
19	**3**	2d. dp blue (Plate 4) (1.3.54)	£1600	50·00	75·00
		a. Imperf three sides (horiz pair)	†	—	
		Wi. Watermark inverted	—	£110	
20		2d. pale blue (Plate 4)	£1600	60·00	
20*a*		2d. blue (Plate 5) (18.8.55)	£2100	£160	£275
		*a*Wi. Watermark inverted	£2250	£325	
21	**1**	1d. red-brown (Die II) (22.2.55)	£225	25·00	40·00
		a. Imperf (Plates 2, 14)			
		Wi. Watermark inverted	£500	75·00	
		(b) Wmk Small Crown, W **2**. *P* 14			
22	**1**	1d. red-brown (Die I) (1.55)	£350	30·00	50·00
		Wi. Watermark inverted	—	95·00	
23	**3**	2d. blue (Plate 4) (22.2.55)	£2100	£140	£200
		Wi. Watermark inverted	—	£250	
23*a*		2d. blue (Plate 5) (5.7.55)	£2100	£140	£175
		b. Imperf (Plate 5)			
		*a*Wi. Watermark inverted	—	£275	
24	**1**	1d red-brown (Die II) (27.2.55)	£290	25·00	35·00
		Wi. Watermark inverted	£450	55·00	
24*a*		1d. dp red-brown (very blue paper) (Die II)	£340	28·00	
25		1d. orange-brown (Die II)	£750	55·00	
		(c) Wmk Large Crown, W **4**. *P* 16			
26	**1**	1d. red-brown (Die II) (15.5.55)	£600	45·00	70·00
		a. Imperf (Plate 7)			
		Wi. Watermark inverted	—	£110	
27	**3**	2d. blue (Plate 5) (20.7.55)	£2600	£160	£275
		a. Imperf	—	£2800	
		Wi. Watermark inverted	—	£350	
		(d) Wmk Large Crown, W **4**. *P* 14.			
29	**1**	1d. red-brown (Die II) (6.55)	£140	5·00	15·00
		a. Imperf (*shades*) (Plates 22, 24, 25, 32, 43)	£1100	£900	
		Wi. Watermark inverted	£450	25·00	
30		1d. brick-red (Die II)	£225	20·00	
31		1d. plum (Die II) (2.56)	£1000	£325	
32		1d. brown-rose (Die II)	£225	22·00	
33		1d. orange-brown (Die II) (3.57)	£340	28·00	
34	**3**	2d. blue (Plate 5) (20.7.55)	£1300	40·00	£100
		Wi. Watermark inverted	—	£120	
35		2d. blue (Plate 6) (2.7.57)	£1400	40·00	90·00
		a. Imperf	—	£3250	
		b. Imperf horiz (vert pair)	†	—	
		Wi. Watermark inverted	—	95·00	
★17/35a		**For well-centred, lightly used**	**+125%**		

1856–58. *Paper no longer blued. (a) Wmk Large Crown, W* **4**. *P* 16.

36	**1**	1d. rose-red (Die II) (26.12.57)	£750	35·00	60·00
36*a*	**3**	2d. blue (Plate 6) (1.2.58)	£3750	£160	£250
		*a*Wi. Watermark inverted	—	£375	
		(b) (Die II) Wmk Large Crown, W **4**. *P* 14			
37	**1**	1d. red-brown (11.56)	£325	70·00	
38		1d. pale red (9.4.57)	40·00	5·00	
		a. Imperf	£600	£500	
39		1d. pale rose (3.57)	45·00	10·00	
40		1d. rose-red (9.57)	28·00	5·00	8·00
		a. Imperf	£650	£500	
		Wi. Watermark inverted	50·00	35·00	
41		1d. dp rose-red (7.57)	50·00	6·00	

1861. *Letters engraved on plate instead of punched (Alphabet IV).*

42	**1**	1d rose-red (Die II) (Plates 50 & 51)	£160	20·00	35·00
		a. Imperf	—	£2000	
		Wi. Watermark inverted	£250	30·00	
★36/42a		**For well-centred, lightly used**	**+125%**		

The original die (Die I) was used to provide roller dies for the laying down of all the line-engraved stamps from 1840 to 1855. In that year a new master die was laid down (by means of a Die I roller die) and the

impression was retouched by hand engraving by William Humphrys. This retouched die, always known to philatelists as Die II, was from that time used for preparing all new roller dies.

One Penny. The numbering of the 1d. plates recommenced at 1 on the introduction of Die II. Plates 1 to 21 were Alphabet II from which a scarce plum shade exists. Corner letters of Alphabet III appear on Plate 22 and onwards.

As an experiment, the corner letters were engraved by hand on Plates 50 and 51 in 1856, instead of being punched (Alphabet IV), but punching was again resorted to from Plate 52 onwards. Plates 50 and 51 were not put into use until 1861.

Two Pence. Unlike the 1d. the old sequence of plate numbers continued. Plates 3 and 4 of the 2d. had corner letters of Alphabet I, Plate 5 Alphabet II and Plate 6 Alphabet III. In Plate 6 the white lines are thinner than before.

In both values, varieties may be found as described in the preceding issues—ivory heads, inverted watermarks, re-entries, and double letters in corners.

The change of perforation from 16 to 14 was decided upon late in 1854 since the closer holes of the former gauge tended to cause the sheets of stamps to break up when handled, but for a time both gauges were in concurrent use. Owing to faulty alignment of the impressions on the plates and to shrinkage of the paper when dampened, badly perforated stamps are plentiful in the line-engraved issues.

5

6

Showing position of the plate number on the 1d. and 2d. values. (Plate 170 shown)

1858–79. *Letters in all four corners. Wmk Large Crown, W* **4**. *Die II (1d. and 2d.). P 14.*

			Un	*Used*	★ *Used on cover*
43	**5**	1d. rose-red (1.4.64)	5·00	1·50	4·00
44		1d. lake-red	5·00	1·50	
		a. Imperf *from*	£800	£625	
		Wi. Watermark inverted *from*	30·00	8·00	
★43/4a		**For well-centred, lightly used**	**+125%**		

Plate	*Un*	*Used*
71	15·00	2·25
72	20·00	2·75
73	15·00	2·25
74	12·00	1·50
76	22·00	1·50
77	£100000	£80000
78	55·00	1·50
79	18·00	1·50
80	12·00	1·50
81	32·00	1·75
82	65·00	2·75
83	80·00	4·25
84	32·00	1·75
85	15·00	1·75
86	18·00	2·75
87	5·00	1·50
88	90·00	5·75
89	22·00	1·50
90	16·00	1·50
91	22·00	3·75
92	10·00	1·50
93	22·00	1·50
94	22·00	3·25
95	15·00	1·50
96	16·00	1·50
97	10·00	2·25
98	10·00	3·75
99	15·00	3·25
100	20·00	1·75
101	28·00	6·25
102	12·00	1·50
103	12·00	2·25
104	16·00	3·25
105	38·00	4·25
106	18·00	1·50
107	22·00	4·00
108	18·00	1·75
109	40·00	2·25
110	12·00	6·25
111	20·00	1·75
112	32·00	1·75
113	10·00	8·00
114	£190	8·50
115	55·00	1·75
116	40·00	6·25
117	10·00	1·50
118	15·00	1·50
119	8·00	1·50
120	5·00	1·50
121	22·00	6·25
122	5·00	1·50
123	8·00	1·50
124	8·00	1·50
125	8·00	1·75
127	20·00	1·75
129	8·00	5·25
130	12·00	1·75
131	40·00	12·00
132	55·00	17·00
133	50·00	6·25
134	5·00	1·50
135	55·00	21·00
136	55·00	16·00
137	10·00	1·75
138	8·00	1·50
139	18·00	12·00
140	8·00	1·50
141	80·00	6·25
142	28·00	19·00
143	18·00	11·00
144	55·00	16·00
145	5·00	1·75
146	8·00	3·75
147	12·00	2·25
148	12·00	2·25
149	10·00	3·75
150	5·00	1·50
151	15·00	6·25
152	12·00	3·50
153	40·00	6·25
154	10·00	1·50
155	10·00	1·75
156	10·00	1·50
157	10·00	1·50
158	5·00	1·50
159	5·00	1·50
160	5·00	1·50
161	18·00	4·25
162	10·00	4·25
163	10·00	2·25
164	10·00	2·25
165	12·00	1·50
166	10·00	3·75
167	8·00	1·50
168	8·00	5·75
169	18·00	4·25
170	8·00	1·50
171	5·00	1·50
172	5·00	1·50
173	28·00	6·25
174	5·00	1·50
175	20·00	2·25
176	15·00	1·75
177	8·00	1·50
178	10·00	2·25
179	10·00	1·75
180	10·00	3·25
181	10·00	1·50
182	55·00	3·25
183	15·00	2·25
184	5·00	1·75
185	10·00	2·25
186	18·00	1·75
187	8·00	1·50
188	12·00	7·50
189	20·00	4·25
190	10·00	3·75
191	5·00	4·25
192	15·00	1·50
193	5·00	1·50
194	10·00	5·25
195	10·00	5·25
196	8·00	3·25
197	10·00	6·25
198	6·00	3·75
199	12·00	3·75
200	12·00	1·50
201	5·00	3·25
202	10·00	5·25
203	5·00	11·00
204	8·00	1·75
205	8·00	2·25
206	8·00	6·25
207	8·00	6·25
208	8·00	11·00
209	10·00	6·25
210	12·00	8·50
211	25·00	16·00
212	10·00	8·00
213	10·00	8·00
214	15·00	14·00
215	15·00	14·00
216	15·00	14·00
217	12·00	4·25
218	8·00	5·25
219	32·00	55·00
220	5·00	4·25
221	18·00	11·00
222	28·00	27·00
223	32·00	45·00
224	38·00	38·00
225	£1100	£375

Error. Imperf. Issued at Cardiff (Plate 116)

			Un	*Used*
44*b*	**5**	1d. rose-red (18.1.70)	£2000	£1250

The following plate numbers are also known imperf and used (No. 44a); 72, 79, 80, 81, 82, 83, 84, 85, 86, 87, 88, 90, 91, 92, 93, 96, 97, 100, 101, 102, 103, 104, 105, 107, 108, 109, 112, 113, 114, 116, 117, 120, 121, 122, 136, 137, 142, 146, 148, 158, 162, 164, 166, 171, 174, 191 and 202.

The numbering of this series of 1d. red plates follows after that of the previous 1d. stamp, last printed from Plate 68.

Plates 69, 70, 75, 126 and 128 were prepared for this issue but rejected owing to defects, and stamps from these plates do not exist, so that specimens which appear to be from these plates (like many of those which optimistic collectors believe to be from Plate 77) bear other plate numbers. Owing to faulty engraving or printing it is not always easy to identify the plate number. Plate 77 was also rejected but some stamps printed from it were used. One specimen is in the Tapling Collection and six or seven others are known. Plates 226 to 228 were made but not used.

Specimens from most of the plates are known with inverted watermark. The variety of watermark described in the General Notes to this section occurs on stamp M A (or M L) on plates up to about 96 (*Prices from £110 used*).

Re-entries in this issue are few, the best being on stamps M K and T K of Plate 71 and on S L and T L, Plate 83.

			Un	*Used*	★ *Used on cover*
45	6	2d. blue (thick lines) (7.58)	£175	6·00	18·00
		a. Imperf (Plate 9)	—	£3250	
		Wi. Watermark inverted	£275	75·00	
		Plate			
		7	£450	25·00	
		8	£475	20·00	
		9	£175	6·00	
		12	£800	55·00	
46		2d. blue (thin lines) (1.7.69)	£180	10·00	20·00
		Wi. Watermark inverted	£225	50·00	
47		2d. dp blue (thin lines)	£175	10·00	
		a. Imperf (Plate 13)	£2250		
		Plate			
		13	£190	10·00	
		14	£225	12·00	
		15	£175	12·00	
★45/7		**For well-centred, lightly used**		+**125**%	

Plates 10 and 11 of the 2d. were prepared but rejected. Plates 13 to 15 were laid down from a new roller impression on which the white lines were thinner.

There are some marked re-entries and repairs, particularly on Plates 7, 8, 9 and 12.

Stamps with inverted watermark may be found and also the T A (T L) and M A (M L) watermark varieties (*see* General Notes to this section).

Though the paper is normally white, some printings showed blueing and stamps showing the "ivory head" may therefore be found.

7

Showing the plate number (9)

9

1870 (1 Oct). *Wmk W* **9**, *extending over three stamps. P* 14.

			Un	*Used*	★ *Used on cover*
48	7	½d. rose-red	55·00	10·00	30·00
49		½d. rose	55·00	10·00	
		a. Imperf (Plates 1, 4, 5, 6, 8, 14) *from*	£1000	£650	
		Wi. Watermark inverted	—	75·00	
		Wj. Watermark reversed	—	60·00	
(49)		Wk. Watermark inverted & reversed	£150	40·00	
		Plate			
		1	£110	50·00	
		3	65·00	18·00	
		4	80·00	12·00	
		5	60·00	10·00	
		6	55·00	10·00	
		8	£100	55·00	
		9	£2250	£350	
		10	80·00	10·00	
		11	55·00	10·00	
		12	55·00	10·00	
		13	55·00	10·00	
		14	55·00	10·00	
		15	65·00	15·00	
		19	£100	28·00	
		20	£110	40·00	
★48/9a		**For well-centred, lightly used**		+**200**%	

The ½d. was printed in sheets of 480 (24 × 20) so that the check letters run from AA/AA to XT/TX.

Plates 2, 7, 16, 17 and 18 were not completed while Plates 21 and 22, though made, were not used.

Owing to the method of perforating, the outer side of stamps in either the A or X row (ie the left or right side of the sheet) is imperf.

Stamps may be found with watermark inverted or reversed, or without watermark, the latter due to misplacement of the paper when printing.

8

Position of plate number

1870 (1 Oct). *Wmk W* **4**. *P* 14.

			Un	*Used*	★ *Used on cover*
51	8	1½d. rose-red	£200	28·00	£175
52		1½d. lake-red	£200	28·00	
		a. Imperf (Plates 1 & 3) *from*	£2000	†	
		Wi. Watermark inverted	—	£140	
		Plate			
		(1)	£400	45·00	
		3	£200	28·00	
		Error of lettering. OP–PC for CP–PC (Plate 1)			
53	8	1½d. rose-red	£4500	£675	
★51/3		**For well-centred, lightly used**		+**125**%	

1860. *Prepared for use but not issued; blued paper. Wmk W* **4**. *P* 14

			Un	*Used*
53*a*	8	1½d. rosy mauve (Plate 1)	£2000	
		b. Error of lettering, OP–PC for CP–PC		

Owing to a proposed change in the postal rates, 1½d. stamps were first printed in 1860, in rosy mauve, No. 53a, but the change was not approved and the greater part of the stock was destroyed.

In 1870 a 1½d. stamp was required and was issued in rose-red.

Plate 1 did not have the plate number in the design of the stamps but on stamps from Plate 3 the number will be found in the frame as shown above.

Plate 2 was defective and was not used.

The error of lettering OP–PC on Plate 1 was apparently not noticed by the printer, and therefore not corrected.

EMBOSSED ISSUES

Volume 1 of the Stanley Gibbons *Great Britian Specialised Catalogue* gives further detailed information on the embossed issues.

PRICES. The prices quoted are for cut-square stamps with average to fine embossing. Stamps with exceptionally clear embossing are worth more.

10

11

12

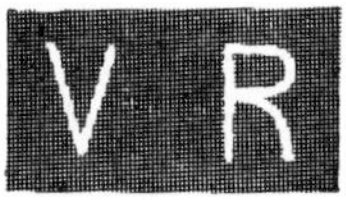

13

Position of die number

(Primary die engraved at the Royal Mint by William Wyon. Stamps printed at Somerset House)

1847–54. *Imperf* (For paper and wmk see footnote).

			Un	*Used*	*Used on cover*
54	**10**	1s. pale green (11.9.47)	£3250	£450	£550
55		1s. green	£3250	£500	
56		1s. dp green	£3750	£550	
		Die 1 (1847)	£3250	£450	
		Die 2 (1854)	£3750	£525	
57	**11**	10d. brown (6.11.48)	£2750	£675	£1100
		Die 1 (1848)	£3000	£725	
		Die 2 (1850)	£2750	£675	
		Die 3 (1853)	£2750	£675	
		Die 4 (1854)	£3000	£725	
		Die 5	£17000		
58	**12**	6d. mauve (1.3.54)	£3000	£525	
59		6d. dull lilac	£3000	£500	£600
60		6d. purple	£3000	£500	
		Wi. Watermark inverted	—	£500	
		Wj. Watermark reversed	£3000	£525	
		Wk. Watermark inverted & reversed	£3000	£500	
61		6d. violet	£4250	£950	

The 1s. and 10d. are on "Dickinson" paper with "silk" threads. The 6d. is on paper watermarked V R in single-lined letters, W **13**, which may be found in four ways—upright, inverted, upright reversed, and inverted reversed.

The die numbers are indicated on the base of the bust. Only Die 1 (1 W W) of the 6d. was used for the adhesive stamps. The 10d. is from Die 1 (W.W.1 on stamps), and Dies 2 to 5 (2W.W., 3W.W., 4W.W. and 5W.W.) but the number and letters on stamps from Die 1 are seldom clear and many specimens are known without any trace of them. Because of this the stamp we previously listed as "No die number" has been deleted. That they are from Die 1 is proved by the existence of blocks showing stamps with and without the die number. The 1s. is from Dies 1 and 2 (W.W.1, W.W.2).

The normal arrangement of the "silk" threads in the paper was in pairs running down each vertical row of the sheets, the space between the threads of each pair being approximately 5 mm and between pairs of threads 20 mm. Varieties due to misplacement of the paper in printing show a single thread on the first stamp from the sheet margin and two threads 20 mm apart on the other stamps of the row. Faulty manufacture is the cause of stamps with a single thread in the middle.

Through bad spacing of the impressions, which were handstruck, all values may be found with two impressions more or less overlapping. Owing to the small margin allowed for variation of spacing, specimens with good margins on all sides are not common.

Double impressions are known of all values.

Later printings of the 6d. had the gum tinted green to enable the printer to distinguish the gummed side of the paper.

SURFACE-PRINTED ISSUES

GENERAL NOTES

Volume 1 of the Stanley Gibbons *Great Britain Specialised Catalogue* gives further detailed information on the surface-printed issues.

"Abnormals". The majority of the great rarities in the surface-printed group of issues are the so-called "abnormals", whose existence is due to the practice of printing six sheets from every plate as soon as made, one of which was kept for record purposes at Somerset House, while the others were perforated and usually issued. If such plates were not used for general production or if, before they came into full use, a change of watermark or colour took place, the six sheets originally printed would differ from the main issue in plate, colour or watermark and, if issued would be extremely rare.

The abnormal stamps of this class listed in this Catalogue and distinguished, where not priced, by an asterisk (*) are:

No.	
78	3d. Plate 3 (with white dots)
152	4d. vermilion, Plate 16
153	4d. sage-green, Plate 17
109	6d. mauve, Plate 10
124/a	6d. pale chestnut & 6d. chestnut, Plate 12
145	6d. pale buff, Plate 13
88	9d. Plate 3 (hair lines)
98	9d. Plate 5 (see footnote to No. 98)
113	10d. Plate 2
91	1s. Plate 3 ("Plate 2")
148/50	1s. green, Plate 14
120	2s. blue, Plate 3

Those which may have been issued, but of which no specimens are known, are $2\frac{1}{2}$d. wmk Anchor, Plates 4 and 5; 3d. wmk Emblems, Plate 5; 3d. wmk Spray, Plate 21, 6d. grey, wmk Spray, Plate 18; 8d. orange, Plate 2; 1s. wmk Emblems, Plate 5; 5s. wmk Maltese Cross, Plate 4.

The 10d. Plate 1, wmk Emblems (No. 99), is sometimes reckoned among the abnormals, but was an error, due to the use of the wrong paper.

Corner Letters. With the exception of the 4d., 6d. and 1s. of 1855–57, the $\frac{1}{2}$d., $1\frac{1}{2}$d., 2d. and 5d. of 1880, the 1d. lilac of 1881 and the £5 (which had letters in lower corners only, and in the reverse order to the normal), all the surface-printed stamps issued prior to 1887 had letters in all four corners, as in the later line-engraved stamps. The arrangement is the same, the letters running in sequence right across and down the sheets, whether these were divided into panes or not. The corner letters existing naturally depend on the number of stamps in the sheet and their arrangement.

Imprimaturs and Imperforate Stamps. The Post Office retained in their records (now in the National Postal Museum) one imperforate sheet from each plate, known as the Imprimatur (or officially approved) sheet. Some stamps were removed from time to time for presentation purposes and have come on to the market, but these imperforates are not listed as they were not issued. Full details can be found in Volume 1 of the *Great Britain Specialised Catalogue*.

However, other imperforate stamps are known to have been issued and these are listed where it has been possible to prove that they do not come from the Imprimatur sheets. It is therefore advisable to purchase these only when accompanied by an Expert Committee certificate of genuineness.

Plate Numbers. All stamps from No. 75 to No. 163 bear in their designs either the plate number or, in one or two earlier instances, some other indication by which one plate can be distinguished from another. With the aid of these and of the corner letters it is thus possible to "reconstruct" a sheet of stamps from any plate of any issue or denomination.

Surface-printing. In this context the traditional designation "surface-printing" is synonymous with typo(graphy)—a philatelic term—or letterpress—the printers' term—as meaning printing from (the surface of) raised type. It is also called relief-printing, as the image is in relief (in French, *en épargne*), unwanted parts of the design having been cut away. Duplicate impressions can be electrotyped or stereotyped from an original die, the resulting *clichés* being locked together to form the printing plate.

Wing Margins. As the vertical gutters (spaces) between the panes, into which sheets of stamps of most values were divided until the introduction of the Imperial Crown watermark, were perforated through the centre with a single row of holes, instead of each vertical row of stamps on the inner side of the panes having its own line of perforation as is now usual, a proportion of the stamps in each sheet have what is called a "wing margin" about 5 mm wide on one or other side.

The stamps with "wing margins" are the watermark Emblems and Spray of Rose series (3d., 6d., 9d., 10d., 1s. and 2s.) with letters D, E, H or I in S.E. corner, and the watermark Garter series (4d. and 8d.) with letters F or G in S.E. corner. Knowledge of this lettering will enable collectors to guard against stamps with wing margin cut down and re-perforated, but note that wing margin stamps of Nos. 62 to 73 are also to be found re-perforated.

PRINTERS. The issues of Queen Victoria, Nos. 62/214, were typo by Thomas De La Rue & Co.

PERFORATIONS. All the surface-printed issues of Queen Victoria are perf 14, with the exception of Nos. 126/9.

14

15 Small Garter

16 Medium Garter

17 Large Garter

1855–57. *No corner letters.*

(a) *Wmk Small Garter, W* **15**. *Highly glazed, deeply blued paper* (31 July 1855)

			Un	*Used*	** Used on cover*
62	**14**	4d. carmine (*shades*)	£2500	£250	£350
		a. Paper slightly blued	£2750	£250	
		b. White paper	£3250	£425	
		Wi. Watermark inverted	—	£350	

(b) *Wmk Medium Garter, W* **16**

(i) *Thick, blued highly glazed paper* (25 February 1856)

63	**14**	4d. carmine (*shades*)	£3000	£250	£350
		a. White paper	£2750		
		Wi. Watermark inverted	—	£325	

(ii) *Ordinary thin white paper* (September 1856)

64	**14**	4d. pale carmine	£2000	£225	£300
		a. Stamp printed double	†	—	
		Wi. Watermark inverted	—	£250	

(iii) *Ordinary white paper, specially prepared ink* (1 November 1856)

65	**14**	4d. rose *or* dp rose	£2000	£225	£325

(c) *Wmk Large Garter, W* **17**. *Ordinary white paper* (January 1857)

66	**14**	4d. rose-carmine	£750	45·00	£110
		a. *Rose*	£650	45·00	
		aWi. Watermark inverted	—	90·00	
		aWj. Watermark inverted & reversed			
		b. Thick glazed paper	£1800	£150	
		bWi. Watermark inverted			
*62/6b		**For well-centred, lightly used**		**+125%**	

18

19

20 Emblems wmk (normal)

20*a* Watermark error, three roses and shamrock

20*b* Watermark error, three roses and thistle

(d) *Wmk Emblems, W* **20**

			Un	*Used*	** Used on cover*
69	**18**	6d. dp lilac (21.10.56)	£625	75·00	
70		6d. pale lilac	£550	55·00	£100
		a. Azure paper	£2750	£425	
		b. Thick paper	£750	£160	
		c. Error. Watermark W **20***a*			
		Wi. Watermark inverted	—	90·00	
		Wj. Watermark reversed			
		Wk. Watermark inverted & reversed			
71	**19**	1s. dp green (1.11.56)	£1400	£190	

72	**19**	1s. green	£700	£160	£190
73		1s. pale green	£700	£160	
		a. Azure paper	—	£575	
		b. Thick paper	—	£180	
		c. Imperf			
		Wi. Watermark inverted	—	£180	
		Wj. Watermark reversed	—	£700	
		Wk. Watermark inverted and reversed			
*69/73b		**For well-centred, lightly used**		+**125**%	

KEY TO SURFACE-PRINTED ISSUES 1855–83

S.G. Nos.	*Description*	*Watermark*	*Date of Issue*
	NO CORNER LETTERS		
62	4d. carmine	Small Garter	31.7.55
63/5	4d. carmine	Medium Garter	25.2.56
66/a	4d. carmine	Large Garter	Jan 1857
69/70	6d. lilac	Emblems	21.10.56
71/3	1s. green	Emblems	1.11.56
	SMALL WHITE CORNER LETTERS		
75/7	3d. carmine	Emblems	1.5.62
78	3d. carmine (dots)	Emblems	Aug 1862
79/82	4d. red	Large Garter	15.1.62
83/5	6d. lilac	Emblems	1.12.62
86/8	9d. bistre	Emblems	15.1.62
89/91	1s. green	Emblems	1.12.62
	LARGE WHITE CORNER LETTERS		
92	3d. rose	Emblems	1.3.65
102/3	3d. rose	Spray	July 1867
93/5	4d. vermilion	Large Garter	4.7.65
96/7	6d. lilac	Emblems	7.3.65
104/7	6d. lilac	Spray	21.6.67
108/9	6d. lilac	Spray	8.3.69
122/4	6d. chestnut	Spray	12.4.72
125	6d. grey	Spray	24.4.73
98	9d. straw	Emblems	30.10.65
110/11	9d. straw	Spray	3.10.67
99	10d. brown	Emblems	11.11.67
112/14	10d. brown	Spray	1.7.67
101	1s. green	Emblems	19.1.65
115/17	1s. green	Spray	13.7.67
118/20*b*	2s. blue	Spray	1.7.67
121	2s. brown	Spray	27.2.80
126/7	5s. rose	Cross	1.7.67
128	10s. grey	Cross	26.9.78
129	£1 brown-lilac	Cross	26.9.78
130, 134	5s. rose	Anchor	25.11.82
131, 135	10s. grey-green	Anchor	Feb 1883
132, 136	£1 brown-lilac	Anchor	Dec 1882
133, 137	£5 orange	Anchor	21.3.82
	LARGE COLOURED CORNER LETTERS		
138/9	$2\frac{1}{2}$d. rosy mauve	Anchor	1.7.75
141	$2\frac{1}{2}$d. rosy mauve	Orb	1.5.76
142	$2\frac{1}{2}$d. blue	Orb	5.2.80
157	$2\frac{1}{2}$d. blue	Crown	23.3.81
143/4	3d. rose	Spray	5.7.73
158	3d. rose	Crown	Jan 1881
159	3d. on 3d. lilac	Crown	1.1.83
152	4d. vermilion	Large Garter	1.3.76
153	4d. sage-green	Large Garter	12.3.77
154	4d. brown	Large Garter	15.8.80
160	4d. brown	Crown	9.12.80
145	6d. buff	Spray	15.3.73
146/7	6d. grey	Spray	20.3.74
161	6d. grey	Crown	1.1.81
162	6d. on 6d. lilac	Crown	1.1.83
156*a*	8d. purple-brown	Large Garter	July 1876
156	8d. orange	Large Garter	11.9.76
148/50	1s. green	Spray	1.9.73
151	1s. brown	Spray	14.10.80
163	1s. brown	Crown	24.5.81

Watermarks:		
	Anchor	W **40, 47**
	Cross	W **39**
	Crown	W **49**
	Emblems	W **20**
	Large Garter	W **17**
	Medium Garter	W **16**
	Orb	W **48**
	Small Garter	W **15**
	Spray	W **33**

21

22

23

24

25 Plate 2

A. White dots added

B. Hair lines

1862–64. *A small uncoloured letter in each corner, the 4d. wmk Large Garter, W* **17**, *the others Emblems, W* **20**.

			Un	*Used*	* *Used on cover*
75	**21**	3d. dp carmine-rose (Plate 2) (1.5.62)	£1500	£160	
76		3d. brt carmine-rose	£800	£140	£300
		Wi. Watermark inverted	—	£190	
77		3d. pale carmine-rose	£800	£160	
		b. Thick paper	—	£225	
		Wj. Watermark reversed			
78		3d. rose (with white dots, Type A, Plate 3) (8.62)	*	£2750	
		a. Imperf (Plate 3)	£2250		
79	**22**	4d. brt red (Plate 3) (15.1.62)	£850	65·00	
80		4d. pale red	£575	45·00	£110
		Wi. Watermark inverted	—	95·00	

81	**22**	4d. brt red (Hair lines, Type B, Plate 4) (16.10.63)	£750	50·00	
82		4d. pale red (Hair lines, Type B, Plate 4)	£650	40·00	£110
		a. Imperf (Plate 4)	£1750		
		Wi. Watermark inverted	—	80·00	
83	**23**	6d. dp lilac (Plate 3) (1.12.62)	£850	70·00	
84		6d. lilac	£725	45·00	90·00
		a. Azure paper	—	£350	
		b. Thick paper	—	80·00	
		c. Error. Watermark W **20***b* (stamp TF)			
		Wi. Watermark inverted	—	80·00	
		Wj. Watermark inverted and reversed			
85		6d. lilac (Hair lines, Plate 4) (20.4.64)	£850	90·00	£150
		a. Imperf (watermark inverted)	£1300		
		Eb. Imperf and watermark upright			
		c. Thick paper	£1300	£100	
		d. Error. Watermark **20***b* (stamp TF)			
		Wi. Watermark inverted	—	£100	
		Wj. Watermark inverted and reversed			
86	**24**	9d. bistre (Plate 2) (15.1.62)	£1500	£175	£300
		Wi. Watermark inverted	—	£200	
		Wj. Watermark reversed	—	£225	
87		9d. straw	£1500	£160	
		a. On azure paper			
		b. Thick paper	£2000	£275	
		c. Error. Watermark W **20***b* (TF)	†	—	
88		9d. bistre (Hair lines, Plate 3) (5.62)	£6500	£2250	
89	**25**	1s. dp green (Plate No. 1 = Plate 2) (1.12.62)	£1000	£140	
90		1s. green (Plate No. 1 = Plate 2)	£850	90·00	£175
		a. "K" in lower left corner in white circle (stamp KD)	£4500	£600	
		aa. "K" normal (stamp KD)	—	£850	
		b. On azure paper			
		c. Thick paper	—	£190	
		ca. Thick paper, "K" in circle as No. 90a	—	£1200	
		Wi. Watermark inverted	—	£120	
		Wj. Watermark reversed			
		Wk. Watermark inverted and reversed	—	£120	
91		1s. dp green (Plate No. 2 = Plate 3)	£12000		
		a. Imperf	£1750		
		aWi. Watermark inverted	£1100		
*75/91		**For well-centred, lightly used**	**+125%**		

The 3d. as Type **21**, but with network background in the spandrels which is found overprinted SPECIMEN, was never issued.

The plates of this issue may be distinguished as follows:

3d.	Plate 2	No white dots.
	Plate 3	White dots as Illustration A.
4d.	Plate 3	No hair lines. Roman I next to lower corner letters.
	Plate 4	Hair lines in corners. (Illustration B.). Roman II.
6d.	Plate 3	No hair lines.
	Plate 4	Hair lines in corners.
9d.	Plate 2	No hair lines.
	Plate 3	Hair lines in corners. Beware of faked lines.
1s.	Plate 2	Numbered 1 on stamps.
	Plate 3	Numbered 2 on stamps & with hair lines.

The 9d. on azure paper (No. 87a) is very rare, only one confirmed example being known.

The variety "K" in circle, No. 90a, is believed to be due to a damaged letter having been cut out and replaced. It is probable that the punch was driven in too deeply, causing the flange to penetrate the surface, producing an indentation showing as an uncoloured circle.

The watermark variety "three roses and a shamrock" illustrated in W **20***a* was evidently due to the substitution of an extra rose for the thistle in a faulty watermark bit. It is found on stamp TA of Plate 4 of the 3d., Plates 1 (No. 70c), 3, 5 and 6 of the 6d., Plate 4 of the 9d. and Plate 4 of the 1s.

A similar variety, W **20***b*, but showing three roses and a thistle is found on stamp T F of the 6d. (Nos. 84/5) and 9d. (Nos. 87, 97/8).

26

27

28
(with hyphen)

28*a*
(without hyphen)

29

30

31

1865–67. *Large uncoloured corner letters. Wmk Large Garter (4d.); others Emblems.*

			Un	Used	* Used on cover
92	**26**	3d. rose (Plate 4) (1.3.65)	£500	55·00	£125
		a. Error. Watermark W **20***a*	£1100	£325	
		b. Thick paper	£600	65·00	
		Wi. Watermark inverted	—	£100	
		Wj. Watermark reversed			
		Wk. Watermark inverted and reversed			
93	**27**	4d. dull vermilion (4.7.65)	£275	30·00	70·00
94		4d. vermilion	£275	30·00	
		a. Imperf (Plates 11, 12)	£575		
		Wi. Watermark inverted	£250	26·00	
95		4d. dp vermilion	£275	28·00	
		Plate			
		7 (1865)	£350	32·00	
		8 (1866)	£300	32·00	
		9 (1867)	£300	30·00	
		10 (1868)	£350	45·00	
		11 (1869)	£300	28·00	
		12 (1870)	£275	30·00	
		13 (1872)	£300	30·00	
		14 (1873)	£350	55·00	
96	**28**	6d. dp lilac (with hyphen) (7.3.65)	£475	60·00	
97		6d. lilac (with hyphen)	£400	45·00	90·00
		a. Thick paper	£500	70·00	
		b. Stamp doubly printed (Plate 6)	—	£5500	
		c. Error. Watermark W **20***a* (Pl 5, 6) *from*	—	£375	
		d. Error. Watermark W **20***b* (Plate 5)			
		Wi. Watermark inverted	—	80·00	
		Wj. Watermark reversed			
		Plate			
		5 (1865)	£400	45·00	
		6 (1867)	£1200	80·00	

			Un	Used	Used on cover
98	**29**	9d. straw (Plate 4) (30.10.65)	£850	£275	£375
		a. Thick paper	£1200	£375	
		b. Error. Watermark W **20***a*	—	£425	
		c. Error. Watermark W **20***b* (stamp TF)			
		Wi. Watermark inverted	—	£300	
99	**30**	10d. red-brown (Plate 1) (11.11.67)		*£13000	
101	**31**	1s. green (Plate 4) (19.1.65)	£775	90·00	£140
		a. Error. Watermark W **20***a*	—	£400	
		b. Thick paper	£900	£175	
		c. Imperf between (vert pair)	—	£4500	
		Wi. Watermark inverted	—	£130	
		Wj. Imperf watermark inverted			
*92/101c		**For well-centred, lightly used**		**+100%**	

From mid-1866 to about the end of 1871 4d. stamps of this issue appeared generally with watermark inverted.

Unused examples of No. 98 from Plate 5 exist, but this was never put to press and all evidence points to such stamps originating from a portion of the Imprimatur sheet which was perforated by De La Rue in 1887 for insertion in albums to be presented to members of the Stamp Committee (*Price* £12000 *un*).

The 10d. stamps, No. 99, were printed in *error* on paper watermarked "Emblems" instead of on "Spray of Rose".

32

33 Spray of Rose

34

1867–80. *Wmk Spray of Rose. W* **33**.

			Un	*Used*	** Used on cover*
102	**26**	3d. dp rose (12.7.67)	£275	30·00	
103		3d. rose	£275	20·00	50·00
		a. Imperf (Plates 5, 6, 8) *from*	£775		
		Wi. Watermark inverted	£400	55·00	
		Plate			
		4 (1867)	£350	75·00	
		5 (1868)	£250	20·00	
		6 (1870)	£275	20·00	
		7 (1871)	£350	25·00	
		8 (1872)	£300	20·00	
		9 (1872)	£300	30·00	
		10 (1873)	£350	60·00	
104	**28**	6d. lilac (with hyphen) (Plate 6) (21.6.67)	£625	45·00	£110
		a. Imperf			
		Wi. Watermark inverted	—	80·00	
105		6d. dp lilac (with hyphen) (Plate 6)	£625	45·00	
106		6d. purple (with hyphen) (Plate 6)	£625	65·00	
107		6d. brt violet (with hyphen) (Plate 6) (22.7.68)	£625	50·00	
108	**28***a*	6d. dull violet (without hyphen) (Plate 8) (8.3.69)	£400	40·00	
		Wi. Watermark inverted	—	80·00	
109		6d. mauve (without hyphen)	£325	40·00	60·00
		a. Imperf (Plate Nos. 8 & 9)	£850	£750	
		Wi. Watermark inverted	—	90·00	
		Plate			
		8 (1869, mauve)	£325	40·00	
		9 (1870, mauve)	£325	40·00	
		10 (1869, mauve)		*£13000	
110	**29**	9d. straw (Plate No. 4) (3.10.67)	£700	£140	£240
		Wi. Watermark inverted	—	£190	
111	**29**	9d. pale straw (Plate No. 4)	£700	£150	
		a. Imperf (Plate 4)	£2100		
112	**30**	10d. red-brown (1.7.67)	£1100	£190	£375
		Wi. Watermark inverted	—	£300	
113		10d. pale red-brown	£1100	£200	
114		10d. dp red-brown	£1300	£210	
		a. Imperf (Plate 1)	£2000		
		Plate			
		1 (1867)	£1100	£190	
		2 (1867)	£13000	£2750	
115	**31**	1s. dp green (13.7.67)	£475	18·00	
117		1s. green	£375	18·00	35·00
		a. Imperf between (horiz pair) (Pl 7)			
		b. Imperf (Plate 4)	£1200	£700	
		Wi. Watermark inverted	£550	60·00	
		Plate			
		4 (1867)	£375	22·00	
		5 (1871)	£425	20·00	
		6 (1871)	£600	18·00	
		7 (1873)	£600	45·00	
118	**32**	2s. dull blue (1.7.67)	£1100	80·00	£375
		Wi. Watermark inverted	—	£200	
119		2s. dp blue	£1100	80·00	
		a. Imperf (Plate 1)	£2250		
120		2s. pale blue	£1700	£140	
		aa. Imperf (Plate 1)	£2000		
120*a*		2s. cobalt	£5500	£1200	
120*b*		2s. milky blue	£3500	£525	
		Plate			
		1 (1867)	£1100	80·00	
		3 (1868)	*	£3250	
121		2s. brown (Plate No. 1) (27.2.80)	£7500	£1500	
		a. Imperf	£4250		
		b. No watermark	†	—	
		Wi. Watermark inverted			
*102/21		**For well-centred, lightly used**		**+75%**	

Examples of the 1s. from Plates 5 and 6 *without* watermark are postal forgeries used at the Stock Exchange Post Office in the early 1870s.

1872–73. *Uncoloured letters in corners. Wmk Spray, W* **33**.

			Un	*Used*	** Used on cover*
122	**34**	6d. dp chestnut (Plate 11) (12.4.72)	£475	28·00	65·00
122*a*		6d. chestnut (Plate 11) (22.5.72)	£400	30·00	
		Wi. Watermark inverted	—	£100	
122*b*		6d. pale chestnut (Plate 11) (1872)	£375	28·00	
123		6d. pale buff (24.10.72)	£400	55·00	£175
		Wi. Watermark inverted	—	£150	
		Plate			
		11 (1872, pale buff)	£400	55·00	
		12 (1872, pale buff)	£850	90·00	
124		6d. chestnut (Plate 12) (1872)	*	£1400	
124*a*		6d. pale chestnut (Plate 12) (1872)	*	£1400	
125		6d. grey (Plate No. 12) (24.4.73)	£800	£140	£190
		a. Imperf	£1500		
		Wi. Watermark inverted	£1200	£160	
*122/5		**For well-centred, lightly used**		**+50%**	

35

36

37

38

39 Maltese Cross

40 Large Anchor

1867–83. *Uncoloured letters in corners.*

(a) *Wmk Maltese Cross, W* **39**. *P* $15\frac{1}{2} \times 15$

			Un	* Used
126	**35**	5s. rose (1.7.67)	£3000	£350
127		5s. pale rose	£3250	£350
		a. Imperf (Plate 1)	£4750	
		Plate		
		1 (1867)	£3000	£350
		2 (1874)	£4000	£425
128	**36**	10s. greenish grey (Plate 1) (26.9.78)	£21000	£1100
129	**37**	£1 brown-lilac (Plate 1) (26.9.78)	£26000	£1600
		(b) *Wmk Anchor, W* **40**. *P* 14. (i) *Blued paper*		
130	**35**	5s. rose (Plate 4) (25.11.82)	£6000	£1200
		Wi. Watermark inverted	—	£2500
131	**36**	10s. grey-green (Plate 1) (2.83)	£25000	£1750
132	**37**	£1 brown-lilac (Plate 1) (12.82)	£31000	£3000
133	**38**	£5 orange (Plate 1) (21.3.82)	£20000	£4500
		(ii) *White paper*		
134	**35**	5s. rose (Plate 4)	£6000	£1200
135	**36**	10s. greenish grey (Plate 1)	£25000	£1750
136	**37**	£1 brown-lilac (Plate 1)	£36000	£2600
137	**38**	£5 orange (Plate 1)	£5500	£1600
*126/37		**For well-centred, lightly used**		**+75%**

41

42

43

44

45

46

47 Small Anchor

48 Orb

1873–80. *Large coloured letters in the corners.*

(a) *Wmk Anchor, W* **47**

			Un	Used	* Used on cover
138	**41**	$2\frac{1}{2}$d. rosy mauve (*blued paper*) (1.7.75)	£450	60·00	
		a. Imperf			
		Wi. Watermark inverted	£600	£130	
139		$2\frac{1}{2}$d. rosy mauve (*white paper*)	£300	50·00	85·00
		Wi. Watermark inverted	£450	75·00	
		Plate			
		1 (*blued paper*) (1875)	£450	60·00	
		1 (*white paper*) (1875)	£300	50·00	
		2 (*blued paper*) (1875)	£3250	£700	
		2 (*white paper*) (1875)	£300	50·00	
		3 (*white paper*) (1875)	£475	55·00	
		3 (*blued paper*) (1875)	—	£2500	
		Error of Lettering L H—F L *for* L H—H L (*Plate* 2)			
140	**41**	$2\frac{1}{2}$d. rosy mauve	£8000	£800	
		(b) *Wmk Orb, W* **48**			
141	**41**	$2\frac{1}{2}$d. rosy mauve (1.5.76)	£275	25·00	55·00
		Wi. Watermark inverted	£350	40·00	
		Plate			
		3 (1876)	£625	55·00	
		4 (1876)	£275	25·00	
		5 (1876)	£275	30·00	
		6 (1876)	£275	25·00	
		7 (1877)	£275	25·00	
		8 (1877)	£275	30·00	
		9 (1877)	£275	25·00	
		10 (1878)	£325	40·00	
		11 (1878)	£275	25·00	
		12 (1878)	£275	30·00	
		13 (1878)	£275	30·00	
		14 (1879)	£275	25·00	
		15 (1879)	£275	25·00	
		16 (1879)	£275	25·00	
		17 (1880)	£700	£140	

142	41	2½d. blue (5.2.80)	£240	20·00	30·00
		Wi. Watermark inverted	£300	32·00	
		Plate			
		17 (1880)	£240	30·00	
		18 (1880)	£275	22·00	
		19 (1880)	£240	20·00	
		20 (1880)	£240	20·00	

(c) *Wmk Spray, W* **33**

143	42	3d. rose (5.7.73)	£240	20·00	40·00
		Wi. Watermark inverted	£325	40·00	
144		3d. pale rose	£240	20·00	
		Plate			
		11 (1873)	£240	20·00	
		12 (1873)	£275	20·00	
		14 (1874)	£300	22·00	
		15 (1874)	£240	20·00	
		16 (1875)	£240	20·00	
		17 (1875)	£275	20·00	
		18 (1875)	£275	20·00	
		19 (1876)	£240	20·00	
		20 (1879)	£240	40·00	
145	43	6d. pale buff (Plate 13) (15.3.73)	*	£5000	
146		6d. dp grey (20.3.74)	£300	35·00	60·00
147		6d. grey	£275	28·00	
		Wi. Watermark inverted	£350	45·00	
		Plate			
		13 (1874)	£275	30·00	
		14 (1875)	£275	30·00	
		15 (1876)	£275	28·00	
		16 (1878)	£275	28·00	
		17 (1880)	£375	55·00	
148	44	1s. dp green (1.9.73)	£400	55·00	
150		1s. pale green	£325	40·00	65·00
		Wi. Watermark inverted	£350	55·00	
		Plate			
		8 (1873)	£400	55·00	
		9 (1874)	£400	55·00	
		10 (1874)	£375	55·00	
		11 (1875)	£375	55·00	
		12 (1875)	£325	40·00	
		13 (1876)	£325	40·00	
		14 (—)	*	£12000	
151		1s. orange-brown (Plate 13) (14.10.80)	£1400	£275	£400
		Wi. Watermark inverted	£1750	£300	

(d) *Wmk Large Garter, W* **17**

152	45	4d. vermilion (1.3.76)	£800	£200	£350
		Wi. Watermark inverted	—	£250	
		Plate			
		15 (1876)	£800	£200	
		16 (1877)	*	£12000	
153		4d. sage-green (12.3.77)	£500	£140	£225
		Wi. Watermark inverted	—	£150	
		Plate			
		15 (1877)	£575	£160	
		16 (1877)	£500	£140	
		17 (1877)	*	£7000	
154		4d. grey-brown (Plate 17) (15.8.80)	£750	£225	£325
		a. Imperf	£2500		
		Wi. Watermark inverted	—	£250	
156	46	8d. orange (Plate 1) (11.9.76)	£650	£175	£240
		Wi. Watermark inverted	—	£190	
*138/56		**For well-centred, lightly used**		+**100%**	

1876 (July). *Prepared for use but not issued.*

156*a*	46	8d. purple-brown (Plate 1)	£3500

49 Imperial Crown

(50)

1880–83. *Wmk Imperial Crown, W* **49**.

			Un	*Used*	* *Used on cover*
157	41	2½d. blue (23.3.81)	£225	12·00	28·00
		Wi. Watermark inverted	£275	25·00	
		Plate			
		21 (1881)	£275	18·00	
		22 (1881)	£225	18·00	
		23 (1881)	£225	12·00	
158	42	3d. rose (3.81)	£275	45·00	60·00
		Wi. Watermark inverted	£600	65·00	
		Plate			
		20 (1881)	£325	60·00	
		21 (1881)	£275	45·00	
159		3d. on 3d. lilac (T **50**) (C.) (Plate 21) (1.1.83)	£275	90·00	£275
		Wi. Watermark inverted			
160	45	4d. grey-brown (8.12.80)	£225	35·00	90·00
		Wi. Watermark inverted	—	90·00	
		Plate			
		17 (1880)	£225	35·00	
		18 (1882)	£225	35·00	
161	43	6d. grey (1.1.81)	£210	38·00	65·00
		Wi. Watermark inverted	—	90·00	
		Plate			
		17 (1881)	£225	38·00	
		18 (1882)	£210	38·00	
162		6d. on 6d. lilac (as T **50**) (C.) (Plate 18) (1.1.83)	£240	90·00	£190
		a. Slanting dots (various) *from*	£290	95·00	
		b. Opt double	—	£5000	
		Wi. Watermark inverted	£375	£130	
163	44	1s. orange-brown (24.5.81)	£300	85·00	£160
		Wi. Watermark inverted	£350	90·00	
		Plate			
		13 (1881)	£350	85·00	
		14 (1881)	£300	85·00	
*157/63		**For well-centred, lightly used**		+**75%**	

The 1s. plate 14 (line perf 14) exists in purple but was not issued in this shade (*Price £2750 unused*). Examples were included in a few of the Souvenir Albums prepared for members of the "Stamp Committee of 1884".

52

53

54

55

56

1880–81. *Wmk Imperial Crown, W* **49**.

			Un	Used	* Used on cover
164	**52**	½d. dp green (14.10.80)	25·00	6·00	12·00
		a. Imperf	£700		
		b. No watermark	£3000		
		Wi. Watermark inverted	—	50·00	
165		½d. pale green	25·00	10·00	
166	**53**	1d. Venetian red (1.1.80)	10·00	6·00	10·00
		a. Imperf	£700		
		Wi. Watermark inverted	—	50·00	
167	**54**	1½d. Venetian red (14.10.80)	£110	25·00	90·00
168	**55**	2d. pale rose (8.12.80)	£125	55·00	90·00
		Wi. Watermark inverted	£225	£100	
168*a*		2d. dp rose	£125	55·00	
169	**56**	5d. indigo (15.3.81)	£400	70·00	£150
		a. Imperf	£1400	£1000	
		Wi. Watermark inverted	—	£1250	
*164/9		**For well-centred, lightly used**		**+75%**	

57

Die I

Die II

1881. *Wmk Imperial Crown, W* **49**. (*a*) *14 dots in each corner, Die I* (12 July).

			Un	Used	* Used on cover
170	**57**	1d. lilac	90·00	18·00	26·00
		Wi. Watermark inverted			
171		1d. pale lilac	90·00	18·00	
		(*b*) *16 dots in each corner, Die* II (13 December)			
172	**57**	1d. lilac	1·50	1·00	2·00
		Wi. Watermark inverted	10·00	6·00	
172*a*		1d. bluish lilac	£200	60·00	
173		1d. dp purple	1·50	75	
		a. Printed both sides	£450	†	
		b. Frame broken at bottom	£525	£225	
		c. Printed on gummed side	£425	†	
		d. Imperf three sides (pair)	£2750	†	
		e. Printed both sides but impression on back inverted	£450	†	
		f. No watermark	£800	†	
		g. Blued paper	£1750		
174		1d. mauve	1·50	75	
		a. Imperf (pair)	£1000		
*170/4		**For well-centred, lightly used**		**+50%**	

1d. stamps with the words "PEARS SOAP" printed on back in *orange, blue* or *mauve price from £375, unused.*

The variety "frame broken at bottom" (No. 173b) shows a white space just inside the bottom frame-line from between the "N" and "E" of "ONE" to below the first "N" of "PENNY", breaking the pearls and cutting into the lower part of the oval below "PEN".

KEY TO SURFACE-PRINTED ISSUES 1880–1900

S.G. Nos.	*Description*	*Date of Issue*
164/5	½d. green	14.10.80
187	½d. slate-blue	1.4.84
197/e	½d. vermilion	1.1.87
213	½d. blue-green	17.4.1900
166	1d. Venetian red	1.1.80
170/1	1d. lilac, Die I	12.7.81
172/4	1d. lilac, Die II	12.12.81
167	1½d. Venetian red	14.10.80
188	1½d. lilac	1.4.84
198	1½d. purple & green	1.1.87
168/a	2d. rose	8.12.80
189	2d. lilac	1.4.84
199/200	2d. green & red	1.1.87
190	2½d. lilac	1.4.84
201	2½d. purple on blue paper	1.1.87
191	3d. lilac	1.4.84
202/4	3d. purple on yellow paper	1.1.87
192	4d. dull green	1.4.84
205/a	4d. green & brown	1.1.87
206	4½d. green and carmine	15.9.92
169	5d. indigo	15.3.81
193	5d. dull green	1.4.84
207	5d. purple & blue, Die I	1.1.87
207a	5d. purple & blue, Die II	1888
194	6d. dull green	1.4.84
208/a	6d. purple on rose-red paper	1.1.87
195	9d. dull green	1.8.83
209	9d. purple & blue	1.1.87
210/b	10d. purple & carmine	24.2.90
196	1s. dull green	1.4.84
211	1s. green	1.1.87
214	1s. green & carmine	11.7.1900
175	2s. 6d. lilac on blued paper	2.7.83
178/9	2s. 6d. lilac	1884
176	5s. rose on blued paper	1.4.84
180/1	5s. rose	1884
177/a	10s. ultramarine on blued paper	1.4.84
182/3a	10s. ultramarine	1884
185	£1 brown-lilac, wmk Crowns	1.4.84
186	£1 brown-lilac, wmk Orbs	2.88
212	£1 green	28.1.91

Note that the £5 value used with the above series is listed as Nos. 133 and 137.

58

59

60

62

63

64

1883–84. *Coloured letters in the corners. Wmk Anchor, W* **40**.

(a) Blued paper

			Un	*Used* ★
175	**58**	2s. 6d. lilac (2.7.83)	£2500	£650
176	**59**	5s. rose (1.4.84)	£4000	£1400
177	**60**	10s. ultramarine (1.4.84)	£13000	£3600
177*a*		10s. cobalt (5.84)	£15000	£5250

(b) White paper

			Un	*Used*
178	**58**	2s. 6d. lilac	£275	80·00
179		2s. 6d. dp lilac	£275	80·00
		a. Error. On blued paper	£1750	£600
		Wi. Watermark inverted	—	£2750
180	**59**	5s. rose	£475	£100
		Wi. Watermark inverted	†	—
181		5s. crimson	£475	£100
182	**60**	10s. cobalt	£14000	£3600
183		10s. ultramarine	£900	£300
183*a*		10s. pale ultramarine	£900	£300
★175/83*a*		**For well-centred, lightly used**		+**50**%

For No. 180 perf 12 *see* second note below No. 196.

65

66

1883 (1 Aug) (9d.) *or* **1884** (1 Apr) (*others*). *Wmk Imperial Crown, W* **49** (*sideways on horiz designs*).

			Un	*Used* ★	*Used on cover*
187	**52**	½d. slate-blue	15·00	5·00	10·00
		a. Imperf	£700		
		Wi. Watermark inverted	—	50·00	
188	**62**	1½d. lilac	75·00	28·00	80·00
		a. Imperf	£700		
		Wi. Watermark inverted	—	80·00	
189	**63**	2d. lilac	£110	55·00	90·00
		a. Imperf	£800		
		Wi. Watermark sideways-inverted			
190	**64**	2½d. lilac	60·00	10·00	20·00
		a. Imperf	£800		
		Wi. Watermark sideways-inverted			
191	**65**	3d. lilac	£140	75·00	£100
		a. Imperf	£800		
		Wi. Watermark inverted	†	—	
192	**66**	4d. dull green	£350	£150	£200
		a. Imperf	£850		
193	**62**	5d. dull green	£350	£150	£200
		a. Imperf	£850		
194	**63**	6d. dull green	£375	£160	£210
		a. Imperf	£850		
		Wi. Watermark sideways-inverted			
195	**64**	9d. dull green (1.8.83)	£700	£325	£775
		Wi. Watermark sideways-inverted	£775	£450	
196	**65**	1s. dull green	£500	£175	£325
		a. Imperf	£1750		
		Wi. Watermark-inverted			
★187/96		**For well-centred, lightly used**	+**100**%		

The above prices are for stamps in the true dull green colour. Stamps which have been soaked, causing the colour to run, are virtually worthless.

Stamps of the above set and No. 180 are also found perf 12; these are official perforations, but were never issued. A second variety of the 5d. is known with a line instead of a stop under the "d" in the value; this was never issued and is therefore only known *unused* (*Price £5500*).

61

Broken frames, Plate 2

1884 (1 Apr). *Wmk Three Imperial Crowns, W* **49**.

			Un	*Used* ★
185	**61**	£1 brown-lilac	£13000	£1200
		a. Frame broken	£19000	£1750
		Wi. Watermark inverted	—	£3250

1888 (Feb). *Watermark Three Orbs, W* **48**.

			Un	*Used*
186	**61**	£1 brown-lilac	£19000	£1750
		a. Frame broken	£26000	£2750
★185/6*a*		**For well-centred, lightly used**		+**50**%

The broken-frame varieties, Nos. 185a and 186a, are on Plate 2 stamps JC and TA, as illustrated. *See also* No. 212a.

71

72

73

74

75

76

77

78

79

80

81

82

Die I

Die II

Die I: Square dots to right of "d".
Die II: Thin vertical lines to right of "d".

1887 (1 Jan)–**92**. *"Jubilee" issue. New types. The bicoloured stamps have the value tablets, or the frames including the value tablets, in the second colour. Wmk Imperial Crown, W* **49** *(Three Crowns on £1).*

			Unmtd Mint	*Mtd Mint*	*Used*
197	**71**	$\frac{1}{2}$d. vermilion	1·40	1·25	75
		a. Printed on gummed side	£1200	£1000	†
		b. Printed both sides			
		c. Doubly printed	—	£5500	
		d. Imperf	—	£1250	
		Wi. Watermark inverted	22·00	18·00	
197*e*		$\frac{1}{2}$d. orange-vermilion	1·40	1·00	50
198	**72**	$1\frac{1}{2}$d. dull purple & pale green	18·00	13·00	5·00
		a. Purple part of design double		—	£3750
		Wi. Watermark inverted	£450	£400	£180
199	**73**	2d. green & scarlet	£350	£300	£180
200		2d. grey-green & carmine	25·00	20·00	9·00
		Wi. Watermark inverted	£550	£500	£190
201	**74**	$2\frac{1}{2}$d. purple/*blue*	18·00	13·00	2·00
		a. Printed on gummed side	£2750	£2500	†
		b. Imperf three sides	—	£2250	
		c. Imperf	—	£2500	
		Ed. Missing "d" in value	†	†	£3000
		Wi. Watermark inverted	£550	£500	
202	**75**	3d. purple/*yellow*	24·00	18·00	2·50
		a. Imperf	—	£3500	
		Wi. Watermark inverted	—	—	£200
203		3d. dp purple/*yellow*	24·00	18·00	2·50
204		3d. purple/*orange* (1891)	£450	£400	£150
205	**76**	4d. green & purple-brown	25·00	20·00	9·50
		aa. Imperf			
		Wi. Watermark inverted	£500	£450	£180
205*a*		4d. green & dp brown	25·00	20·00	9·50
206	**77**	$4\frac{1}{2}$d. green & carmine (15.9.92)	10·00	7·00	28·00
		Wi. Watermark inverted			
206*a*		$4\frac{1}{2}$d. green & dp brt carmine	£500	£450	£300
207	**78**	5d. dull purple & blue (Die I)	£500	£450	45·00
207*a*		5d. dull purple & blue (Die II) (1888)	28·00	22·00	8·50
		Wi. Watermark inverted	—	—	£180
208	**79**	6d. purple/*rose-red*	25·00	20·00	8·50
		Wi. Watermark inverted	£550	£500	£150
208*a*		6d. dp purple/*rose-red*	25·00	20·00	8·50
209	**80**	9d. dull purple & blue	60·00	48·00	30·00
		Wi. Watermark inverted	£600	£550	£190
210	**81**	10d. dull purple & carmine (*shades*) (24.2.90)	45·00	38·00	30·00
		aa. Imperf	—	£4000	
		Wi. Watermark inverted	£700	£650	£350
210*a*		10d. dull purple & dp dull carmine	£450	£350	£150
210*b*		10d. dull purple & scarlet	65·00	50·00	38·00
211	**82**	1s. dull green	£225	£180	50·00
		Wi. Watermark inverted	£450	£400	£190
212	**61**	£1 green (28.1.91)	£2500	£2250	£400
		a. Frame broken	£6000	£5000	£1000
		Wi. Watermark inverted	—	£20000	£2250

*197/212a **For well-centred, lightly used** +**50**%

The broken-frame varieties, No. 212a, are on Plate 2 stamps JC or TA, as illustrated above No. 185.

$\frac{1}{2}$d. stamps with "PEARS SOAP" printed on the back in *orange, blue* or *mauve*, price *from* £375 each.

1900. *Colours changed. Wmk Imperial Crown, W* **49**.

213	**71**	$\frac{1}{2}$d. blue-green (17.4)	1·25	1·25	1·00
		a. Printed on gummed side	—	—	†
		b. Imperf	—	£1750	
		Wi. Watermark inverted	20·00	15·00	
214	**82**	1s. green & carmine (11.7)	55·00	45·00	£100
		Wi. Watermark inverted	£600	£550	£180
		Set of 14		£375	£225

*213/14 **For well-centred, lightly used** +**50**%

The $\frac{1}{2}$d. No. 213, in bright blue, is a colour changeling caused by a constituent of the ink used for some months in 1900.

USED ON COVER PRICES

No. 197	£5	No. 205	£18	No. 209	£55
No. 198	£18	No. 206	£60	No. 210	£60
No. 200	£20	No. 207	£90	No. 211	£80
No. 201	£5	No. 207*a*	£24	No. 213	£5
No. 202	£20	No. 208	£15	No. 214	£250

For full information on all future British issues, collectors should write to the British Post Office Philatelic Bureau, 20 Brandon Street, Edinburgh EH3 5TT

KING EDWARD VII

22 January 1901–6 May 1910

PRINTINGS. Distinguishing De La Rue printings from the provisional printings of the same values made by Harrison & Sons Ltd. or at Somerset House may prove difficult in some cases. For very full guidance Volume 2 of the Stanley Gibbons *Great Britain Specialised Catalogue* should prove helpful.

Note that stamps perforated 15 × 14 must be Harrison; the 2$\frac{1}{2}$d., 3d. and 4d. in this perforation are useful reference material, their shades and appearance in most cases matching the Harrison perf 14 printings.

Except for the 6d. value, all stamps on chalk-surfaced paper were printed by De La Rue.

Of the stamps on ordinary paper, the De La Rue impressions are usually clearer and of a higher finish than those of the other printers. The shades are markedly different except in some printings of the 4d., 6d. and 7d. and in the 5s., 10s. and £1.

Used stamps in good, clean, unrubbed condition and with dated postmarks can form the basis of a useful reference collection, the dates often assisting in the assignment to the printers.

PRICES. For Nos. 215/456a prices are quoted for unmounted mint, mounted mint and used stamps.

USED STAMPS. For well-centred, lightly used examples of King Edward VII stamps, add the following percentages to the used prices quoted below:

De La Rue printings (Nos. 215/66)—3d. values + 35%, 4d. orange + 100%, 6d. + 75%, 7d. & 1s. + 25%, all other values + 50%.

Harrison printings (Nos 267/86)—all values and perforations + 75%.

Somerset House printings (Nos. 287/320)—1s. values + 25%, all other values + 50%.

83

84

85

86

87

88

89

90

91

92

93

94

95

96

97

(Des E. Fuchs)

1902 (1 Jan)–**10**. *Printed by De La Rue & Co. Wmk Imperial Crown W* **49** (*$\frac{1}{2}$d. to 1s. Three Crowns on £1*); *Anchor, W* **40** (*2s. 6d. to 10s.*). *Ordinary paper. P* 14.

				Unmtd mint	*Mtd mint*	*Used*
215	**83**	$\frac{1}{2}$d.	dull blue-green (1.1.02)	1·25	1·00	75
		Wi.	Watermark inverted	£1200	£1100	£550
216		$\frac{1}{2}$d.	blue-green	1·25	1·00	75
217		$\frac{1}{2}$d.	pale yellowish green (26.11.04)	1·25	1·00	75
218		$\frac{1}{2}$d.	yellowish green	1·25	1·00	75
		a.	Booklet pane. Five stamps plus St. Andrew's Cross label (6.06)	£250	£175	
		b.	Doubly printed (bottom row on one pane) (Control H9)	—	£15000	
		Wi.	Watermark inverted	15·00	10·00	5·00
219		1d.	scarlet (1.1.02)	1·25	1·00	75
220		1d.	brt scarlet	1·25	1·00	75
		a.	Imperf (pair)	—	£8500	
		Wi.	Watermark inverted	3·50	2·50	2·50
221	**84**	1$\frac{1}{2}$d.	dull purple & green (21.3.02)	38·00	18·00	10·00
222		1$\frac{1}{2}$d.	slate-purple & green	40·00	20·00	9·00
		Wi.	Watermark inverted	—	—	£375
223		1$\frac{1}{2}$d.	pale dull purple & green (*chalk-surfaced paper*) (8.05)	40·00	25·00	10·00
224		1$\frac{1}{2}$d.	slate-purple & bluish green (*chalk-surfaced paper*)	40·00	25·00	7·00
225	**85**	2d.	yellowish green & carmine-red (25.3.02)	40·00	25·00	10·00

226		2d. grey-green & carmine-red (1904)	45·00	25·00	10·00
227		2d. pale grey-green & carmine-red (*chalk-surfaced paper*) (4.06)	40·00	25·00	12·00
		Wi. Watermark inverted			
228		2d. pale grey-green & scarlet (*chalk-surfaced paper*) (1909)	40·00	22·00	12·00
229		2d. dull blue-green & carmine (*chalk-surfaced paper*) (1907)	80·00	48·00	30·00
230	**86**	$2\frac{1}{2}$d. ultramarine (1.1.02)	12·00	9·00	5·00
231		$2\frac{1}{2}$d. pale ultramarine	12·00	9·00	5·00
		Wi. Watermark inverted	—	—	£700
232	**87**	3d. dull purple/*orange-yellow* (20.3.02)	40·00	22·00	5·00
		Wi. Watermark inverted			
		a. Chalk-surfaced paper (3.06)	£160	90·00	35·00
232*b*		3d. dp purple/*orange-yellow*	40·00	22·00	6·00
232*c*		3d. pale reddish purple/*orange-yellow* (*chalk-surfaced paper*) (3.06)	£150	85·00	25·00
233		3d. dull reddish purple/*yellow* (*lemon back*) (*chalk-surfaced paper*)	£160	90·00	40·00
233*b*	**87**	3d. pale purple/*lemon* (*chalk-surfaced paper*)	35·00	20·00	9·00
234		3d. purple/*lemon* (*chalk-surfaced paper*)	35·00	20·00	9·00
235	**88**	4d. green & grey-brown (27.3.02)	60·00	30·00	18·00
		Wi. Watermark inverted			
236		4d. green & chocolate-brown	60·00	30·00	18·00
		a. Chalk-surfaced paper (1.06)	35·00	22·00	10·00
238		4d. dp green & chocolate-brown (*chalk-surfaced paper*)	35·00	22·00	10·00
239		4d. brown-orange (1.11.09)	£150	£100	90·00
240		4d. pale orange (12.09)	18·00	12·00	10·00
241		4d. orange-red (12.09)	18·00	12·00	10·00
242	**89**	5d. dull purple & ultramarine (14.5.02)	60·00	25·00	9·00
		a. Chalk-surfaced paper (5.06)	60·00	25·00	12·00
244		5d. slate-purple & ultramarine (*chalk-surfaced paper*) (5.06)	60·00	25·00	12·00
		Wi. Watermark inverted	£700	£550	
245	**83**	6d. pale dull purple (1.1.02)	40·00	20·00	9·00
		a. Chalk-surfaced paper (1.06)	40·00	20·00	9·00
246		6d. slate-purple	40·00	20·00	9·00
248		6d. dull purple (*chalk-surfaced paper*) (1.06)	40·00	20·00	9·00
		Wi. Watermark inverted	—	—	£850
249	**90**	7d. grey-black (4.5.10)	10·00	7·00	10·00
249a		7d. dp grey-black	90·00	70·00	70·00
250	**91**	9d. dull purple & ultramarine (7.4.02)	£100	48·00	35·00
		a. Chalk-surfaced paper (6.05)	£120	48·00	38·00
		aWi. Watermark inverted	—	—	£850
251		9d. slate-purple & ultramarine	£100	48·00	35·00
		a. Chalk-surfaced paper (6.05)	£110	48·00	40·00
254	**92**	10d. dull purple & carmine (3.7.02)	£100	48·00	40·00
		a. No cross on crown	£275	£200	£120
		b. Chalk-surfaced paper (9.06)	£110	48·00	30·00
255		10d. slate-purple & carmine (*chalk-surfaced paper*) (9.06)	£100	48·00	38·00
		a. No cross on crown	£240	£175	£120
256		10d. dull purple & scarlet (*chalk-surfaced paper*) (9.10)	£100	45·00	48·00
		a. No cross on crown	£225	£160	£110
257	**93**	1s. dull green & carmine (24.3.02)	£100	42·00	15·00
		a. Chalk-surfaced paper (9.05)	£110	45·00	20·00
259		1s. dull green & scarlet (*chalk-surfaced paper*) (9.10)	£110	45·00	30·00
260	**94**	2s. 6d. lilac (5.4.02)	£240	£125	60·00
		Wi. Watermark inverted	£1100	£850	£550
261		2s. 6d. pale dull purple (*chalk-surfaced paper*) (7.10.05)	£275	£120	£100
		Wi. Watermark inverted	£1100	£850	£550
262	**94**	2s. 6d. dull purple (*chalk-surfaced paper*)	£275	£120	80·00
263	**95**	5s. brt carmine (5.4.02)	£275	£140	80·00
		Wi. Watermark inverted	—	—	£850
264		5s. dp brt carmine	£275	£140	80·00
265	**96**	10s. ultramarine (5.4.02)	£600	£375	£240
266	**97**	£1 dull blue-green (16.6.02)	£1300	£900	£375
		Wi. Watermark inverted	—	£18000	£5500

USED ON COVER PRICES

No. 215	£1	No. 217	£1	No. 219	£1
No. 222	£15	No. 225	£18	No. 230	£12
No. 232	£22	No. 236a	£30	No. 240	£28
No. 242	£38	No. 245	£32	No. 249	£140
No. 250	£140	No. 254	£140	No. 257	£95
No. 260	£550	No. 263	£600		

97*a*

1910 (May). *Prepared for use, by* De La Rue *but not issued. Wmk Imperial Crown, W* **49**. *P*14.

266*a* **97***a* 2d. Tyrian plum £16000 £13000

One example of this stamp is known used, but it was never issued to the public.

1911. *Printed by* Harrison & Sons. *Ordinary paper. Wmk Imperial Crown, W* **49**. (*a*) *P* 14.

			Unmtd mint	*Mtd mint*	*Used*
267	**83**	$\frac{1}{2}$d. dull yellow-green (3.5.11)	2·75	2·00	1·00
		Wi. Watermark inverted	20·00	10·00	5·00
268		$\frac{1}{2}$d. dull green	3·00	2·25	1·00
269		$\frac{1}{2}$d. dp dull green	12·00	8·00	3·00
270		$\frac{1}{2}$d. pale bluish green	50·00	30·00	28·00
		a. Booklet pane. Five stamps plus St. Andrew's Cross label	£300	£240	
		b. Watermark sideways	†	†	£12000
		c. Imperf (pair)	—	£12000	†
271		$\frac{1}{2}$d. brt green (fine impression) (6.11)	£210	£190	£120
272		1d. rose-red (3.5.11)	6·00	4·00	8·00
		Wi. Watermark inverted	20·00	10·00	9·00
		a. No wmk	45·00	40·00	40·00
273		1d. dp rose-red	6·00	4·00	7·00
274		1d. rose-carmine	55·00	40·00	20·00
275		1d. aniline pink (5.11)	£425	£300	£140
275a		1d. aniline rose	£160	£100	90·00
276	**86**	$2\frac{1}{2}$d. brt blue (10.7.11)	55·00	30·00	16·00
		Wi. Watermark inverted	£525	£400	
277	**87**	3d. purple/*lemon* (12.9.11)	70·00	48·00	£130
277a		3d. grey/*lemon*	£3750	£2750	
278	**88**	4d. brt orange (12.7.11)	75·00	42·00	38·00
		(*b*) *P* 15 × 14			
279	**83**	$\frac{1}{2}$d. dull green (30.10.11)	38·00	30·00	35·00
279a		$\frac{1}{2}$d. dp dull green	50·00	30·00	35·00
280		1d. rose-red (4.10.11)	35·00	25·00	18·00
281		1d. rose-carmine	18·00	10·00	9·00
282		1d. pale rose-carmine	22·00	15·00	8·00
283	**86**	$2\frac{1}{2}$d. brt blue (14.10.11)	30·00	15·00	8·00
284		$2\frac{1}{2}$d. dull blue	30·00	15·00	8·00
		Wi. Watermark inverted	—	—	£250
285	**87**	3d. purple/*lemon* (22.9.11)	40·00	25·00	8·00
285a		3d. grey/*lemon*	£3000	£2250	
286	**88**	4d. brt orange (11.11.11)	30·00	19·00	10·00
		Set of 5	£140	90·00	60·00

USED ON COVER PRICES

No. 267	£3	No. 272	£7	No. 276	£20
No. 277	£400	No. 278	£110	No. 279	£65
No. 281	£18	No. 283	£15	No. 285	£18
No. 286	£45				

1911–13. *Printed at Somerset House. Ordinary paper. Wmk as 1902–10. P 14.*

287	**84**	1½d.	reddish puple & brt green (13.7.11)	50·00	30·00	22·00
288		1½d.	dull purple & green	28·00	15·00	15·00
289		1½d.	slate-purple & green (9.12)	32·00	18·00	16·00
290	**85**	2d.	dp dull green & red (8.8.11)	25·00	16·00	9·00
291		2d.	dp dull green & carmine	25·00	16·00	9·00
292		2d.	grey-green & brt carmine (carmine shows clearly on back) (11.3.12)	25·00	16·00	12·00
293	**89**	5d.	dull reddish purple & brt blue (7.8.11)	32·00	18·00	9·00
294		5d.	dp dull reddish purple & brt blue	30·00	15·00	9·00
295	**83**	6d.	royal purple (31.10.11)	50·00	32·00	50·00
296		6d.	brt magenta (*chalk-surfaced paper*) (31.10.11)	£2750	£1900	
297		6d.	dull purple	30·00	18·00	9·00
298		6d.	reddish purple (11.11)	30·00	18·00	12·00
		a.	No cross on crown (*various shades*)	£300	£225	
299		6d.	very deep reddish purple (11.11)	48·00	30·00	26·00
300		6d.	dark purple (3.12)	30·00	20·00	20·00
301		6d.	dull purple "Dickinson" coated paper* (3.13)	£150	£110	95·00
303		6d.	dp plum (*chalk-surfaced paper*) (7.13)	30·00	15·00	50·00
		a.	No cross on crown	£350	£250	
305	**90**	7d.	slate-grey (1.8.12)	12·00	8·00	11·00
306	**91**	9d.	reddish purple & lt blue (24.7.11)	95·00	55·00	40·00
306*a*		9d.	dp dull reddish purple & dp brt blue (9.11)	95·00	55·00	40·00
307		9d.	dull reddish purple & blue (10.11)	65·00	38·00	30·00
307*a*		9d.	dp plum & blue (7.13)	65·00	38·00	40·00
308		9d.	slate-purple & cobalt-blue (3.12)	95·00	70·00	50·00
309	**92**	10d.	dull purple & scarlet (9.10.11)	80·00	55·00	40·00
310		10d.	dull reddish purple & aniline pink	£275	£200	£140
311		10d.	dull reddish purple & carmine (5.12)	65·00	45·00	30·00
		a.	No cross on crown	£700	£500	
312	**93**	1s.	dark green & scarlet (13.7.11)	£110	65·00	35·00
313		1s.	dp green & scarlet (9.10.11)	80·00	45·00	20·00
		Wi.	Wmk inverted	£100	85·00	†
314		1s.	green & carmine (15.4.12)	70·00	35·00	20·00
315	**94**	2s. 6d.	dull greyish purple (15.9.11)	£475	£325	£180
316		2s. 6d.	dull reddish purple	£240	£120	80·00
		Wi.	Watermark inverted	†	†	—
317		2s. 6d.	dark purple	£240	£120	80·00
318	**95**	5s.	carmine (29.2.12)	£300	£175	80·00
319	**96**	10s.	blue (14.1.12)	£625	£425	£300
320	**97**	£1	dp green (3.9.11)	£1400	£900	£400

*No. 301 was on an experimental coated paper which does not respond to the silver test.

USED ON COVER PRICES

No. 288	£32	No. 290	£32	No. 293	£55
No. 297	£65	No. 305	£90	No. 307	£110
No. 311	£120	No. 313	£100		

KING GEORGE V

6 May 1910–20 January 1936

Further detailed information on the issues of King George V will be found in Volume 2 of the Stanley Gibbons *Great Britain Specialised Catalogue.*

PRINTERS. Types **98** to **102** were typographed by Harrison & Sons Ltd, with the exception of certain preliminary printings made at Somerset House and distinguishable by the controls "A.11", "B.11" or "B.12" (the Harrison printings do not have a full stop after the letter). The booklet stamps, Nos. 334/7, and 344/5 were printed by Harrison only.

WATERMARK VARIETIES. Many British stamps to 1967 exist without watermark owing to misplacement of the paper, and with either inverted, reversed, or inverted and reversed watermarks. A proportion of the low-value stamps issued in booklets have the watermark inverted in the normal course of printing.

Low values with *watermark sideways* are normally from stamp rolls used on machines with sideways delivery or, from June 1940, certain booklets.

STAMPS WITHOUT WATERMARK. Stamps found without watermark, due to misplacement of the sheet in relation to the dandy roll, are not listed here but will be found in the *Great Britain Specialised Catalogue.*

The 1½d. and 5d. 1912–22, and 2d. and 2½d., 1924–26, listed here, are from *whole* sheets completely without watermark.

98

99

100 Simple Cypher

For type difference with T **101/2** *see* notes below the latter.

Die A

Die B

Dies of Halfpenny

Die A. The three upper scales on the body of the right hand dolphin form a triangle; the centre jewel of the cross inside the crown is suggested by a comma.

Die B. The three upper scales are incomplete; the centre jewel is suggested by a crescent.

Die A

Die B

Dies of One Penny

Die A. The second line of shading on the ribbon to the right of the crown extends right across the wreath; the line nearest to the crown on the right hand ribbon shows as a short line at the bottom of the ribbon.

Die B. The second line of shading is broken in the middle; the first line is little more than a dot.

(Des Bertram Mackennal and G. W. Eve. Head from photograph by W. and D. Downey. Die eng J.A.C. Harrison)

1911–12. *Wmk Imperial Crown, W* **49**. *P* 15 × 14.

			Unmtd mint	Mtd mint	Used
321	**98**	$\frac{1}{2}$d. pale green (Die A) (22.6.11)	6·00	4·00	1·50
322		$\frac{1}{2}$d. green (Die A) (22.6.11)	5·00	4·00	1·50
		a. Error. Perf 14 (8.11)	—	—	£300
		Wi. Watermark inverted	—	—	£600
323		$\frac{1}{2}$d. bluish green (Die A)	£340	£260	£150
324		$\frac{1}{2}$d. yellow-green (Die B)	12·00	7·00	1·00
325		$\frac{1}{2}$d. brt green (Die B)	7·50	4·00	1·00
		a. Watermark sideways	—	—	£2500
		Wi. Watermark inverted	12·00	7·00	4·00
326		$\frac{1}{2}$d. bluish green (Die B)	£225	£150	90·00
327	**99**	1d. carmine-red (Die A) (22.6.11)	6·00	4·00	2·00
		c. Watermark sideways	†	†	—
		Wi. Watermark inverted	£800	£550	£375
328		1d. pale carmine (Die A) (22.6.11)	15·00	12·00	1·50
		a. No cross on crown	£400	£300	£175
329		1d. carmine (Die B)	10·00	6·00	1·50
		Wi. Watermark inverted	10·00	6·00	2·50
330		1d. pale carmine (Die B)	10·00	6·00	1·50
		a. No cross on crown	£600	£400	£275
331		1d. rose-pink (Die B)	£110	80·00	30·00
332		1d. scarlet (Die B) (6.12)	25·00	15·00	12·00
		Wi. Watermark inverted	25·00	15·00	12·00
333		1d. aniline scarlet (Die B)	£175	£110	70·00

For note on the aniline scarlet No. 333 *see* below No. 343.

1912 (Aug). *Booklet stamps. Wmk Royal Cypher ("Simple"), W* **100**. *P* 15 × 14.

334	**98**	$\frac{1}{2}$d. pale green (Die B)	45·00	28·00	30·00
335		$\frac{1}{2}$d. green (Die B)	45·00	28·00	30·00
		Wi. Watermark inverted	45·00	28·00	30·00
		Wj. Watermark reversed	£400	£350	£170
		Wk. Watermark inverted and reversed	£400	£350	£170
336	**99**	1d. scarlet (Die B)	25·00	20·00	20·00
		Wi. Watermark inverted	25·00	20·00	20·00
		Wj. Watermark reversed	£400	£375	
		Wk. Watermark inverted and reversed	—	—	£110
337		1d. brt scarlet (Die B)	25·00	20·00	20·00

101

102

103 Multiple Cypher

Type differences

$\frac{1}{2}$d. In T **98** the ornament above "P" of "HALFPENNY" has two thin lines of colour and the beard is undefined. In T **101** the ornament has one thick line and the beard is well defined.

1d. In T **99** the body of the lion is unshaded and in T **102** it is shaded.

1912 (1 Jan). *Wmk Imperial Crown, W* **49**. *P* 15 × 14.

338	**101**	$\frac{1}{2}$d. dp green	15·00	10·00	5·00
339		$\frac{1}{2}$d. green	10·00	5·00	1·00
340		$\frac{1}{2}$d. yellow-green	10·00	5·00	1·00
		a. No cross on crown	90·00	60·00	20·00
		Wi. Watermark inverted	£375	£325	£170
341	**102**	1d. brt scarlet	4·00	3·00	1·50
		a. No cross on crown	70·00	50·00	20·00
		b. Printed double, one albino	£150	£110	
		Wi. Watermark inverted	£200	£180	£120
342		1d. scarlet	4·00	3·00	1·50
343		1d. aniline scarlet*	£160	£120	70·00
		a. No cross on crown	£850	£700	

*Our prices for the aniline scarlet 1d. stamps, Nos. 333 and 343, are for the specimens in which the colour is suffused on the surface of the stamp and shows through clearly on the back. Specimens without these characteristics but which show "aniline" reactions under the quartz lamp are relatively common.

1912 (Aug). *Wmk Royal Cypher ("Simple"), W* **100**. *P* 15 × 14.

344	**101**	$\frac{1}{2}$d. green	6·00	5·00	1·50
		a. No cross on crown	90·00	70·00	20·00
		Wi. Watermark inverted	85·00	60·00	20·00
		Wj. Watermark reversed	75·00	45·00	20·00
		Wk. Watermark inverted and reversed	8·00	6·00	3·00
345	**102**	1d. scarlet	7·00	6·00	1·50
		a. No cross on crown	80·00	70·00	20·00
		Wi. Watermark inverted	15·00	10·00	7·00
		Wj. Watermark reversed	25·00	15·00	10·00
		Wk. Watermark inverted and reversed	12·00	7·00	7·00

1912 (Sept–Oct). *Wmk Royal Cypher ("Multiple"), W* **103**. *P* 15 × 14.

346	**101**	$\frac{1}{2}$d. green (Oct)	10·00	9·00	6·00
		a. No cross on crown	90·00	70·00	40·00
		b. Imperf	£150	£100	
		c. Watermark sideways	†	†	£1200
		d. Printed on gummed side	—	—	†
		Wi. Watermark inverted	10·00	7·00	7·00
		Wj. Watermark reversed	10·00	7·00	7·00
		Wk. Watermark inverted and reversed	22·00	15·00	
347		$\frac{1}{2}$d. yellow-green	10·00	8·00	6·00
348		$\frac{1}{2}$d. pale green	15·00	8·00	6·00
349	**102**	1d. brt scarlet	15·00	8·00	6·00
350		1d. scarlet	15·00	8·00	6·00
		a. No cross on crown	£100	80·00	22·00
		b. Imperf	£110	80·00	
		c. Watermark sideways	£110	80·00	80·00
		d. Watermark sideways. No cross on crown	£650	£550	
		Wi. Watermark inverted	15·00	10·00	
		Wj. Watermark reversed	15·00	10·00	
		Wk. Watermark inverted and reversed	£450	£350	£190

104

105

106

107

108

No. 357a

No. 357ab

No. 357ac

Die I

Die II

Two Dies of the 2d.

Die I.— Inner frame-line at top and sides close to solid of background. *Four* complete lines of shading between top of head and oval frame-line. These four lines do *not* extend to the oval itself. White line round "TWOPENCE" thin.

Die II.—Inner frame-line further from solid of background. *Three* lines between top of head and extending to the oval. White line round "TWOPENCE" thicker.

(Des Bertram Mackennal (heads) and G.W. Eve (frames). Coinage head (½, 1½, 2, 3 and 4d.); large medal head (1d., 2½d.); intermediate medal head (5d. to 1s.); small medal head used for fiscal stamps. Dies eng J. A. C. Harrison)

(Typo by Harrison & Sons Ltd., except the 6d. printed by the Stamping Department of the Board of Inland Revenue, Somerset House. The latter also made printings of the following which can only be distinguished by the controls: ½d. B.13; 1½d. A.12; 2d. C.13; 2½d. A.12; 3d. A12, B.13, C.13; 4d. B.13; 5d. B.13; 7d. C.13; 8d. C.13; 9d. agate B.13; 10d. C.13; 1s. C.13)

1912–24. *Wmk Royal Cypher, W* **100**. *Chalk-surfaced paper (6d.). P* 15 × 14.

351	**105**	½d. green (1.13)	1·50	75	50
		a. Partial double print (half of bottom row) (Control G15)	—	£15000	†
		b. Gummed both sides			
		Wi. Watermark inverted	2·75	2·00	1·00
		Wj. Watermark reversed	15·00	10·00	6·00
		Wk. Watermark inverted and reversed	4·00	3·00	2·25
352	**105**	½d. brt green	1·50	75	50
353		½d. dp green	5·00	3·00	1·50
354		½d. yellow-green	6·00	4·25	2·00
355		½d. very yellow (Cyprus) green (1914)	£2500	£1750	†
356		½d. blue-green	40·00	25·00	15·00
357	**104**	1d. brt scarlet (8.10.12)	1·50	75	50
		a. "Q" for "O" (R.1/4) (Control E14)	£175	£150	90·00
		ab. "Q" for "O" (R.4/11) (Control T22)	£250	£300	£110
		ac. Reversed "Q" for "O" (R.15/9) (Control T22)	£325	£250	£150
		ad. Inverted "Q" for "O" (R.20/3)	£400	£325	£160
		b. *Tête-bêche* (pair)	—	£50000	†
		Wi. Watermark inverted	3·00	1·50	40
		Wj. Watermark reversed	14·00	10·00	6·00
		Wk. Watermark inverted and reversed	3·00	1·75	1·25
358		1d. vermilion	3·75	2·25	1·50
359		1d. pale rose-red	12·00	8·00	1·50
360		1d. carmine-red	10·00	6·00	3·00
361		1d. scarlet-vermilion	£110	80·00	25·00
		a. Printed on back†	£225	£175	†
362	**105**	1½d. red-brown (15.10.12)	2·50	1·75	75
		a. "PENCF" (R.15/12)	£225	£180	£125
		b. Booklet pane. Four stamps plus two printed labels (2.24)	£350	£300	
		Wi. Watermark inverted	5·00	2·75	1·00
		Wi. Watermark reversed	14·00	10·00	4·00
		Wk. Watermark inverted and reversed	7·00	6·00	4·00
363		1½d. chocolate-brown	4·50	3·00	1·00
		a. No watermark	£140	£120	90·00
364		1½d. chestnut	4·00	3·00	75
		a. "PENCF" (R.15/12)	£140	£100	80·00
365		1½d. yellow-brown	15·00	10·00	12·00
366	**106**	2d. orange-yellow (Die I) (20.8.12)	8·00	5·00	2·00
367		2d. reddish orange (Die I) (11.13)	4·00	2·00	1·00
368		2d. orange (Die I)	3·00	2·00	1·00
		Wi. Watermark inverted	12·00	8·00	4·50
		Wj. Watermark reversed	10·00	8·00	5·50
		Wk. Watermark inverted and reversed	9·00	6·00	4·00
369		2d. brt orange (Die I)	4·00	2·50	1·50
370		2d. orange (Die II) (9.21)	4·00	3·00	2·75
		Wi. Watermark inverted	18·00	12·00	7·00
		Wj. Watermark inverted and reversed	22·00	18·00	7·00
371	**104**	2½d. cobalt-blue (18.10.12)	11·00	6·00	2·00
371a		2½d. brt blue (1914)	11·00	6·00	2·0
372		2½d. blue	11·00	6·00	2·0
		Wi. Watermark inverted	35·00	25·00	22·0
		Wj. Watermark reversed	18·00	13·00	7·0
		Wk. Watermark inverted and reversed	18·00	13·00	6·5
373		2½d. indigo-blue* (1920)	£1100	£850	£60
373a		2½d. dull Prussian blue* (1921)	£600	£475	£35
374	**106**	3d. dull reddish violet (9.10.12)	11·00	7·00	1·5
375		3d. violet	4·50	3·00	2·0
		Wi. Watermark inverted	55·00	35·00	18·0
		Wj. Watermark reversed	£100	85·00	25·0
		Wk. Watermark inverted and reversed	15·00	11·00	8·0
376		3d. bluish violet (11.13)	6·00	4·00	1·5
377		3d. pale violet	8·00	5·00	1·5
378		4d. dp grey-green (15.1.13)	32·00	22·00	6·0
379		4d. grey-green	11·00	6·00	1·5
		Wi. Watermark inverted	20·00	12·00	14·0
		Wj. Watermark reversed	50·00	35·00	9·0
		Wk. Watermark inverted and reversed	30·00	22·00	6·0
380		4d. pale grey-green	17·00	12·00	3·

381	107	5d. brown (30.6.13)	11·00	5·00	4·00
		Wi. Watermark inverted	£400	£300	£200
		Wj. Watermark inverted and reversed	£140	£120	50·00
		Wk. Watermark reversed	†	†	—
382		5d. yellow-brown	11·00	6·00	4·00
		a. No watermark	£700	£500	
383		5d. bistre-brown	£100	75·00	30·00
384		6d. dull purple (1.8.13)	25·00	15·00	6·00
385		6d. reddish purple	15·00	8·00	3·00
		a. Perf 14 (10.20)	85·00	70·00	£100
		Wi. Watermark inverted	32·00	20·00	16·00
		Wj. Watermark reversed	£575	£425	
		Wk. Watermark inverted and reversed	30·00	18·00	8·00
386		6d. dp reddish purple	30·00	15·00	3·00
387		7d. olive (1.8.13)	17·00	10·00	5·00
		Wi. Watermark inverted	32·00	24·00	22·00
		Wj. Watermark inverted and reversed	£1250	£900	
		Wk. Watermark reversed	†	†	—
388		7d. bronze-green (1915)	60·00	45·00	18·00
389		7d. sage-green (1917)	60·00	45·00	10·00
390		8d. black/*yellow* (1.8.13)	32·00	22·00	9·00
		Wi. Watermark inverted	75·00	60·00	55·00
		Wj. Watermark reversed	90·00	70·00	
		Wk. Watermark inverted and reversed	£1500	£1250	
391		8d. black/*yellow-buff* (*granite*) (5.17)	35·00	25·00	12·00
392	108	9d. agate (30.6.13)	20·00	12·00	4·00
		a. Printed double, one albino			
		Wi. Watermark inverted	70·00	40·00	32·00
		Wj. Watermark inverted and reversed	50·00	35·00	22·00
393		9d. dp agate	22·00	14·00	4·00
393*a*		9d. olive-green (9.22)	£140	80·00	25·00
		aWi. Watermark inverted	£525	£425	£275
		aWj. Watermark inverted and reversed	£450	£350	£250
393*b*		9d. pale olive-green	£160	75·00	25·00
394		10d. turquoise-blue (1.8.13)	18·00	12·00	15·00
		Wi. Watermark inverted	£900	£650	£225
		Wj. Watermark inverted and reversed	£120	£100	40·00
394*a*		10d. dp turquoise-blue	65·00	48·00	18·00
395		1s. bistre (1.8.13)	18·00	12·00	2·00
		Wi. Watermark inverted	£110	75·00	35·00
		Wj. Watermark inverted and reversed	32·00	28·00	16·00
396		1s. bistre-brown	32·00	22·00	7·00
		Set of 15	£275	£160	65·00

Imperf stamps of this issue exist but may be war-time colour trials.

† The impression of No. 361a is set sideways and is very pale.

*No. 373 comes from Control O 20 and also exists on toned paper. No. 373a comes from Control R 21 and also exists on toned paper, but both are unlike the rare Prussian blue shade of the 1935 2½d. Jubilee issue.

Examples of the 2d., T **106** which were in the hands of philatelists, are known bisected in Guernsey from 27 December 1940 to February 1941.

See also Nos. 418/29.

1913 (Aug). *Wmk Royal Cypher ("Multiple"), W* **103**. *P* 15 × 14.

397	105	½d. brt green	£250	£150	£180
		a. Watermark sideways	†	†	£18000
		Wi. Watermark inverted	£450	£300	
398	104	1d. dull scarlet	£350	£225	£225
		Wi. Watermark inverted	£525	£375	

Both these stamps were originally issued in rolls only. Subsequently sheets were found, so that horizontal pairs and blocks are known but are of considerable rarity.

109

A

110 Single Cypher

Major Re-entries on 2s. 6d.

Nos. 400a and 408a

No. 415b

(Des Bertram Mackennal. Dies eng J.A.C. Harrison. Recess)

High values, so-called "Sea Horses" design: T **109**. *Background around portrait consists of horizontal lines, Type A. Wmk Single Cypher, W* **110**. *P* 11 × 12.

1913 (30 June–Aug). *Printed by Waterlow Bros & Layton.*

399	109	2s. 6d. dp sepia-brown	£200	£140	85·00
400		2s. 6d. sepia-brown	£200	£130	75·00
		a. Re-entry (R.2/1)	£950	£700	£450
401		5s. rose-carmine (4 July)	£300	£225	£175
402		10s. indigo-blue (1 Aug)	£600	£350	£275
403		£1 green (1 Aug)	£1800	£1200	£725
404		£1 dull blue-green (1 Aug)	£1800	£1200	£775
★399/404		**For well-centred, lightly used**			+35%

For full information on all future British issues, collectors should write to the British Post Office Philatelic Bureau, 20 Brandon Street, Edinburgh EH3 5TT

1915 (Nov–Dec). *Printed by De la Rue & Co.*

405	**109**	2s. 6d. dp yellow-brown	£225	£150	80·00
		Wi. Watermark inverted	£450	£350	
406		2s. 6d. yellow-brown	£225	£150	75·00
		Wi. Watermark inverted	£400	£300	
		Wj. Watermark reversed	£400	£300	
		Wk. Watermark inverted and reversed	£950	£800	
407		2s. 6d. pale brown (worn plate)	£200	£140	75·00
		Wi. Watermark inverted	£400	£300	
		Wj. Watermark reversed	£450	£350	
408		2s. 6d. sepia (seal-brown)	£225	£150	80·00
		a. Re-entry (R.2/1)	£750	£600	£450
		Wi. Watermark inverted	£400	£300	
		Wj. Watermark reversed	£400	£300	
409		5s. brt carmine	£325	£225	£160
		Wi. Watermark inverted	£950	£750	
		Wj. Watermark reversed	£900	£700	
		Wk. Watermark inverted and reversed	£3000	£2500	†
410		5s. pale carmine (worn plate)	£400	£300	£180
411		10s. dp blue (12.15)	£1400	£950	£450
412		10s. blue	£1200	£800	£400
		Wi. Watermark inverted and reversed	—	—	†
413		10s. pale blue	£1200	£800	£400
*405/13		**For well-centred, lightly used**			**+40%**

1918 (Dec)–**19**. *Printed by Bradbury, Wilkinson & Co, Ltd.*

413*a*	**109**	2s. 6d. olive-brown	£110	65·00	35·00
414		2s. 6d. chocolate-brown	£110	75·00	35·00
415		2s. 6d. reddish brown	£125	80·00	35·00
415*a*		2s. 6d. pale brown	£110	80·00	30·00
		b. Major re-entry (R.1/2)	£650	£500	£275
416		5s. rose-red (1.19)	£225	£170	50·00
417		10s. dull grey-blue (1.19)	£350	£240	95·00
		Set of 4 (inc. no. 403)	£2250	£1500	£800
*413*a*/17		**For well-centred, lightly used**			**+35%**

DISTINGUISHING PRINTINGS. Note that the £1 value was only printed by Waterlow.

Waterlow and De La Rue stamps measure exactly 22 mm vertically. In the De La Rue printings the gum is usually patchy and yellowish, and the colour of the stamp, particularly in the 5s., tends to show through the back. The holes of the perforation are smaller than those of the other two printers, but there is a thick perforation tooth at the top of each vertical side.

In the Bradbury Wilkinson printings the height of the stamp is $22\frac{3}{4}$ or 23 mm. On most of the $22\frac{3}{4}$ mm high stamps a minute coloured guide dot appears in the margin just above the middle of the upper frame-line.

For (1934) re-engraved Waterlow printings *see* Nos. 450/2.

UNITED KINGDOM OF GREAT BRITAIN AND NORTHERN IRELAND

111 Block Cypher **111*a***

The watermark Type **111*a***, as compared with Type **111**, differs as follows: Closer spacing of horizontal rows ($12\frac{1}{2}$ mm instead of $14\frac{1}{2}$ mm). Letters shorter and rounder. Watermark thicker.

(Typo by Waterlow & Sons, Ltd (all values except 6d.) and later, 1934–35, by Harrison & Sons, Ltd (all values). Until 1934 the 6d. was printed at Somerset House where a printing of the $1\frac{1}{2}$d. was also made in 1926 (identifiable only by control E.26). Printings by Harrisons in 1934–35 can be identified, when in mint condition, by the fact that the gum shows a streaky appearance vertically, the Waterlow gum being uniformly applied, but Harrisons also used up the balance of the Waterlow "smooth gum" paper)

1924 (Feb)–**26**. *Wmk Block Cypher, W* **111**. *P* 15 × 14.

418	**105**	$\frac{1}{2}$d. green	60	40	25
		a. Watermark sideways (5.24)	8·00	5·00	2·75
		b. Doubly printed	£9000	£7500	†
		Wi. Watermark inverted	3·50	1·50	60
		Wj. Watermark sideways-inverted			
419	**104**	1d. scarlet	60	40	25
		a. Watermark sideways	20·00	14·00	14·00
		b. Experimental paper, W **111***a* (10.24)	28·00	22·00	
		c. Partial double print, one inverted			
		d. Inverted "Q" for "O" (R.20/3)	£400	£300	
		Wi. Watermark inverted	4·00	2·00	1·00
420	**105**	$1\frac{1}{2}$d. red-brown	60	40	25
		a. *Tête-bêche* (pair)	£400	£300	£525
		b. Watermark sideways (8.24)	12·00	6·00	3·00
		c. Printed on the gummed side	£425	£325	†
		d. Booklet pane. Four stamps plus two printed labels (3.24)	£125	90·00	
		e. Ditto. Watermark sideways	£3750	£3250	
		f. Experimental paper, W **111***a* (10.24)	55·00	40·00	70·00
		g. Double impression	—	£8500	†
		Wi. Watermark inverted	1·25	75	50
		Wj. Watermark sideways-inverted			
421	**106**	2d. orange (Die II) (7.24)	2·50	1·50	1·25
		a. No watermark	£600	£500	
		b. Watermark sideways (7.26)	95·00	60·00	70·00
		c. Partial double print	—	£13000	†
		Wi. Watermark inverted	15·00	9·00	12·00
422	**104**	$2\frac{1}{2}$d. blue (10.24)	6·00	3·25	1·50
		a. No watermark	£900	£650	
		b. Watermark sideways	†	†	£3750
		Wi. Watermark inverted	25·00	18·00	20·00
423	**106**	3d. violet (10.24)	12·00	5·50	1·50
		Wi. Watermark inverted	25·00	15·00	15·00
424		4d. grey-green (11.24)	15·00	7·00	1·25
		a. Printed on the gummed side	£1500	£1200	†
		Wi. Watermark inverted	60·00	40·00	17·00
425	**107**	5d. brown (11.24)	25·00	11·00	2·00
		Wi. Watermark inverted	40·00	30·00	26·00
426		6d. reddish purple (*chalk-surfaced paper*) (9.24)	12·00	7·00	1·75
		Wi. Watermark inverted	30·00	20·00	20·00
		Wj. Watermark inverted and reversed	£140	90·00	
426*a*		6d. purple (6.26)	3·75	2·00	75
		aWi. Watermark inverted	26·00	20·00	20·00
427	**108**	9d. olive-green (12.24)	23·00	7·00	2·50
		Wi. Watermark inverted	55·00	30·00	25·00
428		10d. turquoise-blue (11.24)	50·00	22·00	22·00
		Wi. Watermark inverted	£800	£600	£300
429		1s. bistre-brown (10.24)	30·00	13·00	1·75
		Wi. Watermark inverted	£250	£200	£190
		Set of 12	£150	65·00	32·00

There are numerous shades in this issue.

The 6d. on chalk-surfaced and ordinary papers was printed by both Somerset House and Harrisons. The Harrison printings have streaky gum, differ slightly in shade, and that on chalk-surfaced paper is printed in a highly fugitive ink. The prices quoted are for the commonest (Harrison) printing in each case.

112

(Des H. Nelson. Eng J. A. C. Harrison. Recess Waterlow)

1924–25. British Empire Exhibition. *W* **111**. *P* 14.

(a) Dated "1924" (23.4.24)

430	**112**	1d. scarlet		9·00	6·00	9·00
431		$1\frac{1}{2}$d. brown		16·00	9·00	13·00
			Set of 2	25·00	15·00	22·00
			First Day Cover			£350

(b) Dated "1925" (9.5.25)

432	**112**	1d. scarlet		10·00	10·00	20·00
433		$1\frac{1}{2}$d. brown		40·00	30·00	55·00
			Set of 2	50·00	40·00	75·00
			First Day Cover			£1200

113

114

115

116 St. George and the Dragon

117

(Des J. Farleigh (T **113** and **115**), E. Linzell (T **114**) and H. Nelson (T **116**). Eng C. G. Lewis (T **113**), T.E. Storey (T **115**), both at the Royal Mint; J. A. C. Harrison, of Waterlow (T **114** & **116**). Typo by Waterlow from plates made at the Royal Mint, except T **116**, recess by Bradbury, Wilkinson from die and plate of their own manufacture)

1929 (10 May). **Ninth U.P.U. Congress, London.**

(a) W **111**. *P* 15 × 14

434	**113**	$\frac{1}{2}$d.	green	2·25	2·00	2·00
		a.	Watermark sideways	35·00	26·00	34·00
		Wi.	Watermark inverted	22·00	10·00	8·00
435	**114**	1d.	scarlet	2·25	2·00	2·00
		a.	Watermark sideways	75·00	45·00	48·00
		Wi.	Watermark inverted	22·00	10·00	9·00
436		$1\frac{1}{2}$d.	purple-brown	1·50	1·75	1·50
		a.	Watermark sideways	45·00	26·00	25·00
		b.	Booklet pane. Four stamps plus two printed labels	£190	£170	
		Wi.	Watermark inverted	8·00	3·00	6·00
437	**115**	$2\frac{1}{2}$d.	blue	15·00	10·00	10·00
		Wi.	Watermark inverted	£1000	£700	£425

(b) W **117**. *P* 12

438	**116**	£1	black	£850	£650	£450
			Set of 4 (to $2\frac{1}{2}$d.)	19·00	14·00	14·00
			First Day Cover (4 vals.)			£500
			First Day Cover (5 vals.)			£3250

PRINTERS. All subsequent issues were printed in photogravure by Harrison & Sons, Ltd, *except where otherwise stated.*

118

119

120

121

122

1934–36. *W* **111**. *P* 15 × 14.

439	**118**	$\frac{1}{2}$d.	green (19.11.34)	25	10	25
		a.	Watermark sideways	10·00	7·00	3·50
		b.	Imperf three sides	£1500	£1250	
		Wi.	Watermark inverted	15·00	4·50	1·25
		Wj.	Watermark sideways-inverted	£200	£180	75·00
440	**119**	1d.	scarlet (24.9.34)	35	15	25
		a.	Imperf (pair)	£1250	£950	
		b.	Printed on gummed side	£500	£400	†
		c.	Watermark sideways	20·00	11·00	4·75
		d.	Double impression	†	†	£12500
		e.	Imperf between (pair)	£2500	£1750	
		f.	Imperf (three sides) (pair)	£1500	£1250	
		Wi.	Watermark inverted	12·00	6·50	2·75
		Wj.	Watermark sideways-inverted	80·00	60·00	
441	**118**	$1\frac{1}{2}$d.	red-brown (20.8.34)	25	10	25
		a.	Imperf (pair)	£350	£275	
		b.	Imperf (three sides) (lower stamp in vert pair)	£900	£700	
		c.	Imperf between (horiz pair)			
		d.	Watermark sideways	6·00	6·00	3·50
		e.	Booklet pane. Four stamps plus two printed labels (1.35)	75·00	60·00	
		Wi.	Watermark inverted	2·00	1·25	50
		Wj.	Watermark sideways-inverted			

442	**120**	2d.	orange (21.1.35)	60	30	50
		a.	Imperf (pair)	£1750	£1500	
		b.	Watermark sideways	£120	65·00	55·00
443	**119**	$2\frac{1}{2}$d.	ultramarine (18.3.35)	1·50	1·25	1·00
444	**120**	3d.	violet (18.3.35)	1·75	1·25	1·00
		Wi.	Watermark inverted	—	—	£500
445		4d.	dp grey-green (2.12.35)	2·75	1·75	1·00
		Wi.	Watermark inverted	†	†	—
446	**121**	5d.	yellow-brown (17.2.36)	9·00	6·00	2·50
447	**122**	9d.	dp olive-green (2.12.35)	16·00	12·00	2·00
448		10d.	turquoise-blue (24.2.36)	22·00	15·00	10·00
449		1s.	bistre-brown (24.2.36)	30·00	15·00	1·00
		a.	Double impression	—	—	†
			Set of 11	75·00	48·00	18·00

Owing to the need for wider space for the perforations the size of the designs of the $\frac{1}{2}$d. and 2d. were once, and the 1d. and $1\frac{1}{2}$d. twice reduced from that of the first printings.

The format description, size in millimetres and S.G. catalogue number are given but further details will be found in the *Great Britain Specialised Catalogue, Volume 2.*

Description	*Size*	*S.G. Nos.*	*Date of Issue*
$\frac{1}{2}$d. intermediate format	18.4 × 22.2	–	19.11.34
$\frac{1}{2}$d. small format	17.9 × 21.7	439	1935
1d. large format	18.7 × 22.5	–	24.9.34
1d. intermediate format	18.4 × 22.2	–	1934
1d. small format	17.9 × 21.7	440	1935
$1\frac{1}{2}$d. large format	18.7 × 22.5	–	20.8.34
$1\frac{1}{2}$d. intermediate format	18.4 × 22.2	–	1934
$1\frac{1}{2}$d. small format	17.9 × 21.7	441	1935
2d. intermediate format	18.4 × 22.2	–	21.1.35
2d. small format	18.15 × 21.7	442	1935

There are also numerous minor variations, due to the photographic element in the process.

The $\frac{1}{2}$d. imperf three sides, No. 439b, is known in a block of four, from a sheet, in which the bottom pair is imperf at top and sides.

Examples of 2d., T **120**, which were in the hands of philatelists are known bisected in Guernsey from 27 December 1940 to February 1941.

B

123

(Eng J .A .C. Harrison. Recess Waterlow)

1934 (16 Oct). *T* **109** *(re-engraved). Background around portrait consists of horizontal and diagonal lines, Type B, W* **110**. *P* 11 × 12.

450	**109**	2s. 6d.	chocolate-brown	80·00	55·00	25·00
451		5s.	brt rose-red	£225	£110	70·00
452		10s.	indigo	£350	£275	60·00
			Set of 3	£575	£400	£140

There are numerous other minor differences in the design of this issue.

(Des B. Freedman)

1935 (7 May). **Silver Jubilee.** *W* **111**. *P* 15 × 14.

453	**123**	$\frac{1}{2}$d.	green	75	50	40
		Wi.	Watermark inverted	12·00	6·00	3·00
454		1d.	scarlet	2·00	1·25	1·50
		Wi.	Watermark inverted	12·00	6·00	4·00
455		$1\frac{1}{2}$d.	red-brown	75	50	40
		Wi.	Watermark inverted	4·00	3·00	1·00
456		$2\frac{1}{2}$d.	blue	5·00	4·50	5·50
456*a*		$2\frac{1}{2}$d.	Prussian blue	£4250	£3500	£3500
			Set of 4	7·00	6·00	7·00
			First Day Cover			£500

The 1d., $1\frac{1}{2}$d. and $2\frac{1}{2}$d. values differ from T **123** in the emblem in the panel at right.

Four sheets of No. 456*a*, printed in the wrong shade, were issued in error by the Post Office Stores Department on 25 June 1935. It is known that three from the sheets were sold from the sub-office at 134 Fore Street, Upper Edmonton, London, between that date and 4 July.

KING EDWARD VIII

20 January–10 December 1936

Further detailed information on the stamps of King Edward VIII will be found in Volume 2 of the Stanley Gibbons *Great Britain Specialised Catalogue.*

> **PRICES.** From S.G. 457 prices quoted in the first column are for stamps in unmounted mint condition.

124

125

(Des H. Brown, adapted Harrison using a photo by Hugh Cecil)

1936. *W* **125**. *P* 15 × 14.

457	**124**	$\frac{1}{2}$d.	green (1.9.36)	20	20
		a.	Double impression		
		Wi.	Watermark inverted	8·00	3·25
458		1d.	scarlet (14.9.36)	50	25
		Wi.	Watermark inverted	8·00	3·25
459		$1\frac{1}{2}$d.	red-brown (1.9.36)	25	20
		a.	Booklet pane. Four stamps plus two printed labels (10.36)	50·00	
		Wi.	Watermark inverted	1·50	1·50
460		$2\frac{1}{2}$d.	brt blue (1.9.36)	25	75
			Set of 4	1·00	1·25

First Day Covers

1.9.36	$\frac{1}{2}$d., $1\frac{1}{2}$d., $2\frac{1}{2}$d. *(457, 459/60)*	£140
14.9.36	1d. *(458)*	£170

KING GEORGE VI

11 December 1936–6 February 1952

Further detailed information on the stamps of King George VI will be found in Volume 2 of the Stanley Gibbons *Great Britain Specialised Catalogue.*

126 King George VI and Queen Elizabeth

127

(Des E. Dulac)

1937 (13 May). **Coronation.** *W* **127**. *P* 15 × 14.

461	**126**	1½d. maroon	50	40
		First Day Cover		28·00

128

129

130

King George VI and National Emblems

(Des T **128/9**, E. Dulac (head) and E. Gill (frames). T **130**, E. Dulac (whole stamp))

1937–47. *W* **127**. *P* 15 × 14.

462	**128**	½d. green (10.5.37)	10	15
		a. Watermark sideways (1.38)	25	25
		ab. Booklet pane of 4 (6.40)	25·00	
		Wi. Watermark inverted	8·00	40
463		1d. scarlet (10.5.37)	10	15
		a. Watermark sideways (2.38)	13·00	4·50
		ab. Booklet pane of 4 (6.40)	65·00	
		Wi. Watermark inverted	30·00	2·00
464		1½d. red-brown (30.7.37)	20	15
		a. Watermark sideways (2.38)	80	1·00
		b. Booklet pane. Four stamps plus two printed labels (8.37)	45·00	
		c. Imperf three sides (pair)		
		Wi. Watermark inverted	9·00	70
465		2d. orange (31.1.38)	75	50
		a. Watermark sideways (2.38)	65·00	28·00
		b. Bisected (on cover)	†	22·00
		Wi. Watermark inverted	45·00	4·00
466		2½d. ultramarine (10.5.37)	25	15
		a. Watermark sideways (6.40)	50·00	16·00
		b. *Tête-bêche* (horiz pair)		
		Wi. Watermark inverted	27·00	2·25
467		3d. violet (31.1.38)	3·25	90
468	**129**	4d. grey-green (21.11.38)	50	50
		a. Imperf (pair)	£2000	
		b. Imperf three sides (horiz pair)	£2500	
469		5d. brown (21.11.38)	2·00	60
		a. Imperf (pair)	£2500	
		b. Imperf three sides (horiz pair)	£2000	
470		6d. purple (30.1.39)	1·25	50
471	**130**	7d. emerald-green (27.2.39)	3·25	50
		a. Imperf three sides (horiz pair)	£2000	
472		8d. brt carmine (27.2.39)	3·50	60
473		9d. dp olive-green (1.5.39)	5·50	70
474		10d. turquoise-blue (1.5.39)	5·00	70
		aa. Imperf (pair)	£3500	
474*a*		11d. plum (29.12.47)	2·00	1·75
475		1s. bistre-brown (1.5.39)	5·75	60
		Set of 15	30·00	7·50

For later printings of the lower values in apparently lighter shades and different colours, see Nos. 485/90 and 503/8.

No. 465b was authorised for use in Guernsey from 27 December 1940 until February 1941.

Nos. 468b and 469b are perforated at foot only and each occurs in the same sheet as Nos. 468a and 469a.

No. 471a is also perforated at foot only, but occurs on the top row of a sheet.

First Day Covers

10.5.37	½d., 1d., 2½d. (*462/3, 466*)	4·00
30.7.37	1½d. (*464*)	4·00
31.1.38	2d., 3d. (*465, 467*)	22·00
21.11.38	4d., 5d. (*468/9*)	35·00
30.1.39	6d. (*470*)	35·00
27.2.39	7d., 8d. (*471/2*)	50·00
1.5.39	9d., 10d., 1s. (*473/4, 475*)	£325
29.12.47	11d. (*474a*)	40·00

131

132

133

(Des E. Dulac (T **131**) and Hon. G. R. Bellew (T **132**). Eng J. A. C. Harrison. Recess Waterlow)

1939–48. *W* **133**. *P* 14.

476	**131**	2s. 6d. brown (4.9.39)	38·00	6·50
476*a*		2s. 6d. yellow-green (9.3.42)	7·00	1·25
477		5s. red (21.8.39)	14·00	1·75
478	**132**	10s. dark blue (30.10.39)	£170	21·00
478*a*		10s. ultramarine (30.11.42)	35·00	5·50
478*b*		£1 brown (1.10.48)	10·00	23·00
		Set of 6	£250	55·00

First Day Covers

21.8.39	5s. (*477*)	£375
4.9.39	2s. 6d. brown (*476*)	£800
30.10.39	10s. dark blue (*478*)	£1600
9.3.42	2s. 6d. yellow-green (*476a*)	£1000
30.11.42	10s. ultramarine (*478a*)	£1900
1.10.48	£1 (*478b*)	£190

134 Queen Victoria and King George VI

(Des H. L. Palmer)

1940 (6 May). **Centenary of First Adhesive Postage Stamps.** *W* **127**. *P* 14½ × 14.

479	**134**	½d. green	30	30
480		1d. scarlet	1·00	50
481		1½d. red-brown	30	40
482		2d. orange	50	50
		a. Bisected (on cover)	†	16·00
483		2½d. ultramarine	2·25	90
484		3d. violet	3·00	3·25
		Set of 6	6·50	5·25
		First Day Cover		45·00

No. 482a was authorised for use on Guernsey from 27 December 1940 until February 1941.

1941–42. *Head as Nos. 462/7, but lighter background.* *W* **127**. *P* 15 × 14.

485	**128**	½d. pale green (1.9.41)	20	20
		a. *Tête-bêche* (horiz pair)	£3000	
		b. Imperf (pair)	£1750	
		Wi. Watermark inverted	3·50	20
486		1d. pale scarlet (11.8.41)	20	20
		a. Watermark sideways (10.42)	3·50	5·00
		b. Imperf (pair)	£2500	
		c. Imperf three sides (horiz pair)	£2500	
487		1½d. pale red-brown (28.9.42)	85	55
488		2d. pale orange (6.10.41)	60	50
		a. Watermark sideways (6.42)	22·00	14·00
		b. *Tête-bêche* (horiz pair)	£2500	
		c. Imperf (pair)	£2000	
		d. Imperf pane*	£4500	
		Wi. Watermark inverted	2·75	50
489		2½d. light ultramarine (21.7.41)	25	20
		a. Watermark sideways (8.42)	12·00	10·00
		b. *Tête-bêche* (horiz pair)	£2500	
		c. Imperf (pair)	£2250	
		d. Imperf pane*	£3500	
		e. Imperf three sides (horiz pair)	£3500	
		Wi. Watermark inverted	1·25	75
490		3d. pale violet (3.11.41)	1·75	60
		Set of 6	3·50	2·00

The *tête-bêche* varieties are from defectively made-up stamp booklets.

Nos. 486c and 489e are perforated at foot only and occur in the same sheets as Nos. 486b and 489c.

*BOOKLET ERRORS. Those listed as "imperf panes" show one row of perforations either at the top or at the bottom of the pane of 6.

First Day Covers

21.7.41	2½d. (*489*)	35·00
11.8.41	1d. (*486*)	17·00
1.9.41	½d. (*485*)	17·00
6.10.41	2d. (*488*)	50·00
3.11.41	3d. (*490*)	90·00
28.9.42	1½d. (*487*)	45·00

135

136

(Des H. L. Palmer (T **135**) and R. Stone (T **136**))

1946 (11 June). **Victory.** *W* **127**. *P* 15 × 14.

491	**135**	2½d. ultramarine	30	20
492	**136**	3d. violet	30	20
		Set of 2	60	40
		First Day Cover		60·00

137

138

King George VI and Queen Elizabeth

(Des G. Knipe and Joan Hassall from photographs by Dorothy Wilding)

1948 (26 Apr). **Royal Silver Wedding.** *W* **127**. *P* 15 × 14 (2½*d.*) *or* 14 × 15 (£1).

493	**137**	2½d. ultramarine	30	30
494	**138**	£1 blue	38·00	35·00
		Set of 2	38·00	35·00
		First Day Cover		£350

1948 (10 May). Stamps of 1d. and 2½d. showing seaweed-gathering were on sale at eight Head Post Offices in Great Britain, but were primarily for use in the Channel Islands and are listed there (see Nos. C1/2, after Royal Mail Postage Labels).

139 Globe and Laurel Wreath

140 "Speed"

141 Olympic Symbol

142 Winged Victory

(Des P. Metcalfe (T **139**), A. Games (T **140**), S. D. Scott (T **141**) and E. Dulac (T **142**))

1948 (29 July). **Olympic Games.** *W* **127**. *P* 15 × 14.

495	**139**	2½d. ultramarine	10	10
496	**140**	3d. violet	30	30
497	**141**	6d. brt purple	60	30
498	**142**	1s. brown	1·25	1·50
		Set of 4	2·00	2·00
		First Day Cover		38·00

143 Two Hemispheres

144 U.P.U. Monument, Berne

145 Goddess Concordia, Globe and Points of Compass

146 Posthorn and Globe

(Des Mary Adshead (T **143**), P. Metcalfe (T **144**), H. Fleury (T **145**) and Hon. G. R. Bellew (T **146**))

1949 (10 Oct). **75th Anniv of Universal Postal Union.** *W* **127**. *P* 15 × 14.

499	**143**	2½d.	ultramarine	10	10
500	**144**	3d.	violet	30	40
501	**145**	6d.	brt purple	60	75
502	**146**	1s.	brown	1·25	1·50
			Set of 4	2·00	2·75
			First Day Cover		55·00

1950–52. *4d. as No.* 468 *and others as Nos.* 485/9, *but colours changed. W* **127**. *P* 15 × 14.

503	**128**	½d.	pale orange (3.5.51)	30	30
		a.	Imperf (pair)		
		b.	*Tête-bêche* (horiz pair)	£3000	
		c.	Imperf pane*	£4000	
		Wi.	Watermark inverted	10	30
504		1d.	lt ultramarine (3.5.51)	30	30
		a.	Watermark sideways (5.51)	50	60
		b.	Imperf (pair)	£2000	
		c.	Imperf three sides (horiz pair)	£1500	
		d.	Booklet pane. Three stamps plus three printed labels (3.52)	15·00	
		e.	Ditto. Partial *tête-bêche* pane	£2500	
		Wi.	Watermark inverted	2·25	1·00
505		1½d.	pale green (3.5.51)	35	50
		a.	Watermark sideways (9.51)	2·25	3·00
		Wi.	Watermark inverted	2·50	80
506		2d.	pale red-brown (3.5.51)	35	30
		a.	Watermark sideways (5.51)	1·25	1·40
		b.	*Tête-bêche* (horiz pair)	£3000	
		c.	Imperf three sides (horiz pair)	£1500	
		Wi.	Watermark inverted	3·50	4·50
507		2½d.	pale scarlet (3.5.51)	35	30
		a.	Watermark sideways (5.51)	1·25	1·25
		b.	*Tête-bêche* (horiz pair)		
		Wi.	Watermark inverted	70	60
508	**129**	4d.	lt ultramarine (2.10.50)	2·25	1·50
		a.	Double impression	†	£5000
			Set of 6	3·50	2·75

*BOOKLET ERRORS. Those listed as "imperf panes" show one row of perforations either at the top or at the bottom of the pane of 6.

No. 504c is perforated at foot only and occurs in the same sheet as No. 504b.

No. 506c is also perforated at foot only.

First Day Covers

2.10.50	4d. (*508*)	85·00
3.5.51	½d., 1d., 1½d., 2d., 2½d. (*503/7*)	35·00

147 H.M.S. *Victory*

148 White Cliffs of Dover

149 St. George and the Dragon

150 Royal Coat of Arms

(Des Mary Adshead (T **147**/**8**), P. Metcalfe (T **149**/**50**). Recess Waterlow)

1951 (3 May). *W* **133**. *P* 11 × 12.

509	**147**	2s.	6d. yellow-green	6·00	75
510	**148**	5s.	red	32·00	1·50
511	**149**	10s.	ultramarine	21·00	8·00
512	**150**	£1	brown	32·00	18·00
			Set of 4	80·00	24·00
			First Day Cover		£750

151 "Commerce and Prosperity"

152 Festival Symbol

(Des E. Dulac (T **151**), A. Games (T **152**))

1951 (3 May). **Festival of Britain.** *W* **127**. *P* 15 × 14.

513	**151**	2½d.	scarlet	25	20
514	**152**	4d.	ultramarine	50	45
			Set of 2	75	65
			First Day Cover		30·00

QUEEN ELIZABETH II
6 February 1952

Further detailed information on the stamps of Queen Elizabeth II will be found in Volumes 3, 4 and 5 of the Stanley Gibbons *Great Britain Specialised Catalogue*.

153 Tudor Crown

154

155

156

157

158

159

160

Queen Elizabeth II and National Emblems

I

II

Two types of the 2½d.

Type I:—In the frontal cross of the diadem, the top line is only half the width of the cross.

Type II:—The top line extends to the full width of the cross and there are signs of strengthening in other parts of the diadem.

(Des Enid Marx (T **154**), M. Farrar-Bell (T **155/6**), G. Knipe (T **157**), Mary Adshead (T **158**), E. Dulac (T **159/60**). Portrait by Dorothy Wilding)

1952–54. *W* **153**. *P* 15 × 14.

515	**154**	½d.	orange-red (31.8.53)	10	15
		Wi.	Watermark inverted (3.54)	40	60
516		1d.	ultramarine (31.8.53)	20	20
		a.	Booklet pane. Three stamps plus three printed labels	22·00	
		Wi.	Watermark inverted (3.54)	3·75	1·75
517		1½d.	green (5.12.52)	10	15
		a.	Watermark sideways (15.10.54)	50	70
		b.	Imperf pane*		
		Wi.	Watermark inverted (5.53)	25	40
518		2d.	red-brown (31.8.53)	20	15
		a.	Watermark sideways (8.10.54)	1·00	1·75
		Wi.	Watermark inverted (3.54)	20·00	16·00
519	**155**	2½d.	carmine-red (Type I) (5.12.52)	10	15
		a.	Watermark sideways (15.11.54)	8·50	8·50
		b.	Type II (booklets) (5.53)	1·25	1·00
		bWi.	Watermark inverted (5.53)	15	60
520		3d.	dp lilac (18.1.54)	1·00	75
521	**156**	4d.	ultramarine (2.11.53)	3·00	1·25
522	**157**	5d.	brown (6.7.53)	90	2·75
523		6d.	reddish purple (18.1.54)	3·00	90
		a.	Imperf three sides (pair)		
524		7d.	brt green (18.1.54)	9·00	5·00
525	**158**	8d.	magenta (6.7.53)	1·00	1·00
526		9d.	bronze-green (8.2.54)	22·00	3·75
527		10d.	Prussian blue (8.2.54)	18·00	3·75
528		11d.	brown-purple (8.2.54)	30·00	20·00
529	**160**	1s.	bistre-brown (6.7.53)	1·25	60
530	**159**	1s.	3d. green (2.11.53)	4·50	3·00
531	**160**	1s.	6d. grey-blue (2.11.53)	11·00	3·50
			Set of 17	95·00	42·00

See also Nos. 540/56, 561/6, 570/94 and 599/618*a*.

*BOOKLET ERRORS.—This pane of 6 stamps is *completely* imperf (see No. 540a, etc).

Stamps with *sideways watermark* come from left-side delivery coils and stamps with *inverted watermark* are from booklets.

First Day Covers

5.12.52	1½d., 2½d. (*517, 519*)	8·00
6.7.53	5d., 8d., 1s. (*522, 525, 529*)	40·00
31.8.53	½d., 1d., 2d. (*515/16, 518*)	40·00
2.11.53	4d., 1s. 3d., 1s. 6d. (*521, 530/1*)	£140
18.1.54	3d., 6d., 7d. (*520, 523/4*)	85·00
8.2.54	9d., 10d., 11d. (*526/8*)	£170

161

162

163

164

(Des E. Fuller (2½d.), M. Goaman (4d.), E. Dulac (1s. 3d.), M. Farrar-Bell (1s. 6d.). Portrait (except 1s. 3d.) by Dorothy Wilding)

1953 (3 June). **Coronation.** *W* **153**. *P* 15 × 14.

532	**161**	2½d.	carmine-red	10	50
533	**162**	4d.	ultramarine	40	1·75
534	**163**	1s.	3d. dp yellow-green	3·50	2·75
535	**164**	1s.	6d. dp grey-blue	7·00	3·50
			Set of 4	10·00	7·50
			First Day Cover		50·00

165 St. Edward's Crown

166 Carrickfergus Castle

167 Caernarvon Castle

168 Edinburgh Castle

169 Windsor Castle

(Des L. Lamb. Portait by Dorothy Wilding. Recess Waterlow (until 31.12.57) and De La Rue (subsequently))

1955–58. *W* **165**. *P* 11 × 12.

536	**166**	2s. 6d. black-brown (23.9.55)	10·00	2·00
		a. De La Rue printing (17.7.58)	30·00	2·50
		Wi. Watermark inverted	†	£2000
537	**167**	5s. rose-carmine (23.9.55)	30·00	3·50
		a. De La Rue printing (30.4.58)	75·00	10·00
538	**168**	10s. ultramarine (1.9.55)	80·00	12·00
		a. De La Rue printing. *Dull ultramarine* (25.4.58)	£170	20·00
539	**169**	£1 black (1.9.55)	£130	38·00
		a. De La Rue printing (28.4.58)	£300	60·00
		Set of 4 (Nos. 536/9)	£225	50·00
		Set of 4 (Nos 536a/9a)	£525	85·00
		First Day Cover (538/9)		£500
		First Day Cover (536/7)		£350

See also Nos. 595/8a & 759/62.

On 1 January 1958, the contract for printing the high values, T **166** to **169**, was transferred to De La Rue & Co, Ltd.

The work of the two printers is very similar, but the following notes will be helpful to those attempting to identify Waterlow and De La Rue stamps of the W **165** issue.

The De la Rue sheets are printed in pairs and have a –| or |– shaped guide-mark at the centre of one side-margin, opposite the middle row of perforations, indicating left and right-hand sheets respectively.

The Waterlow sheets have a small circle (sometimes crossed) instead of a "|–" and this is present in both side-margins opposite the 6th row of stamps, though one is sometimes trimmed off. Short dashes are also present in the perforation gutter between the marginal stamps marking the middle of the four sides and a cross is at the centre of the sheet. The four corners of the sheet have two lines forming a right-angle as trimming marks, but some are usually trimmed off. All these gutter marks and sheet-trimming marks are absent in the De La Rue printings.

De La Rue used the Waterlow die and no alterations were made to it, so that no difference exists in the design or its size, but the making of new plates at first resulted in slight but measurable variations in the width of the gutters between stamps, particularly the horizontal, as follows:

	Waterlow	De La Rue
Horiz gutters, mm	3.8 to 4.0	3.4 to 3.8

Later D.L.R. plates were however less distinguishable in this respect.

For a short time in 1959 the D.L.R. 2s. 6d. appeared with one dot in the bottom margin below the first stamp.

It is possible to sort singles with reasonable certainty by general characteristics. The individual lines of the D.L.R. impression are cleaner and devoid of the whiskers of colour of Waterlow's, and the whole impression lighter and softer.

Owing to the closer setting of the horizontal rows the strokes of the perforating comb are closer; this results in the topmost tooth on each side of De La Rue stamps being narrower than the corresponding teeth in Waterlow's which were more than normally broad.

Shades also help. The 2s. 6d. D.L.R. is a warmer, more chocolate shade than the blackish brown of Waterlow; the 5s. a lighter red with less carmine than Waterlow's; the 10s. more blue and less ultramarine; the £1 less intense black.

The paper of D.L.R. printings is uniformly white, identical with that of Waterlow printings from February 1957 onwards, but earlier Waterlow printings are on paper which is creamy by comparison.

In this and later issues of T **166/9** the dates of issue given for changes of watermark or paper are those on which supplies were first sent by the Supplies Department to Postmasters.

1955–58. *W* **165**. *P* 15 × 14.

540	**154**	$\frac{1}{2}$d. orange-red (booklets 8.55, sheets 12.12.55)	10	15
		a. Part perf pane*	£1200	
		Wi. Watermark inverted (9.55)	15	25
541		1d. ultramarine (19.9.55)	25	15
		a. Booklet pane. Three stamps plus three printed labels	13·00	
		b. *Tête-bêche* (horiz pair)		
		Wi. Watermark inverted (9.55)	40	30
542		$1\frac{1}{2}$d. green (booklet 8.55, sheets 11.10.55)	25	25
		a. Watermark sideways (7.3.56)	25	75
		b. *Tête-bêche* (horiz pair)	£900	
		Wi. Watermark inverted (8.55)	20	25
543		2d. red-brown (6.9.55)	20	25
		aa. Imperf between (vert pair)	£1500	
		a. Watermark sideways (31.7.56)	20	60
		ab. Imperf between (horiz pair)	£1500	
		Wi. Watermark inverted (9.55)	12·00	8·50
543*b*		2d. light red-brown (17.10.56)	20	25
		ba. *Tête-bêche* (horiz pair)	£600	
		bb. Imperf pane*		
		bc. Part perf pane*	£1200	
		bWi. Watermark inverted (1.57)	5·00	3·00
		d. Watermark sideways (5.3.57)	9·00	5·50
544	**155**	$2\frac{1}{2}$d. carmine-red (Type I) (28.9.55)	20	25
		a. Watermark sideways (Type I) (23.3.56)	1·25	1·25
		b. Type II (booklets 9.55, sheets 1957)	25	50
		ba. *Tête-bêche* (horiz pair)	£750	
		bb. Imperf pane*	£900	
		bc. Part perf pane*		
		bWi. Watermark inverted (9.55)	25	50
545		3d. dp lilac (17.7.56)	20	25
		aa. *Tête-bêche* (horiz pair)	£750	
		a. Imperf three sides (pair)	£500	
		b. Watermark sideways (22.11.57)	14·00	12·50
		Wi. Watermark inverted (1.10.57)	60	1·00
546	**156**	4d. ultramarine (14.11.55)	1·40	50
547	**157**	5d. brown (21.9.55)	5·50	4·75
548		6d. reddish purple (20.12.55)	4·00	1·00
		aa. Imperf three sides (pair)	£400	
		a. *Deep claret* (8.5.58)	4·00	1·25
		ab. Imperf three sides (pair)	£400	
549		7d. brt green (23.4.56)	50·00	9·00
550	**158**	8d. magenta (21.12.55)	6·00	1·00
551		9d. bronze-green (15.12.55)	23·00	2·75
552		10d. Prussian blue (22.9.55)	19·00	2·75
553		11d. brown-purple (28.10.55)	50	1·50
554	**160**	1s. bistre-brown (3.11.55)	19·00	50
555	**159**	1s. 3d. green (27.3.56)	27·00	1·50
556	**160**	1s. 6d. grey-blue (27.3.56)	19·00	1·50
		Set of 18	£150	23·00

The dates given for Nos. 540/556 are those on which they were first issued by the Supplies Dept to postmasters.

In December 1956 a completely imperforate sheet of No. 543*b* was noticed by clerks in a Kent post office, one of whom purchased it against P.O. regulations. In view of this irregularity we do not consider it properly issued.

Types of 2½d. In this issue, in 1957, Type II formerly only found in stamps from booklets, began to replace Type I on sheet stamps.

*BOOKLET ERRORS. Those listed as "imperf panes" show one row of perforations either at top or bottom of the booklet pane; those as "part perf panes" have one row of 3 stamps imperf on three sides.

For Nos. 542 and 553 in Presentation Pack, see after No. 586.

170 Scout Badge and "Rolling Hitch"

171 "Scouts coming to Britain"

172 Globe within a Compass

(Des Mary Adshead (2½d.), P. Keely (4d.), W. H. Brown (1s. 3d.))

1957 (1 Aug). **World Scout Jubilee Jamboree.** *W* **165**. *P* 15 × 14.

557	**170**	2½d. carmine-red		15	25
558	**171**	4d. ultramarine		50	1·25
559	**172**	1s. 3d. green		5·00	4·75
			Set of 3	5·00	5·50
			First Day Cover		20·00

173

½d.to 1½d., 2½d., 3d. 2d.
Graphite-line arrangements
(Stamps viewed from back)

1957 (12 Sept). **46th Inter-Parliamentary Union Conference.** *W* **165**. *P* 15 × 14.

560	**173**	4d. ultramarine	1·00	1·25
		First Day Cover		90·00

GRAPHITE-LINED ISSUES. These were used in connection with automatic sorting machinery, first introduced experimentally at Southampton.

The graphite lines were printed in black on the back, beneath the gum; two lines per stamp, except for the 2d.

In November 1959 phosphor bands were introduced (see notes after No. 598).

1957 (19 Nov). *Graphite-lined issue. Two graphite lines on the back, except 2d. value, which has one line.* *W* **165**. *P* 15 × 14.

561	**154**	½d. orange-red	20	30
562		1d. ultramarine	20	50
563		1½d. green	30	2·00
		a. Both lines at left	£800	£400
564		2d. light red-brown	2·50	2·25
		a. Line at left	£500	£175
565	**155**	2½d. carmine-red (Type II)	8·00	7·00
566		3d. dp lilac	30	70
		Set of 6	10·50	11·50
		First Day Cover		80·00

No. 564a results from a misplacement of the line and horizontal pairs exist showing one stamp without line. No. 563a results from a similar misplacement.

See also Nos. 587/94.

176 Welsh Dragon

177 Flag and Games Emblem

178 Welsh Dragon

(Des R. Stone (3d.), W. H. Brown (6d.), P. Keely (1s. 3d.))

1958 (18 July). **Sixth British Empire and Commonwealth Games, Cardiff.** *W* **165**. *P* 15 × 14.

567	**176**	3d. dp lilac	15	10
568	**177**	6d. reddish purple	25	45
569	**178**	1s. 3d. green	2·75	2·75
		Set of 3	2·75	2·75
		First Day Cover		60·00

179 Multiple Crowns

1958–65. *W* **179**. *P* 15 × 14.

570	**154**	½d. orange-red (25.11.58)	10	10
		a. Watermark sideways (26.5.61)	10	15

No.	Type		Description	Mint	Used
(570)		c.	Part perf pane*	£1000	
		Wi.	Watermark inverted (11.58)	30	25
		k.	Chalk-surfaced paper (15.7.63)	2·00	2·25
		kWi.	Watermark inverted	2·00	2·25
		l.	Booklet pane. No. 570a × 4	3·00	
		m.	Booklet pane. No. 570k × 3 *se-tenant* with 574k	9·50	
		n.	Booklet pane. No. 570a × 2 *se-tenant* with 574l × 2 (1.7.64)	2·00	
571	**154**	1d.	ultramarine (booklets 11.58, sheets 24.3.59)	10	10
		aa.	Imperf (vert pair from coil)		
		a.	Watermark sideways (26.5.61)	1·00	75
		b.	Part perf pane*	£1200	
		c.	Imperf pane		
		Wi.	Watermark inverted (11.58)	15	20
		l.	Booklet pane. No. 571a × 4	4·25	
		m.	Booklet pane. No. 571a × 2 *se-tenant* with 575a × 2 (1d. values at left) (16.8.65)	9·00	
		ma.	Ditto. 1d. values at right	10·00	
572		$1\frac{1}{2}$d.	green (booklets 12.58, sheets 30.8.60)	10	15
		a.	Imperf three sides (horiz strip of 3)		
		b.	Watermark sideways (26.5.61)	8·00	4·00
		Wi.	Watermark inverted (12.58)	1·00	50
		l.	Booklet pane. No. 572b × 4	30·00	
573		2d.	light red-brown (4.12.58)	10	10
		a.	Watermark sideways (3.4.59)	50	1·00
		Wi.	Watermark inverted (10.4.61)	85·00	35·00
574	**155**	$2\frac{1}{2}$d.	carmine-red (Type II) (booklets 11.58, sheets 15.9.59)	10	10
		a.	Imperf strip of 3		
		b.	*Tête-bêche* (horiz pair)		
		c.	Imperf pane*	£1200	
		Wi.	Watermark inverted (Type II) (11.58)	3·50	1·00
		d.	Watermark sideways (Type I) (10.11.60)	20	30
		da.	Imperf strip of 6		
		e.	Type I (wmk upright) (4.10.61)	15	50
		k.	Chalk-surfaced paper (Type II) (15.7.63)	20	45
		kWi.	Do. Watermark inverted (15.7.63)	20	75
		l.	Watermark sideways (Type II) (1.7.64)	75	1·25
575		3d.	dp lilac (booklets 11.58, sheets 8.12.58)	10	20
		a.	Watermark sideways (24.10.58)	15	25
		b.	Imperf pane*	£850	
		c.	Part perf pane*		
		d.	Phantom "R" (Cyl 41 no dot)	£275	
		Eda.	Do. First retouch	13·00	
		Edb.	Do. Second retouch	13·00	
		e.	Phantom "R" (Cyl 37 no dot)	28·00	
		Eea.	Do. Retouch	9·00	
		Wi.	Watermark inverted (11.58)	15	20
		l.	Booklet pane. No. 575a × 4 (26.5.61)	2·50	
576	**156**	4d.	ultramarine (29.10.58)	50	20
		a.	*Dp ultramarine*†† (28.4.65)	15	10
		ab.	Watermark sideways (31.5.65)	45	35
		ac.	Imperf pane*	£1200	
		ad.	Part perf pane*	£800	
		al.	Booklet pane. No. 576ab × 4 (16.8.65)	2·50	
		aWi.	Watermark inverted (21.6.65)	30	30
577		$4\frac{1}{2}$d.	chestnut (9.2.59)	10	30
		Ea.	Phantom frame	5·00	
578	**157**	5d.	brown (10.11.58)	25	40
579		6d.	dp claret (23.12.58)	40	30
		a.	Imperf three sides (pair)	£450	
		b.	Imperf (pair)	£550	
580		7d.	brt green (26.11.58)	40	60
581	**158**	8d.	magenta (24.2.60)	40	30
582		9d.	bronze-green (24.3.59)	40	50
583		10d.	Prussian blue (18.11.58)	1·00	50
584	**160**	1s.	bistre-brown (30.10.58)	50	30
585	**159**	1s.	3d. green (17.6.59)	25	30
586	**160**	1s.	6d. grey-blue (16.12.58)	4·00	40
			Set of 17 (one of each value)	8·00	4·25
			First Day Cover (577)		£200
			*Presentation Pack***	95·00	

*BOOKLET ERROR. See note after No. 556.

**This was issued in 1960 and comprises Nos. 542, 553, 570/1 and 573/86. It exists in two forms: (a) inscribed "10s 6d" for sale in the U.K.; and (b) inscribed "$1.80" for sale in the U.S.A.

††This "shade" was brought about by making more deeply etched cylinders, resulting in apparent depth of colour in parts of the design. There is no difference in the colour of the ink.

Sideways watermark. The 2d., $2\frac{1}{2}$d., 3d. and 4d. come from coils and the $\frac{1}{2}$d., 1d., $1\frac{1}{2}$d., $2\frac{1}{2}$d., 3d. and 4d. come from booklets. In *coil* stamps the sideways watermark shows the top of the watermark to the left *as seen from the front of the stamp.* In the *booklet* stamps it comes equally to the left or right.

Nos. 570k and 574k only come from 2s. "Holiday Resort" experimental undated booklets issued in 1963, in which one page contained 1 x $2\frac{1}{2}$d. *se-tenant* with 3 x $\frac{1}{2}$d. (*See* No. 570l).

No. 574l comes from coils, and the "Holiday Resort" experimental booklets dated "1964" comprising four panes each containing two of these $2\frac{1}{2}$d. stamps *se-tenant* vertically with two $\frac{1}{2}$d. No. 570a. (*See* No. 570m).

$2\frac{1}{2}$d. imperf. No. 574a comes from a booklet with watermark upright. No. 574da is from a coil with sideways watermark.

No. 574e comes from sheets bearing cylinder number 42 and is also known on vertical delivery coils.

In 1964 No. 575 was printed from cylinder number 70 no dot and dot on an experimental paper which is distinguishable by an additional watermark letter "T" lying on its side, which occurs about four times in the sheet, usually in the side margins, 48,000 sheets were issued.

Phantom "R" varieties

Nos. 575d and 615a (Cyl 41 no dot) — No. 575Eda

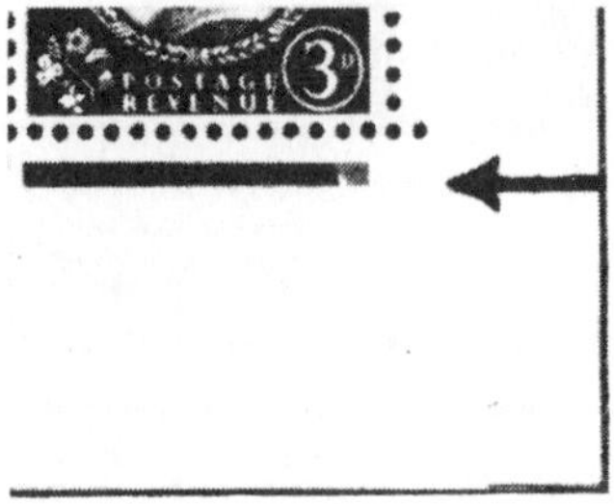

No. 575e (Cyl 37 no dot)

3d. An incomplete marginal rule revealed an "R" on cyls 37 and 41 no dot below R.20/12. It is more noticeable on cyl 41 because of the wider marginal rule. The "R" on cyl 41 was twice retouched, the first being as illustrated here (No. 575Eda) and traces of the "R" can still be seen in the second retouch.

No. 575d is best collected in a block of 4 or 6 with full margins in order to be sure that it is not 615a with phosphor lines removed.

The retouch on cyl 37 is not easily identified: there is no trace of the "R" but the general appearance of that part of the marginal rule is uneven.

Phantom Frame variety

Nos. 577Ea and 616Eba

4½d. An incomplete marginal rule revealed a right-angled shaped frame-line on cyl 8 no dot below R.20/12. It occurs on ordinary and phosphor.

WHITER PAPER. On 18 May 1962 the Post Office announced that a whiter paper was being used for the current issue (including Nos. 595/8). This is beyond the scope of this catalogue, but the whiter papers are listed in Vol. 3 of the Stanley Gibbons *Great Britain Specialised Catalogue*.

1958 (24 Nov)–**61**. *Graphite-lined issue. Two graphite lines on the back, except 2d. value, which has one line. W* **179**. *P* 15 × 14.

587	**154**	½d. orange-red (15.6.59)	6·00	7·50
		Wi. Watermark inverted (4.8.59)	1·25	2·25
588		1d. ultramarine (18.12.58)	1·00	1·50
		a. Misplaced graphite lines (7.61)*	1·00	1·25
		Wi. Watermark inverted (4.8.59)	1·25	2·00
589		1½d. green (4.8.59)	95·00	65·00
		Wi. Watermark inverted (4.8.59)	40·00	40·00
590		2d. lt red-brown (24.11.58)	6·00	3·25
591	**155**	2½d. carmine-red (Type II) (9.6.59)	8·00	10·00
		Wi. Watermark inverted (21.8.59)	48·00	48·00
592		3d. dp lilac (24.11.58)	75	50
		a. Misplaced graphite lines (5.61)*	£375	£350
		Wi. Watermark inverted (4.8.59)	35	60
593	**156**	4d. ultramarine (29.4.59)	3·50	4·50
		a. Misplaced graphite lines (1961)*	£1500	
594		4½d. chestnut (3.6.59)	5·00	4·00
		Set of 8 (cheapest)	60·00	60·00

Nos. 587/9 were only issued in booklets or coils (587/8).

*No. 588a (in coils), and Nos. 592a and 593a (both in sheets) result from the use of a residual stock of graphite-lined paper. As the use of graphite lines had ceased, the register of the lines in relation to the stamps was of no importance and numerous misplacements occurred —two lines close together, one line only, etc. No. 588a refers to two lines at left or right; No. 592a refers to stamps with two lines only at left and both clear of the perforations and No. 593a to stamps with two lines at left (with left line down perforations) and traces of a third line down the opposite perforations.

(Recess D.L.R. (until 31.12.62), then B.W.)

1959–68. *W* **179**. *P* 11 × 12.

595	**166**	2s. 6d. black-brown (22.7.59)	10·00	75
		Wi. Watermark inverted		
		a. B.W. printing (1.7.63)	50	30
		aWi. Watermark inverted	£800	75·00
		k. Chalk-surfaced paper (30.5.68)	50	1·25
596	**167**	5s. scarlet-vermilion (15.6.59)	60·00	2·00
		Wi. Watermark inverted	—	£250
		a. B.W. ptg. *Red (shades)* (3.9.63)	1·00	60
		ab. Printed on the gummed side	£750	
		aWi. Watermark inverted	£225	50·00
597	**168**	10s. blue (21.7.59)	38·00	5·00
		a. B.W. ptg. *Bright ultramarine* (16.10.63)	3·00	3·50
		aWi. Watermark inverted	—	£650
598	**169**	£1 black (23.6.59)	90·00	12·00
		Wi. Watermark inverted	—	£1500
		a. B.W. printing (14.11.63)	8·00	5·50
		aWi. Watermark inverted	—	£2000
		Set of 4 (*Nos.* 595/8)	£170	17·00
		Set of 4 (*Nos.* 595a/8a)	11·00	9·00
		Presentation Pack (1960)*	£475	

The B.W. printings have a marginal Plate Number. They are generally more deeply engraved than the D.L.R. showing more of the Diadem detail and heavier lines on Her Majesty's face. The vertical perf is 11.9 to 12 against D.L.R. 11.8.

*This exists in two forms: (a) inscribed "$6.50" for sale in the U.S.A.; and (b) without price for sale in the U.K.

See also Nos. 759/62.

PHOSPHOR BAND ISSUES. These are printed on the front and are wider than graphite lines. They are not easy to see but show as broad vertical bands at certain angles to the light.

Values representing the rate for printed papers (and when this was abolished in 1968 for second issue class mail) have one band and others two, three or four bands as stated, according to the size and format.

In the small size stamps the bands are on each side with the single band at left (*except where otherwise stated*). In the large-size commemorative stamps the single band may be at left, centre or right, varying in different designs. The bands are vertical on both horizontal and vertical designs *except where otherwise stated*.

The phosphor was originally applied typographically but later usually by photogravure and sometimes using flexography, a typographical process using rubber cylinders.

Three different types of phosphor have been used, distinguishable by the colour emitted under an ultra-violet lamp, the first being green, then blue and now violet. Different sized bands are also known. All these are fully listed in Vol. 3 of the Stanley Gibbons *Great Britain Specialised Catalogue*.

Varieties. Misplaced and missing phosphor bands are known but such varieties are beyond the scope of this Catalogue.

1959 (18 Nov). *Phosphor-Graphite issue. Two phosphor bands on front and two graphite lines on back, except 2d. value, which has one band on front and one line on back. P* 15 × 14. (*a*) *W* **165**.

599	**154**	½d. orange-red	4·00	6·00
600		1d. ultramarine	9·00	7·00
601		1½d. green	2·00	6·00

(*b*) *W* **179**

605	**154**	2d. lt red-brown (1 band)	4·50	4·00
		a. Error. *W* **165**	£170	£170
606	**155**	2½d. carmine-red (Type II)	20·00	13·00
607		3d. dp lilac	9·00	8·00
608	**156**	4d. ultramarine	12·00	25·00
609		4½d. chestnut	35·00	15·00
		Set of 8	80·00	70·00
		Presentation Pack	£200	

Examples of the 2½d., No. 606, exist showing watermark W **165** in error. It is believed that phosphor-graphite stamps of this value with this watermark were not used by the public for postal purposes.

The Presentation Pack was issued in 1960 and comprises two each of Nos. 599/609. It exists in two forms: (a) inscribed "3s 8d" for sale in the U.K. and (b) inscribed "50 c" for sale in the U.S.A.

1960 (22 June)–**67**. *Phosphor issue. Two phosphor bands on front, except where otherwise stated. W* **179**. *P* 15 × 14.

610	**154**	½d.	orange-red	10	15
		a.	Watermark sideways (14.7.61)	10·00	10·00
		Wi.	Watermark inverted (14.8.60)	60	60
		l.	Booklet pane. No. 610a × 4	35·00	
611		1d.	ultramarine	10	10
		a.	Watermark sideways (14.7.61)	35	40
		Wi.	Watermark inverted (14.8.60)	20	30
		l.	Booklet pane. No. 611a × 4	8·00	
		m.	Booklet pane. No. 611a × 2 *se-tenant* with 615d × 2† (16.8.65)	12·50	
		n.	Booklet pane. No. 611a × 2 *se-tenant* with 615b × 2†† (11.67)	7·00	
612		1½d.	green	10	20
		a.	Watermark sideways (14.7.61)	10·00	10·00
		Wi.	Watermark inverted (14.8.60)	9·00	8·00
		l.	Booklet pane. No. 612a × 4	40·00	
613		2d.	lt red-brown (1 band)	22·00	19·00
613*a*		2d.	lt red-brown (2 bands) (4.10.61)	10	10
		aa.	Imperf three sides***		
		ab.	Watermark sideways (6.4.67)	15	60
614	**155**	2½d.	carmine-red (Type II) (2 bands)*	10	50
		Wi.	Watermark inverted (14.8.60)	£170	80·00
614*a*		2½d.	carmine-red (Type II) (1 band) (4.10.61)	50	1·00
		aWi.	Watermark inverted (3.62)	35·00	24·00
614*b*		2½d.	carmine-red (Type I) (1 band) (4.10.61)	32·00	30·00
615		3d.	dp lilac (2 bands)	60	75
		a.	Phantom "R" (Cyl 41 no dot)	28·00	
		Wi.	Watermark inverted (14.8.60)	45	70
		b.	Watermark sideways (14.7.61)	1·75	1·50
		l.	Booklet pane. No. 615b × 4	4·00	
615*c*		3d.	dp lilac (1 band at right) (29.4.65)	50	75
		cEa.	Band at left	50	75
		cWi.	Watermark inverted (band at right) (2.67)	2·25	2·25
		cWia.	Watermark inverted (band at left) (2.67)	24·00	24·00
		d.	Watermark sideways (band at right) (16.8.65)	5·00	4·00
		dEa.	Watermark sideways (band at left)	5·00	4·00
		e.	One centre band (8.12.66)	25	40
		eWi.	Watermark inverted (8.67)	2·25	2·25
		ea.	Wmk sideways (19.6.67)	40	75
616	**156**	4d.	ultramarine	3·00	3·00
		a.	*Dp ultramarine* (28.4.65)	30	30
		aa.	Part perf pane		
		ab.	Watermark sideways (16.8.65)	30	30
		aWi.	Watermark inverted (21.6.65)	25	20
		al.	Booklet pane. No. 616ab × 4	2·50	
616*b*		4½d.	chestnut (13.9.61)	30	30
		Eba.	Phantom frame	13·00	
616*c*	**157**	5d.	brown (9.6.67)	30	50
617		6d.	dp claret (27.6.60)	50	30
617*a*		7d.	brt green (15.2.67)	60	30
617*b*	**158**	8d.	magenta (28.6.67)	20	30
617*c*		9d.	bronze-green (29.12.66)	60	30
617*d*		10d.	Prussian blue (30.12.66)	80	35
617*e*	**160**	1s.	bistre-brown (28.6.67)	40	40
618	**159**	1s.	3d. green	1·75	2·75
618*a*	**160**	1s.	6d. grey-blue (12.12.66)	2·00	1·25
			Set of 17 (one of each value)	7·00	6·50

The automatic facing equipment was brought into use on 6 July 1960 but the phosphor stamps may have been released a few days earlier.

The stamps with watermark sideways are from booklets except Nos. 613ab and 615ea which are from coils. No. 616ab comes from both booklets and coils.

No. 615a. See footnote after No. 586.

*No. 614 with two bands on the creamy paper was originally from cylinder 50 dot and no dot. When the change in postal rates took place in 1965 it was reissued from cylinder 57 dot and no dot on the whiter paper. Some of these latter were also released in error in districts of S.E. London in September 1964. The shade of the reissue is slightly more carmine.

***This comes from the bottom row of a sheet which is imperf at bottom and both sides.

†Booklet pane No. 611m comes in two forms, with the 1d. stamps on the left or on the right. This was printed in this manner to provide for 3d. stamps with only one band.

††Booklet pane No. 611n comes from 2s. booklets of January and March 1968. The two bands on the 3d. stamp were intentional because of the technical difficulties in producing one band and two band stamps *se-tenant*.

The Phosphor-Graphite stamps had the phosphor applied by typography but the Phosphor issue can be divided into those with the phosphor applied typographically and others where it was applied by photogravure. Moreover the photogravure form can be further divided into those which phosphoresce green and others which phosphoresce blue under ultra-violet light. From 1965 violet phosphorescence was introduced in place of the blue. All these are fully listed in Vol. 3 of the Stanley Gibbons *Great Britain Specialised Catalogue*.

Unlike previous one-banded phosphor stamps, No. 615c has a broad band extending over two stamps so that alternate stamps have the band at left or right (same prices either way). No. 615cWi comes from the 10s phosphor booklet of February 1967 and No. 615eWi comes from the 10s. phosphor booklets of August 1967 and February 1968.

Nos. 615a (Phantom "R") and 615Eba (Phantom frame), *see* illustrations following No. 586.

180 Postboy of 1660

181 Posthorn of 1660

(Des R. Stone (3d.), Faith Jaques (1s. 3d.))

1960 (7 July). **Tercentenary of Establishment of General Letter Office.** *W* **179** *(sideways on* 1s. 3d.*). P* 15 × 14 *(3d.) or* 14 × 15 *(1s. 3d.).*

619	**180**	3d.	dp lilac	20	10
620	**181**	1s.	3d. green	3·75	3·75
			Set of 2	3·75	3·75
			First Day Cover		48·00

182 Conference Emblem

(Des R. Stone (emblem, P. Rahikainen))

1960 (19 Sept). **First Anniversary of European Postal and Telecommunications Conference.** *Chalk-surfaced paper. W* **179**. *P* 15 × 14.

621	**182**	6d.	bronze-green & purple	40	60
622		1s.	6d. brown & blue	6·50	5·00
			Set of 2	6·75	5·50
			First Day Cover		40·00

SCREENS. Up to this point all photogravure stamps were printed in a 200 screen (200 dots per linear inch), but all later commemorative stamps are a finer 250 screen. Exceptionally No. 622 has a 200 screen for the portrait and a 250 screen for the background.

184 "Growth of Savings"

183 Thrift Plant

185 Thrift Plant

(Des P. Gauld (2½d.), M. Goaman (others))

1961 (28 Aug). **Centenary of Post Office Savings Bank.** *Chalk-surfaced paper. W* **179** *(sideways on 2½d.) P* 14 × 15 *(2½d.) or* 15 × 14 *(others).*
I. "TIMSON" Machine
II. "THRISSELL" Machine

			I		II	
623	**183**	2½d. black & red	20	20	2·25	2·25
		a. Black omitted	£6000	—	†	
624	**184**	3d. orange-brown & violet	20	20	25	25
		a. Orange-brown omitted	£110	—	£250	—
		x. Perf through side sheet margin	35·00	35·00	†	
		xa. Orange-brown omitted	£400	—	†	
625	**185**	1s. 6d. red & blue	2·75	2·25	†	
		Set of 3	2·75	2·25		
		First Day Cover		60·00		

2½d. TIMSON. Cyls 1E–1F. Deeply shaded portrait (brownish black).
2½d. THRISSELL. Cyls 1D–1B or 1D (dot)–1B (dot). Lighter portrait (grey-black).
3d. TIMSON. Cyls 3D–3E. Clear, well-defined portrait with deep shadows and bright highlights.
3d. THRISSELL. Cyls 3C–3B or 3C (dot)–3B (dot). Dull portrait, lacking in contrast.

Sheet marginal examples *without* single extension perf hole on the short side of the stamp are always "Timson", as are those with large punch-hole *not* coincident with printed three-sided box guide mark.

The 3d. "Timson" perforated completely through the right-hand side margin comes from a relatively small part of the printing perforated on a sheet-fed machine.

Normally the "Timsons" were perforated in the reel, with three large punch-holes in both long margins and the perforations completely through both short margins. Only one punch-hole coincides with the guide-mark.

The "Thrissells" have one large punch-hole in one long margin, coinciding with guide-mark and one short margin imperf (except sometimes for encroachments).

186 C.E.P.T. Emblem

187 Doves and Emblem

188 Doves and Emblem

(Des M. Goaman (doves T. Kurpershoek))

1961 (18 Sept). **European Postal and Telecommunications (C.E.P.T.) Conference, Torquay.** *Chalk-surfaced paper. W* **179**. *P* 15 x 14.

626	**186**	2d. orange, pink & brown	20	15
		a. Orange omitted	£10000	
627	**187**	4d. buff, mauve & ultramarine	20	15
628	**188**	10d. turquoise, pale green & Prussian blue	50	55
		a. Pale green omitted	£3500	
		b. Turquoise omitted	£1800	
		Set of 3	75	75
		First Day Cover		6·00

189 Hammer Beam Roof, Westminster Hall

190 Palace of Westminster

(Des Faith Jaques)

1961 (25 Sept). **Seventh Commonwealth Parliamentary Conference.** *Chalk-surfaced paper. W* **179** *(sideways on 1s. 3d.). P* 15 × 14 *(6d.) or* 14 × 15 *(1s. 3d.).*

629	**189**	6d. purple & gold	25	25
		a. Gold omitted	£450	
630	**190**	1s. 3d. green & blue	2·75	2·50
		a. Blue (Queen's head) omitted	£4500	
		Set of 2	3·00	2·75
		First Day Cover		26·00

191 "Units of Productivity"

192 "National Productivity"

193 "Unified Productivity"

(Des D. Gentleman)

1962 (14 Nov). **National Productivity Year.** *Chalk-surfaced paper. W* **179** *(inverted on 2½d. and 3d.). P* 15 × 14.

631	**191**	2½d.	myrtle-green & carmine-red (*shades*)	20	10
		Ea.	*Blackish olive & carmine-red*	25	15
		p.	One phosphor band. *Blackish olive & carmine-red*	1·00	50
632	**192**	3d.	light blue & violet (*shades*)	25	10
		a.	Lt blue (Queen's head) omitted	£700	
		p.	Three phosphor bands	1·00	50
633	**193**	1s.	3d. carmine, lt blue & dp green	1·75	2·00
		a.	Lt blue (Queen's head) omitted	£3750	
		p.	Three phosphor bands	32·00	22·00
			Set of 3 (Ordinary)	2·00	2·00
			Set of 3 (Phosphor)	32·00	22·00
			First Day Cover (Ordinary)		48·00
			First Day Cover (Phosphor)		85·00

194 Campaign Emblem and Family

195 Children of Three Races

(Des M. Goaman)

1963 (21 Mar). **Freedom from Hunger.** *Chalk-surfaced paper. W* **179** *(inverted). P* 15 × 14.

634	**194**	2½d.	crimson & pink	10	10
		p.	One phosphor band	1·00	1·25
635	**195**	1s.	3d. bistre-brown & yellow	2·00	2·00
		p.	Three phosphor bands	32·00	22·00
			Set of 2 (Ordinary)	2·00	2·00
			Set of 2 (Phosphor)	32·00	22·00
			First Day Cover (Ordinary)		32·00
			First Day Cover (Phosphor)		38·00

196 "Paris Conference"

(Des R. Stone)

1963 (7 May). **Paris Postal Conference Centenary.** *Chalk-surfaced paper. W* **179** *(inverted). P* 15 × 14.

636	**196**	6d.	green & mauve	50	50
		a.	Green omitted	£1300	
		p.	Three phosphor bands	6·50	6·50
			First Day Cover (Ordinary)		14·00
			First Day Cover (Phosphor)		28·00

197 Posy of Flowers

198 Woodland Life

(Des S. Scott (3d.), M. Goaman (4½d.))

1963 (16 May). **National Nature Week.** *Chalk-surfaced paper. W* **179**. *P* 15 × 14.

637	**197**	3d.	yellow, green, brown & black	25	20
		p.	Three phosphor bands	50	60
638	**198**	4½d.	black, blue, yellow, magenta & brown-red	40	50
		p.	Three phosphor bands	2·50	2·50
			Set of 2 (Ordinary)	60	70
			Set of 2 (Phosphor)	3·00	3·00
			First Day Cover (Ordinary)		22·00
			First Day Cover (Phosphor)		27·00

Special First Day of Issue Postmark

	Ordinary	*Phosphor*
London E.C. (Type A)	21·00	27·00

This postmark was used on first day covers serviced by the Philatelic Bureau.

199 Rescue at Sea

200 19th-century Lifeboat

201 Lifeboatmen

(Des D. Gentleman)

1963 (31 May). **Ninth International Lifeboat Conference, Edinburgh.** *Chalk-surfaced paper. W* **179**. *P* 15 × 14.

639	**199**	2½d.	blue, black & red	10	10
		p.	One phosphor band	40	50
640	**200**	4d.	red, yellow, brown, black & blue	40	30
		p.	Three phosphor bands	20	50
641	**201**	1s.	6d. sepia, yellow & grey-blue	2·50	2·75
		p.	Three phosphor bands	48·00	30·00
			Set of 3 (Ordinary)	2·75	2·75
			Set of 3 (Phosphor)	48·00	30·00
			First Day Cover (Ordinary)		30·00
			First Day Cover (Phosphor)		38·00

Special First Day of Issue Postmark

	Ordinary	*Phosphor*
London	50·00	65·00

This postmark was used on first day covers serviced by the Philatelic Bureau.

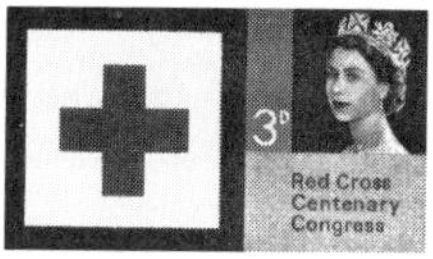

202 Red Cross

203

204

(Des H. Bartram)

1963 (15 Aug). **Red Cross Centenary Congress.** *Chalk-surfaced paper. W* **179**. *P* 15 × 14.

642 **202**	3d.	red & dp lilac	10	10
	a.	Red omitted	£2600	
	p.	Three phosphor bands	60	60
	pa.	Red omitted	£6000	
643 **203**	1s.	3d. red, blue & grey	3·25	2·75
	p.	Three phosphor bands	40·00	38·00
644 **204**	1s.	6d. red, blue & bistre	3·00	2·75
	p.	Three phosphor bands	35·00	30·00
		Set of 3 (Ordinary)	6·00	5·00
		Set of 3 (Phosphor)	70·00	60·00
		First Day Cover (Ordinary)		35·00
		First Day Cover (Phosphor)		65·00

Special First Day of Issue Postmark

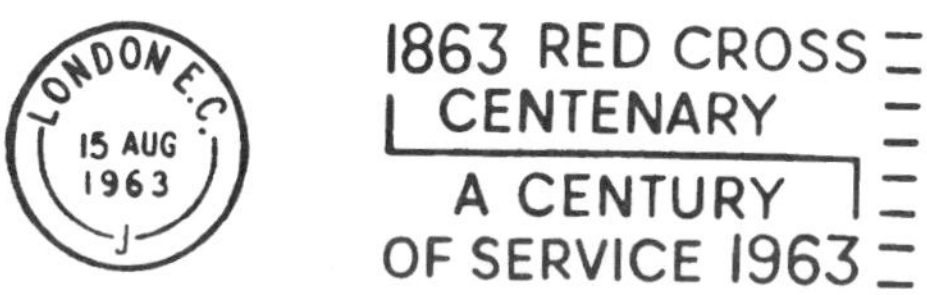

	Ordinary	*Phosphor*
London E.C.	70·00	95·00

This postmark was used on first day covers serviced by the Philatelic Bureau.

205 Commonwealth Cable

(Des P. Gauld)

1963 (3 Dec). **Opening of COMPAC (Trans-Pacific Telephone Cable).** *Chalk-surfaced paper. W* **179**. *P* 15 × 14.

645 **205**	1s.	6d. blue & black	2·25	2·25
	a.	Black omitted	£2400	
	p.	Three phosphor bands	18·00	18·00
		First Day Cover (Ordinary)		22·00
		First Day Cover (Phosphor)		28·00

Special First Day of Issue Postmark

	Ordinary	*Phosphor*
Philatelic Bureau, London E.C.1 (Type A)	30·00	38·00

PRESENTATION PACKS. Special Packs comprising slip-in cards with printed commemorative inscriptions and descriptive notes on the back and with protective covering, were introduced in 1964 with the Shakespeare issue. These are listed and priced.

Issues of 1968–69 (British Paintings to the Prince of Wales Investiture) were also issued in packs with text in German for sale through the Post Office's German Agency and these are also quoted. Subsequently, however, the packs sold in Germany were identical with the normal English version with the addition of a separate printed insert card with German text. These, as also English packs with Japanese and Dutch printed cards for sale in Japan and the Netherlands respectively, are listed in Vols. 3 and 5 of the Stanley Gibbons *Great Britain Specialised Catalogue*.

206 Puck and Bottom (*A Midsummer Night's Dream*)

207 Feste (*Twelfth Night*)

208 Balcony Scene (*Romeo and Juliet*)

209 "Eve of Agincourt" (*Henry V*)

210 Hamlet contemplating Yorick's Skull (*Hamlet*) and Queen Elizabeth II

(Des D. Gentleman. Photo Harrison & Sons (3d., 6d., 1s. 3d., 1s. 6d.). Des C. and R. Ironside. Recess B.W. (2s. 6d.))

1964 (23 Apr). **Shakespeare Festival.** *Chalk-surfaced paper. W* **179**. *P* 11 × 12 (2*s.* 6*d.*) *or* 15 × 14 (*others*).

646 **206**	3d.	yellow-bistre, black & dp violet-blue (*shades*)	10	10
	p.	Three phosphor bands	20	30
647 **207**	6d.	yellow, orange, black & yellow-olive (*shades*)	20	30
	p.	Three phosphor bands	60	90
648 **208**	1s.	3d. cerise, blue-green, black & sepia (*shades*)	90	1·00
	Wi.	Watermark inverted		
	p.	Three phosphor bands	5·75	6·50
	pWi.	Watermark inverted	£110	
649 **209**	1s.	6d. violet, turquoise, black & blue (*shades*)	1·25	1·00
	Wi.	Watermark inverted		
	p.	Three phosphor bands	11·00	6·75
650 **210**	2s.	6d. dp slate-purple (*shades*)	2·00	2·25
	Wi.	Watermark inverted	£325	
		Set of 5 (Ordinary)	4·00	4·25
		Set of 4 (Phosphor)	15·00	13·00
		First Day Cover (Ordinary)		10·00
		First Day Cover (Phosphor)		15·00
		Presentation Pack (Ordinary)	10·00	

The 3d. is known with yellow-bistre missing in the top two-thirds of the figures of Puck and Bottom. This occured in the top row only of a sheet.

Special First Day of Issue Postmark

	Ordinary	Phosphor
Stratford-upon-Avon, Warwicks	13·00	17·00

This postmark was used on first day covers serviced by the Philatelic Bureau, as well as on covers posted at Stratford P.O.

211 Flats near Richmond Park ("Urban Development")

212 Shipbuilding Yards, Belfast ("Industrial Activity")

213 Beddgelert Forest Park, Snowdonia ("Forestry")

214 Nuclear Reactor, Dounreay ("Technological Development")

(Des D. Bailey)

1964 (1 July). **20th International Geographical Congress, London.** *Chalk-surfaced paper. W* **179**. *P* 15 × 14.

651	**211**	2½d.	black, olive-yellow, olive-grey & turquoise-blue	10	10
		p.	One phosphor band	50	40
652	**212**	4d.	orange-brown, red-brown, rose, black & violet	25	25
		a.	Violet omitted	£175	
		c.	Violet and red-brown omitted	£175	
		Wi.	Watermark inverted	£500	
		p.	Three phosphor bands	75	70
653	**213**	8d.	yellow-brown, emerald, green & black ..	60	50
		a.	Green (lawn) omitted	£5500	
		Wi.	Watermark inverted	£275	
		p.	Three phosphor bands	1·75	1·50
654	**214**	1s.	6d. yellow-brown, pale pink, black, & brown	3·25	3·25
		Wi.	Watermark inverted	22·00	
		p.	Three phosphor bands	26·00	21·00
			Set of 4 (Ordinary)	4·00	4·00
			Set of 4 (Phosphor)	26·00	21·00
			First Day Cover (Ordinary)		19·00
			First Day Cover (Phosphor)		29·00
			Presentation Pack (Ordinary)	£100	

A used example of the 4d. is known with the red-brown omitted.

Special First Day of Issue Postmark

	Ordinary	Phosphor
G.P.O. Philatelic Bureau, London E.C.1 (Type B)	25·00	35·00

215 Spring Gentian

216 Dog Rose

217 Honeysuckle

218 Fringed Water Lily

(Des M. and Sylvia Goaman)

1964 (5 Aug). **Tenth International Botanical Congress, Edinburgh.** *Chalk-surfaced paper. W* **179**. *P* 15 × 14.

655	**215**	3d.	violet, blue & sage-green	10	10
		a.	Blue omitted	£4000	
		b.	Sage-green omitted	£4000	
		p.	Three phosphor bands	20	30
656	**216**	6d.	apple-green, rose, scarlet & green	20	20
		Wi.	Watermark inverted		
		p.	Three phosphor bands	2·00	1·50
657	**217**	9d.	lemon, green, lake & rose-red	1·60	2·50
		a.	Green (leaves) omitted	£4000	
		Wi.	Watermark inverted	37·00	
		p.	Three phosphor bands	4·50	3·00
658	**218**	1s.	3d. yellow, emerald, reddish violet & grey-green	2·50	1·90
		a.	Yellow (flowers) omitted	£8000	
		Wi.	Watermark inverted	£240	
		p.	Three phosphor bands	24·00	20·00
			Set of 4 (Ordinary)	4·00	4·00
			Set of 4 (Phosphor)	28·00	22·00
			First Day Cover (Ordinary)		25·00
			First Day Cover (Phosphor)		35·00
			Presentation Pack (Ordinary)	£100	

Special First Day of Issue Postmark

	Ordinary	Phosphor
G.P.O. Philatelic Bureau, London E.C.1 (Type B)	26·00	38·00

219 Forth Road Bridge

220 Forth Road and Railway Bridges

(Des A. Restall)

1964 (4 Sept). **Opening of Forth Road Bridge.** *Chalk-surfaced paper. W* **179**. *P* 15 × 14.

659 **219**	3d.	black, blue & reddish violet	15	10
	p.	Three phosphor bands	50	50
660 **220**	6d.	black, lt blue & carmine-red	45	40
	a.	Lt blue omitted	£1500	£1500
	Wi.	Watermark inverted	2·00	
	p.	Three phosphor bands	4·75	4·75
	pWi.	Watermark inverted		
		Set of 2 (Ordinary)	60	50
		Set of 2 (Phosphor)	5·25	5·25
		First Day Cover (Ordinary)		7·50
		First Day Cover (Phosphor)		11·00
		Presentation Pack (Ordinary)	£250	

Special First Day of Issue Postmarks

	Ordin-ary	*Phos-phor*
G.P.O. Philatelic Bureau, London E.C.1 (Type B)	10·00	15·00
North Queensferry, Fife	22·00	90·00
South Queensferry, West Lothian	18·00	70·00

The Queensferry postmarks were applied to first day covers sent to a temporary Philatelic Bureau at Edinburgh.

221 Sir Winston Churchill

(Des D. Gentleman and Rosalind Dease, from photograph by Karsh)

1965 (8 July). **Churchill Commemoration.** *Chalk-surfaced paper. W* **179**. *P* 15 × 14.

I. "REMBRANDT" Machine

661 **221**	4d.	black & olive-brown	15	10
	Wi.	Watermark inverted	2·25	
	p.	Three phosphor bands	30	30

II. "TIMSON" Machine

661a **221**	4d.	black & olive-brown	50	50

III. "L. & M. 4" Machine

662 –	1s.	3d. black & grey	45	40
	Wi.	Watermark inverted	70·00	
	p.	Three phosphor bands	3·50	3·50
		Set of 2 (Ordinary)	60	50
		Set of 2 (Phosphor)	3·75	3·75
		First Day Cover (Ordinary)		5·00
		First Day Cover (Phosphor)		7·50
		Presentation Pack (Ordinary)	16·00	

The 1s. 3d. shows a closer view of Churchill's head.

Two examples of the 4d. value exist with the Queen's head omitted, one due to something adhering to the cylinder and the other due to a paper fold. The stamp also exists with Churchill's head omitted, also due to a paper fold.

4d. REMBRANDT, Cyls 1A-1B dot and no dot. Lack of shading detail on Churchill's portrait. Queen's portrait appears dull and coarse. This is a rotary machine which is sheet-fed.

4d. TIMSON. Cyls 5A-6B no dot. More detail on Churchill's portrait—furrow on forehead, his left eyebrow fully drawn and more shading on cheek. Queen's portrait lighter and sharper. This is a reel-fed two-colour 12-in. wide rotary machine and the differences in impressions are due to the greater pressure applied by this machine.

1s. 3d. Cyls 1A-1B no dot. The "Linotype and Machinery No. 4" machine is an ordinary sheet-fed rotary press machine. Besides being used for printing the 1s. 3d. stamps it was also employed for overprinting the phosphor bands on both values.

Special First Day of Issue Postmark

	Ordin-ary	*Phos-phor*
G.P.O. Philatelic Bureau, London E.C.1 (Type B)	9·00	12·00

A First Day of Issue handstamp was provided at Bladon, Oxford, for this issue.

222 Simon de Montfort's Seal

223 Parliament Buildings
(after engraving by Hollar, 1647)

(Des S. Black (6d.), R. Guyatt (2s. 6d.))

1965 (19 July). **700th Anniversary of Simon de Montfort's Parliament.** *Chalk-surfaced paper. W* **179**. *P* 15 × 14.

663 **222**	6d.	olive-green	10	10
	p.	Three phosphor bands	1·00	1·00
664 **223**	2s.	6d. black, grey & pale drab	1·25	1·25
	Wi.	Watermark inverted	14·00	
		Set of 2 (Ordinary)	1·25	1·25
		First Day Cover (Ordinary)		11·00
		First Day Cover (Phosphor)		16·00
		Presentation Pack (Ordinary)	35·00	

Special First Day of Issue Postmark

	Ordin-ary
G.P.O. Philatelic Bureau, London E.C.1 (Type B)	13·00

A First Day of Issue handstamp was provided at Evesham, Worcs, for this issue.

224 Bandsmen and Banner

225 Three Salvationists

(Des M. Farrar-Bell (3d.), G. Trenaman (1s. 6d.))

1965 (9 Aug). **Salvation Army Centenary.** *Chalk-surfaced paper. W* **179**. *P* 15 × 14.

665 **224**	3d. indigo, grey-blue, cerise, yellow & brown	10	10
	p. One phosphor band	50	40
666 **225**	1s. 6d. red, blue, yellow & brown	1·00	1·00
	p. Three phosphor bands	3·00	3·25
	Set of 2 (Ordinary)	1·10	1·10
	Set of 2 (Phosphor)	3·50	3·50
	First Day Cover (Ordinary)		21·00
	First Day Cover (Phosphor)		28·00

The Philatelic Bureau did not provide first day cover services for Nos. 665/70.

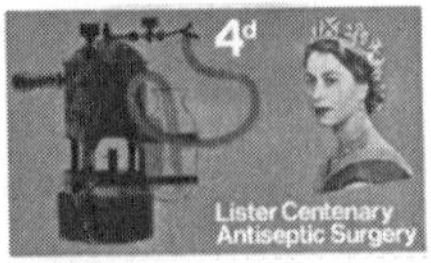

226 Lister's Carbolic Spray

227 Lister and Chemical Symbols

(Des P. Gauld (4d.), F. Ariss (1s.))

1965 (1 Sept). **Centenary of Joseph Lister's Discovery of Antiseptic Surgery.** *Chalk-surfaced paper. W* **179**. *P* 15 × 14.

667 **226**	4d. indigo, brown-red & grey-black	10	10
	a. Brown-red (tube) omitted	£160	
	b. Indigo omitted	£1750	
	p. Three phosphor bands	15	20
	pa. Brown-red (tube) omitted	£1500	
668 **227**	1s. black, purple & new blue	1·00	1·50
	Wi. Watermark inverted	£180	
	p. Three phosphor bands	2·75	2·75
	pWi. Watermark inverted	£180	
	Set of 2 (Ordinary)	1·10	1·50
	Set of 2 (Phosphor)	2·75	2·75
	First Day Cover (Ordinary)		12·00
	First Day Cover (Phosphor)		13·00

228 Trinidad Carnival Dancers

229 Canadian Folk-dancers

(Des D. Gentleman and Rosalind Dease)

1965 (1 Sept). **Commonwealth Arts Festival.** *Chalk-surfaced paper. W* **179**. *P* 15 × 14.

669 **228**	6d. black & orange	10	10
	p. Three phosphor bands	30	30
670 **229**	1s. 6d. black & lt reddish violet	1·25	1·50
	p. Three phosphor bands	2·50	2·50
	Set of 2 (Ordinary)	1·25	1·50
	Set of 2 (Phosphor)	2·75	2·75
	First Day Cover (Ordinary)		15·00
	First Day Cover (Phosphor)		21·00

230 Flight of Supermarine Spitfires

231 Pilot in Hawker Hurricane Mk I

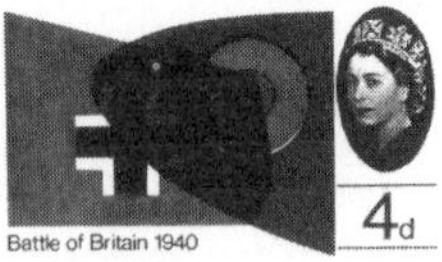

232 Wing-tips of Supermarine Spitfire and Messerschmitt Bf 109

233 Supermarine Spitfires attacking Heinkel HE-111H Bomber

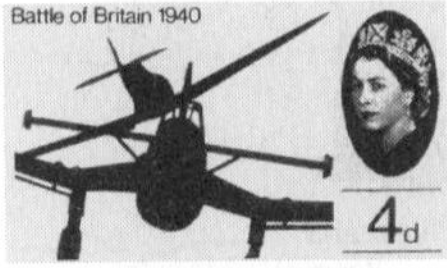

234 Supermarine Spitfire attacking Junkers Ju 87B "Stuka" Dive-bomber

235 Hawker Hurricanes Mk I over Wreck of Dornier Do-17Z Bomber

236 Anti-aircraft Artillery in Action

237 Air-battle over St. Paul's Cathedral

(Des D. Gentleman and Rosalind Dease (4d. × 6 and 1s. 3d.), A. Restall (9d.))

1965 (13 Sept). **25th Anniv of Battle of Britain.** *Chalk-surfaced paper. W* **179**. *P* 15 × 14.

671 **230**	4d. yellow-olive & black	30	35
	a. Block of 6. Nos. 671/6	8·00	9·00
	p. Three phosphor bands	40	50
	pa. Block of 6. Nos. 671p/6p	12·00	14·00
672 **231**	4d. yellow-olive, olive-grey & black	30	35
	p. Three phosphor bands	40	50
673 **232**	4d. red, new blue, yellow-olive, olive-grey & black	30	35
	p. Three phosphor bands	40	50
674 **233**	4d. olive-grey, yellow-olive & black	30	35
	p. Three phosphor bands	40	50
675 **234**	4d. olive-grey, yellow-olive & black	30	35
	p. Three phosphor bands	40	50
676 **235**	4d. olive-grey, yellow-olive, new blue & black	30	3
	a. New blue omitted	†	£350
	p. Three phosphor bands	40	5
677 **236**	9d. bluish violet, orange & slate-purple	1·25	1·2
	Wi. Watermark inverted	25·00	
	p. Three phosphor bands	1·25	8
678 **237**	1s. 3d. lt grey, dp grey, black, lt blue & brt blue	1·25	1·2
	Wi. Watermark inverted	20·00	
	p. Three phosphor bands	1·25	8
	pWi. Watermark inverted	3·00	
	Set of 8 (Ordinary)	9·50	4·2
	Set of 8 (Phosphor)	14·00	4·2
	First Day Cover (Ordinary)		24·0
	First Day Cover (Phosphor)		24·0
	Presentation Pack (Ordinary)	48·00	

Nos. 671/6 were issued together *se-tenant* in blocks of 6 (3 × 2) within the sheet.

No. 676a is only known commercially used on cover from Truro.

Special First Day of Issue Postmark

	Ordinary	Phosphor
G.P.O. Philatelic Bureau, London E.C.1 (Type C)	26·00	26·00

238 Tower and Georgian Buildings

239 Tower and "Nash" Terrace, Regent's Park

(Des C. Abbott)

1965 (8 Oct). **Opening of Post Office Tower.** *Chalk-surfaced paper. W* **179** *(sideways on 3d.). P 14 × 15 (3d.) or 15 × 14 (1s. 3d.).*

679 **238**		3d. olive-yellow, new blue & bronze-green	10	10
	a.	Olive-yellow (Tower) omitted	£650	
	p.	One phosphor band at right	10	10
	pEa.	Band at left	10	10
	pEb.	Horiz pair. Nos. 679p/pEa	20	20
680 **239**		1s. 3d. bronze-green, yellow-green & blue	65	75
	Wi.	Watermark inverted	42·00	
	p.	Three phosphor bands	50	50
	pWi.	Watermark inverted	45·00	
		Set of 2 (Ordinary)	75	85
		Set of 2 (Phosphor)	60	60
		First Day Cover (Ordinary)		7·00
		First Day Cover (Phosphor)		9·00
		Presentation Pack (Ordinary)	3·50	
		Presentation Pack (Phosphor)	3·50	

The one phosphor band on No. 679p was produced by printing broad phosphor bands across alternate vertical perforations. Individual stamps show the band at right or left.

Special First Day of Issue Postmark

	Ordinary	Phosphor
G.P.O. Philatelic Bureau, London E.C.1 (Type C)	8·00	11·00

The Philatelic Bureau did not provide first day cover services for Nos. 681/4.

240 U.N. Emblem

241 I.C.Y. Emblem

(Des J. Matthews)

965 (25 Oct). **20th Anniv of U.N.O. and International Co-operation Year.** *Chalk-surfaced paper. W* **179**. *P 15 × 14.*

81 **240**		3d. black, yellow-orange & lt blue	15	20
	p.	One phosphor band	25	40
32 **241**		1s. 6d. black, brt purple & lt blue	1·10	1·10
	Wi.	Watermark inverted		
	p.	Three phosphor bands	3·50	3·50
		Set of 2 (Ordinary)	1·25	1·25
		Set of 2 (Phosphor)	3·75	3·75
		First Day Cover (Ordinary)		12·00
		First Day Cover (Phosphor)		14·00

242 Telecommunications Network

243 Radio Waves and Switchboard

(Des A. Restall)

1965 (15 Nov). **I.T.U. Centenary.** *Chalk-surfaced paper. W* **179**. *P 15 × 14.*

683 **242**		9d. red, ultramarine, dp slate, violet, black & pink	20	25
	Wi.	Watermark inverted	14·00	
	p.	Three phosphor bands	60	50
	pWi.	Watermark inverted	65·00	
684 **243**		1s. 6d. red, greenish blue, indigo, black & lt pink	1·60	1·50
	a.	Lt pink omitted	£900	
	Wi.	Watermark inverted	50·00	
	p.	Three phosphor bands	5·25	5·25
		Set of 2 (Ordinary)	1·75	1·75
		Set of 2 (Phosphor)	5·75	5·75
		First Day Cover (Ordinary)		16·00
		First Day Cover (Phosphor)		18·00

Originally scheduled for issue on 17 May 1965, supplies from the Philatelic Bureau were sent in error to reach a dealer on that date and another dealer received his supply on 27 May.

244 Robert Burns (after Skirving chalk drawing)

245 Robert Burns (after Nasmyth portrait)

(Des G. Huntly)

1966 (25 Jan). **Burns Commemoration.** *Chalk-surfaced paper. W* **179**. *P 15 × 14.*

685 **244**		4d. black, dp violet-blue & new blue	15	15
	p.	Three phosphor bands	25	25
686 **245**		1s. 3d. black, slate-blue & yellow-orange..	70	70
	p.	Three phosphor bands	2·25	2·25
		Set of 2 (Ordinary)	85	85
		Set of 2 (Phosphor)	2·50	2·50
		First Day Cover (Ordinary)		4·00
		First Day Cover (Phosphor)		5·00
		Presentation Pack (Ordinary)	40·00	

Special First Day of Issue Postmarks
(35 mm diameter)

	Ordin-ary	*Phos-phor*
Alloway, Ayrshire	9·00	9·00
Ayr	9·00	9·00
Dumfries	9·00	9·00
Edinburgh	9·00	9·00
Glasgow	9·00	9·00
Kilmarnock, Ayrshire	10·00	10·00

A special Philatelic Bureau was set up in Edinburgh to deal with first day covers of this issue. The Bureau serviced covers to receive the above postmarks, and other versions were applied locally. The locally applied handstamps were 38–39mm in diameter, the Bureau postmarks, applied by machine, 35mm. The Ayr, Edinburgh, Glasgow and Kilmarnock postmarks are similar in design to that for Alloway. Similar handstamps were also provided at Greenock and Mauchline, but the Bureau did not provide a service for these.

246 Westminster Abbey

247 Fan Vaulting, Henry VII Chapel

(Des Sheila Robinson. Photo Harrison (3d.). Des and eng Bradbury, Wilkinson. Recess (2s. 6d.))

1966 (28 Feb). **900th Anniversary of Westminster Abbey.** *Chalk-surfaced paper* (3d.). *W* **179**. *P* 15 × 14 (3d.) *or* 11 × 12 (2s. 6d.).

687	**246**	3d. black, red-brown & new blue	15	20
		p. One phosphor band	30	30
688	**247**	2s. 6d. black	85	1·10
		Set of 2	1·00	1·25
		First Day Cover (Ordinary)		7·50
		First Day Cover (Phosphor)		11·00
		Presentation Pack (Ordinary)	16·00	

Special First Day of Issue Postmark

	Ordin-ary
G.P.O. Philatelic Bureau, London E.C.1 (Type B)	8·00

The Bureau did not provide a first day cover service for the 3d. phosphor stamp.

248 View near Hassocks, Sussex

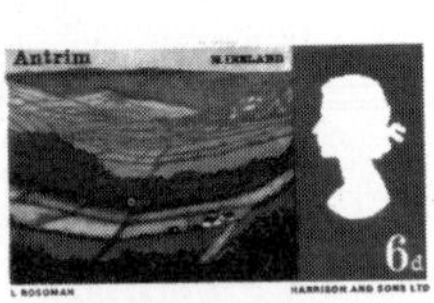

249 Antrim, Northern Ireland

250 Harlech Castle, Wales

251 Cairngorm Mountains, Scotland

(Des L. Rosoman. Queen's portrait, adapted by D. Gentleman from coinage)

1966 (2 May). **Landscapes.** *Chalk-surfaced paper. W* **179**. *P* 15 × 14.

689	**248**	4d. black, yellow-green & new blue	15	15
		p. Three phosphor bands	15	15
690	**249**	6d. black, emerald & new blue	15	15
		Wi. Watermark inverted	6·00	
		p. Three phosphor bands	25	25
		pWi. Watermark inverted	28·00	
691	**250**	1s. 3d. black, greenish yellow & greenish blue	35	35
		p. Three phosphor bands	35	35
692	**251**	1s. 6d. black, orange & Prussian blue	50	50
		Wi. Watermark inverted	10·00	
		p. Three phosphor bands	50	50
		Set of 4 (Ordinary)	1·00	1·00
		Set of 4 (Phosphor)	1·00	1·00
		First Day Cover (Ordinary)		9·50
		First Day Cover (Phosphor)		9·50

Special First Day of Issue Postmark

	Ordin-ary	*Phos-phor*
G.P.O. Philatelic Bureau, London E.C.1 (Type B)	11·00	12·00

First Day of Issue handstamps were provided at Lewes, Sussex; Coleraine, Co. Londonderry; Harlech, Merioneth and Grantown-on-Spey, Morayshire, for this issue.

252 Players with Ball

253 Goalmouth Mêlée

254 Goalkeeper saving Goal

(Des D. Gentleman (4d.), W. Kempster (6d.), D. Caplan (1s. 3d.). Queen' portrait adapted by D. Gentleman from coinage)

1966 (1 June). **World Cup Football Championship.** *Chalk-surface paper. W* **179** (*sideways on 4d.*). *P* 14 × 15 (4*d.*) *or* 15 × 14 (*others*).

693	**252**	4d. red, reddish purple, brt blue, flesh & black	15	1
		p. Two phosphor bands	15	1
694	**253**	6d. black, sepia, red, apple-green & blue	20	2
		a. Black omitted	85·00	
		b. Apple-green omitted	£2000	
		c. Red omitted	£2250	
		Wi. Watermark inverted	2·00	
		p. Three phosphor bands	20	
		pa. Black omitted	£500	

695 **254** 1s. 3d. black, blue, yellow, red & lt yellow-olive 75 75
a. Blue omitted £150
Wi. Watermark inverted .... 80·00
p. Three phosphor bands 75 75
pWi. Watermark inverted .... 1·25
Set of 3 (Ordinary) .... 1·00 1·00
Set of 3 (Phosphor) .... 1·00 1·00
First Day Cover (Ordinary) .... 11·00
First Day Cover (Phosphor) .... 15·00
Presentation Pack (Ordinary) .... 14·00

Special First Day of Issue Postmark

	Ordinary	*Phosphor*
G.P.O. Philatelic Bureau, London E.C.1 (Type C)	12·00	16·00

A First Day of Issue handstamp was provided at Wembley, Middx, for this issue.

255 Black-headed Gull

256 Blue Tit

257 European Robin

258 Blackbird

(Des J. Norris Wood)

1966 (8 Aug). **British Birds.** *Chalk-surfaced paper. W* **179**. *P* 15 × 14.

696 **255** 4d. grey, black, red, emerald-green, brt blue, greenish yellow & bistre 10 15
Wi. Watermark inverted .... 4·00
a. Block of 4. Nos. 696/9 .... 1·00 1·25
ab. Black (value), etc. omitted * *(block of four)* £4000
ac. Black only omitted* £2500
aWi. Watermark inverted *(block of four)* .... 17·00
p. Three phosphor bands 10 15
pWi. Watermark inverted .... 16·00
pa. Block of 4. Nos. 696p/9p .... 1·00 1·00
paWi. Watermark inverted *(block of four)* .... 60·00

697 **256** 4d. black, greenish yellow, grey, emerald-green, brt blue & bistre 10 15
Wi. Watermark inverted .... 4·00
p. Three phosphor bands 10 15
pWi. Watermark inverted .... 16·00

698 **257** 4d. red, greenish yellow, black, grey, bistre, reddish brown & emerald-green 10 15
Wi. Watermark inverted .... 4·00
p. Three phosphor bands 10 15
pWi. Watermark inverted .... 16·00

699 **258** 4d. black, reddish brown, greenish yellow, grey & bistre** 10 15
Wi. Watermark inverted .... 4·00
p. Three phosphor bands 10 15
pWi. Watermark inverted .... 16·00
Set of 4 (Ordinary) .... 1·00 50
Set of 4 (Phosphor) .... 1·00 50
First Day Cover (Ordinary) .... 12·00
First Day Cover (Phosphor) .... 12·00
Presentation Pack (Ordinary) .... 9·00

Nos. 696/9 were issued together *se-tenant* in blocks of four within the sheet.

*In No. 696ab the blue, bistre and reddish brown are also omitted but in No. 696ac only the black is omitted.

**In No. 699 the black was printed over the bistre.

Other colours omitted, and the stamps affected:

d.	Greenish yellow (Nos. 696/9)	£400
e.	Red (Nos. 696 and 698)	£400
f.	Emerald-green (Nos. 696/8)	75·00
pf.	Emerald-green (Nos. 696p/8p)	75·00
g.	Brt blue (Nos. 696/7)	£250
pg.	Brt blue (Nos. 696p and 697p)	£800
h.	Bistre (Nos. 696/9)	90·00
ph.	Bistre (Nos. 696p/9p)	90·00
j.	Reddish brown (Nos. 698/9)	80·00
pj.	Reddish brown (Nos. 698p and 699p)	80·00

The prices quoted are for each stamp.

Special First Day of Issue Postmark

	Ordinary	*Phosphor*
G.P.O. Philatelic Bureau, London E.C.1 (Type C)	13·00	13·00

259 Cup Winners

1966 (18 Aug). **England's World Cup Football Victory.** *Chalk-surfaced paper. W* **179** *(sideways). P* 14 × 15.

700 **259** 4d. red, reddish purple, brt blue, flesh & black 20 20
First Day Cover .... 6·00

These stamps were only put on sale at post offices in England, the Channel Islands and the Isle of Man, and at the Philatelic Bureau in London and also, on 22 August, in Edinburgh on the occasion of the opening of the Edinburgh Festival as well as at Army post offices at home and abroad.

The Philatelic Bureau did not service first day covers for this stamp, but a First Day of Issue handstamp was provided inscribed "Harrow & Wembley" to replace the "Wembley, Middx", postmark of the initial issue.

For full information on all future British issues, collectors should write to the British Post Office Philatelic Bureau, 20 Brandon Street, Edinburgh EH3 5TT

260 Jodrell Bank Radio Telescope

261 British Motor-cars

262 "SRN 6" Hovercraft

263 Windscale Reactor

(Des D. and A. Gillespie (4d., 6d.), A. Restall (others))

1966 (19 Sept). **British Technology.** *Chalk-surfaced paper. W* **179**. *P* 15 × 14.

701	**260**	4d.	black & lemon	15	15
		p.	Three phosphor bands	15	15
702	**261**	6d.	red, dp blue & orange	15	15
		a.	Red (Mini-cars) omitted	£4000	
		b.	Dp blue (Jaguar & inscr) omitted	£2500	
		p.	Three phosphor bands	15	15
703	**262**	1s.	3d. black, orange-red, slate & lt greenish blue	30	40
		p.	Three phosphor bands	45	50
704	**263**	1s.	6d. black, yellow-green, bronze-green, lilac & dp blue	50	45
		p.	Three phosphor bands	65	60
			Set of 4 (Ordinary)	1·00	1·00
			Set of 4 (Phosphor)	1·25	1·25
			First Day Cover (Ordinary)		6·50
			First Day Cover (Phosphor)		7·00
			Presentation Pack (Ordinary)	9·00	

Special First Day of Issue Postmark

	Ordinary	*Phosphor*
G.P.O. Philatelic Bureau, Edinburgh 1 (Type C)	7·50	8·50

264

265

266

267

268

269

All the above show battle scenes and they were issued together *se-tenant* in horizontal strips of six within the sheet.

270 Norman Ship

271 Norman Horsemen attacking Harold's Troops

(All the above are scenes from the Bayeux Tapestry)

(Des D. Gentleman. Photo. Queen's head die-stamped (6d., 1s. 3d.))

1966 (14 Oct). **900th Anniv of Battle of Hastings.** *Chalk-surfaced paper. W* **179** *(sideways on 1s. 3d.). P* 15 × 14.

705	**264**	4d.	black, olive-green, bistre, dp blue, orange, magenta, green, blue & grey	10	15
		a.	Strip of 6. Nos. 705/10	2·25	4·00
		aWi.	Strip of 6. Watermark inverted	45·00	
		Wi.	Watermark inverted	7·00	
		p.	Three phosphor bands	10	25
		pa.	Strip of 6. Nos. 705p/10p	2·25	4·00
		paWi.	Strip of 6. Watermark inverted	20·00	
		pWi.	Watermark inverted	3·00	
706	**265**	4d.	black, olive-green, bistre, dp blue, orange, magenta, green, blue & grey	10	15
		Wi.	Watermark inverted	7·00	
		p.	Three phosphor bands	10	25
		pWi.	Watermark inverted	2·00	
707	**266**	4d.	black, olive-green, bistre, dp blue, orange, magenta, green, blue & grey	10	15
		Wi.	Watermark inverted	7·00	
		p.	Three phosphor bands	10	25
		pWi.	Watermark inverted	3·00	
708	**267**	4d.	black, olive-green, bistre, dp blue, magenta, green, blue & grey	10	15
		Wi.	Watermark inverted	7·00	
		p.	Three phosphor bands	10	25
		pWi.	Watermark inverted	3·00	
709	**268**	4d.	black, olive-green, bistre, dp blue, orange, magenta, green, blue & grey	10	15
		Wi.	Watermark inverted	7·00	
		p.	Three phosphor bands	10	25
		pWi.	Watermark inverted	3·00	
710	**269**	4d.	black, olive-green, bistre, dp blue, orange, magenta, green, blue & grey	10	15
		Wi.	Watermark inverted	7·00	
		p.	Three phosphor bands	10	25
		pWi.	Watermark inverted	3·00	

711	**270**	6d. black, olive-green, violet, blue, green & gold	10	10
		Wi. Watermark inverted	38·00	
		p. Three phosphor bands	10	10
		pWi. Watermark inverted	50·00	
712	**271**	1s. 3d. black, lilac, bronze-green, rosine bistre-brown & gold	20	20
		a. Lilac omitted	£450	
		Wi. Watermark sideways inverted (top of crown pointing to right)*	35·00	
		p. Four phosphor bands	20	20
		pa. Lilac omitted	£650	
		pWi. Watermark sideways inverted (top of crown pointing to right)*	14·00	
		Set of 8 (Ordinary)	2·50	1·50
		Set of 8 (Phosphor)	2·50	1·90
		First Day Cover (Ordinary)		5·00
		First Day Cover (Phosphor)		6·00
		Presentation Pack (Ordinary)	10·00	

*The normal sideways watermark shows the tops of the Crowns pointing to the right, *as seen from the front of the stamp.*

Other colours omitted in the 4d. values and the stamps affected:

b.	Olive-green (Nos. 705/10)	30·00
pb.	Olive-green (Nos. 705p/10p)	30·00
c.	Bistre (Nos. 705/10)	30·00
pc.	Bistre (Nos. 705p/10p)	35·00
d.	Dp blue (Nos. 705/10)	40·00
pd.	Dp blue (Nos. 705p/10p)	40·00
e.	Orange (Nos. 705/7 and 709/10)	30·00
pe.	Orange (Nos. 705p/7p and 709p/10p)	25·00
f.	Magenta (Nos. 705/10)	35·00
pf.	Magenta (Nos. 705p/10p)	35·00
g.	Green (Nos. 705/10)	30·00
pg.	Green (Nos. 705p/10p)	30·00
h.	Blue (Nos. 705/10)	25·00
ph.	Blue (Nos. 705p/10p)	40·00
j.	Grey (Nos. 705/10)	25·00
pj.	Grey (Nos. 705p/10p)	25·00
pk.	Magenta & green (Nos. 705p/10p)	

The prices quoted are for each stamp.

Nos. 705 and 709, with grey and blue omitted, have been seen commercially used, posted from Middleton-in-Teesdale.

The 6d. phosphor is known in a yellowish gold as well as the reddish gold as used in the 1s. 3d.

Three examples of No. 712 in a right-hand top corner block of 10 (2 × 5) are known with the Queen's head omitted as a result of a double paper fold prior to die-stamping. The perforation is normal. Of the other seven stamps, four have the Queen's head misplaced and three are normal.

MISSING GOLD HEADS. The 6d. and 1s. 3d. were also issued with the die-stamped gold head omitted but as these can also be removed by chemical means we are not prepared to list them unless a way is found of distinguishing the genuine stamps from the fakes which will satisfy the Expert Committees.

The same remarks apply to Nos. 713/14.

Special First Day of Issue Postmark

	Ordinary	*Phosphor*
G.P.O. Philatelic Bureau, Edinburgh 1 (Type C)	6·00	7·00

A First Day of Issue handstamp was provided at Battle, Sussex, for this issue.

For full information on all future British issues, collectors should write to the British Post Office Philatelic Bureau, 20 Brandon Street, Edinburgh EH3 5TT

272 King of the Orient

273 Snowman

(Des Tasveer Shemza (3d.), J. Berry (1s. 6d.) (winners of children's design competition). Photo, Queen's head die-stamped)

1966 (1 Dec). **Christmas.** *Chalk-surfaced paper. W* **179** *(sideways on 3d.). P* 14 × 15.

713	**272**	3d. black, blue, green, yellow, red & gold	10	10
		a. Queen's head double	†	—
		b. Green omitted	—	£150
		p. One phosphor band at right	10	10
		pEa. Band at left	10	10
		pEb. Horiz pair. Nos. 713p/pEa	20	20
714	**273**	1s. 6d. blue, red, pink, black & gold	40	40
		a. Pink (hat) omitted	£750	
		Wi. Watermark inverted	13·00	
		p. Two phosphor bands	40	40
		pWi. Watermark inverted	42·00	
		Set of 2 (Ordinary)	50	50
		Set of 2 (Phosphor)	50	50
		First Day Cover (Ordinary)		3·50
		First Day Cover (Phosphor)		3·50
		Presentation Pack (Ordinary)	10·00	

Special First Day of Issue Postmarks

	Ordinary	*Phosphor*
G.P.O. Philatelic Bureau, Edinburgh 1 (Type C)	4·00	4·00
Bethlehem, Llandeilo, Carms (Type C)	5·00	5·00

274 Sea Freight

275 Air Freight

(Des C. Abbott)

1967 (20 Feb). **European Free Trade Association (EFTA).** *Chalk-surfaced paper. W* **179**. *P* 15 × 14.

715	**274**	9d. dp blue, red, lilac, green. brown, new blue, yellow & black	20	20
		a. Black (Queen's head, etc.), brown, new blue & yellow omitted	£650	
		b. Lilac omitted	60·00	
		c. Green omitted	40·00	
		d. Brown omitted	45·00	
		e. New blue omitted	42·00	
		f. Yellow omitted	42·00	
		Wi. Watermark inverted	24·00	
		p. Three phosphor bands	20	20
		pb. Lilac omitted	75·00	
		pc. Green omitted	45·00	
		pd. Brown omitted	45·00	
		pe. New blue omitted	45·00	
		pf. Yellow omitted	75·00	
		pWi. Watermark inverted	12·00	

716 **275**	1s. 6d. violet, red, dp blue, brown, green, blue-grey, new blue, yellow & black		30	30
	a.	Red omitted		
	b.	Dp blue omitted	£250	
	c.	Brown omitted	45·00	
	d.	Blue-grey omitted	45·00	
	e.	New blue omitted	45·00	
	f.	Yellow omitted	45·00	
	p.	Three phosphor bands	30	30
	pa.	Red omitted		
	pb.	Dp blue omitted	£250	
	pc.	Brown omitted	45·00	
	pd.	Blue-grey omitted	45·00	
	pf.	New blue omitted	45·00	
	pWi.	Watermark inverted	25·00	
		Set of 2 (Ordinary)	50	50
		Set of 2 (Phosphor)	50	50
		First Day Cover (Ordinary)		3·50
		First Day Cover (Phosphor)		3·75
		Presentation Pack (Ordinary)	3·50	

Special First Day of Issue Postmark

	Ordinary	*Phosphor*
G.P.O. Philatelic Bureau, Edinburgh 1 (Type C)	4·00	5·00

276 Hawthorn and Bramble

277 Larger Bindweed and Viper's Bugloss

278 Ox-eye Daisy, Coltsfoot and Buttercup

279 Bluebell, Red Campion and Wood Anemone

T **276/9** were issued together *se-tenant* in blocks of four within the sheet.

280 Dog Violet

281 Primroses

(Des Rev. W. Keble Martin (T **276/9**), Mary Grierson (others))

1967 (24 Apr). **British Wild Flowers.** *Chalk-surfaced paper. W* **179**. *P* 15 × 14.

717 **276**	4d. grey, lemon, myrtle-green, red, agate & slate-purple		15	10
	a.	Block of 4. Nos. 717/20	1·40	2·50
	aWi.	Block of 4. Watermark inverted	9·00	
	b.	Grey double*		
	c.	Red omitted	£2000	
	f.	Slate-purple omitted		
	Wi.	Watermark inverted	2·00	
	p.	Three phosphor bands	10	10
	pa.	Block of 4. Nos. 717p/20p	1·00	2·25
	paWi.	Block of 4. Watermark inverted	9·00	
	pd.	Agate omitted	£600	
	pf.	Slate-purple omitted	£150	
	pWi.	Watermark inverted	2·00	
718 **277**	4d. grey, lemon, myrtle-green, red, agate & violet		15	10
	b.	Grey double*		
	Wi.	Watermark inverted	2·00	
	p.	Three phosphor bands	10	10
	pd.	Agate omitted	£600	
	pe.	Violet omitted	£1250	
	pWi.	Watermark inverted	2·00	
719 **278**	4d. grey, lemon, myrtle-green, red & agate		15	10
	b.	Grey double*		
	Wi.	Watermark inverted	2·00	
	p.	Three phosphor bands	10	10
	pd.	Agate omitted	£600	
	pWi.	Watermark inverted	2·00	
720 **279**	4d. grey, lemon, myrtle-green, reddish purple, agate & violet		15	10
	b.	Grey double*		
	c.	Reddish purple omitted	£950	
	Wi.	Watermark inverted	2·00	
	p.	Three phosphor bands	10	10
	pd.	Agate omitted	£450	
	pe.	Violet omitted	£2000	
	pWi.	Watermark inverted	2·00	
721 **280**	9d. lavender-grey, green, reddish violet & orange-yellow		15	1(
	Wi.	Watermark inverted	1·25	
	p.	Three phosphor bands	10	1
722 **281**	1s. 9d. lavender-grey, green, greenish yellow & orange		20	2
	p.	Three phosphor bands	30	2
		Set of 6 (Ordinary)	1·50	6
		Set of 6 (Phosphor)	1·25	6
		First Day Cover (Ordinary)		5·0
		First Day Cover (Phosphor)		6·0
		Presentation Pack (Ordinary)	4·50	
		Presentation Pack (Phosphor)	4·50	

*The double impression of the grey printing affects the Queen head, value and inscription.

Special First Day of Issue Postmark

	Ordinary	*Phosphor*
G.P.O. Philatelic Bureau, Edinburgh 1 (Type C)	6·50	7·00

PHOSPHOR BANDS. Issues from No. 723 are normally with phosph bands only, except for the high values but most stamps have appear with the phosphor bands omitted in error. Such varieties are list under "Ey" numbers and are priced unused only. See also further not after 1971–95 Decimal Machin issue.

PHOSPHORISED PAPER. Following the adoption of phosphor bands t Post Office started a series of experiments involving the addition of t phosphor to the paper coating before the stamps were printed. No. 743c was the first of these experiments to be issued for normal postal use. See also notes after 1971–96 Decimal Machin issue.

PVA GUM. Polyvinyl alcohol was introduced by Harrisons in place of gum arabic in 1968. It is almost invisible except that a small amount of pale yellowish colouring matter was introduced to make it possible to see that the stamps had been gummed. Although this can be distinguished from gum arabic in unused stamps there is, of course, no means of detecting it in used examples. Where the two forms of gum exist on the same stamps, the PVA type are listed under "Ev" numbers, except in the case of the 1d. and 4d. (vermilion), both one centre band, which later appeared with gum arabic and these have "Eg" numbers. "Ev" and "Eg" numbers are priced unused only. All stamps printed from No. 763 onwards were issued with PVA gum only *except where otherwise stated.*

It should be further noted that gum arabic is shiny in appearance, and that, normally, PVA gum has a matt appearance. However, depending upon the qualities of the paper ingredients and the resultant absorption of the gum, occasionally, PVA gum has a shiny appearance. In such cases, especially in stamps from booklets, it is sometimes impossible to be absolutely sure which gum has been used except by testing the stamps chemically which destroys them. Therefore, whilst all gum arabic is shiny it does not follow that all shiny gum is gum arabic.

282

282a

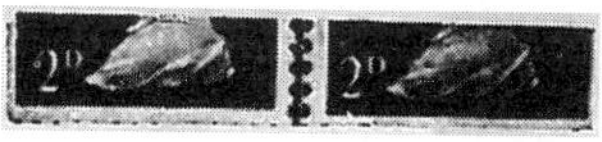

I II

Two types of the 2d.

I. Value spaced away from left side of stamp (cylinders 1 no dot and dot).

II. Value close to left side from new multipositive used for cylinders 5 no dot and dot onwards. The portrait appears in the centre, thus conforming to the other values.

Three types of the Machin head, known as Head A, B or C, are distinguished by specialists. These are illustrated in Vol. 3 of the *Great Britain Specialised Catalogue.*

(Des after plaster cast by Arnold Machin)

1967 (5 June)–**70**. *Chalk-surfaced paper. Two phosphor bands except where otherwise stated. No wmk. PVA gum except Nos. 725m, 728, 729, 731, 731Ea, 740, 742/Ea, 743/a and 744/Ea.*

23	**282**		½d. orange-brown (5.2.68)	10	20
		Ey.	Phosphor omitted	30·00	
24			1d. lt olive (*shades*) (2 bands) (5.2.68)	10	10
		a.	Imperf (coil strip)†	£1100	
		b.	Part perf pane*		
		c.	Imperf pane*	£3750	
		d.	Uncoated paper (1970)**	65·00	
		Ey.	Phosphor omitted	1·00	
24)	**282**	l.	Booklet pane. No. 724 × 2 *se-tenant* with 730 × 2 (6.4.68)	3·00	
(724)	**282**	lEy.	Booklet pane. Phosphor omitted	75·00	
		m.	Booklet pane. No. 724 × 4 *se-tenant* with 734 × 2 (6.1.69)	3·50	
		mEy.	Booklet pane. Phosphor omitted	£160	
		n.	Booklet pane. No. 724 × 6, 734 × 3, 734Eb × 3 & 735 × 3 *se-tenant* (1.12.69)	8·50	
		na.	Booklet pane. Uncoated paper**	£900	
		nEy.	Booklet pane. Phosphor omitted	£150	
725			1d. yellowish olive (1 centre band) (16.9.68)	25	30
		Eg.	Gum arabic (27.8.69)	25	
		l.	Booklet pane. No. 725 × 4 *se-tenant* with 732 × 2	4·00	
		lEy.	Booklet pane. Phosphor omitted	30·00	
		m.	Coil strip. No. 728 × 2 *se-tenant* with 729, 725Eg & 733Eg (27.8.69)	1·25	
726			2d. lake-brown (Type I) (2 bands) (5.2.68)	10	15
		Ey.	Phosphor omitted	30·00	
727			2d. lake-brown (Type II) (2 bands) (1969)	15	15
		Ey.	Phosphor omitted	1·00	
728			2d. lake-brown (Type II) (1 centre band) (27.8.69)	50	75
729			3d. violet (*shades*) (1 centre band) (8.8.67)	10	10
		a.	Imperf (pair)	£550	
		Ey.	Phosphor omitted	1·25	
		Ev.	PVA gum (*shades*) (12.3.68)	10	
		Evy.	Phosphor omitted	2·00	
730			3d. violet (2 bands) (6.4.68)	30	30
		a.	Uncoated paper**	£2000	
731			4d. dp sepia (*shades*) (2 bands)	10	10
		Ey.	Phosphor omitted	1·00	
		Ea.	*Dp olive-brown*	10	15
		Eay.	Phosphor omitted	2·00	
		b.	Part perf pane*	£1000	
		Ev.	PVA gum (*shades*) (22.1.68)	10	
		Evy.	Phosphor omitted	2·00	
732			4d. dp olive-brown (*shades*) (1 centre band) (16.9.68)	10	10
		a.	Part perf pane*	£1000	
		l.	Booklet pane. Two stamps plus two printed labels	1·00	
		lEy.	Booklet pane. Phosphor omitted	60·00	
733			4d. brt vermilion (1 centre band) (6.1.69)	10	10
		a.	*Tête-bêche* (horiz pair)	£2500	
		b.	Uncoated paper**	6·00	
		Ey.	Phosphor omitted	1·25	
		Eg.	Gum arabic (27.8.69)	10	
		Egy.	Phosphor omitted	£1200	
		l.	Booklet pane. Two stamps plus two printed labels (3.3.69)	1·00	
		lEy.	Booklet pane. Phosphor omitted	70·00	
734			4d. brt vermilion (1 band at left) (6.1.69)	1·75	1·50
		a.	Uncoated paper**	£175	
		Eb.	One band at right (1.12.69)	2·00	3·00
		Eba.	Ditto. Uncoated paper**	£175	
735			5d. royal blue (*shades*) (1.7.68)	10	10
		a.	Imperf pane*	£1200	
		b.	Part perf pane*	£800	
		c.	Imperf (pair)††	£200	
		d.	Uncoated paper**	15·00	
		Ey.	Phosphor omitted	2·00	
		Ee.	*Dp blue*	10	15
		Eey.	Phosphor omitted	3·00	
736			6d. brt reddish purple (*shades*) (5.2.68)	20	20
		Ey.	Phosphor omitted	6·50	
		Ea.	*Brt magenta*	3·00	50
		Eb.	*Claret*	50	40
		Eby.	Phosphor omitted	10·00	
737	**282a**		7d. brt emerald (1.7.68)	40	30
		Ey.	Phosphor omitted	55·00	

738	**282a**	8d. brt vermilion (1.7.68)	15	30
		Ey. Phosphor omitted	£400	
739		8d. lt turquoise-blue (6.1.69)	55	60
		Ey. Phosphor omitted	60·00	
740		9d. myrtle-green (8.8.67)	50	30
		Ey. Phosphor omitted	20·00	
		Ev. PVA gum (29.11.68)	50	
		Evy. Phosphor omitted	25·00	
741	**282**	10d. drab (1.7.68)	45	50
		a. Uncoated paper**	23·00	
		Ey. Phosphor omitted	40·00	
742		1s. lt bluish violet (*shades*)	40	30
		Ey. Phosphor omitted	70·00	
		Ea. Pale bluish violet	1·25	30
		Ev. Ditto. PVA gum (26.4.68)	50	
		Evy. Phosphor omitted	3·50	
743		1s. 6d. greenish blue & deep blue (*shades*) (8.8.67)	50	30
		a. Greenish blue omitted	£125	
		Ey. Phosphor omitted	6·00	
		Ev. PVA gum (28.8.68)	60	
		Eva. Greenish blue omitted	80·00	
		Evy. Phosphor omitted	14·00	
		Evb. Prussian blue & indigo	2·25	75
		Evby. Phosphor omitted	11·00	
		c. Phosphorised paper (*Prussian blue & indigo*) (10.12.69)	85	90
		ca. Prussian blue omitted	£400	
744		1s. 9d. dull orange & black (*shades*)	40	30
		Ey. Phosphor omitted	30·00	
		Ea. Brt orange & black	1·50	50
		Ev. PVA gum (*brt orange & black*) (16.11.70)	40	
		Set of 16 (one of each value & colour)	3·00	3·25
		Presentation Pack (one of each value) (1968)	6·00	
		Presentation Pack (German) (1969)	35·00	

*BOOKLET ERRORS. See note after No. 556.

** Uncoated paper. This does not respond to the chalky test, and may be further distinguished from the normal chalk-surfaced paper by the fibres which clearly show on the surface, resulting in the printing impression being rougher, and by the screening dots which are not so evident. The 1d., 4d. and 5d. come from the £1 "Stamps for Cooks" Booklet (1970); the 3d. and 10d. from sheets (1969). The 20p. and 50p. high values (Nos. 830/1) exist with similar errors.

†No. 724a occurs in a vertical strip of four, top stamp perforated on three sides, bottom stamp imperf three sides and the two middle stamps completely imperf.

††No. 735c comes from the original state of cylinder 15 which is identifiable by the screening dots which extend through the gutters of the stamps and into the margins of the sheet. This must not be confused with imperforate stamps from cylinder 10, a large quantity of which was stolen from the printers early in 1970.

The 1d. with centre band and PVA gum (725) only came in the September 1968 10s. booklet (No. XP6). The 1d., 2d. and 4d. with centre band and gum arabic (725Eg, 728 and 733Eg respectively) only came in the coil strip (725m). The 3d. (No. 730) appeared in booklets on 6.4.68, from coils during Dec 68 and from sheets in Jan 1969. The 4d. with one side band at left (734) came from 10s. (band at left) and £1 (band at left or right) booklet *se-tenant* panes, and the 4d. with one side band at right (734Eb) came from the £1 booklet *se-tenant* panes only.

The 4d. (731) in shades of washed-out grey are colour changelings which we understand are caused by the concentrated solvents used in modern dry cleaning methods.

For decimal issue, see Nos. X841, etc.

First Day Covers

5.6.67	4d., 1s., 1s. 9d. (*731, 742, 744*)	1·00
8.8.67	3d., 9d., 1s. 6d. (*729, 740, 743*)	1·00
5.2.68	½d., 1d., 2d., 6d. (*723/4, 726, 736*)	1·00
1.7.68	5d., 7d., 8d., 10d. (*735, 737/8, 741*)	1·00

283 "Master Lambton" (Sir Thomas Lawrence)

284 "Mares and Foals in a Landscape" (George Stubbs)

285 "Children Coming Out of School" (L. S. Lowry)

(Des S. Rose)

1967 (10 July). **British Paintings.** *Chalk-surfaced paper. Two phosphor bands. No wmk. P* 14 × 15 (*4d.*) *or* 15 × 14 (*others*).

748	**283**	4d. rose-red, lemon, brown, black, new blue & gold	10	10
		a. Gold (value & Queen's head) omitted	£200	
		b. New blue omitted	£2500	
		Ey. Phosphor omitted	7·00	
749	**284**	9d. Venetian red, ochre, grey-black, new blue, greenish yellow & black	20	20
		a. Black (Queen's head & value) omitted	£400	
		b. Greenish yellow omitted	£1300	
		Ey. Phosphor omitted	£450	
750	**285**	1s. 6d. greenish yellow, grey, rose, new blue, grey-black & gold	35	25
		a. Gold (Queen's head) omitted	£750	
		b. New blue omitted	£160	
		c. Grey (clouds and shading) omitted	95·00	
		Ey. Phosphor omitted	£300	
		Set of 3	50	50
		First Day Cover		4·00
		Presentation Pack	8·00	

Special First Day of Issue Postmark

G.P.O. Philatelic Bureau, Edinburgh 1 (Type C) .... 4·75

A First Day of Issue handstamp was provided at Bishop Auckland Co. Durham, for this issue.

286 *Gypsy Moth IV*

(Des M. and Sylvia Goaman)

1967 (24 July). **Sir Francis Chichester's World Voyage.** *Chalk-surface paper. Three phosphor bands. No wmk. P* 15 × 14.

751	**286**	1s. 9d. black, brown-red, lt emerald & blue	25	2
		First Day Cover		2·2

Special First Day of Issue Postmarks

G.P.O. Philatelic Bureau, Edinburgh 1 .... 4·50
Greenwich, London SE10 .... 4·50
Plymouth, Devon .... 4·75

The Philatelic Bureau and Greenwich postmarks are similar in design to that for Plymouth. A First Day of Issue handstamp was provided at Chichester, Sussex for this issue.

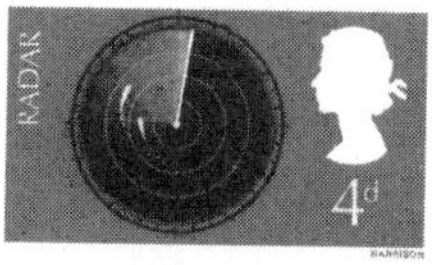

287 Radar Screen

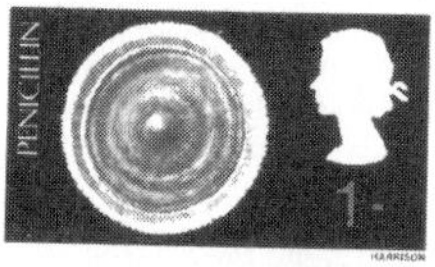

288 *Penicillium notatum*

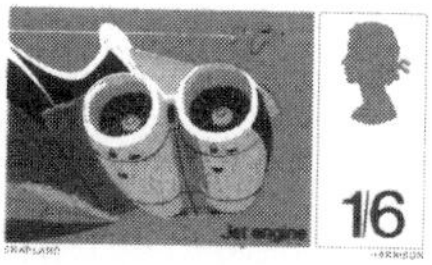

289 Vickers VC-10 Jet Engines

290 Television Equipment

(Des C. Abbott (4d., 1s.), Negus-Sharland team (others))

967 (19 Sept). **British Discovery and Invention.** *Chalk-surfaced paper. Three phosphor bands (4d.) or two phosphor bands (others). W* **179** *(sideways on 1s. 9d.). P* 14 × 15 *(1s. 9d.) or* 15 × 14 *(others).*

2 **287** 4d. greenish yellow, black & vermilion 10 10
  Ey. Phosphor omitted .... 2·00
3 **288** 1s. blue-green, lt greenish blue, slate-purple & bluish violet 10 10
  Wi. Watermark inverted .... 12·00
  Ey. Phosphor omitted .... 9·00
4 **289** 1s. 6d. black, grey, royal blue, ochre & turquoise-blue 25 15
  Wi. Watermark inverted .... 33·00
  Ey. Phosphor omitted £500
5 **290** 1s. 9d. black, grey-blue, pale olive-grey, violet & orange 30 20
  a. Grey-blue omitted ....
  Ey. Phosphor omitted £500
  Set of 4 .... 60 50
  First Day Cover .... 2·50
  Presentation Pack .... 3·00

Special First of Issue Postmark

G.P.O. Philatelic Bureau, Edinburgh (Type C) .... 3·00

TERMARK. All issues from this date are on unwatermarked paper.

291 "The Adoration of the Shepherds" (School of Seville)

292 "Madonna and Child" (Murillo)

293 "The Adoration of the Shepherds" (Louis le Nain)

(Des S. Rose)

1967. Christmas. *Chalk-surfaced paper. One phosphor band (3d.) or two phosphor bands (others). P* 15 × 14 *(1s. 6d.) or* 14 × 15 *(others).*

756 **291** 3d. olive-yellow, rose, blue, black & gold (27.11) 10 10
  a. Gold (value & Queen's head) omitted ... 75·00
  b. Printed on the gummed side £300
  c. Rose omitted ....
  Ey. Phosphor omitted .... 1·00
757 **292** 4d. brt purple, greenish yellow, new blue, grey-black & gold (18.10) 10 10
  a. Gold (value & Queen's head) omitted ... 60·00
  b. Gold ("4D" only) omitted ....
  c. Greenish yellow (Child, robe & Madonna's face) omitted ....
  Ey. Phosphor omitted £100
758 **293** 1s. 6d. brt purple, bistre, lemon, black, orange-red, ultramarine & gold (27.11) .. 35 35
  a. Gold (value & Queen's head) omitted ... £3500
  b. Ultramarine omitted £350
  c. Lemon omitted £10000
  Ey. Phosphor omitted .... 12·00
  Set of 3 .... 50 50
  First Day Covers (2) .... 5·00

Distinct shades exist of the 3d. and 4d. values but are not listable as there are intermediate shades. For the 4d., stamps from one machine show a darker background and give the appearance of the yellow colour being omitted, but this is not so and these should not be confused with the true missing yellow No. 757c.

No. 757b comes from stamps in the first vertical row of a sheet.

Special First Day of Issue Postmarks

G.P.O. Philatelic Bureau, Edinburgh 1 (4d.) (18 Oct.) (Type C) .... 2·50
G.P.O. Philatelic Bureau, Edinburgh 1 (3d., 1s. 6d.) (27 Nov.) (Type C) .... 3·00
Bethlehem, Llandeilo, Carms (4d.) (18 Oct.) (Type C) .. 3·50
Bethlehem, Llandeilo, Carms (3d., 1s. 6d.) (27 Nov.) (Type C) .... 4·00

Gift Pack 1967

1967 (27 Nov). *Comprises Nos.* 715p/22p *and* 748/58.

GP758c	Gift Pack	2·50

(Recess Bradbury, Wilkinson)

1967–68. *No wmk. White paper. P* 11 × 12.

759	**166**	2s. 6d. black-brown (1.7.68)	40	50
760	**167**	5s. red (10.4.68)	1·00	1·00
761	**168**	10s. brt ultramarine (10.4.68)	5·50	7·00
762	**169**	£1 black (4.12.67)	4·50	6·00
		Set of 4	10·00	13·00

PVA GUM. All the following issues from this date have PVA gum *except where footnotes state otherwise.*

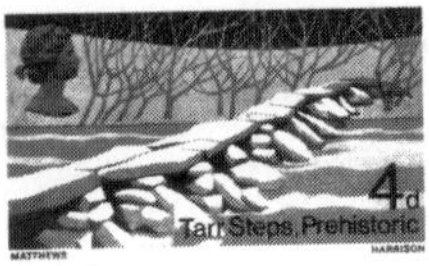

294 Tarr Steps, Exmoor

295 Aberfeldy Bridge

296 Menai Bridge

297 M4 Viaduct

(Des A. Restall (9d.), L. Rosoman (1s. 6d.), J. Matthews (others))

1968 (29 Apr). **British Bridges.** *Chalk-surfaced paper. Two phosphor bands. P* 15 × 14.

763	**294**	4d. black, bluish violet, turquiose-blue & gold	10	10
		a. Printed on gummed side	25·00	
		Ey. Phosphor omitted	2·00	
764	**295**	9d. red-brown, myrtle-green, ultramarine, olive-brown, black & gold	10	10
		a. Gold (Queen's head) omitted	£125	
		b. Ultramarine omitted	†	£3750
		Ey. Phosphor omitted	15·00	
765	**296**	1s. 6d. olive-brown, red-orange, brt green, turquoise-green & gold	20	15
		a. Gold (Queen's head) omitted	£125	
		b. Red-orange (rooftops) omitted	£150	
		Ey. Phosphor omitted	45·00	
766	**297**	1s. 9d. olive-brown, greenish yellow, dull green, dp ultramarine & gold	25	30
		a. Gold (Queen's head) omitted	£150	
		Ey. Phosphor omitted	9·00	
		Set of 4	60	60
		First Day Cover		3·50
		Presentation Pack	2·50	

No 764b is only known on first day covers posted from Canterbury, Kent, or the Philatelic Bureau, Edinburgh.

Special First Day of Issue Postmarks

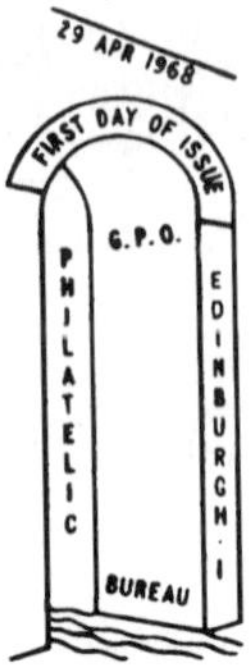

G.P.O. Philatelic Bureau, Edinburgh 1	4·50
Bridge, Canterbury, Kent	4·50
Aberfeldy, Perthshire (Type A) (9d. value only)	12·00
Menai Bridge, Anglesey (Type A) (1s. 6d. value only)	12·00

The Bridge, Canterbury, postmark is similar in design to that for the Philatelic Bureau.

298 "TUC" and Trades Unionists

299 Mrs. Emmeline Pankhurst (statue)

300 Sopwith Camel and English Electric Lightning Fighters

301 Captain Cook's *Endeavour* and Signature

(Des D. Gentleman (4d.), C. Abbott (others))

1968 (29 May). **British Anniversaries.** *Events described on stamp Chalk-surfaced paper. Two phosphor bands. P* 15 × 14.

767	**298**	4d. emerald, olive, blue & black	10	
		Ey. Phosphor omitted	12·00	
768	**299**	9d. reddish violet, bluish grey & black	10	
		Ey. Phosphor omitted	7·00	
769	**300**	1s. olive-brown, blue, red, slate-blue & black	20	
		Ey. Phosphor omitted	10·00	
770	**301**	1s. 9d. yellow-ochre & blackish brown	25	
		Ey. Phosphor omitted	£150	
		Set of 4	60	
		First Day Cover		6
		Presentation Pack	4·00	

Special First Day of Issue Postmarks

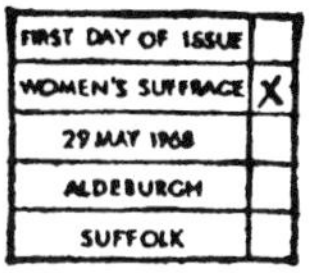

G.P.O. Philatelic Bureau, Edinburgh 1 (Type C) .... 7·50
Manchester (4d. value only) .... 2·00
Aldeburgh, Suffolk (9d. value only) .... 2·25
Hendon, London NW4 (1s. value only) .... 2·25
Whitby, Yorkshire (1s. 9d. value only) .... 2·25

The Philatelic Bureau postmark was used on sets of four, but the other postmarks were only available on single stamps.

302 "Queen Elizabeth I" (unknown artist)

303 "Pinkie" (Lawrence)

304 "Ruins of St. Mary Le Port" (Piper)

305 "The Hay Wain" (Constable)

(Des S. Rose)

1968 (12 Aug). **British Paintings.** *Queen's head embossed. Chalk-surfaced paper. Two phosphor bands. P 15 × 14 (1s. 9d.) or 14 × 15 (others).*

771 **302** 4d. black, vermilion, greenish yellow, grey & gold 10 10
a. Gold (value & Queen's head) omitted ... £125
b. Vermilion omitted* £225
Ec. Embossing omitted .... 80·00
Ey. Phosphor omitted .... 1·50
Eya. Gold (value & Queen's head) & phosphor omitted £175

772 **303** 1s. mauve, new blue, greenish yellow, black, magenta & gold 15 15
a. Gold (value & Queen's head) omitted ... £200
Eb. Gold (value & Queen's head), embossing & phosphor omitted £225
Ec. Embossing omitted ....
Ey. Phosphor omitted .... 7·00

773 **304** 1s. 6d. slate, orange, black, mauve, greenish yellow, ultramarine & gold 20 20
a. Gold (value & Queen's head) omitted ... £100
Eb. Embossing omitted ....
Ey. Phosphor omitted .... 7·00

774 **305** 1s. 9d. greenish yellow, black, new blue, red & gold 25 25
a. Gold (value & Queen's head) & embossing omitted £500
b. Red omitted £10000
Ec. Embossing omitted ....
Ey. Phosphor omitted .... 19·00
Set of 4 .... 60 60
First Day Cover .... 2·75
Presentation Pack .... 2·25
Presentation Pack (German) .... 5·00

No. 774a is only known with the phosphor also omitted.

*The effect of this is to leave the face and hands white and there is more yellow and olive in the costume.

The 4d. also exists with the value only omitted resulting from a colour shift.

Special First Day of Issue Postmark
G.P.O. Philatelic Bureau, Edinburgh 1 (Type C) .... 4·00

Gift Pack 1968

1968 (16 Sept). *Comprises Nos.* 763/74.
GP774*c* Gift Pack .... 8·00
GP774*d* Gift Pack (German) .... 18·00

Collectors Pack 1968

1968 (16 Sept). *Comprises Nos.* 752/8 *and* 763/74.
CP774*e* Collectors Pack .... 8·00

306 Boy and Girl with Rocking Horse

307 Girl with Doll's House

308 Boy with Train Set

(Des Rosalind Dease. Head printed in gold and then embossed)

1968 (25 Nov). **Christmas.** *Chalk-surfaced paper. One centre phosphor band (4d.) or two phosphor bands (others). P 15 × 14 (4d.) or 14 × 15 (others).*

775	**306**	4d. black, orange, vermilion, ultramarine, bistre & gold	10	10
		a. Gold omitted	£2250	
		b. Vermilion omitted*	£275	
		c. Ultramarine omitted	£175	
		Ed. Embossing omitted	6·00	
		Ey. Phosphor omitted	2·00	
776	**307**	9d. yellow-olive, black, brown, yellow, magenta, orange, turquoise-green & gold	15	15
		a. Yellow omitted	65·00	
		b. Turquoise-green (dress) omitted		
		Ec. Embossing omitted	6·00	
		Ey. Phosphor omitted	9·00	
		Eya. Embossing & phosphor omitted	9·00	
777	**308**	1s. 6d. ultramarine, yellow-orange, brt purple, blue-green, black & gold	25	25
		Ea. Embossing omitted		
		Ey. Phosphor omitted	15·00	
		Set of 3	40	40
		First Day Cover		2·25
		Presentation Pack	3·75	
		Presentation Pack (German)	4·00	

*The effect of the missing vermilion is shown on the rocking horse, saddle and faces which appear orange instead of red.

A single used example of the 4d. exists with the bistre omitted.

No. 775c is only known with phosphor also omitted.

Two machines were used for printing for the 4d. value:

Stamps from cylinders 1A–1B–2C–1D–1E in combination with 1F, 2F or 3F (gold) were printed entirely on the Rembrandt sheet-fed machine. They invariably have the Queen's head level with the top of the boy's head and the sheets are perforated through the left side margin.

Stamps from cylinders 2A–2B–3C–2D–2E in combination with 1F, 2F, 3F or 4F (gold) were printed on the reel-fed Thrissell machine in five colours (its maximum colour capacity) and subsequently sheet-fed on the Rembrandt machine for the Queen's head and the embossing. The position of the Queen's head is generally lower than on the stamps printed at one operation but it varies in different parts of the sheet and is not, therefore, a sure indication for identifying single stamps. Another small difference is that the boy's grey pullover is noticeably "moth-eaten" in the Thrissell printings and is normal on the Rembrandt. The Thrissell printings are perforated through the top margin.

Special First Day of Issue Postmarks

G.P.O. Philatelic Bureau, Edinburgh 1 (Type C)	3·00
Bethlehem, Llandeilo, Carms (Type C)	4·50

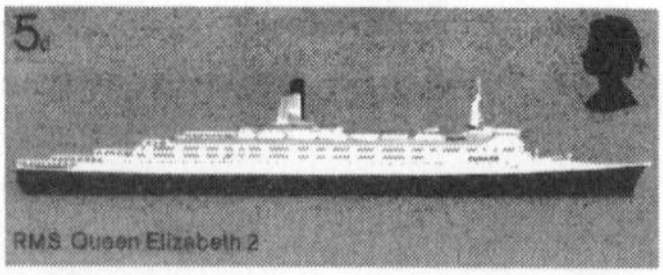

309 *Queen Elizabeth 2*

310 Elizabethan Galleon

311 East Indiaman

312 *Cutty Sark*

313 *Great Britain*

314 *Mauretania I*

(Des D. Gentleman)

1969 (15 Jan). **British Ships.** *Chalk-surfaced paper. Two vertical phosphor bands at right (1s.), one horizontal phosphor band (5d.) or two phosphor bands (9d.). P 15 × 14.*

778	**309**	5d. black, grey, red & turquoise	10	10
		a. Black (Queen's head, value, hull and inscr) omitted	£700	
		b. Grey (decks, etc.) omitted	90·00	
		c. Red omitted	50·00	
		Ey. Phosphor omitted	2·00	
		Eya. Red & phosphor omitted	80·00	
779	**310**	9d. red, blue, ochre, brown, black & grey	10	15
		a. Strip of 3. Nos. 779/81	1·50	2·00
		ab. Red & blue omitted	£1500	
		ac. Blue omitted	£1500	
		Ey. Phosphor omitted	12·00	
		Eya. Strip of 3. Nos. 779/81. Phosphor omitted	40·00	
780	**311**	9d. ochre, brown, black & grey	10	15
		Ey. Phosphor omitted	12·00	
781	**312**	9d. ochre, brown, black & grey	10	15
		Ey. Phosphor omitted	12·00	
782	**313**	1s. brown, black, grey, green & greenish yellow	40	30
		a. Pair. Nos. 782/3	1·25	1·75
		ab. Greenish yellow omitted		
		Ey. Phosphor omitted	28·00	
		Eya. Pair. Nos. 782/3. Phosphor omitted	65·00	
783	**314**	1s. red, black, brown, carmine & grey	40	30
		a. Carmine (hull overlay) omitted	£10000	
		b. Red (funnels) omitted	£10000	
		c. Carmine and red omitted		
		Ey. Phosphor omitted	28·00	
		Set of 6	2·00	1·00
		First Day Cover		5·50
		Presentation Pack	4·00	
		Presentation Pack (German)	19·00	

The 9d. and 1s. values were arranged in horizontal strips of three and pairs respectively throughout the sheet.

No. 779ab is known only with the phosphor also omitted.

Special First Day of Issue Postmark

G.P.O. Philatelic Bureau, Edinburgh 1 (Type C)	6·50

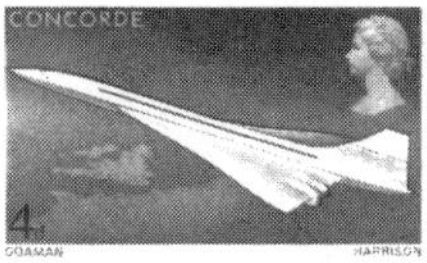

315 Concorde in Flight

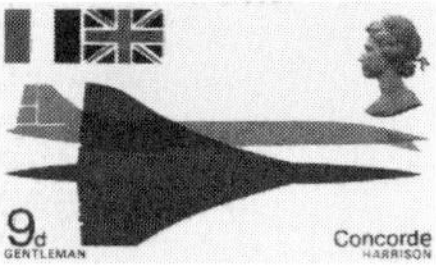

316 Plan and Elevation Views

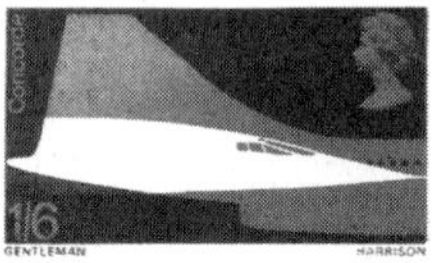

317 Concorde's Nose and Tail

(Des M. and Sylvia Goaman (4d.), D. Gentleman (9d., 1s. 6d.))

969 (3 Mar). **First Flight of Concorde.** *Chalk-surfaced paper. Two phosphor bands. P* 15 × 14.

'84	**315**	4d.	yellow-orange, violet, greenish blue, blue-green & pale green	10	10
		a.	Violet (value etc.) omitted	£225	
		b.	Yellow-orange omitted	£110	
		Ey.	Phosphor omitted	1·00	
		Eya.	Yellow-orange & phosphor omitted	£110	
85	**316**	9d.	ultramarine, emerald, red & grey-blue	20	20
		Ey.	Phosphor omitted	£100	
86	**317**	1s.	6d. deep blue, silver-grey & lt blue	30	30
		a.	Silver-grey omitted	£275	
		Ey.	Phosphor omitted	9·00	
			Set of 3	50	50
			First Day Cover		3·00
			Presentation Pack	3·75	
			Presentation Pack (German)	15·00	

No. 786a affects the Queen's head which appears in the light blue olour.

Special First Day of Issue Postmarks

G.P.O. Philatelic Bureau, Edinburgh (Type C)	3·75
Filton, Bristol (Type C)	4·25

318 Queen Elizabeth II. (See also Type **357**)

)es after plaster cast by Arnold Machin. Recess Bradbury, Wilkinson)

969 (5 Mar). *P* 12.

37	**318**	2s.	6d. brown	50	30
38		5s.	crimson-lake	2·25	60
39		10s.	dp ultramarine	7·00	6·00
90		£1	bluish black	3·00	1·60
			Set of 4	11·50	7·50
			First Day Cover		7·50
			Presentation Pack	18·00	
			Presentation Pack (German)	38·00	

Special First Day of Issue Postmarks

G.P.O. Philatelic Bureau (Type C)	8·00
Windsor, Berks (Type C)	15·00

For decimal issue, see Nos. 829/31*b* and notes after No. 831*b*.

319 Page from *Daily Mail*, and Vickers FB-27 Vimy Aircraft

320 Europa and CEPT Emblems

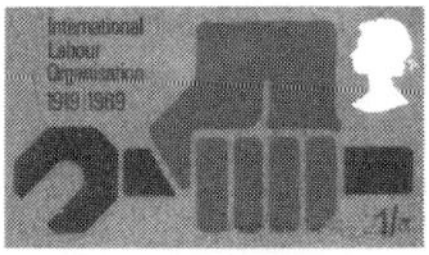

321 ILO Emblem

322 Flags of NATO Countries

323 Vickers FB-27 Vimy Aircraft and Globe showing Flight

(Des P. Sharland (5d., 1s., 1s. 6d.), M. and Sylvia Goaman (9d., 1s. 9d.))

1969 (2 Apr). **Anniversaries.** *Events described on stamps. Chalk-surfaced paper. Two phosphor bands. P* 15 × 14.

791	**319**	5d.	black, pale sage-green, chestnut & new blue	10	10
		Ey.	Phosphor omitted		
792	**320**	9d.	pale turquoise, dp blue, lt emerald-green & black	20	20
		a.	Uncoated paper*	£1500	
		Ey.	Phosphor omitted	18·00	
793	**321**	1s.	brt purple, dp blue & lilac	20	20
		Ey.	Phosphor omitted	7·00	
794	**322**	1s.	6d. red, royal blue, yellow-green, black, lemon & new blue	20	20
		e.	Black omitted	60·00	
		f.	Yellow-green omitted	48·00	
		Ey.	Phosphor omitted	9·00	
		Eya.	Yellow-green & phosphor omitted	55·00	
795	**323**	1s.	9d. yellow-olive, greenish yellow & pale turquoise-green	25	25
		a.	Uncoated paper*	£200	
		Ey.	Phosphor omitted	6·00	
			Set of 5	85	85
			First Day Cover		3·50
			Presentation Pack	2·75	
			Presentation Pack (German)	35·00	

*Uncoated paper. The second note after No. 744 also applies here.

Special First Day of Issue Postmark

G.P.O. Philatelic Bureau, Edinburgh (Type C)	6·00

324 Durham Cathedral

325 York Minster

326 St. Giles' Cathedral, Edinburgh

327 Canterbury Cathedral

328 St. Paul's Cathedral

329 Liverpool Metropolitan Cathedral

(Des P. Gauld)

1969 (28 May). **British Architecture. Cathedrals.** *Chalk-surfaced paper. Two phosphor bands. P* 15 × 14.

796	**324**	5d.	grey-black, orange, pale bluish violet & black	10	10
		a.	Block of 4. Nos. 796/9	85	1·50
		ab.	Block of 4. Uncoated paper†		
		b.	Pale bluish violet omitted	£2250	
797	**325**	5d.	grey-black, pale bluish violet, new blue & black	10	10
		b.	Pale bluish violet omitted	£2500	
798	**326**	5d.	grey-black, purple, green & black	10	10
		c.	Green omitted*	40·00	
799	**327**	5d.	grey-black, green, new blue & black	10	10
800	**328**	9d.	grey-black, ochre, pale drab, violet & black	15	15
		a.	Black (value) omitted	£100	
		Ey.	Phosphor omitted	45·00	
		Eya.	Black and phosphor omitted	£150	
801	**329**	1s.	6d. grey-black, pale turquoise, pale reddish violet, pale yellow-olive & black	15	15
		a.	Black (value) omitted	£1600	
		b.	Black (value) double		
		Ey.	Phosphor omitted	20·00	
			Set of 6	1·00	55
			First Day Cover		4·00
			Presentation Pack	4·00	
			Presentation Pack (German)	16·00	

*The missing green on the roof top is known on R.2/5, R.8/5 and R.10/5 but all are from different sheets and it only occured in part of the printing, being "probably caused by a batter on the impression cylinder". Examples are also known with the green partly omitted.

†Uncoated paper. The second note after No. 744 also applies here.

The 5d. values were issued together *se-tenant* in blocks of four throughout the sheet.

Special First Day of Issue Postmark

G.P.O. Philatelic Bureau, Edinburgh (Type C) .... 6·00

330 The King's Gate, Caernarvon Castle

331 The Eagle Tower, Caernarvon Castle

332 Queen Eleanor's Gate, Caernarvon Castle

333 Celtic Cross, Margam Abbey

334 H.R.H. The Prince of Wales (after photo by G. Argent)

(Des D. Gentleman)

1969 (1 July). **Investiture of H.R.H. The Prince of Wales.** *Chalk-surfaced paper. Two phosphor bands. P* 14 × 15.

802	**330**	5d.	dp olive-grey, lt olive-grey, dp grey, lt grey, red, pale turquoise-green, black & silver	10	10
		a.	Strip of 3. Nos. 802/4	70	1·25
		b.	Black (value & inscr) omitted	£150	
		c.	Red omitted*	£250	
		d.	Dp grey omitted**	90·00	
		e.	Pale turquoise-green omitted	£325	
		Ey.	Phosphor omitted	4·00	
		Eya.	Strip of 3. Nos. 802/4. Phosphor omitted	12·00	
803	**331**	5d.	dp olive-grey, lt olive-grey, dp grey, lt grey, red, pale turquoise-green, black & silver	10	10
		b.	Black (value and inscr) omitted	£150	
		c.	Red omitted*	£250	
		d.	Dp grey omitted**	90·00	
		e.	Pale turquoise-green omitted	£325	
		f.	Light grey (marks on walls, window frames, etc) omitted	†	£7500
		Ey.	Phosphor omitted	3·00	

804	**332**	5d. dp olive-grey, lt olive-grey, dp grey, lt grey, red, pale turquoise-green, black & silver	10	10
		b. Black (value & inscr) omitted	£150	
		c. Red omitted*	£250	
		d. Dp grey omitted**	90·00	
		e. Pale turquoise-green omitted	£325	
		Ey. Phosphor omitted	3·00	
805	**333**	9d. dp grey, lt grey, black & gold	20	10
		Ey. Phosphor omitted	22·00	
806	**334**	1s. blackish yellow-olive & gold	20	10
		Ey. Phosphor omitted	13·00	
		Set of 5	1·00	45
		First Day Cover		1·50
		Presentation Pack†	1·60	
		Presentation Pack (German)	16·00	

The 5d. values were issued together *se-tenant* in strips of three throughout the sheet.

*The 5d. value is also known with the red misplaced downwards and where this occurs the red printing does not take very well on the silver background and in some cases is so faint it could be mistaken for a missing red. However, the red can be seen under a magnifying glass and caution should therefore be exercised when purchasing copies of Nos. 802/4c.

**The deep grey affects the dark portions of the windows and doors.

†In addition to the generally issued Presentation Pack a further pack in different colours and with all texts printed in both English and Welsh was made available exclusively through Education Authorities for free distribution to all schoolchildren in Wales and Monmouthshire (*Price* £4).

No. 803f is only known commercially used on cover.

Special First Day of Issue Postmarks

G.P.O. Philatelic Bureau, Edinburgh 1 (Type C)	4·50
Day of Investiture, Caernarvon	3·00

335 Mahatma Gandhi

(Des B. Mullick)

1969 (13 Aug). **Gandhi Centenary Year.** *Chalk-surfaced paper. Two phosphor bands. P* 15 × 14.

807	**335**	1s. 6d. black, green, red-orange & grey	30	30
		a. Printed on the gummed side	£300	
		Ey. Phosphor omitted	4·00	
		First Day Cover		2·00

Special First Day of Issue Postmark

G.P.O. Philatelic Bureau, Edinburgh (Type C)	2·25

Collectors Pack 1969

1969 (15 Sept). *Comprises Nos.* 775/86 *and* 791/807.

CP807*b*	Collectors Pack	20·00

336 National Giro "G" Symbol

337 Telecommunications—International Subscriber Dialling

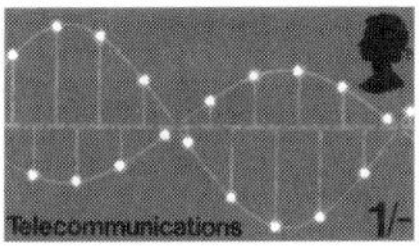

338 Telecommunications—Pulse Code Modulation

339 Postal Mechanisation—Automatic Sorting

(Des D. Gentleman. Litho De La Rue)

1969 (1 Oct). **Post Office Technology Commemoration.** *Chalk-surfaced paper. Two phosphor bands. P* $13\frac{1}{2}$ × 14.

808	**336**	5d. new blue, greenish blue, lavender & black	10	10
		Ey. Phosphor omitted	5·00	
809	**337**	9d. emerald, violet-blue & black	15	15
810	**338**	1s. emerald, lavender & black	15	15
		Ey. Phosphor omitted	£300	
811	**339**	1s. 6d. brt purple, lt blue, grey-blue & black	40	40
		Set of 4	70	70
		First Day Cover		2·25
		Presentation Pack	3·00	

Special First Day of Issue Postmark

G.P.O. Philatelic Bureau, Edinburgh (Type C)	2·75

340 Herald Angel

341 The Three Shepherds

342 The Three Kings

(Des F. Wegner. Queen's head (and stars 4d., 5d. and scroll-work 1s. 6d.) printed in gold and then embossed)

1969 (26 Nov). **Christmas.** *Chalk-surfaced paper. Two phosphor bands (5d., 1s. 6d.) or one centre band (4d.). P* 15 × 14.

812	**340**	4d. vermilion, new blue, orange, brt purple, lt green, bluish violet, blackish brown & gold	10	10
		a. Gold (Queen's head etc.) omitted	£2000	
		Eb. Centre band $3\frac{1}{2}$ mm	25	15

813 **341** 5d. magenta, lt blue, royal blue, olive-brown, green, greenish yellow, red & gold 10 10
a. Lt blue (sheep, etc.) omitted .... 60·00
b. Red omitted* £550
c. Gold (Queen's head) omitted £450
d. Green omitted £200
e. Olive-brown, red & gold omitted £7000
Ef. Embossing omitted .... 22·00
Ey. Phosphor omitted .... 1·50
814 **342** 1s. 6d. greenish yellow, brt purple, bluish violet, dp slate, orange, green, new blue & gold 30 30
a. Gold (Queen's head etc.) omitted ...... 90·00
b. Dp slate (value) omitted £250
c. Greenish yellow omitted £150
d. Bluish violet omitted £300
e. New blue omitted .... 60·00
Ef. Embossing omitted .... 10·00
Ey. Phosphor omitted .... 6·00
Eya. Embossing and phosphor omitted ...... 10·00
Set of 3 .... 45 45
First Day Cover .... 2·50
Presentation Pack .... 2·50

*The effect of the missing red is shown on the hat, leggings and purse which appear as dull orange.

No. 812 has one centre band 8 mm. wide but this was of no practical use in the automatic facing machines and after about three-quarters of the stamps had been printed the remainder were printed with a $3\frac{1}{2}$mm. band (No. 812Eb).

No. 813e was caused by a paper fold and also shows the phosphor omitted.

Used copies of the 5d. have been seen with the olive-brown or greenish yellow (tunic at left) omitted.

Special First Day of Issue Postmarks
P.O. Philatelic Bureau, Edinburgh (Type C) .... 2·75
Bethlehem, Llandeilo, Carms (Type C) .... 3·50

343 Fife Harling

344 Cotswold Limestone

345 Welsh Stucco

346 Ulster Thatch

(Des D. Gentleman (5d., 9d.), Sheila Robinson (1s., 1s. 6d.))

1970 (11 Feb). **British Rural Architecture.** *Chalk-surfaced paper. Two phosphor bands. P* 15 × 14.

815 **343** 5d. grey, grey-black, black, lemon, greenish blue, orange-brown, ultramarine & green 10 10
a. Lemon omitted .... 60·00
b. Grey (Queen's head & cottage shading) omitted £4000
Ey. Phosphor omitted .... 2·00
816 **344** 9d. orange-brown, olive-yellow, brt green, black, grey-black & grey 20 20
Ey. Phosphor omitted .... 7·00
817 **345** 1s. dp blue, reddish lilac, drab & new blue . 20 20
a. New blue omitted .... 55·00
Ey. Phosphor omitted .... 14·00
818 **346** 1s. 6d. greenish yellow, black, turquoise-blue & lilac 35 35
a. Turquoise-blue omitted £4000
Ey. Phosphor omitted .... 3·00
Set of 4 .... 75 75
First Day Cover .... 2·00
Presentation Pack .... 3·25

Used examples of the 5d. have been seen with the greenish blue colour omitted.

Special First Day of Issue Postmark
British Philatelic Bureau, Edinburgh (Type C) .... 2·75

347 Signing the Declaration of Arbroath

348 Florence Nightingale attending Patients

349 Signing of International Co-operative Alliance

350 Pilgrims and *Mayflower*

351 Sir William Herschel, Francis Baily, Sir John Herschel and Telescope

(Des F. Wegner (5d., 9d., and 1s. 6d.), Marjorie Saynor (1s., 1s. 9d.). Queen's head printed in gold and then embossed)

1970 (1 Apr). **Anniversaries.** *Events described on stamps. Chalk-surfaced paper. Two phosphor bands. P* 15 × 14.

819 **347** 5d. black, yellow-olive, blue, emerald, greenish yellow, rose-red, gold & orange-red . 10 10
a. Gold (Queen's head) omitted £400
b. Emerald omitted £100
Ey. Phosphor omitted £300
820 **348** 9d. ochre, dp blue, carmine, black, blue-green, yellow-olive, gold & blue 15 15
a. Ochre omitted £150
Eb. Embossing omitted .... 12·00
Ey. Phosphor omitted .... 3·00
821 **349** 1s. green, greenish yellow, brown, black, cerise, gold & lt blue 25 25
a. Gold (Queen's head) omitted .... 50·00
Eb. Green & embossing omitted .... 75·00
c. Green omitted .... 75·00
d. Brown omitted £100
Ee. Embossing omitted .... 12·00

(821) Ey. Phosphor omitted .... 5·00
Eya. Brown & phosphor omitted £110
Eyb. Embossing & phosphor omitted .... 22·00
822 **350** 1s. 6d. greenish yellow, carmine, dp yellow-olive, emerald, black, blue, gold & sage-green 30 30
a. Gold (Queen's head) omitted .... 75·00
b. Emerald omitted .... 40·00
Ec. Embossing omitted .... 6·00
Ey. Phosphor omitted .... 3·00
823 **351** 1s. 9d. black, slate, lemon, gold & brt purple 30 30
a. Lemon (trousers and document) omitted † —
Eb. Embossing omitted .... 75·00
Ey. Phosphor omitted .... 3·00
Set of 5 .... 1·00 1·00
First Day Cover .... 3·50
Presentation Pack .... 3·25

No. 823a is only known used on first day cover postmarked London WC.

Special First Day of Issue Postmark

British Philatelic Bureau, Edinburgh (Type C) .... 4·00

First Day of Issue handstamps were provided at Billericay, Essex; Boston, Lincs and Rochdale, Lancs for this issue.

352 "Mr. Pickwick and Sam" (*Pickwick Papers*)

353 "Mr. and Mrs. Micawber" (*David Copperfield*)

354 "David Copperfield and Betsy Trotwood" (*David Copperfield*)

355 "Oliver asking for more" (*Oliver Twist*)

356 "Grasmere" (from engraving by J. Farrington, R.A.)

T **352/5** were issued together *se-tenant* in blocks of four throughout the sheet.

(Des Rosalind Dease. Queen's head printed in gold and then embossed)

1970 (3 June). **Literary Anniversaries. Death Centenary of Charles Dickens (novelist)** (*5d.* × 4) **and Birth Bicentenary of William Wordsworth (poet)** (*1s. 6d.*). *Chalk-surfaced paper. Two phosphor bands. P* 14 × 15.

824 **352** 5d. black, orange, silver, gold & magenta 10 10
a. Block of 4. Nos. 824/7 .... 1·00 1·50
ab. Imperf (block of four) £700
ac. Silver (inscr) omitted ....
825 **353** 5d. black, magenta, silver, gold & orange 10 10
826 **354** 5d. black, lt greenish blue, silver, gold & yellow-bistre 10 10
b. Yellow-bistre (value) omitted £1200
827 **355** 5d. black, yellow-bistre, silver, gold & lt greenish blue 10 10
b. Yellow-bistre (background) omitted £3000
c. Lt greenish blue (value) omitted* £400
828 **356** 1s. 6d. yellow-olive, black, silver, gold & bright blue 20 20
a. Gold (Queen's head) omitted £250
b. Silver ("Grasmere") omitted .... 70·00
Ec. Embossing omitted .... 6·00
Ey. Phosphor omitted .... 5·00
Eya. Embossing & phosphor omitted .... 22·00
Set of 5 .... 1·00 55
First Day Cover .... 3·50
Presentation Pack .... 3·25

*No. 827c (unlike No. 826b) comes from a sheet on which the colour was only partially omitted so that, although No. 827 was completely without the light greenish blue colour, it was still partially present on No. 826.

Essays exist of Nos. 824/7 showing the Queen's head in silver and with different inscriptions.

Special First Day of Issue Postmarks

British Philatelic Bureau, Edinburgh (Type C) .... 4·50
Cockermouth, Cumberland (Type C) (No. 828 only) .. 2·50
Rochester, Kent (Type C) (Nos. 824/7) .... 2·50

A First Day of Issue handstamp was provided at Broadstairs, Kent, for this issue.

357 (Value redrawn)

(Des after plaster cast by Arnold Machin. Recess B.W.)

1970 (17 June)–**72**. *Decimal Currency. Chalk-surfaced paper or phosphorised paper* (*10p.*). *P* 12.

829 **357** 10p. cerise .... 1·00 75
830 20p. olive-green 70 15
Ea. Thinner uncoated paper* ....
831 50p. dp ultramarine .... 1·50 40
Ea. Thinner uncoated paper* .... 45·00
831*b* £1 bluish black (6.12.72) .... 3·50 75
Set of 4 .... 6·00 1·75
First Day Cover (829/31) .... 2·00
First Day Cover (831b) .... 2·75
Presentation Pack (829/31) .... 7·50
Presentation Pack (790 (or 831b), 830/1) 8·00

*These are not as apparent as uncoated photogravure issues where there is normally a higher degree of chalk-surfacing. The 20p. is known only as a block of four with Plate No. 5. The 50p. comes from Plate No. 9.

The 10p. on phosphorised paper continued the experiments which started with the Machin 1s. 6d. When the experiment had ended a quantity of the 50p. value was printed on the phosphorised paper to use up the stock. These stamps were issued on 1 February 1973, but they cannot be distinguished from No. 831 by the naked eye. (*Price £2*).

A £1 was also issued in 1970, but it is difficult to distinguish it from the earlier No. 790. In common with the other 1970 values it was issued in sheets of 100.

A whiter paper was introduced in 1973. The £1 appeared on 27 Sept. 1973, the 20p. on 30 Nov. 1973 and the 50p. on 20 Feb. 1974.

Special First Day of Issue Postmarks

British Philatelic Bureau, Edinburgh (Type C) (Nos. 829/31)	2·50
Windsor, Berks (Type C) (Nos. 829/31)	6·00
Philatelic Bureau, Edinburgh (Type E) (No. 831*b*)	5·00
Windsor, Berks (Type E) (No 831*b*)	8·50

358 Runners

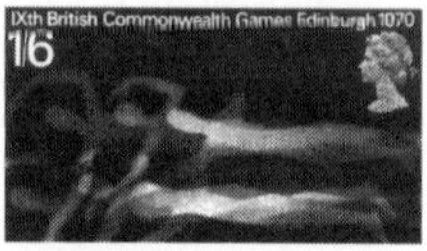

359 Swimmers

360 Cyclists

(Des A. Restall. Litho D.L.R.)

1970 (15 July). **Ninth British Commonwealth Games.** *Chalk-surfaced paper. Two phosphor bands. P* $13\frac{1}{2} \times 14$.

832	**358**	5d.	pink, emerald, greenish yellow & dp yellow-green	10	10
		a.	Greenish yellow omitted	£4500	
		Ey.	Phosphor omitted	£200	
833	**359**	1s.	6d. lt greenish blue, lilac, bistre-brown & Prussian blue	50	50
		Ey.	Phosphor omitted	60·00	
834	**360**	1s.	9d. yellow-orange, lilac, salmon & dp red-brown	50	50
			Set of 3	1·00	1·00
			First Day Cover		2·00
			Presentation Pack	2·75	

Special First Day of Issue Postmark

British Philatelic Bureau, Edinburgh (Type C)	2·75

Collectors Pack 1970

1970 (14 Sept). *Comprises Nos.* 808/28 *and* 832/4.

CP834a	Collectors Pack	22·00

361 1d. Black (1840)

362 1s. Green (1847)

363 4d. Carmine (1855)

(Des D. Gentleman)

1970 (18 Sept). **"Philympia 70" Stamp Exhibition.** *Chalk-surfaced paper. Two phosphor bands. P* $14 \times 14\frac{1}{2}$.

835	**361**	5d.	grey-black, brownish bistre, black & dull purple	10	10
		a.	Grey-black (Queen's head) omitted	£10000	
		Ey.	Phosphor omitted	3·25	
836	**362**	9d.	lt drab, bluish green, stone, black & dull purple	35	35
		Ey.	Phosphor omitted	11·00	
837	**363**	1s.	6d. carmine, lt drab, black & dull purple	40	50
		Ey.	Phosphor omitted	4·00	
			Set of 3	75	90
			First Day Cover		2·00
			Presentation Pack	2·75	

Special First Day of Issue Postmark

British Post Office Philatelic Bureau, Edinburgh (Type D)	2·25

364 Shepherds and Apparition of the Angel

365 Mary, Joseph, and Christ in the Manger

366 The Wise Men bearing gifts

(Des Sally Stiff after De Lisle Psalter. Queen's head printed in gold and then embossed)

1970 (25 Nov). **Christmas.** *Chalk-surfaced paper. One centre phosphor band (4d.) or two phosphor bands (others). P* 14 × 15.

838	**364**	4d.	brown-red, turquoise-green, pale chestnut, brown, grey-black, gold & vermilion	10	10
		Ea.	Embossing omitted	45·00	
		Ey.	Phosphor omitted	60·00	
839	**365**	5d.	emerald, gold, blue, brown-red, ochre, grey-black & violet	10	10
		a.	Gold (Queen's head) omitted	†	£2500
		b.	Emerald omitted	60·00	
		c.	Imperf (pair)	£250	
		Ed.	Embossing omitted	14·00	
		Ey.	Phosphor omitted	3·00	
840	**366**	1s.	6d. gold, grey-black, pale turquoise-green, salmon, ultramarine, ochre & yellow-green	35	35
		a.	Salmon omitted	80·00	
		b.	Ochre omitted	50·00	
		Ec.	Embossing omitted	35·00	
		Ey.	Phosphor omitted	4·00	
		Eya.	Embossing and phosphor omitted		
			Set of 3	50	50
			First Day Cover		1·25
			Presentation Pack	3·25	

Special First Day of Issue Postmarks

British Post Office Philatelic Bureau, Edinburgh (Type D) .... 1·75
Bethlehem, Llandeilo, Carms .... 2·50

(New Currency. 100 new pence = £1)

"X" NUMBERS. The following definitive series has been allocated "X" prefixes to the catalogue numbers to avoid re-numbering all subsequent issues.
NO VALUE INDICATED. Stamps as Types **367**/a inscribed "2nd" or "1st" are listed as Nos. 1445/52, 1511/16, 1663a/6 and 1979.
ELLIPTICAL PERFORATIONS. These were introduced in 1993 and stamps showing them will be found listed as Nos. Y1667 etc.

367

367*a*

Printing differences

Litho **Photo**

(*Illustrations enlarged* × 6)

Litho. Clear outlines to value and frame of stamp.
Photo. Uneven lines to value and frame formed by edges of screen.

Two types of the 3p, 10p and 26p (Nos. X930/c, X886/b and X971/b)

I II

I II

I II

Figures of face value as I (all ptgs of 3p. brt magenta except the multi-value coil No. 930cl and sheets from 21.1.92 onwards, 10p. orange-brown except 1984 "Christmas Heritage" £4 booklet and 26p rosine except 1987 £1.04 barcode booklet.

Figures of face value narrower as in II (from coil No. X930cl and in sheets from 21.1.92 (3p.), 1984 "Christian Heritage" £4 booklet (10p.) or 1987 £1.04 barcode booklet (26p.).

This catalogue includes changes of figure styles on these stamps where there is no other listable difference. Similar changes have also taken place on other values, but only in conjuction with listed colour, paper or perforation changes.

1971 (15 Feb)–**96.** *Decimal Currency. T* **367**. *Chalk-surfaced paper.*

(*a*) *Photo Harrison (except for some printings of Nos.* X879 *and* X913 *in sheets produced by Enschedé and issued on* 12 Dec 1979 (*8p. and* 19 Nov 1991 (*18p.*)). *With phosphor bands. P* 15 × 14.

X841		½p. turquoise-blue (2 bands)	10	10
	a.	Imperf (pair)†	£900	
	l.	Booklet pane. No. X841 × 2 *se-tenant* vert with X849 × 2	5·00	
	lEy.	Booklet pane. Phosphor omitted	£150	
	la.	Booklet pane. No. X841 × 2 *se-tenant* horiz with X849 × 2 (14.7.71)	80	
	laEy.	Booklet pane. Phosphor omitted	£350	
	m.	Booklet pane. No. X841 × 5 plus label	3·50	
	mEy.	Booklet pane. Phosphor omitted	90·00	
	n.	Coil strip. No. X849Eg, X841Eg × 2 and X844Eg × 2	2·00	
	nEy.	Coil strip. Phosphor omitted	30·00	
	nEv.	Coil strip. PVA gum. No. X849, X841 × 2 and X844 × 2 (4.74)	35	
	nEvy.	Coil strip. Phosphor omitted	9·00	
	o.	Booklet pane. No. X841, X851, X852, X852Ea, each × 3 (24.5.72)	12·00	
	oEy.	Booklet pane. Phosphor omitted	£1500	
	p.	Booklet pane. No. X841 × 3, X842 and X852 × 2 (24.5.72)	75·00	
	pEy.	Booklet pane. Phosphor omitted		
	q.	Coil strip. No. X870, X849, X844 and X841 × 2 (3.12.75)	80	
	r.	Booklet pane. No. X841 × 2, X844 × 3 and X870 (10.3.76)	70	
	s.	Booklet pane. No. X841 × 2, X844 × 2, X873 × 2 and X881 × 4 (8½p. values at right) (26.1.77)	2·50	
	sa.	Ditto, but No. X873Ea and 8½p. values at left	2·50	
	t.	Booklet pane. No. X841, X844, X894 × 3 and X902 (14p. value at right) (26.1.81)	2·00	
	tEy.	Booklet pane. Phosphor omitted	35·00	
	ta.	Booklet pane. No. X841, X844, X894Ea × 3 and X902 (14p. value at left)	2·00	
	taEy.	Booklet pane. Phosphor omitted	35·00	
	u.	Booklet pane. No. X841, X857 × 4 and X899 × 3 (12½p. values at left) (1.2.82)	2·50	
	ua.	Ditto, but No. X899Ea and 12½p. values at right	2·50	
	Eg.	Gum arabic (from coil strip, and on 22.9.72 from sheets)	40	
	Egy.	Phosphor omitted	50·00	
X842		½p. turquoise-blue (1 side band at left) (24.5.72)	70·00	35·00
X843		½p. turquoise-blue (1 centre band) (14.12.77)	30	20
	l.	Coil strip. No. X843 × 2, X875 and X845 × 2 (14.12.77)	55	
	m.	Booklet pane. No. X843 × 2, X845 × 2 and X875 plus label (8.2.78)	75	
	mEy.	Booklet pane. Phosphor omitted	25·00	
X844		1p. crimson (2 bands)	10	10
	a.	Imperf (vert coil)		
	b.	Pair, one imperf 3 sides (vert coil)		
	c.	Imperf (pair)		
	l.	Booklet pane. No. X844 × 2 *se-tenant* vert with X848 × 2	5·00	
	m.	Ditto, but *se-tenant* horiz (14.7.71)	80	
	mEy.	Booklet pane. Phosphor omitted	80·00	
	n.	Booklet pane. No. X844 × 2, X876 × 3 and X883 × 3 (9p. values at right) (13.6.77)	4·00	
	na.	Ditto, but No. X876Ea and 9p. values at left	2·50	
	Eg.	Gum arabic (from coil strip)	40	
	Egy.	Phosphor omitted	45·00	

X845	1p. crimson (1 centre band) (14.12.77)	20	20
	l. Booklet pane. No. X879 and X845 × 2 plus label (17.10.79)	70	
	m. Coil strip. No. X879 and X845 × 2 plus 2 labels (16.1.80)	45	
	n. Booklet pane. No. X845 × 2, X860 and X898 each × 3 (5.4.83)	5·00	
	nEy. Booklet pane. Phosphor omitted	16·00	
	p. Booklet pane. No. X845 × 3, X863 × 2 and X900 × 3 (3.9.84)	4·00	
	pEy. Booklet pane. Phosphor omitted	£180	
	q. Booklet pane. No. X845 × 2 and X896 × 4 (29.7.86)	8·00	
	s. Booklet pane. No. X845, X867 × 2 and X900 × 3 (20.10.86)	3·00	
	sa. Ditto, but with vertical edges of pane imperf (29.9.87)	3·00	
	saEy. Booklet pane. Phosphor omitted	£150	
X846	1p. crimson ("all-over") (10.10.79)	20	20
X847	1p. crimson (1 side band at left) (20.10.86)	1·00	1·25
	Ea. Band at right (3.3.87)	2·75	2·75
	l. Booklet pane. No. X847, X901 and X912 × 2 (20.10.86)	3·00	
	lEy. Booklet pane. Phosphor omitted	90·00	
	m. Booklet pane. No. X847Ea, X901 × 2, X912 × 5 and X918 with margins all round (3.3.87)	13·00	
X848	1½p. black (2 bands)	20	15
	a. Uncoated paper*	£110	
	b. Imperf (pair)		
	c. Imperf 3 sides (horiz pair)		
	Ey. Phosphor omitted	10·00	
X849	2p. myrtle-green (2 bands)	20	10
	a. Imperf (horiz pair)	£1250	
	l. Booklet pane. No. X849 × 2, X880 × 2 and X886 × 3 plus label (10p. values at right) (28.8.79)	2·50	
	la. Ditto, but No. X880Ea and 10p. values at left	2·00	
	m. Booklet pane. No. X849 × 3, X889 × 2 and X895 × 2 plus label (12p. values at right) (4.2.80)	2·00	
	mEy. Booklet pane. Phosphor omitted	40·00	
	ma. Booklet pane. No. X849 × 3, X889Ea × 2 and X895 × 2 plus label (12p. values at left)	2·00	
	maEy. Booklet pane. Phosphor omitted	40·00	
	n. Booklet pane. No. X849, X888 × 3, X889Ea and X895 × 4 with margins all round (16.4.80)	3·75	
	nEy. Booklet pane. Phosphor omitted	50·00	
	o. Booklet pane. No. X849 × 6 with margins all round (16.4.80)	80	
	oEy. Booklet pane. Phosphor omitted	50·00	
	p. Booklet pane. No. X849, X857, X898, X899 × 3 and X899Ea × 3 with margins all round (19.5.82)	4·50	
	pEy. Booklet pane. Phosphor omitted	£100	
	Eg. Gum arabic (from coil strip)	2·25	
	Egy. Phosphor omitted	£175	
X850	2p. myrtle-green ("all-over") (10.10.79)	20	15
X851	2½p. magenta (1 centre band)	15	10
	a. Imperf (pair)†	£250	
	Ey. Phosphor omitted	6·50	
	l. Booklet pane. No. X851 × 5 plus label	2·75	
	lEy. Booklet pane. Phosphor omitted	35·00	
	m. Booklet pane. No. X851 × 4 plus two labels	4·00	
	mEy. Booklet pane. Phosphor omitted	75·00	
(X851)	n. Booklet pane. No. X851 × 3, X852Ea × 3 and X855 × 6 (24.5.72)	7·00	
	nEy. Booklet pane. Phosphor omitted		
	Eg. Gum arabic (13.9.72)	15	
X852	2½p. magenta (1 band at left)	1·25	1·75
	l. Booklet pane. No. X852 × 2 and X855 × 4	5·00	
	lEy. Booklet pane. Phosphor omitted	90·00	
	Ea. Band at right (24.5.72)	1·25	2·25
X853	2½p. magenta (2 bands) (21.5.75)	30	75
X854	2½p. rose-red (2 bands) (26.8.81)	50	75
	l. Booklet pane. No. X854 × 3, X862 × 2 and X894 × 3, (11½p. values at left)	5·00	
	la. Ditto, but No. X894Ea and 11½p. values at right	6·50	
X855	3p. ultramarine (2 bands)	20	10
	a. Imperf (coil strip of 5)	£1000	
	b. Imperf (pair)†	£250	
	c. Uncoated paper*	40·00	
	Ey. Phosphor omitted	2·00	
	l. Booklet pane. No. X855 × 5 plus label	2·00	
	lEy. Booklet pane. Phosphor omitted	£250	
	Eg. Gum arabic (23.8.72)	75	
	Egy. Phosphor omitted	7·00	
X856	3p. ultramarine (1 centre band) (10.9.73)	20	25
	a. Imperf (pair)†	£250	
	b. Imperf between (vert pair)†	£375	
	c. Imperf horiz (vert pair)†	£200	
	Eg. Gum arabic	30	
	Egy. Phosphor omitted	75·00	
X857	3p. brt magenta (Type I) (2 bands) (1.2.82)	40	40
X858	3½p. olive-grey (2 bands) (*shades*)	30	30
	a. Imperf (pair)	£350	
	Ey. Phosphor omitted	7·50	
	Eb. Bronze-green (18.7.73)	60	50
	Eby. Phosphor omitted	8·00	
X859	3½p. olive-grey (1 centre band) (24.6.74)	30	15
X860	3½p. purple-brown (1 centre band) (5.4.83)	1·25	1·50
X861	4p. ochre-brown (2 bands)	20	20
	a. Imperf (pair)†	£950	
	Ey. Phosphor omitted	30·00	
	Eg. Gum arabic (1.11.72)	20	
X862	4p. greenish blue (2 bands) (26.8.81)	1·50	1·50
X863	4p. greenish blue (1 centre band) (3.9.84)	1·10	1·10
X864	4p. greenish blue (1 band at right) (8.1.85)	1·75	2·00
	Ea. Band at left	1·75	2·00
	l. Booklet pane. No. X864, X864Ea, X901 × 2, X901Ea × 2, X909 × 2 and X920 with margins all round (8.1.85)	12·50	
	lEy. Booklet pane. Phosphor omitted	£1000	
X865	4½p. grey-blue (2 bands) (24.10.73)	20	25
	a. Imperf (pair)	£300	
	Ey. Phosphor omitted	5·00	
X866	5p. pale violet (2 bands)	20	10
X867	5p. claret (1 centre band) (20.10.86)	1·75	1·75
	Ey. Phosphor omitted	70·00	
X868	5½p. violet (2 bands) (24.10.73)	25	25
X869	5½p. violet (1 centre band) (17.3.75)	20	20
	a. Uncoated paper*	£375	
	Ey. Phosphor omitted	15·00	
X870	6p. lt emerald (2 bands)	30	15
	a. Uncoated paper*	17·00	
	Ey. Phosphor omitted	65·00	
	Eg. Gum arabic (6.6.73)	1·50	
X871	6½p. greenish blue (2 bands) (4.9.74)	45	45
X872	6½p. greenish blue (1 centre band) (24.9.75)	30	15
	a. Imperf (vert pair)	£300	
	b. Uncoated paper*	£160	
	Ey. Phosphor omitted	11·00	
X873	6½p. greenish blue (1 band at right) (26.1.77)	70	75
	Ea. Band at left	70	85

X874	7p. purple-brown (2 bands) (15.1.75)	35	25
	a. Imperf (pair)	£250	
	Ey. Phosphor omitted	1·25	
X875	7p. purple-brown (1 centre band) (13.6.77)	35	20
	a. Imperf (pair)	£100	
	l. Booklet pane. No. X875 and X883, each × 10 (15.11.78)	4·50	
X876	7p. purple-brown (1 band at right) (13.6.77)	60	75
	Ea. Band at left	60	75
X877	7½p. pale chestnut (2 bands)	30	25
	Ey. Phosphor omitted	15·00	
X878	8p. rosine (2 bands) (24.10.73)	25	20
	a. Uncoated paper*	12·00	
X879	8p. rosine (1 centre band) (20.8.79)	25	15
	a. Uncoated paper*	£600	
	b. Imperf (pair)	£600	
	Ey. Phosphor omitted	£275	
	l. Booklet pane. No. X879 and X886, each × 10 (14.11.79)	5·00	
X880	8p. rosine (1 band at right) (28.8.79)	80	80
	Ea. Band at left	80	80
X881	8½p. lt yellowish green (2 bands) (*shades*) (24.9.75)	35	20
	a. Imperf (pair)	£750	
	Eb. Yellowish green (24.3.76)	35	35
X882	9p. yellow-orange and black (2 bands)	60	30
	Ey. Phosphor omitted	75·00	
X883	9p. dp violet (2 bands) (25.2.76)	45	25
	a. Imperf (pair)	£200	
	Ey. Phosphor omitted	2·50	
X884	9½p. purple (2 bands) (25.2.76)	45	30
	Ey. Phosphor omitted	17·00	
X885	10p. orange-brown & chestnut (2 bands) (11.8.71)	40	30
	a. Orange-brown omitted	£150	
	b. Imperf (horiz pair)	£2000	
	Ey. Phosphor omitted	7·50	
X886	10p. orange-brown (Type I) (2 bands) (25.2.76)	40	20
	a. Imperf (pair)	£250	
	b. Type II (4.9.84)	28·00	28·00
	bl. Booklet pane. No. X886b, X901Ea and X909 × 7 with margins all round	29·00	
	blEy. Booklet pane. Phosphor omitted		
X887	10p. orange-brown (Type I) ("all-over") (3.10.79)	30	45
X888	10p. orange-brown (Type I) (1 centre band) (4.2.80)	30	20
	a. Imperf (pair)	£275	
	l. Booklet pane. No. X888 × 9 with margins all round (16.4.80)	2·75	
	lEy. Booklet pane. Phosphor omitted	45·00	
	m. Booklet pane. No. X888 and X895, each × 10 (12.11.80)	6·00	
X889	10p. orange-brown (Type I) (1 band at right) (4.2.80)	85	90
	Ea. Band at left	85	90
X890	10½p. yellow (2 bands) (25.2.76)	50	30
X891	10½p. dp dull blue (2 bands) (26.4.78)	70	45
X892	11p. brown-red (2 bands) (25.2.76)	60	25
	a. Imperf (pair)	£1750	
X893	11½p. drab (1 centre band) (14.1.81)	45	30
	a. Imperf (pair)	£225	
	Ey. Phosphor omitted	5·50	
	l. Booklet pane. No. X893 and X902, each × 10 (11.11.81)	7·00	
X894	11½p. drab (1 band at right) (26.1.81)	60	75
	Ea. Band at left	60	75
	l. Booklet pane. No. X894/Ea, each × 2 & X902 × 6 (6.5.81)	4·00	
X895	12p. yellowish green (2 bands) (4.2.80)	60	40
	l. Booklet pane. No. X895 × 9 with margins all round (16.4.80)	3·00	
	lEy. Booklet pane. Phosphor omitted	40·00	
X896	12p. brt emerald (1 centre band) (29.10.85)	60	40
	a. Imperf (pair)		
	Eu. Underprint Type 4 (29.10.85)	70	
	Ey. Phosphor omitted	8·00	
	l. Booklet pane. No. X896 × 9 with margins all round (18.3.86)	3·00	
	lEy. Booklet pane. Phosphor omitted	£175	
X897	12p. brt emerald (1 band at right) (14.1.86)	90	90
	Ea. Band at left	90	90
	l. Booklet pane. No. X897/Ea, each × 2 and X909 × 6 (12p. values at left) (14.1.86)	6·00	
	la. Ditto, but 12p. values at right	6·00	
	m. Booklet pane. No. X897/Ea, each × 3, X909 × 2 and X919 with margins all round (18.3.86)	14·00	
	mEy. Booklet pane. Phosphor omitted	£1250	
X898	12½p. lt emerald (1 centre band) (27.1.82)	45	25
	a. Imperf (pair)	£100	
	Eu. Underprint Type 1 (10.11.82)	45	
	Eua. Underprint Type 2 (9.11.83)	45	
	Ey. Phosphor omitted	5·50	
	l. Booklet pane. No. X898Eu and X907Eu, each × 10 (10.11.82)	9·00	
X899	12½p. lt emerald (1 band at right) (1.2.82)	60	60
	Ea. Band at left	60	60
	l. Booklet pane. No. X899/Ea, each × 2 and X907 × 6 (1.2.82)††	5·00	
	lEy. Booklet pane. Phosphor omitted		
	m. Booklet pane. No. X899/Ea, each × 3 with margins all round (19.5.82)	2·50	
	mEy. Booklet pane. Phosphor omitted	35·00	
	n. Booklet pane. No. X899/Ea, each × 2, and X908 × 6 (12½p. values at left) (5.4.83)	8·00	
	na. Ditto, but 12½p. values at right	8·00	
X900	13p. pale chestnut (1 centre band) (28.8.84)	45	35
	a. Imperf (pair)	£500	
	Eu. Underprint Type 2 (2.12.86)	45	
	Ey. Phosphor omitted	5·50	
	l. Booklet pane. No. X900 × 9 with margins all round (8.1.85)	3·25	
	lEy. Booklet pane. Phosphor omitted	£350	
	m. Booklet pane. No. X900 × 6 with margins all round (3.3.87)	2·50	
	n. Booklet pane. No. X900 × 4 with margins all round (4.8.87)	2·50	
	o. Booklet pane. No. X900 × 10 with margins all round (4.8.87)	5·00	
X901	13p. pale chestnut (1 band at right) (3.9.84)	60	6
	Ea. Band at left	60	6
	l. Booklet pane. No. X901/Ea, each × 2, and X909 × 6 (13p. values at left)††	6·00	
	la. Ditto, but 13p. values at right	6·00	
	m. Booklet pane. No. X901/Ea, each × 3 with margins all round (4.9.84)	2·50	
	mEy. Booklet pane. Phosphor omitted	£300	
	n. Booklet pane. No. X901Ea and X912 × 5 (20.10.86)	5·00	
	na. Ditto, but with vertical edges of pane imperf (29.9.87)	5·00	
X902	14p. grey-blue (2 bands) (26.1.81)	1·00	4
X903	14p. dp blue (1 centre band) (23.8.88)	60	4
	a. Imperf (pair)	£275	
	Ey. Phosphor omitted	7·00	
	l. Booklet pane. No. X903 × 4 with margins all round	4·50	
	lEy. Booklet pane. Phosphor omitted	40·00	
	m. Booklet pane. No. X903 × 10 with margins all round	8·00	

(X903)	n.	Booklet pane. No. X903 × 4 with horizontal edges of pane imperf (11.10.88)	7·00	
	p.	Booklet pane. No. X903 × 10 with horizontal edges of pane imperf (11.10.88)	9·00	
	pEy.	Booklet pane. Phosphor omitted	£125	
	q.	Booklet pane. No. X903 × 4 with three edges of pane imperf (24.1.89)	20·00	
	qEy.	Booklet pane. Phosphor omitted	30·00	
X904	14p.	dp blue (1 band at right) (5.9.88)	2·75	2·75
	l.	Booklet pane. No. X904 and X914 × 2 plus label	4·50	
	lEy.	Booklet pane. Phosphor omitted	10·00	
	m.	Booklet pane. No. X904 × 2 and X914 × 4 with vertical edges of pane imperf	7·50	
	mEy.	Booklet pane. Phosphor omitted	£650	
X905	15p.	brt blue (1 centre band) (26.9.89)	60	40
	a.	Imperf (pair)	£325	
	Ey.	Phosphor omitted	7·00	
X906	15p.	brt blue (1 band at left) (2.10.89)	2·50	2·25
	Ea.	Band at right (20.3.90)	2·50	2·25
	l.	Booklet pane. No. X906 × 2 and X916 plus label	8·00	
	lEy.	Booklet pane. Phosphor omitted		
	m.	Booklet pane. No. X906Ea, X916, X922, 1446, 1448, 1468Ea, 1470 and 1472 plus label with margins all round (20.3.90)	18·00	
X907	15½p.	pale violet (2 bands) (1.2.82)	60	60
	Eu.	Underprint Type 1 (10.11.82)	60	
	l.	Booklet pane. No. X907 × 6 with margins all round (19.5.82)	3·00	
	lEy.	Booklet pane. Phosphor omitted	75·00	
	m.	Booklet pane. No. X907 × 9 with margins all round (19.5.82)	4·00	
	mEy.	Booklet pane. Phosphor omitted	40·00	
X908	16p.	olive-drab (2 bands) (5.4.83)	1·25	1·25
X909	17p.	grey-blue (2 bands) (3.9.84)	75	75
	Eu.	Underprint Type 4 (4.11.85)	75	
	l.	Booklet pane. No. X909Eu × 3 plus label (4.11.85)	3·00	
	Ela.	Booklet pane. No. X909 × 3 plus label (12.8.86)	3·75	
	lEy.	Booklet pane. Phosphor omitted	50·00	
X910	17p.	dp blue (1 centre band) (4.9.90)	1·00	1·00
	a.	Imperf (pair)		
	Ey.	Phosphor omitted	6·00	
X911	17p.	dp blue (1 band at right) (4.9.90)	1·25	1·25
	Ea.	Band at left	1·25	1·25
	l.	Booklet pane. No. X911 and X911Ea × 2 plus label	3·00	
	lEy.	Booklet pane. Phosphor omitted	50·00	
	m.	Booklet pane. No. X911 × 2 and X917 × 3 plus three labels with vertical edges of pane imperf	4·00	
X912	18p.	dp olive-grey (2 bands) (20.10.86)	75	75
X913	18p.	brt green (1 centre band) (10.9.91)	60	40
	a.	Imperf (pair)	£375	
X914	19p.	brt orange-red (2 bands) (5.9.88)	1·25	1·25
X915	20p.	dull purple (2 bands) (25.2.76)	1·00	50
X916	20p.	brownish black (2 bands) (2.10.89)	1·50	1·75
X917	22p.	brt orange-red (2 bands) (4.9.90)	1·25	1·25
X917a	25p.	rose-red (2 bands) (6.2.96)	60	60
X918	26p.	rosine (Type I) (2 bands) (3.3.87)	8·00	8·00
X919	31p.	purple (2 bands) (18.3.86)	12·00	12·00
X920	34p.	ochre-brown (2 bands) (8.1.85)	8·00	8·00
X921	50p.	ochre-brown (2 bands) (2.2.77)	2·00	50
X922	50p.	ochre (2 bands) (20.3.90)	4·25	4·25

(b) Photo Harrison. On phosphorised paper. P 15 × 14

X924	½p.	turquoise-blue (10.12.80)	10	10
	a.	Imperf (pair)	£130	
	l.	Coil strip. No. X924 and X932 × 3 (30.12.81)	75	
X925	1p.	crimson (12.12.79)	10	10
	a.	Imperf (pair)	£750	
	l.	Coil strip. No. X925 and X932*Ea* × 3 (14.8.84)	80	
	m.	Booklet pane. No. X925 and X969, each × 2 (10.9.91)	1·00	
X926	2p.	myrtle-green (face value as T **367**) (12.12.79)	10	10
	a.	Imperf (pair)	£900	
X927	2p.	dp green (face value as T **367***a*) (26.7.88)	10	10
	a.	Imperf (pair)		
	l.	Booklet pane. No. X927 × 2 and X969 × 4 plus 2 labels with vert edges of pane imperf (10.9.91)	1·50	
X928	2p.	myrtle-green (face value as T **367***a*) (5.9.88)	2·00	2·00
	l.	Coil strip. No. X928 and X932*Ea* × 3	2·25	
X929	2½p.	rose-red (14.1.81)	20	20
	l.	Coil strip. No. X929 and X930 × 3 (6.81)	1·25	
X930	3p.	brt magenta (Type I) (22.10.80)	20	20
	a.	Imperf (horiz pair)	£1000	
	b.	Booklet pane. No. X930, X931 × 2 and X949 × 6 with margins all round (14.9.83)	4·50	
	c.	Type II (10.10.89)	1·00	50
	cl.	Coil strip. No. X930c and X933 × 3	2·75	
X931	3½p.	purple-brown (30.3.83)	45	45
X932	4p.	greenish blue (30.12.81)	40	40
	Ea.	*Pale greenish blue* (14.8.84)	40	40
X933	4p.	new blue (26.7.88)	20	20
	a.	Imperf (pair)		
	l.	Coil strip. No. X933 × 3 and X935 (27.11.90)	1·00	
	m.	Coil strip. No. X933 and X935, each × 2 (1.10.91)	75	
	n.	Coil strip. No. X933 and X935 × 3 (31.1.95)	30	
X934	5p.	pale violet (10.10.79)	30	25
X935	5p.	dull red-brown (26.7.88)	20	20
	a.	Imperf (pair)		
X936	6p.	yellow-olive (10.9.91)	25	25
X937	7p.	brownish red (29.10.85)	1·75	1·75
X938	8½p.	yellowish green (24.3.76)	40	55
X939	10p.	orange-brown (Type I) (11.79)	40	20
X940	10p.	dull orange (Type II) (4.9.90)	30	30
X941	11p.	brown-red (27.8.80)	85	85
X942	11½p.	ochre-brown (15.8.79)	50	45
X943	12p.	yellowish green (30.1.80)	50	50
X944	13p.	olive-grey (15.8.79)	60	45
X945	13½p.	purple-brown (30.1.80)	65	60
X946	14p.	grey-blue (14.1.81)	60	40
X947	15p.	ultramarine (15.8.79)	60	40
X948	15½p.	pale violet (14.1.81)	60	40
	a.	Imperf (pair)	£200	
X949	16p.	olive-drab (30.3.83)	60	30
	a.	Imperf (pair)	£130	
	Eu.	Underprint Type 3 (10.8.83)	75	
	l.	Booklet pane. No. X949 × 9 with margins all round (14.9.83)	3·75	
X950	16½p.	pale chestnut (27.1.82)	85	75
X951	17p.	lt emerald (30.1.80)	70	40
X952	17p.	grey-blue (30.3.83)	60	40
	a.	Imperf (pair)	£275	
	Eu.	Underprint Type 3 (5.3.85)	80	
	l.	Booklet pane. No. X952 × 6 with margins all round (4.9.84)	3·00	
	m.	Booklet pane. No. X952 × 9 with margins all round (8.1.85)	4·50	
X953	17½p.	pale chestnut (30.1.80)	80	80
X954	18p.	dp violet (14.1.81)	80	75
X955	18p.	dp olive-grey (28.8.84)	80	60
	a.	Imperf (pair)	£130	

(X955)	l. Booklet pane. No. X955 × 9 with margins all round (3.3.87)	4·50	
	m. Booklet pane. No. X955 × 4 with margins all round (4.8.87)	3·00	
	n. Booklet pane. No. X955 × 10 with margins all round (4.8.87)	6·50	
X956	19p. brt orange-red (23.8.88)	70	50
	a. Imperf (pair)	£325	
	l. Booklet pane. No. X956 × 4 with margins all round	6·00	
	m. Booklet pane. No. X956 × 10 with margins all round	10 00	
	n. Booklet pane. No. X956 × 4 with horizontal edges of pane imperf (11.10.88)	7·00	
	o. Booklet pane. No. X956 × 10 with horizontal edges of pane imperf (11.10.88)	12·00	
	q. Booklet pane. No. X956 × 4 with three edges of pane imperf (24.1.89)	20·00	
X957	19½p. olive-grey (27.1.82)	1·50	1·50
X958	20p. dull purple (10.10.79)	1·00	30
X959	20p. turquoise-green (23.8.88)	90	60
X960	20p. brownish black (26.9.89)	90	40
	a. Imperf (pair)	£650	
	l. Booklet pane. No. X960 × 5 plus label with vertical edges of pane imperf (2.10.89)	7·00	
X961	20½p. ultramarine (30.3.83)	1·25	1·00
	a. Imperf (pair)	£1100	
X962	22p. blue (22.10.80)	80	45
	a. Imperf (pair)	£200	
X963	22p. yellow-green (28.8.84)	80	55
	a. Imperf (horiz pair)	£900	
X964	22p. brt orange-red (4.9.90)	80	50
	a. Imperf (pair)		
X965	23p. brown-red (30.3.83)	1·00	60
	a. Imperf (horiz pair)	£900	
X966	23p. brt green (23.8.88)	1·00	60
X967	24p. violet (28.8.84)	1·25	1·00
X968	24p. Indian red (26.9.89)	1·60	1·00
	a. Imperf (horiz pair)	£2250	
X969	24p. chestnut (10.9.91)	90	45
	a. Imperf (pair)	£200	
X970	25p. purple (14.1.81)	1·00	1·00
X971	26p. rosine (Type I) (27.1.82)	90	30
	a. Imperf (horiz pair)		
	b. Type II (4.8.87)	3·75	3·75
	bl. Booklet pane. No. X971b × 4 with margins all round	14·00	
X972	26p. drab (Type II) (4.9.90)	1·00	1·00
X973	27p. chestnut (23.8.88)	1·00	1·00
	l. Booklet pane. No. X973 × 4 with margins all round	7·00	
	m. Booklet pane. No. X973 × 4 with horizontal edges of pane imperf (11.10.88)	25·00	
X974	27p. violet (4.9.90)	1·00	1·00
X975	28p. dp violet (30.3.83)	1·00	1·00
	a. Imperf (pair)	£1000	
X976	28p. ochre (23.8.88)	1·00	1·00
X977	28p. dp bluish grey (10.9.91)	1·00	1·00
	a. Imperf (pair)	£1500	
X978	29p. ochre-brown (27.1.82)	1·75	1·00
X979	29p. dp mauve (26.9.89)	1·75	1·00
X980	30p. dp olive-grey (26.9.89)	1·10	1·00
X981	31p. purple (30.3.83)	1·25	1·25
	a. Imperf (pair)	£1000	
X982	31p. ultramarine (4.9.90)	1·25	1·25
X983	32p. greenish blue (23.8.88)	1·25	1·25
	a. Imperf (pair)	£1000	
X984	33p. lt emerald (4.9.90)	1·25	1·25
X985	34p. ochre-brown (28.8.84)	1·25	1·10
X986	34p. dp bluish grey (26.9.89)	1·50	1·25
X987	34p. dp mauve (10.9.91)	1·25	1·25
X988	35p. sepia (23.8.88)	1·50	1·25
	a. Imperf (pair)		
X989	35p. yellow (10.9.91)	1·25	1·00
X990	37p. rosine (26.9.89)	1·50	1·50
X991	39p. bright mauve (10.9.91)	1·50	1·25

(c) Photo Harrison. On ordinary paper. P 15 × 14

X992	50p. ochre-brown (21.5.80)	1·75	80
	a. Imperf (pair)	£600	
X993	75p. grey-black (face value as T **367**a) (26.7.88)	2·25	2·25

(d) Photo Harrison. On ordinary or phosphorised paper. P 15 × 14

X994	50p. ochre (13.3.90)	1·50	60
	a. Imperf (pair)	£850	

(e) Litho J.W. P 14

X996	4p. greenish blue (2 bands) (30.1.80)	20	25
X997	4p. greenish blue (phosphorised paper) (11.81)	35	20
X998	20p. dull purple (2 bands) (21.5.80)	1·10	40
X999	20p. dull purple (phosphorised paper) (11.81)	1·40	40

(f) Litho Questa. P 14 (Nos. X1000, X1003/4 and X1023) or 15 × 14 (others)

X1000	2p. emerald-green (face value as T **367**) (phosphorised paper) (21.5.80)	20	20
	a. Perf 15 × 14 (10.7.84)	30	20
X1001	2p. brt green and dp green (face value as T **367**a) (phosphorised paper) (23.2.88)	1·00	60
X1002	4p. greenish blue (phosphorised paper) (13.5.86)	60	60
X1003	5p. lt violet (phosphorised paper) (21.5.80)	40	20
X1004	5p. claret (phosphorised paper) (27.1.82)	50	20
	a. Perf 15 × 14 (21.2.84)	60	40
X1005	13p. pale chestnut (1 centre band) (9.2.88)	70	7
	l. Booklet pane. No. X1005 × 6 with margins all round	3·50	
X1006	13p. pale chestnut (1 side band at right) (9.2.88)	1·00	1·0
	Ea. Band at left	1·00	1·0
	l. Booklet pane. No. X1006/Ea each × 3, X1010, X1015 and X1021 with margins all round	22·00	
	lEa. Grey-green (on 18p.) ptg double	£1000	
X1007	14p. dp blue (1 centre band) (11.10.88)	1·75	1·7
X1008	17p. dp blue (1 centre band) (19.3.91)	75	7
	Ey. Phosphor omitted	£175	
	l. Booklet pane. No. X1008 × 6 with margins all round	3·50	
	lEy. Booklet pane. Phosphor omitted	£750	
X1009	18p. dp olive-grey (phosphorised paper) (9.2.88)	75	7
	l. Booklet pane. No. X1009 × 9 with margins all round	4·50	
	m. Booklet pane. No. X1009 × 6 with margins all round	3·00	
X1010	18p. dp olive-grey (2 bands) (9.2.88)	5·00	5·0
X1011	18p. brt green (1 centre band) (27.10.92)	1·25	1·2
	l. Booklet pane. No. X1011 × 6 with margins all round	7·50	
X1012	18p. brt green (1 side band at right) (27.10.92)	1·50	1·5
	Ea. Band at left (10.8.93)	2·25	2·2
	l. Booklet pane. No. X1012 × 2, X1018 × 2, X1022 × 2, 1451a, 1514a and centre label with margins all round	10·00	
	m. Booklet pane. No. X1012Ea, X1020, X1022 and 1451aEb, each × 2, with centre label and margins all round (10.8.93)	11·00	
	mEy. Booklet pane. Phosphor omitted		
X1013	19p. brt orange-red (phosphorised paper) (11.10.88)	1·75	1·7
X1014	20p. dull purple (phosphorised paper) (13.5.86)	1·25	1·2
X1015	22p. yellow-green (2 bands) (9.2.88)	8·00	8·(

X1016	22p. brt orange-red (phosphorised paper) (19.3.91)	1·00	1·00
	l. Booklet pane. No. X1016 × 9 with margins all round	5·50	
	m. Booklet pane. No. X1016 × 6, X1019 × 2 and centre label with margins all round .	8·00	
X1017	24p. chestnut (phosphorised paper) (27.10.92)	1·00	80
	l. Booklet pane. No. X1017 × 6 with margins all round	6·00	
X1018	24p. chestnut (2 bands) (27.10.92)	1·25	1·25
X1019	33p. lt emerald (phosphorised paper) (19.3.91)	1·75	1·75
X1020	33p. lt emerald (2 bands) (25.2.92)	1·40	1·40
X1021	34p. ochre-brown (2 bands) (9.2.88)	7·00	7·00
X1022	39p. brt mauve (2 bands) (27.10.92)	2·00	2·00
X1023	75p. black (face value as T **367**) (ordinary paper) (30.1.80)	3·25	1·75
	a. Perf 15 × 14 (21.2.84)	3·75	3·50
X1024	75p. brownish grey and black (face value as T **367**a) (ordinary paper) (23.2.88)	10·00	9·00
	(g) *Litho Walsall. P* 14		
X1050	2p. dp green (phosphorised paper) (9.2.93) ..	1·00	1·00
	l. Booklet pane. No. X1050 × 2 and X1053 × 4 plus 2 labels with vert edges of pane imperf	3·50	
X1051	14p. dp blue (1 side band at right) (25.4.89) ..	3·00	3·00
	Ey. Phosphor omitted	£200	
	l. Booklet pane. No. X1051 × 2 and X1052 × 4 with vertical edges of pane imperf	10·00	
	lEy. Booklet pane. Phosphor omitted	£950	
X1052	19p. brt orange-red (2 bands) (25.4.89)	1·50	1·75
	Ey. Phosphor omitted	£150	
X1053	24p. chestnut (phosphorised paper) (9.2.93) ..	1·25	1·25
X1054	29p. dp mauve (2 bands) (2.10.89)	5·50	5·50
	l. Booklet pane. No. X1054 × 4 with three edges of pane imperf	20·00	
X1055	29p. dp mauve (phosphorised paper) (17.4.90)	6·50	6·50
	l. Booklet pane. No. X1055 × 4 with three edges of pane imperf	24·00	
X1056	31p. ultramarine (phosphorised paper) (17.9.90)	1·75	2·00
	l. Booklet pane. No. X1056 × 4 with horizontal edges of pane imperf	7·00	
X1057	33p. light emerald (phosphorised paper) (16.9.91)	1·25	1·25
	l. Booklet pane. No. X1057 × 4 with horiz edges of pane imperf	5·00	
X1058	39p. brt mauve (phosphorised paper) (16.9.91)	1·75	1·75
	l. Booklet pane. No. X1058 × 4 with horiz edges of pane imperf	7·00	

*See footnote after No. 744.

†These come from sheets with gum arabic.

††Examples of Booklet panes Nos. X899l, X901l and X901la are nown on which the phosphor bands were printed on the wrong alues in error with the result that the side bands appear on the 15½p. r 17p. and the two bands on the 12½p. or 13p. Similarly examples of he 1p. with phosphor band at right instead of left and of the 13p. with and at left instead of right, exist from 50p. booklet pane No. X847l.

Nos. X844a/b come from a strip of eight of the vertical coil. It omprises two normals, one imperforate at sides and bottom, one ompletely imperforate, one imperforate at top, left and bottom and artly perforated at right due to the bottom three stamps being erforated twice. No. X844b is also known from another strip having ne stamp imperforate at sides and bottom.

Nos. X848b/c come from the same sheet, the latter having erforations at the foot of the stamps only.

Multi-value coil strips Nos. X924l, X925l, X928l, X929l, X930cl and 933l/n were produced by the Post Office for use by a large direct mail arketing firm. From 2 September 1981 No. X929l was available from the Philatelic Bureau, Edinburgh, and, subsequently from a number of other Post Office counters. Later multi-value coil strips were sold at the Philatelic Bureau and Post Office philatelic counters.

In addition to booklet pane No. X1012 m No. X1020 also comes from the *se-tenant* pane in the Wales £6 booklet. This pane is listed under No. W49a in the Wales Regional section.

PANES OF SIX FROM STITCHED BOOKLETS. Nos. X841m, X851l/m and X855l include one or two printed labels showing commercial advertisements. These were originally perforated on all four sides, but from the August 1971 editions of the 25p. and 30p. booklets (Nos. DH42, DQ59) and December 1971 edition of the 50p. (No. DT4) the line of perforations between the label and the binding margin was omitted. Similar panes, with the line of perforations omitted, exist for the 3p., 3½p. and 4½p. values (Nos. X856, X858 and X865), but these are outside the scope of this listing as the labels are blank.

PART-PERFORATED SHEETS. Since the introduction of the "Jumelle" press in 1972 a number of part perforated sheets, both definitives and commemoratives, have been discovered. It is believed that these occur when the operation of the press in interrupted. Such sheets invariably show a number of "blind" perforations, where the pins have failed to cut the paper. Our listings of imperforate errors from these sheets are for pairs showing no traces whatsoever of the perforations. Examples showing "blind" perforations are outside the scope of this catalogue.

In cases where perforation varieties affect *se-tenant* stamps, fuller descriptions will be found in Vols. 4 and 5 of the *G.B. Specialised Catalogue*.

WHITE PAPER. From 1972 printings appeared on fluorescent white paper giving a stronger chalk reaction than the original ordinary cream paper.

PHOSPHOR OMITTED ERRORS. These are listed for those stamps or booklet panes which were not subsequently issued on phosphorised paper. The following phosphor omitted errors also exist, but can only be identified by the use of an ultra-violet lamp. Prices quoted are for mint examples:

½p.	X841	(£1)	8½p.	X881	(£1·75)	17p.	X909	(£150)
1p.	X844	(£2)	10p.	X886	(£1)	18p.	X912	(£27)
2p.	X849	(£5)	11p.	X892	(£2·25)	19p.	X914	(£4)
3p.	X857	(£100)	12p.	X895	(£6)	20p.	X916	(£425)
3½p.	X860	(£5·50)	14p.	X902	(£28)	31p.	X919	(£650)
4p.	X863	(£85)	15½p.	X907	(£7)	33p.	X1020	(£450)
5p.	X866	(£200)	16p.	X908	(£100)	34p.	X920	(£750)

No. X909Eu with underprint Type 4 also exists without phosphor (*price* £10).

"ALL-OVER" PHOSPHOR. To improve mechanised handling most commemoratives from the 1972 Royal Silver Wedding 3p. value to the 1979 Rowland Hill Death Centenary set had the phosphor applied by printing cylinder across the entire surface of the stamp, giving a matt effect. Printings of the 1, 2 and 10p. definitives, released in October 1979, also had "all-over" phosphor, but these were purely a temporary expedient pending the adoption of phosphorised paper. Nos. X883, X890 and X921 have been discovered with "all-over" phosphor in addition to the normal phosphor bands. These errors are outside the scope of this catalogue.

PHOSPHORISED PAPER. Following the experiments on Nos. 743c and 829 a printing of the 4½p. definitive was issued on 13 November 1974, which had, in addition to the normal phosphor bands, phosphor included in the paper coating. Because of difficulties in identifying this phosphorised paper with the naked eye this printing is not listed separately in this catalogue.

No. X938 was the first value printed on phosphorised paper without phosphor bands and was a further experimental issue to test the efficacy of this system. From 15 August 1979 phosphorised paper was accepted for use generally, this paper replacing phosphor bands on values other than those required for the second-class rate.

Stamps on phosphorised paper show a shiny surface instead of the matt areas of those printed with phosphor bands.

DEXTRIN GUM. From 1973 printings in photogravure appeared with PVA gum to which dextrin had been added. Because this is virtually colourless a bluish green colouring matter was added to distinguish it from the earlier pure PVA.

The 4p., 5p. (light violet), 20p. and 75p. printed in lithography exist with PVA and PVAD gum. From 1988 Questa printings were with PVAD gum, but did not show the bluish green additive.

VARNISH COATING. Nos. X841 and X883 exist with and without a varnish coating. This cannot easily be detected without the use of an ultra-violet lamp as it merely reduces the fluorescent paper reaction.

POSTAL FORGERIES. In mid-1993 a number of postal forgeries of the 24p. chestnut were detected in the London area. These forgeries, produced by lithography, can be identified by the lack of phosphor in the paper, screening dots across the face value and by the perforations which were applied by a line machine gauging 11.

First Day Covers

15.2.71	$\frac{1}{2}$p., 1p., $1\frac{1}{2}$p., 2p., $2\frac{1}{2}$p., 3p., $3\frac{1}{2}$p., 4p., 5p., 6p., $7\frac{1}{2}$p., 9p. (*X841, X844, X848/9, X851, X855, X858, X861, X866, X870, X877, X882*) (Covers carry "POSTING DELAYED BY THE POST OFFICE STRIKE 1971" cachet)	3·00
11.8.71	10p. (*X885*)	1·25
24.5.72	Wedgwood *se-tenant* pane $\frac{1}{2}$p., $2\frac{1}{2}$p. (*X841p*)	20·00
24.10.73	$4\frac{1}{2}$p., $5\frac{1}{2}$p., 8p. (*X865, X868, X878*)	1·25
4.9.74	$6\frac{1}{2}$p. (*X871*)	1·25
15.1.75	7p. (*X874*)	1·25
24.9.75	$8\frac{1}{2}$p. (*X881*)	1·25
25.2.76	9p., $9\frac{1}{2}$p., 10p., $10\frac{1}{2}$p., 11p., 20p. (*X883/4, X886, X890, X892, X915*)	2·25
2.2.77	50p. (*X921*)	1·25
26.4.78	$10\frac{1}{2}$p. (*X891*)	1·25
15.8.79	$11\frac{1}{2}$p., 13p., 15p. (*X942, X944, X947*)	1·25
30.1.80	4p., 12p., $13\frac{1}{2}$p., 17p., $17\frac{1}{2}$p., 75p. (*X996, X943, X945, X951, X953, X1023*)	2·00
16.4.80	Wedgwood *se-tenant* pane 2p., 10p., 12p. (*X849n*)	2·00
22.10.80	3p., 22p. (*X930, X962*)	1·25
14.1.81	$2\frac{1}{2}$p., $11\frac{1}{2}$p., 14p., $15\frac{1}{2}$p., 18p., 25p. (*X929, X893, X946, X948, X954, X970*)	1·25
27.1.82	5p., $12\frac{1}{2}$p., $16\frac{1}{2}$p., $19\frac{1}{2}$p., 26p., 29p. (*X1004, X898, X950, X957, X971, X978*)	2·00
19.5.82	Stanley Gibbons *se-tenant* pane 2p., 3p., $12\frac{1}{2}$p. (*X849p*)	2·50
30.3.83	$3\frac{1}{2}$p., 16p., 17p., $20\frac{1}{2}$p., 23p., 28p., 31p. (*X931, X949, X952, X961, X965, X975, X981*)	3·00
14.9.83	Royal Mint *se-tenant* pane 3p., $3\frac{1}{2}$p., 16p. (*X930b*)	3·00
28.8.84	13p., 18p., 22p., 24p., 34p. (*X900, X955, X963, X967, X985*)	2·50
4.9.84	Christian Heritage *se-tenant* pane 10p., 13p., 17p. (*X886bl*)	28·00
8.1.85	*The Times se-tenant* pane 4p., 13p., 17p., 34p. (*X864l*)	8·50
29.10.85	7p., 12p. (*X937, X896*)	2·00
18.3.86	British Rail *se-tenant* pane 12p., 17p., 31p. (*X897m*)	9·00
3.3.87	P & O *se-tenant* pane 1p., 13p., 18p., 26p. (*X847m*)	7·50
9.2.88	*Financial Times se-tenant* pane 13p., 18p., 22p., 34p. (*X1006l*)	8·00
23.8.88	14p., 19p., 20p., 23p., 27p., 28p., 32p., 35p. (*X903, X956, X959, X966, X973, X976 X983, X988*)	5·00
26.9.89	15p., 20p., 24p., 29p., 30p., 34p., 37p. (*X905, X960, X968, X979/80, X986, X990*)	4·75
20.3.90†	London Life *se-tenant* pane 15p., (2nd), 20p., (1st), 15p., 20p., 29p. (*X906m*)	7·50
4.9.90	10p., 17p., 22p., 26p., 27p., 31p., 33p. (*X910, X940, X964, X972, X974, X982, X984*)	4·50
19.3.91	Alias Agatha Christie *se-tenant* pane 22p., 33p. (*X1016m*)	8·00
10.9.91	6p., 18p., 24p., 28p., 34p., 35p., 39p. (*X936, X913, X969, X977, X987, X989, X991*)	5·00
27.10.92	Tolkien *se-tenant* pane. 18p., (2nd), 24p., (1st), 39p. (*X1012l*)	4·25
10.8.93	Beatrix Potter *se-tenant* pane 18p., (2nd), 33p., 39p. (*X1012m*)	8·50

Post Office Presentation Packs

15.2.71	P.O. Pack No. 26. $\frac{1}{2}$p. (2 bands), 1p. (2 bands), $1\frac{1}{2}$p. (2 bands), 2p. (2 bands), $2\frac{1}{2}$p. magenta (1 centre band), 3p. ultramarine (2 bands), $3\frac{1}{2}$p. olive-grey (2 bands), 4p. ochre-brown (2 bands), 5p. pale violet (2 bands), 6p. (2 bands), $7\frac{1}{2}$p. (2 bands), 9p. yellow-orange and black (2 bands). (*Nos.* X841, X844, X848/9, X851, X855, X858, X861, X866, X870, X877, X882)	5·00
15.4.71**	"Scandinavia 71". Contents as above	35·00
25.11.71	P.O. Pack No. 37. $\frac{1}{2}$p. (2 bands), 1p. (2 bands), $1\frac{1}{2}$p., (2 bands), 2p. (2 bands), $2\frac{1}{2}$p. magenta (1 centre band), 3p. ultramarine (2 bands) or (1 centre band), $3\frac{1}{2}$p. olive-grey (2 bands) or (1 centre band). 4p. ochre-brown (2 bands), $4\frac{1}{2}$p. (2 bands), 5p. pale violet (2 bands), $5\frac{1}{2}$p. (2 bands) or (1 centre band), 6p. (2 bands), $6\frac{1}{2}$p. (2 bands) or (1 centre band), 7p. (2 bands), $7\frac{1}{2}$p. (2 bands), 8p. (2 bands), 9p. yellow-orange and black (2 bands), 10p. orange-brown and chestnut (2 bands). (*Nos.* X841, X844, X848/9, X851, X855 *or* X856, X858 *or* X859, X861, X865/6, X868 *or* X869, X870, X871 *or* X872, X874, X877/8, X882, X885)	5·00
2.2.77	P.O. Pack No. 90. $\frac{1}{2}$p. (2 bands), 1p. (2 bands), $1\frac{1}{2}$p. (2 bands), 2p. (2 bands), $2\frac{1}{2}$p. magenta (1 centre band), 3p. ultramarine (1 centre band), 5p. pale violet (2 bands), $6\frac{1}{2}$p. (1 centre band), 7p. (2 bands) or (1 centre band), $7\frac{1}{2}$p. (2 bands), 8p. (2 bands), $8\frac{1}{2}$p. (2 bands), 9p. deep violet (2 bands), $9\frac{1}{2}$p. (2 bands), 10p. orange-brown (2 bands), $10\frac{1}{2}$p. yellow (2 bands), 11p. (2 bands), 20p. dull purple (2 bands), 50p. ochre-brown (2 bands). (*Nos.* X841, X844, X848/9, X851, X856, X866, X872, X874 *or* X875, X877/8, X881, X883/4, X886, X890, X892, X915, X921)	5·00

28.10.81 P.O. Pack No. 129a. 10½p. deep dull blue (2 bands), 11½p. (1 centre band), 2½p. (phos paper), 3p. (phos paper), 11½p. (phos paper), 12p. (phos paper), 13p. (phos paper), 13½p. (phos paper), 14p. (phos paper), 15p. (phos paper), 15½p. (phos paper), 17p. light emerald (phos paper), 17½p. (phos paper), 18p. deep violet (phos paper), 22p. blue (phos paper), 25p. (phos paper), 4p. greenish blue (litho, 2 bands), 75p. (litho). (*Nos.* X891, X893, X929/30, X942/8, X951, X953/4, X970, X996, X1023) 16·00

3.8.83 P.O. Pack No. 1. 10p. orange-brown (1 centre band), 12½p. (1 centre band), ½p. (phos paper), 1p. (phos paper), 3p. (phos paper), 3½p. (phos paper), 16p. (phos paper), 16½p. (phos paper), 17p. grey-blue (phos paper), 20½p. (phos paper), 23p. brown-red (phos paper), 26p. rosine (phos paper), 28p. deep violet (phos paper), 31p. purple (phos paper), 50p. (ord paper), 2p. (litho phos paper), 4p. (litho phos paper), 5p. claret (litho phos paper), 20p. (litho phos paper), 75p. (litho). (*Nos.* X888, X898, X924/5, X930/1, X949/50, X952, X961, X965, X971, X975, X981, X992, X997, X999, X1000, X1004, X1023) 22·00

23.10.84 P.O. Pack No. 5. 13p. (1 centre band), ½p. (phos paper), 1p. (phos paper), 3p. (phos paper), 10p. orange-brown (phos paper), 16p. (phos paper), 17p. grey-blue (phos paper), 18p. dp olive-grey (phos paper), 22p. bright green (phos paper), 24p. violet (phos paper), 26p. rosine (phos paper), 28p. deep violet (phos paper), 31p. purple (phos paper), 34p. ochre-brown (phos paper), 50p. (ord paper), 2p. (litho phos paper), 4p. (litho phos paper), 5p. claret (litho phos paper), 20p. (litho phos paper), 75p. (litho). (*Nos.* X900, X924/5, X930, X939, X949, X952, X955, X963, X967, X971, X975, X981, X985, X992, X1000a, X997, X999, X1004a, X1023a) 22·00

3.3.87 P.O. Pack No. 9. 12p. (1 centre band), 13p. (1 centre band), 1p. (phos paper), 3p. (phos paper), 7p. (phos paper), 10p. orange-brown (phos paper), 17p. grey-blue (phos paper), 18p. dp olive-grey (phos paper), 22p. bright green (phos paper), 24p. violet (phos paper), 26p. rosine (phos paper), 28p. deep violet (phos paper), 31p. purple (phos paper), 34p. ochre-brown (phos paper), 50p. (ord paper), 2p. (litho phos paper), 4p. (litho phos paper), 5p. claret (litho phos paper), 20p. (litho phos paper), 75p. (litho). (*Nos.* X896, X900, X925, X930, X937, X939, X952, X955, X963, X967, X971, X975, X981, X985, X992, X997, X999, X1000a, X1004a, X1023a) 20·00

23.8.88 P.O. Pack No. 15. 14p. (1 centre band), 19p. (phos paper), 20p. turquoise-green (phos paper), 23p. bright green (phos paper), 27p. chestnut (phos paper), 28p. ochre (phos paper), 32p. (phos paper), 35p. sepia (phos paper). (*Nos.* X903, X956, X959, X966, X973, X976, X983, X988) 10·00

26.9.89 P.O. Pack No. 19. 15p. (centre band), 20p. brownish black (phos paper), 24p. Indian red (phos paper), 29p. deep mauve (phos paper), 30p. (phos paper), 34p. deep bluish grey (phos paper), 37p. (phos paper). (*Nos.* X905, X960, X968, X979/80, X986, X990) 9·00

4.9.90 P.O. Pack No. 22. 10p. dull orange (phos paper), 17p. (centre band), 22p. bright orange-red (phos paper), 26p. drab (phos paper), 27p. violet (phos paper), 31p. ultramarine (phos paper), 33p. (phos paper). (*Nos.* X910, X940, X964, X972, X974, X982, X984) 7·00

14.5.91 P.O. Pack No. 24. 1p. (phos paper), 2p. (phos paper), 3p. (phos paper), 4p. new blue (phos paper), 5p. dull red-brown (phos paper), 10p. dull orange (phos paper), 17p. (centre band), 20p. turquoise-green (phos paper), 22p. bright orange-red (phos paper), 26p. drab (phos paper), 27p. violet (phos paper), 30p. (phos paper), 31p. ultramarine (phos paper), 32p. (phos paper), 33p. (phos paper), 37p. (phos paper), 50p. (ord paper), 75p. (ord paper). (*Nos.* X910, X925, X927, X930, X933, X935, X940, X959, X964, X972, X974, X980, X982/4, X990, X993/4) 14·00

10.9.91 P.O. Pack No. 25. 6p. (phos paper), 18p. (centre band), 24p. chestnut (phos paper), 28p. deep bluish grey (phos paper), 34p. deep mauve (phos paper), 35p. yellow (phos paper), 39p. (phos paper). (*Nos.* X913, X936, X969, X977, X987, X989, X991) 7·00

**The "Scandinavia 71" was a special pack produced for sale during a visit to six cities in Denmark, Sweden and Norway by a mobile display unit between 15 April and 20 May 1971. The pack gives details of this tour and also lists the other stamps which were due to be issued in 1971, the text being in English. A separate insert gives translations in Danish, Swedish and Norwegian. The pack was also available at the Philatelic Bureau, Edinburgh.

DECIMAL MACHIN INDEX

Those booklet stamps shown below with an * after the catalogue number do not exist with perforations on all four sides, but show one or two sides imperforate.

Val.	*Process*	*Colour*	*Phosphor*	*Cat. No.*	*Source*
½p.	photo	turquoise-blue	2 bands	X841/Eg	(a) with P.V.A. gum—sheets, 5p. m/v coil (X841nEv), 10p. m/v coil (X841q), 10p. booklets (DN46/75, FA1/3), 25p. booklets (DH39/52), 50p. booklets (DT1/12, FB1, FB14/16, FB19/23), £1 Wedgwood booklet (DX1) (b) with gum arabic—sheets, 5p. m/v coil (X841n)
½p.	photo	turquoise-blue	1 band at left	X842	£1 Wedgwood booklet (DX1)
½p.	photo	turquoise-blue	1 centre band	X843	10p. m/v coil (X843l), 10p. booklets (FA4/9)
½p.	photo	turquoise-blue	phos paper	X924	sheets, 12½p. m/v coil (X924l)
1p.	photo	crimson	2 bands	X844/Eg	(a) with P.V.A. gum—sheets, coils, 5p. m/v coil (X841nEv), 10p. m/v coil (X841q), 10p. booklets (DN46/75, FA1/3), 50p. booklets (FB1/8, FB14/16) (b) with gum arabic—coils, 5p. m/v coil (X841n)
1p.	photo	crimson	1 centre band	X845	10p. m/v coils (X843l, X845m), 10p. booklets (FA4/11), 50p. booklets (FB24/30, 34/36, 43/6, 48, 50)
1p.	photo	crimson	"all-over"	X846	sheets
1p.	photo	crimson	phos paper	X925	sheets, coils, 13p. m/v coil (X925l), 50p. booklet (FB59/66)
1p.	photo	crimson	1 band at left	X847	50p. booklets (FB37/42, 47, 49)
1p.	photo	crimson	1 band at right	X847Ea	£5 P. & O. booklet (DX8)
1½p.	photo	black	2 bands	X848	sheets, 10p. booklets (DN46/75)
2p.	photo	myrtle-green	2 bands	X849/Eg	(a) with P.V.A. gum—sheets, 5p. m/v coil (X841nEv), 10p. m/v coil (X841q), 10p. booklets (DN46/75), 50p. booklets (FB9/13), £3 Wedgwood booklet (DX2), £4 SG booklet (DX3) (b) with gum arabic—5p. m/v coil (X841n)
2p.	photo	myrtle-green	"all-over"	X850	sheets
2p.	photo	myrtle-green	phos paper	X926	sheets
2p.	photo	myrtle-green	phos paper	X928	14p. m/v coil (X928l)
2p.	litho	emerald-green	phos paper	X1000/a	sheets
2p.	litho	brt grn & dp grn	phos paper	X1001	sheets
2p.	photo	dp green	phos paper	X927	sheets, £1 booklets (FH23/7)
2p.	litho	dp green	phos paper	X1050*	£1 booklets (FH28/30)
2½p.	photo	magenta	1 centre band	X851/Eg	(a) with P.V.A. gum—sheets, coils, 25p. booklets (DH39/52), 50p. booklets (DT1/12), £1 Wedgwood booklet (DX1) (b) with gum arabic—sheets, coils
2½p.	photo	magenta	1 side band	X852/Ea	(a) band at left—50p. booklets (DT1/12), £1 Wedgwood booklet (DX1) (b) band at right—£1 Wedgwood booklet (DX1)
2½p.	photo	magenta	2 bands	X853	sheets
2½p.	photo	rose-red	phos paper	X929	sheets, 11½p. m/v coil (X929l)
2½p.	photo	rose-red	2 bands	X854	50p. booklets (FB17/18)
3p.	photo	ultramarine	2 bands	X855/Eg	(a) with P.V.A. gum—sheets, coils, 30p. booklets (DQ56/72), 50p. booklets (DT1/12), £1 Wedgwood booklet (DX1) (b) with gum arabic—sheets, coils
3p.	photo	ultramarine	1 centre band	X856/Eg	(a) with P.V.A. gum—sheets, coils, 30p. booklets (DQ73/4), 50p. booklets (DT13/14) (b) with gum arabic—sheets
3p.	photo	brt magenta	phos paper	X930	Type I. sheets, 11½p. m/v coil (X929l), £4 Royal Mint booklet (DX4)
3p.	photo	brt magenta	phos paper	X930c	Type II. sheets (from 21.1.92), 15p. m/v coil (X930cl)
3p.	photo	brt magenta	2 bands	X857	Type I. 50p. booklets (FB19/23), £4 SG booklet (DX3)
3½p.	photo	olive-grey	2 bands	X858/Eb	sheets, coils, 35p. booklets (DP1/3), 50p. booklets (DT13/14)
3½p.	photo	olive-grey	1 centre band	X859	sheets, coils, 35p. booklet (DP4), 85p. booklet (DW1)
3½p.	photo	purple-brown	phos paper	X931	sheets, £4 Royal Mint booklet (DX4)
3½p.	photo	purple-brown	1 centre band	X860	50p. booklets (FB24/6)

Val.	*Process*	*Colour*	*Phosphor*	*Cat. No.*	*Source*
4p.	photo	ochre-brown	2 bands	X861/Eg	(a) with P.V.A. gum—sheets. (b) with gum arabic—sheets
4p.	litho	greenish blue	2 bands	X996	sheets
4p.	photo	greenish blue	2 bands	X862	50p. booklets (FB17/18)
4p.	litho	greenish blue	phos paper	X997 X1002	sheets J.W. ptg. sheets Questa ptg.
4p.	photo	greenish blue	phos paper	X932 X932Ea	$12\frac{1}{2}$p. m/v coil (X924l) 13p. m/v coil (X925l), 14p. m/v coil (X928l)
4p.	photo	greenish blue	1 centre band	X863	50p. booklets (FB27/30)
4p.	photo	greenish blue	1 side band	X864/Ea	(a) band at right—£5 Times booklet (DX6) (b) band at left—£5 Times booklet (DX6)
4p.	photo	new blue	phos paper	X933	sheets, 15p. m/v coil (X930cl), 17p. m/v coil (X933l), 18p. m/v coil (X933m), 19p m/v coil (X933n)
$4\frac{1}{2}$p.	photo	grey-blue	2 bands	X865	sheets, coils, 45p. booklets (DS1/2), 85p. booklet (DW1)
5p.	photo	pale violet	2 bands	X866	sheets
5p.	photo	pale violet	phos paper	X934	sheets
5p.	litho	lt violet	phos paper	X1003	sheets
5p.	litho	claret	phos paper	X1004/a	sheets
5p.	photo	claret	1 centre band	X867	50p. booklets (FB35/36, 43/6, 48, 50)
5p.	photo	dull red-brown	phos paper	X935	sheets, 17p. m/v coil (X933l), 18p. m/v coil (X933m), 19p m/v coil (X933n)
$5\frac{1}{2}$p.	photo	violet	2 bands	X868	sheets
$5\frac{1}{2}$p.	photo	violet	1 centre band	X869	sheets
6p.	photo	lt emerald	2 bands	X870/Eg	(a) with P.V.A. gum—sheets, 10p. m/v coil (X841q), 10p. booklets (FA1/3) (b) with gum arabic—sheets
6p.	photo	yellow-olive	phos paper	X936	sheets
$6\frac{1}{2}$p.	photo	greenish blue	2 bands	X871	sheets
$6\frac{1}{2}$p.	photo	greenish blue	1 centre band	X872	sheets, coils, 65p. booklet (FC1)
$6\frac{1}{2}$p.	photo	greenish blue	1 side band	X873/Ea	(a) band at right—50p. booklet (FB1A). (b) band at left—50p. booklet (FB1B)
7p.	photo	purple-brown	2 bands	X874	sheets
7p.	photo	purple-brown	1 centre band	X875	sheets, coils, 10p. m/v coil (X843l), 10p. booklets (FA4/9), 70p. booklets (FD1/7), £1.60 Christmas booklet (FX1)
7p.	photo	purple-brown	1 side band	X876/Ea	(a) band at right—50p. booklets (FB2A/8A) (b) band at left—50p. booklets (FB2B/8B)
7p.	photo	brownish red	phos paper	X937	sheets
$7\frac{1}{2}$p.	photo	pale chestnut	2 bands	X877	sheets
8p.	photo	rosine	2 bands	X878	sheets
8p.	photo	rosine	1 centre band	X879	sheets, coils, 10p. m/v coil (X845m), 10p. booklets (FA10/11), 80p. booklet (FE1), £1.80 Christmas booklet (FX2)
8p.	photo	rosine	1 side band	X880/Ea	(a) band at right—50p. booklets (FB9A/10A) (b) band at left—50p. booklets (FB9B/10B)
$8\frac{1}{2}$p.	photo	lt yellowish green	2 bands	X881	sheets, coils, 50p. booklet (FB1), 85p. booklet (FF1)
$8\frac{1}{2}$p.	photo	yellowish green	phos paper	X938	sheets
9p.	photo	yellow-orange & black	2 bands	X882	sheets
9p.	photo	dp violet	2 bands	X883	sheets, coils, 50p. booklet (FB2/8), 90p. booklets (FG1/8), £1.60 Christmas booklet (FX1)
$9\frac{1}{2}$p.	photo	purple	2 bands	X884	sheets
10p.	recess	cerise	phos paper	829	sheets
10p.	photo	orange-brown & chestnut	2 bands	X885	sheets
10p.	photo	orange-brown	2 bands	X886	Type I. sheets, 50p. booklets (FB9/10), £1.80 Christmas booklet (FX2)
10p.	photo	orange-brown	2 bands	X886b	Type II. £4 Christian Heritage booklet (DX5)
10p.	photo	orange-brown	"all-over"	X887	Type I. sheets, coils, £1 booklet (FH1)
10p.	photo	orange-brown	phos paper	X939	Type I. sheets

Val.	*Process*	*Colour*	*Phosphor*	*Cat. No.*	*Source*
10p.	photo	orange-brown	1 centre band	X888	Type I. sheets, coils, £1 booklets (FH2/4), £2.20 Christmas booklet (FX3), £3 Wedgwood booklet (DX2)
10p.	photo	orange-brown	1 side band	X889/Ea	Type I. (a) band at right—50p. booklets (FB11A/13A) (b) band at left—50p. booklets (FB11B/13B), £3 Wedgwood booklet (DX2)
10p.	photo	dull orange	phos paper	X940	sheets
10½p.	photo	yellow	2 bands	X890	sheets
10½p.	photo	dp dull blue	2 bands	X891	sheets
11p.	photo	brown-red	2 bands	X892	sheets
11p.	photo	brown-red	phos paper	X941	sheets
11½p.	photo	ochre-brown	phos paper	X942	sheets
11½p.	photo	drab	1 centre band	X893	sheets, coils, £1.15 booklets (F1/4), £2.55 Christmas booklet (FX4)
11½p.	photo	drab	1 side band	X894/Ea	(a) band at right—50p. booklets (FB14A/18A), £1.30 booklets (FL1/2) (b) band at left—50p. booklets FB14B/18B), £1.30 booklets (FL1/2)
12p.	photo	yellowish green	phos paper	X943	sheets, coils, £1.20 booklets (FJ1/3)
12p.	photo	yellowish green	2 bands	X895	50p. booklets (FB11/13), £2.20 Christmas booklet (FX3), £3 Wedgwood booklet (DX2)
12p.	photo	brt emerald	1 centre band	X896	sheets, coils, 50p. booklet (FB34), £1.20 booklets (FJ4/6), £5 British Rail booklet (DX7)
12p.	photo	brt emerald	1 side band	X897/Ea	(a) band at right—£1.50 booklets (FP1/2), £5 British Rail booklet (DX7) (b) band at left—£1.50 booklets (FP1/2), £5 British Rail booklet (DX7)
12p.	photo	brt emerald	1 centre band Underprint T.4	X896Eu	sheets
12½p.	photo	lt emerald	1 centre band	X898	sheets, coils, 50p. booklets (FB24/6), £1.25 booklets (FK1/8), £4 SG booklet (DX3)
12½p.	photo	lt emerald	1 centre band Underprint T.1	X898Eu	£2.80 Christmas booklet (FX5)
12½p.	photo	lt emerald	1 centre band Underprint T.2	X898Eua	£2.50 Christmas booklet (FX6)
12½p.	photo	lt emerald	1 side band	X899/Ea	(a) band at right—50p. booklets (FB19A/23A), £1.43 booklets (FN1/6), £1.46 booklets (FO1/3), £4 SG booklet (DX3), £4 Royal Mint booklet (DX4) (b) band at left—50p. booklets (FB19B/23B), £1.43 booklets (FN1/6), £1.46 booklets (FO1/3), £4 SG booklet (DX3), £4 Royal Mint booklet (DX4)
13p.	photo	olive-grey	phos paper	X944	sheets
13p.	photo	pale chestnut	1 centre band	X900	sheets, coils, 50p. booklets (FB27/30, 35/6, 43/6, 48, 50), 52p. booklet (GA1), £1.30 booklets (FL3/14, GI1), £5 Times booklet (DX6), £5 P & O booklet (DX8)
13p.	photo	pale chestnut	1 centre band Underprint T.2	X900Eu	£1.30 Christmas booklet (FX9)
13p.	photo	pale chestnut	1 side band	X901/Ea	(a) band at right—50p. booklets (FB37/42, 47, 49), £1.54 booklets (FQ1/4), £4 Christian Heritage booklet (DX5), £5 Times booklet (DX6), £5 P & O booklet (DX8) (b) band at left—£1 booklets (FH6/13), £1.54 booklets (FQ1/4), £4 Christian Heritage booklet (DX5), £5 Times booklet (DX6)
13p.	litho	pale chestnut	1 centre band	X1005	£5 Financial Times booklet (DX9)
13p.	litho	pale chestnut	1 side band	X1006/Ea	£5 Financial Times booklet (DX9)
13½p.	photo	purple-brown	phos paper	X945	sheets
14p.	photo	grey-blue	phos paper	X946	sheets, coils, £1.40 booklets (FM1/4)
14p.	photo	grey-blue	2 bands	X902	50p. booklets (FB14/16), £1.30 booklets (FL1/2), £2.55 Christmas booklet (FX4)
14p.	photo	dp blue	1 centre band	X903	sheets, coils, 56p. booklets (GB1/4), £1.40 booklets (FM5/6, GK1, 3)
14p.	photo	dp blue	1 band at right	X904	50p. booklets (FB51/4), £1 booklets (FH14/15)
14p.	litho	dp blue	1 centre band	X1007	£1.40 booklets (GK2, 4)
14p.	litho	dp blue	1 band at right	X1051*	£1 booklet (FH16)
15p.	photo	ultramarine	phos paper	X947	sheets
15p.	photo	brt blue	1 centre band	X905	sheets, coils

Val. Process	*Colour*	*Phosphor*	*Cat. No.*	*Source*
15p. photo	brt blue	1 side band	X906/Ea	(a) band at left—50p. booklet (FB55) (b) band at right—£5 London Life booklet (DX11)
$15\frac{1}{2}$p. photo	pale violet	phos paper	X948	sheets, coils, £1.55 booklets (FR1/6)
$15\frac{1}{2}$p. photo	pale violet	2 bands	X907	£1.43 booklets (FN1/6), £4 SG booklet (DX3)
$15\frac{1}{2}$p. photo	pale violet	2 bands Underprint T.1	X907Eu	£2.80 Christmas booklet (FX5)
16p. photo	olive-drab	phos paper	X949	sheets, coils, £1.60 booklets (FS1, 3/4), £4 Royal Mint booklet (DX4)
16p. photo	olive-drab	phos paper Underprint T.3	X949Eu	£1.60 booklet (FS2)
16p. photo	olive-drab	2 bands	X908	£1.46 booklets (FO1/3)
$16\frac{1}{2}$p. photo	pale chestnut	phos paper	X950	sheets
17p. photo	lt emerald	phos paper	X951	sheets
17p. photo	grey-blue	phos paper	X952	sheets, coils, £1 booklet (FH5), £1.70 booklets (FT1, 3 & 5/7), £4 Christian Heritage booklet (DX5), £5 Times booklet (DX6), £5 British Rail booklet (DX7)
17p. photo	grey-blue	phos paper Underprint T.3	X952Eu	£1.70 booklet (FT2)
17p. photo	grey-blue	2 bands	X909	50p. booklet (FB33), £1.50 booklets (FP1/3), £1.54 booklets (FQ1/4), £4 Christian Heritage booklet (DX5), £5 Times booklet (DX6), £5 British Rail booklet (DX7)
17p. photo	grey-blue	2 bands Underprint T.4	X909Eu	50p. booklets (FB31/3)
17p. photo	dp blue	1 centre band	X910	sheets, coils
17p. photo	dp blue	1 side band	X911/Ea	(a) band at right—50p. booklet (FB57/8), £1 booklet (FH21/2) (b) band at left—50p. booklet (FB57/8)
17p. litho	dp blue	1 centre band	X1008	£6 Alias Agatha Christie booklet (DX12)
$17\frac{1}{2}$p. photo	pale chestnut	phos paper	X953	sheets
18p. photo	dp violet	phos paper	X954	sheets
18p. photo	dp olive-grey	phos paper	X955	sheets, coils, 72p. booklet (GC1), £1.80 booklets (FU1/8, GN1), £5 P & O booklet (DX8)
18p. photo	dp olive-grey	2 bands	X912	50p. booklets (FB37/42, 47, 49), £1 booklet (FH6/13), £5 P & O booklet (DX8)
18p. litho	dp olive-grey	phos paper	X1009	£5 Financial Times booklet (DX9)
18p. litho	dp olive-grey	2 bands	X1010	£5 Financial Times booklet (DX9)
18p. photo	brt green	1 centre band	X913	sheets, coils
18p. litho	brt green	1 centre band	X1011	£6 Tolkien booklet (DX14)
18p. litho	brt green	1 side band	X1012/Ea	(a) band at right—£6 Tolkien booklet (DX14). (b) band at left—£6 (£5.64 Beatrix Potter booklet (DX15)).
19p. photo	brt orange-red	phos paper	X956	sheets, coils, 76p. booklets (GD1/4), £1.90 booklets (FV1/2, GO1, 3)
19p. photo	brt orange-red	2 bands	X914	50p. booklets (FB51/4), £1 booklets (FH14/15, 17)
19p. litho	brt orange-red	phos paper	X1013	£1.90 booklets (GO2, 4)
19p. litho	brt orange-red	2 bands	X1052*	£1 booklet (FH16)
$19\frac{1}{2}$p. photo	olive-grey	phos paper	X957	sheets
20p. recess	olive-green	none	830	sheets
20p. photo	dull purple	2 bands	X915	sheets
20p. photo	dull purple	phos paper	X958	sheets
20p. litho	dull purple	2 bands	X998	sheets
20p. litho	dull purple	phos paper	X999 X1014	sheets J.W. ptg. sheets Questa ptg.
20p. photo	turquoise-green	phos paper	X959	sheets
20p. photo	brownish black	phos paper	X960	sheets, coils, £1 booklet (FH18)
20p. photo	brownish black	2 bands	X916	50p. booklet (FB55), £5 London Life booklet (DX11)
$20\frac{1}{2}$p. photo	ultramarine	phos paper	X961	sheets
22p. photo	blue	phos paper	X962	sheets
22p. photo	yellow-green	phos paper	X963	sheets

Val.	Process	Colour	Phosphor	Cat. No.	Source
22p.	litho	yellow-green	2 bands	X1015	£5 Financial Times booklet (DX9)
22p.	photo	brt orange-red	2 bands	X917*	£1 booklet (FH21/2)
22p.	photo	brt orange-red	phos paper	X964	sheets, coils
22p.	litho	brt orange-red	phos paper	X1016	£6 Alias Agatha Christie booklet (DX12)
23p.	photo	brown-red	phos paper	X965	sheets
23p.	photo	brt green	phos paper	X966	sheets
24p.	photo	violet	phos paper	X967	sheets
24p.	photo	Indian red	phos paper	X968	sheets
24p.	photo	chestnut	phos paper	X969	sheets, coils, 50p. booklets (FB59/66), £1 booklets (FH23/7)
24p.	litho	chestnut	phos paper	X1017 X1053*	£6 Tolkien booklet (DX14) (Questa ptg) £1 booklet (FH28/30) Walsall ptg
24p.	litho	chestnut	2 bands	X1018	£6 Tolkien booklet (DX14)
25p.	photo	purple	phos paper	X970	sheets
25p.	photo	rose-red	2 bands	X917a	coils
26p.	photo	rosine	phos paper	X971	Type I. sheets
26p.	photo	rosine	2 bands	X918	Type I. £5 P & O booklet (DX8)
26p.	photo	rosine	phos paper	X971b	Type II. £1.04 booklet (GE1)
26p.	photo	drab	phos paper	X972	sheets
27p.	photo	chestnut	phos paper	X973	sheets, £1.08 booklets (GF1/2)
27p.	photo	violet	phos paper	X974	sheets
28p.	photo	dp violet	phos paper	X975	sheets
28p.	photo	ochre	phos paper	X976	sheets
28p.	photo	dp bluish grey	phos paper	X977	sheets
29p.	photo	ochre-brown	phos paper	X978	sheets
29p.	photo	dp mauve	phos paper	X979	sheets
29p.	litho	dp mauve	2 bands	X1054*	£1.16 booklet (GG1)
29p.	litho	dp mauve	phos paper	X1055*	£1.16 booklet (GG2)
30p.	photo	dp olive-grey	phos paper	X980	sheets
31p.	photo	purple	phos paper	X981	sheets
31p.	photo	purple	2 bands	X919	£5 British Rail booklet (DX7)
31p.	photo	ultramarine	phos paper	X982	sheets
31p.	litho	ultramarine	phos paper	X1056*	£1.24 booklet (GH1)
32p.	photo	greenish blue	phos paper	X983	sheets
33p.	photo	lt emerald	phos paper	X984	sheets, coils
33p.	litho	lt emerald	phos paper	X1019	£6 Alias Agatha Christie booklet (DX12)
33p.	litho	lt emerald	phos paper	X1057*	£1.32 booklet (GJ1)
33p.	litho	lt emerald	2 bands	X1020	£6 Wales booklet (DX13), £6 (£5.64) Beatrix Potter booklet (DX15)
34p.	photo	ochre-brown	phos paper	X985	sheets
34p.	photo	ochre-brown	2 bands	X920	£5 Times booklet (DX6)
34p.	litho	ochre-brown	2 bands	X1021	£5 Financial Times booklet (DX9)
34p.	photo	dp bluish grey	phos paper	X986	sheets
34p.	photo	dp mauve	phos paper	X987	sheets
35p.	photo	sepia	phos paper	X988	sheets
35p.	photo	yellow	phos paper	X989	sheets
37p.	photo	rosine	phos paper	X990	sheets
39p.	photo	brt mauve	phos paper	X991	sheets, coils
39p.	litho	brt mauve	phos paper	X1058*	78p. booklet (GD4a), £1.56 booklet (G L1)
39p.	litho	brt mauve	2 bands	X1022	£6 Tolkien booklet (DX14), £6 (£5.64) Beatrix Potter booklet (DX15)
50p.	recess	dp ultramarine	none or phos paper	831/Ea	sheets

Val.	Process	Colour	Phosphor	Cat. No.	Source
50p.	photo	ochre-brown	2 bands	X921	sheets
50p.	photo	ochre-brown	none	X992	sheets
50p.	photo	ochre	2 bands	X922	£5 London Life (DX11)
50p.	photo	ochre	none or phos paper	X994	sheets
75p.	litho	black	none	X1023/a	sheets
75p.	litho	brownish grey & black	none	X1024	sheets
75p.	photo	grey-black	none	X993	sheets
£1	recess	bluish black	none	831*b*	sheets
£1	photo	brt yellow-green & blackish olive	none	1026	sheets
£1.30	photo	drab & dp greenish blue	none	1026*b*	sheets
£1.33	photo	pale mauve & grey-black	none	1026*c*	sheets
£1.41	photo	drab & dp greenish blue	none	1026*d*	sheets
£1.50	photo	pale mauve & grey-black	none	1026*e*	sheets
£1.60	photo	pale drab & dp greenish blue	none	1026*f*	sheets
£2	photo	lt emerald & purple-brown	none	1027	sheets
£5	photo	salmon & chalky blue	none	1028	sheets

For 1st and 2nd class no value indicated (NVI) stamps, see Nos. 1445/52, 1511/16, 1663*a*/6 and 1979.
For table covering Machin stamps with elliptical perforations see after Nos. Y1667, etc, in 1993.

DECIMAL MACHIN MULTI-VALUE COIL INDEX

The following is a simplified checklist of multi-value coils, to be used in conjunction with the main listing as details of stamps listed there are not repeated.

Strip Value	Date	Contents	Cat No.
5p.	15.2.71	½p. × 2, 1p. × 2, 2p.	X841n
10p.	3.12.75	½p. × 2, 1p., 2p., 6p.	X841q
10p.	14.12.77	½p. × 2, 1p. × 2, 7p.	X843l
10p.	16.1.80	1p. × 2, 8p. plus 2 labels	X845m
11½p.	6.81	2½p., 3p. × 3	X929l
12½p.	30.12.81	½p., 4p. × 3	X924l
13p.	14.8.84	1p., 4p. × 3	X925l
14p.	5.9.88	2p., 4p. × 3	X928l
15p.	10.10.89	3p., 4p. × 3	X930cl
17p.	27.11.90	4p. × 3, 5p.	X933l
18p.	1.10.91	4p. × 2, 5p. × 2	X933m
19p.	31.1.95	4p., 5p. × 3	X933n

Decimal Machin Booklet Pane Guide

Abbreviations used in the diagrams: 2B = 2 bands, CB = centre band, LB = left band and RB = right band. The shaded squares represent printed labels. Panes completed by unprinted white labels are outside the scope of this catalogue.

Unless otherwise stated the panes were printed in photogravure. Some panes exist in photogravure and lithography and these are separately identified and listed. **Imperforate or straight edges.** These are described under the appropriate illustration and listed as complete panes.

2	2
½	½

X841l
(2 bands)

2	½
2	½

X841la
(2 bands)

½	½	½
	½	½

X841m
(2 bands)

2½ RB	½ 2B	2½ LB	2½ CB
2½ RB	½ 2B	2½ LB	2½ CB
2½ RB	½ 2B	2½ LB	2½ CB

X841o
£1 Wedgwood

½ 2B	2½ LB
½ 2B	2½ LB
½ 2B	½ LB

X841p
£1 Wedgwood

½	½
6	1
1	1

X841r
(2 bands)

½ 2B	½ 2B
1 2B	8½ 2B
1 2B	8½ 2B
6½ RB	8½ 2B
6½ RB	8½ 2B

X841s

½ 2B	½ 2B
8½ 2B	1 2B
8½ 2B	1 2B
8½ 2B	6½ LB
8½ 2B	6½ LB

X841sa

11½ RB	½ 2B
11½ RB	1 2B
11½ RB	14 2B

X841t

½ 2B	11½ LB
1 2B	11½ LB
14 2B	11½ LB

X841ta

½ 2B	3 2B
12½ RB	3 2B
12½ RB	3 2B
12½ RB	3 2B

X841u

3 2B	½ 2B
3 2B	12½ LB
3 2B	12½ LB
3 2B	12½ LB

X841ua

½	
½	1
7	1

X843m
(centre band)

1	1
1½	1½

X844l
(2 bands)

1½	1
1½	1

X844m
(2 bands)

1 2B	1 2B
7 RB	9 2B
7 RB	9 2B
7 RB	9 2B

X844n

1 2B	1 2B
9 2B	7 LB
9 2B	7 LB
9 2B	7 LB

X844na

	1
8	1

X845l
(centre band)

1	1
3½	12½
3½	12½
3½	12½

X845n
(centre band)

1	1
1	13
4	13
4	13

X845p
(centre band)

1	1
12	12
12	12

X845q
(centre band)

1	13
5	13
5	13

X845s/sa
(centre band)
X845sa imperf
at left and right

1 LB	13 RB
18 2B	18 2B

X847l

13 RB	18 2B	18 2B
1 RB	18 2B	26 2B
13 RB	18 2B	18 2B

X847m
£5 P & O

	2 2B
2 2B	10 2B
8 RB	10 2B
8 RB	10 2B

X849l

2 2B	
10 2B	2 2B
10 2B	8 LB
10 2B	8 LB

X849la

	2 RB
2 2B	2 2B
10 RB	12 2B
10 RB	12 2B

X849m

2 2B	
2 2B	2 2B
12 2B	10 LB
12 2B	10 LB

X849ma

12 2B	10 LB	10 CB
12 2B	2 2B	10 CB
12 2B	12 2B	10 CB

X849n
£3 Wedgwood

2	2
2	2
2	2

X849o
(2 bands)
£3 Wedgwood

12½ RB	12½ LB	12½ CB
12½ RB	3 2B	12½ LB
12½ RB	2 2B	12½ LB

X849p
£4 Stanley Gibbons

2½	2½	2½
	2½	2½

X851l
(centre band)

	2½	2½
	2½	2½

X851m
(centre band)

2½ CB	2½ RB	3 2B	3 2B
2½ CB	2½ RB	3 2B	3 2B
2½ CB	2½ RB	3 2B	3 2B

X851n
£1 Wedgwood

3 2B	3 2B	2½ LB
3 2B	3 2B	2½ LB

X852l

4 2B	4 2B
11½ RB	2½ 2B
11½ RB	2½ 2B
11½ RB	2½ 2B

X854l

4 2B	4 2B
2½ 2B	11½ LB
2½ 2B	11½ LB
2½ 2B	11½ LB

X854la

3	3	3
	3	3

X855l
(2 bands)

13 RB	17 2B	13 LB
4 RB	34 2B	4 LB
13 RB	17 2B	13 LB

X864l
£5 The Times

9 2B	9 2B	9 2B	9 2B	9 2B	9 2B	9 2B	9 2B	9 2B	9 2B
7 CB	7 CB	7 CB	7 CB	7 CB	7 CB	7 CB	7 CB	7 CB	7 CB

X875l
Christmas 1978

10 2B	10 2B	10 2B	10 2B	10 2B	10 2B	10 2B	10 2B	10 2B	10 2B
8 CB	8 CB	8 CB	8 CB	8 CB	8 CB	8 CB	8 CB	8 CB	8 CB

X879l
Christmas 1979

17 2B	17 2B	17 2B
10 2B	17 2B	13 LB
17 2B	17 2B	17 2B

X886bl
£4 Christian Heritage

10	10	10
10	10	10
10	10	10

X888l
(centre band)
£3 Wedgwood

12 2B	12 2B	12 2B	12 2B	12 2B	12 2B	12 2B	12 2B	12 2B	12 2B
10 CB	10 CB	10 CB	10 CB	10 CB	10 CB	10 CB	10 CB	10 CB	10 CB

X888m
Christmas 1980

14 2B	14 2B	14 2B	14 2B	14 2B	14 2B	14 2B	14 2B	14 2B	14 2B
11½ CB	11½ CB	11½ CB	11½ 2B	11½ CB	11½ CB	11½ CB	11½ CB	11½ CB	11½ CB

X893l
Christmas 1981

14 2B	14 2B	14 2B	14 2B	14 2B
14 2B	11½ LB	11½ RB	11½ LB	11½ RB

X894l
Margin at left or right

12	12	12
12	12	12
12	12	12

X895l
(2 bands)
£3 Wedgwood

12	12	12
12	12	12
12	12	12

X896l
(centre band)
£5 British Rail

17 2B	17 2B	17 2B	17 2B	17 2B
12 LB	12 RB	12 LB	12 RB	17 2B

X897l

17 2B	17 2B	17 2B	17 2B	17 2B
17 2B	12 LB	12 RB	12 LB	12 RB

X897la

12 RB	17 2B	12 LB
12 RB	31 2B	12 LB
12 RB	17 2B	12 LB

X897m
£5 British Rail

15½ 2B	15½ 2B	15½ 2B	15½ 2B	15½ 2B	15½ 2B	15½ 2B	15½ 2B	15½ 2B	15½ 2B
12½ CB	12½ CB	12½ CB	12½ CB	12½ CB	12½ CB	12½ CB	12½ CB	12½ CB	12½ CB

X898l
Christmas 1982

15½ 2B	15½ 2B	15½ 2B	15½ 2B	15½ 2B
15½ 2B	12½ LB	12½ RB	12½ LB	12½ RB

X899l
Margin at left or right

12½ RB	12½ LB
12½ RB	12½ LB
12½ RB	12½ LB

X899m
£4 Stanley Gibbons
£4 Royal Mint

16 2B	16 2B	16 2B	16 2B	16 2B
12½ LB	12½ RB	12½ LB	12½ RB	16 2B

X899n

16 2B	16 2B	16 2B	16 2B	16 2B
16 2B	12½ LB	12½ RB	12½ LB	12½ RB

X899na

13	13	13
13	13	13
13	13	13

X900l
(centre band)
£5 The Times
£5 P & O

13	13
13	13
13	13

X900m, (photo), X1005l (litho)
(centre band)
£5 P & O (X900m)
£5 Financial Times (X1005l)

13	13
13	13

X900n
(centre band)
52p. Barcode Booklet

13	13	13	13	13
13	13	13	13	13

X900o
(centre band)
£1.30 Barcode Booklet

17 2B	17 2B	17 2B	17 2B	17 2B
13 LB	13 RB	13 LB	13 RB	17 2B

X901l

17 2B	17 2B	17 2B	17 2B	17 2B
17 2B	13 LB	13 RB	13 LB	13 RB

X901la

13 RB	13 LB
13 RB	13 LB
13 RB	13 LB

X901m
£4 Christian Heritage

13 LB	18 2B
18 2B	18 2B
18 2B	18 2B

X901n/na
X901na imperf at
left and right

14	14
14	14

X903l
(centre band)
56p. Barcode Booklet

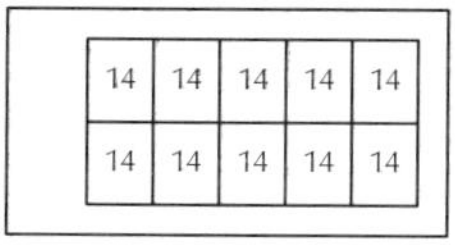

X903m
(centre band)
£1.40 Barcode Booklet

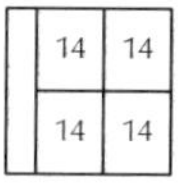

X903n, X903q
(centre band)
56p. Barcode Booklet
X903n imperf at top
and bottom
X903q imperf 3 sides

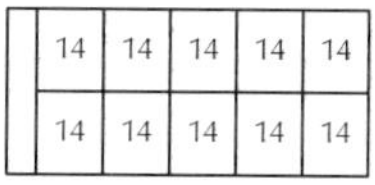

X903p
(centre band)
£1.40 Barcode Booklet
Imperf at top
and bottom

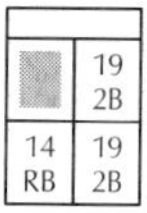

X904l

X904m, (photo)
X1051l (litho)
imperf at left
and right

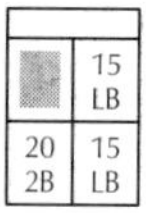

X906l

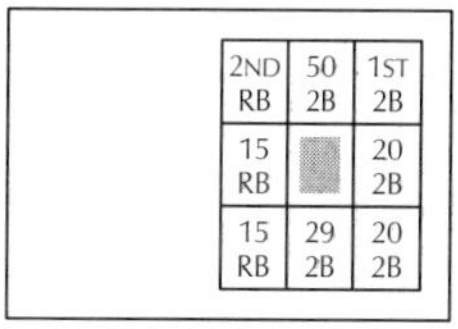

X906m
£5 London Life
The stamps in the bottom row are
Penny Black Anniversary definitives
(Nos. 1468Ea, 1470 and 1472)

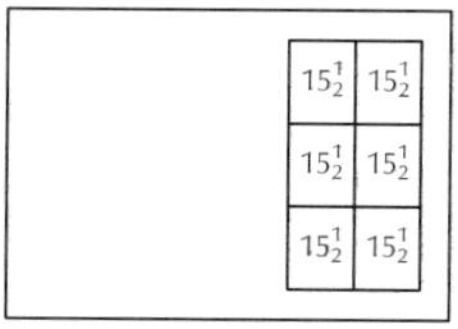

X907l
(2 bands)
£4 Stanley Gibbons

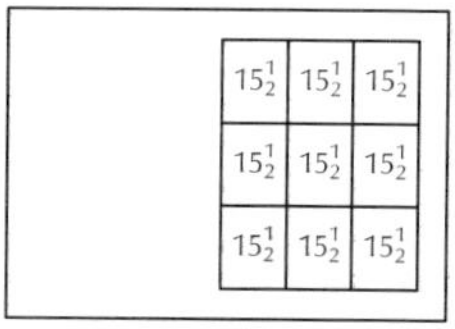

X907m
(2 bands)
£4 Stanley Gibbons

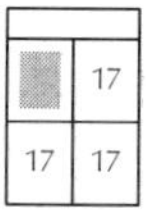

X909l
(2 bands)
and underprint
X909 Ela (as X909l
but without
underprint)

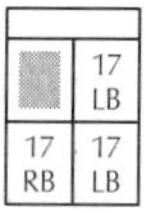

X911l

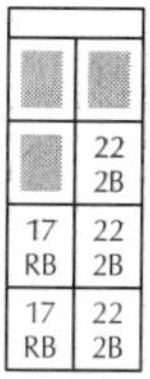

X911m
Imperf at left
and right

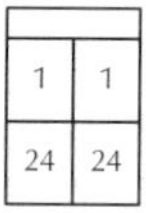

X925m
(phosphorised paper)

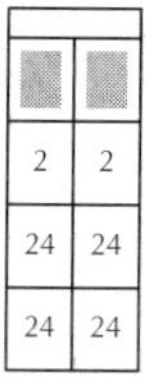

X927l (photo)
X1050l (litho)
(phosphorised paper)
Imperf at left and
right

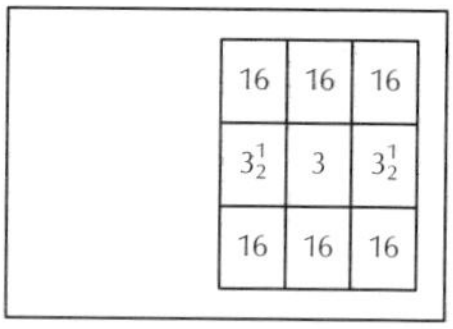

X930b
(phosphorised paper)
£4 Royal Mint

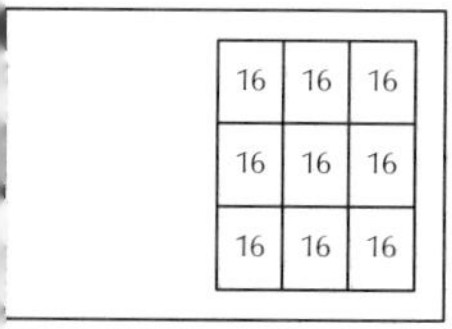

X949l
(phosphorised paper)
£4 Royal Mint

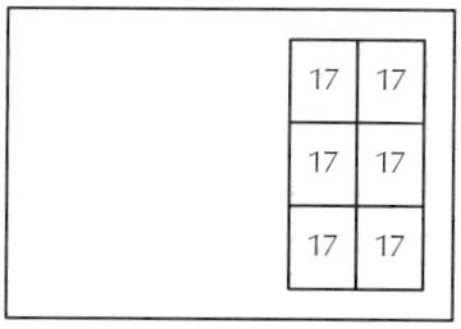

X925l
(phosphorised paper)
£4 Christian Heritage
£5 The Times
£5 British Rail
X1008l
(centre band)
£6 Agatha Christie

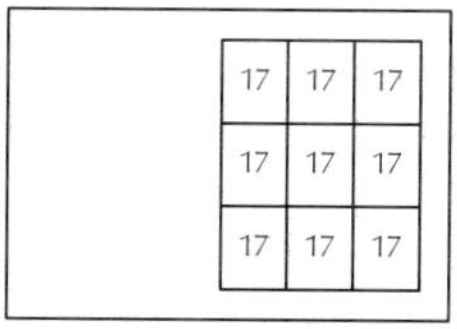

X952m
(phosphorised paper)
£5 The Times
£5 British Rail

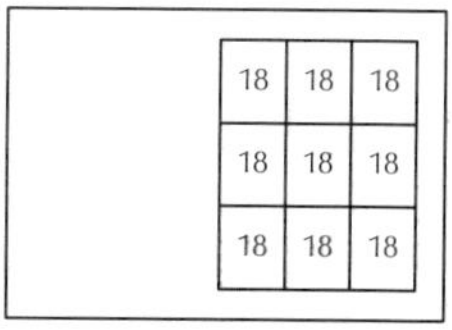

X955l (photo), X1009l (litho)
(phosphorised paper)
£5 P & O (X955l)
£5 Financial Times (X1009l)

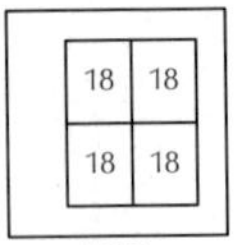

X955m
(phosphorised paper)
72p. Barcode Booklet

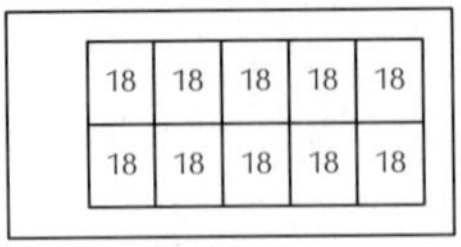

X955n
(phosphorised paper)
£1.80 Barcode Booklet

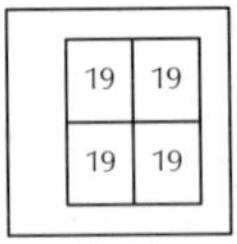

X956l
(phosphorised paper)
76p. Barcode Booklet

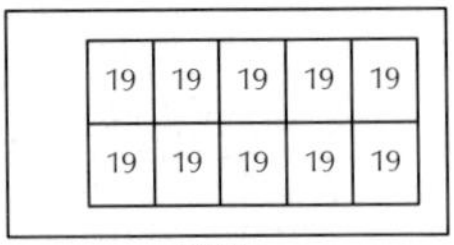

X956m
(phosphorised paper)
£1.90 Barcode Booklet

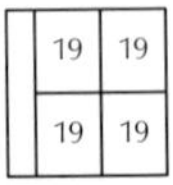

X956n, X956q
(phosphorised paper)
76p. Barcode Booklet
X956n imperf at top and bottom
X956q imperf on three sides

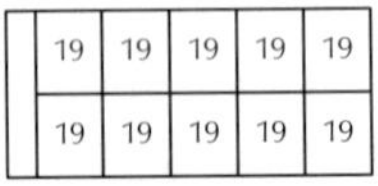

X956o
(phosphorised paper)
£1.90 Barcode Booklet
Imperf at top and bottom

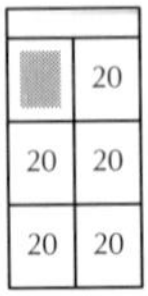

X960l
(phosphorised paper)
Imperf at left and right

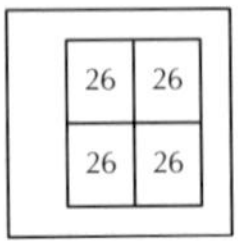

X971bl
(phosphorised paper)
£1.04 Barcode Booklet

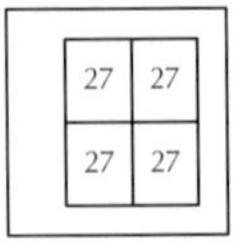

X973l
(phosphorised paper)
£1.08 Barcode Booklet

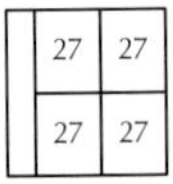

X973m
(phosphorised paper)
£1.08 Barcode Booklet
imperf at top and bottom

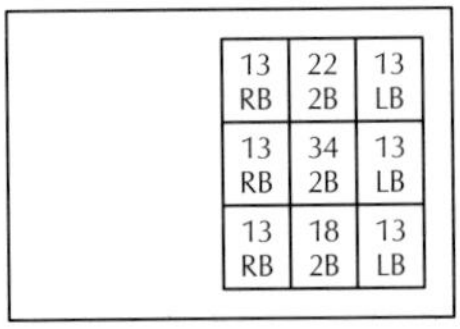

X1006l (litho)
£5 Financial Times

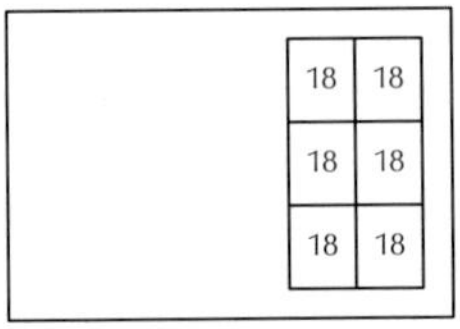

X1009m (litho)
(phosphorised paper)
£5 Financial Times
X1011l (litho)
(centre band)
£6 Tolkien

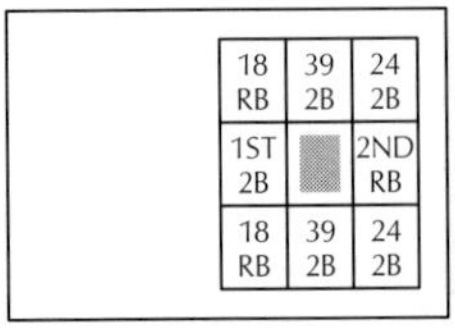

X1012l (litho)
£6 Tolkien

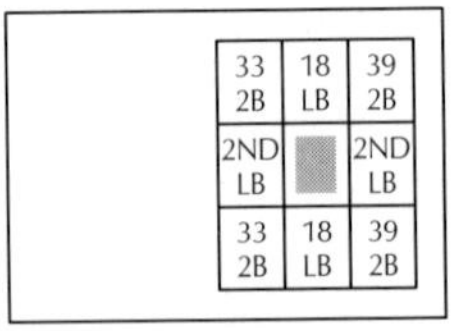

X1012m (litho)
£6 (£5.64) Beatrix Potter

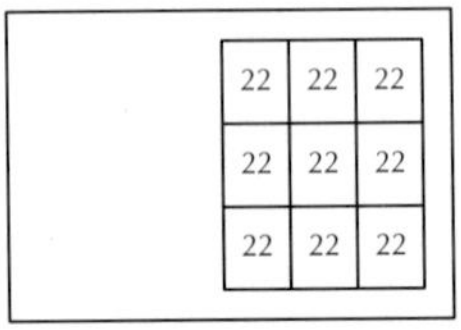

X1016l (litho)
(phosphorised paper)
£6 Agatha Christie

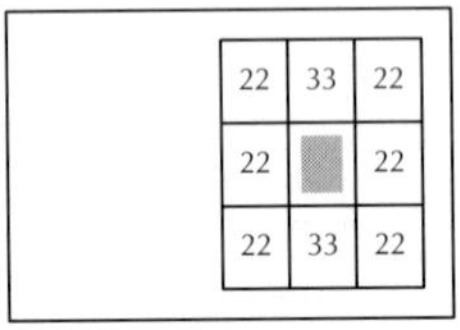

X1016m (litho)
(phosphorised paper)
£6 Agatha Christie

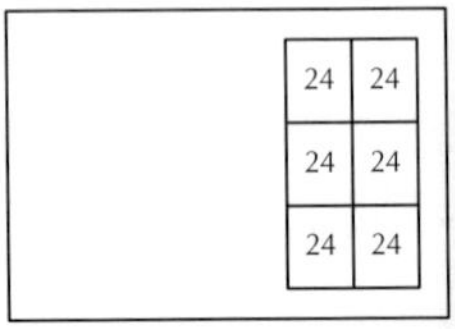

X1017l (litho)
(phosphorised paper)
£6 Tolkien

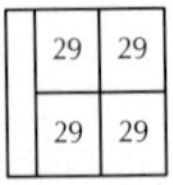

X1054l (litho), X1055l (litho)
(X1054l 2 bands)
(X1055l phosphorised paper)
£1.16 Barcode Booklet
Imperf on three sides

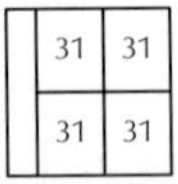

X1056l (litho)
(phosphorised paper)
£1.24 Barcode Booklet
Imperf at top and bottom

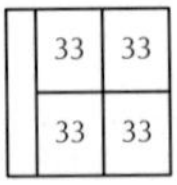

X1057l
(phosphorised paper)
£1.32 Barcode Booklet
Imperf top and bottom

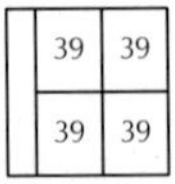

X1058l
(phosphorised paper)
£1.56 Barcode Booklet
Imperf top and bottom

368 "A Mountain Road" (T. P. Flanagan)

369 "Deer's Meadow" (Tom Carr)

371 John Keats (150th Death Anniv)

372 Thomas Gray (Death Bicentenary)

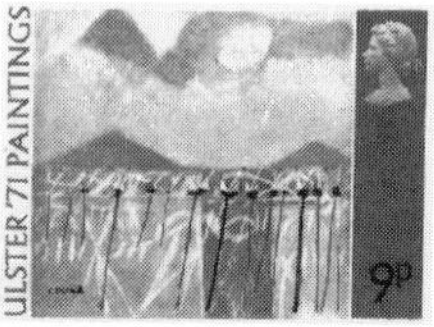

370 "Slieve na brock" (Colin Middleton)

373 Sir Walter Scott (Birth Bicentenary)

1971 (16 June). **"Ulster 1971" Paintings.** *Chalk-surfaced paper. Two phosphor bands. P 15 × 14.*

881	**368**	3p. yellow-buff, pale yellow, Venetian red, black, blue & drab	10	10
		Ey. Phosphor omitted	3·00	
882	**369**	7½p. olive-brown, brownish grey, pale olive-grey, dp blue, cobalt & grey-blue	50	50
		a. Pale olive-grey omitted*	60·00	
		Ey. Phosphor omitted	15·00	
883	**370**	9p. greenish yellow, orange, grey, lavender-grey, bistre, black, pale ochre-brown & ochre-brown	50	50
		a. Orange omitted	£1500	
		Ey. Phosphor omitted	15·00	
		Set of 3	1·00	1·00
		First Day Cover		3·00
		Presentation Pack	5·00	

A used example of the 3p. has been seen with the Venetian red omitted.

*This only affects the boulder in the foreground, which appears whitish and it only applied to some stamps in the sheet.

Special First Day of Issue Postmarks

British Post Office Philatelic Bureau, Edinburgh (Type D, see Introduction)	3·25
Belfast	5·00

First Day of Issue handstamps, in the same design as that for Belfast, were provided at Armagh, Ballymena, Coleraine, Cookstown, Enniskillen, Londonderry, Newry, Omagh and Portadown for this issue.

(Des Rosalind Dease. Queen's head printed in gold and then embossed)

1971 (28 July). **Literary Anniversaries.** *Chalk-surfaced paper. Two phosphor bands. P 15 × 14.*

884	**371**	3p. black, gold & greyish blue	10	10
		a. Gold (Queen's head) omitted	90·00	
		Ey. Phosphor omitted	3·00	
885	**372**	5p. black, gold & yellow-olive	50	50
		a. Gold (Queen's head) omitted	£160	
		Ey. Phosphor omitted	25·00	
886	**373**	7½p. black, gold & yellow-brown	50	50
		Eb. Embossing omitted	30·00	
		Ey. Phosphor omitted	15·00	
		Set of 3	1·00	1·00
		First Day Cover		4·00
		Presentation Pack	5·00	

Special First Day of Issue Postmarks

British Post Office Philatelic Bureau, Edinburgh (Type D, see Introduction)	4·50
London EC	7·50

374 Servicemen and Nurse of 1921

375 Roman Centurion

376 Rugby Football, 1871

(Des F. Wegner)

1971 (25 Aug). **British Anniversaries.** *Events described on stamps. Chalk-surfaced paper. Two phosphor bands. P* 15 × 14.

887	**374**	3p. red-orange, grey, dp blue, olive-green, olive-brown, black, rosine & violet-blue	10	10
		a. Dp blue omitted*	£600	
		b. Red-orange (nurse's cloak) omitted	£275	
		c. Olive-brown (faces, etc.) omitted	£160	
		d. Black omitted	£10000	
		Ey. Phosphor omitted	1·75	
888	**375**	7½p. grey, yellow-brown, vermilion, mauve, grey-black, black, silver, gold & ochre	50	50
		a. Grey omitted	75·00	
		Ey. Phosphor omitted	8·00	
889	**376**	9p. new blue, myrtle-green, grey-black, lemon, olive-brown, magenta & yellow-olive	50	50
		a. Olive-brown omitted	£110	
		b. New blue omitted	£2500	
		c. Myrtle-green omitted	£2250	
		Ey. Phosphor omitted	£400	
		Set of 3	1·00	1·00
		First Day Cover		3·00
		Presentation Pack	5·00	

*The effect of the missing deep blue is shown on the sailor's uniform, which appears as grey.

Used examples have been seen of the 3p. with grey omitted and of the 9p. with the lemon (jerseys) omitted.

Special First Day of Issue Postmarks

British Post Office Philatelic Bureau, Edinburgh (Type D, see Introduction)	4·00
Maidstone	15·00
Twickenham	16·00
York	16·00

377 Physical Sciences Building, University College of Wales, Aberystwyth

378 Faraday Building, Southampton University

379 Engineering Department, Leicester University

380 Hexagon Restaurant, Essex University

(Des N. Jenkins)

1971 (22 Sept). **British Architecture. Modern University Buildings.** *Chalk-surfaced paper. Two phosphor bands. P* 15 × 14.

890	**377**	3p. olive-brown, ochre, lemon, black & yellow-olive	10	10
		a. Lemon omitted		
		b. Black (windows) omitted	£10000	
		Ey. Phosphor omitted	4·50	
891	**378**	5p. rose, black, chestnut & lilac	20	20
		Ey. Phosphor omitted	55·00	
892	**379**	7½p. ochre, black & purple-brown	50	50
		Ey. Phosphor omitted	9·00	
893	**380**	9p. pale lilac, black, sepia-brown & dp blue	90	90
		Ey. Phosphor omitted	12·00	
		Set of 4	1·50	1·50
		First Day Cover		4·00
		Presentation Pack	5·50	

Mint examples of the 5p. exist with a larger "P" following the face value

Special First Day of Issue Postmarks

British Post Office Philatelic Bureau, Edinburgh (Type D, see Introduction)	4·50
Aberystwyth	13·50
Colchester	13·50
Leicester	13·50
Southampton	13·50

Collectors Pack 1971

1971 (29 Sept). *Comprises Nos.* 835/40 *and* 881/93.
CP893*a* Collectors Pack .... 25·00

381 "Dream of the Wise Men"

382 "Adoration of the Magi"

383 "Ride of the Magi"

HAVE YOU READ THE NOTES AT THE BEGINNING OF THIS CATALOGUE?
These often provide answers to the enquiries we receive.

(Des Clarke-Clements-Hughes design team, from stained-glass windows, Canterbury Cathedral. Queen's head printed in gold and then embossed)

1971 (13 Oct). **Christmas.** *Ordinary paper. One centre phosphor band* ($2\frac{1}{2}$*p.*) *or two phosphor bands (others). P* 15 × 14.

894	**381**	$2\frac{1}{2}$p.	new blue, black, lemon, emerald, reddish violet, carmine-red, carmine-rose & gold	10	10
		a.	Imperf (pair)	£400	
		Eb.	Embossing omitted		
895	**382**	3p.	black, reddish violet, lemon, new blue, carmine-rose, emerald, ultramarine & gold	10	10
		a.	Gold (Queen's head) omitted	£500	
		b.	Carmine-rose omitted	£1750	
		c.	Lemon omitted	60·00	
		d.	New blue omitted	†	£7000
		Ee.	Embossing omitted	7·00	
		Ey.	Phosphor omitted	2·25	
		Eya.	Embossing and phosphor omitted	60·00	
896	**383**	$7\frac{1}{2}$p.	black, lilac, lemon, emerald, new blue, rose, green & gold	90	90
		a.	Gold (Queen's head) omitted	80·00	
		b.	Lilac omitted	£400	
		c.	Emerald omitted	£200	
		Ed.	Embossing omitted	35·00	
		Ee.	Embossing double	35·00	
		Ey.	Phosphor omitted	8·00	
		Eya.	Embossing and phosphor omitted	23·00	
			Set of 3	1·00	1·00
			First Day Cover		4·00
			Presentation Pack	4·50	

The 3p. is known with reddish violet and embossing omitted, used in Llandudno and with lemon and carmine-rose both omitted used in Falkirk. The $7\frac{1}{2}$p. is known in used condition showing the lemon omitted.

Special First Day of Issue Postmarks

British Post Office Philatelic Bureau, Edinburgh (Type D, see Introduction)	4·50
Bethlehem, Llandeilo, Carms	7·50
Canterbury	8·00

WHITE CHALK-SURFACED PAPER. From No. 897 all issues, with the exception of Nos. 940/8, were printed on fluorescent white paper, giving a stronger chalk reaction than the original cream paper.

384 Sir James Clark Ross

385 Sir Martin Frobisher

386 Henry Hudson

387 Capt. Scott

(Des Marjorie Saynor. Queen's head printed in gold and then embossed)

1972 (16 Feb). **British Polar Explorers.** *Two phosphor bands. P* 14 × 15.

897 **384**	3p.	yellow-brown, indigo, slate-black, flesh, lemon, rose, brt blue & gold	10	10
	a.	Gold (Queen's head) omitted	60·00	
	b.	Slate-black (hair, etc.) omitted	£2250	
	c.	Lemon omitted	£2000	
	Ed.	Embossing omitted	30·00	
	Ee.	Gold (Queen's head) & embossing omitted	75·00	
	Ey.	Phosphor omitted	2·00	
	Eya.	Embossing and phosphor omitted	23·00	
898 **385**	5p.	salmon, flesh, purple-brown, ochre, black & gold	20	20
	a.	Gold (Queen's head) omitted	90·00	
	Eb.	Embossing omitted	15·00	
	Ey.	Phosphor omitted	9·00	
	Eya.	Gold and phosphor omitted	£110	
	Eyb.	Embossing and phosphor omitted		
899 **386**	$7\frac{1}{2}$p.	reddish violet, blue, dp slate, yellow-brown, buff, black & gold	50	50
	a.	Gold (Queen's head) omitted	£200	
	Ey.	Phosphor omitted	16·00	
900 **387**	9p.	dull blue, ultramarine, black, greenish yellow, pale pink, rose-red & gold	90	90
	Ey.	Phosphor omitted	£275	
		Set of 4	1·50	1·50
		First Day Cover		6·00
		Presentation Pack	5·00	

An example of the 3p. is known used on piece with the flesh colour omitted.

Special First Day of Issue Postmarks

Philatelic Bureau, Edinburgh	7·50
London WC	9·50

388 Statuette of Tutankhamun

389 19th-century Coastguard

390 Ralph Vaughan Williams and Score

(Des Rosalind Dease (3p.), F. Wegner ($7\frac{1}{2}$p.), C. Abbott (9p.). Queen's head printed in gold and then embossed ($7\frac{1}{2}$p., 9p.))

1972 (26 Apr). **General Anniversaries.** *Events described on stamps. Two phosphor bands. P* 15 × 14.

901 **388**	3p.	black, grey, gold, dull bistre-brown, blackish brown, pale stone & lt brown	10	10
902 **389**	$7\frac{1}{2}$p.	pale yellow, new blue, slate-blue, violet-blue, slate & gold	50	50
	Ea.	Embossing omitted		
	Ey.	Phosphor omitted	£250	
903 **390**	9p.	bistre-brown, black, sage-green, dp slate, yellow-ochre, brown & gold	50	50
	a.	Gold (Queen's head) omitted	£1250	
	b.	Brown (facial features) omitted	£750	
	c.	Deep slate omitted		
	Ed.	Embossing omitted		
	Ey.	Phosphor omitted	25·00	
		Set of 3	1·00	1·00
		First Day Cover		3·00
		Presentation Pack	4·50	

Special First Day of Issue Postmarks

Philatelic Bureau, Edinburgh	3·50
London EC	4·75

391 St. Andrew's, Greensted-juxta-Ongar, Essex

392 All Saints, Earls Barton, Northants

393 St. Andrew's, Letheringsett, Norfolk

394 St. Andrew's, Helpringham, Lincs

395 St. Mary the Virgin, Huish Episcopi, Somerset

(Des R. Maddox. Queen's head printed in gold and then embossed)

1972 (21 June). **British Architecture. Village Churches.** *Ordinary paper. Two phosphor bands. P 14 × 15.*

904 **391** 3p. violet-blue, black, lt yellow-olive, emerald-green, orange-vermilion & gold 10 10
 a. Gold (Queen's head) omitted .... 75·00
 Eb. Embossing omitted .... 23·00
 Ey. Phosphor omitted .... 3·00
 Eya. Gold (Queen's head) & phosphor omitted £110
 Eyb. Embossing & phosphor omitted .... 12·00

905 **392** 4p. dp yellow-olive, black, emerald, violet-blue, orange-vermilion and gold 20 20
 a. Gold (Queen's head) omitted £2500
 b. Violet-blue omitted £110
 Ec. Embossing omitted .... 8·00
 Ey. Phosphor omitted .... 12·00

906 **393** 5p. dp emerald, black, royal blue, lt yellow-olive, orange-vermilion & gold 20 25
 a. Gold (Queen's head) omitted £150
 Eb. Embossing omitted .... 30·00
 Ey. Phosphor omitted .... 18·00

907 **394** 7½p. orange-red, black, dp yellow-olive, royal blue, lt emerald & gold 70 80
 Ey. Phosphor omitted .... 11·00

908 **395** 9p. new blue, black, emerald-green, dp yellow-olive, orange-vermilion & gold ... 75 90
 Ea. Embossing omitted .... 12·00
 Ey. Phosphor omitted .... 17·00
 Set of 5 .... 1·75 2·00
 First Day Cover .... 5·00
 Presentation Pack .... 5·50

Nos. 905a and 906a only exist with the phosphor omitted.

An example of the 3p. is known used on piece with the orange-vermilion omitted.

Special First Day of Issue Postmarks

Philatelic Bureau, Edinburgh .... 5·50
Canterbury .... 7·00

"Belgica '72" Souvenir Pack

1972 (24 June). *Comprises Nos. 894/6 and 904/8.*
CP908*b* Souvenir Pack .... 7·00

This pack was specially produced for sale at the "Belgica '72" Stamp Exhibition, held in Brussels between 24 June and 9 July. It contains information on British stamps with a religious theme with text in English, French and Flemish, and was put on sale at Philatelic Bureaux in Britain on 26 June.

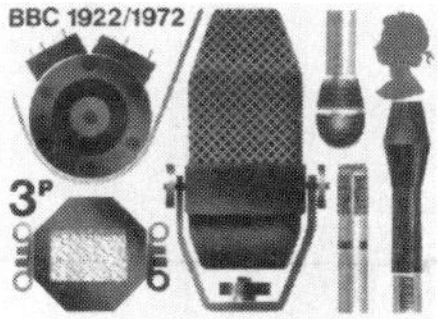

396 Microphones, 1924–69

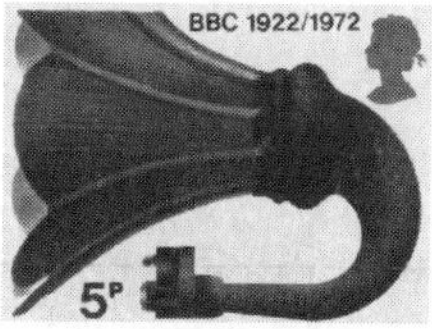

387 Horn Loudspeaker

398 T.V. Camera, 1972

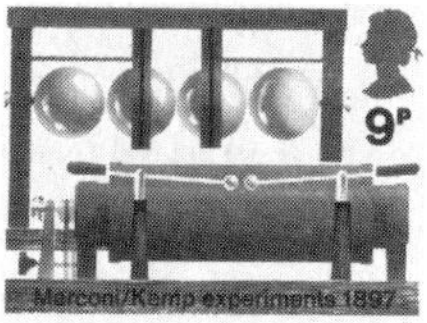

399 Oscillator and Spark Transmitter, 1897

(Des D. Gentleman)

1972 (13 Sept). **Broadcasting Anniversaries. 75th Anniv of Marconi and Kemp's Radio Experiments** (*9p.*), **and 50th Anniv of Daily Broadcasting by the B.B.C.** (*others*). *Two phosphor bands. P 15 × 14.*

909 **396** 3p. pale brown, black, grey, greenish yellow & brownish slate 10 10
 a. Greenish yellow (terminals) omitted £2000

910 **397**	5p.	brownish slate, lake-brown, salmon, lt brown, black & red-brown	15	20
	Ey.	Phosphor omitted	3·25	
	Eya.	Phosphor on back but omitted on front	38·00	
911 **398**	7½p.	lt grey, slate, brownish slate, magenta & black	75	75
	a.	Brownish slate (Queen's head) omitted	†	£2000
	Ey.	Phosphor omitted	7·00	
912 **399**	9p.	lemon, brown, brownish slate, dp brownish slate, bluish slate & black	75	75
	a.	Brownish slate (Queen's head) omitted	£1500	
	Ey.	Phosphor omitted	12·00	
		Set of 4	1·50	1·50
		First Day Cover		4·00
		Presentation Pack	3·75	

In addition to the generally issued Presentation Pack a further pack exists inscribed "1922–1972". This pack of stamps commemorating the 50th Anniversary of the B.B.C. was specially produced as a memento of the occasion for the B.B.C. staff. It was sent with the good wishes of the Chairman and Board of Governors, the Director-General and Board of Management. The pack contains Nos. 909/11 only (*Price* £35).

No. 911a is only found in first day covers posted from the Philatelic Bureau in Edinburgh.

Special First Day of Issue Postmarks

Philatelic Bureau, Edinburgh .... 4·75
London W1 .... 9·50

400 Angel holding Trumpet

401 Angel playing Lute

402 Angel playing Harp

(Des Sally Stiff. Photo and embossing)

1972 (18 Oct). **Christmas.** *One centre phosphor band* (2½*p*.) *or two phosphor bands (others). P* 14 × 15.

913 **400**	2½p.	cerise, pale reddish brown, yellow-orange, orange-vermilion, lilac, gold, red-brown & dp grey	10	15
	a.	Gold omitted	£250	
	Eb.	Embossing omitted	9·00	
	c.	Dp grey omitted		
	Ey.	Phosphor omitted	7·00	
914 **401**	3p.	ultramarine, lavender, lt turquoise-blue, brt green, gold, red-brown & bluish violet	10	15
	a.	Red-brown omitted	£500	
	b.	Brt green omitted	70·00	
	c.	Bluish violet omitted	75·00	
	Ed.	Embossing omitted	5·00	
	Ey.	Phosphor omitted	3·00	
	Eya.	Embossing and phosphor omitted	8·00	
915 **402**	7½p.	dp brown, pale lilac, lt cinnamon, ochre, gold, red-brown & blackish violet	90	8(
	a.	Ochre omitted	55·00	
	Eb.	Embossing omitted	10·00	
	Ey.	Phosphor omitted	7·00	
	Eya.	Embossing and phosphor omitted	20·00	
		Set of 3	1·00	1·0
		First Day Cover		3·0
		Presentation Pack	2·75	

The gold printing on the 3p. is from two cylinders: 1E and 1F. Examples have been seen with the gold of the 1F cylinder omitted, but these are difficult to detect on single stamps.

Special First Day of Issue Postmarks

Philatelic Bureau, Edinburgh .... 3·50
Bethlehem, Llandeilo, Carms .... 5·50

403 Queen Elizabeth and Duke of Edinburgh

404 "Europe"

(Des J. Matthews from photo by N. Parkinson)

1972 (20 Nov). **Royal Silver Wedding.** *"All-over" phosphor (3p.) or without phosphor (20p.) P 14 × 15.*

I. "REMBRANDT" Machine

916	**403**	3p. brownish black, dp blue & silver	25	25
		a. Silver omitted	£300	
917		20p. brownish black, reddish purple & silver	1·00	1·00

II. "JUMELLE" Machine

918	**403**	3p. brownish black, dp blue & silver	20	25
		Set of 2	1·25	1·25
		Gutter Pair (No. 918)	1·00	
		Traffic Light Gutter Pair	20·00	
		First Day Cover		2·00
		Presentation Pack	2·50	
		Presentation Pack (Japanese)	3·50	
		Souvenir Book	3·00	

The souvenir book is a twelve-page booklet containing photographs)f the Royal Wedding and other historic events of the royal family and ıccompanying information.

The 3p. "JUMELLE" has a lighter shade of the brownish black than he 3p. "REMBRANDT". It also has the brown cylinders less deeply ·tched, which can be distinguished in the Duke's face which is slightly ghter, and in the Queen's hair where the highlights are sharper.

p. "REMBRANDT". Cyls. 3A–1B–11C no dot. Sheets of 100 (10 x 10).
p. "JUMELLE". Cyls. 1A–1B–3C dot and no dot. Sheets of 100 (two anes 5 x 10, separated by gutter margin).

Special First Day of Issue Postmarks

Philatelic Bureau, Edinburgh	3·75
Windsor, Berks	7·50

ollectors Pack 1972

972 (20 Nov). *Comprises Nos. 897/917.*

P918*a*	Collectors Pack	25·00

(Des P. Murdoch)

973 (3 Jan). **Britain's Entry into European Communities.** *Two phosphor bands. P 14 × 15.*

19	**404**	3p. dull orange, brt rose-red, ultramarine, lt lilac & black	10	10
20		5p. new blue, brt rose-red, ultramarine, cobalt-blue & black	25	50
		a. Pair. Nos. 920/1	1·25	1·50
21		5p. lt emerald-green, brt rose-red, ultramarine, cobalt-blue & black	25	50
		Set of 3	1·25	1·00
		First Day Cover		3·00
		Presentation Pack	2·50	

Nos. 920/1 were printed horizontally *se-tenant* throughout the sheet.

Special First Day of Issue Postmark

Philatelic Bureau, Edinburgh	4·00

405 Oak Tree

(Des D. Gentleman)

1973 (28 Feb). **Tree Planting Year. British Trees (1st issue).** *Two phosphor bands. P 15 × 14.*

922	**405**	9p. brownish black, apple-green, dp olive, sepia, blackish green & brownish grey	50	50
		a. Brownish black (value & inscr) omitted	£400	
		b. Brownish grey (Queen's head) omitted	£250	
		Ey. Phosphor omitted	80·00	
		First Day Cover		2·50
		Presentation Pack	2·50	

See also No. 949.

Special First Day of Issue Postmark

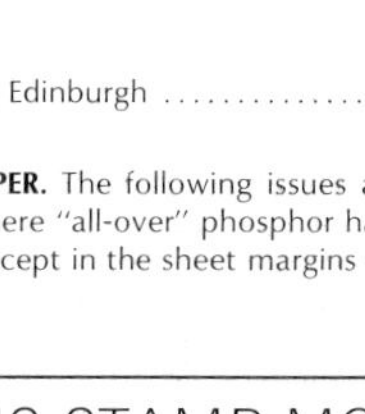

Philatelic Bureau, Edinburgh	4·50

CHALK-SURFACED PAPER. The following issues are printed on chalk-surfaced paper but where "all-over" phosphor has been applied there is no chalk reaction except in the sheet margins outside the phosphor area.

406 David Livingstone

407 H. M. Stanley

T **406**/**7** were printed together, horizontally *se-tenant* within the sheet

408 Sir Francis Drake

409 Walter Raleigh

410 Charles Sturt

(Des Marjorie Saynor. Queen's head printed in gold and then embossed)

1973 (18 Apr). **British Explorers.** *"All-over" phosphor. P* 14 × 15.

923	**406**	3p. orange-yellow, lt orange-brown, grey-black, lt turquoise-blue, turquoise-blue & gold	25	20
		a. Pair. Nos. 923/4	1·00	1·25
		b. Gold (Queen's head) omitted	40·00	
		c. Turquoise-blue (background & inscr) omitted	£350	
		d. Lt orange-brown omitted	£300	
		Ee. Embossing omitted	22·00	
924	**407**	3p. orange-yellow, lt orange-brown, grey-black, lt turquoise-blue, turquoise-blue & gold	25	20
		b. Gold (Queen's head) omitted	40·00	
		c. Turquoise-blue (background & inscr) omitted	£350	
		d. Lt orange-brown omitted	£300	
		Ee. Embossing omitted	22·00	
925	**408**	5p. lt flesh, chrome-yellow, orange-yellow, sepia, brownish grey, grey-black, violet-blue & gold	20	30
		a. Gold (Queen's head) omitted	90·00	
		b. Grey-black omitted	£500	
		c. Sepia omitted	£450	
		Ed. Embossing omitted	8·00	
926	**409**	7½p. lt flesh, reddish brown, sepia, ultramarine, grey-black, brt lilac & gold	20	30
		a. Gold (Queen's head) omitted	£1750	
		b. Ultramarine (eyes) omitted	£2500	
927	**410**	9p. flesh, pale stone, grey-blue, grey-black, brown-grey, Venetian red, brown-red & gold	25	40
		a. Gold (Queen's head) omitted	90·00	
		b. Brown-grey printing double ... *from*	£800	
		c. Grey-black omitted	£1000	
		d. Brown-red (rivers on map) omitted	£500	
		Ee. Embossing omitted	25·00	
		Set of 5	1·50	1·25
		First Day Cover		4·50
		Presentation Pack	3·50	

Caution is needed when buying missing gold heads in this issue as they can be removed by using a hard eraser, etc., but this invariably affects the "all-over" phosphor. Genuine examples have the phosphor intact. Used examples off cover cannot be distinguished as much of the phosphor is lost in the course of floating.

In the 5p. value the missing grey-black affects the doublet, which appears as brownish grey, and the lace ruff, which is entirely missing. The missing sepia affects only Drake's hair, which appears much lighter.

The double printing of the brown-grey (cylinder 1F) on the 9p., is a most unusual type of error to occur in a multicoloured photogravure issue. Two sheets are known and it is believed that they stuck to the cylinder and went through a second time. This would result in the following two sheets missing the colour but at the time of going to press this error has not been reported. The second print is slightly askew and more prominent in the top half of the sheets. Examples from the upper part of the sheet showing a clear double impression of the facial features are worth a substantial premium over the price quoted.

Special First Day of Issue Postmark

Philatelic Bureau, Edinburgh .... 7·50

First Day of Issue handstamps were provided at Blantyre, Glasgow, and Denbigh for this issue.

411

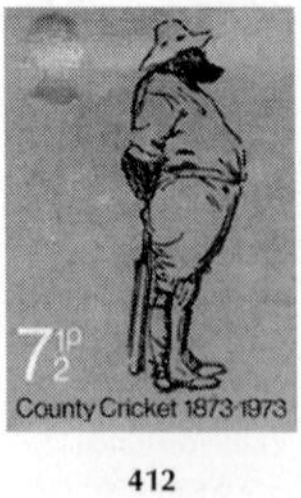

412

413

(T **411**/**13** show sketches of W.G. Grace by Harry Furniss)

(Des E. Ripley. Queen's head printed in gold and then embossed)

1973 (16 May). **County Cricket 1873–1973.** *"All-over" phosphor. P* 14 × 15.

928 **411** 3p. black, ochre & gold 10 10
a. Gold (Queen's head) omitted £1800
Eb. Embossing omitted .... 10·00
929 **412** 7½p. black, light sage-green & gold 80 70
Eb. Embossing omitted .... 19·00
930 **413** 9p. black, cobalt & gold .... 1·00 90
Eb. Embossing omitted .... 60·00
Set of 3 .... 1·75 1·50
First Day Cover .... 3·50
Presentation Pack .... 3·50
Souvenir Book .... 6·25
P.H.Q. Card (No. 928) .... 48·00 £140

The souvenir book is a 24-page illustrated booklet containing a history of County Cricket with text by John Arlott.

The P.H.Q. card did not become available until mid-July. The used price quoted is for an example used in July or August 1973.

Special First Day of Issue Postmarks

Philatelic Bureau, Edinburgh .... 4·25
Lords, London NW .... 7·00

414 "Self-portrait" (Reynolds)

415 "Self-portrait" (Raeburn)

416 "Nelly O'Brien" (Reynolds)

417 "Rev. R. Walker (The Skater)" (Raeburn)

(Des S. Rose. Queen's head printed in gold and then embossed)

1973 (4 July). **British Paintings. 250th Birth Anniv of Sir Joshua Reynolds and 150th Death Anniv of Sir Henry Raeburn.** *"All-over" phosphor. P* 14 × 15.

931 **414** 3p. rose, new blue, jet-black, magenta, greenish yellow, black, ochre & gold ... 10 10
a. Gold (Queen's head) omitted .... 60·00
Ec. Gold (Queen's head) & embossing omitted .... 65·00
932 **415** 5p. cinnamon, greenish yellow, new blue, lt magenta, black, yellow-olive & gold 20 25
a. Gold (Queen's head) omitted .... 75·00
b. Greenish yellow omitted £350
Ec. Embossing omitted .... 18·00
933 **416** 7½p. greenish yellow, new blue, lt magenta, black, cinnamon & gold 55 50
a. Gold (Queen's head) omitted .... 75·00
b. Cinnamon omitted £4000
Ec. Embossing omitted .... 15·00
934 **417** 9p. brownish rose, black, dull rose, pale yellow, brownish grey, pale blue & gold 60 60
b. Brownish rose omitted .... 30·00
Ec. Embossing omitted £100
Set of 4 .... 1·25 1·25
First Day Cover .... 2·75
Presentation Pack .... 2·75

Special First Day of Issue Postmark

Philatelic Bureau, Edinburgh .... 4·50

418 Court Masque Costumes

419 St. Paul's Church, Covent Garden

420 Prince's Lodging, Newmarket **421** Court Masque Stage Scene

T **418/19** and T **420/1** were printed horizontally *se-tenant* within the sheet.

(Des Rosalind Dease. Litho and typo B.W.)

1973 (15 Aug). **400th Birth Anniv of Inigo Jones (architect and designer).** *"All-over" phosphor. P* 15 × 14.

935	**418**	3p.	dp mauve, black & gold	10	15
		a.	Pair. Nos. 935/6	35	40
		Eab.	Dp mauve ptg double (pair)		
		Ec.	9 mm. phosphor band*	12·00	
936	**419**	3p.	dp brown, black & gold	10	15
937	**420**	5p.	blue, black & gold	40	45
		a.	Pair. Nos. 937/8	1·50	1·50
		Ec.	9 mm. phosphor band*	15·00	
938	**421**	5p.	grey-olive, black & gold	40	45
			Set of 4	1·60	1·10
			First Day Cover		2·75
			Presentation Pack	3·75	
			P.H.Q. Card (No. 936)	£150	95·00

*On part of the printings for both values the "all-over" phosphor band missed the first vertical row and a 9 mm. phosphor band was applied to correct this.

Special First Day of Issue Postmark

Philatelic Bureau, Edinburgh .... 4·50

422 Palace of Westminster seen from Whitehall

423 Palace of Westminster seen from Millbank

(Des R. Downer. Recess and typo B.W.)

1973 (12 Sept). **19th Commonwealth Parliamentary Conference.** *"All-over" phosphor. P* 15 × 14.

939	**422**	8p.	black, brownish grey & stone	50	60
940	**423**	10p.	gold & black	50	40
			Set of 2	1·00	1·00
			First Day Cover		2·50
			Presentation Pack	2·50	
			Souvenir Book	5·00	
			P.H.Q. Card (No. 939)	40·00	90·00

The souvenir book is a twelve-page booklet containing a history of the Palace of Westminster.

Special First Day of Issue Postmark

Philatelic Bureau, Edinburgh .... 3·50

424 Princess Anne and Capt. Mark Phillips

(Des C. Clements and E. Hughes from photo by Lord Litchfield)

1973 (14 Nov). **Royal Wedding.** *"All-over" phosphor. P* 15 × 14.

941	**424**	3½p.	dull violet & silver	10	10
		a.	Imperf (horiz pair)	£1000	
942		20p.	dp brown & silver	90	90
		a.	Silver omitted	£1200	
			Set of 2	1·00	1·00
			Set of 2 Gutter Pairs	4·00	
			Set of 2 Traffic Light Gutter Pairs	95·00	
			First Day Cover		2·50
			Presentation Pack	2·50	
			P.H.Q. Card (No. 941)	7·50	20·00

Special First Day of Issue Postmarks

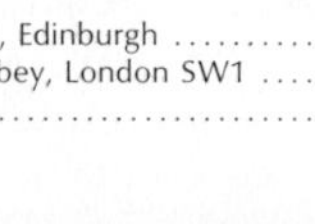

Philatelic Bureau, Edinburgh .... 3·00
Westminster Abbey, London SW1 .... 6·00
Windsor, Berks .... 6·00

425

426

427

428

429

T **425/9** depict the carol "Good King Wenceslas" and were printed horizontally *se-tenant* within the sheet.

430 Good King Wenceslas, the Page and Peasant

(Des D. Gentleman)

1973 (28 Nov). **Christmas.** *One centre phosphor band (3p.) or "all-over" phosphor (3½p.). P* 15 × 14.

943	**425**	3p.	grey-black, blue, brownish grey, lt brown, brt rose-red, turquoise-green, salmon-pink & gold	15	15
		a.	Strip of 5. Nos. 943/7	2·75	3·00
		b.	Imperf (horiz strip of 5)	£1250	
		Eg.	Gum arabic	20	
		Ega.	Strip of 5. Nos. 943Eg/7Eg	2·75	
		Egb.	Imperf (strip of 5. Nos. 943Eg/7Eg)		
944	**426**	3p.	grey-black, violet-blue, slate, brown, rose-red, rosy mauve, turquoise-green, salmon-pink & gold	15	15
		a.	Rosy mauve omitted	£625	
		Eg.	Gum arabic	20	
945	**427**	3p.	grey-black, violet-blue, slate, brown, rose-red, rosy mauve, turquoise-green, salmon-pink & gold	15	15
		a.	Rosy mauve omitted	£625	
		Eg.	Gum arabic	20	
946	**428**	3p.	grey-black, violet-blue, slate, brown, rose-red, rosy mauve, turquoise-green, salmon-pink & gold	15	15
		a.	Rosy mauve omitted	£625	
		Eg.	Gum arabic	20	
947	**429**	3p.	grey-black, violet-blue, slate, brown, rose-red, rosy mauve, turquoise-green, salmon-pink & gold	15	15
		a.	Rosy mauve omitted	£625	
		Eg.	Gum arabic	20	
948	**430**	3½p.	salmon-pink, grey-black, red-brown, blue, turquoise-green, brt rose-red, rosy mauve, lavender-grey & gold	15	15
		a.	Imperf (pair)	£400	
		b.	Grey-black (value, inscr, etc.) omitted	75·00	
		c.	Salmon-pink omitted	70·00	
		d.	Blue (leg, robes) omitted	£130	
		e.	Rosy mauve (robe at right) omitted	80·00	
		f.	Blue and rosy mauve omitted	£250	
		g.	Brt rose-red (King's robe) omitted	75·00	
		h.	Red-brown (logs, basket, etc.) omitted		
		i.	Turquoise-green (leg, robe, etc.) omitted	£2000	
		j.	Gold (background) omitted	†	£750
			Set of 6	2·75	80
			First Day Cover		3·50
			Presentation Pack	3·25	

Examples of No. 948j are only known used on covers from Gloucester. The 3½p. has also been seen with the lavender-grey omitted used on piece.

The 3p. and 3½p. are normally with PVA gum with added dextrin, but the 3½p. also exists with normal PVA gum.

Special First Day of Issue Postmarks

Philatelic Bureau, Edinburgh	3·75
Bethlehem, Llandeilo, Carms	7·50

Collectors Pack 1973

1973 (28 Nov). *Comprises Nos.* 919/48.

CP948*k*	Collectors Pack	23·00

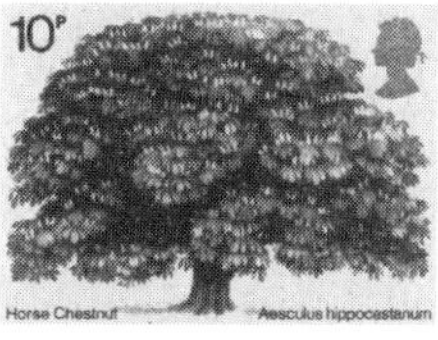

431 Horse Chestnut

(Des D. Gentleman)

1974 (27 Feb). **British Trees (2nd issue).** *"All-over" phosphor. P* 15 × 14.

949	**431**	10p.	lt emerald, brt green, greenish yellow, brown-olive, black & brownish grey	50	50
			Gutter Pair	3·00	
			Traffic Light Gutter Pair	60·00	
			First Day Cover		2·50
			Presentation Pack	2·25	
			P.H.Q. Card	£110	70·00

Special First Day of Issue Postmark

Philatelic Bureau, Edinburgh .... 4·50

432 First Motor Fire-engine, 1904

433 Prize-winning Fire-engine, 1863

434 First Steam Fire-engine, 1830

435 Fire-engine, 1766

(Des D. Gentleman)

1974 (24 Apr). **Bicentenary of the Fire Prevention (Metropolis) Act.** *"All-over" phosphor. P* 15 × 14.

950	**432**	3½p.	grey-black, orange-yellow, greenish yellow, dull rose, ochre & grey	10	10
		a.	Imperf (pair)	£800	
951	**433**	5½p.	greenish yellow, dp rosy magenta, orange-yellow, lt emerald, grey-black & grey	25	25
952	**434**	8p.	greenish yellow, lt blue-green, lt greenish blue, lt chestnut, grey-black & grey	35	35
953	**435**	10p.	grey-black, pale reddish brown, lt brown, orange-yellow & grey	40	40
			Set of 4	1·00	1·00
			Set of 4 Gutter Pairs	4·00	
			Set of 4 Traffic Light Gutter Pairs	60·00	
			First Day Cover		3·50
			Presentation Pack	3·00	
			P.H.Q. Card (No. 950)	£120	70·00

The 3½p. exists with ordinary PVA gum.

Special First Day of Issue Postmark

Philatelic Bureau, Edinburgh .... 4·50

436 P & O Packet, *Peninsular*, 1888

437 Farman H.F. III Biplane, 1911

438 Airmail-blue Van and Postbox, 1930

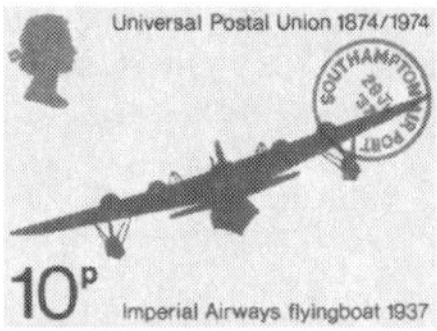

439 Imperial Airways Short S.21 Flying Boat *Maia* 1937

(Des Rosalind Dease)

1974 (12 June). **Centenary of Universal Postal Union.** *"All-over" phosphor. P* 15 × 14.

954	**436**	3½p.	dp brownish grey, brt mauve, grey-black & gold	10	10
955	**437**	5½p.	pale orange, lt emerald, grey-black & gold	20	25
956	**438**	8p.	cobalt, brown, grey-black & gold	30	35
957	**439**	10p.	dp brownish grey, orange, grey-black & gold	50	40
			Set of 4	1·00	1·00
			Set of 4 Gutter Pairs	4·00	
			Set of 4 Traffic Light Gutter Pairs	45·00	
			First Day Cover		2·50
			Presentation Pack	2·00	

Special First Day of Issue Postmark

Philatelic Bureau, Edinburgh .... 4·50

440 Robert the Bruce

441 Owain Glyndwr

442 Henry the Fifth

443 The Black Prince

(Des F. Wegner)

1974 (10 July). **Medieval Warriors.** *"All-over" phosphor. P* 15 × 14.

958	**440**	4½p.	greenish yellow, vermilion, slate-blue, red-brown, reddish brown, lilac-grey & gold	10	10
959	**441**	5½p.	lemon, vermilion, slate-blue, red-brown, reddish brown, olive-drab & gold	20	20
960	**442**	8p.	dp grey, vermilion, greenish yellow, new blue, red-brown, dp cinnamon & gold	50	40
961	**443**	10p.	vermilion, greenish yellow, new blue, red-brown, reddish brown, lt blue & gold	55	40
			Set of 4	1·25	1·00
			Set of 4 Gutter Pairs	6·00	
			Set of 4 Traffic Light Gutter Pairs	65·00	
			First Day Cover		3·50
			Presentation Pack	4·00	
			P.H.Q. Cards (set of 4)	30·00	22·00

Special First Day of Issue Postmark

Philatelic Bureau, Edinburgh .... 5·00

444 Churchill in Royal Yacht Squadron Uniform

445 Prime Minister, 1940

446 Secretary for War and Air, 1919

447 War Correspondent, South Africa, 1899

(Des C. Clements and E. Hughes)

1974 (9 Oct). **Birth Centenary of Sir Winston Churchill.** *"All-over" phosphor. P* 14 × 15.

962	**444**	4½p.	Prussian blue, pale turquoise-green & silver	15	15
963	**445**	5½p.	sepia, brownish grey & silver	30	25
964	**446**	8p.	crimson, lt claret & silver	60	50
965	**447**	10p.	lt brown, stone & silver	65	50
			Set of 4	1·50	1·50
			Set of 4 Gutter Pairs	4·50	
			Set of 4 Traffic Light Gutter Pairs	40·00	
			First Day Cover		3·50
			Presentation Pack	2·00	
			Souvenir Book	2·75	
			P.H.Q. Card (No. 963)	6·00	12·00

The souvenir book consists of an illustrated folder containing a biography of Sir Winston.

Nos. 962/5 come with PVA gum containing added dextrin, but the 8p. also exists with normal PVA.

Special First Day of Issue Postmarks

Philatelic Bureau, Edinburgh .... 5·50
Blenheim, Woodstock, Oxford .... 6·50
House of Commons, London SW .... 6·50

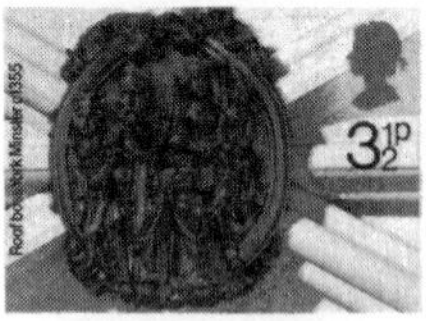

448 "Adoration of the Magi" (York Minster, *circa* 1355)

449 "The Nativity" (St. Helen's Church, Norwich, *circa* 1480)

450 "Virgin and Child" (Ottery St. Mary Church, *circa* 1350)

451 "Virgin and Child" (Worcester Cathedral, *circa* 1224)

(Des Peter Hatch Partnership)

1974 (27 Nov). **Christmas. Church Roof Bosses.** *One phosphor band (3½p.) or "all-over" phosphor (others). P 15 × 14.*

966	**448**	3½p.	gold, lt new blue, lt brown, grey-black & lt stone	10	10
		a.	Lt stone (background shading) omitted	£10000	
		Ey.	Phosphor omitted	9·00	
967	**449**	4½p.	gold, yellow-orange, rose-red, lt brown, grey-black & lt new blue	10	10
968	**450**	8p.	blue, gold, lt brown, rose-red, dull green & grey-black	45	45
969	**451**	10p.	gold, dull rose, grey-black, lt new blue, pale cinnamon & lt brown	50	50
			Set of 4	1·00	1·00
			Set of 4 Gutter Pairs	4·00	
			Set of 4 Traffic Light Gutter Pairs	40·00	
			First Day Cover		2·50
			Presentation Pack	1·75	

The phosphor band on the 3½p. was first applied down the centre of the stamp but during the printing this was deliberately placed to the right between the roof boss and the value; however, intermediate positions, due to shifts, are known.

Two used examples of the 3½p. have been reported with the light brown colour omitted.

Special First Day of Issue Postmarks

Philatelic Bureau, Edinburgh	3·75
Bethlehem, Llandeilo, Carms	6·50

Collectors Pack 1974

1974 (27 Nov). *Comprises Nos.* 949/69.

CP969*a*	Collectors Pack	8·50

452 Invalid in Wheelchair

(Des P. Sharland)

1975 (22 Jan). **Health and Handicap Funds.** *"All-over" phosphor. P* 15 × 14.

970	**452**	4½p.	+ 1½p. azure & grey-blue	25	25
			Gutter Pair	50	
			Traffic Light Gutter Pair	1·00	
			First Day Cover		1·25

Special First Day of Issue Postmark

Philatelic Bureau, Edinburgh	2·75

453 "Peace—Burial at Sea"

454 "Snowstorm—Steamer off a Harbour's Mouth"

455 "The Arsenal, Venice"

456 "St. Laurent"

(Des S. Rose)

1975 (19 Feb). **Birth Bicentenary of J. M. W. Turner (painter).** *"All-over" phosphor. P* 15 × 14.

971	**453**	4½p.	grey-black, salmon, stone, blue & grey	10	10
972	**454**	5½p.	cobalt, greenish yellow, lt yellow-brown, grey-black & rose	15	15
973	**455**	8p.	pale yellow-orange, greenish yellow, rose, cobalt & grey-black	40	40

974	**456**	10p. dp blue, lt yellow-ochre, lt brown, dp cobalt & grey-black	45	45
		Set of 4	1·00	1·00
		Set of 4 Gutter Pairs	2·50	
		Set of 4 Traffic Light Gutter Pairs	7·00	
		First Day Cover		3·00
		Presentation Pack	2·50	
		P.H.Q. Card (No. 972)	35·00	11·00

Special First Day of Issue Postmarks

Philatelic Bureau, Edinburgh	4·50
London WC	6·50

457 Charlotte Square, Edinburgh

458 The Rows, Chester

T **457**/**8** were printed horizontally *se-tenant* within the sheet.

459 Royal Observatory, Greenwich

460 St. George's Chapel, Windsor

461 National Theatre, London

(Des P. Gauld)

1975 (23 Apr). **European Architectural Heritage Year.** *"All-over" phosphor. P* 15 × 14.

975	**457**	7p. greenish yellow, brt orange, grey-black, red-brown, new blue, lavender & gold	30	30
		a. Pair. Nos. 975/6	80	90
976	**458**	7p. grey-black, greenish yellow, new blue, brt orange, red-brown & gold	30	30
977	**459**	8p. magenta, dp slate, pale magenta, lt yellow-olive, grey-black & gold	20	25
978	**460**	10p. bistre-brown, greenish yellow, dp slate, emerald-green, grey-black & gold	20	25
979	**461**	12p. grey-black, new blue, pale magenta & gold	20	35
		Set of 5	1·25	1·25
		Set of 5 Gutter Pairs	4·00	
		Set of 5 Traffic Light Gutter Pairs	16·00	
		First Day Cover		4·25
		Presentation Pack	3·50	
		P.H.Q. Cards (Nos. 975/7)	8·00	11·00

Special First Day of Issue Postmark

Philatelic Bureau, Edinburgh	6·50

462 Sailing Dinghies

463 Racing Keel Yachts

464 Cruising Yachts

465 Multihulls

(Des A. Restall. Recess and photo)

1975 (11 June). **Sailing.** *"All-over" phosphor. P* 15 × 14.

980	**462**	7p. black, bluish violet, scarlet, orange-vermilion, orange & gold	20	20
981	**463**	8p. black, orange-vermilion, orange, lavender, brt mauve, brt blue, dp ultramarine & gold	35	30
		a. Black omitted	55·00	
982	**464**	10p. black, orange, bluish emerald, lt olive-drab, chocolate & gold	40	30
983	**465**	12p. black, ultramarine, turquoise-blue, rose, grey, steel-blue & gold	45	35
		Set of 4	1·25	1·00
		Set of 4 Gutter Pairs	2·50	
		Set of 4 Traffic Light Gutter Pairs	24·00	
		First Day Cover		2·50
		Presentation Pack	1·50	
		P.H.Q. Card (No. 981)	4·50	10·00

On No. 981a the recess-printed black colour is completely omitted.

Special First Day of Issue Postmark

Philatelic Bureau, Edinburgh .... 3·50

A First Day of Issue handstamp was provided at Weymouth for this issue.

466 Stephenson's *Locomotion*, 1825

467 *Abbotsford*, 1876

468 *Caerphilly Castle*, 1923

469 High Speed Train, 1975

(Des B. Craker)

1975 (13 Aug). **150th Anniv of Public Railways.** *"All-over" phosphor. P* 15 × 14.

984	**466**	7p.	red-brown, grey-black, greenish yellow, grey & silver	20	20
985	**467**	8p.	brown, orange-yellow, vermilion, grey-black, grey & silver	45	35
986	**468**	10p.	emerald-green, grey-black, yellow-orange, vermilion, grey & silver	50	40
987	**469**	12p.	grey-black, pale lemon, vermilion, blue, grey & silver	55	45
			Set of 4	1·50	1·25
			Set of 4 Gutter Pairs	3·00	
			Set of 4 Traffic Light Gutter Pairs	11·00	
			First Day Cover		3·50
			Presentation Pack	2·75	
			Souvenir Book	3·00	
			P.H.Q. Cards (set of 4)	55·00	22·00

The souvenir book is an eight-page booklet containing a history of the railways.

Special First Day of Issue Postmarks

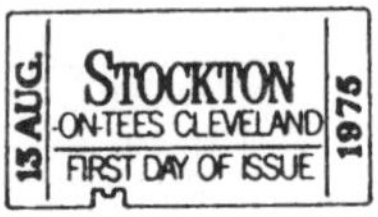

Philatelic Bureau, Edinburgh	5·00
Darlington, Co. Durham	9·00
Shildon, Co. Durham	9·00
Stockton-on-Tees, Cleveland	9·00

470 Palace of Westminster

(Des R. Downer)

1975 (3 Sept). **62nd Inter-Parliamentary Union Conference.** *"All-over" phosphor. P* 15 × 14.

988	**470**	12p.	lt new blue, black, brownish grey & gold	50	50
			Gutter Pair	1·00	
			Traffic Light Gutter Pair	3·00	
			First Day Cover		1·25
			Presentation Pack	1·25	

Special First Day of Issue Postmark

Philatelic Bureau, Edinburgh .... 2·75

471 Emma and Mr. Woodhouse (*Emma*)

472 Catherine Morland (*Northanger Abbey*)

473 Mr. Darcy (*Pride and Prejudice*)

474 Mary and Henry Crawford (*Mansfield Park*)

(Des Barbara Brown)

1975 (22 Oct). **Birth Bicentenary of Jane Austen (novelist).** *"All-over" phosphor. P* 14 × 15.

989	**471**	8½p.	blue, slate, rose-red, lt yellow, dull green, grey-black & gold	20	20
990	**472**	10p.	slate, brt magenta, grey, lt yellow, grey-black & gold	25	25
991	**473**	11p.	dull blue, pink, olive-sepia, slate, pale-greenish yellow, grey-black & gold	30	30
992	**474**	13p.	brt magenta, lt new blue, slate, buff, dull blue-green, grey-black & gold	35	35
			Set of 4	1·00	1·00
			Set of 4 Gutter Pairs	2·50	
			Set of 4 Traffic Light Gutter Pairs	7·00	
			First Day Cover		2·50
			Presentation Pack	2·25	
			P.H.Q. Cards (set of 4)	20·00	16·00

Special First Day of Issue Postmark

Philatelic Bureau, Edinburgh	3·75
Steventon, Basingstoke, Hants	4·50

475 Angels with Harp and Lute

476 Angel with Mandolin

477 Angel with Horn

478 Angel with Trumpet

(Des R. Downer)

1975 (26 Nov). **Christmas.** *One phosphor band* (6½*p.*), *phosphor-inked background* (8½*p.*), *"all-over" phosphor (others). P* 15 × 14.

993	**475**	6½p.	bluish violet, brt reddish violet, light lavender & gold	20	15
994	**476**	8½p.	turquoise-green, brt emerald-green, slate, lt turquoise-green & gold	20	20
995	**477**	11p.	vermilion, cerise, pink & gold	30	35
996	**478**	13p.	drab, brown, brt orange, buff & gold	40	40
			Set of 4	1·00	1·00
			Set of 4 Gutter Pairs	2·50	
			Set of 4 Traffic Light Gutter Pairs	7·00	
			First Day Cover		2·50
			Presentation Pack	2·00	

The 6½p. exists with both ordinary PVA gum and PVA containing added dextrin.

Special First Day of Issue Postmarks

Philatelic Bureau, Edinburgh	2·75
Bethlehem, Llandeilo, Dyfed	3·75

Collectors Pack 1975

1975 (26 Nov). *Comprises Nos.* 970/96.

CP996*a*	Collectors Pack	7·50

479 Housewife

480 Policeman

481 District Nurse

482 Industrialist

(Des P. Sharland)

1976 (10 Mar). **Telephone Centenary.** *"All-over" phosphor. P* 15 × 14.

997	**479**	8½p.	greenish blue, dp rose, black & blue	20	20
		a.	Dp rose (vase and picture frame) omitted	£2000	
998	**480**	10p.	greenish blue, black & yellow-olive	25	25
999	**481**	11p.	greenish blue, dp rose, black & brt mauve	30	30
1000	**482**	13p.	olive-brown, dp rose, black & orange-red	35	35
			Set of 4	1·00	1·00
			Set of 4 Gutter Pairs	2·50	
			Set of 4 Traffic Light Gutter Pairs	7·00	
			First Day Cover		2·50
			Presentation Pack	2·00	

Special First Day of Issue Postmark

Philatelic Bureau, Edinburgh .... 2·75

483 Hewing Coal (Thomas Hepburn)

484 Machinery (Robert Owen)

485 Chimney Cleaning (Lord Shaftesbury)

486 Hands clutching Prison Bars (Elizabeth Fry)

(Des D. Gentleman)

1976 (28 Apr). **Social Reformers.** *"All-over" phosphor. P* 15 × 14.

1001	**483**	8½p.	lavender-grey, grey-black, black & slate-grey	20	20
1002	**484**	10p.	lavender-grey, grey-black, grey & slate-violet	25	25
1003	**485**	11p.	black, slate-grey & drab	30	30
1004	**486**	13p.	slate-grey, black & dp dull green	35	35
			Set of 4	1·00	1·00
			Set of 4 Gutter Pairs	2·50	
			Set of 4 Traffic Light Gutter Pairs	7·00	
			First Day Cover		2·50
			Presentation Pack	2·25	
			P.H.Q. Card (No. 1001)	5·00	7·50

Special First Day of Issue Postmark

Philatelic Bureau, Edinburgh .... 2·75

487 Benjamin Franklin (bust by Jean-Jacques Caffieri)

(Des P. Sharland)

1976 (2 June). **Bicentenary of American Revolution.** *"All-over" phosphor. P* 14 × 15.

1005	**487**	11p.	pale bistre, slate-violet, pale blue-green, black & gold	50	5
			Gutter Pair	1·00	
			Traffic Light Gutter Pair	2·00	
			First Day Cover		1·5
			Presentation Pack	1·25	
			P.H.Q. Card	3·00	8·5

Special First Day of Issue Postmark

Philatelic Bureau, Edinburgh .... 2·00

488 "Elizabeth of Glamis"

489 "Grandpa Dickson"

490 *"Rosa Mundi"*

491 "Sweet Briar"

(Des Kristin Rosenberg)

1976 (30 June). **Centenary of Royal National Rose Society.** *"All-over" phosphor. P* 14 × 15.

1006	**488**	8½p.	brt rose-red, greenish yellow, emerald, grey-black & gold	20	20
1007	**489**	10p.	greenish yellow, brt green, reddish brown, grey-black & gold	30	30
1008	**490**	11p.	brt magenta, greenish yellow, emerald, grey-blue, grey-black & gold	55	50
1009	**491**	13p.	rose-pink, lake-brown, yellow-green, pale greenish yellow, grey-black & gold	60	40
			a. Value omitted*	£20000	
			Set of 4	1·50	1·25
			Set of 4 Gutter Pairs	3·00	
			Set of 4 Traffic Light Gutter Pairs	9·00	
			First Day Cover		2·50
			Presentation Pack	2·25	
			P.H.Q. Cards (set of 4)	28·00	11·00

*During repairs to the cylinder the face value on R.1/9 was temporarily covered with copper. This covering was inadvertently left in place during printing, but the error was discovered before issue and most examples were removed from the sheets. Two mint and one used examples have so far been reported, but only one of the mint remains in private hands.

Special First Day of Issue Postmark

Philatelic Bureau, Edinburgh .... 3·75

492 Archdruid

493 Morris Dancing

494 Scots Piper

495 Welsh Harpist

(Des Marjorie Saynor)

1976 (4 Aug). **British Cultural Traditions.** *"All-over" phosphor. P* 14 × 15.

1010	**492**	8½p.	yellow, sepia, brt rose, dull ultramarine, black & gold	20	20
1011	**493**	10p.	dull ultramarine, brt rose-red, sepia, greenish yellow, black & gold	25	25
1012	**494**	11p.	bluish green, yellow-brown, yellow-orange, black, brt rose-red & gold	30	30
1013	**495**	13p.	dull violet-blue, yellow-orange, yellow, black, bluish green & gold	35	35
			Set of 4	1·00	1·00
			Set of 4 Gutter Pairs	2·50	
			Set of 4 Traffic Light Gutter Pairs	8·50	
			First Day Cover		2·50
			Presentation Pack	2·00	
			P.H.Q. Cards (set of 4)	14·00	10·00

The 8½p. and 13p. commemorate the 800th anniversary of the Royal National Eisteddfod.

Special First Day of Issue Postmarks

Philatelic Bureau, Edinburgh .... 2·75
Cardigan, Dyfed .... 3·75

496 Woodcut from *The Canterbury Tales*

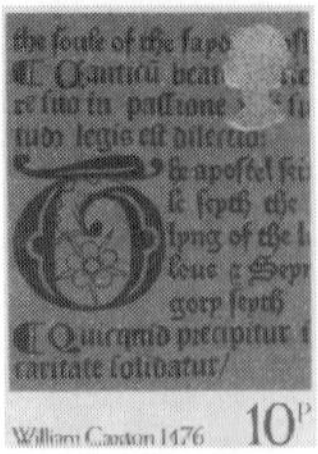

497 Extract from *The Tretyse of Love*

498 Woodcut from *The Game and Playe of Chesse*

499 Early Printing Press

(Des R. Gay. Queen's head printed in gold and then embossed)

1976 (29 Sept). **500th Anniv of British Printing.** *"All-over" phosphor. P* 14 × 15.

1014	**496**	$8\frac{1}{2}$p.	black, lt new blue & gold	20	20
1015	**497**	10p.	black, olive-green & gold	25	25
1016	**498**	11p.	black, brownish grey & gold	30	30
1017	**499**	13p.	chocolate, pale ochre & gold	35	35
			Set of 4	1·00	1·00
			Set of 4 Gutter Pairs	2·50	
			Set of 4 Traffic Light Gutter Pairs	7·00	
			First Day Cover		2·50
			Presentation Pack	2·50	
			P.H.Q. Cards (set of 4)	10·00	10·00

Special First Day of Issue Postmarks

Philatelic Bureau, Edinburgh	2·75
London SW1	3·50

500 Virgin and Child

501 Angel with Crown

502 Angel appearing to Shepherds

503 The Three Kings

(Des Enid Marx)

1976 (24 Nov). **Christmas. English Medieval Embroidery.** *One phosphor band* ($6\frac{1}{2}$*p.*) *or "all-over" phosphor (others). P* 15 × 14.

1018	**500**	$6\frac{1}{2}$p.	blue, bistre-yellow, brown & orange	15	15
			a. Imperf (pair)	£400	
1019	**501**	$8\frac{1}{2}$p.	sage-green, yellow, brown-ochre, chestnut & olive-black	20	20
1020	**502**	11p.	dp magenta, brown-orange, new blue, black & cinnamon	35	35
			a. Uncoated paper*	60·00	30·00
1021	**503**	13p.	bright purple, new blue, cinnamon, bronze-green & olive-grey	40	40
			Set of 4	1·00	1·00
			Set of 4 Gutter Pairs	2·50	
			Set of 4 Traffic Light Gutter Pairs	6·50	
			First Day Cover		2·50
			Presentation Pack	2·25	
			P.H.Q. Cards (set of 4)	3·00	8·00

*See footnote after No. 744.

Special First Day of Issue Postmarks

Philatelic Bureau, Edinburgh	2·75
Bethlehem, Llandeilo, Dyfed	3·50

Collectors Pack 1976

1976 (24 Nov). *Comprises Nos.* 997/1021.

CP1021a	Collectors Pack	10·00

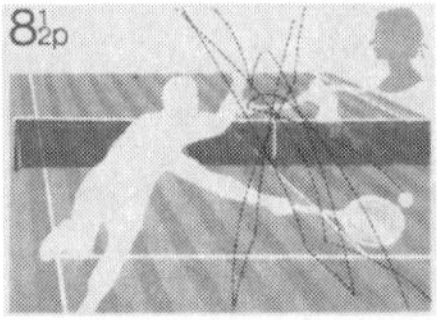

504 Lawn Tennis

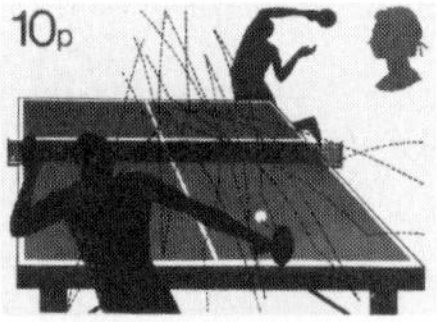

505 Table Tennis

506 Squash

507 Badminton

(Des A. Restall)

1977 (12 Jan). **Racket Sports.** *Phosphorised paper. P* 15 × 14.

1022	**504**	$8\frac{1}{2}$p.	emerald-green, black, grey & bluish green	20	20
		a.	Imperf (horiz pair)	£850	
1023	**505**	10p.	myrtle-green, black, grey-black & dp blue-green	35	25
1024	**506**	11p.	orange, pale yellow, black, slate-black & grey	40	30
1025	**507**	13p.	brown, grey-black, grey & brt reddish violet	45	35
			Set of 4	1·25	1·00
			Set of 4 Gutter Pairs	2·50	
			Set of 4 Traffic Light Gutter Pairs	6·50	
			First Day Cover		2·50
			Presentation Pack	2·00	
			P.H.Q. Cards (set of 4)	6·00	9·50

Special First Day of Issue Postmark

Philatelic Bureau, Edinburgh .... 2·75

508

1977 (2 Feb)–**87**. *P* 14 × 15.

1026	**508**	£1 brt yellow-green & blackish olive	3·00	20
		a. Imperf (pair)	£650	
1026*b*		£1.30 pale drab & dp greenish blue (3.8.83)	5·50	5·00
1026*c*		£1.33 pale mauve & grey-black (28.8.84)	6·00	6·00
1026*d*		£1.41 pale drab & dp greenish blue (17.9.85)	7·00	6·00
1026*e*		£1.50 pale mauve & grey-black (2.9.86)	5·50	4·00
1026*f*	**508**	£1.60 pale drab & dp greenish blue (15.9.87)	5·50	6·00
1027		£2 light emerald & purple-brown	5·50	75
1028		£5 salmon & chalky blue	13·00	2·00
		a. Imperf (vert pair)	£2750	
		Set of 8	45·00	27·00
		Set of 8 Gutter Pairs	£100	
		Set of 8 Traffic Light Gutter Pairs	£150	
		First Day Cover (1026, 1027/8)		8·00
		First Day Cover (1026*b*)		5·50
		First Day Cover (1026*c*)		6·00
		First Day Cover (1026*d*)		6·00
		First Day Cover (1026*e*)		4·00
		First Day Cover (1026*f*)		6·00
		Presentation Pack (1026, 1027/8)	22·00	
		Presentation Pack (1026*f*)	13·00	

Special First Day of Issue Postmarks
(for illustrations see Introduction)

Philatelic Bureau, Edinburgh (Type F) (£1, £2, £5)	8·50
Windsor, Berks (Type F) (£1, £2, £5)	22·00
Philatelic Bureau, Edinburgh (Type F) (£1.30)	5·50
Windsor, Berks (Type F) (£1.30)	8·00
British Philatelic Bureau, Edinburgh (Type F) (£1.33)	5·00
Windsor, Berks (Type F) (£1.33)	7·00
British Philatelic Bureau, Edinburgh (Type G) (£1.41)	5·50
Windsor, Berks (Type G) (£1.41)	7·00
British Philatelic Bureau, Edinburgh (Type G) (£1.50)	5·00
Windsor, Berks (Type G) (£1.50)	7·00
British Philatelic Bureau, Edinburgh (Type G) (£1.60)	4·50
Windsor, Berks (Type G) (£1.60)	6·00

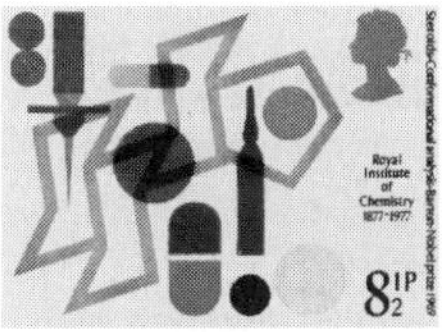

509 Steroids—Conformational Analysis

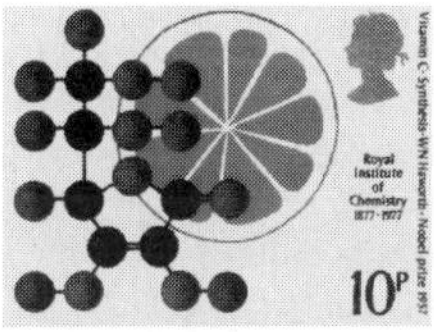

510 Vitamin C—Synthesis

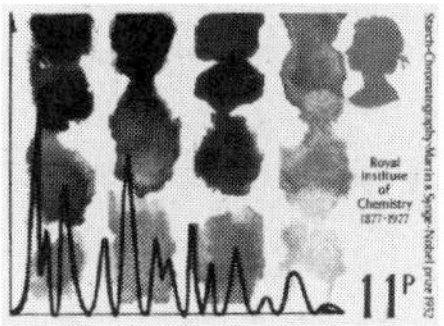

511 Starch—Chromatography

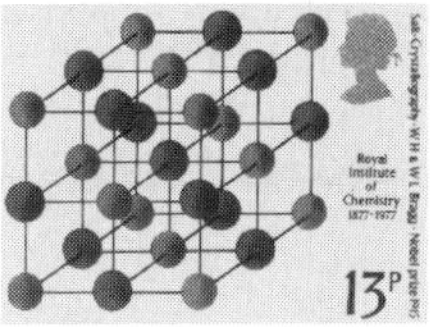

512 Salt—Crystallography

(Des J. Karo)

1977 (2 Mar). **Royal Institute of Chemistry Centenary.** *"All-over" phosphor. P* 15 × 14.

1029	**509**	$8\frac{1}{2}$p.	rosine, new blue, olive-yellow, brt mauve, yellow-brown, black & gold	20	20
		a.	Imperf (horiz pair)	£850	
1030	**510**	10p.	brt orange, rosine, new blue, brt blue, black & gold	30	30

1031	**511**	11p.	rosine, greenish yellow, new blue, dp violet, black & gold	30	30
1032	**512**	13p.	new blue, brt green, black & gold	30	30
			Set of 4	1·00	1·00
			Set of 4 Gutter Pairs	2·50	
			Set of 4 Traffic Light Gutter Pairs	6·00	
			First Day Cover		2·50
			Presentation Pack	2·50	
			P.H.Q. Cards (set of 4)	7·00	10·00

Special First Day of Issue Postmark

Philatelic Bureau, Edinburgh .... 3·00

513

514

515

516

T **513**/**16** differ in the decorations of "ER".

(Des R. Guyatt)

1977 (11 May–15 June). **Silver Jubilee.** *"All-over" phosphor. P* 15 × 14.

1033	**513**	8½p.	blackish green, black, silver, olive-grey & pale turquoise-green	20	20
			a. Imperf (pair)	£700	
1034		9p.	maroon, black, silver, olive-grey & lavender (15 June)	25	25
1035	**514**	10p.	blackish blue, black, silver, olive-grey & ochre	25	25
			a. Imperf (horiz pair)	£1300	
1036	**515**	11p.	brown-purple, black, silver, olive-grey & rose-pink	30	30
			a. Imperf (horiz pair)	£1300	
1037	**516**	13p.	sepia, black, silver, olive-grey & bistre-yellow	40	40
			a. Imperf (pair)	£1000	
			Set of 5	1·25	1·25
			Set of 5 Gutter Pairs	2·75	
			Set of 5 Traffic Light Gutter Pairs	4·50	
			First Day Covers (2)		3·50
			Presentation Pack (Nos. 1033, 1035/7)	2·00	
			Souvenir Book	4·00	
			P.H.Q. Cards (set of 5)	9·50	9·00

The souvenir book is a 16-page booklet containing a history of the Queen's reign.

Special First Day of Issue Postmarks

Philatelic Bureau, Edinburgh (1033, 1035/7) (11 May)	2·50
Philatelic Bureau, Edinburgh (1034) (15 June)	1·75
Windsor, Berks (1033, 1035/7) (11 May)	3·00
Windosr, Berks (1034) (15 June)	1·75

517 "Gathering of Nations"

(Des P. Murdoch. Recess and photo)

1977 (8 June). **Commonwealth Heads of Government Meeting, London.** *"All-over" phosphor. P* 14 × 15.

1038	**517**	13p.	black, blackish green, rose-carmine & silver	50	50
			Gutter Pair	1·00	
			Traffic Light Gutter Pair	1·25	
			First Day Cover		1·50
			Presentation Pack	1·00	
			P.H.Q. Card	2·25	4·50

Special First Day of Issue Postmarks

Philatelic Bureau, Edinburgh .... 1·75
London SW .... 1·75

518 Hedgehog

519 Brown Hare

520 Red Squirrel

521 Otter

522 Badger

T **518/22** were printed horizontally *se-tenant* within the sheet.

(Des P. Oxenham)

1977 (5 Oct). **British Wildlife.** *"All-over" phosphor. P* 14 × 15.

1039 **518** 9p. reddish brown, grey-black, pale lemon, brt turquoise-blue, brt magenta & gold 25 20
a. Horiz strip of 5. Nos. 1039/43 .... 1·75 2·00
b. Imperf (vert pair) £600
c. Imperf (horiz pair. Nos. 1039/40) £1000

1040 **519** 9p. reddish brown, grey-black, pale lemon, brt turquoise-blue, brt magenta & gold 25 20
1041 **520** 9p. reddish brown, grey-black, pale lemon, brt turquoise-blue, brt magenta & gold 25 20
1042 **521** 9p. reddish brown, grey-black, pale lemon, brt turquoise-blue, brt magenta & gold 25 20
1043 **522** 9p. grey-black, reddish brown, pale lemon, brt turquoise-blue, brt magenta & gold 25 20
Set of 5 .... 1·75 1·00
Gutter Strip of 10 .... 3·75
Traffic Light Gutter Strip of 10 .... 4·00
First Day Cover .... 2·75
Presentation Pack .... 2·50
P.H.Q. Cards (set of 5) .... 4·00 5·00

Special First Day of Issue Postmark

Philatelic Bureau, Edinburgh .... 3·50

523 "Three French Hens, Two Turtle Doves and a Partridge in a Pear Tree"

524 "Six Geese-a-laying, Five Gold Rings, Four Colly Birds"

525 "Eight Maids-a-milking, Seven Swans a-swimming"

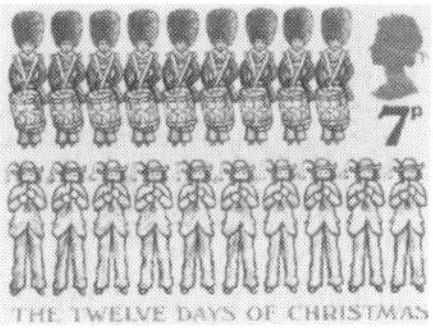

526 "Ten Pipers piping, Nine Drummers drumming"

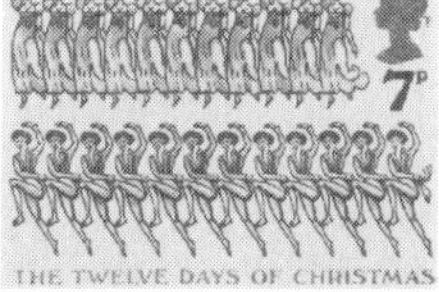

527 "Twelve Lords a-leaping, Eleven Ladies dancing"

T **523/7** depict the card "The Twelve Days of Christmas" and were printed horizontally *se-tenant* within the sheet.

528 "A Partridge in a Pear Tree"

(Des D. Gentleman)

1977 (23 Nov). **Christmas.** *One centre phosphor band (7p.) or "all-over" phosphor (9p.). P 15 × 14.*

1044	**523**	7p.	slate, grey, brt yellow-green, new blue, rose-red & gold	15	15
		a.	Horiz strip of 5. Nos. 1044/8	1·00	1·50
		ab.	Imperf (strip of 5. Nos. 1044/8)	£1100	
1045	**524**	7p.	slate, brt yellow-green, new blue & gold	15	15
1046	**525**	7p.	slate, grey, brt yellow-green, new blue, rose-red & gold	15	15
1047	**526**	7p.	slate, grey, brt yellow-green, new blue, rose-red & gold	15	15
1048	**527**	7p.	slate, grey, brt yellow-green, new blue, rose-red & gold	15	15
1049	**528**	9p.	pale brown, pale orange, brt emerald, pale greenish yellow, slate-black & gold	20	20
		a.	Imperf (pair)	£800	
			Set of 6	1·00	85
			Set of 6 Gutter Pairs	2·50	
			Traffic Light Gutter Pairs	4·50	
			First Day Cover		2·50
			Presentation Pack	2·25	
			P.H.Q. Cards (set of 6)	3·25	4·00

Special First Day of Issue Postmarks

Philatelic Bureau, Edinburgh	3·75
Bethlehem, Llandeilo, Dyfed	4·75

Collectors Pack 1977

1977 (23 Nov). *Comprises Nos.* 1022/5 *and* 1029/49.

CP1049*b*	Collectors Pack	6·50

529 Oil—North Sea Production Platform

530 Coal—Modern Pithead

531 Natural Gas—Flame Rising from Sea

532 Electricity—Nuclear Power Station and Uranium Atom

(Des P. Murdoch)

1978 (25 Jan). **Energy Resources.** *"All-over" phosphor. P* 14 × 15.

1050	**529**	9p.	dp brown, orange-vermilion, grey-black, greenish yellow, rose-pink, new blue & silver	25	20
1051	**530**	$10\frac{1}{2}$p.	lt emerald-green, grey-black, red-brown, slate-grey, pale apple-green & silver	25	30
1052	**531**	11p.	greenish blue, brt violet, violet-blue, blackish brown, grey-black & silver	30	30
1053	**532**	13p.	orange-vermilion, grey-black, dp brown, greenish yellow, lt brown, lt blue & silver	30	30
			Set of 4	1·00	1·00
			Set of 4 Gutter Pairs	2·50	
			Set of 4 Traffic Light Gutter Pairs	4·00	
			First Day Cover		1·50
			Presentation Pack	2·00	
			P.H.Q. Cards (set of 4)	3·00	4·00

Special First Day of Issue Postmark

Philatelic Bureau, Edinburgh	5·00

533 The Tower of London

534 Holyroodhouse

535 Caernarvon Castle

536 Hampton Court Palace

(Des R. Maddox (stamps), J. Matthews (miniature sheet))

1978 (1 Mar). **British Architecture. Historic Buildings.** *"All-over" phosphor. P* 15 × 14.

1054	**533**	9p.	black, olive-brown, new blue, brt green, lt yellow-olive & rose-red	25	20
1055	**534**	$10\frac{1}{2}$p.	black, brown-olive, orange-yellow, brt green, lt yellow-olive & violet-blue	25	30
1056	**535**	11p.	black, brown-olive, violet-blue, brt green, lt yellow-olive & dull blue	30	30
1057	**536**	13p.	black, orange-yellow, lake-brown, brt green & lt yellow-olive	30	30
			Set of 4	1·00	1·00
			Set of 4 Gutter Pairs	2·50	
			Set of 4 Traffic Light Gutter Pairs	4·00	
			First Day Cover		1·50
			Presentation Pack	2·00	
			P.H.Q. Cards (set of 4)	2·50	4·00
MS1058			121 × 89 mm. Nos. 1054/7 (*sold at* $53\frac{1}{2}$*p.*)	1·25	1·50
			a. Imperforate	£4250	
			b. Lt yellow-olive (Queen's head) omitted	£3500	
			c. Rose-red (Union Jack on 9p.) omitted	£2500	
			d. Orange-yellow omitted	£2500	
			e. New blue (Union Jack on 9p.) omitted	£10000	
			First Day Cover		2·50

The premium on No. **MS**1058 was used to support the London 1980 International Stamp Exhibition.

No. **MS**1058d is most noticeable on the $10\frac{1}{2}$p. (spheres absent on towers) and around the roadway and arch on the 13p.

Special First Day of Issue Postmarks

Philatelic Bureau, Edinburgh (stamps)	2·75
Philatelic Bureau, Edinburgh (miniature sheet)	4·50
London EC (stamps)	2·75
London EC (miniature sheet)	4·50

537 State Coach

538 St. Edward's Crown

HAVE YOU READ THE NOTES AT THE BEGINNING OF THIS CATALOGUE?

These often provide answers to the enquiries we receive.

539 The Sovereign's Orb

540 Imperial State Crown

(Des J. Matthews)

1978 (31 May). **25th Anniv of Coronation.** *"All-over" phosphor. P* 14 × 15.

1059	**537**	9p.	gold & royal blue	20	20
1060	**538**	$10\frac{1}{2}$p.	gold & brown-lake	25	30
1061	**539**	11p.	gold & dp dull green	30	30
1062	**540**	13p.	gold & reddish violet	35	30
			Set of 4	1·00	1·00
			Set of 4 Gutter Pairs	2·50	
			Set of 4 Traffic Light Gutter Pairs	4·00	
			First Day Cover		1·50
			Presentation Pack	2·25	
			Souvenir Book	4·00	
			P.H.Q. Cards (set of 4)	2·50	4·00

The souvenir book is a 16-page booklet illustrated with scenes from the Coronation.

Special First Day of Issue Postmarks

Philatelic Bureau, Edinburgh	2·75
London SW1	2·75

541 Shire Horse

542 Shetland Pony

543 Welsh Pony

544 Thoroughbred

(Des P. Oxenham)

1978 (5 July). **Horses.** *"All-over" phosphor. P* 15 × 14.

1063	**541**	9p.	black, pale reddish brown, grey-black, greenish yellow, lt blue, vermilion & gold	20	20
1064	**542**	$10\frac{1}{2}$p.	pale chestnut, magenta, brownish grey, greenish yellow, greenish blue, grey-black & gold	35	25
1065	**543**	11p.	reddish brown, black, lt green, greenish yellow, bistre, grey-black & gold	40	30
1066	**544**	13p.	reddish brown, pale reddish brown, emerald, greenish yellow, grey-black & gold	45	35
			Set of 4	1·25	1·00
			Set of 4 Gutter Pairs	2·50	
			Set of 4 Traffic Light Gutter Pairs	4·00	
			First Day Cover		1·50
			Presentation Pack	2·25	
			P.H.Q. Cards (set of 4)	2·50	5·00

Special First Day of Issue Postmarks

Philatelic Bureau, Edinburgh	2·75
Peterborough	3·50

545 "Penny-farthing" and 1884 Safety Bicycle

546 1920 Touring Bicycles

547 Modern Small-wheel Bicycles

548 1978 Road-racers

(Des F. Wegner)

1978 (2 Aug). **Centenaries of Cyclists Touring Club and British Cycling Federation.** *"All-over" phosphor. P* 15 × 14.

1067	**545**	9p.	brown, dp dull blue, rose-pink, pale olive, grey-black & gold	20	20
			a. Imperf (pair)	£350	
1068	**546**	$10\frac{1}{2}$p.	olive, pale yellow-orange, orange-vermilion, rose-red, lt brown, grey-black & gold	25	25
1069	**547**	11p.	orange-vermilion, greenish blue, lt brown, pale greenish yellow, dp grey, grey-black & gold	30	30
1070	**548**	13p.	new blue, orange-vermilion, lt brown, olive-grey, grey-black & gold	35	35
			a. Imperf (pair)	£750	
			Set of 4	1·00	1·00
			Set of 4 Gutter Pairs	2·50	
			Set of 4 Traffic Light Gutter Pairs	4·00	
			First Day Cover		1·50
			Presentation Pack	2·00	
			P.H.Q. Cards (set of 4)	1·50	3·25

Special First Day of Issue Postmarks

Philatelic Bureau, Edinburgh	2·75
Harrogate, North Yorkshire	2·75

549 Singing Carols round the Christmas Tree

550 The Waits

551 18th-century Carol Singers

552 "The Boar's Head Carol"

(Des Faith Jaques)

1978 (22 Nov). **Christmas.** *One centre phosphor band (7p.) or "all-over" phosphor (others). P* 15 × 14.

1071	**549**	7p.	brt green, greenish yellow, magenta, new blue, black & gold	20	2(
			a. Imperf (vert pair)	£350	
1072	**550**	9p.	magenta, greenish yellow, new blue, sage-green, black & gold	25	2:
			a. Imperf (pair)	£750	
1073	**551**	11p.	magenta, new blue, greenish yellow, yellow-brown, black & gold	30	3(
			a. Imperf (horiz pair)	£750	

1074	**552**	13p.	salmon-pink, new blue, greenish yellow, magenta, black & gold	35	35
			Set of 4	1·00	1·00
			Set of 4 Gutter Pairs	2·50	
			Set of 4 Traffic Light Gutter Pairs	3·00	
			First Day Cover		1·50
			Presentation Pack	1·75	
			P.H.Q. Cards (set of 4)	1·50	4·00

Special First Day of Issue Postmarks

Philatelic Bureau, Edinburgh	1·75
Bethlehem, Llandeilo, Dyfed	2·50

Collectors Pack 1978

1978 (22 Nov). *Comprises Nos.* 1050/7 *and* 1059/74.

CP1074*a*	Collectors Pack	7·00

553 Old English Sheepdog

554 Welsh Springer Spaniel

555 West Highland Terrier

556 Irish Setter

(Des P. Barrett)

1979 (7 Feb). **Dogs.** *"All-over" phosphor. P* 15 × 14.

1075	**553**	9p.	grey-black, sepia, turquoise-green, pale greenish yellow, pale greenish blue & grey	20	20
1076	**554**	10½p.	grey-black, lake-brown, apple-green, pale greenish yellow, pale greenish blue & grey	40	30
1077	**555**	11p.	grey-black, claret, yellowish green, pale greenish yellow, cobalt & grey	40	30
		a.	Imperf (horiz pair)	£900	
1078	**556**	13p.	grey-black, lake-brown, green, pale greenish yellow & dp turquoise-blue	40	30
			Set of 4	1·25	1·00
			Set of 4 Gutter Pairs	2·50	
			Set of 4 Traffic Light Gutter Pairs	3·75	
			First Day Cover		1·50
			Presentation Pack	2·25	
			P.H.Q. Cards (set of 4)	3·00	5·00

Special First Day of Issue Postmarks

Philatelic Bureau, Edinburgh	2·00
London SW	2·75

557 Primrose

558 Daffodil

559 Bluebell

560 Snowdrop

(Des P. Newcombe)

1979 (21 Mar). **Spring Wild Flowers.** *"All-over" phosphor. P* 14 × 15.

1079	**557**	9p.	slate-black, dp brown, pale greenish yellow, dp olive, pale new blue & silver	20	20
		a.	Imperf (pair)	£400	
1080	**558**	10½p.	greenish yellow, grey-green, steel-blue, slate-black, new blue & silver	40	30
		a.	Imperf (vert pair)	£1500	
1081	**559**	11p.	slate-black, dp brown, ultramarine, lt greenish blue, pale greenish yellow & silver	40	30
		a.	Imperf (horiz pair)	£1200	
1082	**560**	13p.	slate-black, indigo, grey-green, sepia, ochre & silver	40	30
		a.	Imperf (horiz pair)	£750	
			Set of 4	1·25	1·00
			Set of 4 Gutter Pairs	2·50	
			Set of 4 Traffic Light Gutter Pairs	3·75	
			First Day Cover		1·50
			Presentation Pack	2·00	
			P.H.Q. Cards (set of 4)	2·00	4·00

Special First Day of Issue Postmark

Philatelic Bureau, Edinburgh	2·00	

Special First Day of Issue Postmarks

Philatelic Bureau, Edinburgh	2·75
London SW	2·75

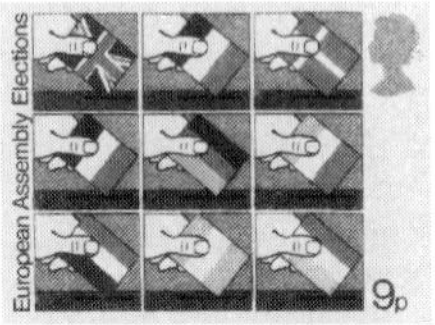

561

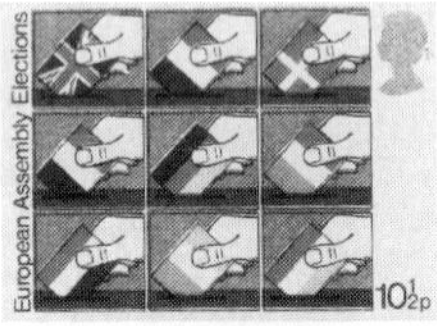

562

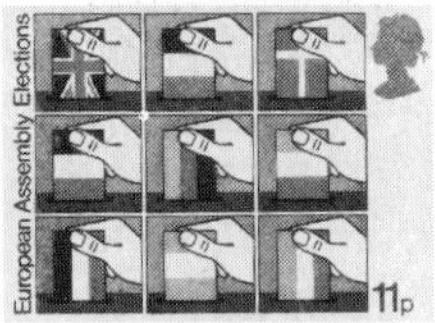

563

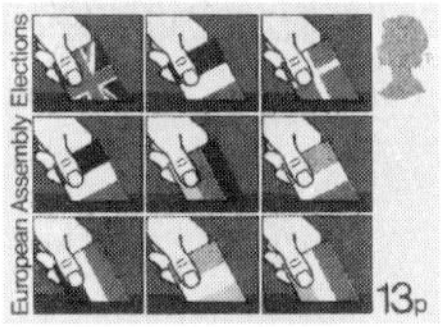

564

T **561/4** show Hands placing National Flags in Ballot Boxes.

(Des S. Cliff)

1979 (9 May). **First Direct Elections to European Assembly.** *Phosphorised paper. P* 15 × 14.

1083	**561**	9p. grey-black, vermilion, cinnamon, pale greenish yellow, pale turquoise-green & dull ultramarine	20	20
1084	**562**	10½p. grey-black, vermilion, cinnamon, pale greenish yellow, dull ultramarine, pale turquoise-green & chestnut	30	30
1085	**563**	11p. grey-black, vermilion, cinnamon, pale greenish yellow, dull ultramarine, pale turquoise-green & grey-green	30	30
1086	**564**	13p. grey-black, vermilion, cinnamon, pale greenish yellow, dull ultramarine, pale turquoise-green & brown	30	30
		Set of 4	1·00	1·00
		Set of 4 Gutter Pairs	2·50	
		Set of 4 Traffic Light Gutter Pairs	3·75	
		First Day Cover		1·50
		Presentation Pack	2·00	
		P.H.Q. Cards (set of 4)	1·50	3·50

565 "Saddling 'Mahmoud' for the Derby, 1936" (Sir Alfred Munnings)

566 "The Liverpool Great National Steeple Chase, 1839" (aquatint by F. C. Turner)

567 "The First Spring Meeting, Newmarket, 1793" (J. N. Sartorius)

568 "Racing at Dorsett Ferry, Windsor, 1684" (Francis Barlow)

(Des S. Rose)

1979 (6 June). **Horseracing Paintings. Bicentenary of the Derby (9p.).** *"All-over" phosphor. P* 15 × 14.

1087	**565**	9p. lt blue, red-brown, rose-pink, pale greenish yellow, grey-black & gold	25	25
1088	**566**	10½p. bistre-yellow, slate-blue, salmon-pink, lt blue, grey-black & gold	30	30
1089	**567**	11p. rose, vermilion, pale greenish yellow, new blue, grey-black & gold	30	30
1090	**568**	13p. bistre-yellow, rose, turquoise, grey-black & gold	30	30
		Set of 4	1·10	1·10
		Set of 4 Gutter Pairs	2·50	
		Set of 4 Traffic Light Gutter Pairs	3·75	
		First Day Cover		1·75
		Presentation Pack	2·00	
		P.H.Q. Cards (set of 4)	1·50	3·00

Special First Day of Issue Postmarks

Philatelic Bureau, Edinburgh .... 2·75
Epsom, Surrey .... 2·75

569 *The Tale of Peter Rabbit* (Beatrix Potter)

570 *The Wind in the Willows* (Kenneth Grahame)

571 *Winnie-the-Pooh* (A. A. Milne)

572 *Alice's Adventures in Wonderland* (Lewis Carroll)

(Des E. Hughes)

1979 (11 July). **International Year of the Child. Children's Book Illustrations.** *"All-over" phosphor. P* 14 × 15.

1091	**569**	9p.	dp bluish green, grey-black, bistre-brown, brt rose, greenish yellow & silver	25	20
1092	**570**	10½p.	dull ultramarine, grey-black, olive-brown, brt rose, yellow-orange, pale greenish yellow & silver	30	35
1093	**571**	11p.	drab, grey-black, greenish yellow, new blue, yellow-orange, agate & silver	35	40
1094	**572**	13p.	pale greenish yellow, grey-black, brt rose, dp bluish green, olive-brown, new blue & silver	50	45
			Set of 4	1·25	1·25
			Set of 4 Gutter Pairs	3·00	
			Set of 4 Traffic Light Gutter Pairs	4·75	
			First Day Cover		2·25
			Presentation Pack	2·25	
			P.H.Q. Cards (set of 4)	2·50	3·00

Special First Day of Issue Postmark

Philatelic Bureau, Edinburgh .... 2·50

First Day of Issue handstamps were provided at Hartfield, East Sussex and Stourbridge, West Midlands for this issue.

573 Sir Rowland Hill

574 Postman, *circa* 1839

575 London Postman, *circa* 1839

576 Woman and Young Girl with Letters, 1840

(Des E. Stemp)

1979 (22 Aug–24 Oct). **Death Centenary of Sir Rowland Hill.** *"All-over" phosphor. P* 14 × 15.

1095	**573**	10p.	grey-black, brown-ochre, myrtle-green, pale greenish yellow, rosine, brt blue & gold	25	25
			a. Imperf (horiz pair)		
1096	**574**	11½p.	grey-black, brown-ochre, brt blue, rosine, bistre-brown, pale greenish yellow & gold	30	35
1097	**575**	13p.	grey-black, brown-ochre, brt blue, rosine, bistre-brown, pale greenish yellow & gold	35	40
1098	**576**	15p.	grey-black, brown-ochre, myrtle-green, bistre-brown, rosine, pale greenish yellow & gold	50	40
			Set of 4	1·25	1·25
			Set of 4 Gutter Pairs	2·50	
			Set of 4 Traffic Light Gutter Pairs	3·75	
			First Day Cover		1·50
			Presentation Pack	2·00	
			P.H.Q. Cards (set of 4)	1·50	3·00

MS1099	89 × 121 mm. Nos. 1095/8 (*sold at* $59\frac{1}{2}$p.) (24 Oct)	1·25	1·25
	a. Imperforate	£1000	
	b. Brown-ochre (15p. background, etc.) omitted	£750	
	c. Gold (Queen's head) omitted	£175	
	d. Brown-ochre, myrtle-green & gold omitted	£3000	
	e. Brt blue (13p. background, etc.) omitted	£900	
	f. Myrtle-green (10p. (background), 15p.) omitted	£1200	
	g. Pale greenish yellow omitted	£140	
	h. Rosine omitted	£500	
	i. Bistre-brown omitted	£650	
	j. Grey-black and pale greenish yellow omitted	£10000	
	First Day Cover		1·75

The premium on No. **MS**1099 was used to support the London 1980 International Stamp Exhibition.

Examples of No. **MS**1099 showing face values on the stamps of 9p., $10\frac{1}{2}$p., 11p. and 13p., with a sheet price of $53\frac{1}{2}$p., were prepared, but not issued.

Special First Day of Issue Postmarks

Philatelic Bureau, Edinburgh (stamps) (22 Aug)	1·75
Philatelic Bureau, Edinburgh (miniature sheet) (24 Oct)	2·00
London EC (stamps) (22 Aug)	1·75
London EC (miniature sheet) (24 Oct)	2·00

First Day of Issue handstamps were provided at Kidderminster, Worcs on 22 August (pictorial) and 24 October (Type C) and at Sanquhar, Dumfriesshire on 22 August and 24 October (both Type C).

577 Policeman on the Beat

578 Policeman directing Traffic

579 Mounted Policewoman

580 River Patrol Boat

(Des B. Sanders)

1979 (26 Sept). **150th Anniv of Metropolitan Police.** *Phosphorised paper. P* 15 × 14.

1100	**577**	10p.	grey-black, red-brown, emerald, greenish yellow, brt blue & magenta	25	25
1101	**578**	$11\frac{1}{2}$p.	grey-black, brt orange, purple-brown, ultramarine, greenish yellow & dp bluish green	30	35
1102	**579**	13p.	grey-black, red-brown, magenta, olive-green, greenish yellow & dp dull blue	35	40
1103	**580**	15p.	grey-black, magenta, brown, slate-blue, dp brown & greenish black	50	40
			Set of 4	1·25	1·25
			Set of 4 Gutter Pairs	2·50	
			Set of 4 Traffic Light Gutter Pairs	3·75	
			First Day Cover		1·50
			Presentation Pack	2·00	
			PHQ Cards (set of 4)	1·50	3·00

Special First Day of Issue Postmarks

Philatelic Bureau, Edinburgh	1·75
London SW	1·75

581 The Three Kings

582 Angel appearing to the Shepherds

583 The Nativity

584 Mary and Joseph travelling to Bethlehem

585 The Annunciation

(Des F. Wegner)

1979 (21 Nov). **Christmas.** *One centre phosphor band* (8p.) *or phosphorised paper (others). P* 15 × 14.

1104	**581**	8p.	blue, grey-black, ochre, slate-violet & gold	20	20
			a. Imperf (pair)	£500	
1105	**582**	10p.	brt rose-red, grey-black, chestnut, chrome-yellow, dp violet & gold	25	25
			a. Imperf between (vert pair)	£450	
			b. Imperf (pair)	£600	
1106	**583**	11½p.	orange-vermilion, steel-blue, drab, grey-black, dp blue-green & gold	30	35
1107	**584**	13p.	brt blue, orange-vermilion, bistre, grey-black & gold	40	40
1108	**585**	15p.	orange-vermilion, blue, bistre, grey-black, green & gold	50	45
			Set of 5	1·50	1·50
			Set of 5 Gutter Pairs	3·00	
			Set of 5 Traffic Light Gutter Pairs	3·75	
			First Day Cover		1·75
			Presentation Pack	2·25	
			P.H.Q. Cards (set of 5)	1·50	3·50

Special First Day of Issue Postmarks

Philatelic Bureau, Edinburgh	2·00
Bethlehem, Llandeilo, Dyfed	2·00

Collectors Pack 1979

1979 (21 Nov). *Comprises Nos.* 1075/98 *and* 1100/8.

CP1108a	Collectors Pack	8·50

586 Common Kingfisher

587 Dipper

588 Moorhen

589 Yellow Wagtails

(Des M. Warren)

1980 (16 Jan). **Centenary of Wild Bird Protection Act.** *Phosphorised paper. P* 14 × 15.

1109	**586**	10p.	brt blue, brt yellow-green, vermilion, pale greenish yellow, grey-black & gold	25	25
1110	**587**	11½p.	sepia, grey-black, dull ultramarine, vermilion, grey-green, pale greenish yellow & gold	40	35
1111	**588**	13p.	emerald-green, grey-black, brt blue, vermilion, pale greenish yellow & gold	50	40
1112	**589**	15p.	greenish yellow, brown, lt green, slate-blue, grey-black & gold	55	45
			Set of 4	1·50	1·25
			Set of 4 Gutter Pairs	3·00	
			First Day Cover		1·75
			Presentation Pack	2·00	
			P.H.Q. Cards (set of 4)	1·50	3·00

Special First Day of Issue Postmarks

Philatelic Bureau, Edinburgh	2·00
Sandy, Beds	2·00

590 *Rocket* approaching Moorish Arch, Liverpool

591 First and Second Class Carriages passing through Olive Mount Cutting

592 Third Class Carriage and Cattle Truck crossing Chat Moss

593 Horsebox and Carriage Truck near Bridgewater Canal

594 Goods Truck and Mail-Coach at Manchester

T **590/4** were printed together, *se-tenant*, in horizontal strips of 5 throughout the sheet.

(Des D. Gentleman)

1980 (12 Mar). **150th Anniv of Liverpool and Manchester Railway.** *Phosphorised paper. P* 15 x 14.

1113	**590**	12p.	lemon, lt brown, rose-red, pale blue & grey-black	25	25
		a.	Strip of 5. Nos. 1113/17	1·50	1·60
		ab.	Imperf (horiz strip of 5. Nos. 1113/17)	£1200	
		ac.	Lemon omitted (horiz strip of 5. Nos. 1113/17)	£7500	
1114	**591**	12p.	rose-red, lt brown, lemon, pale blue & grey-black	25	25
1115	**592**	12p.	pale blue, rose-red, lemon, lt brown & grey-black	25	25
1116	**593**	12p.	lt brown, lemon, rose-red, pale blue & grey-black	25	25
1117	**594**	12p.	lt brown, rose-red, pale blue, lemon & grey-black	25	25
			Set of 5	1·50	1·10
			Gutter Block of 10	3·25	
			First Day Cover		1·50
			Presentation Pack	2·75	
			P.H.Q. Cards (set of 5)	1·50	3·75

Special First Day of Issue Postmarks

Philatelic Bureau, Edinburgh	2·00
Liverpool	2·00
Manchester	2·00

595 Montage of London Buildings

During the printing of No. 1118 the die was re-cut resulting in the following two types:

Type I (original). Top and bottom lines of shading in portrait oval broken. Hatched shading below left arm of Tower Bridge and hull of ship below right arm. Other points: Hatched shading on flag on Westminster Abbey, bottom right of Post Office Tower and archway of entrance to Westminster Abbey.

Type II (re-engraved). Lines in oval unbroken. Solid shading on bridge and ship. Also solid shading on flag, Post Office Tower and archway.

(Des J. Matthews. Recess)

1980 (9 Apr–7 May). **"London 1980" International Stamp Exhibition.** *Phosphorised paper. P* $14\frac{1}{2} \times 14$.

1118 **595**	50p. agate (I)	1·50	1·25
	Ea. Type II	1·50	1·50
	Gutter Pair	3·00	
	First Day Cover		1·50
	Presentation Pack	2·00	
	P.H.Q. Card	50	1·75
MS1119	90 × 123 mm. No. 1118 (*sold at 75p.*) (7 May)	1·50	1·50
	a. Error. Imperf	£700	
	First Day Cover		1·75

Examples of No 1118 are known in various shades of green. Such shades result from problems with the drying of the printed sheets on the press, but are not listed as similar colours can be easily faked.

Special First Day of Issue Postmarks

Philatelic Bureau, Edinburgh (stamp) (9 Apr.)	2·00
Philatelic Bureau, Edinburgh (miniature sheet) (7 May)	2·00
London SW (stamp) (9 Apr.)	2·00
London SW (miniature sheet) (7 May)	2·00

596 Buckingham Palace

597 The Albert Memorial

598 Royal Opera House

599 Hampton Court

600 Kensington Palace

(Des Sir Hugh Casson)

1980 (7 May). **London Landmarks.** *Phosphorised paper. P* 14×15.

1120 **596**	$10\frac{1}{2}$p. grey, pale blue, rosine, pale greenish yellow, yellowish green & silver	25	25
1121 **597**	12p. grey-black, bistre, rosine, yellowish green, pale greenish yellow & silver	30	30
	a. Imperf (vert pair)	£550	
1122 **598**	$13\frac{1}{2}$p. grey-black, pale salmon, pale olive-green, slate-blue & silver	35	35
	a. Imperf (pair)	£550	
1123 **599**	15p. grey-black, pale salmon, slate-blue, dull yellowish green, olive-yellow & silver	40	40
1124 **600**	$17\frac{1}{2}$p. grey, slate-blue, red-brown, sepia, yellowish green, pale greenish yellow & silver	40	40
	a. Silver (Queen's head) omitted	£175	
	Set of 5	1·50	1·50
	Set of 5 Gutter Pairs	3·00	
	First Day Cover		1·75
	Presentation Pack	2·50	
	P.H.Q. Cards (set of 5)	1·50	3·00

No. 1124a shows the Queen's head in pale greenish yellow, this colour being printed beneath the silver for technical reasons.

Special First Day of Issue Postmarks

Philatelic Bureau, Edinburgh	2·25
Kingston-upon-Thames	2·25

601 Charlotte Brontë (*Jane Eyre*)

602 George Eliot (*The Mill on the Floss*)

603 Emily Brontë (*Wuthering Heights*)

604 Mrs. Gaskell (*North and South*)

T **601/4** show authoresses and scenes from their novels. T **601/2** also include the "Europa" C.E.P.T. emblem.

(Des Barbara Brown)

1980 (9 July). **Famous Authoresses.** *Phosphorised paper. P* 15 × 14.

1125	**601**	12p.	red-brown, brt rose, brt blue, greenish yellow, grey & gold	30	30
		Ea.	Missing "p" in value (R.4/6)	25·00	
1126	**602**	$13\frac{1}{2}$p.	red-brown, dull vermilion, pale blue, pale greenish yellow, grey & gold	35	35
		a.	Pale blue omitted	£1750	
1127	**603**	15p.	red-brown, vermilion, blue, lemon, grey & gold	40	45
1128	**604**	$17\frac{1}{2}$p.	dull vermilion, slate-blue, ultramarine, pale greenish yellow, grey & gold	60	60
		a.	Imperf and slate-blue omitted (pair)	£700	
			Set of 4	1·50	1·50
			Set of 4 Gutter Pairs	3·00	
			First Day Cover		1·50
			Presentation Pack	2·50	
			P.H.Q. Cards (set of 4)	1·50	3·00

Special First Day of Issue Postmarks

Philatelic Bureau, Edinburgh	1·75
Haworth, Keighley, W. Yorks	1·75

605 Queen Elizabeth the Queen Mother

(Des J. Matthews from photograph by N. Parkinson)

1980 (4 Aug). **80th Birthday of Queen Elizabeth the Queen Mother.** *Phosphorised paper. P* 14 × 15.

1129	**605**	12p.	brt rose, greenish yellow, new blue, grey & silver	75	75
		a.	Imperf (horiz pair)	£1200	
			Gutter Pair	1·50	
			First Day Cover		1·00
			P.H.Q. Card	50	1·25

Special First Day of Issue Postmarks

Philatelic Bureau, Edinburgh	1·75
Glamis Castle, Forfar	1·75

606 Sir Henry Wood

607 Sir Thomas Beecham

608 Sir Malcolm Sargent

609 Sir John Barbirolli

(Des P. Gauld)

1980 (10 Sept). **British Conductors.** *Phosphorised paper. P* 14 × 15.

1130	**606**	12p.	slate, rose-red, greenish yellow, bistre & gold	30	30
1131	**607**	$13\frac{1}{2}$p.	grey-black, vermilion, greenish yellow, pale carmine-rose & gold	35	40
1132	**608**	15p.	grey-black, brt rose-red, greenish yellow, turquoise-green & gold	45	45
1133	**609**	$17\frac{1}{2}$p.	black, brt rose-red, greenish yellow, dull violet-blue & gold	55	50
			Set of 4	1·50	1·50
			Set of 4 Gutter Pairs	3·00	
			First Day Cover		1·50
			Presentation Pack	2·00	
			P.H.Q. cards (set of 4)	1·50	2·50

Special First Day of Issue Postmarks

Philatelic Bureau, Edinburgh .... 2·00
London SW .... 2·00

610 Running

611 Rugby

612 Boxing

613 Cricket

(Des R. Goldsmith. Litho Questa)

1980 (10 Oct). **Sport Centenaries.** *Phosphorised paper. P* 14 × 14½.

1134	**610**	12p. pale new blue, greenish yellow, magenta, lt brown, reddish purple & gold	30	30
		a. Gold (Queen's head) omitted	£10000	
1135	**611**	13½p. pale new blue, olive-yellow, brt purple, orange-vermilion, blackish lilac & gold .	35	40
1136	**612**	15p. pale new blue, greenish yellow, brt purple, chalky blue & gold	40	40
		a. Gold (Queen's head) omitted	£10000	
1137	**613**	17½p. pale new blue, greenish yellow, magenta, dp olive, grey-brown & gold	60	55
		Set of 4	1·50	1·50
		Set of 4 Gutter Pairs	3·00	
		First Day Cover		1·50
		Presentation Pack	2·00	
		P.H.Q. Cards (set of 4)	1·50	2·50

Centenaries:—12p. Amateur Athletics Association; 13½p. Welsh Rugby Union; 15p. Amateur Boxing Association; 17½p. First England–Australia Test Match.

Nos. 1134a and 1136a were caused by paper folds.

Special First Day of Issue Postmarks

Philatelic Bureau, Edinburgh .... 2·00
Cardiff .... 2·00

614 Christmas Tree

615 Candles

616 Apples and Mistletoe

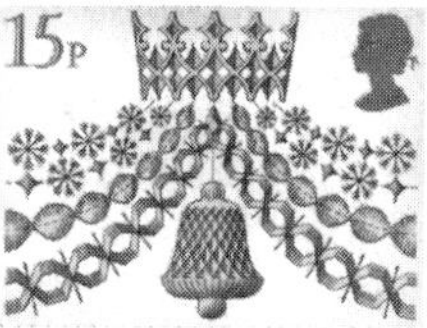

617 Crown, Chains and Bell

618 Holly

(Des J. Matthews)

1980 (19 Nov). **Christmas.** *One centre phosphor band* (10p.) *or phosphorised paper* (*others*). *P* 15 × 14.

1138	**614**	10p. black, turquoise-green, greenish yellow, vermilion & blue	25	25
		a. Imperf (horiz pair)	£950	
1139	**615**	12p. grey, magenta, rose-red, greenish grey & pale orange	30	35
1140	**616**	13½p. grey-black, dull yellow-green, brown, greenish yellow & pale olive-bistre	35	40
1141	**617**	15p. grey-black, bistre-yellow, brt orange, magenta & new blue	40	40

1142 **618** $17\frac{1}{2}$p.	black, vermilion, dull yellowish green & greenish yellow	50	40
	Set of 5	1·60	1·60
	Set of 5 Gutter Pairs	3·25	
	First Day Cover		1·60
	Presentation Pack	2·25	
	P.H.Q. Cards (set of 5)	1·50	2·50

Special First Day of Issue Postmarks

Philatelic Bureau, Edinburgh	2·00
Bethlehem, Llandeilo, Dyfed	2·50

Collectors Pack 1980

1980 (19 Nov). *Comprises Nos.* 1109/18 *and* 1120/42.

CP1142*a*	Collectors Pack	10·00

619 St. Valentine's Day

620 Morris Dancers

621 Lammastide

622 Medieval Mummers

T **619/20** also include the "Europa" C.E.P.T. emblem.

(Des F. Wegner)

1981 (6 Feb). **Folklore.** *Phosphorised paper. P* 15 × 14.

1143 **619** 14p.	cerise, green, yellow-orange, salmon-pink, black & gold	35	35
1144 **620** 18p.	dull ultramarine, lemon, lake-brown, brt green, black & gold	45	50
1145 **621** 22p.	chrome-yellow, rosine, brown, new blue, black & gold	60	60
1146 **622** 25p.	brt blue, red-brown, brt rose-red, greenish yellow, black & gold	75	70
	Set of 4	2·00	2·00
	Set of 4 Gutter Pairs	4·00	
	First Day Cover		2·00
	Presentation Pack	2·50	
	P.H.Q. Cards (set of 4)	1·50	2·50

Special First Day of Issue Postmarks

Philatelic Bureau, Edinburgh	2·00
London WC	2·00

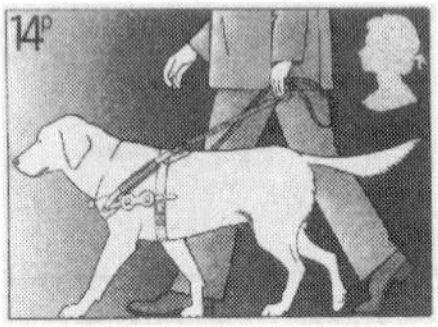

623 Blind Man with Guide Dog

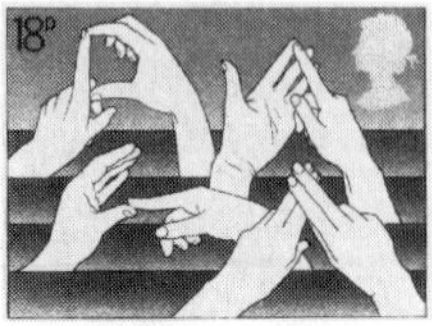

624 Hands spelling "Deaf" in Sign Language

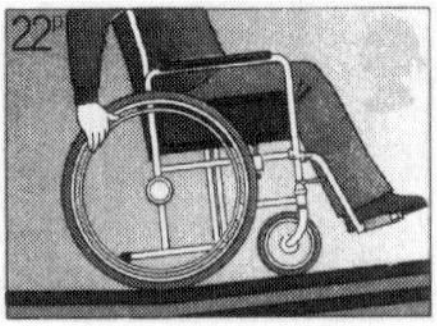

625 Disabled Man in Wheelchair

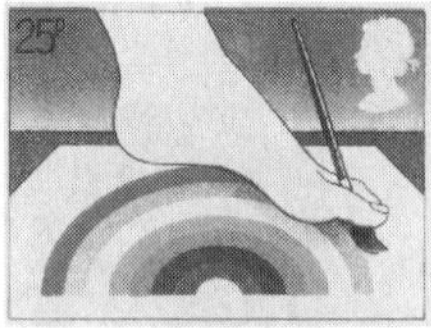

626 Disabled Artist painting with Foot

(Des J. Gibbs)

1981 (25 Mar). **International Year of the Disabled.** *Phosphorised paper. P* 15 × 14.

1147 **623** 14p.	drab, greenish yellow, brt rose-red, dull purple & silver	35	35
	a. Imperf (pair)	£750	
1148 **624** 18p.	dp blue-green, brt orange, dull vermilion, grey-black & silver	45	50
1149 **625** 22p.	brown-ochre, rosine, purple-brown, greenish blue, black & silver	60	60
1150 **626** 25p.	vermilion, lemon, pale salmon, olive-brown, new blue, black & silver	75	70
	Set of 4	2·00	2·00
	Set of 4 Gutter Pairs	4·00	
	First Day Cover		2·00
	Presentation Pack	2·50	
	P.H.Q. Cards (set of 4)	1·50	2·75

All known examples of No. 1147*a* are creased.

Special First Day of Issue Postmarks

Philatelic Bureau, Edinburgh	2·00
Windsor	2·00

627 *Aglais urticae*

628 *Maculinea arion*

629 *Inachis io*

630 *Carterocephalus palaemon*

(Des G. Beningfield)

1981 (13 May). **Butterflies.** *Phosphorised paper. P* 14 × 15.

1151	**627**	14p.	greenish yellow, yellow-green, brt rose, brt blue, emerald & gold	35	35
			a. Imperf (pair)	£950	
1152	**628**	18p.	black, greenish yellow, dull yellowish green, brt mauve, brt blue, brt green & gold	60	50
1153	**629**	22p.	black, greenish yellow, bronze-green, rosine, ultramarine, lt green & gold	70	65
1154	**630**	25p.	black, greenish yellow, bronze-green, brt rose-red, ultramarine, brt emerald & gold	80	75
			Set of 4	2·25	2·00
			Set of 4 Gutter Pairs	4·50	
			First Day Cover		2·25
			Presentation Pack	2·50	
			P.H.Q. Cards (set of 4)	2·00	3·00

Special First Day of Issue Postmarks

Philatelic Bureau, Edinburgh	2·75
London SW	2·50

631 Glenfinnan, Scotland

632 Derwentwater, England

633 Stackpole Head, Wales

634 Giant's Causeway, Northern Ireland

635 St. Kilda, Scotland

(Des M. Fairclough)

1981 (24 June). **50th Anniv of National Trust for Scotland. British Landscapes.** *Phosphorised paper. P* 15 × 14.

1155	**631**	14p.	lilac, dull blue, reddish brown, bistre-yellow, black & gold	30	30
1156	**632**	18p.	bottle green, brt blue, brown, bistre-yellow, black & gold	40	40
1157	**633**	20p.	dp turquoise-blue, dull blue, greenish yellow, reddish brown, black & gold	50	50
1158	**634**	22p.	chrome-yellow, reddish brown, new blue, yellow-brown, black & gold	60	60
1159	**635**	25p.	ultramarine, new blue, olive-green, olive-grey & gold	70	70
			Set of 5	2·25	2·25
			Set of 5 Gutter Pairs	4·50	
			First Day Cover		2·25
			Presentation Pack	2·75	
			P.H.Q. Cards (set of 5)	2·00	2·75

Special First Day of Issue Postmarks

Philatelic Bureau, Edinburgh	2·75
Glenfinnan	3·50
Keswick	3·50

636 Prince Charles and Lady Diana Spencer

(Des J. Matthews from photograph by Lord Snowdon)

1981 (22 July). **Royal Wedding.** *Phosphorised paper. P* 14 × 15.

1160	**636**	14p.	grey-black, greenish yellow, brt rose-red, ultramarine, pale blue, blue & silver	2·00	1·75
1161		25p.	drab, greenish yellow, brt rose-red, ultramarine, grey-brown, grey-black & silver	3·00	2·25
			Set of 2	5·00	4·00
			Set of 2 Gutter Pairs	10·00	
			First Day Cover		5·00
			Presentation Pack	5·00	
			Souvenir Book	6·00	
			P.H.Q. Cards (set of 2)	3·00	4·50

The souvenir book is a 12-page illustrated booklet with a set of mint stamps in a sachet attached to the front cover.

Special First Day of Issue Postmarks

Philatelic Bureau, Edinburgh	5·50
Caernarfon, Gwynedd	5·50
London EC	5·50

637 "Expeditions"

638 "Skills"

639 "Service"

640 "Recreation"

(Des P. Sharland. Litho J.W.)

1981 (12 Aug). **25th Anniv of Duke of Edinburgh Award Scheme.** *Phosphorised paper. P* 14.

1162	**637**	14p.	greenish yellow, magenta, pale new blue, black, emerald & silver	35	35
1163	**638**	18p.	greenish yellow, magenta, pale new blue, black, cobalt & gold	50	50
1164	**639**	22p.	greenish yellow, magenta, pale new blue, black, red-orange & gold	60	60
1165	**640**	25p.	brt orange, mauve, pale new blue, black, flesh & bronze	70	70
			Set of 4	2·00	2·00
			Set of 4 Gutter Pairs	4·00	
			First Day Cover		2·00
			Presentation Pack	2·50	
			P.H.Q. Cards (set of 4)	1·60	2·25

Special First Day of Issue Postmarks

Philatelic Bureau, Edinburgh	2·50
London W2	2·75

Special First Day of Issue Postmarks

Philatelic Bureau, Edinburgh	2·50
Hull	2·75

641 Cockle-dredging from *Linsey II*

642 Hauling in Trawl Net

643 Lobster Potting

644 Hoisting Seine Net

(Des B. Sanders)

1981 (23 Sept). **Fishing Industry.** *Phosphorised paper. P* 15 × 14.

1166	**641**	14p.	slate, greenish yellow, magenta, new blue, orange-brown, olive-grey & bronze-green	35	35
1167	**642**	18p.	slate, greenish yellow, brt crimson, ultramarine, black & greenish slate	50	50
1168	**643**	22p.	grey, greenish yellow, brt rose, dull ultramarine, reddish lilac & black	60	60
1169	**644**	25p.	grey, greenish yellow, brt rose, cobalt & black	70	65
			Set of 4	2·00	2·00
			Set of 4 Gutter Pairs	4·00	
			First Day Cover		2·00
			Presentation Pack	2·50	
			P.H.Q. Cards (set of 4)	2·00	2·50

Nos. 1166/9 were issued on the occasion of the centenary of the Royal National Mission to Deep Sea Fishermen.

645 Father Christmas

646 Jesus Christ

647 Flying Angel

648 Joseph and Mary arriving at Bethlehem

649 Three Kings approaching Bethlehem

(Des Samantha Brown ($11\frac{1}{2}$p.), Tracy Jenkins (14p.), Lucinda Blackmore (18p.), Stephen Moore (22p.), Sophie Sharp (25p.))

1981 (18 Nov). **Christmas. Children's Pictures.** *One phosphor band* (*$11\frac{1}{2}$p.*) *or phosphorised paper (others). P* 15 × 14.

1170	**645**	$11\frac{1}{2}$p.	ultramarine, black, red, olive-bistre, brt green & gold	30	30
1171	**646**	14p.	bistre-yellow, brt magenta, blue, greenish blue, brt green, black & gold	40	40
1172	**647**	18p.	pale blue-green, bistre-yellow, brt magenta, ultramarine, black & gold	50	50
1173	**648**	22p.	dp turquoise-blue, lemon, magenta, black & gold	60	60

1174	**649**	25p.	royal blue, lemon, brt magenta, black & gold	70	70
			Set of 5	2·25	2·25
			Set of 5 Gutter Pairs	4·50	
			First Day Cover		2·25
			Presentation Pack	3·00	
			P.H.Q. Cards (set of 5)	2·00	3·50

Special First Day of Issue Postmarks

Philatelic Bureau, Edinburgh	2·50
Bethlehem, Llandeilo, Dyfed	2·75

Collectors Pack 1981

1981 (18 Nov). *Comprises Nos.* 1143/74.

CP1174a	Collectors Pack	16·00

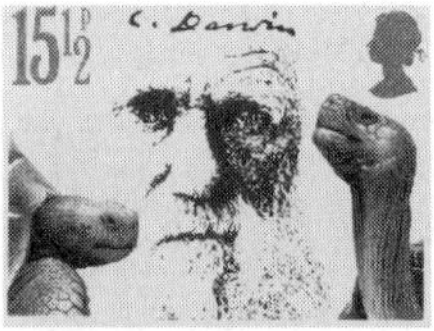

650 Charles Darwin and Giant Tortoises

651 Darwin and Marine Iguanas

652 Darwin, Cactus Ground Finch and Large Ground Finch

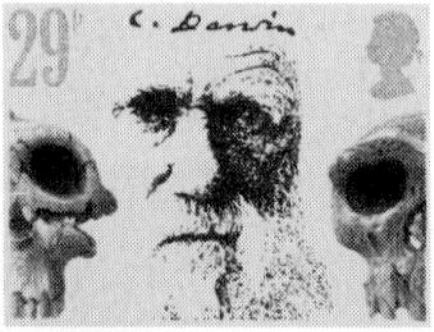

653 Darwin and Prehistoric Skulls

(Des D. Gentleman)

1982 (10 Feb). **Death Centenary of Charles Darwin.** *Phosphorised paper. P* 15 × 14.

1175	**650**	15½p.	dull purple, drab, bistre, black & grey-black	35	35
1176	**651**	19½p.	violet-grey, bistre-yellow, slate-black, red-brown, grey-black & black	60	60
1177	**652**	26p.	sage green, bistre-yellow, orange, chalky blue, grey-black, red-brown & black	70	70
1178	**653**	29p.	grey-brown, yellow-brown, brown-ochre, black & grey-black	75	75
			Set of 4	2·25	2·25
			Set of 4 Gutter Pairs	4·50	
			First Day Cover		2·25
			Presentation Pack	3·00	
			P.H.Q. Cards (set of 4)	2·50	6·50

Special First Day of Issue Postmarks

Philatelic Bureau, Edinburgh	2·25
Shrewsbury	2·25

654 Boys' Brigade

655 Girls' Brigade

656 Boy Scout Movement

657 Girl Guide Movement

(Des B. Sanders)

1982 (24 Mar). **Youth Organizations.** *Phosphorised paper. P* 15 × 14.

1179	**654**	15½p.	gold, greenish yellow, pale orange, mauve, dull blue & grey-black	35	35
1180	**655**	19½p.	gold, greenish yellow, pale orange, brt rose, dp ultramarine, olive-bistre & grey-black	60	50
1181	**656**	26p.	gold, greenish yellow, olive-sepia, rosine, dp blue, dp dull green & grey-black	85	75
1182	**657**	29p.	gold, yellow, dull orange, cerise, dull ultramarine, chestnut & grey-black	1·00	90
			Set of 4	2·50	2·25
			Set of 4 Gutter Pairs	5·00	
			First Day Cover		2·25
			Presentation Pack	3·50	
			P.H.Q. Cards (set of 4)	2·50	6·50

Nos. 1179/82 were issued on the occasion of the 75th anniversary of the Boy Scout Movement; the 125th birth anniversary of Lord Baden-Powell and the centenary of the Boys' Brigade (1983).

Special First Day of Issue Postmarks

Edinburgh Philatelic Bureau	2·25
Glasgow	2·25
London SW	2·25

658 Ballerina

659 Harlequin

660 Hamlet

661 Opera Singer

(Des A. George)

1982 (28 Apr). **Europa. British Theatre.** *Phosphorised paper. P* 15 × 14.

1183	**658**	15½p.	carmine-lake, greenish blue, greenish yellow, grey-black, bottle green & silver	35	35
1184	**659**	19½p.	rosine, new blue, greenish yellow, black, ultramarine & silver	60	50
1185	**660**	26p.	carmine-red, brt rose-red, greenish yellow, black, dull ultramarine, lake-brown & silver	90	75
1186	**661**	29p.	rose-red, greenish yellow, brt blue, grey-black & silver	1·25	90
			Set of 4	2·75	2·25
			Set of 4 Gutter Pairs	5·50	
			First Day Cover		2·25
			Presentation Pack	3·25	
			P.H.Q. Cards (set of 4)	2·50	6·50

Special First Day of Issue Postmarks

Philatelic Bureau, Edinburgh	2·25
Stratford-upon-Avon	2·25

662 Henry VIII and *Mary Rose*

663 Admiral Blake and *Triumph*

664 Lord Nelson and H.M.S. *Victory*

665 Lord Fisher and H.M.S. *Dreadnought*

666 Viscount Cunningham and H.M.S. *Warspite*

(Des Marjorie Saynor. Eng C. Slania. Recess and photo)

1982 (16 June). **Maritime Heritage.** *Phosphorised paper. P* 15 × 14.

1187	**662**	15½p.	black, lemon, brt rose, pale orange, ultramarine & grey	35	35
		a.	Imperf (pair)	£750	
1188	**663**	19½p.	black, greenish yellow, brt rose-red, pale orange, ultramarine & grey	60	60
1189	**664**	24p.	black, orange-yellow, brt rose-red, lake-brown, dp ultramarine & grey	70	70

1190 **665** 26p. black, orange-yellow, brt rose, lemon, ultramarine & grey 80 80
a. Imperf (pair) ....
1191 **666** 29p. black, olive-yellow, brt rose, orange-yellow, ultramarine & grey 90 90
Set of 5 .... 3·00 3·00
Set of 5 Gutter Pairs .... 6·00
First Day Cover .... 3·00
Presentation Pack .... 3·75
P.H.Q. Cards (set of 5) .... 3·00 6·50

Nos. 1187/91 were issued on the occasion of Maritime England Year, the Bicentenary of the Livery Grant by the City of London to the Worshipful Company of Shipwrights and the raising of the *Mary Rose* from Portsmouth Harbour.

Several used examples of the 15½p. have been seen with the black recess (ship and waves) omitted.

Special First Day of Issue Postmarks

Philatelic Bureau, Edinburgh .... 3·50
Portsmouth .... 3·25

667 "Strawberry Thief" (William Morris)

668 Untitled (Steiner and Co)

669 "Cherry Orchard" (Paul Nash)

670 "Chevron" (Andrew Foster)

(Des Peter Hatch Partnership)

1982 (23 July). **British Textiles.** *Phosphorised paper. P* 14 × 15.
1192 **667** 15½p. blue, olive-yellow, rosine, dp blue-green, bistre & Prussian blue 35 35
a. Imperf (horiz pair) £950
1193 **668** 19½p. olive-grey, greenish yellow, brt magenta, dull green, yellow-brown & black .. 55 55
a. Imperf (vert pair) £1500
1194 **669** 26p. brt scarlet, dull mauve, dull ultramarine & brt carmine 70 70
1195 **670** 29p. bronze-green, orange-yellow, turquoise-green, stone, chestnut & sage-green ... 90 90
Set of 4 .... 2·25 2·25
Set of 4 Gutter Pairs .... 4·50
First Day Cover .... 2·50
Presentation Pack .... 3·25
P.H.Q. Cards (set of 4) .... 3·00 6·50

Nos. 1192/5 were issued on the occasion of the 250th birth anniversary of Sir Richard Arkwright (inventor of spinning machine).

Special First Day of Issue Postmarks

Philatelic Bureau, Edinburgh .... 3·00
Rochdale .... 3·00

671 Development of Communications

672 Modern Technological Aids

(Des Delaney and Ireland)

1982 (8 Sept). **Information Technology.** *Phosphorised paper. P* 14 × 15.
1196 **671** 15½p. black, greenish yellow, brt rose-red, bistre-brown, new blue & lt ochre 45 50
a. Imperf (pair) £200
1197 **672** 26p. black, greenish yellow, brt rose-red, olive-bistre, new blue & lt olive-grey ... 80 85
a. Imperf (pair) £1300
Set of 2 .... 1·25 1·25
Set of 2 Gutter Pairs .... 2·50
First Day Cover .... 1·50
Presentation Pack .... 2·00
P.H.Q. cards (set of 2) .... 1·50 4·50

Special First Day of Issue Postmarks

Philatelic Bureau, Edinburgh	2·00
London WC	2·00

673 Austin "Seven" and "Metro"

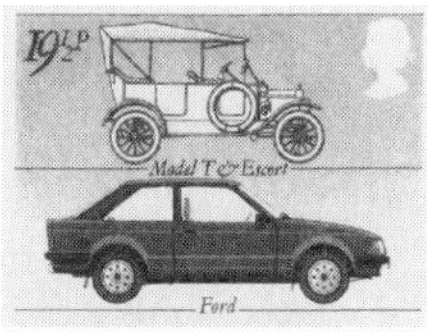

674 Ford "Model T" and "Escort"

675 Jaguar "SS 1" and "XJ6"

676 Rolls-Royce "Silver Ghost" and "Silver Spirit"

(Des S. Paine. Litho Questa)

1982 (13 Oct). **British Motor Cars.** *Phosphorised paper. P* 14½ × 14.

1198 **673** 15½p.	slate, orange-vermilion, brt orange, drab, yellow-green, olive-yellow, bluish grey & black	50	50
1199 **674** 19½p.	slate, brt orange, olive-grey, rose-red, dull vermilion, grey & black	70	70
Ea.	Rose-red, grey and black ptgs double	£600	
1200 **675** 26p.	slate, red-brown, brt orange, turquoise-green, myrtle-green, dull blue-green, grey & olive	90	90
1201 **676** 29p.	slate, brt orange, carmine-red, reddish purple, grey & black	1·25	1·25
Ea.	Black ptg quadruple	£400	
Eb.	Brt orange, carmine-red, grey and black ptgs double	£750	
	Set of 4	3·00	3·00
	Set of 4 Gutter Pairs	6·00	
	First Day Cover		3·00
	Presentation Pack	3·75	
	P.H.Q. cards (set of 4)	3·00	7·00

Special First Day of Issue Postmarks

Philatelic Bureau, Edinburgh	3·50
Birmingham	3·50
Crewe	3·50

677 "While Shepherds Watched"

678 "The Holly and the Ivy"

679 "I Saw Three Ships"

680 "We Three Kings"

681 "Good King Wenceslas"

(Des Barbara Brown)

1982 (17 Nov). **Christmas. Carols.** *One phosphor band* (12½p.) *or phosphorised paper (others). P* 15 × 14.

1202 **677** 12½p.	black, greenish yellow, brt scarlet, steel blue, red-brown & gold	30	30
1203 **678** 15½p.	black, bistre-yellow, brt rose-red, brt blue, brt green & gold	40	40
a.	Imperf (pair)	£950	

1204 **679** 19½p. black, bistre-yellow, brt rose-red, dull blue, dp brown & gold 70 70
a. Imperf (pair) £1300
1205 **680** 26p. black, bistre-yellow, brt magenta, brt blue, chocolate, gold & orange-red 80 80
1206 **681** 29p. black, bistre-yellow, magenta, brt blue, chestnut, gold & brt magenta 90 90
Set of 5 .... 2·75 2·75
Set of 5 Gutter Pairs .... 5·50
First Day Cover .... 2·75
Presentation Pack .... 3·25
P.H.Q. cards (set of 5) .... 3·00 7·00

Special Day of Issue Postmarks

Philatelic Bureau, Edinburgh .... 3·00
Bethlehem, Llandeilo, Dyfed .... 3·25

Collectors Pack 1982

1982 (17 Nov). *Comprises Nos.* 1175/1206.
CP1206*a* Collectors Pack .... 21·00

682 Salmon

683 Pike

684 Trout

685 Perch

(Des A. Jardine)

1983 (26 Jan). **British River Fishes.** *Phosphorised paper. P* 15 × 14.
1207 **682** 15½p. grey-black, bistre-yellow, brt purple, new blue & silver 35 35
a. Imperf (pair) £1300
1208 **683** 19½p. black, bistre-yellow, olive-bistre, dp claret, silver & dp bluish green 65 55
1209 **684** 26p. grey-black, bistre-yellow, chrome-yellow, magenta, silver & pale blue 80 70
a. Imperf (pair) £850
1210 **685** 29p. black, greenish yellow, brt carmine, new blue & silver .... 1·00 90
Set of 4 .... 2·50 2·25
Set of 4 Gutter Pairs .... 5·00
First Day Cover .... 2·50
Presentation Pack .... 3·00
P.H.Q. Cards (set of 4) .... 3·00 6·50

All known examples of No. 1209a are creased.

Special First Day of Issue Postmarks

Philatelic Bureau, Edinburgh .... 2·50
Peterborough .... 2·50

686 Tropical Island

687 Desert

688 Temperate Farmland

689 Mountain Range

(Des D. Fraser)

1983 (9 Mar). **Commonwealth Day. Geographical Regions.** *Phosphorised paper. P* 14 × 15.
1211 **686** 15½p. greenish blue, greenish yellow, brt rose, lt brown, grey-black, dp claret & silver 35 35
1212 **687** 19½p. brt lilac, greenish yellow, magenta, dull blue, grey-black, dp dull blue & silver . 55 55
1213 **688** 26p. lt blue, greenish yellow, brt magenta, new blue, grey-black, violet & silver ... 70 70
1214 **689** 29p. dull violet-blue, reddish violet, slate-lilac, new blue, myrtle-green, black & silver 90 90
Set of 4 .... 2·25 2·25
Set of 4 Gutter Pairs .... 4·50
First Day Cover .... 2·50
Presentation Pack .... 3·25
P.H.Q. Cards (set of 4) .... 3·00 6·50

Special First Day of Issue Postmarks

Philatelic Bureau, Edinburgh	2·50
London SW	2·50

690 Humber Bridge

691 Thames Flood Barrier

692 *Iolair* (oilfield emergency support vessel)

(Des M. Taylor)

1983 (25 May). **Europa. Engineering Achievements.** *Phosphorised paper. P* 15 × 14.

1215	**690**	16p.	silver, orange-yellow, ultramarine, black & grey	45	45
1216	**691**	20½p.	silver, greenish yellow, brt purple, blue, grey-black & grey	95	1·10
1217	**692**	28p.	silver, lemon, brt rose-red, chestnut, dull ultramarine, black & grey	1·10	1·25
			Set of 3	2·25	2·50
			Set of 3 Gutter Pairs	4·50	
			First Day Cover		2·50
			Presentation Pack	3·50	
			P.H.Q. Cards (set of 3)	2·50	6·00

Special First Day of Issue Postmarks

Philatelic Bureau, Edinburgh	2·50
Hull	2·50

693 Musketeer and Pikeman, The Royal Scots (1633)

694 Fusilier and Ensign, The Royal Welch Fusiliers (mid-18th century)

695 Riflemen, 95th Rifles (The Royal Green Jackets) (1805)

695 Sergeant (khaki service) and Guardsman (full dress), The Irish Guards (1900)

697 Paratroopers, The Parachute Regiment (1983)

(Des E. Stemp)

1983 (6 July). **British Army Uniforms.** *Phosphorised paper. P* 14 × 15.

1218	**693**	16p.	black, buff, dp brown, slate-black, rose-red, gold & new blue	40	40
1219	**694**	20½p.	black, buff, greenish yellow, slate-black, brown-rose, gold & brt blue	70	70
1220	**695**	26p.	black, buff, slate-purple, green, bistre & gold	85	85
		a.	Imperf (pair)	£1300	
1221	**696**	28p.	black, buff, lt brown, grey, dull rose, gold & new blue	85	85
1222	**697**	31p.	black, buff, olive-yellow, grey, dp magenta, gold & new blue	1·10	1·10
			Set of 5	3·50	3·50
			Set of 5 Gutter Pairs	7·00	
			First Day Cover		3·25
			Presentation Pack	4·50	
			P.H.Q. Cards (set of 5)	3·00	6·00

Nos. 1218/22 were issued on the occasion of the 350th anniversary of the Royal Scots, the senior line regiment of the British Army.

Special First Day of Issue Postmarks

Philatelic Bureau, Edinburgh	3·50
Aldershot	4·00

698 20th-century Garden, Sissinghurst

699 19th-century Garden, Biddulph Grange

700 18th-century Garden, Blenheim

701 17th-century Garden, Pitmedden

(Des Liz Butler. Litho J.W.)

1983 (24 Aug). **British Gardens.** *Phosphorised paper. P* 14.

1223	**698** 16p.	greenish yellow, brt purple, new blue, black, brt green & silver	40	40
1224	**699** 20½p.	greenish yellow, brt purple, new blue, black, brt green & silver	50	50
1225	**700** 28p.	greenish yellow, brt purple, new blue, black, brt green & silver	90	90
1226	**701** 31p.	greenish yellow, brt purple, new blue, black, brt green & silver	1·00	1·00
		Set of 4	2·50	2·50
		Set of 4 Gutter Pairs	5·00	
		First Day Cover		2·75
		Presentation Pack	3·50	
		P.H.Q. Cards (set of 4)	3·00	6·00

Nos. 1223/6 were issued on the occasion of the death bicentenary of "Capability" Brown (landscape gardener).

For full information on all future British issues, collectors should write to the British Post Office Philatelic Bureau, 20 Brandon Street, Edinburgh EH3 5TT

Special First Day of Issue Postmarks

Philatelic Bureau, Edinburgh	3·50
Oxford	3·50

702 Merry-go-round

703 Big Wheel, Helter-skelter and Performing Animals

704 Side Shows

705 Early Produce Fair

(Des A. Restall)

1983 (5 Oct). **British Fairs.** *Phosphorised paper. P* 15 × 14.

1227	**702** 16p.	grey-black, greenish yellow, orange-red, ochre & turquoise-blue	40	40
1228	**703** 20½p.	grey-black, yellow-ochre, yellow-orange, brt magenta, violet & black	65	65
1229	**704** 28p.	grey-black, bistre-yellow, orange-red, violet & yellow-brown	85	85
1230	**705** 31p.	grey-black, greenish yellow, red, dp turquoise-green, slate-violet & brown	90	90
		Set of 4	2·50	2·50
		Set of 4 Gutter Pairs	5·00	
		First Day Cover		2·75
		Presentation Pack	3·50	
		P.H.Q. Cards (set of 4)	3·00	6·00

Special First Day of Issue Postmarks

Philatelic Bureau, Edinburgh	3·50
Nottingham	3·50

706 "Christmas Post" (pillar-box)

707 "The Three Kings" (chimney-pots)

708 "World at Peace" (Dove and Blackbird)

709 "Light of Christmas" (street lamp)

710 "Christmas Dove" (hedge sculpture)

(Des T. Meeuwissen)

1983 (16 Nov). **Christmas.** *One phosphor band* (12½p.) *or phosphorised paper (others). P* 15 × 14.

1231	**706**	12½p.	black, greenish yellow, brt rose-red, brt blue, gold & grey-black	30	30
			a. Imperf (horiz pair)	£750	
1232	**707**	16p.	black, greenish yellow, brt rose, pale new blue, gold & brown-purple	35	35
			a. Imperf (pair)	£850	
1233	**708**	20½p.	black, greenish yellow, brt rose, new blue, gold & blue	60	60
1234	**709**	28p.	black, lemon, brt carmine, bluish violet, gold, dp turquoise-green & purple	70	80
1235	**710**	31p.	black, greenish yellow, brt rose, new blue, gold, green & brown-olive	85	1·00
			Set of 5	2·50	2·75
			Set of 5 Gutter Pairs	5·00	
			First Day Cover		2·75
			Presentation Pack	3·50	
			P.H.Q. Cards (set of 5)	3·00	6·00

Special First Day of Issue Postmarks

Philatelic Bureau, Edinburgh	3·00
Bethlehem, Llandeilo, Dyfed	3·00

Collectors Pack 1983

1983 (16 Nov). *Comprises Nos.* 1207/35.

CP1235*a*	Collectors Pack	35·00

711 Arms of the College of Arms

712 Arms of King Richard III (founder)

713 Arms of the Earl Marshal of England

714 Arms of the City of London

(Des J. Matthews)

1984 (17 Jan). **500th Anniv of College of Arms.** *Phosphorised paper. P* 14½.

1236	**711**	16p.	black, chrome-yellow, reddish brown, scarlet-vermilion, brt blue & grey-black	40	40
1237	**712**	20½p.	black, chrome-yellow, rosine, brt blue & grey-black	60	60
1238	**713**	28p.	black, chrome-yellow, rosine, brt blue, dull green & grey-black	85	85
1239	**714**	31p.	black, chrome-yellow, rosine, brt blue & grey-black	95	95
			a. Imperf (horiz pair)	£1800	
			Set of 4	2·50	2·50
			Set of 4 Gutter Pairs	5·00	
			First Day Cover		2·50
			Presentation Pack	3·50	
			P.H.Q. Cards	3·00	6·00

Special First Day of Issue Postmarks

Philatelic Bureau, Edinburgh	3·00
London EC	3·50

715 Highland Cow

716 Chillingham Wild Bull

717 Hereford Bull

718 Welsh Black Bull

719 Irish Moiled Cow

(Des B. Driscoll)

1984 (6 Mar). **British Cattle.** *Phosphorised paper. P* 15 × 14.

1240 **715** 16p. grey-black, bistre-yellow, rosine, yellow-orange, new blue & pale drab 40 40
1241 **716** 20½p. grey-black, greenish yellow, magenta, bistre, dull blue-green, pale drab & lt green 65 65
1242 **717** 26p. black, chrome-yellow, rosine, reddish brown, new blue & pale drab 70 70
1243 **718** 28p. black, greenish yellow, brt carmine, orange-brown, dp dull blue & pale drab 70 70
1244 **719** 31p. grey-black, bistre-yellow, rosine, red-brown, lt blue & pale drab 90 90
Set of 5 .... 3·00 3·00
Set of 5 Gutter Pairs .... 6·00
First Day Cover .... 3·00
Presentation Pack .... 4·25
P.H.Q. Cards (set of 5) .... 3·00 6·00

Nos. 1240/4 were issued on the occasion of the centenary of the Highland Cattle Society and the bicentenary of the Royal Highland and Agricultural Society of Scotland.

Special First Day of Issue Postmarks

Philatelic Bureau, Edinburgh .... 3·75
Oban, Argyll .... 3·75

720 Garden Festival Hall, Liverpool

721 Milburngate Centre, Durham

722 Bush House, Bristol

723 Commercial Street Development, Perth

(Des R. Maddox and Trickett and Webb Ltd)

1984 (10 Apr). **Urban Renewal.** *Phosphorised paper. P* 15 × 14.

1245 **720** 16p. brt emerald, greenish yellow, cerise, steel-blue, black, silver & flesh 40 40
1246 **721** 20½p. brt orange, greenish yellow, dp dull blue, yellowish green, azure, black & silver 60 60
a. Imperf (horiz pair) £1000
1247 **722** 28p. rosine, greenish yellow, Prussian blue, pale blue-green, black & silver 90 90
1248 **723** 31p. blue, greenish yellow, cerise, grey-blue, brt green, black & silver 90 90
a. Imperf (pair) £1000
Set of 4 .... 2·50 2·50
Set of 4 Gutter Pairs .... 5·00
First Day Cover .... 3·00
Presentation Pack .... 3·50
P.H.Q. Cards (set of 4) .... 3·00 6·00

Nos. 1245/8 were issued on the occasion of 150th anniversaries of the Royal Institute of British Architects and the Chartered Institute of Building, and to commemorate the first International Gardens Festival, Liverpool.

Special First Day of Issue Postmarks

Philatelic Bureau, Edinburgh .... 3·50
Liverpool .... 3·75

724 C.E.P.T. 25th Anniversary Logo

725 Abduction of Europa

(Des J. Larrivière (T **724**), F. Wegner (T **725**))

1984 (15 May). **25th Anniv of C.E.P.T. ("Europa")** (*T* **724**) **and Second Elections to European Parliament** (*T* **725**). *Phosphorised paper. P* 15 × 14.

1249	**724**	16p. greenish slate, dp blue & gold		90	90
		a. Horiz pair. Nos. 1249/50		1·75	1·75
		ab. Imperf (horiz pair)		£1300	
1250	**725**	16p. greenish slate, dp blue, black & gold		90	90
1251	**724**	20½p. Venetian red, dp magenta & gold		1·60	1·60
		a. Horiz pair. Nos. 1251/2		3·25	3·25
		ab. Imperf (horiz pair)			
1252	**725**	20½p. Venetian red, dp magenta, black & gold		1·60	1·60
		Set of 4		4·50	4·50
		Set of 2 Gutter Blocks of 4		9·00	
		First Day Cover			4·50
		Presentation Pack		5·00	
		P.H.Q. Cards (set of 4)		3·00	6·00

Nos. 1249/50 and 1251/2 were each printed together, *se-tenant*, in horizontal pairs throughout the sheets.

Special First Day of Issue Postmarks

Philatelic Bureau, Edinburgh	4·75
London SW	4·75

726 Lancaster House

(Des P. Hogarth)

1984 (5 June). **London Economic Summit Conference.** *Phosphorised paper. P* 14 × 15.

1253	**726**	31p. silver, bistre-yellow, brown-ochre, black, rosine, brt blue & reddish lilac	1·00	1·00
		Gutter Pair	2·00	
		First Day Cover		2·00
		P.H.Q. Card	1·00	2·75

Special First Day of Issue Postmarks

Philatelic Bureau, Edinburgh	2·50
London SW	2·50

727 View of Earth from "Apollo 11"

728 Navigational Chart of English Channel

729 Greenwich Observatory

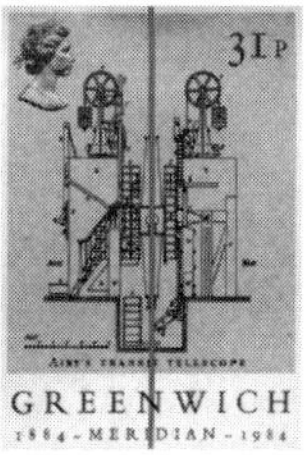

730 Sir George Airy's Transit Telescope

(Des H. Waller. Litho Questa)

1984 (26 June). **Centenary of the Greenwich Meridian.** *Phosphorised paper. P* 14 × 14½.

1254 **727**	16p.	new blue, greenish yellow, magenta, black, scarlet & blue-black	40	40
1255 **728**	20½p.	olive-sepia, lt brown, pale buff, black & scarlet	65	65
1256 **729**	28p.	new blue, greenish yellow, scarlet, black & brt purple	85	90
1257 **730**	31p.	dp blue, cobalt, scarlet & black	90	1·10
		Set of 4	2·50	2·75
		Set of 4 Gutter Pairs	5·00	
		First Day Cover		2·75
		Presentation Pack	3·75	
		P.H.Q. Cards (set of 4)	3·00	6·00

On Nos. 1254/7 the Meridian is represented by a scarlet line.

Special First Day of Issue Postmarks

Philatelic Bureau, Edinburgh	3·50
London SE10	3·50

731 Bath Mail Coach, 1784

732 Attack on Exeter Mail, 1816

733 Norwich Mail in Thunderstorm, 1827

734 Holyhead and Liverpool Mails leaving London, 1828

735 Edinburgh Mail Snowbound, 1831

(Des K. Bassford and S. Paine. Eng C. Slania. Recess and photo)

1984 (31 July). **Bicentenary of First Mail Coach Run, Bath and Bristol to London.** *Phosphorised paper. P* 15 × 14.

1258 **731**	16p.	pale stone, black, grey-black & brt scarlet	60	40
		a. Horiz strip of 5. Nos. 1258/62	2·75	2·75
1259 **732**	16p.	pale stone, black, grey-black & brt scarlet	60	40
1260 **733**	16p.	pale stone, black, grey-black & brt scarlet	60	40
1261 **734**	16p.	pale stone, black, grey-black & brt scarlet	60	40
1262 **735**	16p.	pale stone, black, grey-black & brt scarlet	60	40
		Set of 5	2·75	1·75
		Gutter Block of 10	5·50	
		First Day Cover		2·75
		Presentation Pack	3·75	
		Souvenir Book	6·00	
		P.H.Q. Cards (set of 5)	3·00	6·50

Nos. 1258/62 were printed together, *se-tenant*, in horizontal strips of 5 throughout the sheet.

The souvenir book is a 24-page illustrated booklet with a set of mint stamps in a sachet attached to the front cover.

Special First Day of Issue Postmarks

Philatelic Bureau, Edinburgh	3·25
Bristol	3·50

736 Nigerian Clinic

737 Violinist and Acropolis, Athens

738 Building Project, Sri Lanka

739 British Council Library, Middle East

(Des F. Newell and J. Sorrell)

1984 (25 Sept). **50th Anniv of the British Council.** *Phosphorised paper. P 15 × 14.*

1263	**736**	17p. grey-green, greenish yellow, brt purple, dull blue, black, pale green & yellow-green	50	50
1264	**737**	22p. crimson, greenish yellow, brt rose-red, dull green, black, pale drab & slate-purple	65	65
1265	**738**	31p. sepia, olive-bistre, red, black, pale stone & olive-brown	90	90
1266	**739**	34p. steel blue, yellow, rose-red, new blue, black, azure & pale blue	1·00	1·00
		Set of 4	2·75	2·75
		Set of 4 Gutter Pairs	5·50	
		First Day Cover		2·75
		Presentation Pack	3·50	
		P.H.Q. Cards (set of 4)	3·00	6·00

Special First Day of Issue Postmarks

Philatelic Bureau, Edinburgh	3·25
London SW	3·50

740 The Holy Family

741 Arrival in Bethlehem

742 Shepherd and Lamb

743 Virgin and Child

744 Offering of Frankincense

(Des Yvonne Gilbert)

1984 (20 Nov). **Christmas.** *One phosphor band (13p.) or phosphorised paper (others). P 15 × 14.*

1267	**740**	13p. pale cream, grey-black, bistre-yellow, magenta, red-brown & lake-brown	30	30
		Eu. Underprint Type 4	45	
1268	**741**	17p. pale cream, grey-black, yellow, magenta, dull blue & dp dull blue	50	50
		a. Imperf (pair)		
1269	**742**	22p. pale cream, grey-black, olive-yellow, brt magenta, brt blue & brownish grey	60	60
1270	**743**	31p. pale cream, grey-black, bistre-yellow, magenta, dull blue & lt brown	95	95
1271	**744**	34p. pale cream, olive-grey, bistre-yellow, magenta, turquoise-green & brown-olive	1·00	1·00
		Set of 5	3·00	3·00
		Set of 5 Gutter Pairs	6·00	
		First Day Cover		3·00
		Presentation Pack	3·75	
		P.H.Q. Cards (set of 5)	3·00	6·00

Examples of No. 1267Eu from the 1984 Christmas booklet (No. FX7) show a random pattern of blue double-lined stars printed on the reverse over the gum.

Special First Day of Issue Postmarks

Philatelic Bureau, Edinburgh	3·75
Bethlehem, Llandeilo, Dyfed	3·75

Collectors Pack 1984

1984 (20 Nov). *Comprises Nos.* 1236/71.

CP1271a	Collectors Pack	35·00

Post Office Yearbook

1984. *Comprises Nos.* 1236/71 *in 24-page hardbound book with slip case, illustrated in colour* .... 75·00

745 "The Flying Scotsman"

746 "The Golden Arrow"

747 "The Cheltenham Flyer"

748 "The Royal Scot"

749 "The Cornish Riviera"

(Des T. Cuneo)

1985 (22 Jan). **Famous Trains.** *Phosphorised paper. P* 15 × 14.

1272	**745**	17p.	black, lemon, magenta, dull blue, grey-black & gold	50	50
		a.	Imperf (pair)	£1800	
1273	**746**	22p.	black, greenish yellow, brt rose, dp dull blue, grey-black & gold	85	70
1274	**747**	29p.	black, greenish yellow, magenta, blue, grey-black & gold	1·00	90
1275	**748**	31p.	black, bistre-yellow, brt magenta, new blue, slate-black & gold	1·25	1·00
1276	**749**	34p.	black, greenish yellow, brt rose, blue, slate-black & gold	1·40	1·10
			Set of 5	4·50	4·00
			Set of 5 Gutter Pairs	9·00	
			First Day Cover		5·00
			Presentation Pack	5·25	
			P.H.Q. Cards (set of 5)	4·00	11·00

Nos. 1272/6 were issued on the occasion of the 150th anniversary of the Great Western Railway Company.

Special First Day of Issue Postmarks

Philatelic Bureau, Edinburgh	6·00
Bristol	6·25

750 *Bombus terrestris* (bee)

751 *Coccinella septempunctata* (ladybird)

752 *Decticus verrucivorus* (bush-cricket)

753 *Lucanus cervus* (stag beetle)

754 *Anax imperator* (dragonfly)

(Des G. Beningfield)

1985 (12 Mar). **Insects.** *Phosphorised paper. P* 14 × 15.

1277	**750**	17p.	black, greenish yellow, magenta, blue, azure, gold & slate-black	40	40
1278	**751**	22p.	black, greenish yellow, brt rose-red, dull blue-green, slate-black & gold	60	60
1279	**752**	29p.	black, greenish yellow, brt rose, greenish blue, grey-black, gold & bistre-yellow	80	80
1280	**753**	31p.	black, greenish yellow, rose, pale new blue & gold	90	90
1281	**754**	34p.	black, greenish yellow, magenta, greenish blue, grey-black & gold	90	90
			Set of 5	3·25	3·25
			Set of 5 Gutter Pairs	6·50	
			First Day Cover		3·50
			Presentation Pack	4·00	
			P.H.Q. Cards (set of 5)	3·00	6·50

Nos. 1277/81 were issued on the occasion of the centenaries of the Royal Entomological Society of London's Royal Charter, and of the Selborne Society.

Special First Day of Issue Postmarks

Philatelic Bureau, Edinburgh	4·50
London SW	4·50

755 "Water Music" (George Frederick Handel)

756 "The Planets Suite" (Gustav Holst)

757 "The First Cuckoo" (Frederick Delius)

758 "Sea Pictures" (Edward Elgar)

(Des W. McLean)

1985 (14 May). **Europa. European Music Year. British Composers.** *Phosphorised paper. P* 14 × 14½.

1282	**755**	17p.	black, brt yellow-green, dp magenta, new blue, grey & gold	65	65
			a. Imperf (vert pair)		
1283	**756**	22p.	black, greenish yellow, brt magenta, new blue, grey-black & gold	90	90
			a. Imperf (pair)	£1300	
1284	**757**	31p.	black, greenish yellow, magenta, greenish blue, grey-black & gold	1·40	1·40
1285	**758**	34p.	black, olive-yellow, bistre, turquoise-blue, slate & gold	1·50	1·50
			Set of 4	4·00	4·00
			Set of 4 Gutter Pairs	8·00	
			First Day Cover		4·00
			Presentation Pack	4·50	
			P.H.Q. Cards (set of 4)	3·00	6·00

Nos. 1282/5 were issued on the occasion of the 300th birth anniversary of Handel.

Special First Day of Issue Postmarks

Philatelic Bureau, Edinburgh	4·00
Worcester	4·00

759 R.N.L.I. Lifeboat and Signal Flags

760 Beachy Head Lighthouse and Chart

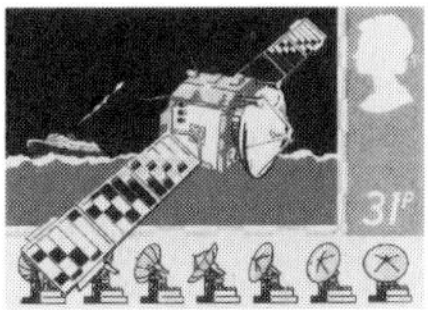

761 "Marecs A" Communications Satellite and Dish Aerials

762 Buoys

(Des F. Newell and J. Sorrell. Litho J.W.)

1985 (18 June). **Safety at Sea.** *Phosphorised paper. P* 14.

1286	**759**	17p.	black, azure, emerald, ultramarine, orange-yellow, vermilion, brt blue & chrome-yellow	50	50
1287	**760**	22p.	black, azure, emerald, ultramarine, orange-yellow, vermilion, brt blue & chrome-yellow	65	65
1288	**761**	31p.	black, azure, emerald, ultramarine, orange-yellow, vermilion & brt blue	1·10	1·10
1289	**762**	34p.	black, azure, emerald, ultramarine, orange-yellow, vermilion, brt blue & chrome-yellow	1·10	1·10
			Set of 4	3·00	3·00
			Set of 4 Gutter Pairs	6·00	
			First Day Cover		3·50
			Presentation Pack	4·25	
			P.H.Q. Cards (set of 4)	3·00	6·00

Nos. 1286/9 were issued on the occasion of the bicentenary of the unimmersible lifeboat and the 50th anniversary of radar.

Special First Day of Issue Postmarks

Philatelic Bureau, Edinburgh	3·50
Eastbourne	3·50

HAVE YOU READ THE NOTES AT THE BEGINNING OF THIS CATALOGUE?

These often provide answers to the enquiries we receive.

763 Datapost Motorcyclist, City of London

764 Rural Postbus

765 Parcel Delivery in Winter

766 Town Letter Delivery

(Des P. Hogarth)

1985 (30 July). **350 Years of Royal Mail Public Postal Service.** *Phosphorised paper. P* 14 × 15.

1290	**763**	17p.	black, greenish yellow, brt carmine, greenish blue, yellow-brown, grey-black & silver	50	50
		a.	Imperf on 3 sides (vert pair)	£1300	
		Eu.	Underprint Type 5	70	
1291	**764**	22p.	black, greenish yellow, cerise, steel-blue, lt green, grey-black & silver	65	65
1292	**765**	31p.	black, greenish yellow, brt carmine, dull blue, drab, grey-black & silver	1·10	1·10
		a.	Imperf (vert pair)	£1300	
1293	**766**	34p.	black, greenish yellow, cerise, ultramarine, lt brown, grey-black & silver	1·10	1·10
		a.	Imperf between (vert pair)		
			Set of 4	3·00	3·00
			Set of 4 Gutter Pairs	6·00	
			First Day Cover		3·25
			Presentation Pack	4·25	
			P.H.Q. Cards (set of 4)	3·00	6·00

No. 1290a shows perforation indentations at right, but is imperforate at top, bottom and on the left-hand side.

Examples of No. 1290Eu from the 1985 £1.70 booklet (sold at £1.53) (No. FT4) show a blue double-lined D in a random pattern, on the reverse over the gum.

Special First Day of Issue Postmarks

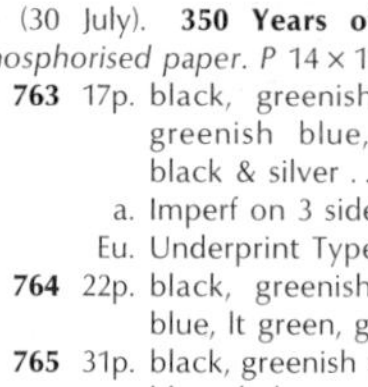

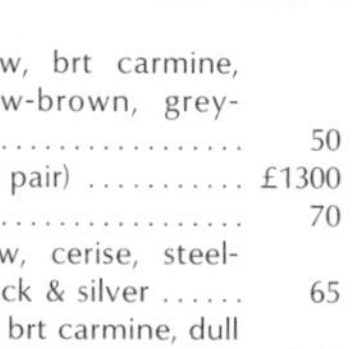

Philatelic Bureau, Edinburgh	3·50
Bagshot, Surrey	3·50

767 King Arthur and Merlin

768 Lady of the Lake

769 Queen Guinevere and Sir Lancelot

770 Sir Galahad

(Des Yvonne Gilbert)

1985 (3 Sept). **Arthurian Legends.** *Phosphorised paper. P* 15 × 14.

1294	**767**	17p.	grey-black, lemon, brown-lilac, ultramarine, grey-black & silver	50	50
		a.	Imperf (pair)	£1800	
1295	**768**	22p.	black, lemon, brown-lilac, pale blue, grey-black, silver & grey-black	65	75
1296	**769**	31p.	black, lemon, magenta, turquoise-blue, grey-black, silver & grey-black	1·10	1·10
1297	**770**	34p.	grey, lemon, magenta, new blue, grey-black, silver & grey-black	1·10	1·25
			Set of 4	3·00	3·25
			Set of 4 Gutter Pairs	6·00	
			First Day Cover		3·50
			Presentation Pack	5·00	
			P.H.Q. Cards (set of 4)	3·00	6·00

Nos. 1294/7 were issued on the occasion of the 500th anniversary of the printing of Sir Thomas Malory's *Morte d'Arthur*.

Special First Day of Issue Postmarks

Philatelic Bureau, Edinburgh	3·50
Tintagel, Cornwall	3·50

771 Peter Sellers (from photo by Bill Brandt)

772 David Niven (from photo by Cornell Lucas)

773 Charlie Chaplin (from photo by Lord Snowdon)

774 Vivien Leigh (from photo by Angus McBean)

775 Alfred Hitchcock (from photo by Howard Coster)

(Des K. Bassford)

1985 (8 Oct). **British Film Year.** *Phosphorised paper. P* $14\frac{1}{2}$.

1298	**771**	17p. grey-black, olive-grey, gold & silver		50	50
1299	**772**	22p. black, brown, gold & silver		75	75
1300	**773**	29p. black, lavender, gold & silver		1·10	1·10
1301	**774**	31p. black, pink, gold & silver		1·25	1·25
1302	**775**	34p. black, greenish blue, gold & silver		1·40	1·40
		Set of 5		4·50	4·50
		Set of 5 Gutter Pairs		9·00	
		First Day Cover			4·75
		Presentation Pack		6·50	
		Souvenir Book		7·50	
		P.H.Q. Cards (set of 5)		3·00	6·00

The souvenir book is a 24-page illustrated booklet with a set of mint stamps in a sachet attached to the front cover.

Special First Day of Issue Postmarks

Philatelic Bureau, Edinburgh	5·00
London WC	5·00

776 Principal Boy

777 Genie

778 Dame

779 Good Fairy

780 Pantomime Cat

(Des A. George)

1985 (19 Nov). **Christmas. Pantomine Characters.** *One phosphor band* (*12p.*) *or phosphorised paper* (*others*). *P* 15 × 14.

1303	**776**	12p. new blue, greenish yellow, brt rose, gold, grey-black & silver	35	30
		a. Imperf (pair)	£1300	
		Eu. Underprint Type 4	40	
1304	**777**	17p. emerald, greenish yellow, brt rose, new blue, black, gold & silver	45	40
		a. Imperf (pair)	£1800	
1305	**778**	22p. brt carmine, greenish yellow, pale new blue, grey, gold & silver	70	80
1306	**779**	31p. brt orange, lemon, rose, slate-purple, silver & gold	95	1·00
1307	**780**	34p. brt reddish violet, brt blue, brt rose, black, grey-brown, gold & silver	1·00	1·10
		Set of 5	3·00	3·25
		Set of 5 Gutter Pairs	6·00	
		First Day Cover		3·75
		Presentation Pack	4·50	
		P.H.Q. Cards (set of 5)	3·00	6·00
		Christmas Folder (contains No. 1303 × 50)	20·00	

Examples of No. 1303Eu from the 1985 Christmas booklet (No. FX8) show a random pattern of blue double-lined stars printed on the reverse over the gum.

Special First Day of Issue Postmarks

Philatelic Bureau, Edinburgh .... 4·00
Bethlehem, Llandeilo, Dyfed .... 4·00

Collectors Pack 1985

1985 (19 Nov). *Comprises Nos.* 1272/1307.
CP1307*a* Collectors Pack .... 35·00

Post Office Yearbook

1985. *Comprises Nos.* 1272/1307 *in 32-page hardbound book with slip case, illustrated in colour* .... 75·00

781 Light Bulb and North Sea Oil Drilling Rig (Energy)

782 Thermometer and Pharmaceutical Laboratory (Health)

783 Garden Hoe and Steelworks (Steel)

784 Loaf of Bread and Cornfield (Agriculture)

(Des K. Bassford. Litho Questa)

1986 (14 Jan). **Industry Year.** *Phosphorised paper. P* $14\frac{1}{2} \times 14$.

1308	**781**	17p.	gold, black, magenta, greenish yellow & new blue	45	45
1309	**782**	22p.	gold, pale turquoise-green, black, magenta, greenish yellow & blue	60	60
1310	**783**	31p.	gold, black, magenta, greenish yellow & new blue	90	90
1311	**784**	34p.	gold, black, magenta, greenish yellow & new blue	1·10	1·10
			Set of 4	2·75	2·75
			Set of 4 Gutter Pairs	5·50	
			First Day Cover		3·25
			Presentation Pack	4·00	
			P.H.Q. Cards (set of 4)	3·00	6·00

Special First Day of Issue Postmarks

Philatelic Bureau, Edinburgh .... 3·50
Birmingham .... 3·50

785 Dr. Edmond Halley as Comet

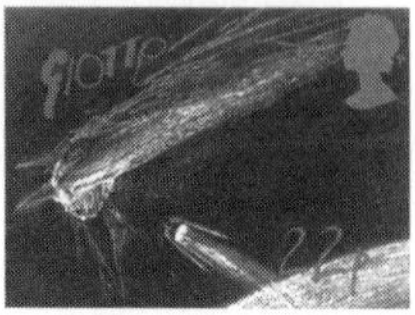

786 *Giotto* Spacecraft approaching Comet

787 "Maybe Twice in a Lifetime"

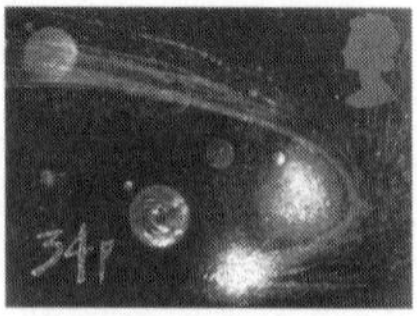

788 Comet orbiting Sun and Planets

(Des R. Steadman)

1986 (18 Feb). **Appearance of Halley's Comet.** *Phosphorised paper. P* 15×14.

1312	**785**	17p.	black, bistre, rosine, blue, grey-black, gold & dp brown	45	45
1313	**786**	22p.	orange-vermilion, greenish yellow, brt purple, new blue, black & gold	70	70
1314	**787**	31p.	black, greenish yellow, brt purple, dp turquoise-blue, grey-black & gold	1·10	1·10
1315	**788**	34p.	blue, greenish yellow, magenta, dp turquoise-blue, black & gold	1·10	1·10
			Set of 4	3·00	3·00
			Set of 4 Gutter Pairs	6·00	
			First Day Cover		4·00
			Presentation Pack	4·75	
			P.H.Q. Cards (set of 4)	4·00	6·00

Special First Day of Issue Postmarks

Philatelic Bureau, Edinburgh	4·25
London SE10	4·25

791 Barn Owl

792 Pine Marten

789 Queen Elizabeth in 1928, 1942 and 1952

790 Queen Elizabeth in 1958, 1973 and 1982

T **789/90** were printed horizontally *se-tenant* within the sheet

793 Wild Cat

794 Natterjack Toad

(Des J. Matthews)

1986 (21 Apr). **60th Birthday of Queen Elizabeth II.** *Phosphorised paper. P* 15 × 14.

1316	**789**	17p.	grey-black, turquoise-green, brt green, green & dull blue	70	40
			a. Pair. Nos. 1316/17	1·40	1·40
1317	**790**	17p.	grey-black, dull blue, greenish blue & indigo	70	40
1318	**789**	34p.	grey-black, dp dull purple, yellow-orange & red	1·50	1·50
			a. Pair. Nos. 1318/19	3·00	3·00
1319	**790**	34p.	grey-black, olive-brown, yellow-brown, olive-grey & red	1·50	1·50
			Set of 4	4·00	4·00
			Set of 2 Gutter Blocks of 4	8·00	
			First Day Cover		4·50
			Presentation Pack	5·00	
			Souvenir Book	7·50	
			P.H.Q. Cards (set of 4)	3·00	6·00

The souvenir book is a special booklet, fully illustrated and containing a mint set of stamps.

Special First Day of Issue Postmarks

Philatelic Bureau, Edinburgh	4·75
Windsor	4·75

(Des K. Lilly)

1986 (20 May). **Europa. Nature Conservation – Endangered Species.** *Phosphorised paper. P* $14\frac{1}{2} \times 14$.

1320	**791**	17p.	gold, greenish yellow, rose, yellow-brown, olive-grey, new blue & black	50	50
1321	**792**	22p.	gold, greenish yellow, reddish brown, olive-yellow, turquoise-blue, grey-black & black	90	75
1322	**793**	31p.	gold, brt yellow-green, magenta, lt brown, ultramarine, olive-brown & black	1·25	1·10
1323	**794**	34p.	gold, greenish yellow, brt rose-red, brt green, grey-black & black	1·50	1·25
			Set of 4	3·75	3·25
			Set of 4 Gutter Pairs	7·50	
			First Day Cover		4·50
			Presentation Pack	4·50	
			P.H.Q. Cards (set of 4)	3·00	6·00

Special First Day of Issue Postmarks

Philatelic Bureau, Edinburgh	4·75
Lincoln	4·75

795 Peasants working in Fields

796 Freemen working at Town Trades

801 Weightlifting

802 Rifle Shooting

797 Knight and Retainers

798 Lord at Banquet

803 Hockey

(Des Tayburn Design Consultancy)

1986 (17 Jun). **900th Anniv of Domesday Book.** *Phosphorised paper. P* 15 × 14.

1324	**795**	17p.	yellow-brown, vermilion, lemon, brt emerald, orange-brown, grey & brownish grey	50	50
1325	**796**	22p.	yellow-ochre, red, greenish blue, chestnut, grey-black & brownish grey	75	75
1326	**797**	31p.	yellow-brown, vermilion, green, Indian red, grey-black & brownish grey	1·10	1·10
1327	**798**	34p.	yellow-ochre, bright scarlet, grey-brown, new blue, lake-brown, grey-black & grey	1·25	1·25
			Set of 4	3·25	3·25
			Set of 4 Gutter Pairs	6·50	
			First Day Cover		4·00
			Presentation Pack	4·50	
			P.H.Q. Cards (set of 4)	3·00	6·00

Special First Day of Issue Postmarks

Philatelic Bureau, Edinburgh	4·25
Gloucester	4·25

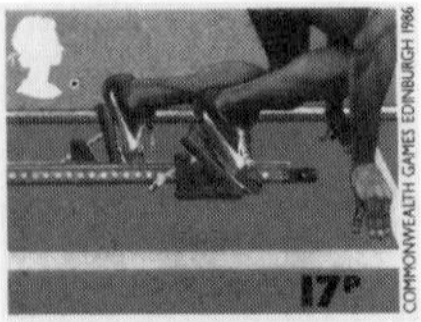

799 Athletics

800 Rowing

(Des N. Cudworth)

1986 (15 July). **Thirteenth Commonwealth Games, Edinburgh and World Hockey Cup for Men, London** (34*p*.). *Phosphorised paper. P* 15 × 14.

1328	**799**	17p.	black, greenish yellow, orange-vermilion, ultramarine, chestnut & emerald	50	50
1329	**800**	22p.	black, lemon, scarlet, new blue, royal blue, chestnut & dp ultramarine	70	70
1330	**801**	29p.	grey-black, greenish yellow, scarlet, new blue, brown-ochre, brown-rose & pale chestnut	90	90
1331	**802**	31p.	black, greenish yellow, rose, blue, dull yellow-green, chestnut & yellow-green	1·10	1·10
1332	**803**	34p.	black, lemon, scarlet, brt blue, brt emerald, red-brown & vermilion	1·25	1·25
		a.	Imperf (pair)	£1300	
			Set of 5	4·00	4·00
			Set of 5 Gutter Pairs	8·00	
			First Day Cover		4·25
			Presentation Pack	5·25	
			P.H.Q. Cards (set of 5)	4·00	6·00

No. 1332 also commemorates the centenary of the Hockey Association.

Special First Day of Issue Postmarks

Philatelic Bureau, Edinburgh	4·50
Head Post Office, Edinburgh	4·50

For full information on all future British issues, collectors should write to the British Post Office Philatelic Bureau, 20 Brandon Street, Edinburgh EH3 5TT

804 **805**

Prince Andrew and Miss Sarah Ferguson (from photo by Gene Nocon)

(Des J. Matthews)

1986 (22 July). **Royal Wedding.** *One phosphor band* (12*p.*) *or phosphorised paper* (17*p.*). *P* 14 × 15.

1333 **804** 12p. lake, greenish yellow, cerise, ultramarine, black & silver 60 60

1334 **805** 17p. steel blue, greenish yellow, cerise, ultramarine, black & gold 90 90

a. Imperf (pair) £850

Set of 2 .... 1·50 1·50

Set of 2 Gutter Pairs .... 3·00

First Day Cover .... 2·50

Presentation Pack .... 2·00

P.H.Q. Cards (set of 2) .... 1·50 5·00

Special First Day of Issue Postmarks

Philatelic Bureau, Edinburgh .... 2·75
London, SW1 .... 2·75

806 Stylised Cross on Ballot Paper

(Des J. Gibbs. Litho Questa)

1986 (19 Aug). **32nd Commonwealth Parliamentary Association Conference.** *Phosphorised paper. P* $14 \times 14\frac{1}{2}$.

1335 **806** 34p. pale grey-lilac, black, vermilion, yellow & ultramarine .... 1·25 1·25

Gutter Pair .... 2·50

First Day Cover .... 2·00

P.H.Q. Card .... 1·00 2·50

Special First Day of Issue Postmarks

Philatelic Bureau, Edinburgh .... 2·25
London, SW1 .... 2·25

807 Lord Dowding and Hawker Hurricane Mk I

808 Lord Tedder and Hawker Typhoon IB

809 Lord Trenchard and De Havilland D.H.9A

810 Sir Arthur Harris and Avro Type 683 Lancaster

811 Lord Portal and De Havilland D.H.98 Mosquito

(Des B. Sanders)

1986 (16 Sept). **History of the Royal Air Force.** *Phosphorised paper. P* $14\frac{1}{2}$.

1336 **807** 17p. pale blue, greenish yellow, brt rose, blue, black & grey-black 50 40

a. Imperf (pair) £950

1337 **808** 22p. pale turquoise-green, greenish yellow, magenta, new blue, black & grey-black 75 85

a. Face value omitted* £400

b. Queen's head omitted* £400

1338	**809**	29p.	pale drab, olive-yellow, magenta, blue, grey-black & black	1·00	1·00
1339	**810**	31p.	pale flesh, greenish yellow, magenta, ultramarine, black & grey-black	1·25	1·10
1340	**811**	34p.	buff, greenish yellow, magenta, blue, grey-black & black	1·50	1·25
			Set of 5	4·50	4·25
			Set of 5 Gutter Pairs	9·00	
			First Day Cover		5·00
			Presentation Pack	6·00	
			P.H.Q. Cards (set of 5)	4·00	6·50

Nos. 1336/40 were issued to celebrate the 50th anniversary of the first R.A.F. Commands.

*Nos. 1337a/b come from three consecutive sheets on which the stamps in the first vertical row are without the face value and those in the second vertical row the Queen's head.

Special First Day of Issue Postmarks

Philatelic Bureau, Edinburgh	5·25
Farnborough	5·25

812 The Glastonbury Thorn

813 The Tanad Valley Plygain

814 The Hebrides Tribute

815 The Dewsbury Church Knell

816 The Hereford Boy Bishop

(Des Lynda Gray)

1986 (18 Nov–2 Dec). **Christmas. Folk Customs.** *One phosphor band (12p., 13p.) or phosphorised paper (others). P* 15 × 14.

1341	**812**	12p.	gold, greenish yellow, vermilion, dp brown, emerald & dp blue (2.12)	50	50
		a.	Imperf (pair)	£900	
1342		13p.	dp blue, greenish yellow, vermilion, dp brown, emerald & gold	30	30
		Eu.	Underprint Type 4 (2.12)	50	
1343	**813**	18p.	myrtle-green, yellow, vermilion, dp blue, black, reddish brown & gold	45	45
1344	**814**	22p.	vermilion, olive-bistre, dull blue, dp brown, dp green & gold	65	65
1345	**815**	31p.	dp brown, yellow, vermilion, violet, dp dull green, black & gold	80	80
1346	**816**	34p.	violet, lemon, vermilion, dp dull blue, reddish brown & gold	90	90
			Set of 6	3·25	3·25
			Set of 6 Gutter Pairs	6·50	
			First Day Covers (2)		5·25
			Presentation Pack (Nos. 1342/6)	5·00	
			P.H.Q. Cards (Nos. 1342/6) (Set of 5)	3·00	6·00
			Christmas Folder (contains No. 1342Eu × 36)	17·00	

No. 1341 represented a discount of 1p., available between 2 and 24 December 1986, on the current second class postage rate.

Special First Day of Issue Postmarks

Philatelic Bureau, Edinburgh (Nos. 1342/6) (18 Nov)	4·50
Bethlehem, Llandeilo, Dyfed (Nos. 1342/6) (18 Nov)	4·50
Philatelic Bureau, Edinburgh (No. 1341) (2 Dec)	1·50

Collectors Pack 1986

1986 (18 Nov). *Comprises Nos.* 1308/40 *and* 1342/6.
CP1346*a* Collectors Pack .... 35·00

Post Office Yearbook

1986 (18 Nov). *Comprises Nos.* 1308/46 *in 32-page hardbound book with slip case, illustrated in colour* .... 65·00

817 North American Blanket Flower

818 Globe Thistle

819 *Echeveria*

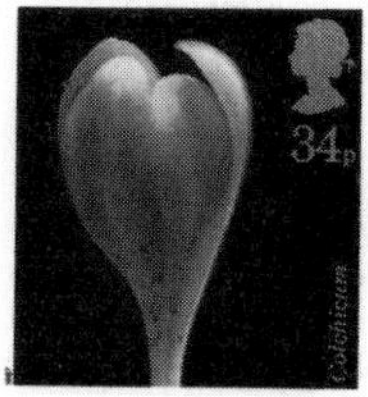

820 Autumn Crocus

(Adapted J. Matthews)

1987 (20 Jan). **Flower Photographs by Alfred Lammer.** *Phosphorised paper. P* $14\frac{1}{2} \times 14$.

1347	**817**	18p.	silver, greenish yellow, rosine, dp green & black	50	50
1348	**818**	22p.	silver, greenish yellow, new blue, greenish blue & black	80	70
1349	**819**	31p.	silver, greenish yellow, scarlet, blue-green, dp green & black	1·25	1·10
			a. Imperf (pair)	£1600	
1350	**820**	34p.	silver, greenish yellow, magenta, dull blue, dp green & black	1·40	1·25
			Set of 4	3·50	3·25
			Set of 4 Gutter Pairs	7·00	
			First Day Cover		4·25
			Presentation Pack	4·75	
			P.H.Q. Cards (set of 4)	3·00	6·00

Special First Day of Issue Postmarks

Philatelic Bureau, Edinburgh	4·75
Richmond, Surrey	4·75

821 *The Principia Mathematica*

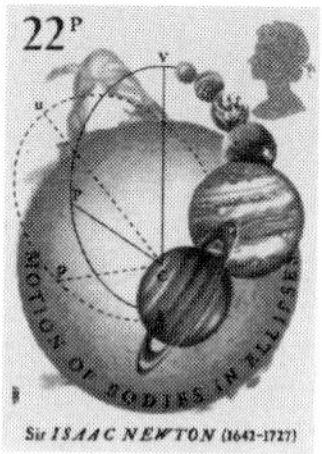

822 *Motion of Bodies in Ellipses*

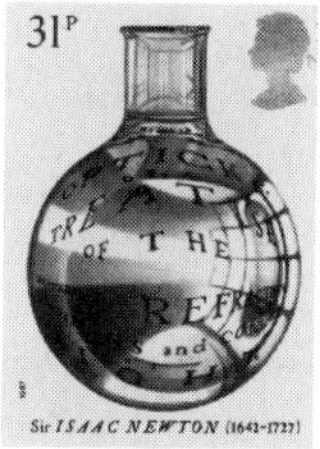

823 *Optick Treatise*

824 *The System of the World*

(Des Sarah Godwin)

1987 (24 Mar). **300th Anniv of "The Principia Mathematica" by Sir Isaac Newton.** *Phosphorised paper. P* 14×15.

1351	**821**	18p.	black, greenish yellow, cerise, blue-green, grey-black & silver	50	50
1352	**822**	22p.	black, greenish yellow, brt orange, blue, brt emerald, silver & bluish violet	70	70
1353	**823**	31p.	black, greenish yellow, scarlet, new blue, bronze-green, silver & slate-green	1·10	1·10
1354	**824**	34p.	black, greenish yellow, red, brt blue, grey-black & silver	1·25	1·25
			Set of 4	3·25	3·25
			Set of 4 Gutter Pairs	6·50	
			First Day Cover		3·50
			Presentation Pack	4·50	
			P.H.Q. Cards (set of 4)	3·00	6·00

Special First Day of Issue Postmarks

Philatelic Bureau, Edinburgh	4·00
Woolsthorpe, Lincs	4·00

825 Willis Faber and Dumas Building, Ipswich

826 Pompidou Centre, Paris

827 Staatsgalerie, Stuttgart

828 European Investment Bank, Luxembourg

(Des B. Tattersfield)

1987 (12 May). **Europa. British Architects in Europe.** *Phosphorised paper. P* 15 × 14.

1355	**825**	18p.	black, bistre-yellow, cerise, brt blue, dp grey & grey-black	50	50
1356	**826**	22p.	black, greenish yellow, carmine, brt blue, dp grey & grey-black	70	70
1357	**827**	31p.	grey-black, bistre-yellow, cerise, brt blue, brt green, black & dull violet	1·10	1·10
			a. Imperf (horiz pair)	£1000	
1358	**828**	34p.	black, greenish yellow, cerise, brt blue, grey-black & dp grey	1·25	1·25
			Set of 4	3·25	3·25
			Set of 4 Gutter Pairs	6·50	
			First Day Cover		3·50
			Presentation Pack	4·50	
			P.H.Q. Cards (set of 4)	3·00	6·00

Special First Day of Issue Postmarks

Philatelic Bureau, Edinburgh	4·00
Ipswich	4·00

829 Brigade Members with Ashford Litter, 1887

830 Bandaging Blitz Victim, 1940

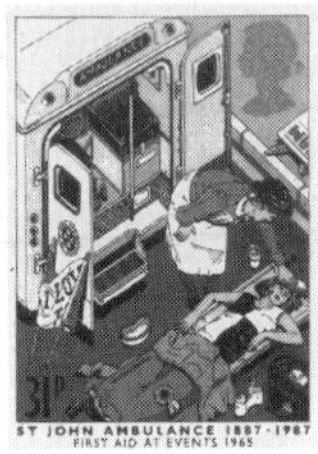

831 Volunteer with fainting Girl, 1965

832 Transport of Transplant Organ by Air Wing, 1987

(Des Debbie Cook. Litho Questa)

1987 (16 June). **Centenary of St. John Ambulance Brigade.** *Phosphorised paper. P* 14 × $14\frac{1}{2}$.

1359	**829**	18p.	new blue, greenish yellow, magenta, black, silver & pink	50	50
			Ea. Black ptg double	†	£250
			Eb. Black ptg triple	†	£750
1360	**830**	22p.	new blue, greenish yellow, magenta, black, silver & cobalt	65	65
1361	**831**	31p.	new blue, greenish yellow, magenta, black, silver & bistre-brown	1·10	1·10
1362	**832**	34p.	new blue, greenish yellow, magenta, black, silver & greenish grey	1·10	1·10
			Set of 4	3·00	3·00
			Set of 4 Gutter Pairs	6·00	
			First Day Cover		3·50
			Presentation Pack	4·50	
			P.H.Q. Cards (set of 4)	3·00	6·00

Special First Day of Issue Postmarks

Philatelic Bureau, Edinburgh	4·00
London, EC1	4·00

833 Arms of the Lord Lyon King of Arms

834 Scottish Heraldic Banner of Prince Charles

837 Crystal Palace, "Monarch of the Glen" (Landseer) and Grace Darling

838 *Great Eastern, Beeton's Book of Household Management* and Prince Albert

835 Arms of Royal Scottish Academy of Painting, Sculpture and Architecture

836 Arms of Royal Society of Edinburgh

839 Albert Memorial, Ballot Box and Disraeli

840 Diamond Jubilee Emblem, Newspaper Placard for Relief of Mafeking and Morse Key

(Des J. Matthews)

1987 (21 July). **300th Anniv of Revival of Order of the Thistle.** *Phosphorised paper. P* 14½.

1363	**833**	18p.	black, lemon, scarlet, blue, dp green, slate & brown	50	50
1364	**834**	22p.	black, greenish yellow, carmine, new blue, dp green, grey & lake-brown	65	65
1365	**835**	31p.	black, greenish yellow, scarlet, new blue, dull green, grey & grey-black	1·10	1·10
1366	**836**	34p.	black, greenish yellow, scarlet, dp ultramarine, dull green, grey & yellow-brown	1·10	1·10
			Set of 4	3·00	3·00
			Set of 4 Gutter Pairs	6·00	
			First Day Cover		4·25
			Presentation Pack	4·50	
			P.H.Q. Cards (set of 4)	3·00	6·00

Special First Day of Issue Postmarks

Philatelic Bureau, Edinburgh	4·75
Rothesay, Isle of Bute	4·75

(Des M. Dempsey. Eng C. Slania. Recess and photo)

1987 (8 Sept). **150th Anniv of Queen Victoria's Accession.** *Phosphorised paper. P* 15 × 14.

1367	**837**	18p.	pale stone, dp blue, lemon, rose, greenish blue, brown-ochre & grey-black	50	50
1368	**838**	22p.	pale stone, dp brown, lemon, rose, grey-black & brown-ochre	75	75
1369	**839**	31p.	pale stone, dp lilac, lemon, cerise, brown-ochre, greenish blue & grey-black	1·10	1·10
1370	**840**	34p.	pale stone, myrtle-green, yellow-ochre, reddish brown & brown-ochre	1·25	1·25
			Set of 4	3·25	3·25
			Set of 4 Gutter Pairs	6·50	
			First Day Cover		4·25
			Presentation Pack	4·75	
			P.H.Q. Cards (set of 4)	3·00	6·00

Special First Day of Issue Postmarks

Philatelic Bureau, Edinburgh	4·75
Newport, Isle of Wight	4·75

841 Pot by Bernard Leach

842 Pot by Elizabeth Fritsch

843 Pot by Lucie Rie

844 Pot by Hans Coper

(Des T. Evans)

1987 (13 Oct). **Studio Pottery.** *Phosphorised paper. P* $14\frac{1}{2} \times 14$.

1371	**841**	18p.	gold, lemon, lt red-brown, chestnut, lt grey & black	50	50
1372	**842**	26p.	blue over silver, yellow-orange, brt purple, lavender, bluish violet, grey-brown & black	70	70
1373	**843**	31p.	rose-lilac over silver, greenish yellow, cerise, new blue, grey-lilac & black	1·10	1·10
1374	**844**	34p.	copper, yellow-brown, reddish brown, grey-lilac & black	1·25	1·25
			Set of 4	3·25	3·25
			Set of 4 Gutter Pairs	6·50	
			First Day Cover		3·50
			Presentation Pack	4·50	
			P.H.Q. Cards (set of 4)	3·00	6·00

Special First Day of Issue Postmarks

Philatelic Bureau, Edinburgh	4·00
St. Ives, Cornwall	4·00

845 Decorating the Christmas Tree

846 Waiting for Father Christmas

847 Sleeping Child and Father Christmas in Sleigh

848 Child reading

849 Child playing Recorder and Snowman

(Des M. Foreman)

1987 (17 Nov). **Christmas.** *One phosphor band* (13p.) *or phosphorised paper* (*others*). *P* 15 × 14.

1375	**845**	13p.	gold, greenish yellow, rose, greenish blue & black	30	30
		Eu.	Underprint Type 4	50	
1376	**846**	18p.	gold, greenish yellow, brt purple, greenish blue, brt blue & black	50	50
1377	**847**	26p.	gold, greenish yellow, brt purple, new blue, brt blue & black	75	75
1378	**848**	31p.	gold, greenish yellow, scarlet, brt magenta, dull rose, greenish blue & black	95	1·10
1379	**849**	34p.	gold, greenish yellow, dull rose, greenish blue, brt blue & black	1·10	1·25
			Set of 5	3·25	3·50
			Set of 5 Gutter Pairs	6·50	
			First Day Cover		4·25
			Presentation Pack	4·50	
			P.H.Q. Cards (set of 5)	3·00	6·00
			Christmas Folder (contains No. 1375Eu × 36)	15·00	

Examples of the 13p. value from special folders, containing 36 stamps and sold for £4.60, show a blue underprint of double-lined stars printed on the reverse over the gum.

Special First Day of Issue Postmarks

Philatelic Bureau, Edinburgh	4·75
Bethlehem, Llandeilo, Dyfed	4·75

Collectors Pack 1987

1987 (17 Nov). *Comprises Nos.* 1347/79.
CP1379*a* Collectors Pack ... 38·00

Post Office Yearbook

1987 (17 Nov). *Comprises Nos.* 1347/79 *in 32-page hardbound book with slip case, illustrated in colour* .... 40·00

850 Bull-rout (Jonathan Couch)

851 Yellow Waterlily (Major Joshua Swatkin)

852 Whistling ("Bewick's") Swan (Edward Lear)

853 *Morchella esculenta* (James Sowerby)

854 Revd William Morgan (Bible translator, 1588)

855 William Salesbury (New Testament translator, 1567)

856 Bishop Richard Davies (New Testament translator, 1567)

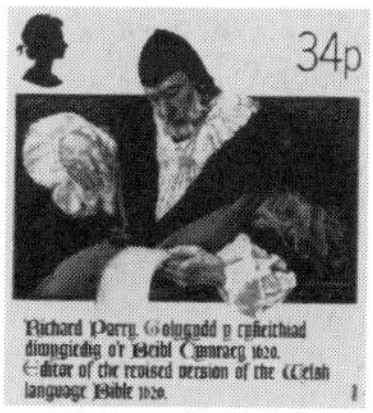

857 Bishop Richard Parry (editor of Revised Welsh Bible, 1620)

(Des. E. Hughes)

1988 (19 Jan). **Bicentenary of Linnean Society. Archive Illustrations.** *Phosphorised paper. P* 15 × 14.

1380	**850**	18p.	grey-black, stone, orange-yellow, brt purple, olive-bistre & gold	60	45
1381	**851**	26p.	black, stone, bistre-yellow, dull orange, greenish blue, gold & pale bistre	80	70
1382	**852**	31p.	black, stone, greenish yellow, rose-red, dp blue, gold & olive-bistre	1·25	1·10
		a.	Imperf (horiz pair)	£1300	
1383	**853**	34p.	black, stone, yellow, pale bistre, olive-grey, gold & olive-bistre	1·25	1·10
			Set of 4	3·50	3·00
			Set of 4 Gutter Pairs	7·00	
			First Day Cover		3·50
			Presentation Pack	4·50	
			P.H.Q. Cards (set of 4)	3·00	6·00

Special First Day of Issue Postmarks

Philatelic Bureau, Edinburgh .... 4·00
London, W1 .... 4·00

(Des K. Bowen)

1988 (1 Mar). **400th Anniv of Welsh Bible.** *Phosphorised paper. P* $14\frac{1}{2}$ × 14.

1384	**854**	18p.	grey-black, greenish yellow, cerise, blue, black & emerald	45	45
		a.	Imperf (pair)	£1300	
1385	**855**	26p.	grey-black, yellow, brt rose-red, turquoise-blue, black & orange	70	70
1386	**856**	31p.	black, chrome-yellow, carmine, new blue, grey-black & blue	1·10	1·10
1387	**857**	34p.	grey-black, greenish yellow, cerise, turquoise-green, black & brt violet	1·10	1·10
			Set of 4	3·00	3·00
			Set of 4 Gutter Pairs	6·00	
			First Day Cover		4·00
			Presentation Pack	4·50	
			P.H.Q. Cards (set of 4)	3·00	6·00

Special First Day of Issue Postmarks

Philatelic Bureau, Edinburgh .... 4·75
Ty Mawr, Wybrnant, Gwynedd .... 4·75

858 Gymnastics (Centenary of British Amateur Gymnastics Association)

859 Downhill Skiing (Ski Club of Great Britain)

860 Tennis (Centenary of Lawn Tennis Association)

861 Football (Centenary of Football League)

(Des. J. Sutton)

1988 (22 Mar). **Sports Organizations.** *Phosphorised paper. P* 14½.

1388	**858**	18p.	violet-blue, greenish yellow, rosine, brt rose, new blue & silver	45	45
1389	**859**	26p.	violet-blue, greenish yellow, vermilion, carmine, yellow-orange & silver	70	70
1390	**860**	31p.	violet-blue, greenish yellow, rose, blue, pale greenish blue, silver & brt orange	1·10	1·10
1391	**861**	34p.	violet-blue, greenish yellow, vermilion, blue, brt emerald, silver & pink	1·10	1·10
			Set of 4	3·00	3·00
			Set of 4 Gutter Pairs	6·00	
			First Day Cover		4·00
			Presentation Pack	4·50	
			P.H.Q. Cards (set of 2)	2·25	5·00

Special First Day of Issue Postmarks

Philatelic Bureau, Edinburgh	4·50
Wembley	4·50

862 *Mallard* and Mailbags on Pick-up Arms

863 Loading Transatlantic Mail on Liner *Queen Elizabeth*

864 Glasgow Tram No. 1173 and Pillar Box

865 Imperial Airways Handley Page H.P.45 *Horatius* and Airmail Van

(Des M. Dempsey)

1988 (10 May). **Europa. Transport and Mail Services in 1930s.** *Phosphorised paper. P* 15 × 14.

1392	**862**	18p.	brown, yellow, rose-red, dull blue, dp brown, reddish violet & black	50	50
1393	**863**	26p.	brown, yellow, orange-vermilion, dull blue, violet-blue, brt emerald & black	80	80
1394	**864**	31p.	brown, yellow-orange, carmine, dull purple, violet-blue, brt green & black	1·10	1·10
1395	**865**	34p.	brown, orange-yellow, carmine-rose, bluish violet, brt blue, sepia & black	1·25	1·25
			Set of 4	3·25	3·25
			Set of 4 Gutter Pairs	6·50	
			First Day Cover		3·50
			Presentation Pack	4·50	
			P.H.Q. Cards (set of 4)	2·00	5·00

Special First Day of Issue Postmarks

Philatelic Bureau, Edinburgh	4·00
Glasgow	4·00

866 Early Settler and Sailing Clipper

867 Queen Elizabeth II with British and Australian Parliament Buildings

868 W.G. Grace (cricketer) and Tennis Racquet

868 Shakespeare, John Lennon (entertainer) and Sydney Opera House

(Des G. Emery. Litho Questa)

1988 (21 June). **Bicentenary of Australian Settlement.** *Phosphorised paper. P* $14\frac{1}{2}$.

1396	**866**	18p.	dp ultramarine, orange-yellow, scarlet, black, bluish grey & emerald	60	60
			a. Horiz pair. Nos. 1396/7	1·25	1·25
1397	**867**	18p.	dp ultramarine, orange-yellow, black, bluish grey & emerald	60	60
1398	**868**	34p.	dp ultramarine, orange-yellow, scarlet, black, bluish grey & emerald	1·10	1·10
			a. Horiz pair. Nos. 1398/9	2·40	2·40
1399	**869**	34p.	dp ultramarine, orange-yellow, black, bluish grey & emerald	1·10	1·10
			Set of 4	3·25	3·25
			Set of 2 Gutter Blocks of 4	6·50	
			First Day Cover		3·50
			Presentation Pack	4·50	
			Souvenir Book	6·00	
			P.H.Q. Cards (set of 4)	2·00	5·00

Nos. 1396/7 and 1398/9 were each printed together, *se-tenant*, in horizontal pairs throughout the sheets, each pair showing a background design of the Australian flag.

The 40 page souvenir book contains the British and Australian sets which were issued on the same day in similar designs.

Special First Day of Issue Postmarks

Philatelic Bureau, Edinburgh	4·00
Portsmouth	4·00

870 Spanish Galeasse off The Lizard

871 English Fleet leaving Plymouth

872 Engagement off Isle of Wight

873 Attack of English Fire-ships, Calais

874 Armada in Storm, North Sea

(Des G. Evernden)

1988 (19 July). **400th Anniv of Spanish Armada.** *Phosphorised paper. P* 15 × 14.

1400	**870**	18p.	slate-black, yellow-orange, brt carmine, brt blue, turquoise-blue, yellow-green & gold	65	65
			a. Horiz strip of 5. Nos. 1400/4	2·75	2·75
1401	**871**	18p.	slate-black, yellow-orange, brt carmine, brt blue, turquoise-blue, yellow-green & gold	65	65
1402	**872**	18p.	slate-black, yellow-orange, brt carmine, brt blue, turquoise-blue, yellow-green & gold	65	65
1403	**873**	18p.	slate-black, yellow-orange, brt carmine, brt blue, turquoise-blue, yellow-green & gold	65	65
1404	**874**	18p.	slate-black, yellow-orange, brt carmine, brt blue, turquoise-blue, yellow-green & gold	65	65
			Set of 5	2·75	2·75
			Gutter block of 10	5·50	
			First Day Cover		3·25
			Presentation Pack	4·00	
			P.H.Q. Cards (set of 5)	2·50	5·50

Nos. 1400/4 were printed together, *se-tenant*, in horizontal strips of 5 througout the sheet, forming a composite design.

Special First Day of Issue Postmarks

Philatelic Bureau, Edinburgh	3·50
Plymouth	3·50

875 "The Owl and the Pussy-cat"

876 "Edward Lear as a Bird" (self-portrait)

877 "Cat" (from alphabet book)

878 "There was a Young Lady whose Bonnet . . ." (limerick)

(Des M. Swatridge and S. Dew)

1988 (6–27 Sept). **Death Centenary of Edward Lear (artist and author).** *Phosphorised paper. P* 15 × 14.

1405	**875**	19p. black, pale cream & carmine	50	50
1406	**876**	27p. black, pale cream & yellow	65	80
1407	**877**	32p. black, pale cream & emerald	1·10	1·10
1408	**878**	35p. black, pale cream & blue	1·10	1·25
		Set of 4	3·00	3·25
		Set of 4 Gutter Pairs	6·00	
		First Day Cover		4·00
		Presentation Pack	4·50	
		P.H.Q. Cards (set of 4)	2·00	5·00
MS1409		22 × 90 mm. Nos. 1405/8 (*sold at* £1.35) (27 Sept)	8·00	7·00
		First Day Cover		7·00

The premium on No. **MS**1409 was used to support the "Stamp World London 90" International Stamp Exhibition.

Special First Day of Issue Postmarks

Philatelic Bureau, Edinburgh (stamps) (6 Sept)	4·50
Philatelic Bureau, Edinburgh (miniature sheet) (27 Sept)	7·50
London N7 (stamps) (6 Sept)	4·50
London N22 (miniature sheet) (27 Sept)	7·50

879 Carrickfergus Castle

880 Caernarfon Castle

881 Edinburgh Castle

882 Windsor Castle

(Des from photos by Prince Andrew, Duke of York. Eng C. Matthews. Recess Harrison)

1988 (18 Oct). *Ordinary paper. P* 15 × 14.

1410	**879**	£1 dp green	3·00	50
1411	**880**	£1.50 maroon	4·50	1·25
1412	**881**	£2 indigo	6·50	1·75
1413	**882**	£5 dp brown	15·00	3·50
		Set of 4	26·00	6·25
		Set of 4 Gutter Pairs	50·00	
		First Day Cover		45·00
		Presentation Pack	28·00	

For similar designs, but with silhouette of Queen's head see Nos. 1611/14 and 1993/6.

Special First Day of Issue Postmarks
(For illustrations see Introduction)

Philatelic Bureau, Edinburgh (Type H)	50·00
Windsor, Berkshire (Type I)	50·00

883 Journey to Bethlehem

884 Shepherds and Star

885 Three Wise Men

886 Nativity

887 The Annunciation

(Des L. Trickett)

1988 (15 Nov). **Christmas. Christmas Cards.** *One phosphor band (14p.) or phosphorised paper (others). P* 15 × 14.

1414	**883**	14p.	gold, orange-yellow, brt mauve, bluish violet, brt blue & grey-black	35	35
			a. Error. "13p" instead of "14p"	£5500	
			b. Imperf (pair)	£750	
1415	**884**	19p.	gold, yellow-orange, brt violet, ultramarine, rose-red, grey-black & brt blue	40	45
			a. Imperf (pair)	£600	
1416	**885**	27p.	gold, red, dp lavender, dp lilac, emerald, grey-black & brt blue	70	70
1417	**886**	32p.	gold, orange-yellow, brt rose, dp mauve, violet, grey-black & brt blue	90	1·00
1418	**887**	35p.	gold, green, reddish violet, brt blue, brt purple & grey-black	1·00	1·10
			Set of 5	3·00	3·25
			Set of 5 Gutter Pairs	6·00	
			First Day Cover		4·25
			Presentation Pack	4·25	
			P.H.Q. Cards (set of 5)	2·50	5·25

Examples of No. 1414a were found in some 1988 Post Office Yearbooks.

Special First Day of Issue Postmarks

Philatelic Bureau, Edinburgh	4·50
Bethlehem, Llandeilo, Dyfed	4·50

Collectors Pack 1988

1988 (15 Nov). *Comprises Nos.* 1380/1408, 1414/18.

CP1418*a* Collectors Pack .... 32·00

Post Office Yearbook

1988 (15 Nov). *Comprises Nos.* 1380/1404, **MS**1409, 1414/18 *in 32-page hardbound book with slip case, illustrated in colour* . 40·00

888 Atlantic Puffin

889 Avocet

890 Oystercatcher

891 Northern Gannet

(Des D. Cordery)

1989 (17 Jan). **Centenary of Royal Society for the Protection of Birds.** *Phosphorised paper. P* 14 × 15.

1419	**888**	19p.	grey, orange-yellow, orange-red, dull ultramarine, grey-black & silver	45	45
1420	**889**	27p.	grey, bistre, rose, steel-blue, lavender, silver & grey-black	1·25	1·10
1421	**890**	32p.	grey, bistre, scarlet, orange-red, lavender, silver & black	1·25	1·10
1422	**891**	35p.	grey, lemon, rose-carmine, green, new blue, silver & black	1·50	1·25
			Set of 4	4·00	3·50
			Set of 4 Gutter Pairs	8·00	
			First Day Cover		4·50
			Presentation Pack	4·50	
			P.H.Q. Cards (set of 4)	2·50	5·00

Special First Day of Issue Postmarks

Philatelic Bureau, Edinburgh	4·75
Sandy, Bedfordshire	4·75

892 Rose

893 Cupid

894 Yachts

895 Fruit

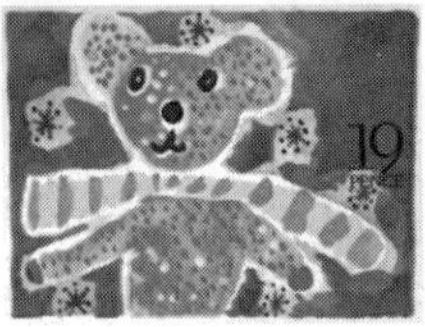

896 Teddy Bear

(Des P. Sutton)

1989 (31 Jan). **Greetings Stamps.** *Phosphorised paper. P* 15 × 14.

1423	**892**	19p.	black, greenish yellow, brt rose, red, new blue, lt green & gold	6·25	4·50
			a. Booklet pane. Nos. 1423/7 × 2 plus 12 half stamp-size labels	55·00	
1424	**893**	19p.	black, greenish yellow, brt rose, red, new blue, lt green & gold	6·25	4·50
1425	**894**	19p.	black, greenish yellow, brt rose, red, new blue, lt green & gold	6·25	4·50
1426	**895**	19p.	black, greenish yellow, brt rose, red, new blue, lt green & gold	6·25	4·50
1427	**896**	19p.	black, greenish yellow, brt rose, red, new blue, lt green & gold	6·25	4·50
			Set of 5	28·00	20·00
			First Day Cover		20·00

Nos. 1423/7 were only issued in £1.90 booklets.

Special First Day of Issue Postmarks

Philatelic Bureau, Edinburgh	20·00
Lover, Salisbury, Wilts	20·00

897 Fruit and Vegetables

898 Meat Products

899 Dairy Products

900 Cereal Products

(Des Sedley Place Ltd)

1989 (7 Mar). **Food and Farming Year.** *Phosphorised paper. P* $14 \times 14\frac{1}{2}$.

1428	**897**	19p.	brownish grey, greenish yellow, rose, new blue, black, pale grey & emerald	50	50
1429	**898**	27p.	brownish grey, greenish yellow, brt carmine, new blue, black, pale grey & brt orange	80	80
1430	**899**	32p.	brownish grey, greenish yellow, rose-red, new blue, black, pale grey & bistre-yellow	1·10	1·10
1431	**900**	35p.	brownish grey, greenish yellow, brt carmine, new blue, black, pale grey & brown-red	1·25	1·25
			Set of 4	3·25	3·25
			Set of 4 Gutter Pairs	6·50	
			First Day Cover		4·25
			Presentation Pack	4·50	
			P.H.Q. Cards (set of 4)	2·00	5·00

Special First Day of Issue Postmarks

Philatelic Bureau, Edinburgh	4·50
Stoneleigh, Kenilworth, Warwicks	4·50

For full information on all future British issues, collectors should write to the British Post Office Philatelic Bureau, 20 Brandon Street, Edinburgh EH3 5TT

901 Mortar Board (150th Anniv of Public Education in England)

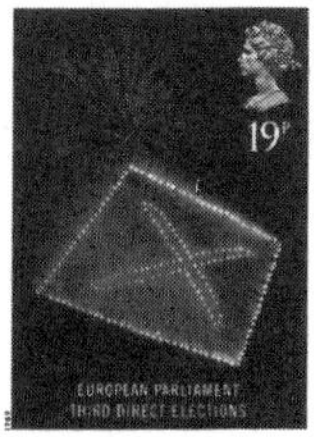

902 Cross on Ballot Paper (3rd Direct Elections to European Parliament)

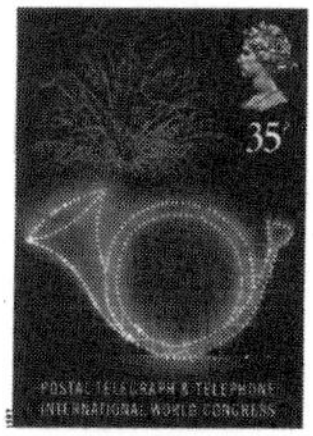

903 Posthorn (26th Postal, Telegraph and Telephone International Congress, Brighton)

904 Globe (Inter-Parliamentary Union Centenary Conference, London)

(Des Lewis Moberly from firework set-pieces. Litho Questa)

1989 (11 Apr). **Anniversaries.** *Phosphorised paper. P* $14 \times 14\frac{1}{2}$.

1432	**901**	19p.	new blue, greenish yellow, magenta & black	1·25	1·25
			a. Horiz pair. Nos. 1432/3	2·50	2·50
1433	**902**	19p.	new blue, greenish yellow, magenta & black	1·25	1·25
1434	**903**	35p.	new blue, greenish yellow, magenta & black	1·75	1·75
			a. Horiz pair. Nos. 1434/5	3·50	3·50
1435	**904**	35p.	new blue, greenish yellow, magenta & black	1·75	1·75
			Set of 4	5·50	5·50
			Set of 2 Gutter Strips of 4	11·00	
			First Day Cover		6·00
			Presentation Pack	6·50	
			P.H.Q. Cards (set of 4)	2·00	7·00

Nos. 1432/3 and 1434/5 were each printed together, *se-tenant*, in horizontal pairs throughout the sheets.

Stamps as No. 1435, but inscribed "ONE HUNDREDTH CONFERENCE" were prepared, but not issued.

Special First Day of Issue Postmarks

Philatelic Bureau, Edinburgh	6·50
London SW	6·50

905 Toy Train and Airplane

906 Building Bricks

907 Dice and Board Games

908 Toy Robot, Boat and Doll's House

(Des D. Fern)

1989 (16 May). **Europa. Games and Toys.** *Phosphorised paper. P* 14×15.

1436	**905**	19p.	black, greenish yellow, vermilion, blue-green, blue, gold & pale ochre	50	50
1437	**906**	27p.	black, greenish yellow, reddish orange, blue-green, blue & gold	90	90
1438	**907**	32p.	black, greenish yellow, orange-red, blue-green, blue, gold & pale ochre	1·25	1·25
1439	**908**	35p.	black, greenish yellow, reddish orange, blue-green, blue, gold & stone	1·40	1·40
			Set of 4	3·50	3·50
			Set of 4 Gutter Pairs	7·00	
			First Day Cover		4·25
			Presentation Pack	4·50	
			P.H.Q. Cards (set of 4)	2·00	5·00

Special First Day of Issue Postmarks

Philatelic Bureau, Edinburgh	4·50
Leeds	4·50

909 Ironbridge, Shropshire

910 Tin Mine, St. Agnes Head, Cornwall

911 Cotton Mills, New Lanark, Strathclyde

912 Pontcysyllte Aqueduct, Clwyd

912a Horizontal versions of T **909/12**

(Des R. Maddox)

1989 (4–25 July). **Industrial Archaeology.** *Phosphorised paper. P* 14 × 15.

1440	**909**	19p.	black, bistre-yellow, rose-red, apple-green, lt blue, grey-black & emerald ...	50	50
1441	**910**	27p.	black, bistre-yellow, rose-red, apple-green, lt blue, grey-black & dull blue ..	80	80
1442	**911**	32p.	black, yellow-orange, apple-green, yellow, dull blue, grey-black & dp reddish violet	1·00	1·00
1443	**912**	35p.	black, yellow, brt rose, apple-green, dull blue, grey-black & vermilion	1·10	1·10
			Set of 4	3·00	3·00
			Set of 4 Gutter Pairs	6·50	
			First Day Cover		4·25
			Presentation Pack	4·50	
			P.H.Q. Cards (set of 4)	2·00	5·00
MS1444	**912***a*		122 × 90 mm. As Nos. 1440/3, but horizontal. Each black, olive-yellow, brt rose-red, dull blue, apple-green, grey-black & vermilion (*sold at* £1.40) (25 July)	6·50	5·50
			First Day Cover		5·50

The premium on No. **MS**1444 was used to support the "Stamp World London 90" International Stamp Exhibition.

Special First Day of Issue Postmarks

Philatelic Bureau, Edinburgh (stamps) (4 July)	4·50
Philatelic Bureau, Edinburgh (miniature sheet) (25 July)	6·00
Telford (stamps) (4 July)	4·50
New Lanark (miniature sheet) (25 July)	6·00

913

914

1989 (22 Aug)–**93**. *Booklet Stamps.*

(a) *Photo Harrison. P* 15 x 14.

1445	**913**	(2nd)	brt blue (1 centre band)	1·00	35
			a. Booklet pane. No. 1445 × 10 with horizontal edges of pane imperf	6·00	
			b. Booklet pane. No. 1445 × 4 with three edges of pane imperf (28.11.89)	24·00	
1446		(2nd)	brt blue (1 band at right) (20.3.90)	2·50	2·50

1447 **914** (1st) brownish black (phosphorised paper) .. 1·25 60
a. Booklet pane. No. 1447 × 10 with horizontal edges of pane imperf .... 8·00
b. Booklet pane. No. 1447 × 4 with three edges of pane imperf (5.12.89) .... 24·00
1448 (1st) brownish black (2 phosphor bands) (20.3.90) .... 2·50 2·50
First Day Cover (Nos. 1445, 1447) ...... 3·50

(*b*) *Litho Walsall. P* 14

1449 **913** (2nd) brt blue (1 centre band) .... 1·00 1·00
a. Imperf between (vert pair) ....
b. Booklet pane. No. 1449 × 4 with three edges of pane imperf .... 3·50
c. Booklet pane. No. 1449 × 4 with horiz edges of pane imperf (6.8.91) .... 3·00
d. Booklet pane. No. 1449 × 10 with horiz edges of pane imperf (6.8.91) .... 6·00
1450 **914** (1st) blackish brown (2 phosphor bands) ... 2·50 2·00
a. Booklet pane. No. 1450 × 4 with three edges of pane imperf .... 9·00
Ey. Phosphor omitted ....

(*c*) *Litho Questa. P* 15 × 14.

1451 **913** (2nd) brt blue (1 centre band) (19.9.89) ..... 1·00 1·00
1451*a* (2nd) brt blue (1 band at right) (25.2.92) .... 2·00 2·00
aEb. Band at left (10.8.93) .... 2·00 2·00
aEy. Phosphor omitted ....
al. Booklet pane. Nos. 1451aEb and 1514*a*, each × 3, with margins all round (10.8.93) .... 6·00
1452 **914** (1st) brownish black (phosphorised paper) (19.9.89) .... 1·50 1·50

Nos. 1445, 1447 and 1449/52 were initially sold at 14p. (2nd) and 19p. (1st), but these prices were later increased to reflect new postage rates.

Nos. 1446 and 1448 come from the *se-tenant* pane in the London Life £5 Booklet. This pane is listed under No. X906m in the Decimal Machin section.

No. 1451a comes from the *se-tenant* panes in the Wales and Tolkien £6 booklet. These panes are listed under Nos. X1012l and W49a (Wales Regionals). No. 1451aEb comes from the £6 (£5.64) Beatrix Potter booklet.

Nos. 1445, 1447 and 1449/50 do not exist perforated on all four sides, but come with either one or two adjacent sides imperforate.

No. 1450Ey comes from a pane in which one stamp was without phosphor bands due to a dry print.

For illustrations showing the differences between photogravure and lithography see above Type **367**.

For similar designs, but in changed colours, see Nos. 1511/16 and for those with elliptical perforations, Nos. 1663a/6 and 1979.

Special First Day of Issue Postmarks
(for illustrations see Introduction)

Philatelic Bureau, Edinburgh (Type G) (in red) ...... 4·25
Windsor, Berks (Type G) (in red) .... 4·25

915 Snowflake (× 10)

916 *Calliphora erythrocephala* (× 5) (fly)

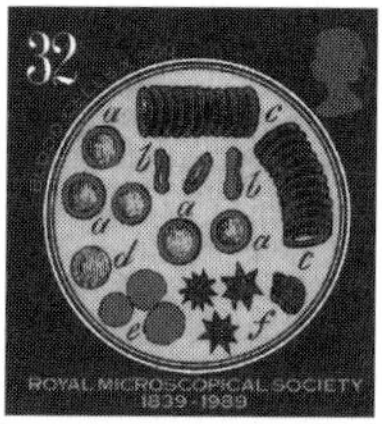

917 Blood Cells (× 500)

918 Microchip (× 600)

(Des K. Bassford. Litho Questa)

1989 (5 Sept). **150th Anniv of Royal Microscopical Society** *Phosphorised paper. P* $14\frac{1}{2}$ × 14.

1453 **915** 19p. gold, lemon, pale blue, grey, black & grey-black 50 50
1454 **916** 27p. gold, lemon, drab, black & grey-black . 85 85
1455 **917** 32p. gold, lemon, orange-vermilion, flesh, black & grey-black .... 1·25 1·25
1456 **918** 35p. gold, lemon, black, brt green & grey-black .... 1·40 1·40
Set of 4 .... 3·50 3·50
Set of 4 Gutter Pairs .... 7·00
First Day Cover .... 4·25
Presentation Pack .... 4·00
P.H.Q. Cards (set of 4) .... 2·00 5·00

Special First Day of Issue Postmarks

Philatelic Bureau, Edinburgh .... 4·50
Oxford .... 4·50

919 Royal Mail Coach

920 Escort of Blues and Royals

HAVE YOU READ THE NOTES AT THE BEGINNING OF THIS CATALOGUE?
These often provide answers to the enquiries we receive.

921 Lord Mayor's Coach

922 Passing St. Paul's

923 Blues and Royals Drum Horse

(Des P. Cox)

1989 (17 Oct). **Lord Mayor's Show, London.** *Phosphorised paper. P* 14 × 15.

1457	**919**	20p.	gold, lemon, rose, orange, pale blue & black	75	80
		a.	Horiz strip of 5. Nos. 1457/61	3·25	3·50
		ab.	Imperf (horiz strip of 5. Nos. 1457/61)	£5000	
		ac.	Imperf (horiz strip of 4. Nos. 1457/60)	£2000	
		ad.	Imperf (horiz strip of 3. Nos. 1457/9)	£950	
1458	**920**	20p.	gold, lemon, rose, orange, pale blue & black	75	80
1459	**921**	20p.	gold, lemon, rose, orange, pale blue & black	75	80
1460	**922**	20p.	gold, lemon, rose, orange, pale blue & black	75	80
1461	**923**	20p.	gold, lemon, rose, orange, pale blue & black	75	80
			Set of 5	3·25	3·50
			Gutter Strip of 10	6·50	
			First Day Cover		3·75
			Presentation Pack	4·50	
			P.H.Q. Cards (set of 5)	2·50	5·00

Nos. 1457/61 were printed together, *se-tenant*, in horizontal strips of 5 throughout the sheet. This issue commemorates the 800th anniversary of the installation of the first Lord Mayor of London.

Nos. 1457ab/ad come from a sheet partly imperf at left.

Special First Day of Issue Postmarks

Philatelic Bureau, Edinburgh	4·00
London, EC4	4·00

924 14th-century Peasants from Stained-glass Window

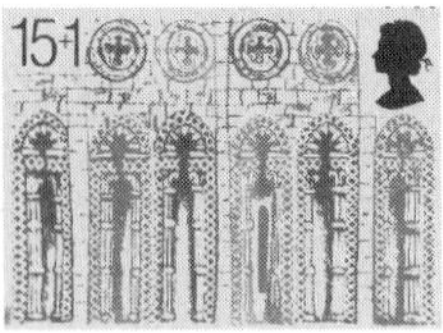

925 Arches and Roundels, West Front

926 Octagon Tower

927 Arcade from West Transept

928 Triple Arch from West Front

(Des D. Gentleman)

1989 (14 Nov). **Christmas. 800th Anniv of Ely Cathedral.** *One phosphor band (15p., 15p. + 1p.) or phosphorised paper (others). P* 15 × 14.

1462	**924**	15p.	gold, silver & blue	35	35
1463	**925**	15p.	+ 1p. gold, silver & blue	50	40
		a.	Imperf (pair)	£1300	
1464	**926**	20p.	+ 1p. gold, silver & rosine	60	50
		a.	Imperf (pair)	£1300	
1465	**927**	34p.	+ 1p. gold, silver & emerald	1·25	1·40
1466	**928**	37p.	+ 1p. gold, silver & yellow-olive	1·25	1·40
			Set of 5	3·50	3·50
			Set of 5 Gutter Pairs	7·00	
			First Day Cover		4·00
			Presentation Pack	4·50	
			P.H.Q. Cards (set of 5)	2·50	5·00

Special First Day of Issue Postmarks

Philatelic Bureau, Edinburgh	4·50
Bethlehem, Llandeilo, Dyfed	4·50
Ely	4·50

Collectors Pack 1989

1989 (14 Nov). *Comprises Nos.* 1419/22, 1428/43 *and* 1453/66.

CP1466*a*	Collectors Pack	35·00

Post Office Yearbook

1989 (14 Nov). *Comprises Nos. 1419/22, 1428/44 and 1453/66 in hardbound book with slip case, illustrated in colour* . 40·00

929 Queen Victoria and Queen Elizabeth II

(Des J. Matthews (after Wyon and Machin)

1990 (10 Jan–12 June). **150th Anniv of the Penny Black.**

(a) *Photo Harrison. P* 15 × 14.

1467	**929**	15p.	brt blue (1 centre band)	50	50
		a.	Imperf (pair)	£1250	
		l.	Booklet pane. No. 1467 × 10 with horizontal edges of pane imperf (30.1.90)	7·50	
1468		15p.	brt blue (1 side band at left) (30.1.90)	2·50	2·50
		Ea.	Band at right (20.3.90)	1·50	1·75
		l.	Booklet pane. No. 1468 × 2 and 1470 plus label	5·00	
1469		20p.	brownish black & cream (phosphorised paper)	75	75
		a.	Imperf (pair)	£900	
		l.	Booklet pane. No. 1469 × 5 plus label with vertical edges of pane imperf (30.1.90)	7·00	
		m.	Booklet pane. No. 1469 × 10 with horizontal edges of pane imperf (30.1.90)	9·00	
		n.	Booklet pane. No. 1469 × 6 with margins all round (20.3.90)	2·50	
		r.	Booklet pane. No. 1469 × 4 with three edges of pane imperf (17.4.90)	6·00	
1470		20p.	brownish black & cream (2 bands) (30.1.90)	1·75	1·50
1471		29p.	dp mauve (phosphorised paper)	1·25	1·25
1472		29p.	dp mauve (2 bands) (20.3.90)	8·00	8·00
1473		34p.	dp bluish grey (phosphorised paper)	1·50	1·25
1474		37p.	rosine (phosphorised paper)	1·50	1·50

(b) *Litho Walsall. P* 14 *(from booklets)*

1475	**929**	15p.	brt blue (1 centre band) (30.1.90)	1·00	70
		l.	Booklet pane. No. 1475 × 4 with three edges of pane imperf	7·50	
		m.	Booklet pane. No. 1475 × 10 with three edges of pane imperf (12.6.90)	8·00	
1476		20p.	brownish black & cream (phosphorised paper) (30.1.90)	1·25	80
		l.	Booklet pane. No. 1476 × 5 plus label with vertical edges of pane imperf	7·00	
		m.	Booklet pane. No. 1476 × 4 with three edges of pane imperf	7·50	
		n.	Booklet pane. No. 1476 × 10 with three edges of pane imperf (12.6.90)	10·00	

(c) *Litho Questa. P* 15 × 14

1477	**929**	15p.	brt blue (1 centre band) (17.4.90)	1·50	1·50
1478		20p.	brownish black (phosphorised paper) (17.4.90)	1·50	1·50
			Set of 5 (Nos. 1467, 1469, 1471, 1473/4)	4·50	4·75
			First Day Cover (Nos. 1467, 1469, 1471, 1473/4)		5·00
			Presentation Pack (Nos. 1467, 1469, 1471, 1473/4)	5·75	

Nos. 1475/6 do not exist perforated on all four sides, but come with either one or two adjacent sides imperforate.

Nos. 1468, 1468Ea, 1470, 1472 and 1475/8 were only issued in stamp booklets. Nos. 1468Ea, 1470 and 1472 occur in the *se-tenant* pane from the 1990 London Life £5 booklet. This pane is listed as No. X906m.

For illustrations showing the difference between photogravure and lithography see beneath Type **367**.

For No. 1469 in miniature sheet see No. **MS**1501.

Special First Day of Issue Postmark

Philatelic Bureau, Edinburgh (in red) . . . . 5·00
Windsor, Berks (Type G, see Introduction) (in red) . 5·00

930 Kitten

931 Rabbit

932 Duckling

933 Puppy

(Des T. Evans. Litho Questa)

1990 (23 Jan). **150th Anniv of Royal Society for Prevention of Cruelty to Animals.** *Phosphorised paper. P* $14 \times 14\frac{1}{2}$.

1479	**930**	20p.	new blue, greenish yellow, brt magenta, black & silver	65	70
		a.	Silver (Queen's head and face value) omitted	£175	
1480	**931**	29p.	new blue, greenish yellow, brt magenta, black & silver	1·25	1·10
		a.	Imperf (horiz pair)	£2500	
1481	**932**	34p.	new blue, greenish yellow, brt magenta, black & silver	1·50	1·25
		a.	Silver (Queen's head and face value) omitted	£350	
1482	**933**	37p.	new blue, greenish yellow, brt magenta, black & silver	1·60	1·40
			Set of 4	4·50	4·00
			Set of 4 Gutter Pairs	9·00	
			First Day Cover		4·25
			Presentation Pack	5·00	
			P.H.Q. Cards (set of 4)	2·50	5·50

Special First Day of Issue Postmarks

Philatelic Bureau, Edinburgh .... 4·50
Horsham .... 4·50

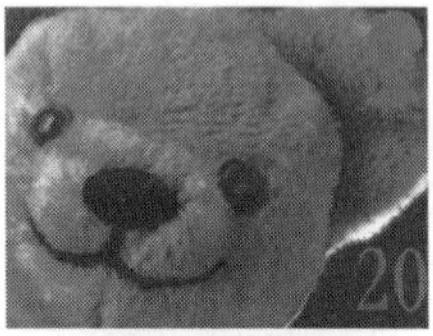

934 Teddy Bear

935 Dennis the Menace

936 Punch

937 Cheshire Cat

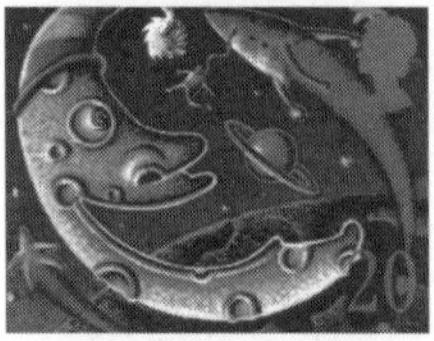

938 The Man in the Moon

939 The Laughing Policeman

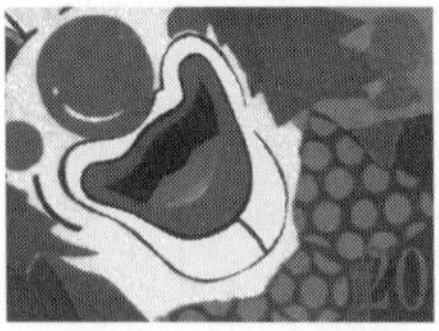

940 Clown

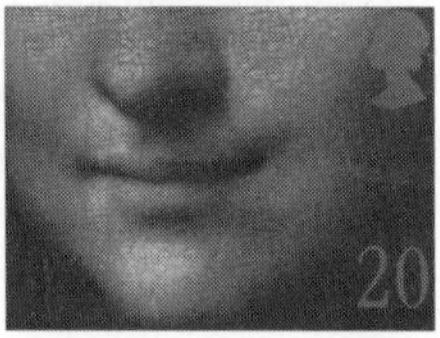

941 Mona Lisa

942 Queen of Hearts

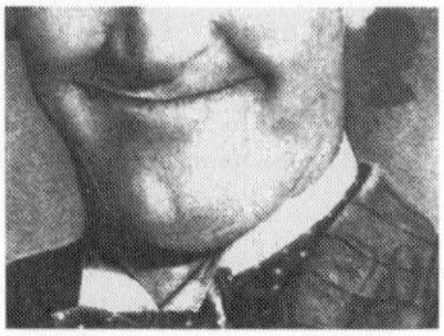

943 Stan Laurel (comedian)

(Des Michael Peters and Partners Ltd)

1990 (6 Feb). **Greetings Stamps. "Smiles".** *Two phosphor bands. P* 15 × 14.

1483	**934**	20p.	gold, greenish yellow, brt rose-red, new blue & grey-black	3·25	2·50
			a. Booklet pane. Nos. 1483/92 with margins all round	28·00	
1484	**935**	20p.	gold, greenish yellow, brt rose-red, new blue, dp blue & grey-black	3·25	2·50
1485	**936**	20p.	gold, greenish yellow, brt rose-red, new blue, dp blue & grey-black	3·25	2·50
1486	**937**	20p.	gold, greenish yellow, brt rose-red, new blue & grey-black	3·25	2·50
1487	**938**	20p.	gold, greenish yellow, brt rose-red, new blue & grey-black	3·25	2·50
1488	**939**	20p.	gold, greenish yellow, brt rose-red, new blue & grey-black	3·25	2·50
1489	**940**	20p.	gold, greenish yellow, brt rose-red, new blue & grey-black	3·25	2·50
1490	**941**	20p.	gold, greenish yellow, brt rose-red, new blue & grey-black	3·25	2·50
1491	**942**	20p.	gold, greenish yellow, brt rose-red, new blue & grey-black	3·25	2·50
1492	**943**	20p.	gold & grey-black	3·25	2·50
			Set of 10	28·00	22·00
			First Day Cover		24·00

Nos. 1483/92 were only issued in £2 booklets. The design of Nos. 1483, 1485/7, 1489 and 1492 extend onto the pane margin.

For Types **934**/**43** inscribed (1st), see Nos. 1550/59.

Special First Day of Issue Postmarks

Philatelic Bureau, Edinburgh .... 25·00
Giggleswick, North Yorkshire .... 25·00

944 Alexandra Palace ("Stamp World London 90" Exhibition)

945 Glasgow School of Art

946 British Philatelic Bureau, Edinburgh

947 Templeton Carpet Factory, Glasgow

(Des P. Hogarth)

1990 (6–20 Mar). **Europa** (*Nos.* 1493 *and* 1495) **and "Glasgow 1990 European City of Culture"** (*Nos.* 1494 *and* 1496). *Phosphorised paper. P* 14 × 15.

1493	**944**	20p.	silver, lemon, flesh, grey-brown, blue, grey-black & black	50	50
		a.	Booklet pane. No. 1493 × 4 with margins all round (20 Mar)	2·00	
1494	**945**	20p.	silver, greenish yellow, dull orange, blue, grey-black & black	50	50
1495	**946**	29p.	silver, stone, orange, olive-sepia, grey-blue, grey-black & black	1·10	1·10
1496	**947**	37p.	silver, greenish-yellow, brt emerald, salmon, olive-sepia, brt blue & black	1·25	1·25
			Set of 4	3·00	3·00
			Set of 4 Gutter Pairs	6·00	
			First Day Cover		4·25
			Presentation Pack	4·00	
			P.H.Q. Cards (set of 4)	2·50	5·25

Special First Day of Issue Postmarks

Philatelic Bureau, Edinburgh	4·50
Glasgow	4·50

948 Export Achievement Award

949 Technological Achievement Award

(Des S. Broom. Litho Questa)

1990 (10 Apr). **25th Anniv of Queen's Awards for Export and Technology.** *P* 14 × 14½.

1497	**948**	20p.	new blue, greenish yellow, magenta, black & silver	75	75
		a.	Horiz pair. Nos. 1497/8	1·50	1·50
1498	**949**	20p.	new blue, greenish yellow, magenta, black & silver	75	75
1499	**948**	37p.	new blue, greenish yellow, magenta, black & silver	1·40	1·40
		a.	Horiz pair. Nos. 1499/500	2·75	2·75
1500	**949**	37p.	new blue, greenish yellow, magenta, black & silver	1·40	1·40
			Set of 4	3·75	3·75
			Set of 2 Gutter Strips of 4	7·50	
			First Day Cover		4·50
			Presentation Pack	4·00	
			P.H.Q. Cards (set of 4)	2·50	5·25

Nos. 1497/8 and 1499/1500 were each printed together, *se-tenant*, in horizontal pairs throughout the sheets.

Special First Day of Issue Postmarks

Philatelic Bureau, Edinburgh	4·75
London, SW	4·75

949*a*

(Des Sedley Place Design Ltd. Eng C. Matthews. Recess and photo Harrison)

1990 (3 May). **"Stamp World 90" International Stamp Exhibition.** *Sheet* 122 × 89 *mm containing No.* 1469. *Phosphorised paper. P* 15 × 14.

MS1501 **949***a*	20p.	brownish black & cream (*sold at* £1)	4·25	4·25
	a.	Error. Imperf	£6500	
	b.	Black (recess-printing) omitted	£7500	
	c.	Black (recess-printing) inverted	£7500	
		First Day Cover		5·00
		Souvenir Book (*Nos.* 1467, 1469, 1471, 1473/4 *and* **MS**1501)	18·00	

The premium on No. **MS**1501 was used to support the "Stamp World London '90" International Stamp Exhibition. In No. **MS**1501 only the example of the 20p. is perforated.

No. **MS**1501b shows an albino impression on the reverse. The 1d. black and Seahorse background are omitted due to one sheet becoming attached to the underside of another prior to recess-printing.

No. **MS**1501c shows the recess part of the design inverted in relation to the photogravure of Type **929**.

Special First Day of Issue Postmarks

Philatelic Bureau, Edinburgh (in red)	5·00
City of London (in red)	5·00

A First Day of Issue handstamp as Type B was provided at Alexandra Palace; London N22 for this issue.

950 Cycad and Sir Joseph Banks Building

951 Stone Pine and Princess of Wales Conservatory

952 Willow Tree and Palm House

953 Cedar Tree and Pagoda

(Des P. Leith)

1990 (5 June). **150th Anniv of Kew Gardens.** *Phosphorised paper. P* 14 × 15.

1502	**950**	20p.	black, brt emerald, pale turquoise-green, lt brown & lavender	50	50
1503	**951**	29p.	black, brt emerald, turquoise-green, reddish orange & grey-black	80	80
1504	**952**	34p.	Venetian red, brt green, cobalt, dull purple, turquoise-green & yellow-green	1·10	1·25
1505	**953**	37p.	pale violet-blue, brt emerald, red-brown, steel-blue & brown-rose	1·25	1·40
			Set of 4	3·25	3·50
			Set of 4 Gutter Pairs	6·50	
			First Day Cover		4·50
			Presentation Pack	4·00	
			P.H.Q. Cards (set of 4)	2·50	5·00

Special First Day of Issue Postmarks

Philatelic Bureau, Edinburgh	4·75
Kew, Richmond	4·75

954 Thomas Hardy and Clyffe Clump, Dorset

(Des J. Gibbs)

1990 (10 July). **150th Birth Anniv of Thomas Hardy (author).** *Phosphorised paper. P* 14 × 15.

1506	**954**	20p.	vermilion, greenish yellow, pale lake-brown, dp brown, lt red-brown & black	75	75
			a. Imperf (pair)	£950	
			Gutter Pair	1·50	
			First Day Cover		2·00
			Presentation Pack	1·75	
			P.H.Q. Card	75	2·00

Special First Day of Issue Postmarks

Philatelic Bureau, Edinburgh	2·25
Dorchester	2·25

955 Queen Elizabeth the Queen Mother

956 Queen Elizabeth

957 Elizabeth, Duchess of York **958** Lady Elizabeth Bowes-Lyon

(Des J. Gorham from photographs by N. Parkinson (20p.), Dorothy Wilding (29p.), B. Park (34p.), Rita Martin (37p.))

1990 (2 Aug). **90th Birthday of Queen Elizabeth the Queen Mother.** *Phosphorised paper. P* 14 × 15.

1507	**955**	20p.	silver, greenish yellow, magenta, turquoise-blue & grey-black	70	70
1508	**956**	29p.	silver, indigo & grey-blue	1·00	1·00
1509	**957**	34p.	silver, lemon, red, new blue & grey-black	1·50	1·50
1510	**958**	37p.	silver, sepia & stone	1·75	1·75
			Set of 4	4·50	4·50
			Set of 4 Gutter Pairs	9·00	
			First Day Cover		4·75
			Presentation Pack	4·75	
			P.H.Q. Cards (set of 4)	2·50	5·50

Special First Day of Issue Postmarks

Philatelic Bureau, Edinburgh	5·00
Westminster, SW1	5·00

1990 (7 Aug)–**92**. *Booklet stamps. As T* **913/14**, *but colours changed.*

(a) Photo Harrison. P 15 × 14

1511	**913**	(2nd)	dp blue (1 centre band)	90	90
			a. Booklet pane. No. 1511 × 10 with horiz edges of pane imperf	7·00	
1512	**914**	(1st)	brt orange-red (phosphorised paper)	80	80
			a. Booklet pane. No. 1512 × 10 with horiz edges of pane imperf	5·25	

(b) Litho Questa. P 15 × 14

1513	**913**	(2nd)	dp blue (1 centre band)	1·60	1·60
1514	**914**	(1st)	brt orange-red (phosphorised paper)	75	75
1514*a*		(1st)	brt orange-red (2 bands) (25.2.92)	2·00	2·00

(c) Litho Walsall. P 14

1515	**913**	(2nd)	dp blue (1 centre band)	80	80
			a. Booklet pane. No. 1515 × 4 with horiz edges of pane imperf	3·00	
			b. Booklet pane. No. 1515 × 10 with horiz edges of pane imperf	6·00	
1516	**914**	(1st)	brt orange-red (phosphorised paper)	80	80
			a. Booklet pane. No. 1516 × 4 with horiz edges of pane imperf	2·50	
			b. Booklet pane. No. 1516 × 10 with horiz edges of pane imperf	5·25	
			c. Perf 13	2·25	2·25
			ca. Booklet pane. No. 1516c × 4 with horiz edges of pane imperf	10·00	
			First Day Cover (Nos. 1515/16)		3·50

Nos. 1511/14 and 1515/16 were initially sold at 15p. (2nd) and 20p. (1st), but these prices were later increased to reflect new postage rates.

No. 1514a comes from the *se-tenant* panes in the £6 Wales, £6 Tolkien and £5.64 Beatrix Potter booklets. These panes are listed under Nos. X1012l, 1451a l and W49a (Wales Regionals).

No. 1516c was caused by the use of an incorrect perforation comb.

Nos. 1511/12 and 1515/16 do not exist with perforations on all four sides, but come with either the top or the bottom edge imperforate.

For similar stamps with elliptical perforations see Nos. 1663a/6.

Special First Day of Issue Postmarks
(For illustration see Introduction)

Philatelic Bureau, Edinburgh (Type G)	3·50
Windsor, Berks (Type G)	3·50

959 Victoria Cross

960 George Cross

961 Distinguished Service Cross and Distinguished Service Medal

962 Military Cross and Military Medal

963 Distinguished Flying Cross and Distinguished Flying Medal

(Des J. Gibbs and J. Harwood)

1990 (11 Sept). **Gallantry Awards.** *Phosphorised paper. P* 14 × 15 (*vert*) *or* 15 × 14 (*horiz*).

1517	**959**	20p.	grey-black, pale stone, stone, bistre-brown & brt carmine	80	80
1518	**960**	20p.	grey-black, pale stone, flesh, grey & ultramarine	80	80
1519	**961**	20p.	grey-black, pale stone, flesh, pale blue & ultramarine	80	80
		a.	Imperf (pair)		
1520	**962**	20p.	grey-black, pale stone, ochre, pale blue, ultramarine, scarlet & violet	80	80
1521	**963**	20p.	grey-black, pale stone, yellow-brown, bluish grey & purple	80	80
			Set of 5	3·50	3·50
			Set of 5 Gutter Pairs	7·00	
			First Day Cover		3·75
			Presentation Pack	4·00	
			P.H.Q. Cards (set of 5)	3·00	5·50

Special First Day of Issue Postmarks

Philatelic Bureau, Edinburgh	4·25
Westminster, SW1	4·25

964 Armagh Observatory, Jodrell Bank Radio Telescope and La Palma Telescope

965 Newton's Moon and Tides Diagram and Early Telescopes

966 Greenwich Old Observatory and Early Astronomical Equipment

967 Stonehenge, Gyroscope and Navigation by Stars

(Des J. Fisher. Litho Questa)

1990 (16 Oct). **Astronomy.** *Phosphorised paper. P* 14 × 14½.

1522	**964**	22p.	cream, grey, dull blue-green, slate-blue, blue-green, orange-red, gold & black	50	40
		a.	Gold (Queen's head) omitted	£350	
1523	**965**	26p.	black, yellow, dull purple, pale cream, brown-rose, new blue, greenish yellow, vermilion & gold	80	90
1524	**966**	31p.	black, cream, pale cream, yellow-orange, salmon, lemon, vermilion & gold	1·00	1·00
1525	**967**	37p.	black, pale buff, olive-bistre, pale cream, pale flesh, flesh, grey, rose-red & gold	1·10	1·10
			Set of 4	3·00	3·00
			Set of 4 Gutter Pairs	6·00	
			First Day Cover		4·25
			Presentation Pack	4·00	
			P.H.Q. Cards (set of 4)	2·50	5·50

Special First Day of Issue Postmarks

Philatelic Bureau, Edinburgh	4·25
Armagh	4·25

968 Building a Snowman

969 Fetching the Christmas Tree

970 Carol Singing

971 Tobogganing

972 Ice-skating

(Des J. Gorham and A. Davidson)

1990 (13 Nov). **Christmas.** *One phosphor band* (17p.) *or phosphorised paper* (*others*). *P* 15 × 14.

1526	**968**	17p.	gold, greenish yellow, rose, new blue & grey-black	45	35
			a. Booklet pane of 20	9·00	
1527	**969**	22p.	gold, greenish yellow, magenta, new blue & black	55	65
			a. Imperf (horiz pair)	£450	
1528	**970**	26p.	gold, olive-yellow, pale magenta, agate, new blue, dull violet-blue & black	80	80
1529	**971**	31p.	gold, greenish yellow, brt rose-red, dull mauve, new blue, turquoise-blue & grey-black	1·00	1·00
1530	**972**	37p.	gold, greenish yellow, rose, new blue & slate-green	1·10	1·10
			Set of 5	3·50	3·50
			Set of 5 Gutter Pairs	7·00	
			First Day Cover		4·50
			Presentation Pack	4·25	
			P.H.Q. Cards (set of 5)	3·25	6·00

Booklet pane No. 1526a has the horizontal edges of the pane imperforate.

Special First Day of Issue Postmarks

Philatelic Bureau, Edinburgh	4·50
Bethlehem, Llandeilo, Dyfed	4·50

Collectors Pack 1990

1990 (13 Nov). *Comprises Nos.* 1479/82, 1493/1510 *and* 1517/30.

CP1530*a* Collectors Pack	45·00

Post Office Yearbook

1990 (13 Nov). *Comprises Nos.* 1479/82, 1493/1500, 1502/10, 1517/30 *in hardbound book with slip case, illustrated in colour* . 50·00

973 "King Charles Spaniel"

974 "A Pointer"

975 "Two Hounds in a Landscape"

976 "A Rough Dog"

977 "Fino and Tiny"

(Des Carroll, Dempsey and Thirkell Ltd)

1991 (8 Jan). **Dogs. Paintings by George Stubbs.** *Phosphorised paper. P* 14 × 14½.

1531	**973**	22p.	gold, greenish yellow, magenta, new blue, black & drab	75	75
			a. Imperf (pair)	£400	
1532	**974**	26p.	gold, greenish yellow, magenta, new blue, black & drab	90	80
1533	**975**	31p.	gold, greenish yellow, magenta, new blue, black & drab	1·00	85
			a. Imperf (pair)	£950	
1534	**976**	33p.	gold, greenish yellow, magenta, new blue, black & drab	1·10	95
1535	**977**	37p.	gold, greenish yellow, magenta, new blue, black & drab	1·25	1·10
			Set of 5	4·50	4·00
			Set of 5 Gutter Pairs	9·00	
			First Day Cover		4·25
			Presentation Pack	5·00	
			P.H.Q. Cards (set of 5)	3·25	6·00

Special First Day of Issue Postmarks

Philatelic Bureau, Edinburgh	4·50
Birmingham	4·50

978 Thrush's Nest

979 Shooting Star and Rainbow

980 Magpies and Charm Bracelet

981 Black Cat

982 Common Kingfisher with Key

983 Mallard and Frog

984 Four-leaf Clover in Boot and Match Box

985 Pot of Gold at End of Rainbow

986 Heart-shaped Butterflies

987 Wishing Well and Sixpence

(Des T. Meeuwissen)

1991 (5 Feb). **Greetings Stamps. "Good Luck".** *Two phosphor bands. P* 15 × 14.

1536 **978** (1st) silver, greenish yellow, magenta, new blue, olive-brown & black .... 1·40 1·40
a. Booklet pane. Nos. 1536/45 plus 12 half stamp-size labels with margins on 3 sides .... 12·50

1537 **979** (1st) silver, greenish yellow, magenta, new blue, olive-brown & black .... 1·40 1·40
1538 **980** (1st) silver, greenish yellow, magenta, new blue, olive-brown & black .... 1·40 1·40
1539 **981** (1st) silver, greenish yellow, magenta, new blue, olive-brown & black .... 1·40 1·40
1540 **982** (1st) silver, greenish yellow, magenta, new blue, olive-brown & black .... 1·40 1·40
1541 **983** (1st) silver, greenish yellow, magenta, new blue, olive-brown & black .... 1·40 1·40
1542 **984** (1st) silver, greenish yellow, magenta, new blue, olive-brown & black .... 1·40 1·40
1543 **985** (1st) silver, greenish yellow, magenta, new blue, olive-brown & black .... 1·40 1·40
1544 **986** (1st) silver, greenish yellow, magenta, new blue, olive-brown & black .... 1·40 1·40
1545 **987** (1st) silver, greenish yellow, magenta, new blue, olive-brown & black .... 1·40 1·40
Set of 10 .... 12·50 12·50
First Day Cover .... 13·00

Nos. 1536/45 were only issued in £2.20 booklets (sold at £2.40 from 16 September 1991). The backgrounds of the stamps form a composite design.

Special First Day of Issue Postmarks

Philatelic Bureau, Edinburgh .... 14·00
Greetwell, Lincs .... 14·00

988 Michael Faraday (inventor of electric motor) (Birth Bicentenary)

989 Charles Babbage (computer science pioneer) (Birth Bicentenary)

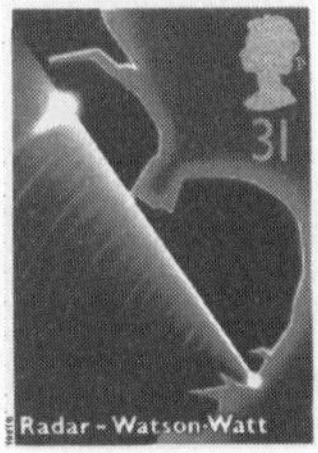

990 Radar Sweep of East Anglia (50th Anniv of Operational Radar Network)

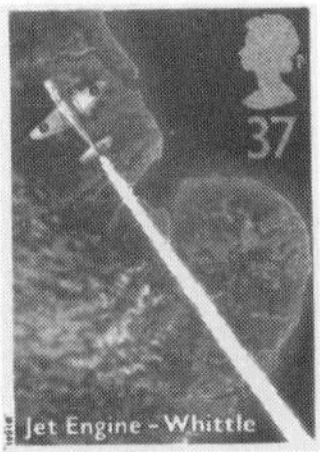

991 Gloster Whittle E28/39 Airplane over East Anglia (50th Anniv of First Flight of Sir Frank Whittle's Jet Engine)

(Des P. Till (Nos. 1546/7), J. Harwood (Nos. 1548/9))

1991 (5 Mar). **Scientific Achievements.** *Phosphorised paper. P* 14 × 15.

1546	**988**	22p. silver, olive-brown, greenish yellow, magenta, slate-blue, grey & black	65	65
		a. Imperf (pair)	£325	
1547	**989**	22p. silver, chrome-yellow, red, grey-black, brownish grey & sepia	65	65
1548	**990**	31p. silver, dp turquoise-green, violet-blue, steel-blue & dp dull blue	95	95
1549	**991**	37p. silver, olive-bistre, rose-red, turquoise-blue, new blue & grey-black	1·10	1·10
		Set of 4	3·00	3·00
		Set of 4 Gutter Pairs	6·00	
		First Day Cover		4·00
		Presentation Pack	3·75	
		P.H.Q. Cards (set of 4)	3·00	5·50

Special First Day of Issue Postmarks

Philatelic Bureau, Edinburgh .... 4·25
South Kensington, London, SW7 .... 4·25

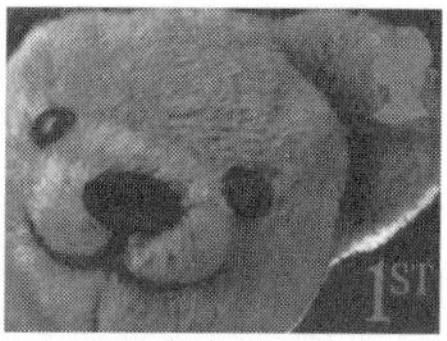

992 Teddy Bear

1991 (26 Mar). **Greeting Stamps.** *As Nos.* 1483/92, *but inscribed "1st" as T* **992**. *Two phosphor bands. P* 15 × 14.

1550	**992**	(1st) gold, greenish yellow, brt rose-red, new blue & grey-black	90	90
		a. Booklet pane. Nos. 1550/9 plus 12 half stamp-size labels with margins on 3 sides	8·00	
1551	**935**	(1st) gold, greenish yellow, brt rose-red, new blue, dp blue & grey-black	90	90
1552	**936**	(1st) gold, greenish yellow, brt rose-red, new blue, dp blue & grey-black	90	90
1553	**937**	(1st) gold, greenish yellow, bright rose-red, new blue & grey-black	90	90
1554	**938**	(1st) gold, greenish yellow, brt rose-red, new blue & grey-black	90	90
1555	**939**	(1st) gold, greenish yellow, brt rose-red, new blue & grey-black	90	90
1556	**940**	(1st) gold, greenish yellow, brt rose-red, new blue & grey-black	90	90
1557	**941**	(1st) gold, greenish yellow, brt rose-red, new blue & grey-black	90	90
1558	**942**	(1st) gold, greenish yellow, brt rose-red, new blue & grey-black	90	90
1559	**943**	(1st) gold & grey-black	90	90
		Set of 10	8·00	8·00
		First Day Cover		9·00

Nos. 1550/9 were only issued in £2.20 booklets (sold at £2.40 from 16 September 1991 and at £2.50 from 1 November 1993). The designs of Nos. 1550, 1552/4, 1556 and 1559 extend onto the pane margin.

Special First Day of Issue Postmarks

Philatelic Bureau, Edinburgh .... 10·00
Laugherton, Lincs .... 10·00

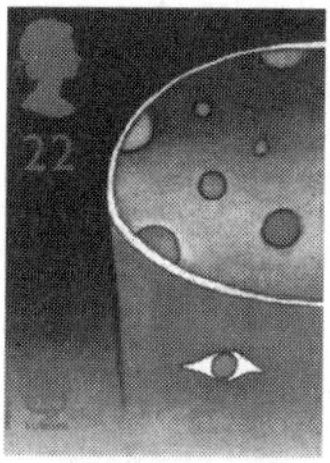

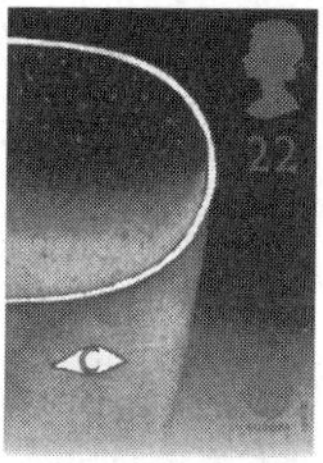

993 **994**
Man Looking at Space

995 **996**
Space Looking at Man

(Des J.-M. Folon)

1991 (23 Apr). **Europa. Europe in Space.** *Phosphorised paper. P* 14 × 15.

1560	**993**	22p. silver-mauve, greenish yellow, scarlet, violet-blue, brt blue, brt green & black	55	55
		a. Horiz pair. Nos. 1560/1	1·10	1·10
1561	**994**	22p. silver-mauve, greenish yellow, scarlet, violet-blue, brt blue & black	55	55
1562	**995**	37p. silver-mauve, bistre-yellow, dull vermilion, blue & black	1·10	1·10
		a. Horiz pair. Nos. 1562/3	2·25	2·25
1563	**996**	37p. silver-mauve, bistre-yellow, dull vermilion, blue & black	1·10	1·10
		Set of 4	3·00	3·00
		Set of 2 Gutter Strips of 4	6·00	
		First Day Cover		4·00
		Presentation Pack	4·00	
		P.H.Q. Cards (set of 4)	3·00	5·50

Nos. 1560/1 and 1562/3 were each printed together, *se-tenant*, in horizontal pairs throughout the sheets, each pair forming a composite design.

Special First Day of Issue Postmarks

Philatelic Bureau, Edinburgh	4·50
Cambridge	4·50

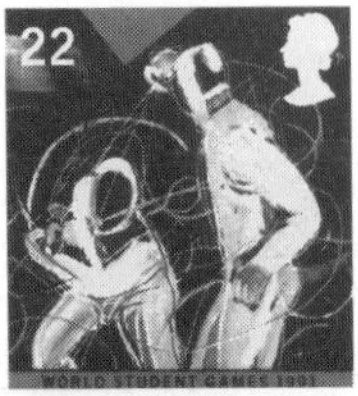

997 Fencing

998 Hurdling

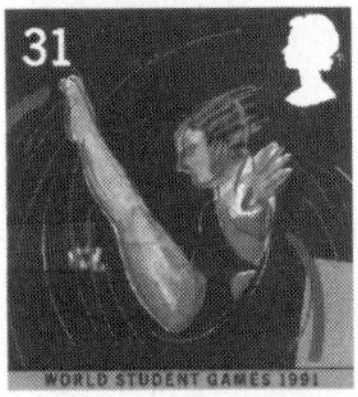

999 Diving

1000 Rugby

(Des Huntley Muir Partners)

1991 (11 June). **World Student Games, Sheffield** (*Nos.* 1564/6) **and World Cup Rugby Championship, London** (*No.* 1567). *Phosphorised paper. P* $14\frac{1}{2} \times 14$.

1564	**997**	22p.	black, greenish yellow, vermilion, brt orange, ultramarine & grey	50	50
1565	**998**	26p.	pale blue, greenish yellow, red, brt blue & black	80	80
1566	**999**	31p.	brt blue, bistre-yellow, rose, vermilion, new blue & black	95	95
1567	**1000**	37p.	yellow-orange, greenish yellow, rose, brt blue, emerald & black	1·10	1·10
			Set of 4	3·00	3·00
			Set of 4 Gutter Pairs	6·00	
			First Day Cover		4·00
			Presentation Pack	4·00	
			P.H.Q. Cards (set of 4)	3·00	5·50

Special First Day of Issue Postmarks

Philatelic Bureau, Edinburgh	4·50
Sheffield	4·50

1001 "Silver Jubilee"

1002 "Mme Alfred Carrière"

1003 *Rosa moyesii*

1004 "Harvest Fayre"

1005 "Mutabilis"

(Des Yvonne Skargon. Litho Questa)

1991 (16 July). **9th World Congress of Roses, Belfast.** *Phosphorised paper. P* $14\frac{1}{2} \times 14$.

1568	**1001**	22p.	new blue, greenish yellow, magenta, black & silver	75	50
		a.	Silver (Queen's head) omitted	£750	
		Eb.	Black printing double	—	£1500
1569	**1002**	26p.	new blue, greenish yellow, magenta, black & silver	90	80
1570	**1003**	31p.	new blue, greenish yellow, magenta, black & silver	1·00	85
1571	**1004**	33p.	new blue, greenish yellow, magenta, black & silver	1·10	95
1572	**1005**	37p.	new blue, greenish yellow, magenta, black & silver	1·25	1·25
			Set of 5	4·50	4·00
			Set of 5 Gutter Pairs	9·00	
			First Day Cover		4·50
			Presentation Pack	4·50	
			P.H.Q. Cards (set of 5)	3·25	7·00

Special First Day of Issue Postmarks

Philatelic Bureau, Edinburgh	5·00
Belfast	5·00

1006 Iguanodon

1007 Stegosaurus

1008 Tyrannosaurus

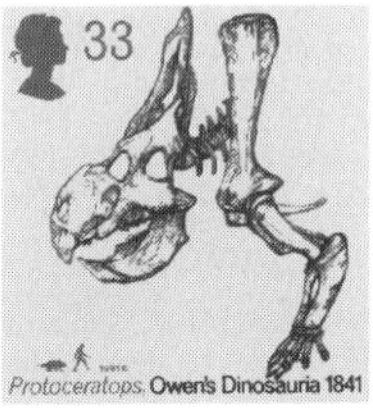

1009 Protoceratops

1010 Triceratops

(Des B. Kneale)

1991 (20 Aug). **150th Anniversary of Dinosaurs' Identification by Owen.** *Phosphorised paper. P* $14\frac{1}{2} \times 14$

1573	**1006**	22p.	grey, pale blue, magenta, brt blue, dull violet & grey-black	75	50
		a.	Imperf (pair)	£1000	
1574	**1007**	26p.	grey, greenish yellow, pale emerald, brt blue-green, pale brt blue, grey-black & black	90	1·00
1575	**1008**	31p.	grey, lt blue, magenta, brt blue, pale blue, brown & grey-black	1·10	1·10
1576	**1009**	33p.	grey, dull rose, pale brt blue, brt rose-red, yellow-orange, grey-black & black	1·40	1·10
1577	**1010**	37p.	grey, greenish yellow, turquoise-blue, dull violet, yellow-brown & black	1·50	1·25
			Set of 5	5·00	4·50
			Set of 5 Gutter Pairs	10·00	
			First Day Cover		5·00
			Presentation Pack	5·50	
			P.H.Q. Cards (set of 5)	3·25	6·00

Special First Day of Issue Postmarks

Philatelic Bureau, Edinburgh	6·00
Plymouth	6·00

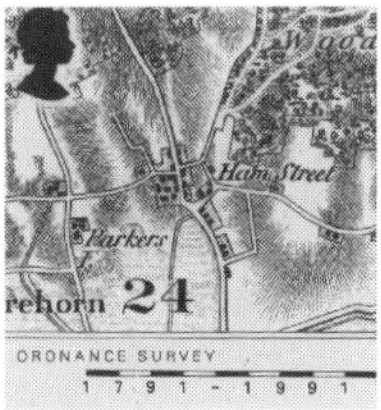

1011 Map of 1816

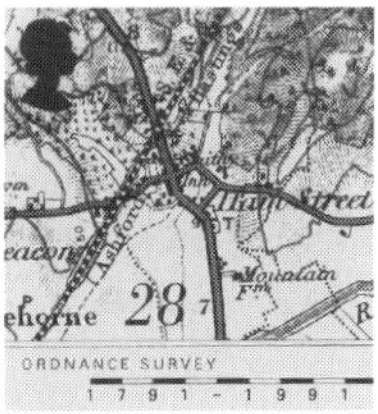

1012 Map of 1906

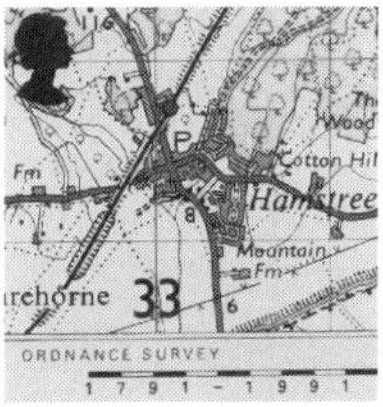

1013 Map of 1959

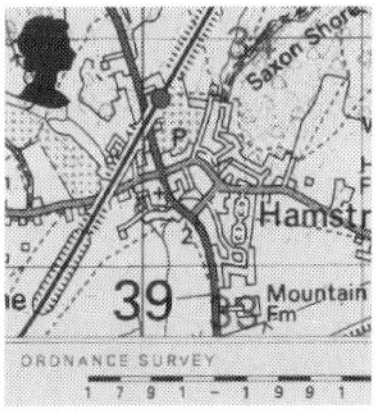

1014 Map of 1991

(Des H. Brown. Recess and litho Harrison (24p.), litho Harrison (28p.), Questa (33p., 39p.))

1991 (17 Sept). **Bicentenary of Ordnance Survey. Maps of Hamstreet, Kent.** *Phosphorised paper. P* $14\frac{1}{2} \times 14$.

1578	**1011**	24p.	black, magenta & cream	50	50
		Ea.	Black (litho) printing treble & magenta printing double	£950	
		Eb.	Black (litho) & magenta printing double		
1579	**1012**	28p.	black, brt yellow-green, new blue, reddish orange, magenta, olive-sepia & cream	80	85
1580	**1013**	33p.	dull blue-green, orange-brown, magenta, olive-grey, greenish yellow, vermilion, greenish grey, pale blue, blue, dull orange, apple green & black	95	1·00
1581	**1014**	39p.	black, magenta, greenish yellow & new blue	1·10	1·25
			Set of 4	3·00	3·25
			Set of 4 Gutter Pairs	6·00	
			First Day Cover		4·25
			Presentation Pack	4·00	
			P.H.Q. Cards (set of 4)	3·00	6·00

Mint examples of Type **1012** exist with a face value of 26p.

Special First Day of Issue Postmarks

Philatelic Bureau, Edinburgh .... 4·50
Southampton .... 4·50

1015 Adoration of the Magi

1016 Mary and Jesus in the Stable

1017 The Holy Family and Angel

1018 The Annunciation

1019 The Flight into Egypt

(Des D. Driver)

1991 (12 Nov). **Christmas. Illuminated Letters from "Acts of Mary and Jesus" Manuscript in Bodleian Library, Oxford.** *One phosphor band (18p.) or phosphorised paper (others). P* 15 × 14.

1582	**1015**	18p.	steel-blue, greenish yellow, rose-red, orange-red, black & gold	70	40
			a. Imperf (pair)	£1750	
			b. Booklet pane of 20	8·25	
1583	**1016**	24p.	brt rose-red, greenish yellow, vermilion, slate-blue, yellow-green, grey-black & gold	80	50
1584	**1017**	28p.	reddish brown, bistre-yellow, orange-vermilion, orange-red, dp dull blue, grey-black & gold	85	1·00
1585	**1018**	33p.	green, greenish yellow, red, orange-red, blue, grey & gold	95	1·10
1586	**1019**	39p.	orange-red, greenish yellow, orange-vermilion, dp dull blue, olive-sepia, black & gold	1·10	1·40
			Set of 5	4·00	4·00
			Set of 5 Gutter Pairs	8·00	
			First Day Cover		4·50
			Presentation Pack	4·25	
			P.H.Q. Cards (set of 5)	3·00	6·00

Booklet pane No. 1582b has margins at left, top and bottom.

Special First Day of Issue Postmarks

Philatelic Bureau, Edinburgh .... 5·00
Bethlehem, Landeilo, Dyfed .... 5·00

Collectors Pack 1991

1991 (12 Nov). *Comprises Nos.* 1531/5, 1546/9 *and* 1560/86.
CP1586*a* Collectors Pack .... 45·00

Post Office Yearbook

1991 (13 Nov). *Comprises Nos.* 1531/5, 1546/9 *and* 1560/86 *in hardbound book with slip case, illustrated in colour* . 50·00

1020 Fallow Deer in Scottish Forest

1021 Hare on North Yorkshire Moors

1022 Fox in the Fens

1023 Redwing and Home Counties Village

1024 Welsh Mountain Sheep in Snowdonia

(Des J. Gorham and K. Bowen)

1992 (14 Jan-25 Feb). **The Four Seasons. Wintertime.** *One phosphor band (18p.) or phosphorised paper (others). P* 15 × 14.

1587	**1020**	18p.	silver, greenish yellow, grey, dull rose, new blue & black	45	50
1588	**1021**	24p.	silver, lemon, rose, blue & grey-black	60	65
			a. Imperf (pair)	£300	
1589	**1022**	28p.	silver, greenish yellow, bright rose, steel-blue & grey-black	80	75
1590	**1023**	33p.	silver, greenish yellow, brt orange, brt purple, greenish blue & grey	95	90
1591	**1024**	39p.	silver, yellow, yellow-orange, grey, vermilion, new blue & black	1·10	1·10
			a. Booklet pane. No. 1591 × 4 with margins all round (25 Feb)	3·25	
			Set of 5	3·50	3·50
			Set of 5 Gutter Pairs	7·00	
			First Day Cover		3·75
			Presentation Pack	4·25	
			P.H.Q. Cards (set of 5)	3·00	7·00

Booklet pane No. 1591a comes from the £6 "Cymru–Wales" booklet.

Special First Day of Issue Postmarks

Philatelic Bureau, Edinburgh	4·25
Brecon	4·25

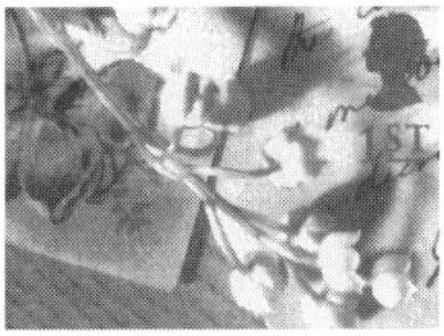

1025 Flower Spray

1026 Double Locket

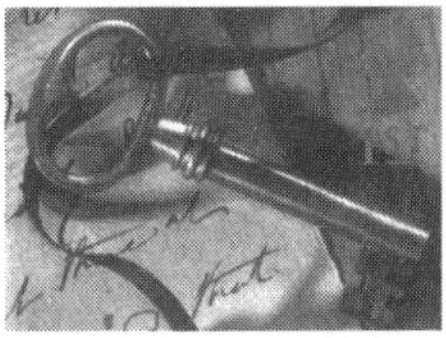

1027 Key

1028 Model Car and Cigarette Cards

1029 Compass and Map

1030 Pocket Watch

1031 1854 1d. Red Stamp and Pen

1032 Pearl Necklace

1033 Marbles

1034 Bucket, Spade and Starfish

(Des Trickett and Webb Ltd)

1992 (28 Jan). **Greetings Stamps. "Memories".** *Two phosphor bands. P* 15 × 14.

1592	**1025**	(1st)	gold, greenish yellow, magenta, ochre, lt blue & grey-black	80	80
			a. Booklet pane. Nos. 1592/1601 plus 12 half stamp-size labels with margins on 3 sides	7·00	
1593	**1026**	(1st)	gold, greenish yellow, magenta, ochre, lt blue & grey-black	80	80
1594	**1027**	(1st)	gold, greenish yellow, magenta, ochre, lt blue & grey-black	80	80
1595	**1028**	(1st)	gold, greenish yellow, magenta, ochre, lt blue & grey-black	80	80
1596	**1029**	(1st)	gold, greenish yellow, magenta, ochre, lt blue & grey-black	80	80
1597	**1030**	(1st)	gold, greenish yellow, magenta, ochre, lt blue & grey-black	80	80
1598	**1031**	(1st)	gold, greenish yellow, magenta, ochre, lt blue & grey-black	80	80
1599	**1032**	(1st)	gold, greenish yellow, magenta, ochre, lt blue & grey-black	80	80
1600	**1033**	(1st)	gold, greenish yellow, magenta, ochre, lt blue & grey-black	80	80
1601	**1034**	(1st)	gold, greenish yellow, magenta, ochre, lt blue & grey-black	80	80
			Set of 10	7·00	7·00
			First Day Cover		8·50
			Presentation Pack	8·00	

Nos. 1592/1601 were only issued in £2.40 booklets (sold at £2.50 from 1 November 1993 and at £2.60 from 8 July 1996). The backgrounds of the stamps form a composite design.

Special First Day of Issue Postmarks

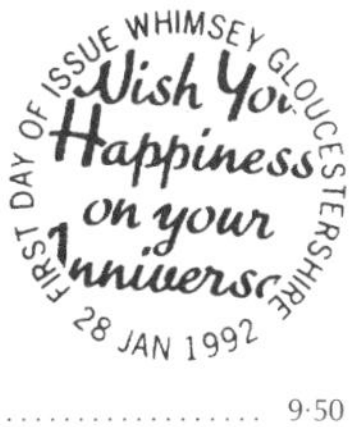

Philatelic Bureau, Edinburgh	9·50
Whimsey, Gloucestershire	9·50

1035 Queen Elizabeth in Coronation Robes and Parliamentary Emblem

1036 Queen Elizabeth in Garter Robes and Archiepiscopal Arms

1037 Queen Elizabeth with Baby Prince Andrew and Royal Arms

1038 Queen Elizabeth at Trooping the Colour and Service Emblems

1039 Queen Elizabeth and Commonwealth Emblem

(Des Why Not Associates. Litho Questa)

1992 (6 Feb). **40th Anniv of Accession.** *Two phosphor bands. P* $14\frac{1}{2} \times 14$.

1602	**1035**	24p.	new blue, greenish yellow, magenta, black, silver & gold	1·40	1·40
		a.	Horiz strip of 5. Nos. 1602/6	6·00	6·00
1603	**1036**	24p.	new blue, greenish yellow, magenta, black, silver & gold	1·40	1·40
1604	**1037**	24p.	new blue, greenish yellow, magenta, black & silver	1·40	1·40
1605	**1038**	24p.	new blue, greenish yellow, magenta, black, silver & gold	1·40	1·40
1606	**1039**	24p.	new blue, greenish yellow, magenta, black, silver & gold	1·40	1·40
			Set of 5	6·00	6·00
			Gutter Block of 10	12·00	
			First Day Cover		6·50
			Presentation Pack	6·50	
			P.H.Q. Cards (set of 5)	3·50	7·00

Nos. 1602/6 were printed together, *se-tenant*, in horizontal strips of five throughout the sheet.

Special First Day of Issue Postmarks

Philatelic Bureau, Edinburgh	7·00
Buckingham Palace, London SW1	7·00

1040 Tennyson in 1888 and "The Beguiling of Merlin" (Sir Edward Burne-Jones)

1041 Tennyson in 1856 and "April Love" (Arthur Hughes)

1042 Tennyson in 1864 and "I am Sick of the Shadows" (John Waterhouse)

1043 Tennyson as a Young Man and "Mariana" (Dante Gabriel Rossetti)

(Des Irene von Treskow)

1992 (10 Mar). **Death Centenary of Alfred, Lord Tennyson (poet).** *Phosphorised paper. P* $14\frac{1}{2} \times 14$.

1607	**1040**	24p.	gold, greenish yellow, magenta, new blue & black	50	50
1608	**1041**	28p.	gold, greenish yellow, magenta, new blue & black	65	65
1609	**1042**	33p.	gold, greenish yellow, magenta, new blue & black	1·10	1·10
1610	**1043**	39p.	gold, greenish yellow, magenta, new blue, bistre & black	1·10	1·10
			Set of 4	3·00	3·00
			Set of 4 Gutter Pairs	6·00	
			First Day Cover		3·50
			Presentation Pack	3·75	
			P.H.Q. Cards (set of 4)	2·50	5·00

Special First Day of Issue Postmarks

Philatelic Bureau, Edinburgh	3·75
Isle of Wight	3·75

For full information on all future British issues, collectors should write to the British Post Office Philatelic Bureau, 20 Brandon Street, Edinburgh EH3 5TT

1044 Carrickfergus Castle

Elliptical hole in vertical perforations

CASTLE

Harrison Plates (Nos. 1611/14)

CASTLE

Enschedé Plates (Nos. 1993/6)

(Des from photos by Prince Andrew, Duke of York. Eng C. Matthews. Recess Harrison)

1992 (24 Mar)–**95**. *Designs as Nos.* 1410/13, *but showing Queen's head in silhouette as T* **1044**. *P* 15 × 14 (*with one elliptical hole on each vertical side*).

1611	**1044**	£1 bottle green & gold†	4·50	1·50
1612	**880**	£1.50 maroon & gold†	3·25	2·25
1613	**881**	£2 indigo & gold†	4·50	3·00
1613*a*	**1044**	£3 reddish violet & gold† (22.8.95)	6·50	4·50
1614	**882**	£5 dp brown & gold†	11·00	7·50
		a. Gold† (Queen's head) omitted	£275	
		Set of 5	27·00	18·00
		Set of 5 Gutter Pairs	55·00	
		First Day Cover (Nos. 1611, 1612, 1613, 1614)		30·00
		First Day Cover (No. 1613a)		7·00
		Presentation Pack (Nos. 1611/13, 1614)	23·00	
		Presentation Pack (No. 1613a)	7·00	
		P.H.Q. Cards†† (Nos. 1611/13, 1614)	1·40	
		P.H.Q. Cards (No. 1613a)	40	7·50

†The Queen's head on these stamps is printed in optically variable ink which changes colour from gold to green when viewed from different angles.

††The P.H.Q. cards for this issue did not appear until 16 February 1993. They do not exist used on the first day of issue of Nos. 1611/13 and 1614.

The £1.50 (5 March 1996), £2 (2 May 1996) and £5 (17 September 1996) subsequently appeared on PVA (white gum) instead of the tinted PVAD previously used.

Special First Day of Issue Postmarks
(for illustrations see Introduction)

Philatelic Bureau, Edinburgh (Type H) (£1, £1.50, £2, £5)	32·00
Windsor, Berkshire (Type I) (£1, £1.50, £2, £5)	32·00
Philatelic Bureau, Edinburgh (Type H) (£3)	12·00
Carrickfergus, Antrim (as Type I) (£3)	15·00

1045 British Olympic Association Logo (Olympic Games, Barcelona)

1046 British Paralympic Association Symbol (Paralympics '92, Barcelona)

1047 *Santa Maria* (500th Anniv of Discovery of America by Columbus)

1048 *Kaisei* (Japanese cadet brigantine) (Grand Regatta Columbus, 1992)

1049 British Pavilion, "EXPO '92", Seville

(Des K. Bassford (Nos. 1615/16, 1619), K. Bassford and S. Paine. Eng C. Matthews (Nos. 1617/18). Litho Questa (Nos. 1615/16, 1619) or recess and litho Harrison (Nos. 1617/18))

1992 (7 Apr). **Europa. International Events.** *Phosphorised paper.* P 14 × 14½.

1615	**1045**	24p. new blue, lemon, magenta & black	65	65
		a. Horiz pair. Nos. 1615/16	1·25	1·25
1616	**1046**	24p. new blue, lemon, magenta & black	65	65
1617	**1047**	24p. black, grey, carmine, cream & gold	65	65
1618	**1048**	39p. black, grey, carmine, cream & gold	1·10	1·10
1619	**1049**	39p. new blue, lemon, magenta & black	1·10	1·10
		Set of 5	3·75	3·75
		Set of 3 Gutter Pairs and a Gutter Strip of 4	7·50	
		First Day Cover		4·50
		Presentation Pack	4·25	
		PHQ Cards (set of 5)	3·00	6·00

Nos. 1615/16 were printed together, *se-tenant*, throughout the sheet.

No. 1617 is known with the cream omitted used from Cornwall in September 1992.

Special First Day of Issue Postmarks

Philatelic Bureau, Edinburgh	4·75
Liverpool	4·75

1050 Pikeman

1051 Drummer

1052 Musketeer

1053 Standard Bearer

(Des J. Sancha)

1992 (16 June). **350th Anniv of the Civil War.** *Phosphorised paper. P* $14\frac{1}{2} \times 14$.

1620	**1050**	24p.	black, stone, bistre, scarlet, indigo, grey-green & yellow-ochre	55	55
		a.	Imperf (pair)		
1621	**1051**	28p.	black, yellow-ochre, ochre, rose-pink, blue, dull yellow-green & slate-lilac	70	70
1622	**1052**	33p.	black, ochre, pale orange, lemon, reddish orange, new blue & olive-green	1·00	1·00
1623	**1053**	39p.	black, yellow-ochre, yellow, greenish yellow, vermilion, indigo & orange-brown	1·10	1·10
			Set of 4	3·00	3·00
			Set of 4 Gutter Pairs	6·00	
			First Day Cover		4·00
			Presentation Pack	3·75	
			P.H.Q. Cards (set of 4)	2·00	5·00

Special First Day of Issue Postmarks

Philatelic Bureau, Edinburgh	4·25
Banbury, Oxfordshire	4·25

1054 *The Yeomen of the Guard*

1055 *The Gondoliers*

1056 *The Mikado*

1057 *The Pirates of Penzance*

1058 *Iolanthe*

(Des Lynda Gray)

1992 (21 July). **150th Birth Anniv of Sir Arthur Sullivan (composer). Gilbert and Sullivan Operas.** *One phosphor band* (18p.) *or phosphorised paper (others). P* $14\frac{1}{2} \times 14$.

1624	**1054**	18p.	bluish violet, bistre-yellow, scarlet, stone, blue & grey-black	40	45
1625	**1055**	24p.	purple-brown, lemon, scarlet, stone, blue, olive-bistre & black	55	55
		a.	Imperf (pair)	£250	
1626	**1056**	28p.	rose-red, lemon, stone, new blue, bluish violet, brt emerald & black	70	70

1627	**1057**	33p.	blue-green, orange-yellow, scarlet, olive-bistre, blue, brown-purple & black	1·10	1·10
1628	**1058**	39p.	dp blue, lemon, scarlet, stone, lavender, olive-bistre & lake-brown	1·25	1·25
			Set of 5	3·50	3·50
			Set of 5 Gutter Pairs	7·00	
			First Day Cover		4·75
			Presentation Pack	4·00	
			P.H.Q. Cards (set of 5)	2·25	6·00

Special First Day of Issue Postmarks

Philatelic Bureau, Edinburgh	5·00
Birmingham	5·00

1059 "Acid Rain Kills"

1060 "Ozone Layer"

1061 "Greenhouse Effect"

1062 "Bird of Hope"

(Des Christopher Hall (24p.), Lewis Fowler (28p.), Sarah Warren (33p.), Alice Newton-Mold (39p.). Adapted Trickett and Webb Ltd)

1992 (15 Sept). **Protection of the Environment. Children's Paintings.** *Phosphorised paper. P* 14 × 14½.

1629	**1059**	24p.	emerald, greenish yellow, pale olive-yellow, brt carmine & black	60	45
1630	**1060**	28p.	vermilion, lemon, brt blue, new blue, brt green, ultramarine & black	85	90
1631	**1061**	33p.	greenish blue, greenish yellow, brt rose-red, brt green, emerald, blue & black	90	1·00
1632	**1062**	39p.	emerald, greenish yellow, brt magenta, brt orange, brt blue & black	1·00	1·00
			Set of 4	3·00	3·00
			Set of 4 Gutter Pairs	6·00	
			First Day Cover		3·75
			Presentation Pack	3·50	
			P.H.Q. Cards (set of 4)	2·00	5·50

Special First Day of Issue Postmarks

Philatelic Bureau, Edinburgh (in green)	4·00
Torridon (in green)	4·00

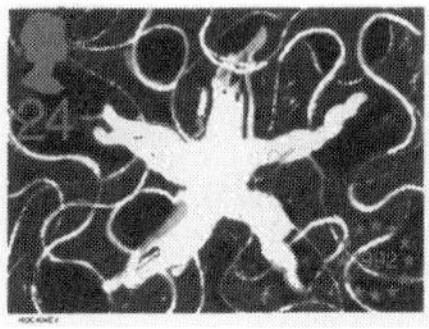

1063 European Star

(Des D. Hockney)

1992 (13 Oct). **Single European Market.** *Phosphorised paper. P* 15 × 14.

1633	**1063**	24p.	gold, greenish yellow, brt magenta, dull ultramarine & black	75	75
			Gutter Pair	1·50	
			First Day Cover		1·50
			Presentation Pack	1·40	
			P.H.Q. Card	60	1·60

Special First Day of Issue Postmarks

Philatelic Bureau, Edinburgh	1·75
Westminster	1·75

1064 "Angel Gabriel", St. James's, Pangbourne

1065 "Madonna and Child", St. Mary's, Bibury

1066 "King with Gold", Our Lady and St. Peter, Leatherhead

1067 "Shepherds", All Saints, Porthcawl

1068 "Kings with Frankincense and Myrrh", Our Lady and St. Peter, Leatherhead

(Des Carroll, Dempsey and Thirkell Ltd from windows by Karl Parsons (18, 24, 33p.) and Paul Woodroffe (28p. 39p.))

1992 (10 Nov). **Christmas. Stained Glass Windows.** *One centre band (18p.) or phosphorised paper (others). P* 15 × 14.

1634	**1064**	18p.	black, greenish yellow, mauve, ultramarine, brt emerald & gold	40	40
			a. Booklet pane of 20	7·50	
1635	**1065**	24p.	black, greenish yellow, brt purple, ultramarine, new blue, brt greenish yellow & gold	65	65
1636	**1066**	28p.	black, lemon, rosine, ultramarine, reddish lilac, red-orange & gold	80	80
1637	**1067**	33p.	brt ultramarine, greenish yellow, rosine, brown, yellow-orange, black & gold	95	95
1638	**1068**	39p.	black, lemon, rosine, brt blue, dp violet, yellow-orange & gold	1·10	1·10
			Set of 5	3·50	3·50
			Set of 5 Gutter Pairs	7·00	
			First Day Cover		4·25
			Presentation Pack	4·00	
			P.H.Q. Cards (set of 5)	2·25	5·50

Booklet pane No. 1634a comes from a special £3.60 Christmas booklet and has margins at left, top and bottom.

Special First Day of Issue Postmarks

Philatelic Bureau, Edinburgh	4·50
Bethlehem, Llandeilo, Dyfed	4·50
Pangbourne	4·50

Collectors Pack 1992

1992 (10 Nov). *Comprises Nos.* 1587/91, 1602/10 *and* 1615/38.
CP1638*a* Collectors Pack .... 40·00

Post Office Yearbook

1992 (11 Nov). *Comprises Nos.* 1587/91, 1602/10 *and* 1615/38 *in hardbound book with slip case, illustrated in colour* . 45·00

1069 Mute Swan Cob and St. Catherine's Chapel, Abbotsbury

1070 Cygnet and Decoy

1071 Swans and Cygnet

1072 Eggs in Nest and Tithe Barn, Abbotsbury

1073 Young Swan and the Fleet

(Des D. Gentleman)

1993 (19 Jan). **600th Anniv of Abbotsbury Swannery.** *One phosphor band (18p.) or phosphorised paper (others). P* 14 × 15.

1639	**1069**	18p.	gold, greenish yellow, bistre, green, vermilion & black	1·50	60
1640	**1070**	24p.	gold, cream, brt green, grey-brown, dull blue & grey-black	1·00	1·00
1641	**1071**	28p.	gold, greenish grey, yellow-brown, myrtle-green, brown, vermilion & black	1·25	1·40

1642	**1072**	33p.	gold, ochre, apple-green, olive-brown, brt orange & grey-black	1·50	1·75
1643	**1073**	39p.	gold, cream, brt green, cobalt, lt brown & black	2·00	2·00
			Set of 5	6·50	6·00
			Set of 5 Gutter Pairs	13·00	
			First Day Cover		6·50
			Presentation Pack	7·00	
			P.H.Q. Cards (set of 5)	2·25	7·00

Special First Day of Issue Postmarks

Philatelic Bureau, Edinburgh	7·00
Abbotsbury, Dorset	7·00

1074 Long John Silver and Parrot (*Treasure Island*)

1075 Tweedledum and Tweedledee (*Alice Through the Looking-Glass*)

1076 William (*William* books)

1077 Mole and Toad (*The Wind in the Willows*)

1078 Teacher and Wilfrid ("The Bash Street Kids")

1079 Peter Rabbit and Mrs. Rabbit (*The Tale of Peter Rabbit*)

1080 Snowman (*The Snowman*) and Father Christmas (*Father Christmas*)

1081 The Big Friendly Giant and Sophie (*The BFG*)

1082 Bill Badger and Rupert Bear

1083 Aladdin and the Genie

(Des Newell and Sorell)

1993 (2 Feb–10 Aug). **Greetings Stamps. "Gift Giving".** *Two phosphor bands. P* 15 × 14 (*with one elliptical hole in each horizontal side*).

1644	**1074**	(1st)	gold, greenish yellow, magenta, pale brown, lt blue & black	85	85
			a. Booklet pane. Nos. 1644/53	7·50	
1645	**1075**	(1st)	gold, cream & black	85	85
1646	**1076**	(1st)	gold, greenish yellow, magenta, cream, new blue & black	85	85
1647	**1077**	(1st)	gold, greenish yellow, magenta, cream, new blue & black	85	85
1648	**1078**	(1st)	gold, greenish yellow, magenta, cream, new blue & black	85	85
1649	**1079**	(1st)	gold, greenish yellow, magenta, cream, new blue & black	85	85
			a. Booklet pane. No. 1649 × 4 with margins all round (10 Aug)	3·00	
1650	**1080**	(1st)	gold, greenish yellow, magenta, cream, new blue & black	85	85
1651	**1081**	(1st)	gold, greenish yellow, magenta, cream, new blue & black	85	85
1652	**1082**	(1st)	gold, greenish yellow, magenta, cream, new blue & black	85	85
1653	**1083**	(1st)	gold, greenish yellow, magenta, cream, new blue & black	85	85
			Set of 10	7·50	7·50
			First Day Cover		8·00
			Presentation Pack	8·00	
			P.H.Q. Cards (set of 10)	3·00	8·50

Nos. 1644/53 were issued in £2.40 booklets (sold at £2.50 from 1 November 1993), together with a pane of 20 half stamp-sized labels. The stamps and labels were affixed to the booklet cover by a common gutter margin.

Booklet pane No. 1649a comes from the £6 (£5.64) Beatrix Potter booklet.

Special First Day of Issue Postmarks

Philatelic Bureau, Edinburgh (No. 1644a) (2 Feb) ... 9·00
Greetland (No. 1644a) (2 Feb) .... 9·00
Philatelic Bureau, Edinburgh (No. 1649a) (10 Aug) .. 5·00
Keswick (No. 1649a) (10 Aug) .... 5·00

1084 Decorated Enamel Dial

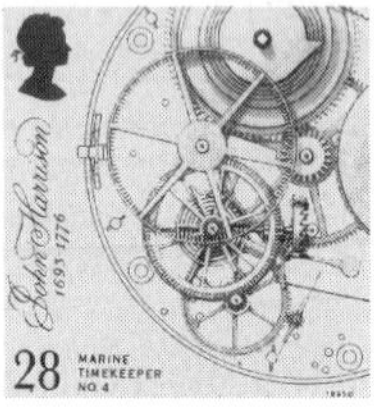

1085 Escapement, Remontoire and Fusée

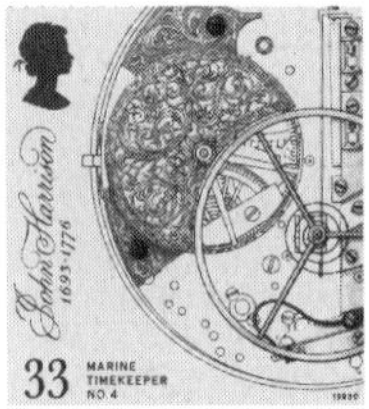

1086 Balance, Spring and Temperature Compensator

1087 Back of Movement

(Des H. Brown and D. Penny. Litho Questa)

1993 (16 Feb). **300th Birth Anniv of John Harrison (inventor of the marine chronometer). Details of "H4" Clock.** *Phosphorised paper. P* $14\frac{1}{2} \times 14$.

1654	**1084**	24p.	new blue, greenish yellow, magenta, black, grey-black & pale cream	50	50
1655	**1085**	28p.	new blue, greenish yellow, magenta, black, grey-black & pale cream	80	80
1656	**1086**	33p.	new blue, greenish yellow, magenta, black, grey-black & pale cream	95	95
1657	**1087**	39p.	new blue, greenish yellow, magenta, black, grey-black & pale cream	1·10	1·10
			Set of 4	3·00	3·00
			Set of 4 Gutter Pairs	6·00	
			First Day Cover		4·00
			Presentation Pack	4·00	
			P.H.Q. Cards (set of 4)	2·00	4·50

Special First Day of Issue Postmarks

Philatelic Bureau, Edinburgh .... 4·00
Greenwich .... 4·00

1088 Britannia

(Des B. Craddock, adapted Roundel Design Group. Litho (silver die-stamped, Braille symbol for "10" embossed) Questa)

1993 (2 Mar). *Granite paper. P* $14 \times 14\frac{1}{2}$ *(with two elliptical holes on each horizontal side).*

1658	**1088**	£10	greenish grey, rosine, yellow, new blue, reddish violet, vermilion, violet, brt green & silver	15·00	6·00
			a. Silver omitted		
			First Day Cover		25·00
			Presentation Pack	15·00	
			P.H.Q. Card	35	25·00

The paper used for No. 1658 contains fluorescent coloured fibres which, together with the ink used on the shield, react under U.V. light.

Special First Day of Issue Postmarks

Philatelic Bureau, Edinburgh .... 27·00
Windsor .... 27·00

1089 *Dendrobium hellwigianum*

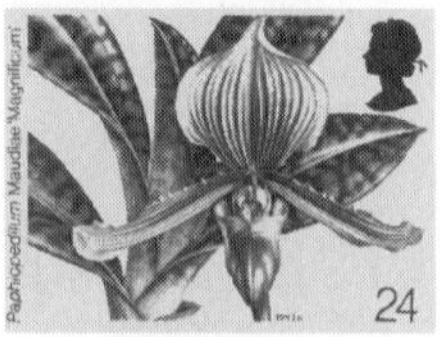

1090 *Paphiopedilum Maudiae "Magnificum"*

1091 *Cymbidium lowianum*

1092 *Vanda* Rothschildiana

1093 *Dendrobium vexillarius* var *albiviride*

(Des Pandora Sellars)

1993 (16 Mar). **14th World Orchid Conference, Glasgow.** *One phosphor band* (18p.) *or phosphorised paper* (*others*). *P* 15 × 14.

1659	**1089**	18p.	green, greenish yellow, magenta, pale blue, apple-green & slate	40	40
		a.	Imperf (pair)	£900	
1660	**1090**	24p.	green, greenish yellow, brt green & grey-black	65	65
1661	**1091**	28p.	green, greenish yellow, red, brt turquoise-blue & drab	90	90
1662	**1092**	33p.	green, greenish yellow, pale magenta, brt violet, brt green & grey	1·10	1·00
1663	**1093**	39p.	green, greenish yellow, red, pale olive-yellow, brt green, violet & grey-black	1·40	1·25
			Set of 5	4·00	3·50
			Set of 5 Gutter Pairs	8·00	
			First Day Cover		4·50
			Presentation Pack	4·50	
			P.H.Q. Cards (*set of 5*)	2·25	5·00

Special First Day of Issue Postmarks

Philatelic Bureau, Edinburgh	4·50
Glasgow	4·50

FLUORESCENT PHOSPHOR BANDS. Following the introduction of new automatic sorting machinery in 1991 it was found necessary to substantially increase the signal emitted by the phosphor bands. This was achieved by adding a fluorescent element to the phosphor which appears yellow under U.V. light. This combination was first used on an experimental sheet printing of the 18p., No. X913, produced by Enschedé in 1991. All values with phosphor bands from the elliptical perforations issue, including the No Value Indicated design, originally showed this yellow fluor.

From mid-1995 printings of current sheet and booklet stamps began to appear with the colour of the fluorescent element changed to blue. As such differences in fluor colour can only be identified by use of a U.V. lamp they are outside the scope of this catalogue, but full details will be found in the *Great Britain Specialised Catalogue Volume 4.*

The first commemorative/special stamp issue to show the change to blue fluor was the Centenary of Rugby League set, Nos. 1891/5.

COMPUTER-ENGRAVED CYLINDERS. In 1991 Enschedé introduced a new method of preparing photogravure cylinders for Great Britain stamps. This new method utilised computer-engraving instead of the traditional acid-etching and produced cylinders without the minor flaws which had long been a feature of the photogravure process. Such cylinders were first used on Great Britain stamps for the printing of the 18p. released on 19 November 1991 (see No. X913).

Harrison and Sons continued to use the acid-etching method until mid-1996 after which most Machin values, including N.V.I.'s, were produced from computer-engraved cylinders using a very similar process to that of Enschedé. Some values exist in versions from both cylinder production methods and can often be identified by minor differences. Such stamps are, however, outside the scope of this listing, but full details can be found in the current edition of the *Great Britain Specialised Catalogue Volume 4.*

For commemorative stamps the final Harrison issue to use computer-engraved cylinders was the Centenary of Cinema set (Nos. 1920/4).

When Walsall introduced photogravure printing in 1997 their cylinders were produced using a similar computer-engraved process.

1993 (6 Apr)–**97**. *Booklet Stamps. As T* **913/14,** *but P* 15 × 14 (*with one elliptical hole on each vertical side*).

(*a*) *Photo Harrison* (*No.* 1664), *Harrison or Walsall* (*others*)

1663*a*	**913**	(2nd)	brt blue (1 centre band) (7.9.93)	30	35
1664	**914**	(1st)	brt orange-red (phosphorised paper)	60	55
1664*a*		(1st)	brt orange-red (2 phosphor bands) (4.4.95)	40	45

(*b*) *Litho Questa, Walsall or Enschedé* (*No.* 1666ma)

1665	**913**	(2nd)	brt blue (1 centre band)	30	35
		Ey.	Phosphor omitted		
1666	**914**	(1st)	brt orange-red (2 phosphor bands)	40	45
		Ey.	Phosphor omitted		
		l.	Booklet pane. No. 1666 × 4 plus commemorative label at left (27.7.94)	5·00	
		la.	Ditto, but with commemorative label at right (16.5.95)	1·50	
		lEy.	Phosphor omitted		
		m.	Pane. No. 1666 with margins all round (roul 8 across top corners of pane) (17.8.94)	40	
		ma.	Ditto, but roul 10 across top corners of pane (2.97)	40	

Nos. 1663*a*/6 were issued in booklet panes showing perforations on all four edges.

On 6 September 1993 Nos. 1665/6 printed in lithography by Questa were made available in sheets from post offices in Birmingham, Coventry, Falkirk and Milton Keynes. These sheet stamps became available nationally on 5 October 1993. On 29 April 1997 No. 1663*a* printed in photogravure by Walsall became available in sheets. On the same date Nos. 1663*a* and 1666*a* were issued in coils printed by Harrison.

Nos. 1663a/6 occur from the following Barcode booklets:

No. 1663a (Harrison) – Nos. HA7/8, HC14/15, HC17, HC19; (Walsall) – HA12; No. 1664, – Nos. HB5, HD9, HD20; No. 1664a (Harrison) – Nos. HD24, HD27, HD29/33, HD35, HD39, HD45; (Walsall) – No. HB14; No. 1665 (Questa) – Nos. HC9, HC11, HC13, HC16, HC18, HC20; (Walsall) – Nos. HA9/11, HC12; No. 1666 (Questa) – Nos. HB7, HD11, HD21, HD26; (Walsall) – Nos. HB6, HB8/13, HB15, HD10, HD12/19, HD22/3, HD25, HD28, HD34, HD36/8, HD40, HD44.

No. 1666l includes a commemorative label for the 300th anniversary of the Bank of England and No. 1666la exists with labels for the birth centenary of R. J. Mitchell, 70th birthday of Queen Elizabeth II, "Hong Kong '97" International Stamp Exhibition or Commonwealth Heads of Government Meeting, Edinburgh.

No. 1666m, printed by Questa, was provided by the Royal Mail for inclusion in single pre-packed greetings cards. The pane shows large margins at top and sides with lines of roulette gauging 8 stretching from the bottom corners to the mid point of the top edge. Examples included with greetings cards show the top two corners of the pane folded over. Unfolded examples were available from the British Philatelic Bureau and from other Post Office philatelic outlets. The scheme was originally limited to Boots and their logo appeared on the pane margin. Other card retailers subsequently participated and later supplies omitted the logo.

A further printing by Enschedé in 1997 showed the roulettes gauging 10 (No. 1666ma).

In mid-1994 a number of postal forgeries of the 2nd bright blue printed in lithography were detected after having been rejected by the sorting equipment. These show the Queen's head in bright greenish blue, have a fluorescent, rather than a phosphor, band and show matt, colourless gum on the reverse. These forgeries come from booklets of ten which also have forged covers.

For 1st in gold see No. 1979.

1993 (27 Apr)–**97**. *As Nos.* X841, *etc, but P* 15 × 14 (*with one elliptical hole on each vertical side*).

(a) *Photo Enschedé*: – 20*p*. (Y1674), 29*p*., 35*p*. (Y1682), 36*p*., 38*p*., 41*p*. (Y1688), 43*p*. (Y1690)
Harrison: – 19*p*., 20*p*. (Y1675/*b*), 25*p*. (Y1676), 26*p*., 35*p*. (Y1683), 41*p*. (Y1689), 43*p*. (Y1691)
Enschedé or Harrison: – 1*p*., 2*p*., 4*p*., 5*p*., 6*p*., 10*p*., 25*p*. (Y1677), 30*p*., 31*p*., 37*p*., 39*p*., 50*p*., 63*p*., £1
Enschedé, Harrison or Walsall: – 37*p*., 63*p*.

Y1667	**367**	1p.	crimson (2 bands) (8.6.93)	10	10
Y1668		2p.	dp green (2 bands) (11.4.95)	10	10
Y1669		4p.	new blue (2 bands) (14.12.93)	10	10
Y1670		5p.	dull red-brown (2 bands) (8.6.93)	10	10
Y1671		6p.	yellow-olive (2 bands)	10	15
Y1672		10p.	dull orange (2 bands) (8.6.93)	15	20
Y1673		19p.	bistre (1 centre band) (26.10.93)	30	35
		a.	Imperf (pair)	£350	
		Ey.	Phosphor omitted		
Y1674		20p.	turquoise-green (2 bands) (14.12.93)	50	50
Y1675		20p.	brt green (1 centre band) (25.6.96)	30	35
		a.	Imperf (horiz pair)		
Y1675*b*		20p.	brt green (1 band at right) (23.9.97)	1·00	1·00
		bl.	Booklet pane. Nos. Y1675*b* and Y1678, each × 3 with margins all round	4·00	
Y1676		25p.	rose-red (phosphorised paper) (26.10.93)	70	70
		a.	Imperf (pair)		
		l.	Booklet pane. No. Y1676 × 2 plus 2 labels (1.11.93)	1·25	
Y1677		25p.	rose-red (2 bands) (20.12.94)	60	60
		l.	Booklet pane. No. Y1677 × 2 plus 2 labels (6.6.95)	80	
Y1678		26p.	red-brown (2 bands) (25.6.96)	40	45
Y1679		29p.	grey (2 bands) (26.10.93)	70	70
Y1680		30p.	dp olive-grey (2 bands) (27.7.93)	45	50
Y1681		31p.	dp mauve (2 bands) (25.6.96)	50	55
Y1682		35p.	yellow (2 bands) (17.8.93)	80	80
Y1683		35p.	yellow (phosphorised paper) (1.11.93)	80	80
Y1684		36p.	brt ultramarine (26.10.93)	80	80
Y1685		37p.	brt mauve (2 bands) (25.6.96)	60	65
Y1686		38p.	rosine (2 bands) (26.10.93)	80	80
		a.	Imperf (pair)	£200	
Y1687		39p.	brt magenta (2 bands) (25.6.96)	60	65
Y1688		41p.	grey-brown (2 bands) (26.10.93)	90	90
Y1689		41p.	drab (phosphorised paper) (1.11.93)	90	90
Y1690		43p.	dp olive-brown (2 bands) (25.6.96)	65	70
Y1691		43p.	sepia (2 bands) (8.7.96)	65	70
Y1692		50p.	ochre (2 bands) (14.12.93)	75	80
		a.	Imperf (pair)		
Y1693		63p.	lt emerald (2 bands) (25.6.96)	95	1·00
Y1694		£1	bluish violet (2 bands) (22.8.95)	1·50	1·60

(*b*) *Litho Walsall* (37*p*., 60*p*., 63*p*.), *Questa or Walsall* (25*p*., 35*p*., 41*p*.), *Questa* (*others*)

Y1743	**367**	1p.	lake (2 bands) (8.7.96)	10	10
		l.	Booklet pane. Nos. Y1743 × 2, Y1751 and Y1753 × 3 plus 2 labels	1·50	
Y1748		6p.	yellow-olive (2 bands) (26.7.94)	6·00	6·00
		l.	Booklet pane. Nos. Y1748, Y1750 and Y1752 × 4 with margins all round	9·00	
		la.	6p. value misplaced		
Y1749		10p.	dull orange (2 bands) (25.4.95)	3·00	3·00
		l.	Booklet pane. Nos. Y1749, Y1750/Ea, Y1752 × 2, Y1754/5, Y1757*Ea* and centre label with margins all round	10·00	
Y1750		19p.	bistre (1 band at left) (26.7.94)	1·00	1·00
		Ea.	Band at right (25.4.95)	1·00	1·00
		l.	Booklet pane. Nos. Y1750/Ea, each × 3 with margins all round (25.4.95)	6·00	

Y1751	**367**	20p.	brt yellow-green (1 centre band) (8.7.96)	30	35
		Ey.	Phosphor omitted		
		l.	Booklet pane. Nos. Y1751 and Y1753 × 7	3·00	
		lEy.	Booklet pane. Phosphor omitted		
Y1752		25p.	red (2 bands) (1.11.93)	60	60
		l.	Booklet pane. Nos. Y1752, NI72, S84 and W73, each × 2, with centre label and margins all round (14.5.96)	3·00	
Y1753		26p.	chestnut (2 bands) (8.7.96)	40	45
		Ey.	Phosphor omitted		
Y1754		30p.	olive-grey (2 bands) (25.4.95)	2·00	2·00
Y1755		35p.	yellow (2 bands) (1.11.93)	80	80
Y1756		37p.	brt mauve (2 bands) (8.7.96)	60	65
Y1757		41p.	drab (2 bands) (1.11.93)	65	70
		Ea.	*Grey-brown* (25.4.95)	2·00	2·00
		Ey.	Phosphor omitted		
Y1758		60p.	dull blue-grey (2 bands) (9.8.94)	90	95
Y1759		63p.	lt emerald (2 bands) (8.7.96)	95	1·00
			P.H.Q. Card (No. Y1694)	40	2·75

No. Y1694 is printed in Iriodin ink which gives a shiny effect to the solid part of the background behind the Queen's head.

No. Y1748la shows the 6p. value printed 22 mm to the left so that its position on the booklet pane is completely blank except for the phosphor bands. Other more minor misplacements exist.

For 26*p.* in gold see No. 1978.

First Day Covers

26.10.93	19p., 25p., 29p., 36p., 38p., 41p. (Y1673, Y1676, Y1679, Y1684, Y1686, Y1688)	4·50
9.8.94	60p. (Y1758)	2·00
25.4.95	National Trust *se-tenant* pane 10p., 19p., 25p., 30p., 35p., 41p. (Y1749l)	4·25
22.8.95	£1 (Y1694)	2·75
14.5.96	European Football Championship *se-tenant* pane 25p. × 8 (Y1752l)	6·50
25.6.96	20p., 26p., 31p., 37p., 39p., 43p., 63p. (Y1675, Y1678, Y1681, Y1685, Y1687, Y1690, Y1693)	5·50

Post Office Presentation Packs

26.10.93	P.O. Pack No. 30. 19p. (1 centre band), 25p. (phos paper), 29p., 36p., 38p., 41p. grey-brown (*Nos.* Y1673, Y1676, Y1679, Y1684, Y1686, Y1688)	5·00
21.11.95	P.O. Pack No. 34. 1p. (photo), 2p., 4p., 5p., 6p. (photo), 10p. (photo), 19p. (1 centre band), 20p. turquoise-green, 25p. (photo) (2 bands), 29p., 30p. (photo), 35p. (photo) (2 bands), 36p., 38p., 41p. grey-brown, 50p., 60p., £1 (*Nos.* Y1667/74, Y1677, Y1679/80, Y1682, Y1684, Y1686, Y1688, Y1692, Y1694, Y1758)	8·25
25.6.96	P.O. Pack No. 35. 20p. brt green (1 centre band), 26p. (photo), 31p., 37p. (photo), 39p., 43p. deep olive-brown, 63p. (photo) (*Nos.* Y1675, Y1678, Y1681, Y1685, Y1687, Y1690, Y1693).	4·50

DECIMAL MACHIN WITH ELLIPTICAL PERFORATIONS INDEX

Val.	*Process and Printer*	*Colour*	*Phosphor*	*Cat No.*	*Source*
1p.	photo Enschedé or Harrison	crimson	2 bands	Y1667	sheets
1p.	litho Questa	lake	2 bands	Y1743	£1 booklet (FH41)
2p.	photo Enschedé or Harrison	dp green	2 bands	Y1668	sheets
4p.	photo Enschedé or Harrison	new blue	2 bands	Y1669	sheets
5p.	photo Enschedé or Harrison	dull red-brown	2 bands	Y1670	sheets
6p.	photo Enschedé or Harrison	yellow-olive	2 bands	Y1671	sheets
6p.	litho Questa	yellow-olive	2 bands	Y1748	£6.04 Northern Ireland booklet (DX16)
10p.	photo Enschedé or Harrison	dull orange	2 bands	Y1672	sheets
10p.	litho Questa	dull orange	2 bands	Y1749	£6 National Trust booklet (DX17)
19p.	photo Harrison	bistre	1 centre band	Y1673	sheets, coils
19p.	litho Questa	bistre	1 band at left	Y1750	£6.04 Northern Ireland booklet (DX16), £6 National Trust booklet (DX17)
19p.	litho Questa	bistre	1 band at right	Y1750Ea	£6 National Trust booklet (DX17)
20p.	photo Enschedé	turquoise-green	2 bands	Y1674	sheets
20p.	photo Harrison	brt green	1 centre band	Y1675	sheets
20p.	litho Questa	brt yellow-green	1 centre band	Y1751	£1 booklet (FH41), £2 booklet (FW9)
20p.	photo Harrison	brt green	1 band at right	Y1675*b*	£6.15 B.B.C. booklet (DX19)
25p.	photo Harrison	rose-red	phos paper	Y1676	sheets, coils, 50p booklets (FB67/73), £1 booklets (FH33/7), £2 booklets (FW1/5)
25p	litho Walsall or Questa	red	2 bands	Y1752	£1 booklets (FH31/2) (Walsall), (FH40) (Questa), £2 booklet (FW8) (Questa), £6.04 Northern Ireland booklet (DX16) (Questa), £6 National Trust booklet (DX17) (Questa), £6.84 European Football Championship (DX18) (Questa)
25p.	photo Harrison or Enschedé	rose-red	2 bands	Y1677	sheets (Harrison or Enschedé), coils (Harrison), 50p booklets (FB74/5) (Harrison), £1 booklets (FH38/9) (Harrison), £2 booklets (FW6/7) (Harrison)
25p.	photo Harrison	gold	2 bands	1978	sheets, £6.15 B.B.C. booklet (DX19)
26p.	photo Harrison	red-brown	2 bands	Y1678	sheets, £6.15 B.B.C. booklet (DX19)
26p.	litho Questa	chestnut	2 bands	Y1753	£1 booklet (FH41), £2 booklet (FW9)
29p.	photo Enschedé	grey	2 bands	Y1679	sheets
30p.	photo Enschedé or Harrison	dp olive-grey	2 bands	Y1680	sheets
30p.	litho Questa	olive-grey	2 bands	Y1754	£6 National Trust booklet (DX17)
31p.	photo Enschedé or Harrison	dp mauve	2 bands	Y1681	sheets
35p.	photo Enschedé	yellow	2 bands	Y1682	sheets
35p.	photo Harrison	yellow	phos paper	Y1683	coils
35p.	litho Walsall or Questa	yellow	2 bands	Y1755	£1.40 booklets (GK5/6) (Walsall), £6 National Trust booklet (DX17) (Questa)
36p.	photo Enschedé	brt ultramarine	2 bands	Y1684	sheets
37p.	photo Enschedé, Harrison or Walsall	brt mauve	2 bands	Y1685	sheets (Enschedé or Harrison), coils (Harrison), £1.48 booklet (GL3) (Walsall)
37p.	litho Walsall	brt mauve	2 bands	Y1756	£1.48 booklets (GL1/2)
38p.	photo Enschedé	rosine	2 bands	Y1686	sheets
39p.	photo Enschedé or Harrison	brt magenta	2 bands	Y1687	sheets
41p.	photo Enschedé	grey-brown	2 bands	Y1688	sheets
41p.	photo Harrison	drab	phos paper	Y1689	coils
41p.	litho Walsall	drab	2 bands	Y1757	£1.64 booklets (GN1/3)
41p.	litho Questa	grey-brown	2 bands	Y1757*Ea*	£6 National Trust booklet (DX17)
43p.	photo Enschedé	dp olive-brown	2 bands	Y1690	sheets
43p.	photo Harrison	sepia	2 bands	Y1691	sheets, coils
50p.	photo Enschedé or Harrison	ochre	2 bands	Y1692	sheets
60p.	litho Walsall	dull blue-grey	2 bands	Y1758	£2.40 booklets (GQ1/4)
63p.	photo Enschedé, Harrison or Walsall	lt emerald	2 bands	Y1693	sheets (Enschedé or Harrison), coils (Harrison), £2.52 booklet (GR3) (Walsall)
63p.	litho Walsall	lt emerald	2 bands	Y1759	£2.52 booklets (GR1/2)
£1	photo Enschedé or Harrison	bluish violet	2 bands	Y1694	sheets

1094 "Family Group" (bronze sculpture) (Henry Moore)

1095 "Kew Gardens" (lithograph) (Edward Bawden)

1096 "St. Francis and the Birds" (Stanley Spencer)

1097 "Still Life: Odyssey I" (Ben Nicholson)

(Des. A. Dastor)

1993 (11 May). **Europa. Contemporary Art.** *Phosphorised paper.* P 14 × 14½.

1767	**1094**	24p.	brownish grey, lemon, magenta, turquoise-blue & grey-black	50	50
1768	**1095**	28p.	brownish grey, buff, lt green, yellow-brown, brt orange, new blue & grey-black	80	80
1769	**1096**	33p.	brownish grey, cream, greenish yellow, magenta, new blue & grey-black	95	95
1770	**1097**	39p.	brownish grey, cream, yellow-ochre, rose-lilac, red, lt blue & grey-black	1·10	1·10
			Set of 4	3·00	3·00
			Set of 4 Gutter Pairs	6·00	
			First Day Cover		4·00
			Presentation Pack	3·50	
			PHQ Cards (set of 4)	2·00	4·50

Special First Day of Issue Postmarks

British Philatelic Bureau, Edinburgh	4·00
London SW	4·00

1098 Emperor Claudius (from gold coin)

1099 Emperor Hadrian (bronze head)

1100 Goddess Roma (from gemstone)

1101 Christ (Hinton St. Mary mosaic)

(Des J. Gibbs)

1993 (15 June). **Roman Britain.** *Phosphorised paper with two phosphor bands.* P 14 × 14½.

1771	**1098**	24p.	black, pale orange, lt brown & silver	50	50
1772	**1099**	28p.	black, greenish yellow, brt rose-red, silver, brt blue & grey-black	80	80
1773	**1100**	33p.	black, greenish yellow, brt rose-red, silver & grey	95	95
1774	**1101**	39p.	black, greenish yellow, rosine, silver, pale violet & grey	1·10	1·10
			Set of 4	3·00	3·00
			Set of 4 Gutter Pairs	6·00	
			First Day Cover		4·00
			Presentation Pack	3·50	
			PHQ Cards (set of 4)	1·40	4·00

Special First Day of Issue Postmarks

British Philatelic Bureau, Edinburgh	4·00
Caerllion	4·00

1102 *Midland Maid* and other Narrow Boats, Grand Junction Canal

1103 *Yorkshire Lass* and other Humber Keels, Stainforth and Keadby Canal

1104 *Valley Princess* and other Horse-drawn Barges, Brecknock and Abergavenny Canal

1105 Steam Barges, including *Pride of Scotland,* and Fishing Boats, Crinan Canal

(Des T. Lewery. Litho Questa)

1993 (20 July). **Inland Waterways.** *Two phosphor bands. P* $14\frac{1}{2} \times 14$.

1775	**1102**	24p.	new blue, greenish yellow, brt magenta, black, blue, vermilion, brownish grey & sage-green	50	50
1776	**1103**	28p.	new blue, greenish yellow, brt magenta, black, blue, bluish grey, vermilion & sage-green	80	80
1777	**1104**	33p.	new blue, greenish yellow, brt magenta, black, blue, vermilion, greenish grey & sage-green	95	95
1778	**1105**	39p.	new blue, greenish yellow, brt magenta, black, blue, vermilion, sage-green & dull mauve	1·10	1·10
			Set of 4	3·00	3·00
			Set of 4 Gutter Pairs	6·00	
			First Day Cover		4·00
			Presentation Pack	3·50	
			PHQ Cards (set of 4)	1·40	4·50

Nos. 1775/8 commemorate the bicentenary of the Acts of Parliament authorising the canals depicted.

Special First Day of Issue Postmarks

British Philatelic Bureau, Edinburgh	4·00
Gloucester	4·00

1106 Horse Chestnut

1107 Blackberry

1108 Hazel

1109 Rowan

1110 Pear

(Des Charlotte Knox)

1993 (14 Sept). **The Four Seasons. Autumn. Fruits and Leaves.** *One phosphor band (18p.) or phosphorised paper (others). P* 15 × 14.

1779	**1106**	18p.	black, greenish yellow, cerise, brt green, gold & chestnut	40	40
1780	**1107**	24p.	black, lemon, cerise, myrtle-green, gold, brt green & brown	65	65
1781	**1108**	28p.	grey, lemon, emerald, lake-brown & gold	90	80
1782	**1109**	33p.	grey-black, greenish yellow, rosine, lt green, gold & brown	1·10	95
1783	**1110**	39p.	myrtle-green, greenish yellow, rosine, olive-sepia, gold, apple-green & dp myrtle-green	1·40	1·10
			Set of 5	4·00	3·50
			Set of 5 Gutter Pairs	8·00	
			First Day Cover		4·50
			Presentation Pack	4·25	
			PHQ Cards (set of 5)	1·50	5·00

Special First Day of Issue Postmarks

British Philatelic Bureau, Edinburgh	4·50
Taunton	4·50

1111 *The Reigate Squire*

1112 *The Hound of the Baskervilles*

1113 *The Six Napoleons*

1114 *The Greek Interpreter*

1115 *The Final Problem*

(Des A. Davidson. Litho Questa)

1993 (12 Oct). **Sherlock Holmes. Centenary of the Publication of "The Final Problem".** *Phosphorised paper. P* 14 × 14½.

1784	**1111**	24p. new blue, greenish yellow, magenta, black & gold	90	90
		a. Horiz strip of 5. Nos. 1784/8	4·00	4·00
1785	**1112**	24p. new blue, greenish yellow, magenta, black & gold	90	90
1786	**1113**	24p. new blue, greenish yellow, magenta, black & gold	90	90
1787	**1114**	24p. new blue, greenish yellow, magenta, black & gold	90	90
1788	**1115**	24p. new blue, greenish yellow, magenta, black & gold	90	90
		Set of 5	4·00	4·00
		Gutter strip of 10	8·00	
		First Day Cover		4·75
		Presentation Pack	4·50	
		PHQ Cards (set of 5)	1·50	5·50

Nos. 1785/8 were printed together, *se-tenant*, in horizontal strips of 5 throughout the sheet.

Special First Day of Issue Postmarks

British Philatelic Bureau, Edinburgh	5·00
London NW1	5·00

A First Day of Issue handstamp was provided at Autumn Stampex, London SW1, for this issue.

1116

(Des J. Matthews. Litho Walsall)

1993 (19 Oct) *Self-adhesive Booklet Stamp. Two phosphor bands. Die-cut P* 14 × 15 *(with one elliptical hole on each vertical side).*

1789	**1116**	(1st) orange-red	1·00	1·00
		Ey. Phosphor omitted		
		a. Booklet pane. No. 1789 × 20	15·00	
		aEy. Booklet pane. Phosphor omitted		
		First Day Cover (No. 1789)		3·25
		Presentation Pack (No. 1789a)	12·00	
		PHQ Card	30	3·25

No. 1789 was initially sold at 24p. which was increased to 25p. from November 1993. It was only issued in booklets containing 20 stamps, each surrounded by die-cut perforations.

For similar 2nd and 1st designs printed in photogravure by Enschedé see Nos. 1976/7.

Special First Day of Issue Postmarks

British Philatelic Bureau, Edinburgh	3·50
Newcastle upon Tyne	3·50

1117 Bob Cratchit and Tiny Tim

1118 Mr. and Mrs. Fezziwig

1119 Scrooge

1120 The Prize Turkey

1121 Mr. Scrooge's Nephew

(Des Q. Blake)

1993 (9 Nov). **Christmas. 150th Anniv of Publication of "A Christmas Carol" by Charles Dickens.** *One phosphor band* (19*p.*) *or phosphorised paper* (*others*). *P* 15 × 14.

1790	**1117**	19p.	new blue, yellow, magenta, salmon, brt emerald & grey-black	40	40
			a. Imperf (pair)		
1791	**1118**	25p.	yellow-orange, brown-lilac, steel-blue, lake-brown, lt green, grey-black & black	65	65
1792	**1119**	30p.	cerise, bistre-yellow, dull blue, brown-rose, pale green, grey-black & black	80	80
1793	**1120**	35p.	dp turquoise-green, lemon, vermilion, dull ultramarine, Indian red, bluish grey & black	95	95
1794	**1121**	41p.	reddish purple, lemon, purple, lt blue, salmon, brt green & black	1·10	1·10
			Set of 5	3·50	3·50
			Set of 5 Gutter Pairs	7·25	
			First Day Cover		4·50
			Presentation Pack	4·00	
			PHQ Cards (set of 5)	1·90	5·25

Special First Day of Issue Postmarks

British Philatelic Bureau, Edinburgh	4·50
Bethlehem, Llandeilo	4·50

A First Day of Issue handstamp (pictorial) was provided at the City of London for this issue.

Collectors Pack 1993

1993 (9 Nov). *Comprises Nos.* 1639/43, 1654/7, 1659/63, 1767/88 *and* 1790/4.

CP1794a Collectors Pack .... 40·00

Post Office Yearbook

1993 (9 Nov). *Comprises Nos.* 1639/43, 1654/7, 1659/63, 1767/88 *and* 1790/4 *in hardbound book with slip case, illustrated in colour* .... 45·00

1122 Class "5" No. 44957 and Class "B1" No. 61342 on West Highland Line

1123 Class "A1" No. 60149 *Amadis* at Kings Cross

1124 Class "4" No. 43000 on Turntable at Blyth North

1125 Class "4" No. 42455 near Wigan Central

1126 Class "Castle" No. 7002 *Devizes Castle* on Bridge crossing Worcester and Birmingham Canal

(Des B. Delaney)

1994 (18 Jan). **The Age of Steam. Railway Photographs by Colin Gifford.** *One phosphor band* (19*p.*) *or phosphorised paper with two bands* (*others*). *P* $14\frac{1}{2}$.

1795	**1122**	19p.	dp blue-green, grey-black & black	45	40
1796	**1123**	25p.	slate-lilac, grey-black & black	75	65
1797	**1124**	30p.	lake-brown, grey-black & black	90	80
1798	**1125**	35p.	dp claret, grey-black & black	1·10	95
1799	**1126**	41p.	indigo, grey-black & black	1·25	1·10
			Set of 5	4·00	3·50
			Set of 5 Gutter Pairs	8·00	
			First Day Cover		4·50
			Presentation Pack	4·25	
			PHQ Cards (set of 5)	1·90	5·25

Nos. 1796/9 are on phosphorised paper and also show two phosphor bands.

Special First Day of Issue Postmarks

Philatelic Bureau, Edinburgh	4·50
York	4·50

A First Day of Issue handstamp (pictorial) was provided at Bridge of Orchy for this issue.

1127 Dan Dare and the Mekon

1128 The Three Bears

1129 Rupert Bear

1130 Alice *(Alice in Wonderland)*

1131 Noggin and the Ice Dragon

1132 Peter Rabbit posting Letter

1133 Red Riding Hood and Wolf

1134 Orlando the Marmalade Cat

1135 Biggles

1136 Paddington Bear on Station

(Des Newell and Sorrell)

1994 (1 Feb). **Greetings Stamps. "Messages".** *Two phosphor bands. P* 15 × 14 *(with one elliptical hole on each vertical side).*

1800	**1127**	(1st)	gold, greenish yellow, brt purple, bistre-yellow, new blue & black	40	45
			a. Booklet pane. Nos. 1800/9	4·00	
1801	**1128**	(1st)	gold, greenish yellow, brt purple, bistre-yellow, new blue & black	40	45
1802	**1129**	(1st)	gold, greenish yellow, brt purple, bistre-yellow, new blue & black	40	45
1803	**1130**	(1st)	gold, bistre-yellow & black	40	45
1804	**1131**	(1st)	gold, greenish yellow, brt purple, bistre-yellow, new blue & black	40	45
1805	**1132**	(1st)	gold, greenish yellow, brt purple, bistre-yellow, new blue & black	40	45
1806	**1133**	(1st)	gold, greenish yellow, brt purple, bistre-yellow, new blue & black	40	45
1807	**1134**	(1st)	gold, greenish yellow, brt purple, bistre-yellow, new blue & black	40	45
1808	**1135**	(1st)	gold, greenish yellow, brt purple, bistre-yellow, new blue & black	40	45
1809	**1136**	(1st)	gold, greenish yellow, brt purple, bistre-yellow, new blue & black	40	45
			Set of 10	4·00	4·50
			First Day Cover		7·50
			Presentation Pack	11·00	
			PHQ Cards (set of 10)	4·25	10·00

Nos. 1800/9 were issued in £2.50 stamp booklets (sold at £2.60 from 8 July 1996), together with a pane of 20 half stamp-sized labels. The stamps and labels were attached to the booklet cover by a common gutter margin.

Special First Day of Issue Postmarks

British Philatelic Bureau, Edinburgh	8·00
Penn, Wolverhampton	8·00

1137 Castell Y Waun (Chirk Castle), Clwyd, Wales

1138 Ben Arkle, Sutherland, Scotland

1139 Mourne Mountains, County Down, Northern Ireland

1140 Dersingham, Norfolk. England

1141 Dolwyddelan, Gwynedd, Wales

1144 "Wish You were Here!"

1145 Punch and Judy Show

1146 "The Tower Crane" Machine

1994 (1 Mar–26 July). **25th Anniv of Investiture of the Prince of Wales. Paintings by Prince Charles.** *One phosphor band (19p.) or phosphorised paper (others). P* 15 × 14.

1810	**1137**	19p.	grey-black, greenish yellow, magenta, new blue, black & silver	40	40
1811	**1138**	25p.	grey-black, orange-yellow, brt magenta, new blue, silver & black	75	75
1812	**1139**	30p.	grey-black, greenish yellow, magenta, new blue, silver & black	1·00	1·00
		a.	Booklet pane. No. 1812 × 4 with margins all round (26 July)	3·50	
1813	**1140**	35p.	grey-black, greenish yellow, magenta, new blue, silver & black	1·10	1·10
1814	**1141**	41p.	grey-black, lemon, magenta, new blue, silver & black	1·25	1·25
			Set of 5	4·00	4·00
			Set of 5 Gutter Pairs	8·00	
			First Day Cover		4·50
			Presentation Pack	4·50	
			PHQ Cards (set of 5)	1·90	5·25

Booklet pane No. 1812a comes from the £6.04 "Northern Ireland" booklet.

Special First Day of Issue Postmarks

British Philatelic Bureau, Edinburgh	4·75
Caernarfon	4·75

1142 Bather at Blackpool **1143** "Where's my Little Lad?"

(Des M. Dempsey and B. Dare. Litho Questa)

1994 (12 Apr). **Centenary of Picture Postcards.** *One side band (19p.) or two phosphor bands (others). P* 14 × 14½.

1815	**1142**	19p.	new blue, greenish yellow, magenta & black	40	40
1816	**1143**	25p.	new blue, greenish yellow, magenta & black	65	65
1817	**1144**	30p.	new blue, greenish yellow, magenta & black	80	80
1818	**1145**	35p.	new blue, greenish yellow, magenta & black	95	95
1819	**1146**	41p.	new blue, greenish yellow, magenta & black	1·10	1·10
			Set of 5	3·50	3·50
			Set of 5 Gutter Pairs	7·25	
			First Day Cover		4·00
			Presentation Pack	4·00	
			PHQ Cards (set of 5)	1·90	5·25

Special First Day of Issue Postmarks

British Philatelic Bureau, Edinburgh	4·00
Blackpool	4·00

1147 British Lion and French Cockerel over Tunnel

1149 Groundcrew replacing Smoke Canisters on Douglas Boston of 88 Sqn

1150 H.M.S. *Warspite* (battleship) shelling Enemy Positions

1148 Symbolic Hands over Train

1151 Commandos landing on Gold Beach

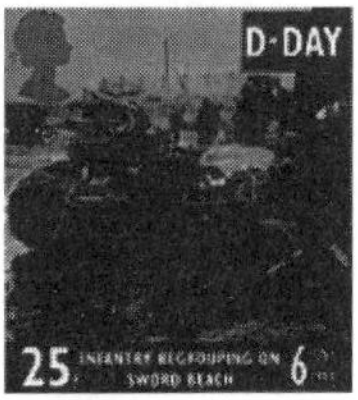

1152 Infantry regrouping on Sword Beach

(Des G. Hardie (T **1147**), J.-P. Cousin (T **1148**))

1994 (3 May) **Opening of Channel Tunnel.** *Phosphorised paper. P* 14 × 14½.

1820	**1147**	25p.	ultramarine, brt orange, scarlet, new blue, emerald, turquoise-blue & silver	60	60
		a.	Horiz pair. Nos. 1820/1	1·25	1·25
1821	**1148**	25p.	ultramarine, scarlet, new blue, emerald & silver	60	60
1822	**1147**	41p.	new blue, brt orange, scarlet, turquoise-blue, emerald, ultramarine & silver	1·40	1·40
		a.	Horiz pair. Nos. 1822/3	2·75	2·75
		ab.	Imperf (horiz pair)	£700	
1823	**1148**	41p.	ultramarine, scarlet, new blue, emerald & silver	1·40	1·40
			Set of 4	3·50	3·50
			First Day Cover		5·00
			Presentation Pack	4·00	
			Souvenir Book	25·00	
			PHQ Cards (set of 4)	1·75	4·50

Nos. 1820/1 and 1822/3 were printed together, *se-tenant,* in horizontal pairs throughout the sheets.

Stamps in similar designs were also issued by France. These are included in the souvenir book.

Special First Day of Issue Postmarks

British Philatelic Bureau, Edinburgh	5·00
Folkestone	5·00

1153 Tank and Infantry advancing, Ouistreham

(Des K. Bassford from contemporary photographs. Litho Questa)

1994 (6 June). **50th Anniv of D-Day.** *Two phosphor bands. P* 14½ × 14.

1824	**1149**	25p.	pink, greenish yellow, blackish lilac, slate-black, brt scarlet & silver-grey	80	80
		a.	Horiz strip of 5. Nos. 1824/8	3·50	3·50
1825	**1150**	25p.	pink. greenish yellow, blackish lilac, slate-black, brt scarlet & silver-grey	80	80
1826	**1151**	25p.	pink, greenish yellow, blackish lilac, slate-black, brt scarlet & silver-grey	80	80
1827	**1152**	25p.	pink. greenish yellow, blackish lilac, slate-black, brt scarlet & silver-grey	80	80
1828	**1153**	25p.	pink, greenish yellow, blackish lilac, slate-black, brt scarlet & silver-grey	80	80
			Set of 5	3·50	3·50
			Gutter block of 10	7·00	
			First Day Cover		4·00
			Presentation Pack	3·75	
			PHQ Cards (set of 5)	2·00	5·00

Nos. 1824/8 were printed together, *se-tenant,* in horizontal strips of 5 throughout the sheet.

Special First Day of Issue Postmarks

British Philatelic Bureau, Edinburgh .... 4·00
Portsmouth .... 4·00

1154 The Old Course, St. Andrews

1155 The 18th Hole, Muirfield

1156 The 15th Hole ("Luckyslap"), Carnoustie

1157 The 8th Hole ("The Postage Stamp"), Royal Troon

1158 The 9th Hole, Turnberry

(Des P. Hogarth)

1994 (5 July). **Scottish Golf Courses.** *One phosphor band* (19p.) *or phosphorised paper* (others). *P* $14\frac{1}{2} \times 14$.

1829 **1154** 19p. yellow-green, olive-grey, orange-vermilion, apple-green, blue & grey-black 55 55
1830 **1155** 25p. yellow-green, lemon, brt orange, apple-green, blue, magenta & grey-black 80 80
1831 **1156** 30p. yellow-green, yellow, rosine, emerald, blue-green, new blue & grey-black ... 1·00 1·00
1832 **1157** 35p. yellow-green, yellow, rosine, apple-green, new blue, dull blue & grey-black 1·25 1·25
1833 **1158** 41p. yellow-green, lemon, magenta, apple-green, dull blue, new blue & grey-black 1·40 1·40

Set of 5 .... 4·75 4·75
Set of 5 Gutter Pairs .... 9·00
First Day Cover .... 4·75
Presentation Pack .... 4·75
PHQ Cards (set of 5) .... 2·25 5·75

Nos. 1829/33 commemorate the 250th anniversary of golf's first set of rules produced by the Honourable Company of Edinburgh Golfers.

Special First Day of Issue Postmarks

British Philatelic Bureau, Edinburgh .... 5·00
Turnberry .... 5·00

1159 Royal Welsh Show, Llanelwedd

1160 All England Tennis Championships, Wimbledon

1161 Cowes Week

1162 Test Match, Lord's

1163 Braemar Gathering

(Des M. Cook)

1994 (2 Aug). **The Four Seasons. Summertime.** *One phosphor band* (19p.) *or phosphorised paper* (others). *P* 15×14.

1834 **1159** 19p. black, greenish yellow, brt magenta, brown, yellow-brown & new blue 50 50
1835 **1160** 25p. black, greenish yellow, magenta, reddish violet, yellow-green, myrtle-green & new blue 70 70
1836 **1161** 30p. black, greenish yellow, brt magenta, yellow-ochre, dp slate-blue, blue-green & blue 90 80

1837	**1162**	35p.	black, greenish yellow, magenta, slate-lilac, yellow-green, dp bluish green & brt blue	1·00	90
1838	**1163**	41p.	black, greenish yellow, brt magenta, dp claret, lt brown, myrtle-green & brt blue	1·10	1·00
			Set of 5	3·75	3·50
			Set of 5 Gutter Pairs	7·50	
			First Day Cover		4·25
			Presentation Pack	4·00	
			PHQ Cards (set of 5)	1·90	5·25

Special First Day of Issue Postmarks

British Philatelic Bureau, Edinburgh .... 4·25
Wimbledon .... 4·25

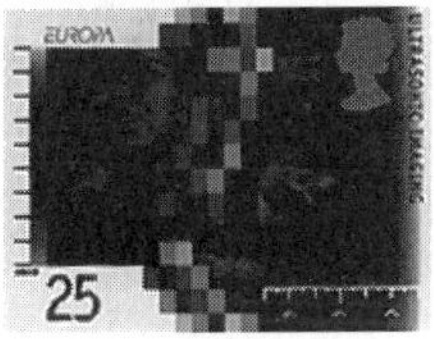

1164 Ultrasonic Imaging

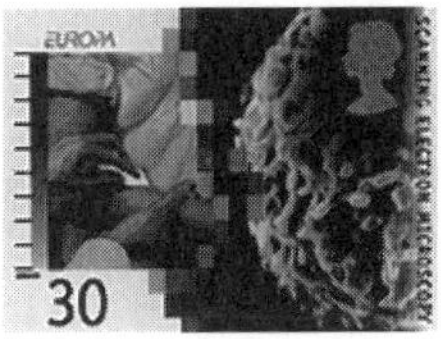

1165 Scanning Electron Microscopy

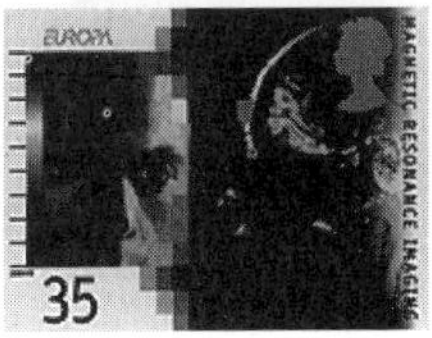

1166 Magnetic Resonance Imaging

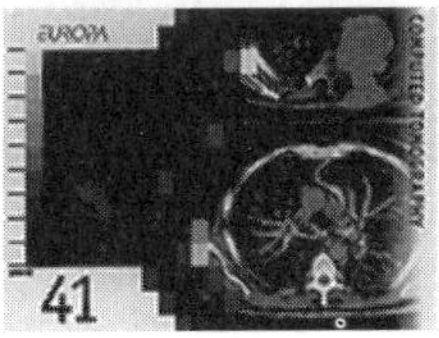

1167 Computed Tomography

(Des P. Vermier and J.-P. Tibbles. Photo Enschedé)

1994 (27 Sept). **Europa. Medical Discoveries.** *Phosphorised paper. P* 14 × 14½.

1839	**1164**	25p.	greenish yellow, brt magenta, new blue, black & silver	65	65
		a.	Imperf (vert pair)		
1840	**1165**	30p.	greenish yellow, brt magenta, new blue, black & silver	85	85
1841	**1166**	35p.	greenish yellow, brt magenta, new blue, black & silver	90	90
1842	**1167**	41p.	greenish yellow, brt magenta, new blue, black & silver	1·00	1·00
			Set of 4	3·00	3·00
			Set of 4 Gutter Pairs	6·00	
			First Day Cover		4·00
			Presentation Pack	4·00	
			PHQ Cards (set of 4)	1·50	3·50

Special First Day of Issue Postmarks

British Philatelic Bureau, Edinburgh .... 4·00
Cambridge .... 4·00

1168 Mary and Joseph

1169 Three Wise Men

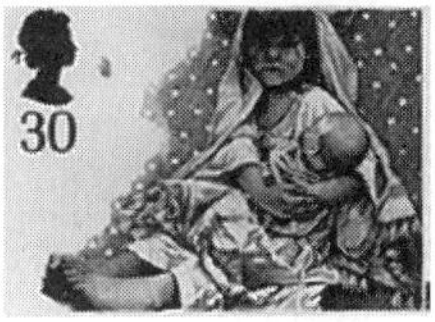

1170 Mary with Doll

1171 Shepherds

1172 Angels

(Des Yvonne Gilbert)

1994 (1 Nov). **Christmas. Children's Nativity Plays.** *One phosphor band (19p.) or phosphorised paper (others). P* 15 × 14.

1843	**1168**	19p.	turquoise-green, greenish yellow, brt magenta, new blue, dull blue & grey-black	50	50
		a.	Imperf (pair)	£200	
1844	**1169**	25p.	orange-brown, greenish yellow, brt magenta, new blue, lt blue, bistre & grey-black	70	70
1845	**1170**	30p.	lt brown, greenish yellow, brt magenta, blue, turquoise-blue, new blue & brownish grey	80	80
1846	**1171**	35p.	dp grey-brown, greenish yellow, brt magenta, turquoise-blue, dull violet-blue, ochre & brown	90	90
1847	**1172**	41p.	blue, greenish yellow, brt magenta, turquoise-blue, lt blue & dp grey	1·00	1·00
			Set of 5	3·50	3·50
			Set of 5 Gutter Pairs	7·00	
			First Day Cover		4·25
			Presentation Pack	4·00	
			PHQ Cards (set of 5)	1·90	5·25

Special First Day of Issue Postmarks

British Philatelic Bureau, Edinburgh	4·25
Bethlehem, Llandeilo	4·25

Collectors Pack 1994

1994 (14 Nov). *Comprises Nos.* 1795/1847

CP1847a Collectors Pack	40·00

Post Office Yearbook

1994 (14 Nov). *Comprises Nos.* 1795/9 *and* 1810/47 *in hardbound book with slip case, illustrated in colour* ... 45·00

1173 Sophie (black cat)

1174 Puskas (Siamese) and Tigger (tabby)

1175 Chloe (ginger cat)

1176 Kikko (tortoiseshell) and Rosie (Abyssinian)

1177 Fred (black and white cat)

(Des Elizabeth Blackadder. Litho Questa)

1995 (17 Jan). **Cats.** *One phosphor band* (19p.) *or two phosphor bands* (*others*). *P* $14\frac{1}{2} \times 14$.

1848	**1173**	19p.	new blue, greenish yellow, magenta, black & brown-red	60	60
1849	**1174**	25p.	new blue, greenish yellow, magenta, black & dull yellow-green	75	75
1850	**1175**	30p.	new blue, greenish yellow, magenta, black & yellow-brown	1·00	1·00
1851	**1176**	35p.	new blue, greenish yellow, magenta, black & yellow	1·10	1·10
1852	**1177**	41p.	new blue, greenish yellow, magenta, black & reddish orange	1·25	1·25
			Set of 5	4·25	4·25
			Set of 5 Gutter Pairs	8·50	
			First Day Cover		4·50
			Presentation Pack	4·50	
			PHQ Cards (set of 5)	2·50	6·00

Special First Day of Issue Postmarks

British Philatelic Bureau, Edinburgh	4·75
Kitts Green	4·75

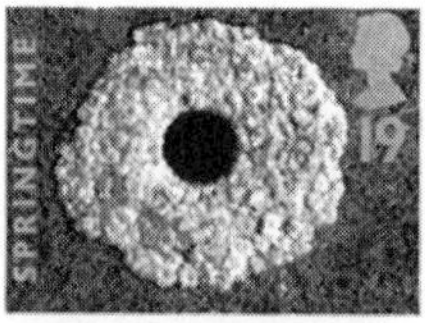

1178 Dandelions

1179 Chestnut Leaves

1180 Garlic Leaves

1181 Hazel Leaves

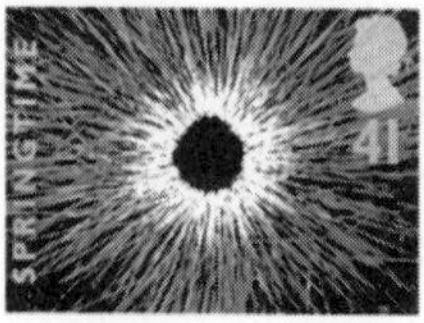

1182 Spring Grass

1995 (14 Mar). **The Four Seasons. Springtime. Plant Sculptures by Andy Goldsworthy.** *One phosphor band* (19p.) *or two phosphor bands* (*others*). *P* 15×14.

1853	**1178**	19p.	silver, greenish yellow, magenta, green & grey-black	55	55
1854	**1179**	25p.	silver, greenish yellow, magenta, new blue & black	65	65
1855	**1180**	30p.	silver, greenish yellow, magenta, new blue & black	90	90

1856	**1181**	35p. silver, greenish yellow, magenta, new blue & black	1·00	1·00
1857	**1182**	41p. silver, greenish yellow, magenta, new blue, blue-green & black	1·10	1·10
		Set of 5	3·75	3·75
		Set of 5 Gutter Pairs	7·50	
		First Day Cover		4·00
		Presentation Pack	4·00	
		PHQ Cards (set of 5)	2·25	5·25

Special First Day of Issue Postmarks

British Philatelic Bureau, Edinburgh .... 4·25
Springfield .... 4·25

1183 "La Danse a la Campagne" (Renoir)

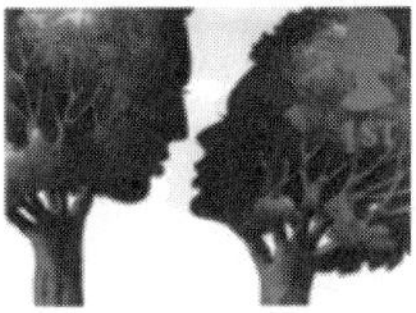

1184 "Troilus and Criseyde" (Peter Brookes)

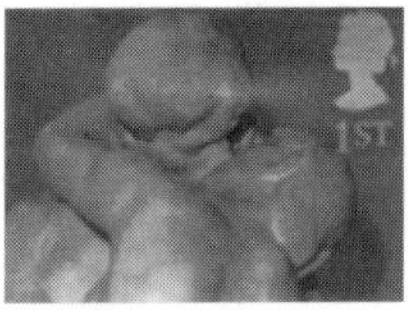

1185 "The Kiss" (Rodin)

1186 "Girls on the Town" (Beryl Cook)

1187 "Jazz" (Andrew Mockett)

1188 "Girls performing a Kathal Dance" (Aurangzeb period)

1189 "Alice Keppel with her Daughter" (Alice Hughes)

1190 "Children Playing" (L. S. Lowry)

1191 "Circus Clowns" (Emily Firmin and Justin Mitchell)

1192 Decoration from "All the Love Poems of Shakespeare" (Eric Gill)

(Des Newell and Sorrell. Litho Walsall)

1995 (21 Mar). **Greetings Stamps. "Greetings in Art".** *Two phosphor bands.* P $14\frac{1}{2} \times 14$ (*with one elliptical hole on each vertical side*).

1858	**1183**	(1st) greenish yellow, new blue, magenta, black & silver	40	45
		a. Booklet pane. Nos. 1858/67	4·00	
		ab. Silver (Queen's head and "1ST") and phosphor omitted	£4250	
1859	**1184**	(1st) greenish yellow, new blue, magenta, black & silver	40	45
1860	**1185**	(1st) greenish yellow, new blue, magenta, black & silver	40	45
1861	**1186**	(1st) greenish yellow, new blue, magenta, black & silver	40	45
1862	**1187**	(1st) greenish yellow, new blue, magenta, black & silver	40	45
1863	**1188**	(1st) greenish yellow, new blue, magenta, black & silver	40	45
1864	**1189**	(1st) purple-brown & silver	40	45
1865	**1190**	(1st) greenish yellow, new blue, magenta, black & silver	40	45
1866	**1191**	(1st) greenish yellow, new blue, magenta, black & silver	40	45
1867	**1192**	(1st) black, greenish yellow & silver	40	45
		Set of 10	4·00	4·25
		First Day Cover		7·00
		Presentation Pack	4·25	
		PHQ Cards (set of 10)	3·75	8·75

Nos. 1858/67 were issued in £2.50 stamp booklets (sold at £2.60 from 8 July 1996), together with a pane of 20 half stamp-sized labels. The stamps and labels were attached to the booklet cover by a common gutter margin.

Special First Day of Issue Postmarks

British Philatelic Bureau, Edinburgh .... 7·50
Lover .... 7·50

1193 Fireplace Decoration, Attingham Park, Shropshire

1194 Oak Seedling

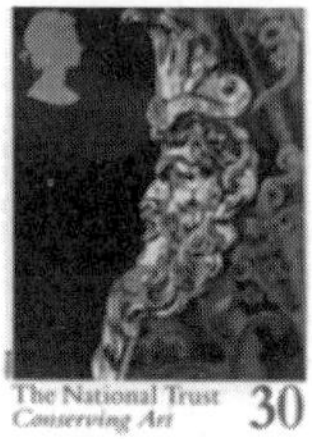

1195 Carved Table Leg, Attingham Park

1196 St. David's Head, Dyfed, Wales

1197 Elizabethan Window, Little Moreton Hall, Cheshire

(Des T. Evans)

1995 (11–25 Apr). **Centenary of The National Trust.** *One phosphor band* (19*p*.), two phosphor bands (25*p*, 35*p*) *or phosphorised paper* (30*p*, 41p). *P* 14 × 15.

1868	**1193**	19p.	grey-green, stone, grey-brown, grey-black & gold	55	55
1869	**1194**	25p.	grey-green, greenish yellow, magenta, new blue, gold & black	65	65
		a.	Booklet pane. No. 1869 × 6 with margins all round (25 Apr)	3·50	
1870	**1195**	30p.	grey-green, greenish yellow, magenta, new blue, gold, black & slate-black	80	80
1871	**1196**	35p.	grey-green, greenish yellow, magenta, blue, gold & black	90	90
1872	**1197**	41p.	grey-green, greenish yellow, brt green, slate-green, gold, blackish brown & black	1·10	1·10
			Set of 5	3·50	3·50
			Set of 5 Gutter Pairs	7·00	
			First Day Cover		3·75
			Presentation Pack	3·75	
			PHQ Cards (set of 5)	1·90	5·25

Booklet pane No. 1869a comes from the £6 "National Trust" booklet.

Special First Day of Issue Postmarks

British Philatelic Bureau, Edinburgh	4·00
Alfriston	4·00

1198 British Troops and French Civilians celebrating

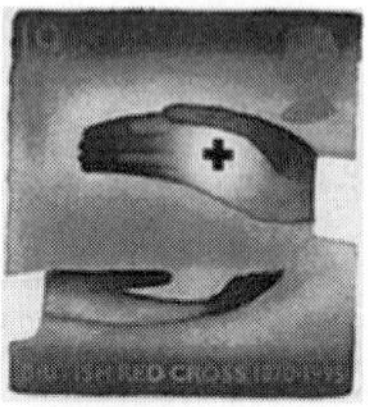

1199 Symbolic Hands and Red Cross

1200 St. Paul's Cathedral and Searchlights

1201 Symbolic Hand releasing Peace Dove

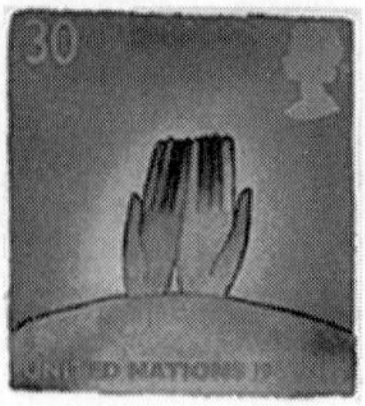

1202 Symbolic Hands

(Des J. Gorham (Nos. 1873, 1875), J-M. Folon (others))

1995 (2 May). **Europa. Peace and Freedom.** *One phosphor band* (*Nos.* 1873/4) *or two phosphor bands* (*others*). *P* $14\frac{1}{2}$ × 14.

1873	**1198**	19p.	silver, bistre-brown & grey-black	50	50
1874	**1199**	19p.	silver, bistre-yellow, brt rose-red, vermilion, brt blue & slate-blue	50	50
1875	**1200**	25p.	silver, blue & grey-black	65	65

1876 **1201** 25p. silver, vermilion, brt blue & grey-black ... 65 65
a. Imperf (vert pair) ...
1877 **1202** 30p. silver, bistre-yellow, brt magenta pale greenish blue, grey-black & flesh ... 75 75
Set of 5 ... 2·75 2·75
Set of 5 Gutter Pairs ... 5·50
First Day Cover ... 3·00
Presentation Pack ... 3·00
PHQ Cards (set of 5) ... 1·90 4·50

Nos. 1873 and 1875 commemorate the 50th anniversary of the end of the Second World War, No. 1874 the 125th anniversary of the British Red Cross Society and Nos. 1876/7 the 50th anniversary of the United Nations.

Nos. 1876/7 include the "EUROPA" emblem.

Special First Day of Issue Postmarks

British Philatelic Bureau, Edinburgh ... 3·00
London SW ... 3·00

A First Day of Issue handstamp (pictorial) was provided at London EC4 for this issue.

1203 *The Time Machine*

1204 *The First Men in the Moon*

1205 *The War of the Worlds*

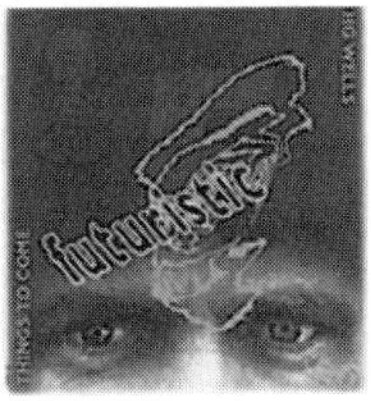

1206 *The Shape of Things to Come*

(Des Siobhan Keaney. Litho Questa)

1995 (6 June). **Science Fiction. Novels by H. G. Wells.** *Two phosphor bands. P* $14\frac{1}{2} \times 14$.

1878 **1203** 25p. new blue, greenish yellow, magenta, black & rosine ... 65 65
1879 **1204** 30p. new blue, greenish yellow, black, rosine & violet ... 85 85
1880 **1205** 35p. rosine, greenish yellow, violet, black & lt blue-green ... 90 90
1881 **1206** 41p. new blue, greenish yellow, magenta, black & rosine ... 1·00 1·00
Set of 4 ... 3·00 3·00
Set of 4 Gutter Pairs ... 6·50
First Day Cover ... 3·50
Presentation Pack ... 3·50
PHQ Cards (set of 4) ... 1·50 4·50

Nos. 1878/81 commemorate the centenary of publication of Wells's *The Time Machine*.

Special First Day of Issue Postmarks

British Philatelic Bureau, Edinburgh ... 3·50
Wells ... 3·50

1207 The Swan, 1595

1208 The Rose, 1592

1209 The Globe, 1599

1210 The Hope, 1613

1211 The Globe, 1614

(Des C. Hodges. Litho Walsall)

1995 (8 Aug). **Reconstruction of Shakespeare's Globe Theatre.** *Two phosphor bands. P* $14\frac{1}{2}$.

1882	**1207**	25p.	brownish grey, black, magenta, new blue & greenish yellow	65	65
		a.	Horiz strip of 5. Nos. 1882/6	3·00	3·00
1883	**1208**	25p.	brownish grey, black, magenta, new blue & greenish yellow	65	65
1884	**1209**	25p.	brownish grey, black, magenta, new blue & greenish yellow	65	65
1885	**1210**	25p.	brownish grey, black, magenta, new blue & greenish yellow	65	65
1886	**1211**	25p.	brownish grey, black, magenta, new blue & greenish yellow	65	65
			Set of 5	3·00	3·00
			Gutter Strip of 10	6·00	
			First Day Cover		3·25
			Presentation Pack	3·25	
			PHQ Cards (set of 5)	1·90	4·75

Nos. 1882/6 were issued together, *se-tenant*, in horizontal strips of 5 throughout the sheet with the backgrounds forming a composite design.

Special First Day of Issue Postmarks

British Philatelic Bureau, Edinburgh	3·50
Stratford-upon-Avon	3·50

1212 Sir Rowland Hill and Uniform Penny Postage Petition

1213 Hill and Penny Black

1214 Guglielmo Marconi and Early Wireless

1215 Marconi and Sinking of *Titanic* (liner)

(Des The Four Hundred, Eng C. Slania. Recess and litho Harrison)

1995 (5 Sept). **Pioneers of Communications.** *One phosphor band* (19p.) *or phosphorised paper (others). P* $14\frac{1}{2} \times 14$.

1887	**1212**	19p.	silver, red & black	55	55
1888	**1213**	25p.	silver, brown & black	80	80
		a.	Silver (Queen's head and face value) omitted	£200	
1889	**1214**	41p.	silver, grey-green & black	1·10	1·10
1890	**1215**	60p.	silver, dp ultramarine & black	1·50	1·50
			Set of 4	3·50	3·50
			Set of 4 Gutter Pairs	7·00	
			First Day Cover		3·75
			Presentation Pack	3·75	
			PHQ Cards (set of 4)	1·50	4·75

Nos. 1887/8 mark the birth bicentenary of Sir Rowland Hill and Nos. 1889/90 the centenary of the first radio transmissions.

Special First Day of Issue Postmarks

British Philatelic Bureau, Edinburgh	4·00
London EC	4·00

1216 Harold Wagstaff

1217 Gus Risman

1218 Jim Sullivan

1219 Billy Batten

1220 Brian Bevan

(Des C. Birmingham)

1995 (3 Oct). **Centenary of Rugby League**. *One phosphor band* (19p.) *or two phosphor bands* (*others*). *P* $14\frac{1}{2} \times 14$.

1891	**1216**	19p.	blue, greenish yellow, magenta, new blue, grey-black & black	45	45
1892	**1217**	25p.	slate-purple, greenish yellow, magenta, new blue, grey-black & black	60	60
1893	**1218**	30p.	slate-green, greenish yellow, brt purple, new blue, grey-black & black	70	70
1894	**1219**	35p.	slate-black, greenish yellow, magenta, new blue & black	95	95
1895	**1220**	41p.	bluish grey, orange-yellow, magenta, new blue, grey-black & black	1·25	1·25
			Set of 5	3·50	3·50
			Set of 5 Gutter Pairs	7·00	
			First Day Cover		3·75
			Presentation Pack	3·75	
			PHQ Cards (set of 5)	1·90	5·25

Special First Day of Issue Postmarks

British Philatelic Bureau, Edinburgh	3·75
Huddersfield	3·75

A First Day of Issue handstamp (pictorial) was provided at Headingly, Leeds for this issue.

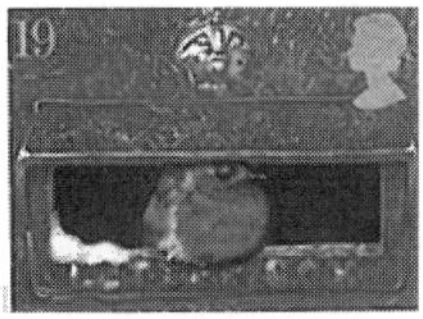

1221 European Robin in Mouth of Pillar Box

1222 European Robin on Railings and Holly

1223 European Robin on Snow-covered Milk Bottles

1224 European Robin on Road Sign

NEW INFORMATION

The editor is always interested to correspond with people who have new information that will improve or correct the Catalogue.

1225 European Robin on Door Knob and Christmas Wreath

(Des K. Lilly)

1995 (30 Oct). **Christmas. Christmas Robins.** *One phosphor band* (19p.) *or two phosphor bands* (*others*). *P* 15 × 14.

1896	**1221**	19p.	silver, greenish yellow, vermilion, orange-vermilion, bistre & black	45	45
1897	**1222**	25p.	silver, greenish yellow, scarlet, pale blue, ochre & black	60	60
1898	**1223**	30p.	silver, greenish yellow, rose-carmine, lt green, olive-brown & grey	80	80
1899	**1224**	41p.	silver, greenish yellow, rose-red, dull blue, bistre & black	1·10	1·10
1900	**1225**	60p.	silver, orange-yellow, red-orange, bistre & black	1·50	1·50
			Set of 5	4·00	4·00
			Set of 5 Gutter Pairs	8·00	
			First Day Cover		4·25
			Presentation Pack	4·25	
			PHQ Cards (set of 5)	1·90	5·75

Special First Day of Issue Postmarks

British Philatelic Bureau, Edinburgh	4·50
Bethlehem, Llandeilo	4·50

Collectors Pack 1995

1995 (30 Oct). *Comprises Nos.* 1848/1900

CP1900*a* Collectors Pack	32·00

Post Office Yearbook

1995 (30 Oct). *Comprises Nos.* 1848/57 *and* 1868/1900 *in hardback book with slip case, illustrated in colour* .... 40·00

1226 Opening Lines of "To a Mouse" and Fieldmouse

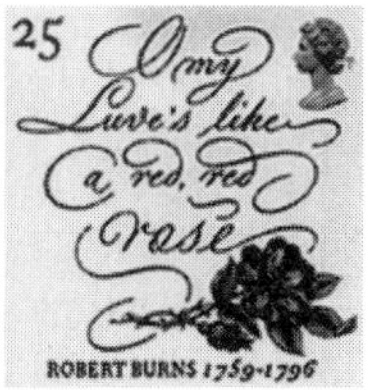

1227 "O my Luve's like a red, red rose" and Wild Rose

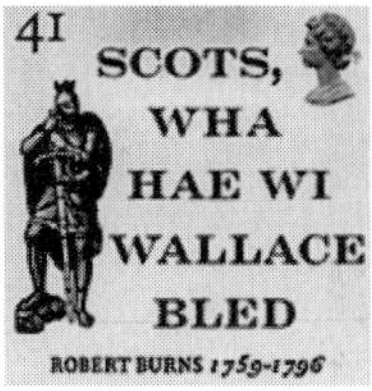

1228 "Scots, wha hae wi Wallace bled" and Sir William Wallace

1229 "Auld Lang Syne" and Highland Dancers

(Des Tayburn Design Consultancy. Litho Questa)

1996 (25 Jan). **Death Bicentenary of Robert Burns (Scottish poet).** *One phosphor band (19p.) or two phosphor bands (others). P* $14\frac{1}{2}$.

1901	**1226**	19p.	cream, bistre-brown & black	55	55
1902	**1227**	25p.	cream, bistre-brown, black, magenta, bistre-yellow & new blue	80	80
1903	**1228**	41p.	cream, bistre-brown, black, magenta, bistre-yellow & new blue	1·10	1·10
1904	**1229**	60p.	cream, bistre-brown, black, magenta, bistre-yellow & new blue	1·50	1·50
			Set of 4	3·50	3·50
			Set of 4 Gutter Pairs	7·00	
			First Day Cover		3·75
			Presentation Pack	3·75	
			PHQ Cards (set of 4)	1·50	4·75

Special First Day of Issue Postmarks

British Philatelic Bureau, Edinburgh	4·00
Dumfries	4·00

1230 "MORE! LOVE" (Mel Calman)

1231 "Sincerely" (Charles Barsotti)

1232 "Do you have something for the HUMAN CONDITION?" (Mel Calman)

1233 "MENTAL FLOSS" (Leo Cullum)

1234 "4.55 P.M." (Charles Barsotti)

1235 "Dear lottery prize winner" (Larry)

1236 "I'm writing to you because...." (Mel Calman)

1237 "FETCH THIS, FETCH THAT" (Charles Barsotti)

1238 "My day starts before I'm ready for it" (Mel Calman)

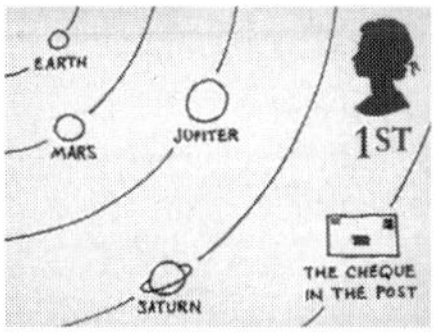

1239 "THE CHEQUE IN THE POST" (Jack Ziegler)

(Des M. Wolff. Litho Walsall)

1996 (26 Feb–11 Nov). **Greetings Stamps. Cartoons.** *"All-over" phosphor. P* $14\frac{1}{2} \times 14$ *(with one elliptical hole on each vertical side).*

1905	**1230**	(1st)	black & bright mauve	40	45
		a.	Booklet pane. Nos. 1905/14	4·00	
		p.	Two phosphor bands (11 Nov)	40	45
		pa.	Booklet pane. Nos. 1905p/14p	4·00	
1906	**1231**	(1st)	black & blue-green	40	45
		p.	Two phosphor bands (11 Nov)	40	45
1907	**1232**	(1st)	black & new blue	40	45
		p.	Two phosphor bands (11 Nov)	40	45
1908	**1233**	(1st)	black & brt violet	40	45
		p.	Two phosphor bands (11 Nov)	40	45
1909	**1234**	(1st)	black & vermilion	40	45
		p.	Two phosphor bands (11 Nov)	40	45
1910	**1235**	(1st)	black & new blue	40	45
		p.	Two phosphor bands (11 Nov)	40	45
1911	**1236**	(1st)	black & vermilion	40	45
		p.	Two phosphor bands (11 Nov)	40	45
1912	**1237**	(1st)	black & brt violet	40	45
		p.	Two phosphor bands (11 Nov)	40	45
1913	**1238**	(1st)	black & blue-green	40	45
		p.	Two phosphor bands (11 Nov)	40	45
1914	**1239**	(1st)	black & brt mauve	40	45
		p.	Two phosphor bands (11 Nov)	40	45
			Set of 10 (Nos. 1905/14)	4·00	4·50
			Set of 10 (Nos. 1905p/14p)	4·00	4·50
			First Day Cover (1905/14)		6·50
			Presentation Pack (1905/14)	4·25	
			PHQ Cards (set of 10)	3·75	8·75

Nos. 1905/14 were issued in £2.50 stamp booklets (sold at £2.60 from 8 July 1996), together with a pane of twenty half stamp-sized labels. The stamps and labels were attached to the booklet cover by a common gutter margin.

Special First Day of Issue Postmarks

British Philatelic Bureau, Edinburgh	6·75
Titterhill, Haytons Bent, Ludlow	6·75

1240 "Muscovy Duck"

1241 "Lapwing"

1242 "White-fronted Goose"

1243 "Bittern"

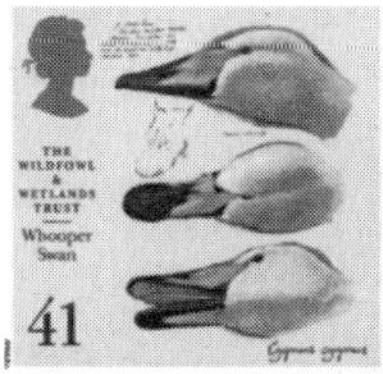

1244 "Whooper Swan"

(Des Moseley Webb)

1996 (12 Mar). **50th Anniv of the Wildfowl and Wetlands Trust. Bird Paintings by C. F. Tunnicliffe.** *One phosphor band* (19p.) *or phosphorised paper* (others). *P* 14 × 14½.

1915	**1240**	19p.	sepia, orange-yellow, brown, pale buff, grey & gold	40	40
1916	**1241**	25p.	bistre-brown, greenish yellow, magenta, new blue, pale buff, gold & black	60	60
1917	**1242**	30p.	bistre-brown, greenish yellow, magenta, new blue, pale buff, gold & grey-black	70	70
1918	**1243**	35p.	sepia, pale orange, lake-brown, brown-olive, pale buff, gold & grey-black	95	95
1919	**1244**	41p.	sepia, greenish yellow, magenta, new blue, pale buff, gold & grey-black	1·25	1·25
			Set of 5	3·50	3·50
			Set of 5 Gutter Pairs	7·00	
			First Day Cover		3·75
			Presentation Pack	3·75	
			PHQ Cards (*set of 5*)	1·90	5·25

Special First Day of Issue Postmarks

British Philatelic Bureau, Edinburgh	4·00
Slimbridge, Gloucester	4·00

1245 The Odeon, Harrogate

1246 Laurence Olivier and Vivien Leigh in *Lady Hamilton* (film)

1247 Old Cinema Ticket

1248 Pathé News Still

1249 Cinema Sign, The Odeon, Manchester

(Des The Chase)

1996 (16 Apr). **Centenary of Cinema.** *One phosphor band* (19*p*.) *or two phosphor bands* (*others*). *P* 14 × 14½.

1920	**1245**	19p.	black, greenish yellow, silver, brt magenta & new blue	40	40
1921	**1246**	25p.	black, greenish yellow, silver, brt magenta & new blue	60	60
1922	**1247**	30p.	black, greenish yellow, silver, brt magenta & new blue	70	70
1923	**1248**	35p.	black, red & silver	95	95
1924	**1249**	41p.	black, greenish yellow, silver, brt magenta & new blue	1·25	1·25
			Set of 5	3·50	3·50
			Set of 5 Gutter Pairs	7·00	
			First Day Cover		3·75
			Presentation Pack	3·75	
			PHQ Cards (set of 5)	1·90	5·25

Special First Day of Issue Postmarks

British Philatelic Bureau, Edinburgh	4·00
London, WC2	4·00

(Des H. Brown. Litho Questa)

1996 (14 May). **European Football Championship.** *One phosphor band* (19*p*.) *or two phosphor bands* (*others*). *P* 14½ × 14.

1925	**1250**	19p.	vermilion, black, pale grey & grey	40	40
			a. Booklet pane. No. 1925 × 4 with margins all round	1·50	
1926	**1251**	25p.	brt emerald, black, pale grey & grey	60	60
			a. Booklet pane. No. 1926 × 4 with margins all round	2·25	
1927	**1252**	35p.	orange-yellow, black, pale grey & grey	1·10	1·10
			a. Booklet pane. Nos. 1927/9, each × 2, with margins all round	6·50	
1928	**1253**	41p.	new blue, black, pale grey & grey	1·10	1·10
1929	**1254**	60p.	brt orange, black, pale grey & grey	1·50	1·50
			Set of 5	4·25	4·25
			Set of 5 Gutter Pairs	8·50	
			First Day Cover		4·50
			Presentation Pack	4·50	
			PHQ Cards (set of 5)	1·90	5·75

Special First Day of Issue Postmarks

British Philatelic Bureau, Edinburgh	4·75
Wembley	4·75

1250 Dixie Dean

1251 Bobby Moore

1252 Duncan Edwards

1253 Billy Wright

1254 Danny Blanchflower

1255 Athlete on Starting Blocks

1256 Throwing the Javelin

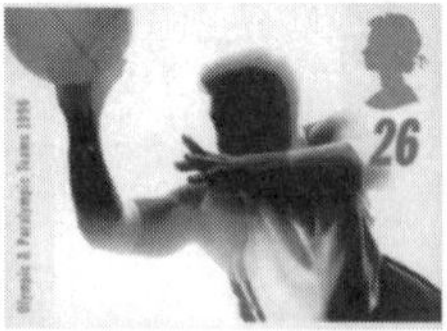

1257 Basketball

1258 Swimming

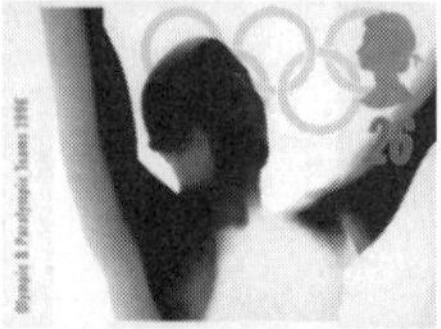

1259 Athlete celebrating and Olympic Rings

(Des N. Knight. Litho Questa)

1996 (9 July). **Olympic and Paralympic Games, Atlanta.** *Two phosphor bands. P* 14½ × 14.

1930	**1255**	26p.	greenish grey, silver, rosine, black, magenta, bistre-yellow & new blue ...	65	65
		a.	Horiz strip of 5. Nos. 1930/4	3·00	
1931	**1256**	26p.	greenish grey, silver, rosine, black, magenta, bistre-yellow & new blue ...	65	65
1932	**1257**	26p.	greenish grey, silver, rosine, black, magenta, bistre-yellow & new blue ...	65	65
1933	**1258**	26p.	greenish grey, silver, rosine, black, magenta, bistre-yellow & new blue ...	65	65
1934	**1259**	26p.	greenish grey, silver, rosine, black, magenta, bistre-yellow & new blue ...	65	65
			Set of 5	3·00	3·00
			Gutter Strip of 10	6·00	
			First Day Cover		3·25
			Presentation Pack	3·25	
			PHQ Cards (set of 5)	1·90	4·75

Nos. 1930/4 were printed together, *se-tenant*, in horizontal strips of 5 throughout the sheet.

Special First Day of Issue Postmarks

British Philatelic Bureau, Edinburgh	3·50
Much Wenlock	3·50

1264 Dame Marea Hartman (sports administrator)

(Des Stephanie Nash)

1996 (6 Aug). **Europa. Famous Women.** *One phosphor band (20p.) or two phosphor bands (others). P* 14½.

1935	**1260**	20p.	dull blue-green, brownish grey & black	50	50
1936	**1261**	26p.	dull mauve, brownish grey & black ...	70	70
		a.	Imperf (horiz pair)		
1937	**1262**	31p.	bronze, brownish grey & black	90	90
1938	**1263**	37p.	silver, brownish grey & black	1·10	1·10
1939	**1264**	43p.	gold, brownish grey & black	1·25	1·25
			Set of 5	4·00	4·00
			Set of 5 Gutter Pairs	8·00	
			First Day Cover		4·25
			Presentation Pack	4·25	
			PHQ Cards (set of 5)	1·90	5·25

Nos. 1936/7 include the "EUROPA" emblem.

Special First Day of Issue Postmarks

British Philatelic Bureau, Edinburgh	4·50
Fowey	4·50

1260 Prof. Dorothy Hodgkin (scientist)

1261 Dame Margot Fonteyn (ballerina)

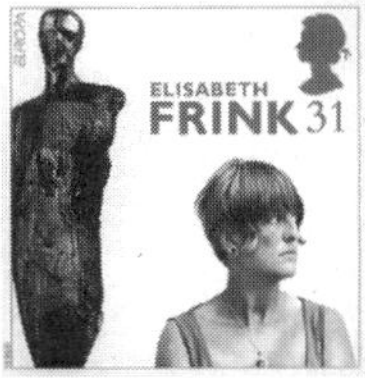

1262 Dame Elisabeth Frink (sculptress)

1263 Dame Daphne du Maurier (novelist)

1265 *Muffin the Mule*

1266 *Sooty*

1267 *Stingray*

1268 *The Clangers*

1269 *Dangermouse*

(Des Tutssels. Photo Enschedé)

1996 (3 Sept)–**97**. **50th Anniv of Children's Television.** *One phosphor band (20p.) or two phosphor bands (others). P* $14\frac{1}{2} \times 14$.

1940	**1265**	20p.	dp claret, black, magenta, rosine & greenish yellow	50	50
		a.	Perf 15 × 14 (23.9.97)	1·00	1·00
		ab.	Booklet pane. No. 1940a × 4 with margins all round	4·00	
1941	**1266**	26p.	brt blue, black, dp grey-blue, magenta & greenish yellow	70	70
1942	**1267**	31p.	greenish blue, black, new blue, magenta & greenish yellow	90	90
1943	**1268**	37p.	dull violet-blue, black, new blue, magenta & greenish yellow	1·10	1·10
1944	**1269**	43p.	brt purple, black, new blue, magenta & greenish yellow	1·25	1·25
			Set of 5	4·00	4·00
			Set of 5 Gutter Pairs	8·00	
			First Day Cover		4·25
			Presentation Pack	4·25	
			PHQ Cards (set of 5)	1·90	5·25

No. 1940a comes from the 1997 £6.15 B.B.C. stamp booklet.

Special First Day of Issue Postmarks

British Philatelic Bureau, Edinburgh	4·50
Alexandra Palace, London	4·50

1270 Triumph TR3

1271 MG TD

1272 Austin-Healey 100

1273 Jaguar XK120

1274 Morgan Plus 4

(Des S. Clay)

1996 (1 Oct). **Classic Sports Cars.** *One phosphor band (20p.) or two phosphor bands (others). P* $14\frac{1}{2}$.

1945	**1270**	20p.	silver, greenish yellow, brt scarlet, vermilion, new blue & black	40	40
1946	**1271**	26p.	silver, greenish yellow, magenta, greenish blue & black	55	55
		a.	Imperf (pair)		
1947	**1272**	37p.	silver, greenish yellow, brt magenta, dp turquoise-blue, new blue & black	75	75
		a.	Imperf (pair)		
1948	**1273**	43p.	silver, greenish yellow, magenta, greenish blue & black	90	90
		a.	Imperf (horiz pair)		
1949	**1274**	63p.	silver, greenish yellow, magenta, greenish blue, stone & black	1·25	1·25
			Set of 5	3·50	3·50
			Set of 5 Gutter Pairs	7·00	
			First Day Cover		3·75
			Presentation Pack	3·75	
			PHQ Cards (set of 5)	1·90	5·75

On Nos. 1946/9 the left-hand phosphor band on each stamp is three times the width of that on the right.

Special First Day of Issue Postmarks

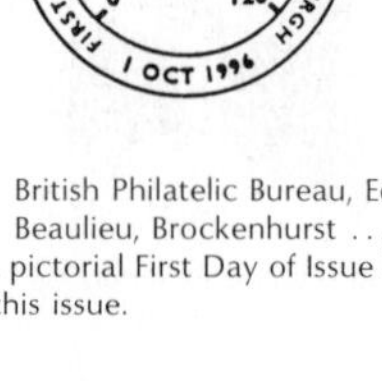

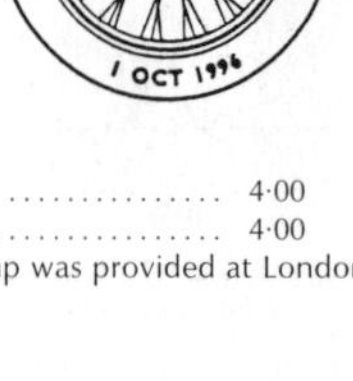

British Philatelic Bureau, Edinburgh	4·00
Beaulieu, Brockenhurst	4·00

A pictorial First Day of Issue handstamp was provided at London E1 for this issue.

1275 The Three Kings

1276 The Annunciation

1277 The Journey to Bethlehem

1278 The Nativity

1279 The Shepherds

(Des Laura Stoddart)

1996 (28 Oct). **Christmas.** *One phosphor band (2nd class) or two phosphor bands (others). P 15 × 14.*

1950	**1275**	(2nd)	gold, greenish yellow, magenta, blue, black & lt brown	40	40
1951	**1276**	(1st)	gold, yellow, cerise, new blue, black & lt brown	55	55
1952	**1277**	31p.	gold, orange-yellow, cerise, blue, black & lt brown	65	65
1953	**1278**	43p.	gold, greenish yellow, magenta, new blue, grey-black & lt brown	90	90
1954	**1279**	63p.	gold, greenish yellow, magenta, new blue, black & lt brown	1·25	1·25
			Set of 5	3·25	3·25
			Set of 5 Gutter Pairs	6·50	
			First Day Cover		3·50
			Presentation Pack	3·50	
			PHQ Cards (set of 5)	1·90	5·50

Special First Day of Issue Postmarks

British Philatelic Bureau, Edinburgh .... 3·75
Bethlehem, Llandeilo .... 3·75

Collectors Pack 1996

1996 (28 Oct). *Comprises Nos.* 1901/4 *and* 1915/54
CP1954a Collectors Pack .... 30·00

Post Office Yearbook

1996 (28 Oct). *Comprises Nos.* 1901/4 *and* 1915/54 *in hardback book* with slip case, illustrated in colour .... 40·00

1280 *Gentiana acaulis* (Georg Ehret)

1281 *Magnolia grandiflora* (Ehret)

1282 *Camellia japonica* (Alfred Chandler)

1283 *Tulipa* (Ehret)

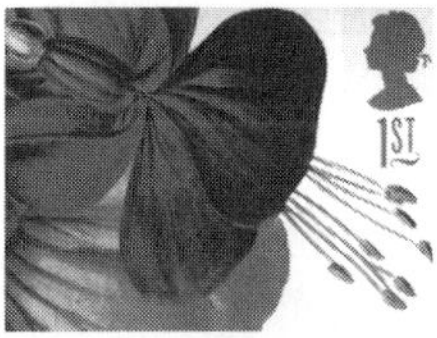

1284 *Fuchsia "Princess of Wales"* (Augusta Withers)

1285 *Tulipa gesneriana* (Ehret)

1286 *Guzmania splendens* (Charlotte Sowerby)

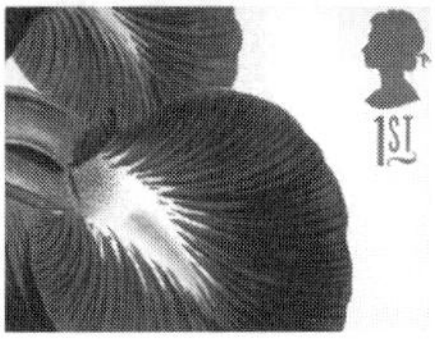

1287 *Iris latifolia* (Ehret)

1288 *Hippeastrum rutilum* (Pierre-Joseph Redoute)

1289 *Passiflora coerulea* (Ehret)

(Des Tutssels. Litho Walsall)

1997 (6 Jan). **Greeting Stamps. 19th-century Flower Paintings.** *Two phosphor bands. P* 14½ × 14 (*with one elliptical hole on each vertical side*).

1955	**1280**	(1st)	greenish yellow, new blue, magenta, black, blue-green & gold	40	45
		a.	Booklet pane. Nos. 1955/64	4·00	
		ab.	Gold, blue-green and phosphor omitted		
1956	**1281**	(1st)	greenish yellow, new blue, magenta, black, blue-green & gold	40	45
1957	**1282**	(1st)	greenish yellow, new blue, magenta, black, blue-green & gold	40	45
1958	**1283**	(1st)	greenish yellow, new blue, magenta, black, blue-green & gold	40	45
1959	**1284**	(1st)	greenish yellow, new blue, magenta, black, blue-green & gold	40	45
1960	**1285**	(1st)	greenish yellow, new blue, magenta, black, blue-green & gold	40	45
1961	**1286**	(1st)	greenish yellow, new blue, magenta, black, blue-green & gold	40	45
1962	**1287**	(1st)	greenish yellow, new blue, magenta, black, blue-green & gold	40	45
1963	**1288**	(1st)	greenish yellow, new blue, magenta, black, blue-green & gold	40	45
1964	**1289**	(1st)	greenish yellow, new blue, magenta, black, blue-green & gold	40	45
			Set of 10	4·00	4·50
			First Day Cover		7·50
			Presentation Pack	4·50	
			PHQ Cards (set of 10)	3·75	7·50

Nos. 1955/64 were issued in £2.60 stamp booklets together with a pane of twenty half-sized labels. The stamps and labels were attached to the booklet cover by a common gutter margin.

Special First Day of Issue Postmarks

British Philatelic Bureau, Edinburgh	8·00
Kew, Richmond, Surrey	8·00

1290 "King Henry VIII"

1291 "Catherine of Aragon"

1292 "Anne Boleyn"

1293 "Jane Seymour"

1294 "Anne of Cleves"

1295 "Catherine Howard"

1296 "Catherine Parr"

(Des Kate Stephens from contemporary paintings)

1997 (21 Jan). *450th Death Anniv of King Henry VIII. Two phosphor bands. P* 15 (*No.* 1965) *or* 14 × 15 (*others*).

1965	**1290**	26p.	gold, greenish yellow, brt purple, new blue and black	40	45
		a.	Imperf (pair)		
1966	**1291**	26p.	gold, greenish yellow, brt carmine, new blue and black	40	45
		a.	Horiz strip of 6. Nos. 1966/71	2·75	3·00
1967	**1292**	26p.	gold, greenish yellow, brt carmine, new blue and black	40	45
1968	**1293**	26p.	gold, greenish yellow, brt carmine, new blue and black	40	45
1969	**1294**	26p.	gold, greenish yellow, brt carmine, new blue and black	40	45
1970	**1295**	26p.	gold, greenish yellow, brt carmine, new blue and black	40	45
1971	**1296**	26p.	gold, greenish yellow, brt carmine, new blue and black	40	45
			Set of 7	2·75	3·00
			Set of 1 Gutter Pair and a Gutter Strip of 12	5·75	
			First Day Cover		6·00
			Presentation Pack	3·25	
			PHQ Cards (set of 7)	2·50	5·50

Nos. 1966/71 were printed together, *se-tenant*, in horizontal strips of six throughout the sheet.

Special First Day of Issue Postmarks

British Philatelic Bureau, Edinburgh	4·50
Hampton Court, East Molesey	4·50

1297 St. Columba in Boat

1298 St. Columba on Iona

1299 St. Augustine with King Ethelbert

1300 St. Augustine with Model of Cathedral

(Des Claire Melinsky. Litho Enschedé)

1997 (11 Mar). *Religious Anniversaries. Two phosphor bands. P* 14½.

1972	**1297**	26p.	greenish yellow, magenta, new blue, grey-black and gold	40	45
			a. Imperf (pair)		
1973	**1298**	37p.	greenish yellow, magenta, new blue, grey-black and gold	60	65
1974	**1299**	43p.	greenish yellow, magenta, new blue, grey-black and gold	65	70
1975	**1300**	63p.	greenish yellow, magenta, new blue, grey-black and gold	95	1·00
			Set of 4	2·50	2·75
			Set of 4 Gutter Pairs	5·25	
			First Day Cover		4·25
			Presentation Pack	3·00	
			PHQ Cards (set of 4)	1·50	4·25

Nos. 1972/3 commemorate the 1400th death anniversary of St. Columba and Nos. 1974/5 the 1400th anniversary of the arrival of St. Augustine of Canterbury in Kent.

Special First Day of Issue Postmarks

British Philatelic Bureau, Edinburgh	4·50
Isle of Iona	4·50

1301

1302

(Des J. Matthews. Photo Enschedé)

1997 (18 Mar). **Self-adhesive Coil Stamps**. *One centre phosphor band* (2nd) *or two phosphor bands* (1st). *P* 14 × 15 *die-cut (with one elliptical hole on each vertical side)*.

1976	**1301**	(2nd)	bright blue	30	35
1977	**1302**	(1st)	bright orange-red	40	45
			Set of 2	70	80
			First Day Cover		1·50
			Presentation Pack	1·40	

Nos. 1976/7, which were initially sold at 20p. and 26p, were in rolls of 100 with the stamps separate on the backing paper.

Special First Day of Issue Postmarks

British Philatelic Bureau, Edinburgh	1·75
Glasgow	1·75

(Photo Harrison (No. 1978), Harrison or Walsall (No. 1979))

1997 (21 April–23 Sept). **Royal Golden Wedding (1st issue)**. *Designs as T* **367** *and* **914** *but colours changed. Two phosphor bands. P* 15 × 14 *(with one elliptical hole on each vertical edge)*.

1978	**367**	26p.	gold	40	45
			a. Imperf (horiz pair)		
			l. Booklet pane. Nos. 1978/9, each x 4, and centre label with margins all round (23 Sept)	3·50	
1979	**914**	(1st)	gold	40	45
			Set of 2	80	90
			First Day Cover		1·50
			Presentation Pack	1·40	

See also Nos. 2011/14.

Special First Day of Issue Postmarks

British Philatelic Bureau, Edinburgh (Type G)	1·75
Windsor, Berks (Type G)	1·75

1303 *Dracula*

1304 *Frankenstein*

1305 *Dr. Jekyll and Mr. Hyde*

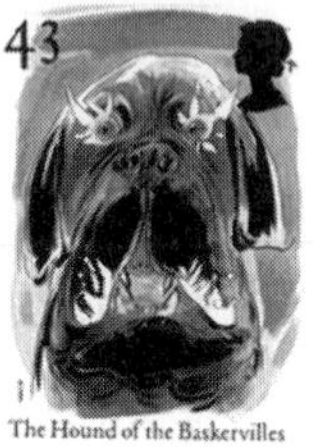

1306 *The Hound of the Baskervilles*

(Des I. Pollock. Photo Walsall)

1997 (13 May). **Tales and Legends. Horror Stories**. *Two phosphor bands. P* 14 × 15.

1980	**1303**	26p.	grey-black, black, new blue, magenta and greenish yellow	40	45
1981	**1304**	31p.	grey-black, black, new blue, magenta and greenish yellow	50	55
1982	**1305**	37p.	grey-black, black, new blue, magenta and greenish yellow	60	65
1983	**1306**	43p.	grey-black, black, new blue, magenta and greenish yellow	65	70
			Set of 4	2·10	2·40
			Set of 4 Gutter Pairs	4·50	5·00
			First Day Cover		3·00
			Presentation Pack	2·50	
			PHQ Cards (set of 4)	1·50	4·50

Nos. 1980/3 commemorate the birth bicentenary of Mary Shelley (creator of Frankenstein) with the 26p. and 31p. values incorporating the "EUROPA" emblem.

Each value has features printed in fluorescent ink which are visible under ultra-violet light.

Special First Day of Issue Postmarks

British Philatelic Bureau, Edinburgh	3·25
Whitby	3·25

1307 Reginald Mitchell and Supermarine Spitfire MkIIA

1308 Roy Chadwick and Avro Lancaster MkI

1309 Ronald Bishop and De Havilland Mosquito B MkXVI

1310 George Carter and Gloster Meteor F Mk8

1311 Sir Sidney Camm and Hawker Hunter FGA Mk9

(Des Turner Duckworth)

1997 (10 June). **British Aircraft Designers**. *One phosphor band* (20p.) *or two phosphor bands (others). P* 15 × 14.

1984	**1307**	20p.	silver, greenish yellow, magenta, new blue, black and grey	30	35
1985	**1308**	26p.	silver, greenish yellow, magenta, new blue, black and grey	40	45
1986	**1309**	37p.	silver, greenish yellow, magenta, new blue, black and grey	60	65
1987	**1310**	43p.	silver, greenish yellow, magenta, new blue, black and grey	65	70
1988	**1311**	63p.	silver, greenish yellow, magenta, new blue, black and grey	95	1·00
			Set of 5	3·00	3·25
			Set of 5 Gutter Pairs	6·25	6·75
			First Day Cover		3·75
			Presentation Pack	3·25	
			PHQ Cards (set of 5)	1·90	5·75

Special First Day of Issue Postmarks

British Philatelic Bureau, Edinburgh	4·00
Duxford, Cambridge	4·00

1312 Carriage Horse and Coachman

1313 Lifeguards Horse and Trooper

1314 Blues and Royals Drum Horse and Drummer

1315 Duke of Edinburgh's Horse and Groom

(Des J.-L. Benard. Litho Walsall)

1997 (8 July). **"All the Queen's Horses". 50th Anniv of the British Horse Society**. *One phosphor band* (20p.) *or two phosphor bands (others)*. P $14\frac{1}{2}$.

1989	**1312**	20p.	scarlet-vermilion, black, magenta, new blue and greenish yellow	30	35
1990	**1313**	26p.	scarlet-vermilion, black, magenta, new blue and greenish yellow	40	45
1991	**1314**	43p.	scarlet-vermilion, black, magenta, new blue and greenish yellow	65	70
1992	**1315**	63p.	scarlet-vermilion, black, magenta, new blue and greenish yellow	95	1·00
			Set of 4	2·25	2·50
			Set of 4 Gutter Pairs	4·75	5·25
			First Day Cover		3·25
			Presentation Pack	2·75	
			PHQ Cards (set of 4)	1·50	4·75

Special First Day of Issue Postmarks

British Philatelic Bureau, Edinburgh	3·50
Windsor, Berks	3·50

NEW INFORMATION

The editor is always interested to correspond with people who have new information that will improve or correct the Catalogue.

CASTLE

Harrison plates (Nos. 1611/14)

CASTLE

Enschedè plates (Nos. 1993/6)

Differences between Harrison and Enschedé:
Harrison - "C" has top serif and tail of letter points to right. "A" has flat top. "S" has top and bottom serifs.
Enschedé - "C" has no top serif and tail of letter points upwards. "A" has pointed top. "S" has no serifs.

(Des from photos by Prince Andrew, Duke of York. Eng Inge Madle Recess (Queen's head by silk screen process) Enschedé)

1997 (29 July). *Designs as Nos.* 1612/14 *with Queen's head in silhouette as T* **1044**, *but re-engraved with differences in inscription as shown above. P* 15 × 14 *(with one elliptical hole on each vertical side).*

1993	**880**	£1.50, deep claret and gold†	2·25	2·40
1994	**881**	£2 indigo and gold†	3·00	3·25
1995	**1044**	£3 violet and gold†	4·50	4·75
1996	**882**	£5 deep brown and gold†	7·50	7·75
		a. Gold† (head) omitted		
		Set of 4	17·00	18·00
		Set of 4 Gutter Pairs	35·00	38·00

† The Queen's head on these stamps is printed in optically variable ink which changes colour from gold to green when viewed from different angles.

No. 1996a occurs on R. 5/8 and R. 6/8 from some sheets.

1316 Haroldswick, Shetland

1317 Painswick, Gloucestershire

1318 Beddgelert, Gwynedd

1319 Ballyroney, County Down

(Des T. Millington. Photo Enschedé)

1997 (12 Aug). **Sub-Post Offices**. *One phosphor band (20p.) or two phosphor bands (others). P* $14\frac{1}{2}$.

1997	**1316**	20p.	greenish yellow, bright magenta, new blue, grey-black, rosine and blue-green	30	35
1998	**1317**	26p.	greenish yellow, bright magenta, new blue, grey-black, rosine and blue-green	40	45
1999	**1318**	43p.	greenish yellow, bright magenta, new blue, grey-black, rosine and blue-green	65	70
2000	**1319**	63p.	greenish yellow, bright magenta, new blue, grey-black, rosine and blue-green	95	1·00
			Set of 4	2·25	2·50
			Set of 4 Gutter Pairs	4·75	5·25
			First Day Cover		3·25
			Presentation Pack	2·75	
			PHQ Cards (set of 4)	1·50	4·75

Nos. 1997/2000 were issued on the occasion of the Centenary of the National Federation of Sub-Postmasters.

Special First Day of Issue Postmarks

British Philatelic Bureau, Edinburgh	3·50
Wakefield	3·50

1320 *Noddy*

1321 *Famous Five*

1322 *Secret Seven*

1323 *Faraway Tree*

1324 *Malory Towers*

(Des C. Birmingham. Photo Enschedé)

1997 (9 Sept). **Birth Centenary of Enid Blyton (children's author)**. *One phosphor band (20p.) or two phosphor bands (others). P* $14 \times 14\frac{1}{2}$.

2001	**1320**	20p.	greenish yellow, magenta, new blue, grey-black and deep grey-blue	30	35
2002	**1321**	26p.	greenish yellow, magenta, new blue, grey-black and deep grey-blue	40	45
2003	**1322**	37p.	greenish yellow, magenta, new blue, grey-black and deep grey-blue	60	65
2004	**1323**	43p.	greenish yellow, magenta, new blue, grey-black and deep grey-blue	65	70
2005	**1324**	63p.	greenish yellow, magenta, new blue, grey-black and deep grey-blue	95	1·00
			Set of 5	3·00	3·25
			Set of 5 Gutter Pairs	6·25	6·75
			First Day Cover		3·75
			Presentation Pack	3·25	
			PHQ Cards (set of 5)	1·90	5·75

Special First Day of Issue Postmarks

British Philatelic Bureau, Edinburgh	4·00
Beaconsfield	4·00

1325 Children and Father Christmas pulling Cracker

1326 Father Christmas with Traditional Cracker

1327 Father Christmas riding Cracker

1328 Father Christmas on Snowball

1329 Father Christmas and Chimney

(Des J. Gorham and M. Thomas (No. 2007), J. Gorham (others))

1997 (27 Oct). **Christmas. 150th Anniv of the Christmas Cracker**. *One phosphor band (2nd class) or two phosphor bands (others). P 15 × 14.*

2006	**1325**	(2nd)	gold, greenish yellow, bright magenta, new blue and grey-black	30	35
			a. Imperf (pair)	£1100	
2007	**1326**	(1st)	gold, greenish yellow, bright magenta, new blue and grey-black	40	45
2008	**1327**	31p.	gold, greenish yellow, bright magenta, new blue, bright blue and grey-black	50	55
2009	**1328**	43p.	gold, greenish yellow, bright magenta, pale new blue and grey-black	65	70
2010	**1329**	63p.	gold, greenish yellow, bright magenta, new blue and grey-black	95	1·00
			Set of 5	2·75	3·00
			Set of 5 Gutter Pairs	5·75	6·25
			First Day Cover		3·75
			Presentation Pack	3·25	
			PHQ Cards (set of 5)	1·90	5·75

Special First Day of Issue Postmarks

British Philatelic Bureau, Edinburgh	4·00
Bethlehem, Llandeilo	4·00

1330 Wedding Photograph, 1947

1331 Queen Elizabeth II and Prince Philip, 1997

(Des D. Driver (20p., 43p.), Lord Snowdon (26p., 63p.))

1997 (13 Nov). **Royal Golden Wedding (2nd issue)**. *One phosphor band (20p.) or two phosphor bands (others). P 15.*

2011	**1330**	20p.	gold, yellow-brown and grey-black	30	35
2012	**1331**	26p.	gold, bistre-yellow, magenta, new blue, grey-black and greenish grey	40	45
2013	**1330**	43p.	gold, bluish green and grey-black	65	70
2014	**1331**	63p.	gold, bistre-yellow, magenta, new blue, grey-black and lavender-grey	95	1·00
			Set of 4	2·25	2·50
			Set of 4 Gutter Pairs	4·75	5·25
			First Day Cover		3·25
			Presentation Pack	2·75	
			PHQ Cards (set of 4)	1·50	4·75

Special First Day of Issue Postmarks

British Philatelic Bureau, Edinburgh	3·50
London, SW1	3·50

Collectors Pack 1997

1997 (27 Oct). *Comprises Nos.* 1965/75, 1980/92 *and* 1997/2014

CP2014a Collectors Pack ... 24·00

Post Office Yearbook

1997 (27 Oct). *Comprises Nos.* 1965/75, 1980/92 *and* 1997/2014 *in hardback book with slip case* ... 35·00

1332 Common Dormouse

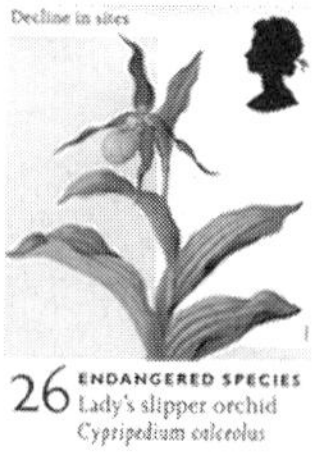

1333 Lady's Slipper Orchid

1334 Song Thrush

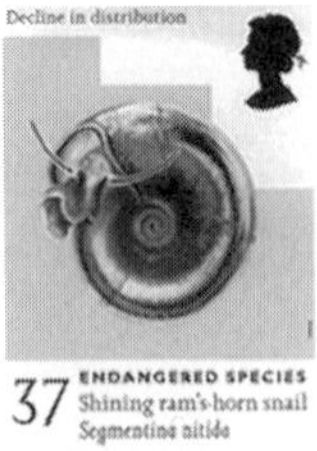

1335 Shining Ram's-horn Snail

1338 Diana, Princess of Wales (photo by Lord Snowdon)

1339 At British Lung Foundation Function, April 1997 (photo by John Stillwell)

1336 Mole Cricket

1337 Devil's Bolete

1340 Wearing Tiara, 1991 (photo by Lord Snowdon)

1341 On Visit to Birmingham, October 1995 (photo by Tim Graham)

(Des R. Maude. Litho Questa)

1998 (20 Jan). **Endangered Species**. *One side phosphor band* (20p.) *or two phosphor bands (others). P* 14 × 14½.

2015	**1332**	20p.	black, new blue, magenta, greenish yellow, deep blue and pale lavender-grey	30	35
2016	**1333**	26p.	black, new blue, magenta, greenish yellow, deep blue and pale yellow-olive	40	45
2017	**1334**	31p.	black, new blue, magenta, greenish yellow, deep blue and pale bluish grey	50	55
2018	**1335**	37p.	black, new blue, magenta, greenish yellow, deep blue and pale greenish grey	60	65
2019	**1336**	43p.	black, new blue, magenta, greenish yellow, deep blue and pale dull mauve	65	70
2020	**1337**	63p.	black, new blue, magenta, greenish yellow, deep blue and pale grey-brown	95	1·00
			Set of 6	3·50	3·75
			Set of 6 *Gutter Pairs*	7·25	7·50
			First Day Cover		4·50
			Presentation Pack	3·75	4·00
			PHQ Cards (set of 6)	2·25	2·40

Special First Day of Issue Postmarks

British Philatelic Bureau, Edinburgh	4·75
Selborne, Alton	4·75

1342 In Evening Dress, 1987 (photo by Terence Donavan)

(Des B. Robinson)

1998 (3 Feb). **Diana, Princess of Wales Commemoration**. *Two phosphor bands. P* 14 × 15.

2021	**1338**	26p.	purple, greenish yellow, magenta, new blue and black	40	45
			a. Horiz strip of 5. Nos. 2021/5	2·00	
2022	**1339**	26p.	purple, greenish yellow, magenta, new blue and black	40	45
2023	**1340**	26p.	purple, greenish yellow, magenta, new blue and black	40	45
2024	**1341**	26p.	purple, greenish yellow, magenta, new blue and black	40	45
2025	**1342**	26p.	purple, greenish yellow, magenta, new blue and black	40	45
			Set of 5	2·00	2·10
			Gutter Strip of 10	4·25	4·50
			First Day Cover		3·00
			Presentation Pack	2·50	
			Presentation Pack (Welsh)	2·50	

Nos. 2021/5 were printed together, *se-tenant*, in horizontal strips of five throughout the sheet.

In addition to the generally issued Presentation Pack a further pack with all text printed in English and Welsh was available.

Special First Day of Issue Postmarks

British Philatelic Bureau, Edinburgh	3·25
Kensington, London	3·25

1343 Lion of England and Griffin of Edward III

1344 Falcon of Plantagenet and Bull of Clarence

1345 Lion of Mortimer and Yale of Beaufort

1346 Greyhound of Richmond and Dragon of Wales

1347 Unicorn of Scotland and Horse of Hanover

(Des J. Matthews. Recess and litho Harrison)

1998 (24 Feb). **650th Anniv of the Order of the Garter. The Queen's Beasts.** *Two phosphor bands. P* 15 × 14.

2026	**1343**	26p.	silver, green, bright blue, carmine-red, vermilion, lemon, grey-black and black	40	45
			a. Horiz strip of 5. Nos. 2026/30	2·00	
2027	**1344**	26p.	silver, green, bright blue, carmine-red, vermilion, lemon, grey, grey-black and black	40	45
2028	**1345**	26p.	silver, green, bright blue, carmine-red, vermilion, lemon, grey, grey-black and black	40	45
2029	**1346**	26p.	silver, green, bright blue, carmine-red, vermilion, lemon, grey, grey-black and black	40	45
2030	**1347**	26p.	silver, green, bright blue, vermilion, lemon, grey, grey-black and black	40	45
			Set of 5	2·00	2·10
			Gutter Block of 10	4·25	4·50
			First Day Cover		3·00
			Presentation Pack	2·50	
			PHQ Cards (set of 5)	1·90	4·75

Nos. 2026/30 were printed together, *se-tenant*, in horizontal strips of five throughout the sheet.

The phosphor bands on Nos 2026/30 are only half the height of the stamps and do not cover the silver parts of the designs.

Special First Day of Issue Postmarks

British Philatelic Bureau, Edinburgh	3·25
London SW1	3·25

ROYAL MAIL POSTAGE LABELS

These imperforate labels were issued as an experiment by the Post Office. Special microprocessor controlled machines were installed at post offices in Cambridge, London, Shirley (Southampton) and Windsor to provide an after-hours sales service to the public. The machines printed and dispensed the labels according to the coins inserted and the buttons operated by the customer. Values were initially available in ½p. steps to 16p. and in addition, the labels were sold at philatelic counters in two packs containing either 3 values (3½, 12½, 16p.) or 32 values (½p. to 16p.).

From 28 August 1984 the machines were adjusted to provide values up to 17p. After 31 December 1984 labels including ½p. values were withdrawn. The machines were taken out of service on 30 April 1985.

Machine postage-paid impression in red on phosphorised paper with grey-green background design. No watermark. Imperforate.

1984 (1 May–28 Aug).

Set of 32 (½p. to 16p.)	17·00	25·00
Set of 3 (3½p., 12½p., 16p.)	3·00	3·50
Set of 3 on First Day Cover (1.5.84)		6·50
Set of 2 (16½p., 17p.) (28.8.84)	4·50	4·50

REGIONAL ISSUES

I. CHANNEL ISLANDS

C **1** Gathering Vraic

C **2** Islanders gathering Vraic

(Des J. R. R. Stobie (1d.) or from drawing by E. Blampied (2½d.). Photo Harrison)

1948 (10 May). *Third Anniv of Liberation. W* **127** *of Great Britain. P* 15 × 14.

C1	C **1**	1d. scarlet	20	20
C2	C **2**	2½d. ultramarine	30	30
		First Day Cover		26·00

PRINTERS (£.s.d. stamps of all regions):—Photo Harrison & Sons. Portrait by Dorothy Wilding Ltd.

DATES OF ISSUE. Conflicting dates of issue have been announced for some of the regional issues, partly explained by the stamps being released on different dates by the Philatelic Bureau in Edinburgh or the Philatelic Counter in London and in the regions. We have adopted the practice of giving the earliest known dates, since once released the stamps could have been used anywhere in the U.K.

II. NORTHERN IRELAND

N **1**

N **2**

N **3**

(Des W. Hollywood (3d., 4d., 5d.), L. Pilton (6d., 9d.), T. Collins (1s. 3d., 1s. 6d.))

1958–67. *W* **179**. *P* 15 × 14.

NI1	N **1**	3d. deep lilac (18.8.58)	20	10
		p. One centre phosphor band (9.6.67)	20	15
NI2		4d. ultramarine (7.2.66)	20	15
		p. Two phosphor bands (10.67)	20	15
NI3	N **2**	6d. deep claret (29.9.58)	20	20
NI4		9d. bronze-green (2 phosphor bands) (1.3.67)	30	70
NI5	N **3**	1s. 3d. green (29.9.58)	30	70
NI6		1s. 6d. grey-blue (2 phosphor bands) (1.3.67)	30	70
		Ey. Phosphor omitted	£200	

First Day Covers

18.8.58	3d. (*NI1*)	28·00
29.9.58	6d., 1s. 3d. (*NI3, NI5*)	32·00
7.2.66	4d. (*NI2*)	7·00
1.3.67	9d., 1s. 6d. (*NI4, NI6*)	2·50

For Nos. NI1, NI3 and NI5 in Presentation Pack, see below Wales No. W6.

1968–69. *No watermark. Chalk-surfaced paper. One centre phosphor band (Nos.* NI8/9) *or two phosphor bands (others). Gum arabic (No.* NI7) *or PVA gum (others). P* 15 × 14.

NI 7	N **1**	4d. dp brt blue (27.6.68)	20	15
		Ev. PVA gum* (23.10.68)	10·00	
NI 8		4d. olive-sepia (4.9.68)	20	15
		Ey. Phosphor omitted		
NI 9		4d. brt vermilion (26.2.69)	20	20
		Ey. Phosphor omitted	4·50	
NI10		5d. royal blue (4.9.68)	20	20
		Ey. Phosphor omitted	25·00	
NI11	N **3**	1s. 6d. grey-blue (20.5.69)	2·50	3·25
		Ey. Phosphor omitted	£500	

4.9.68	*First Day Cover (NI8, NI10)*	1·75
	Presentation Pack (containing Nos. NI1p, NI4/6, NI8/10) (9.12.70)	3·25

*No. NI7Ev was never issued in Northern Ireland. After No. NI7 (gum arabic) had been withdrawn from Northern Ireland but whilst still on sale at the philatelic counters elsewhere, about fifty sheets with PVA gum were sold over the London Philatelic counter on 23 October, 1968, and some were also on sale at the British Philatelic Exhibition Post Office.

For full information on all future British issues, collectors should write to the British Post Office Philatelic Bureau, 20 Brandon Street, Edinburgh EH3 5TT

N **4**

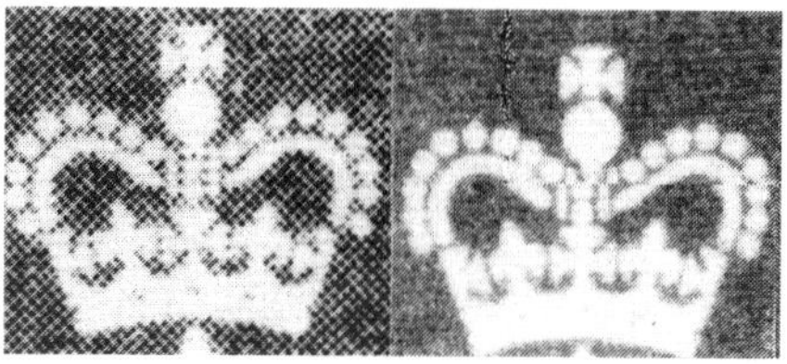

I II

Redrawn design of Type N 4 (litho ptgs.)

Two Types of Crown

Type I:–Crown with all pearls individually drawn.

Type II:–Crown with clear outlines, large pearls and strong white line below them. First 3 pearls at left are joined, except on Nos. NI39 and NI49.

The following stamps printed in lithography show a screened background behind and to the left of the emblem: 11½p., 12½p., 14p. (No. NI38), 15½p., 16p., 18p. (No. NI45), 19½p., 22p. (No. NI53) and 28p. (No. NI62). The 13p. and 17p. (No. NI43) also showed screened backgrounds in Type I, but changed to solid backgrounds for Type II. The 31p. had a solid background in Type I, but changed to a screened background for Type II. All other values printed in lithography have solid backgrounds.

(Des J. Matthews after plaster cast by Arnold Machin)

1971 (7 July)–**93**. *Decimal Currency. Chalk-surfaced paper. Type* N **4**.

(a) *Photo Harrison. With phosphor bands. P* 15 × 14.

NI12	2½p.	brt magenta (1 centre band)	80	25
NI13	3p.	ultramarine (2 bands)	40	15
	Ey.	Phosphor omitted	50·00	
NI14	3p.	ultramarine (1 centre band) (23.1.74)	20	15
NI15	3½p.	olive-grey (2 bands) (23.1.74)	20	20
NI16	3½p.	olive-grey (1 centre band) (6.11.74)	20	25
NI17	4½p.	grey-blue (2 bands) (6.11.74)	25	25
NI18	5p.	reddish violet (2 bands)	1·50	1·50
NI19	5½p.	violet (2 bands) (23.1.74)	20	20
	Ey.	Phosphor omitted	£225	
NI20	5½p.	violet (1 centre band) (21.5.75)	20	20
NI21	6½p.	greenish blue (1 centre band) (14.1.76).	20	20
NI22	7p.	purple-brown (1 centre band) (18.1.78)	35	25
NI23	7½p.	chestnut (2 bands)	2·25	2·25
	Ey.	Phosphor omitted	55·00	
NI24	8p.	rosine (2 bands) (23.1.74)	30	30
	Ey.	Phosphor omitted	75·00	
NI25	8½p.	yellow-green (2 bands) (14.1.76)	30	30
NI26	9p.	dp violet (2 bands) (18.1.78)	30	30
	Ey.	Phosphor omitted	25·00	
NI27	10p.	orange-brown (2 bands) (20.10.76)	35	35
NI28	10p.	orange-brown (1 centre band) (23.7.80)	35	35
NI29	10½p.	steel-blue (2 bands) (18.1.78)	50	50
NI30	11p.	scarlet (2 bands) (20.10.76)	50	50
	Ey.	Phosphor omitted	4·50	

(b) *Photo Harrison. On phosphorised paper. P* 15 × 14.

NI31	12p.	yellowish green (23.7.80)	50	50
NI32	13½p.	purple-brown (23.7.80)	70	80
NI33	15p.	ultramarine (23.7.80)	70	70

(c) *Litho Questa (Type* II, *unless otherwise stated). P* 14 (11½*p.,* 12½*p.,* 14*p.* (*No.* NI38), 15½*p.,* 16*p.,* 18*p.* (*No.* NI45), 19½*p.,* 20½*p.,* 22*p.* (*No.* NI53), 26*p.* (*No.* NI60), 28*p.* (*No.* NI62)) *or* 15 × 14 (*others*)

NI34	11½p.	drab (Type I) (1 side band) (8.4.81)	70	70
NI35	12p.	brt emerald (1 side band) (7.1.86)	70	70
NI36	12½p.	lt emerald (Type I) (1 side band) (24.2.82)	60	60
	a.	Perf 15 × 14 (28.2.84)	4·25	4·25
NI37	13p.	pale chestnut (Type I) (1 side band) (23.10.84)	1·25	70
	Ea.	Type II (28.11.86)	1·00	50
	Ey.	Phosphor omitted (Type I)		
NI38	14p.	grey-blue (Type I) (phosphorised paper) (8.4.81)	70	60
NI39	14p.	dp blue (1 centre band) (8.11.88)	70	60
NI40	15p.	brt blue (1 centre band) (28.11.89)	70	60
NI41	15½p.	pale violet (Type I) (phosphorised paper) (24.2.82)	80	65
NI42	16p.	drab (Type I) (phosphorised paper) (27.4.83)	1·00	1·00
	a.	Perf 15 × 14 (28.2.84)	9·50	8·00
NI43	17p.	grey-blue (Type I) (phosphorised paper) (23.10.84)	1·00	80
	Ea.	Type II (9.9.86)	£100	45·00
NI44	17p.	dp blue (1 centre band) (4.12.90)	70	70
NI45	18p.	dp violet (Type I) (phosphorised paper) (8.4.81)	90	90
NI46	18p.	dp olive-grey (phosphorised paper) (6.1.87)	80	80
NI47	18p.	brt green (1 centre band) (3.12.91)	70	70
	a.	Perf 14 (31.12.92*)	1·25	1·25
NI48	18p.	brt green (1 side band) (10.8.93)	2·00	2·00
	l.	Booklet pane. Nos. NI48, NI59, S61, S71, W49Eb and W60 with margins all round	6·00	
NI49	19p.	brt orange-red (phosphorised paper) (8.11.88)	80	70
NI50	19½p.	olive-grey (Type I) (phosphorised paper) (24.2.82)	1·75	2·25
NI51	20p.	brownish black (phosphorised paper) (28.11.89)	80	70
NI52	20½p.	ultramarine (Type I) (phosphorised paper) (27.4.83)	4·00	4·00
NI53	22p.	blue (Type I) (phosphorised paper) (8.4.81)	1·00	1·10
NI54	22p.	yellow-green (Type I) (phosphorised paper) (23.10.84)	1·00	1·10
NI55	22p.	brt orange-red (phosphorised paper) (4.12.90)	1·00	85
NI56	23p.	brt green (phosphorised paper) (8.11.88)	1·00	1·10
NI57	24p.	Indian red (phosphorised paper) (28.11.89)	1·00	1·10
NI58	24p.	chestnut (phosphorised paper) (3.12.91)	90	75
NI59	24p.	chestnut (2 bands) (10.8.93)	2·00	2·00
NI60	26p.	rosine (Type I) (phosphorised paper) (24.2.82)	1·10	1·40
	a.	Perf 15 × 14 (Type II) (27.1.87)	2·00	2·00
NI61	26p.	drab (phosphorised paper) (4.12.90)	1·00	1·00
NI62	28p.	dp violet-blue (Type I) (phosphorised paper) (27.4.83)	1·10	1·10
	a.	Perf 15 × 14 (Type II) (27.1.87)	1·10	1·10
NI63	28p.	dp bluish grey (phosphorised paper) (3.12.91)	1·10	1·10
NI64	31p.	brt purple (Type I) (phosphorised paper) (23.10.84)	1·40	1·40
	Ea.	Type II (14.4.87)	1·75	1·75
NI65	32p.	greenish blue (phosphorised paper) (8.11.88)	1·25	1·25
NI66	34p.	dp bluish grey (phosphorised paper) (28.11.89)	1·40	1·40
NI67	37p.	rosine (phosphorised paper) (4.12.90)	1·40	1·40
NI68	39p.	brt mauve (phosphorised paper) (3.12.91)	1·40	1·40

*Earliest known date of use.

No. NI47a was caused by the use of a reserve perforating machine for some printings in the second half of 1992.

Nos. NI48 and NI59 only come from booklets.

From 1972 printing were made on fluorescent white paper and from 1973 most printings had dextrin added to the PVA gum (see notes after 1971 Decimal Machin issue).

First Day Covers

7.7.71	2½p., 3p., 5p., 7½p. (*NI12/13, NI18, NI23*)	2·50
23.1.74	3p., 3½p., 5½p., 8p. (*NI14/15, NI19, NI24*)	1·50
6.11.74	4½p. (*NI17*)	1·25
14.1.76	6½p., 8½p. (*NI21, NI25*)	1·25
20.10.76	10p., 11p. (*NI27, NI30*)	1·25
18.1.78	7p., 9p., 10½p. (*NI22, NI26, NI29*)	2·00
23.7.80	12p., 13½p., 15p. (*NI31/3*)	2·25
8.4.81	11½p., 14p., 18p., 22p. (*NI34, NI38, NI45, NI53*)	2·25
24.2.82	12½p., 15½p., 19½p., 26p. (*NI36, NI41, NI50, NI60*)	2·50
27.4.83	16p., 20½p., 28p. (*NI42, NI52, NI62*)	2·75
23.10.84	13p., 17p., 22p., 31p. (*NI37, NI43, NI54, NI64*)	2·50
7.1.86	12p. (*NI35*)	1·50
6.1.87	18p. (*NI46*)	1·50
8.11.88	14p., 19p., 23p., 32p. (*NI39, NI49, NI56, NI65*)	2·25
28.11.89	15p., 20p., 24p., 34p. (*NI40, NI51, NI57, NI66*)	2·50
4.12.90	17p., 22p., 26p., 37p. (*NI44, NI55, NI61, NI67*)	3·25
3.12.91	18p., 24p., 28p., 39p. (*NI47, NI58, NI63, NI68*)	3·25

Presentation Packs

7.7.71	2½p., 3p. (2 bands), 5p., 7½p. (*Nos.* NI12/13, NI18, NI23)	4·25
29.5.74	3p. (1 centre band), 3½p. (2 bands) *or* (1 centre band), 5½p. (2 bands) *or* (1 centre band), 8p. (*Nos.* NI14, NI15 *or* NI16, NI19 *or* NI20, NI24). The 4½p. (No. NI17) was added later	2·50
20.10.76	6½p., 8½p., 10p. (2 bands), 11p. (*Nos.* NI21, NI25, NI27, NI30)	2·00
28.10.81	7p., 9p., 10½p., 12p. (photo), 13½p., 15p. (photo), 11½p., 14p. grey-blue, 18p. dp violet, 22p. blue (*Nos.* NI22, NI26, NI29, NI31/4, NI38, NI45, NI53)	7·50
3.8.83	10p. (1 centre band), 12½p., 16p., 20½p., 26p. rosine, 28p. dp violet-blue (*Nos.* NI28, NI36, NI42, NI52, NI60, NI62)	7·50
23.10.84	10p. (1 centre band) 13p., 16p., 17p. grey-blue, 22p. yellow-green, 26p. rosine, 28p. dp violet-blue, 31p. (*Nos.* NI28, NI37, NI42a, NI43, NI54, NI60, NI62, NI64)	12·00
3.3.87	12p. (litho), 13p., 17p. grey-blue, 18p. dp olive-grey, 22p. yellow-green, 26p. rosine, 28p. dp violet-blue, 31p. (*Nos.* NI35, NI37, NI43, NI46, NI54, NI60a, NI62a, NI64)	7·50

Presentation Packs for Northern Ireland, Scotland and Wales

8.11.88	14p. dp blue, 19p., 23p., 32p. (*Nos.* NI39, NI49, NI56, NI65), 14p. (1 centre band), 19p. (phosphorised paper), 23p. (phosphorised paper), 32p. (*Nos.* S54, S62, S67, S77), 14p. dp blue, 19p., 23p., 32p. (*Nos.* W40, W50, W57, W66)	8·00
28.11.89	15p. (litho), 20p., 24p. Indian red, 34p. (*Nos.* NI40, NI51, NI57, NI66), 15p. (litho), 20p., 24p. Indian red, 34p. (*Nos.* S56, S64, S69, S78), 15p. (litho), 20p., 24p. Indian red, 34p. (*Nos.* W41, W52, W58, W67)	8·00
4.12.90	17p. dp blue, 22p. brt orange-red, 26p. drab, 37p., (*Nos.* NI44, NI55, NI61, NI67), 17p. dp blue, 22p. brt orange-red, 26p. drab, 37p. (*Nos.* S58, S66, S73, S79), 17p. dp blue, 22p. brt orange-red, 26p. drab, 37p. (*Nos.* W45, W56, W62, W68)	8·00
3.12.91	18p. brt green, 24p. chestnut, 28p. dp bluish grey, 39p. (*Nos.* NI47, NI58, NI63, NI68), 18p. brt green, 24p. chestnut, 28p. dp bluish grey, 39p. (*Nos.* S60, S70, S75, S80), 18p. brt green, 24p. chestnut, 28p. dp bluish grey, 39p. (*Nos.* W48, W59, W64, W69)	6·00

(Des J. Matthews after plaster cast by Arnold Machin)

1993 (7 Dec)–**97**. *Chalk-surfaced paper. P 15 × 14 (with one elliptical hole on each vertical side). (a) Litho Questa*

NI69 **N 4**	19p.	bistre (1 centre band)	40	40
NI70	19p.	bistre (1 band at left) (26.7.94)	2·25	2·25
	a.	Booklet pane. Nos. NI70 × 2, NI72 × 4, NI74, NI76 and centre label with margins all round	6·50	
	aEy.	Booklet pane. Phosphor omitted		
	b.	Booklet pane. Nos. NI70, NI72, NI74 and NI76 with margins all round	3·50	
	Ec.	Band at right (25.4.95)	2·00	2·00
	d.	Booklet pane. Nos. NI70Ec, NI72, S82, S84, W71 and W73 with margins all round (25.4.95)	7·00	
	da.	Part perf pane*		
NI71	20p.	brt green (1 centre band) (23.7.96)	30	35
NI72	25p.	red (2 bands)	50	50
NI73	26p.	red-brown (2 bands) (23.7.96)	40	45
NI74	30p.	dp olive-grey (2 bands)	60	60
NI75	37p.	brt mauve (2 bands) (23.7.96)	60	65
NI76	41p.	grey-brown (2 bands)	90	90
NI77	63p.	lt emerald (2 bands) (23.7.96)	95	1·00

(b) *Photo Walsall* (20*p.*, 63*p.*), *Harrison or Walsall* (26*p.*, 37*p.*)

NI78 **N 4**	20p.	bright green (1 centre band) (1.7.97)	30	35
NI79	26p.	chestnut (2 bands) (1.7.97)	40	45
	l.	Booklet pane. Nos. NI79/80, S91/2 and W80/1 with margins all round (23.9.97)	2·75	
NI80	37p.	bright mauve (2 bands) (1.7.97)	60	65
NI81	63p.	light emerald (2 bands) (1.7.97)	95	1·00

* No. NI70da, which comes from the 1995 National Trust £6 booklet, shows the top two values in the pane of 6 (Nos. S82, S84) completely imperforate and the two Wales values below partly imperforate.

No. NI70 only comes from booklets.

No. NI79l, printed by Harrison, comes from the 1997 B.B.C. £6.15 booklet.

First Day Covers

7.12.93	19p., 25p., 30p., 41p. (*NI69, NI72, NI74, NI76*)	4·50
26.7.94	Northern Ireland *se-tenant* pane 19p., 25p., 30p., 41p. (*NI70a*)	6·00
23.7.96	20p., 26p., 37p., 63p. (*NI71, NI73, NI75, NI77*)	3·25

Presentation Packs for Northern Ireland, Scotland and Wales

7.12.93	19p., 25p., 30p., 41p., each × 3 (*Nos.* NI69, NI72, NI74, NI76, S81, S84, S86, S88, W70, W73, W75, W77)	8·00
23.7.96	20p., 26p., 37p., 63p., each × 3 (*Nos.* NI71, NI73, NI75, NI77, S83, S85, S87, S89, W72, W74, W76, W78)	7·00

III. SCOTLAND

S 1

S 2

S 3

(Des. G. Huntly (3d., 4d., 5d.), J. Fleming (6d., 9d.), A. Imrie (1s., 3d., 1s. 6d.))

1958–67. *W* **179**. *P* 15 × 14.

S1	S **1**	3d. dp lilac (18.8.58)	20	15
		p. Two phosphor bands (29.1.63)	13·00	1·25
		pa. One side phosphor band (30.4.65)	20	25
		pb. One centre phosphor band (9.11.67)	20	15
S2		4d. ultramarine (7.2.66)	20	10
		p. Two phosphor bands	20	20
S3	S **2**	6d. dp claret (29.9.58)	20	15
		p. Two phosphor bands (29.1.63)	20	25
S4		9d. bronze-green (2 phosphor bands) (1.3.67)	30	30
S5	S **3**	1s. 3d. green (29.9.58)	30	30
		p. Two phosphor bands (29.1.63)	30	30
S6		1s. 6d. grey-blue (2 phosphor bands) (1.3.67)	35	30

First Day Covers

18.8.58	3d. (*S1*)	11·00
29.9.58	6d., 1s. 3d. (*S3, S5*)	22·00
7.2.66	4d. (*S2*)	7·00
1.3.67	9d., 1s. 6d. (*S4, S6*)	2·50

The one phosphor band on No. S1pa was produced by printing broad phosphor bands across alternate vertical perforations. Individual stamps show the band at right or left (same prices either way).

For Nos. S1, S3 and S5 in Presentation Pack, see below Wales No. W6.

1967–70. *No watermark. Chalk-surfaced paper. One centre phosphor band (S7, S9/10) or two phosphor bands (others). Gum arabic (Nos. S7, S8) or PVA gum (others). P* 15 × 14.

S 7	S **1**	3d. dp lilac (16.5.68)	10	15
		Ey. Phosphor omitted	6·00	
		Ev. PVA gum	10	
		Eya. Phosphor omitted (No. S7Ev)	3·00	
S 8		4d. dp brt blue (28.11.67)	10	15
		Ey. Phosphor omitted	8·00	
		Ev. PVA gum (25.7.68)	10	
S 9		4d. olive-sepia (4.9.68)	10	10
		Ey. Phosphor omitted	2·50	
S10		4d. brt vermilion (26.2.69)	10	10
		Ey. Phosphor omitted	2·50	
S11		5d. royal blue (4.9.68)	20	10
		Ey. Phosphor omitted	50·00	
S12	S **2**	9d. bronze-green (28.9.70)	5·00	6·50
		Ey. Phosphor omitted	£200	
S13	S **3**	1s. 6d. grey-blue (12.12.68)	1·40	1·00
		Ey. Phosphor omitted	£120	

4.9.68	*First Day Cover (S9, S11)*	1·75
	Presentation Pack (containing Nos. S3, S5p., S7, S9/13) (9.12.70)	10·00

S **4**

I II

Redrawn design of Type S 4 (litho ptgs.)

The introduction of the redrawn lion took place in 1983 when Waddington's had the contract and therefore the 13, 17, 22 and 31p. exist in both types and perforated 14. The Questa printings, perforated 15 × 14, are all Type II.

The Types of Lion.

Type I:–The eye and jaw appear larger and there is no line across the bridge of the nose.

Type II:–The tongue is thick at the point of entry to the mouth and the eye is linked to the background by a solid line.

The following stamps printed in lithography show a screened background behind and to the left of the emblem: $12\frac{1}{2}$p., $15\frac{1}{2}$p., 16p., $19\frac{1}{2}$p., 28p. (Nos. S50 and S74) and 31p. (Nos. S51 and S76). The 13p. and 17p. (No. S43) also showed screened backgrounds for both Type I and II of the John Waddington printings, but changed to solid backgrounds for the Questa Type II. All other values printed in lithography have solid backgrounds.

(Des J. Matthews after plaster cast by Arnold Machin)

1971 (7 July)–**93**. *Decimal Currency. Chalk-surfaced paper. Type* S **4**.

(a) *Photo Harrison. With phosphor bands. P* 15 × 14.

S14	$2\frac{1}{2}$p. brt magenta (1 centre band)	25	15
	Ey. Phosphor omitted	4·50	
	Eg. Gum arabic (22.9.72)	20	
S15	3p. ultramarine (2 bands)	30	15
	Ey. Phosphor omitted	10·00	
	Eg. Gum arabic (14.12.72)	30	
	Ega. Imperf (pair)	£400	
S16	3p. ultramarine (1 centre band) (23.1.74)	15	15
S17	$3\frac{1}{2}$p. olive-grey (2 bands) (23.1.74)	20	20
	Ey. Phosphor omitted	50·00	
S18	$3\frac{1}{2}$p. olive-grey (1 centre band) (6.11.74)	20	20
S19	$4\frac{1}{2}$p. grey-blue (2 bands) (6.11.74)	25	20
S20	5p. reddish violet (2 bands)	1·00	1·00
S21	$5\frac{1}{2}$p. violet (2 bands) (23.1.74)	20	20
S22	$5\frac{1}{2}$p. violet (1 centre band) (21.5.75)	20	20
	a. Imperf (pair)	£350	
S23	$6\frac{1}{2}$p. greenish blue (1 centre band) (14.1.76).	20	20
S24	7p. purple-brown (1 centre band) (18.1.78)	25	25
S25	$7\frac{1}{2}$p. chestnut (2 bands)	1·25	1·25
	Ey. Phosphor omitted	4·50	
S26	8p. rosine (2 bands) (23.1.74)	30	40
S27	$8\frac{1}{2}$p. yellow-green (2 bands) (14.1.76)	30	30
S28	9p. dp violet (2 bands) (18.1.78)	30	30
S29	10p. orange-brown (2 bands) (20.10.76)	35	30

S30	10p.	orange-brown (1 centre band) (23.7.80)	35	35
S31	10½p.	steel-blue (2 bands) (18.1.78)	50	35
S32	11p.	scarlet (2 bands) (20.10.76)	50	35
		Ey. Phosphor omitted	1·75	

(b) Photo Harrison. On phosphorised paper. P 15 × 14

S33	12p.	yellowish green (23.7.80)	50	30
S34	13½p.	purple-brown (23.7.80)	70	65
S35	15p.	ultramarine (23.7.80)	60	45

(c) Litho J.W. (Type I unless otherwise stated). One side phosphor band (11½p., 12p., 12½p., 13p.) or phosphorised paper (others). P 14

S36	11½p.	drab (8.4.81)	80	60
		Ey. Phosphor omitted	£700	
S37	12p.	brt emerald (Type II) (7.1.86)	1·75	1·50
S38	12½p.	lt emerald (24.2.82)	60	50
S39	13p.	pale chestnut (Type I) (23.10.84)	70	50
		Ea. Type II (1.85)	6·00	1·00
S40	14p.	grey-blue (8.4.81)	60	50
S41	15½p.	pale violet (24.2.82)	70	65
S42	16p.	drab (Type II) (27.4.83)	70	55
S43	17p.	grey-blue (Type I) (23.10.84)	3·50	2·25
		Ea. Type II (1.85)	1·25	1·00
S44	18p.	dp violet (8.4.81)	80	80
S45	19½p.	olive-grey (24.2.82)	1·75	1·75
S46	20½p.	ultramarine (Type II) (27.4.83)	4·00	4·00
S47	22p.	blue (8.4.81)	90	1·25
S48	22p.	yellow-green (Type I) (23.10.84)	2·25	2·00
		Ea. Type II (1.86)	50·00	28·00
S49	26p.	rosine (24.2.82)	1·10	1·25
S50	28p.	dp violet-blue (Type II) (27.4.83)	1·10	1·10
S51	31p.	brt purple (Type I) (23.10.84)	2·00	1·75
		Ea. Type II (11.85*)	95·00	60·00

(d) Litho Questa (Type II). P 15 × 14

S52	12p.	brt emerald (1 side band) (29.4.86)	2·00	1·75
S53	13p.	pale chestnut (1 side band) (4.11.86)	70	50
S54	14p.	dp blue (1 centre band) (8.11.88)	50	50
		l. Booklet pane. No. S54 × 6 with margins all round (21.3.89)	2·75	
S55	14p.	dp blue (1 side band) (21.3.89)	80	1·00
		l. Booklet pane. No. S55 × 5, S63 × 2, S68 and centre label with margins all round	16·00	
		la. Error. Booklet pane imperf		
S56	15p.	brt blue (1 centre band) (28.11.89)	70	55
		a. Imperf (three sides) (block of four)	£275	
S57	17p.	grey-blue (phosphorised paper) (29.4.86)	4·25	2·25
S58	17p.	dp blue (1 centre band) (4.12.90)	60	60
S59	18p.	dp olive-grey (phosphorised paper) (6.1.87)	80	80
S60	18p.	brt green (1 centre band) (3.12.91)	70	70
		a. Perf 14 (26.9.92*)	1·00	75
S61	18p.	brt green (1 side band) (10.8.93)	2·00	2·00
S62	19p.	brt orange-red (phosphorised paper) (8.11.88)	80	65
		l. Booklet pane. No. S62 × 9 with margins all round (21.3.89)	5·50	
		m. Booklet pane. No. S62 × 6 with margins all round (21.3.89)	3·50	
S63	19p.	brt orange-red (2 bands) (21.3.89)	1·50	1·50
S64	20p.	brownish black (phosphorised paper) (28.11.89)	80	60
S65	22p.	yellow-green (phosphorised paper) (27.1.87)	90	90
S66	22p.	brt orange-red (phosphorised paper) (4.12.90)	1·00	75
S67	23p.	brt green (phosphorised paper) (8.11.88)	1·00	1·10
S68	23p.	brt green (2 bands) (21.3.89)	12·00	11·00
S69	24p.	Indian red (phosphorised paper) (28.11.89)	1·00	1·00
S70	24p.	chestnut (phosphorised paper) (3.12.91)	75	75
		a. Perf 14 (10.92*)	1·50	1·25
S71	24p.	chestnut (2 bands) (10.8.93)	2·00	2·00
S72	26p.	rosine (phosphorised paper) (27.1.87)	2·50	2·50
S73	26p.	drab (phosphorised paper) (4.12.90)	1·00	1·00
S74	28p.	dp violet-blue (phosphorised paper) (27.1.87)	1·10	1·10
S75	28p.	dp bluish grey (phosphorised paper) (3.12.91)	1·10	1·10
		a. Perf 14 (18.2.93*)	3·25	3·25
S76	31p.	brt purple (phosphorised paper) (29.4.86)	1·75	1·75
S77	32p.	greenish blue (phosphorised paper) (8.11.88)	1·25	1·25
S78	34p.	dp bluish grey (phosphorised paper) (28.11.89)	1·40	1·40
S79	37p.	rosine (phosphorised paper) (4.12.90)	1·40	1·40
S80	39p.	brt mauve (phosphorised paper) (3.12.91)	1·40	1·40
		a. Perf 14 (11.92)	2·25	2·25

*Earliest known date of use.

Nos. S55, S61, S63, S68 and S71 only come from booklets.

No. S56a occured in the second vertical row of two sheets. It is best collected as a block of four including the left-hand vertical pair imperforate on three sides.

Nos. S60a, S70a, S75a and S80a were caused by the use of a reserve perforating machine for some printings in the second half of 1992.

From 1972 printings were on fluorescent white paper. From 1973 most printings had dextrin added to the PVA gum (see notes after the 1971 Decimal Machin issue).

First Day Covers

7.7.71	2½p., 3p., 5p., 7½p. (*S14/15, S20, S25*)	2·50
23.1.74	3p., 3½p., 5½p., 8p. (*S16/17, S21, S26*)	1·50
6.11.74	4½p. (*S19*)	1·25
14.1.76	6½p., 8½p. (*S23, S27*)	1·25
20.10.76	10p., 11p. (*S29, S32*)	1·25
18.1.78	7p., 9p., 10½p. (*S24, S28, S31*)	2·00
23.7.80	12p., 13½p., 15p. (*S33/5*)	2·25
8.4.81	11½p., 14p., 18p., 22p. (*S36, S40, S44, S47*)	2·25
24.2.82	12½p., 15½p., 19½p., 26p. (*S38, S41, S45, S49*)	2·50
27.4.83	16p., 20½p., 28p. (*S42, S46, S50*)	2·75
23.10.84	13p., 17p., 22p., 31p. (*S39, S43, S48, S51*)	2·50
7.1.86	12p. (*S37*)	1·50
6.1.87	18p. (*S59*)	1·50
8.11.88	14p., 19p., 23p., 32p. (*S54, S62, S67, S77*)	2·25
21.3.89	Scots Connection *se-tenant* pane 14p., 19p., 23p. (*S55l*)	8·00
28.11.89	15p., 20p., 24p., 34p. (*S56, S64, S69, S78*)	2·50
4.12.90	17p., 22p., 26p., 37p. (*S58, S66, S73, S79*)	3·25
3.12.91	18p., 24p., 28p., 39p. (*S60, S70, S75, S80*)	3·25

Presentation Packs

7.7.71	2½p., 3p. (2 bands), 5p., 7½p. (*Nos.* S14/15, S20, S25)	4·25
29.5.74	3p. (1 centre band), 3½p. (2 bands) *or* (1 centre band), 5½p. (2 bands) *or* (1 centre band), 8p. (*Nos.* S16, S17 *or* S18, S21 *or* S22, S26). The 4½p. (No. S19) was added later	2·50
20.10.76	6½p., 8½p., 10p. (2 bands), 11p. (*Nos.* S23, S27, S29, S32)	2·00
28.10.81	7p., 9p., 10½p., 12p. (photo), 13½p., 15p. (photo), 11½p., 14p. grey-blue, 18p. dp violet, 22p. blue (*Nos.* S24, S28, S31, S33/6, S40, S44, S47)	7·50
3.8.83	10p. (1 centre band), 12½p., 16p., 20½p., 26p. (J.W.), 28p. (J.W.), (*Nos.* S30, S38, S42, S46, S49/50)	8·00
23.10.84	10p. (1 centre band), 13p. (J.W.), 16p., 17p. (J.W.), 22p. yellow-green, 26p. (J.W.), 28p. (J.W.), 31p. (J.W.) (*Nos.* S30, S39, S42/3, S48/51)	11·00
3.3.87	12p. (litho), 13p. (Questa), 17p. grey-blue (Questa), 18p. dp olive-grey, 22p. yellow-green, 26p. rosine (Questa), 28p. dp violet-blue (Questa), 31p. (Questa) (*Nos.* S52/3, S57, S59, S65, S72, S74, S76)	8·00

Presentation Packs containing stamps of Northern Ireland, Scotland and Wales are listed after those for Northern Ireland.

1977–78 EXPERIMENTAL MACHINE PACKETS. These are small cartons containing loose stamps for sale in vending machines. The experiment was confined to the Scottish Postal Board area, where six vending machines were installed, the first becoming operational in Dundee about February 1977.

The cartons carry labels inscribed "ROYAL MAIL STAMPS", their total face value (30p. or 60p.) and their contents.

At first the 30p. packet contained two 6½p. and two 8½p. Scottish Regional stamps and the 60p. packet had four of each. The stamps could be in pairs or blocks, but also in strips or singles.

With the change in postal rates on 13 June 1977 these packets were withdrawn on 11 June and on 13 June the contents were changed, giving three 7p. and one 9p. for the 30p. packet and double this for the 60p. packet. However, this time ordinary British Machin stamps were used. Moreover the Edinburgh machine, situated in an automatic sorting area, was supplied with 7p. stamps with two phosphor bands instead of the new centre band 7p. stamps, despite instructions having been given to withdraw the two band stamps. However, the demand for these packets was too great to be filled and by 27 June the machine was closed down. It was brought back into use on 16 August 1977, supplying 7p. stamps with the centre band.

The 6½p. and 8½p. Scottish Regional packets were put on sale at the Edinburgh Philatelic Bureau in June 1977 and withdrawn in April 1978. The packets with the 7p. and 9p. Machin stamps were put on sale at the Bureau in June 1977 and withdrawn in December 1978.

Such machine packets are outside the scope of this catalogue.

(Des J. Matthews after plaster cast by Arnold Machin)

1993 (7 Dec)–**97**. *Chalk-surfaced paper. P* 15 × 14 (*with one elliptical hole on each vertical side*). (a) *Litho Questa*

S81	S **4**	19p. bistre (1 centre band)	40	40
S82		19p. bistre (1 band at right) (25.4.95)	2·25	2·25
S83		20p. brt green (1 centre band) (23.7.96)	30	35
S84		25p. red (2 bands)	50	50
S85		26p. red-brown (2 bands) (23.7.96)	40	45
S86		30p. dp olive-grey (2 bands)	60	60
S87		37p. brt mauve (2 bands) (23.7.96)	60	65
S88		41p. grey-brown (2 bands)	90	90
S89		63p. lt emerald (2 bands) (23.7.96)	95	1·00

(b) *Photo Walsall* (20*p*., 63*p*.), *Harrison or Walsall* (26*p*., 37*p*.)

S90	S **4**	20p. bright green (1 centre band) (1.7.97)	30	35
S91		26p. chestnut (2 bands) (1.7.97)	40	45
S92		37p. bright mauve (2 bands) (1.7.97)	60	65
S93		63p. light emerald (2 bands) (1.7.97)	95	1·00

No. S82 only comes from booklets.

First Day Covers

7.12.93	19p., 25p., 30p., 41p. (S81, S84, S86, S88)	4·50
23.7.96	20p., 26p., 37p., 63p. (S83, S85, S87, S89)	3·25

For Presentation Pack containing stamps of Northern Ireland, Scotland and Wales see after No. NI81 of Northern Ireland.

IV. WALES

From the inception of the Regional stamps, the Welsh versions were tendered to members of the public at all Post Offices within the former County of Monmouthshire but the national alternatives were available on request. Offices with a Monmouthshire postal address but situated outside the County, namely Beachley, Brockweir, Redbrook, Sedbury, Tutshill, Welsh Newton and Woodcroft, were not supplied with the Welsh Regional stamps.

With the re-formation of Counties, Monmouthshire became known as Gwent and was also declared to be part of Wales. From 1 July 1974, therefore, except for the offices mentioned above, only Welsh Regional stamps were available at the offices under the jurisdiction of Newport, Gwent.

W **1**

W **2**

W **3**

(Des R. Stone)

1958–67. *W* **179**. *P* 15 × 14.

W1	W **1**	3d. dp lilac (18.8.58)	20	10
		p. One centre phosphor band (16.5.67)	20	15
W2		4d. ultramarine (7.2.66)	20	15
		p. Two phosphor bands (10.67)	20	15
W3	W **2**	6d. dp claret (29.9.58)	40	20
W4		9d. bronze-green (2 phosphor bands) (1.3.67)	40	40
		Ey. Phosphor omitted	£325	
W5	W **3**	1s. 3d. green (29.9.58)	30	30
W6		1s. 6d. grey-blue (2 phosphor bands) (1.3.67)	35	40
		Ey. Phosphor omitted	45·00	

First Day Covers

18.8.58	3d. (*W1*)	11·00
29.9.58	6d., 1s. 3d. (*W3, W5*)	22·00
7.2.66	4d. (*W2*)	7·00
1.3.67	9d., 1s. 6d. (*W4, W6*)	2·50
	*Presentation Pack**	£100

*This was issued in 1960 and comprises Guernsey No. 7, Jersey No. 10, Isle of Man No. 2, Northern Ireland Nos. NI1, NI3 and NI5, Scotland Nos. S1, S3 and S5 and Wales Nos. W1, W3 and W5 together with a 6-page printed leaflet describing the stamps. There exist two forms: (*a*) inscribed "7s.3d." for sale in the U.K.; and (*b*) inscribed "$1.20" for sale in the U.S.A.

1967–69. *No wmk. Chalk-surfaced paper. One centre phosphor band* (W7, W9/10) *or two phosphor bands (others). Gum arabic (3d.) or PVA gum (others). P* 15 × 14.

W 7	W **1**	3d. dp lilac (6.12.67)	20	10
		Ey. Phosphor omitted	50·00	
W 8		4d. ultramarine (21.6.68)	20	10
W 9		4d. olive-sepia (4.9.68)	20	10
W10		4d. brt vermilion (26.2.69)	20	20
		Ey. Phosphor omitted	1·75	
W11		5d. royal blue (4.9.68)	20	10
		Ey. Phosphor omitted	2·25	
W12	W **3**	1s. 6d. grey-blue (1.8.69)	3·00	3·75

4.9.68	*First Day Cover (W9, W11)*	1·75
	Presentation Pack (containing Nos. W4, W6/7, W9/11) (9.12.70)	3·75

W **4** With "p"

I II

Redrawn design of Type W 4 (litho ptgs.)

Two Types of Dragon

Type I:–The eye is complete with white dot in the centre. Wing-tips, tail and tongue are thin.

Type II:–The eye is joined to the nose by a solid line. Tail, wing-tips, claws and tongue are wider than in Type I.

The following stamps printed in lithography show a screened background behind and to the left of the emblem: $11\frac{1}{2}$p., $12\frac{1}{2}$p., 14p. (No. W39), $15\frac{1}{2}$p., 16p., 18p. (No. W46), $19\frac{1}{2}$p., 22p. (No. W54) and 28p. (No. W63). The 13p. and 17p. (No. W44) also show screened backgrounds in Type I, but changed to solid backgrounds for Type II. All other values printed in lithography have solid backgrounds.

(Des J. Matthews after plaster cast by Arnold Machin)

1971 (7 July)–**93**. *Decimal Currency. Chalk-surfaced paper. Type* W **4**.

(*a*) *Photo Harrison. With phosphor bands. P* 15 × 14.

W13	$2\frac{1}{2}$p. brt magenta (1 centre band)	20	15
	Ey. Phosphor omitted	7·50	
	Eg. Gum arabic (22.9.72)	20	
	Ega. Imperf (pair)	£350	
W14	3p. ultramarine (2 bands)	25	15
	Ey. Phosphor omitted	20·00	
	Eg. Gum arabic (6.6.73)	30	
	Eya. Phosphor omitted (No. W14Eg)	12·00	
W15	3p. ultramarine (1 centre band) (23.1.74)	20	20
W16	$3\frac{1}{2}$p. olive-grey (2 bands) (23.1.74)	20	25
W17	$3\frac{1}{2}$p. olive-grey (1 centre band) (6.11.74)	20	25
W18	$4\frac{1}{2}$p. grey-blue (2 bands) (6.11.74)	25	20
W19	5p. reddish violet (2 bands)	1·00	1·00
	Ey. Phosphor omitted	15·00	
W20	$5\frac{1}{2}$p. violet (2 bands) (23.1.74)	20	25
	Ey. Phosphor omitted	£160	
W21	$5\frac{1}{2}$p. violet (1 centre band) (21.5.75)	20	25
	a. Imperf (pair)	£400	
W22	$6\frac{1}{2}$p. greenish blue (1 centre band) (14.1.76)	20	20
W23	7p. purple-brown (1 centre band) (18.1.78)	25	25
W24	$7\frac{1}{2}$p. chestnut (2 bands)	1·25	1·50
	Ey. Phosphor omitted	95·00	
W25	8p. rosine (2 bands) (23.1.74)	30	30
	Ey. Phosphor omitted	£650	
W26	$8\frac{1}{2}$p. yellow-green (2 bands) (14.1.76)	30	30
W27	9p. dp violet (2 bands) (18.1.78)	30	30
W28	10p. orange-brown (2 bands) (20.10.76)	35	30
W29	10p. orange-brown (1 centre band) (23.7.80)	35	30
W30	$10\frac{1}{2}$p. steel-blue (2 bands) (18.1.78)	50	50
W31	11p. scarlet (2 bands) (20.10.76)	50	50

(b) Photo Harrison. On phosphorised paper. P 15 × 14

W32	12p. yellowish green (23.7.80)	50	45
W33	13½p. purple-brown (23.7.80)	60	70
W34	15p. ultramarine (23.7.80)	60	50

(c) Litho Questa (Type II unless otherwise stated). P 14 (11½p., 12½p., 14p. (No. W39), 15½p., 16p., 18p. (No. W46), 19½p., 20½p., 22p. (No. W54), 26p. (No. W61), 28p. (No. W63)) or 15 × 14 (others)

W35	11½p. drab (Type I) (1 side band) (8.4.81)	85	60
W36	12p. brt emerald (1 side band) (7.1.86)	1·25	1·10
W37	12½p. lt emerald (Type I) (1 side band) (24.2.82)	80	60
	a. Perf 15 × 14 (10.1.84)	6·00	6·00
W38	13p. pale chestnut (Type I) (1 side band) (23.10.84)	50	35
	Ea. Type II (1.87)	1·75	1·25
W39	14p. grey-blue (Type I) (phosphorised paper) (8.4.81)	65	50
W40	14p. dp blue (1 centre band) (8.11.88)	55	50
W41	15p. brt blue (1 centre band) (28.11.89)	50	50
	Ey. Phosphor omitted		
W42	15½p. pale violet (Type I) (phosphorised paper) (24.2.82)	80	65
W43	16p. drab (Type I) (phosphorised paper) (27.4.83)	1·75	1·25
	a. Perf 15 × 14 (10.1.84)	1·75	1·50
W44	17p. grey-blue (Type I) (phosphorised paper) (23.10.84)	90	70
	Ea. Type II (18.8.86)	30·00	20·00
W45	17p. dp blue (1 centre band) (4.12.90)	70	55
	Ey. Phosphor omitted	18·00	
W46	18p. dp violet (Type I) (8.4.81)	80	75
W47	18p. dp olive-grey (phosphorised paper) (6.1.87)	80	70
W48	18p. brt green (1 centre band) (3.12.91)	55	55
	Ey. Phosphor omitted	£180	
	a. Booklet pane. No. W48 × 6 with margins all round (25.2.92)	2·75	
	aEy. Phosphor omitted		
	b. Perf 14 (12.1.93*)	1·25	1·00
W49	18p. brt green (1 side band at right) (25.2.92)	2·00	2·00
	a. Booklet pane. No. X1020 × 2, 1451*a*, 1514*a*, W49 × 2, W60 × 2 and centre label with margins all round	10·00	
	aEy. Phosphor omitted		
	Eb. Band at left (10.8.93)	2·00	2·00
W50	19p. brt orange-red (phosphorised paper) (8.11.88)	85	60
W51	19½p. olive-grey (Type I) (phosphorised paper) (24.2.82)	2·00	2·00
W52	20p. brownish black (phosphorised paper) (28.11.89)	80	80
W53	20½p. ultramarine (Type I) (phosphorised paper) (27.4.83)	4·00	4·00
W54	22p. blue (Type I) (phosphorised paper) (8.4.81)	1·10	1·10
W55	22p. yellow-green (Type I) (phosphorised paper) (23.10.84)	90	1·25
W56	22p. brt orange-red (phosphorised paper) (4.12.90)	80	70
W57	23p. brt green (phosphorised paper) (8.11.88)	90	1·25
W58	24p. Indian red (phosphorised paper) (28.11.89)	1·00	1·25
W59	24p. chestnut (phosphorised paper) (3.12.91)	90	90
	a. Booklet pane. No. W59 × 6 with margins all round (25.2.92)	4·75	
	b. Perf 14 (14.9.92*)	1·40	1·00
W60	24p. chestnut (2 bands) (25.2.92)	1·25	1·25
W61	26p. rosine (Type I) (phosphorised paper) (24.2.82)	1·10	1·40
	a. Perf 15 × 14 (Type II) (27.1.87)	4·75	5·00
W62	26p. drab (phosphorised paper) (4.12.90)	1·00	1·00
W63	28p. dp violet-blue (Type I) (phosphorised paper) (27.4.83)	1·10	1·25
	a. Perf 15 × 14 (Type II) (27.1.87)	1·10	1·10
W64	28p. dp bluish grey (phosphorised paper) (3.12.91)	1·10	1·10
W65	31p. brt purple (Type I) (phosphorised paper) (23.10.84)	1·25	1·25
W66	32p. greenish blue (phosphorised paper) (8.11.88)	1·25	1·25
W67	34p. dp bluish grey (phosphorised paper) (28.11.89)	1·10	1·40
W68	37p. rosine (phosphorised paper) (4.12.90)	1·10	1·40
W69	39p. brt mauve (phosphorised paper) (3.12.91)	1·10	1·40

*Earliest known date of use.

Nos. W48b and W59b were caused by the use of a reserve perforating machine for some printings in the second half of 1992.

Nos. W49, W49Eb and W60 only come from booklets.

From 1972 printings were on fluorescent white paper. From 1973 most printings had dextrin added to the PVA gum (see notes after 1971 Decimal Machin issue).

First Day Covers

7.7.71	2½p., 3p., 5p., 7½p., (*W13/14, W19, W24*)	2·50
23.1.74	3p., 3½p., 5½p., 8p. (*W15/16, W20, W25*)	1·50
6.11.74	4½p. (*W18*)	1·25
14.1.76	6½p., 8½p. (*W22, W26*)	1·25
20.10.76	10p., 11p. (*W28, W31*)	1·25
18.1.78	7p., 9p., 10½p (*W23, W27, W30*)	2·00
23.7.80	12p., 13½p., 15p. (*W32/4*)	2·25
8.4.81	11½p., 14p., 18p., 22p. (*W35, W39, W46, W54*)	2·25
24.2.82	12½p., 15½p., 19½p., 26p. (*W37, W42, W51, W61*)	2·50
27.4.83	16p., 20½p., 28p. (*W43, W53, W63*)	6·00
23.10.84	13p., 17p., 22p., 31p. (*W38, W44, W55, W65*)	2·75
7.1.86	12p. (*W36*)	1·50
6.1.87	18p. (*W47*)	1·50
8.11.88	14p., 19p., 23p., 32p. (*W40, W50, W57, W66*)	2·25
28.11.89	15p., 20p., 24p., 34p. (*W41, W52, W58, W67*)	2·50
4.12.90	17p., 22p., 26p., 37p (*W45, W56, W62, W68*)	3·25
3.12.91	18p., 24p., 28p., 39p. (*W48, W59, W64, W69*)	3·25
25.2.92	Cymru–Wales *se-tenant* pane 18p., (2nd), 24p., (1st), 33p. (*W49a*)	9·00

Presentation Packs

7.7.71	2½p., 3p. (2 bands), 5p., 7½p., (*Nos.* W13/14, W19, W24)	4·25
29.5.74	3p. (1 centre band), 3½p. (2 bands) *or* (1 centre band), 5½p. (2 bands) *or* (1 centre band), 8p. (*Nos.* W15, W16 or W17, W20 *or* W21, W25). The 4½p. (No. W18) was added later	2·50
20.10.76	6½p., 8½p., 10p. (2 bands), 11p. (*Nos.* W22, W26, W28, W31)	2·00
28.10.81	7p., 9p., 10½p., 12p. (photo), 13½p., 15p. (photo), 11½p., 14p. grey-blue, 18p. dp violet, 22p. blue (*Nos.* W23, W27, W30, W32/5, W39, W46, W54)	7·50
3.8.83	10p. (1 centre band), 12½p., 16p., 20½p., 26p. rosine, 28p. dp violet-blue (*Nos.* W29, W37, W43, W53, W61, W63)	8·00
23.10.84	10p. (1 centre band), 13p., 16p., 17p. grey-blue, 22p. yellow-green, 26p. rosine, 28p. dp violet-blue, 31p. (*Nos.* W29, W38, W43a, W44, W55, W61, W63, W65)	11·00
3.3.87	12p. (litho), 13p., 17p., grey-blue, 18p. dp olive-grey, 22p. yellow-green, 26p. rosine, 28p. dp violet-blue, 31p. (*Nos.* W36, W38, W44, W47, W55, W61a, W63a, W65)	10·00

Presentation Packs containing stamps of Northern Ireland, Scotland and Wales are listed after those for Northern Ireland.

(Des J. Matthews after plaster cast by Arnold Machin. Litho Questa)

1993 (7 Dec)–**96**. *Chalk-surfaced paper. P* 15 × 14 (*with one elliptical hole on each vertical side*).

W70	W **4**	19p. bistre (1 centre band)	40	40
W71		19p. bistre (1 band at right) (25.4.95)	2·25	2·25
W72		20p. brt green (1 centre band) (23.7.96)	40	40
W73		25p. red (2 bands)	50	50
W74		26p. red-brown (2 bands) (23.7.96)	50	50
W75		30p. dp olive-grey (2 bands)	60	60
W76		37p. brt mauve (2 bands) (23.7.96)	75	75
W77		41p. grey-brown (2 bands)	90	90
W78		63p. lt emerald (2 bands) (23.7.96)	1·40	1·40

No. W71 only comes from booklets.

First Day Covers

7.12.93	19p., 25p., 30p., 41p. (*W70, W73, W75, W77*)	4·50
23.7.96	20p., 26p., 37p., 63p., (*W72, W74, W76, W78*)	3·25

For Presentation Pack containing stamps of Northern Ireland, Scotland and Wales see after No. NI81 of Northern Ireland.

W **5** Without "p"

(Photo Walsall (20p., 63p.), Harrison or Walsall (26p., 37p.))

1997 (1 July). *Chalk-surfaced paper. P* 15 × 14 (*with one elliptical hole on each vertical side*).

W79	W **5**	20p. brt green (1 centre band)	30	35
W80		26p. chestnut (2 bands)	40	45
W81		37p. brt mauve (2 bands)	60	65
W82		63p. lt emerald (2 bands)	95	1·00

First Day Cover

1.7.97	20p., 26p., 37p., 63p. (*W79/82*)	3·25

Presentation Pack

1.7.97	20p., 26p., 37p., 63p. (*Nos.* W79/82)	2·75

V. GUERNSEY

War Occupation Issues

BISECTS. On 24 December 1940 authority was given, by Post Office notice, that prepayment of penny postage could be effected by using half a British 2d. stamp, diagonally bisected. Such stamps were first used on 27 December 1940.

The 2d. stamps generally available were those of the Postal Centenary issue, 1940 (S.G. 482) and the first colour of the King George VI issue (S.G. 465). These are listed under Nos. 482a and 465b. A number of the 2d. King George V, 1912–22, and of the King George V photogravure stamp (S.G. 442) which were in the hands of philatelists, were also bisected and used.

1

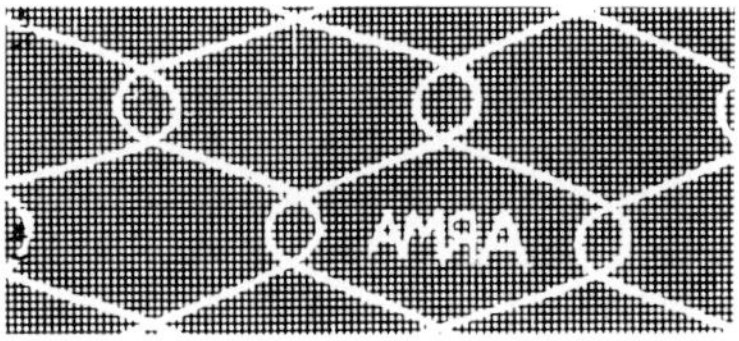

1a Loops (*half actual size*)

(Des E. W. Vaudin. Typo Guernsey Press Co Ltd)

1941–44. *Rouletted.* (a) *White paper. No wmk.*

1	**1**	½d. light green (7.4.41)	2·75	2·00
		a. *Emerald-green* (6.41)	3·25	2·25
		b. *Bluish green* (11.41)	40·00	22·00
		c. *Brt green* (2.42)	24·00	10·00
		d. *Dull green* (9.42)	3·75	3·50
		e. *Olive-green* (2.43)	29·00	18·00
		f. *Pale yellowish green* (7.43 and later) (*shades*)	2·50	2·25
		g. Imperf (pair)	£150	
		h. Imperf between (horiz pair)	£600	
		i. Imperf between (vert pair)	£700	
2		1d. scarlet (18.2.41)	2·00	1·00
		a. *Pale vermilion* (7.43)	2·00	1·50
		b. *Carmine* (1943)	2·50	3·00
		c. Imperf (pair)	£150	75·00
		d. Imperf between (horiz pair)	£600	
		da. Imperf vert (centre stamp of horiz strip of 3)		
		e. Imperf between (vert pair)	£700	
		f. Printed double (scarlet shade)	75·00	
3		2½d. ultramarine (12.4.44)	4·00	4·00
		a. *Pale ultramarine* (7.44)	4·00	4·00
		b. Imperf (pair)	£350	
		c. Imperf between (horiz pair)	£800	
		Set of 3	9·00	7·50

First Day Covers

7.4.41	½d.	6·50
18.2.41	1d.	7·00
12.4.44	2½d.	23·00

(b) *Bluish French bank-note paper. W* **1**a (*sideways*)

4	**1**	½d. bright green (11.3.42)	18·00	19·00
5		1d. scarlet (9.4.42)	9·00	21·00
		Set of 2	27·00	45·00

First Day Covers

11.3.42	½d.	80·00
9.4.42	1d.	45·00

The dates given for the shades of Nos. 1/3 are the months in which they were printed as indicated on the printer's imprints. Others are issue dates.

Regional Issues

2

3

(Des E. A. Piprell. Portrait by Dorothy Wilding Ltd. Photo Harrison & Sons)

1958 (18 Aug)–**67**. *W* **179** *of Great Britain. P* 15 × 14.

6	**2**	2½d. rose-red (8.6.64)	35	40
7	**3**	3d. dp lilac	35	30
		p. One centre phosphor band (24.5.67)	20	20
8		4d. ultramarine (7.2.66)	25	30
		p. Two phosphor bands (24.10.67)	20	20
		Set of 3 (*cheapest*)	70	75

First Day Covers

18.8.58	3d.	17·00
8.6.64	2½d.	22·00
7.2.66	4d.	7·50

For No. 7 in Presentation Pack, see Regional Issues below Wales No. W6.

1968–69. *No wmk. Chalk-surfaced paper. PVA gum**. *One centre phosphor band (Nos. 10/11) or two phosphor bands (others). P* 15 × 14.

9	**3**	4d. pale ultramarine (16.4.68)	10	25
		Ey. Phosphor omitted	40·00	
10		4d. olive-sepia (4.9.68)	15	20
		Ey. Phosphor omitted	40·00	
11		4d. brt vermilion (26.2.69)	15	30
12		5d. royal blue (4.9.68)	15	30
		Set of 4	40	95

First Day Cover

4.9.68	4d., 5d.	1·75

No. 9 was not issued in Guernsey until 22 April.

*PVA Gum. See note after No. 722 of Great Britain.

VI. ISLE OF MAN

Although specifically issued for use in the Isle of Man, these issues were also valid for use throughout Great Britain.

DATES OF ISSUE. The note at the beginning of Northern Ireland also applies here.

Nos. 8/11 and current stamps of Great Britain were withdrawn from sale on the island from 5 July 1973 when the independent postal administration was established but remained valid for use there for a time. They also remained on sale at the Philatelic Sales counters in the United Kingdom until 4 July 1974.

1

2

(Des J. Nicholson. Portrait by Dorothy Wilding Ltd. Photo Harrison)

1958 (18 Aug)–**68**. *W* **179**. *P* 15 × 14.

1	**1**	$2\frac{1}{2}$d. carmine-red (8.6.64)	55	90
2	**2**	3d. dp lilac	20	10
		a. Chalk-surfaced paper (17.5.63)	10·00	8·50
		p. One centre phosphor band (27.6.68)	20	40
3		4d. ultramarine (7.2.66)	1·60	1·25
		p. Two phosphor bands (5.7.67)	20	25
		Set of 3 (cheapest)	75	1·00

First Day Covers

18.8.58	3d.	28·00
8.6.64	$2\frac{1}{2}$d.	28·00
7.2.66	4d.	7·50

No. 2a was released in London sometime after 17 May 1963, this being the date of issue in Douglas.

For No. 2 in Presentation Pack, see Regional Issues below Wales No. W6.

1968–69. *No wmk. Chalk-surfaced paper. PVA gum. One centre phosphor band (Nos. 5/6) or two phosphor bands (others). P* 15 × 14.

4	**2**	4d. blue (24.6.68)	20	25
5		4d. olive-sepia (4.9.68)	20	30
		Ey. Phosphor omitted	20·00	
6		4d. brt vermilion (26.2.69)	50	70
7		5d. royal blue (4.9.68)	50	70
		Ey. Phosphor omitted	£150	
		Set of 4	1·00	1·60

First Day Cover

4.9.68	4d., 5d.	2·00

3

(Des J. Matthews. Portrait after plaster cast by Arnold Machin. Photo Harrison)

1971 (7 July). *Decimal Currency. Chalk-surfaced paper. One centre phosphor band ($2\frac{1}{2}$p.) or two phosphor bands (others). P* 15 × 14.

8	**3**	$2\frac{1}{2}$p. brt magenta	20	15
		Ey. Phosphor omitted	£1500	
9	**3**	3p. ultramarine	20	15
10		5p. reddish violet	50	60
		Ey. Phosphor omitted	£250	
11		$7\frac{1}{2}$p. chestnut	50	75
		Set of 4	1·10	1·25
		Presentation Pack	2·00	

First Day Cover

7.7.71	$2\frac{1}{2}$p., 3p., 5p., $7\frac{1}{2}$p.	2·50

All values exist with PVA gum on ordinary cream paper and the $2\frac{1}{2}$p. and 3p. also on fluorescent white paper.

VII. JERSEY

War Occupation Issues

(Des Major N. V. L. Rybot. Typo *Evening Post*, Jersey)

1941–43. *White paper (thin to thick). No wmk. P* 11.

1	**1**	$\frac{1}{2}$d. brt green (29.1.42)	3·75	3·00
		a. Imperf between (vert pair)	£700	
		b. Imperf between (horiz pair)	£600	
		c. Imperf (pair)	£200	
		d. On greyish paper (1.43)	5·00	5·75
2		1d. scarlet (1.4.41)	4·00	3·00
		a. Imperf between (vert pair)	£700	
		b. Imperf between (horiz pair)	£600	
		c. Imperf (pair)	£225	
		d. On chalk-surfaced paper	40·00	38·00
		e. On greyish paper (1.43)	5·00	5·75

First Day Covers

29.1.42	$\frac{1}{2}$d.	7·00
1.4.41	1d.	7·00

2 Old Jersey Farm

3 Portelet Bay

4 Corbière Lighthouse

5 Elizabeth Castle

6 Mont Orgueil Castle

7 Gathering Vraic (seaweed)

(Des E. Blampied. Eng H. Cortot. Typo French Govt Ptg Works, Paris)

1943–44. *No wmk. P 13½.*

3	**2**	½d. green (1 June)	8·00	7·25
		a. Rough, grey paper (6.10.43)	8·50	8·50
4	**3**	1d. scarlet (1 June)	2·25	1·00
		a. On newsprint (28.2.44)	2·50	2·00
5	**4**	1½d. brown (8 June)	4·00	4·00
6	**5**	2d. orange-yellow (8 June)	5·25	4·00
7	**6**	2½d. blue (29 June)	2·00	1·75
		a. On newsprint (25.2.44)	1·40	2·25
		ba. Thin paper*	£200	
8	**7**	3d. violet (29 June)	1·40	3·75
		Set of 6	20·00	20·00
		First Day Covers (3)		70·00

*On No. 7ba the design shows clearly through the back of the stamp.

Regional Issues

8

9

(Des. E. Blampied (T **8**), W. Gardner (T **9**). Potrait by Dorothy Wilding Ltd. Photo Harrison & Sons)

1958 (18 Aug)–**67**. *W* **179** *of Great Britain. P* 15 × 14.

9	**8**	2½d. carmine-red (8.6.64)	35	60
		a. Imperf three sides (pair)	£2000	
10	**9**	3d. dp lilac	35	30
		p. One centre phosphor band (9.6.67)	20	20
11		4d. ultramarine (7.2.66)	25	30
		p. Two phosphor bands (5.9.67)	20	25
		Set of 3 (cheapest)	60	1·00

First Day Covers

18.8.58	3d.	17·00
8.6.64	2½d.	22·00
7.2.66	4d.	7·50

For No.10 in Presentation Pack, see Regional Issues below Wales No. W6.

1968–69. *No wmk. Chalk-surfaced paper. PVA gum*. One centre phosphor band (4d. values) or two phosphor bands (5d.). P 15 × 14.*

12	**9**	4d. olive-sepia (4.9.68)	20	25
		Ey. Phosphor omitted	£750	
13		4d. brt vermilion (26.2.69)	20	35
14		5d. royal blue (4.9.68)	20	50
		Set of 3	50	1·00

First Day Cover

4.9.68	4d., 5d.	1·75

*PVA Gum. See note after No. 722 of Great Britain.

POSTAGE DUE STAMPS

PERFORATIONS. All postage due stamps to No. D101 are perf 14 × 15.

WATERMARK. The watermark always appears sideways and this is the "normal" listed in this Catalogue for Nos. D1/D68. Varieties occur as follows. The point of identification is which way the top of the crown points, but (where they occur) the disposition of the letters needs to be noted also.

The meaning of the terms is given below: (1) as described and illustrated in the Catalogue, i.e. as read through the front of the stamp, and (2) what is seen during watermark detection when the stamp is face down and the back is under examination.

Watermark	*Crown pointing*	*Letters reading*
	(1) As described	
Sideways	left	upwards
Sideways-inverted	right	downwards
Sideways and reversed	left	downwards, back to front
Sideways-inverted and reversed	right	upwards, back to front
	(2) As detected (stamp face down)	
Sideways	right	upwards, back to front
Sideways-inverted	left	downwards, back to front
Sideways and reversed	right	downwards
Sideways-inverted and reversed	left	upwards

D **1**

D **2**

(Des G. Eve. Typo Somerset House (early trial printings of ½d., 1d., 2d. and 5d.; all printings of 1s.) or Harrison (later printings of all values except 1s.))

1914 (20 Apr)–**22**. *W* **100** *(Simple Cypher) sideways-inverted on 1½d., 4d. and 1s. and sideways on others.*

			Unmtd mint	*Mtd mint*	*Used*
D1	**D 1**	½d. emerald	1·00	50	50
		Wi. Watermark sideways-inverted	1·50	75	75
		Wj. Watermark sideways and reversed	15·00	10·00	12·00
		Wk. Watermark sideways-inverted and reversed			
D2		1d. carmine	1·50	50	50
		a. *Pale carmine*	1·50	75	75
		Wi. Watermark sideways-inverted	1·50	75	75
		Wj. Watermark sideways-inverted and reversed	12·00	10·00	10·00
D3		1½d. chestnut (1922)	£140	70·00	20·00
		Wi. Watermark sideways	95·00	40·00	12·00
D4		2d. agate	1·50	50	70
		Wi. Watermark sideways-inverted	2·25	1·50	1·50
		Wj. Watermark sideways-inverted and reversed	8·00	5·00	5·00
D5		3d. violet (1918)	20·00	2·50	1·00
		a. *Bluish violet*	20·00	3·50	3·50
		Wi. Watermark sideways-inverted	20·00	7·50	2·00
		Wj. Watermark sideways-inverted and reversed			
D6		4d. dull grey-green (12.20)	£125	40·00	5·00
		Wi. Watermark sideways	80·00	10·00	15·00
D7		5d. brownish cinnamon	10·00	5·00	3·25
		Wi. Watermark sideways-inverted	30·00	15·00	15·00
D8		1s. brt blue (1915)	£125	40·00	5·00
		a. *Dp brt blue*	£125	40·00	5·00
		Wi. Watermark sideways	70·00	20·00	20·00
		Wj. Watermark sideways-inverted and reversed			
		Set of 8	£250	90·00	28·00

The 1d. is known bisected and used to make up a 1$\frac{1}{2}$d. rate on understamped letters from Ceylon (1921) or Tasmania (1922, Palmers Green), and to pay $\frac{1}{2}$d. on a returned printed paper matter envelope at Kilburn, London (1923). The 2d. was bisected and used as 1d. at Christchurch, Malvern, Streatham and West Kensington all in 1921.

1924. *As 1914–23, but on thick chalk-surfaced paper.*

D9	D 1	1d. carmine	7·50	2·25	3·50

(Typo Waterlow and (from 1934) Harrison)

1924–31. *W* **111** (*Block Cypher*) *sideways.*

D10	D 1	$\frac{1}{2}$d. emerald (6.25)	2·50	90	75
		Wi. Watermark sideways-inverted	5·00	2·50	1·25
D11		1d. carmine (4.25)	2·50	60	60
		Wi. Watermark sideways-inverted	—	—	10·00
D12		1$\frac{1}{2}$d. chestnut (10.24)	90·00	40·00	18·00
		Wi. Watermark sideways-inverted	—	—	30·00
D13		2d. agate (7.24)	9·00	1·00	40
		Wi. Watermark sideways-inverted	—	—	10·00
D14		3d. dull violet (10.24)	10·00	1·50	40
		a. Printed on gummed side	£100	60·00	†
		b. Experimental paper W **111a**	50·00	35·00	30·00
		Wi. Watermark sideways-inverted	9·00	4·00	1·50
D15		4d. dull grey-green (10.24)	32·00	13·00	3·00
		Wi. Watermark sideways-inverted	35·00	15·00	25·00
D16		5d. brownish cinnamon (1.31)	65·00	29·00	22·00
D17		1s. dp blue (9.24)	16·00	8·50	75
		Wi. Watermark sideways-inverted			
D18	D 2	2s. 6d. purple/*yellow* (5.24)	£170	40·00	2·00
		Wi. Watermark sideways-inverted			
		Set of 9	£350	£120	45·00

The 2d. is known bisected to make up the 2$\frac{1}{2}$d. rate at Perranwell Station, Cornwall, in 1932.

1936–37. *W* **125** (E 8 R) *sideways.*

			Unmtd mint	*Used*
D19	D 1	$\frac{1}{2}$d. emerald (6.37)	7·50	7·00
D20		1d. carmine (5.37)	1·50	1·50
D21		2d. agate (5.37)	7·00	9·00
D22		3d. dull violet (3.37)	1·50	1·60
D23		4d. dull grey-green (12.36)	23·00	23·00
D24		5d. brownish cinnamon (11.36)	40·00	22·00
		a. *Yellow-brown* (1937)	16·00	21·00
D25		1s. dp blue (12.36)	11·00	7·00
D26	D 2	2s. 6d. purple/*yellow* (5.37)	£250	8·00
		Set of 8	£300	70·00

The 1d. is known bisected (Solihull, 3 July 1937).

1937–38. *W* **127** (G VI R) *sideways.*

D27	D 1	$\frac{1}{2}$d. emerald (5.38)	8·00	4·50
D28		1d. carmine (5.38)	2·50	50
		Wi. Watermark sideways-inverted	£125	
D29		2d. agate (5.38)	2·50	50
		Wi. Watermark sideways-inverted	10·00	
D30		3d. violet (12.37)	12·00	90
		Wi. Watermark sideways-inverted	25·00	
D31		4d. dull grey-green (9.37)	65·00	10·00
		Wi. Watermark sideways-inverted	£125	
D32		5d. yellow-brown (11.38)	12·00	1·50
		Wi. Watermark sideways-inverted	35·00	
D33		1s. dp blue (10.37)	60·00	1·50
		Wi. Watermark sideways-inverted	55·00	
D34	D 2	2s. 6d. purple/*yellow* (9.38)	60·00	2·50
		Set of 8	£200	19·00

The 2d. is known bisected in June 1951 (Boreham Wood, Harpenden and St. Albans) and on 30 October 1954 (Harpenden).

DATES OF ISSUE. The dates for Nos. D35/68 are those on which stanps were first issued by the Supplies Department to postmasters.

1951–52. *Colours changed and new value* (1$\frac{1}{2}$*d.*). *W* **127** (G VI R) *sideways.*

D35	D 1	$\frac{1}{2}$d. orange (18.9.51)	1·00	2·50
D36		1d. violet-blue (6.6.51)	1·50	1·25
		Wi. Watermark sideways-inverted		
D37		1$\frac{1}{2}$d. green (11.2.52)	1·75	2·50
		Wi. Watermark sideways-inverted	8·50	
D38		4d. blue (14.8.51)	30·00	11·00
D39		1s. ochre (6.12.51)	35·00	13·00
		Wi. Watermark sideways-inverted		
		Set of 5	60·00	22·00

The 1d. is known bisected (Dorking, 1952, and Camberley, 6 April 1954).

1954–55. *W* **153** (*Mult Tudor Crown and* E 2 R) *sideways.*

D40	D 1	$\frac{1}{2}$d. orange (8.6.55)	6·00	4·50
		Wi. Watermark sideways-inverted	10·00	
D41		2d. agate (28.7.55)	4·00	4·00
		Wi. Watermark sideways-inverted		
D42		3d. violet (4.5.55)	50·00	32·00
D43		4d. blue (14.7.55)	18·00	19·00
		a. Imperf (pair)	£225	
D44		5d. yellow-brown (19.5.55)	25·00	9·50
D45	D 2	2s. 6d. purple/*yellow* (11.54)	£100	3·00
		Wi. Watermark sideways-inverted		
		Set of 6	£190	65·00

1955–57. *W* **165** (*Mult St. Edward's Crown and* E 2 R) *sideways.*

D46	D 1	$\frac{1}{2}$d. orange (16.7.56)	1·25	2·25
		Wi. Watermark sideways-inverted	10·00	
D47		1d. violet-blue (7.6.56)	5·50	1·50
D48		1$\frac{1}{2}$d. green (13.2.56)	5·50	5·00
		Wi. Watermark sideways-inverted	12·00	
D49		2d. agate (22.5.56)	40·00	3·25
D50		3d. violet (5.3.56)	6·00	1·25
		Wi. Watermark sideways-inverted	25·00	
D51		4d. blue (24.4.56)	21·00	3·75
		Wi. Watermark sideways-inverted	30·00	
D52		5d. brown-ochre (23.3.56)	32·00	2·00
D53		1s. ochre (22.11.55)	70·00	2·00
		Wi. Watermark sideways-inverted		
D54	D 2	2s. 6d. purple/*yellow* (28.6.57)	£140	8·00
		Wi. Watermark sideways-inverted		
D55		5s. scarlet/*yellow* (25.11.55)	80·00	25·00
		Wi. Watermark sideways-inverted		
		Set of 10	£350	48·00

The 1d. is known bisected in June 1957 (London S.E.D.O.), the 2d. in June 1956, the 3d. in April/May 1957 (London S.E.D.O.) and the 4d. in April 1957 (Poplar).

1959–63. *W* **179** (*Mult St. Edward's Crown*) *sideways.*

D56	D 1	$\frac{1}{2}$d. orange (18.10.61)	10	1·00
		Wi. Watermark sideways-inverted	1·50	
D57		1d. violet-blue (9.5.60)	10	50
		Wi. Watermark sideways-inverted	15·00	
D58		1$\frac{1}{2}$d. green (5.10.60)	90	2·75
D59		2d. agate (14.9.59)	1·25	50
		Wi. Watermark sideways-inverted	45·00	
D60		3d. violet (24.3.59)	40	30
		Wi. Watermark sideways-inverted	10·00	
D61		4d. blue (17.12.59)	40	30
		Wi. Watermark sideways-inverted	30·00	
D62		5d. yellow-brown (6.11.61)	45	75
		Wi. Watermark sideways-inverted	5·00	
D63		6d. purple (29.3.62)	60	30
		Wi. Watermark sideways-inverted	35·00	

D64	D **1**	1s. ochre (11.4.60)	1·40	30
		Wi. Watermark sideways-inverted	5·00	
D65	D **2**	2s. 6d. purple/*yellow* (11.5.61)	4·25	45
		Wi. Watermark sideways-inverted	7·50	
D66		5s. scarlet/*yellow* (8.5.61)	8·00	1·00
		Wi. Watermark sideways-inverted	12·00	
D67		10s. blue/*yellow* (2.9.63)	10·00	5·00
		Wi. Watermark sideways-inverted	30·00	
D68		£1 black/*yellow* (2.9.63)	45·00	8·00
		Set of 13	65·00	19·00

Whiter paper. The note after No. 586 also applies to Postage Due stamps.

The 1d. is known bisected (Newbury, Dec. 1962 and Mar. 1963).

1968–69. *Typo. No wmk. Chalk-surfaced paper.*

D69	D **1**	2d. agate (11.4.68)	20	60
		Ev. PVA gum (26.11.68)	75	
D70		3d. violet (9.9.68)	25	60
D71		4d. blue (6.5.68)	25	60
		Ev. PVA gum	£1500	
D72		5d. orange-brown (3.1.69)	5·00	6·00
D73		6d. purple (9.9.68)	60	90
D74		1s. ochre (19.11.68)	2·00	1·40
		Set of 6	7·50	9·00

The 2d. and 4d. exist with gum arabic and PVA gum; the remainder with PVA gum only.

1968–69. *Photo. No wmk. Chalk-surfaced paper. PVA gum.*

D75	D **1**	4d. blue (12.6.69)	5·00	5·00
D76		8d. red (3.10.68)	1·00	1·00

Nos. D75/6 are smaller, $21\frac{1}{2} \times 17\frac{1}{2}$mm.

D **3**

D **4**

(Des J. Matthews. Photo Harrison)

1970 (17 June)–**75.** *Decimal Currency. Chalk-surfaced paper.*

D77	D **3**	½p. turquoise-blue (15.2.71)	10	20
D78		1p. dp reddish purple (15.2.71)	10	15
D79		2p. myrtle-green (15.2.71)	10	15
D80		3p. ultramarine (15.2.71)	15	15
D81		4p. yellow-brown (15.2.71)	15	15
D82		5p. violet (15.2.71)	20	20
D83		7p. red-brown (21.8.74)	35	45
D84	D **4**	10p. carmine	30	20
D85		11p. slate-green (18.6.75)	60	60
D86		20p. olive-brown	60	50
D87		50p. ultramarine	1·50	50
D88		£1 black	3·50	75
D89		£5 orange-yellow and black (2.4.73)	35·00	2·00
		Set of 13	38·00	5·00
		Presentation Pack (Nos. D77/82, D84, D86/8, (3.11.71)	11·00	
		Presentation Pack (Nos. D77/88) (30.3.77)	6·00	

Later printings were on fluorescent white paper, some with dextrin added to the PVA gum (see notes after X1058).

D **5**

D **6**

(Des Sedley Place Design Ltd. Photo Harrison)

1982 (9 June). *Chalk-surfaced paper.*

D 90	D **5**	1p. lake	10	10
D 91		2p. brt blue	20	10
D 92		3p. dp mauve	10	15
D 93		4p. dp blue	10	20
D 94		5p. sepia	20	20
D 95	D **6**	10p. lt brown	20	25
D 96		20p. olive-green	40	30
D 97		25p. dp greenish blue	50	70
D 98		50p. grey-black	1·00	75
D 99		£1 red	2·00	50
D100		£2 turquoise-blue	4·50	50
D101		£5 dull orange	12·00	50
		Set of 12	19·00	3·75
		Set of 12 Gutter Pairs	40·00	
		Presentation Pack	20·00	

D **7**

(Des Sedley Place Design Ltd. Litho Questa)

1994 (15 Feb). *P* 15 × 14 (*with one elliptical hole on each vertical side*).

D102	D **7**	1p. red, yellow & black	10	10
D103		2p. magenta, purple & black	10	10
D104		5p. yellow, red-brown & black	10	10
D105		10p. yellow, emerald & black	15	20
D106		20p. blue-green, violet & black	30	35
D107		25p. cerise, rosine & black	40	45
D108		£1 violet, magenta & black	1·50	1·60
D109		£1.20, greenish blue, blue-green & black	1·75	1·90
D110		£5 greenish black, blue-green & black	7·50	7·75
		Set of 9	11·50	12·50
		First Day Cover		12·50
		Presentation Pack	12·00	

Special First Day of Issue Postmark

London EC3 .... 16·00

Following changes in the method of collecting money due on unpaid or underpaid mail the use of postage due stamps was restricted from April 1995 to mail addressed to business customers and to Customs/V.A.T. charges levied by the Royal Mail on behalf of the Customs and Excise.

OFFICIAL STAMPS

In 1840 the 1d. black (Type **1**), with "V R" in the upper corners, was prepared for official use, but was never issued for postal purposes. Obliterated specimens are those which were used for experimental trials of obliterating inks, or those that passed through the post by oversight.

V **1**

1840. *Prepared for use but not issued; "V" "R" in upper corners. Imperf.*

			Un	*Used*	*Used on cover*
V1	V **1**	1d. black	£6000	£6000	

The following Official stamps would be more correctly termed Departmental stamps as they were exclusively for the use of certain government departments. Until 1882 official mail used ordinary postage stamps purchased at post offices, the cash being refunded once a quarter. Later the government departments obtained Official stamps by requisition.

Official stamps were on sale to the public for a short time at Somerset House but they were not sold from post offices. The system of only supplying the Government departments with stamps was open to abuse so that all official stamps were withdrawn on 13 May 1904.

OVERPRINTS, PERFORATIONS, WATERMARKS. All official stamps were overprinted by Thomas De La Rue & Co. and are perf 14. Except for the 5s., and 10s. on Anchor, they are on Crown watermarked paper unless otherwise stated.

INLAND REVENUE

These stamps were used by revenue officials in the provinces, mail to and from Head Office passing without a stamp. The London Office used these stamps only for foreign mail.

I.R.

OFFICIAL

(O **1**)

I. R.

OFFICIAL

(O **2**)

Optd with Types O **1** *(½d. to 1s.) or* O **2** *(others)*

1882–1901. *Stamps of Queen Victoria. (a) Issues of 1880–81.*

			Un	*★ Used*	*Used on cover*
O1	½d.	dp green (1.11.82)	12·00	3·00	45·00
O2	½d.	pale green	12·00	3·00	
O3	1d.	lilac (Die II) (1.10.82)	1·50	65	12·00
	a.	Optd in blue-black	60·00	35·00	
	b.	"OFFICIAL" omitted	—	£2250	
	Wi.	Watermark inverted	—	£600	
O4	6d.	grey (Plate 18) (3.11.82)	75·00	20·00	

No. O3 with the lines of the overprint transposed is an essay.

(b) Issues of 1884–88.

			Un	*★ Used*	*Used on cover*
O 5	½d.	slate-blue (8.5.85)	25·00	15·00	85·00
O 6	2½d.	lilac (12.3.85)	£120	40·00	£600
O 7	1s.	dull green (12.3.85)	£2500	£450	
O 8	5s.	rose (*blued paper*) (12.3.85)	£2750	£475	
O 9	5s.	rose (3.90)	£1300	£400	
	a.	Raised stop after "R"	£1600	£400	
	b.	Optd in blue-black	£2000	£450	
O 9*c*	10s.	cobalt (*blued paper*) (12.3.85)	£5000	£800	
O 9*d*	10s.	ultramarine (*blued paper*) (12.3.85)	£5000	£1600	
O10	10s.	ultramarine (3.90)	£2500	£525	
	a.	Raised stop after "R"	£3250	£550	
	b.	Optd in blue-black	£3500	£700	
O11	£1	brown-lilac (watermark Crowns) (12.3.85)	£20000		
	a.	Frame broken	£25000		
O12	£1	brown-lilac (watermark Orbs) (3.90)	£27500		
	a.	Frame broken	£30000		

(c) Issues of 1887–92

			Un	*★ Used*	*Used on cover*
O13	½d.	vermilion (15.5.88)	1·50	50	25·00
	a.	Without "I.R."	£2000		
	b.	Imperf	£1200		
	c.	Opt double (imperf)	£1500		
O14	2½d.	purple/*blue* (2.92)	50·00	4·00	£200
O15	1s.	dull green (9.89)	£225	25·00	£1000
O16	£1	green (6.92)	£3750	£500	
	a.	No stop after "R"	—	£850	
	b.	Frame broken	£6000	£1000	

Nos. O3, O13, O15 and O16 may be found with two varieties of overprint, *thin* letters, and from 1894 printings, *thicker* letters.

(d) Issues of 1887 and 1900

			Un	*★ Used*	*Used on cover*
O17	½d.	blue-green (4.01)	4·00	3·00	95·00
O18	6d.	purple/*rose-red* (1.7.01)	£100	22·00	
O19	1s.	green and carmine (12.01)	£800	£175	
★O1/19		**For well-centred, lightly used**		**+35%**	

1902–04. *Stamps of King Edward VII. Ordinary paper.*

			Un	*★ Used*	*Used on cover*
O20	½d.	blue-green (4.2.02)	17·00	1·50	90·00
O21	1d.	scarlet (4.2.02)	10·00	70	45·00
O22	2½d.	ultramarine (19.2.02)	£450	90·00	
O23	6d.	pale dull purple (14.3.04)	£85000	£65000	
O24	1s.	dull green & carmine (29.4.02)	£550	95·00	
O25	5s.	brt carmine (29.4.02)	£4000	£1500	
	a.	Raised stop after "R"	£4750	£1600	
O26	10s.	ultramarine (29.4.02)	£15000	£9500	
	a.	Raised stop after "R"	£18000	£12000	
O27	£1	blue-green (29.4.02)	£12000	£7000	

OFFICE OF WORKS

These were issued to Head and Branch (local) offices in London and to Branch (local) offices at Birmingham, Bristol, Edinburgh, Glasgow, Leeds, Liverpool, Manchester and Southampton. The overprints on stamps of value 2d. and upwards were created later in 1902, the 2d. for registration fees and the rest for overseas mail.

O. W.

OFFICIAL

(O **3**)

Optd with Type O **3**

1896 (24 Mar)–**02**. *Stamps of Queen Victoria.*

		Un	Used	★ Used on cover
O31	$\frac{1}{2}$d. vermilion	90·00	40·00	£250
O32	$\frac{1}{2}$d. blue-green (2.02)	£150	75·00	
O33	1d. lilac (Die II)	£150	40·00	£275
O34	5d. dull purple & blue (II) (29.4.02)	£800	£175	
O35	10d. dull purple & carmine (28.5.02)	£1400	£275	

1902 (11 Feb)–**03**. *Stamps of King Edward VII. Ordinary paper.*

		Un	Used	Used on cover
O36	$\frac{1}{2}$d. blue-green (8.02)	£350	80·00	£850
O37	1d. scarlet	£350	80·00	£200
O38	2d. yellowish green & carmine-red (29.4.02)	£600	80·00	£1100
O39	$2\frac{1}{2}$d. ultramarine (29.4.02)	£700	£250	
O40	10d. dull purple & carmine (28.5.03)	£5000	£1500	
★O31/40	**For well-centred, lightly used**		**+25%**	

ARMY

Letters to and from the War Office in London passed without postage. The overprinted stamps were distributed to District and Station Paymasters nationwide, including Cox and Co., the Army Agents, who were paymasters to the Household Division.

(O 4)	(O 5)	(O 6)
ARMY OFFICIAL	ARMY OFFICIAL	ARMY OFFICIAL

1896 (1 Sept)–**01**. *Stamps of Queen Victoria optd with Type O* **4** *($\frac{1}{2}$d., 1d.) or O* **5** *($2\frac{1}{2}$d., 6d.).*

O41	$\frac{1}{2}$d. vermilion	1·50	75	25·00
	a. "OFFICIAI" (R.13/7)	35·00	16·00	
	b. Lines of opt transposed	£1000		
	Wi. Watermark inverted	£170	75·00	
O42	$\frac{1}{2}$d. blue-green (6.00)	1·75	4·00	
	Wi. Watermark inverted	£130	60·00	
O43	1d. lilac (Die II)	1·50	75	35·00
	a. "OFFICAI" (R.13/7)	35·00	20·00	
O44	$2\frac{1}{2}$d. purple/*blue*	4·00	3·00	£300
O45	6d. purple/*rose-red* (20.9.01)	16·00	10·00	£500

Nos. O41a and O43a occur in sheets overprinted by Forme 1.

1902-03. *Stamps of King Edward VII optd with Type O* **4** *(Nos. O48/50) or Type O* **6** *(O52). Ordinary paper.*

O48	$\frac{1}{2}$d. blue-green (11.2.02)	2·00	65	60·00
O49	1d. scarlet (11.2.02)	1·50	55	60·00
	a. "ARMY" omitted	†	—	
O50	6d. pale dull purple (23.8.02)	70·00	32·00	
O52	6d. pale dull purple (12.03)	£850	£300	

GOVERNMENT PARCELS

These stamps were issued to all departments, including Head Office, for use on parcels weighing over 3 lb. Below this weight government parcels were sent by letter post to avoid the 55% of the postage paid from accruing to the railway companies, as laid down by parcel-post regulations. Most government parcels stamps suffered heavy postmarks in use.

GOVT
PARCELS

(O 7)

Optd as Type O **7**

1883 (1 Aug)–**86**. *Stamps of Queen Victoria.*

		Un	★ Used
O61	$1\frac{1}{2}$d. lilac (1.5.86)	£100	25·00
	a. No dot under "T"	£130	28·00
	b. Dot to left of "T"	£100	28·00
O62	6d. dull green (1.5.86)	£800	£275
O63	9d. dull green	£650	£180
O64	1s. orange-brown (watermark Crown, Pl 13)	£425	70·00
	a. No dot under "T"	£475	80·00
	b. Dot to left of "T"	£475	80·00
O64c	1s. orange-brown (Pl 14)	£750	£110
	ca. No dot under "T"	£825	£100
	cb. Dot to left of "T"		

1887–90. *Stamps of Queen Victoria.*

O65	$1\frac{1}{2}$d. dull purple & pale green (29.10.87)	14·00	2·00
	a. No dot under "T"	18·00	6·00
	b. Dot to right of "T"	16·00	5·00
	c. Dot to left of "T"	16·00	5·00
O66	6d. purple/*rose-red* (19.12.87)	28·00	10·00
	a. No dot under "T"	30·00	12·00
	b. Dot to right of "T"	30·00	12·00
	c. Dot to left of "T"	30·00	11·00
O67	9d. dull purple & blue (21.8.88)	55·00	15·00
O68	1s. dull green (25.3.90)	£120	70·00
	a. No dot under "T"	£140	75·00
	b. Dot to right of "T"	£140	75·00
	c. Dot to left of "T"	£160	80·00
	d. Optd in blue-black		

1891–1900 *Stamps of Queen Victoria.*

O69	1d. lilac (Die II) (18.6.97)	28·00	8·00
	a. No dot under "T"	30·00	20·00
	b. Dot to left of "T"	30·00	20·00
	c. Opt inverted	£1000	£850
	d. Ditto. Dot to left of "T"	£900	£500
	Wi. Watermark inverted	—	75·00
O70	2d. grey-green & carmine (24.10.91)	45·00	7·00
	a. No dot under "T"	50·00	8·00
	b. Dot to left of "T"	50·00	9·00
O71	$4\frac{1}{2}$d. green & carmine (29.9.92)	£100	75·00
	b. Dot to right of "T"		
	Wi. Watermark inverted		
O72	1s. green & carmine (11.00)	£160	50·00
	a. Opt inverted	†	£4000
★O61/72	**For well-centred lightly used**		**+100%**

1902. *Stamps of King Edward VII. Ordinary paper.*

O74	1d. scarlet (30.10.02)	17·00	6·00
O75	2d. yellowish green & carmine-red (29.4.02)	65·00	18·00
O76	6d. pale dull purple (19.2.02)	£100	18·00
	a. Opt double, one albino	£4500	
O77	9d. dull purple & ultramarine (28.8.02)	£225	50·00
O78	1s. dull green & carmine (17.12.02)	£350	85·00

The "no dot under T" variety occured on R.12/3 and 20/2. The "dot to left of T" comes four times in the sheet on R.2/7, 6/7, 7/9 and 12/9. The best example of the "dot to right of T" is on R.20/1. All three varieties were corrected around 1897.

BOARD OF EDUCATION

BOARD

OF

EDUCATION

(O **8**)

Optd with Type O **8**

1902 (19 Feb). *Stamps of Queen Victoria.*

		Un	Used	Used on cover
O81	5d. dull purple & blue (II)	£575	£120	
O82	1s. green & carmine	£1000	£400	

1902 (19 Feb)–**04** *Stamps of King Edward VII. Ordinary paper.*

O83	½d. blue-green	20·00	8·00	£275
O84	1d. scarlet	20·00	7·00	£300
O85	2½d. ultramarine	£550	60·00	
O86	5d. dull purple & ultramarine (6.2.04)	£2250	£1000	
O87	1s. dull green & carmine (23.12.02)	£40000	£30000	

ROYAL HOUSEHOLD

R.H.

OFFICIAL

(O **9**)

1902. *Stamps of King Edward VII optd with Type O* **9**. *Ordinary paper.*

O91	½d. blue-green (29.4.02)	£150	95·00	£600
O92	1d. scarlet (19.2.02)	£130	85·00	£400

ADMIRALTY

ADMIRALTY OFFICIAL (O **10**)

ADMIRALTY OFFICIAL (O **11**) (with different "M")

1903 (1 Apr). *Stamps of King Edward VII optd with Type O* **10**. *Ordinary paper.*

O101	½d. blue-green	10·00	4·00	
O102	1d. scarlet	5·00	2·50	£200
O103	1½d. dull purple & green	60·00	45·00	
O104	2d. yellowish green & carmine-red	£110	55·00	
O105	2½d. ultramarine	£130	45·00	
O106	3d. purple/*yellow*	£110	40·00	

1903–04. *Stamps of King Edward VII optd with Type O* **11**. *Ordinary paper.*

O107	½d. blue-green (9.03)	9·00	5·00	£300
O108	1d. scarlet (12.03)	8·00	4·50	60·00
O109	1½d. dull purple & green (2.04)	£220	85·00	
O110	2d. yellowish green & carmine-red (3.04)	£425	£110	
O111	2½d. ultramarine (3.04)	£550	£300	
O112	3d. dull purple/*orange-yellow* (12.03)	£375	95·00	

Stamps of various issues perforated with a Crown and initials ("H.M.O.W.", "O.W.", "B.T." or "S.O.") or with initials only ("H.M.S.O." or "D.S.I.R.") have also been used for official purposes, but these are outside the scope of this catalogue.

POSTAL FISCAL STAMPS

PRICES. Prices in the used column are for stamps with genuine postal cancellations dated from the time when they were authorised for use as postage stamps. Beware of stamps with fiscal cancellations removed and fraudulent postmarks applied.

VALIDITY. The 1d. surface-printed stamps were authorised for postal use from 1 June 1881 and at the same time the 1d. postage issue, No. 166, was declared valid for fiscal purposes. The 3d. and 6d. values together with the embossed issues were declared valid for postal purposes by another Act effective from 1 January 1883.

SURFACE-PRINTED ISSUES

(Typo Thomas De La Rue & Co.)

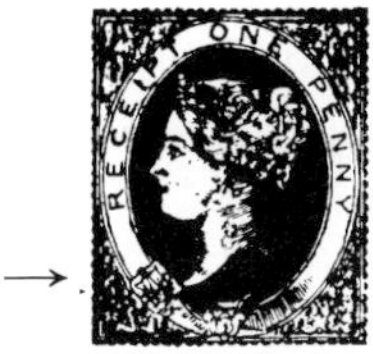

F **1** Rectangular Buckle

F **2**

F **3** Octagonal Buckle

F **4**

F **5** Double-lined Anchor

F **6** Single-lined Anchor

1853–57. P $15\frac{1}{2} \times 15$. (a) *Wmk* F **5** (*inverted*) (1853–55).

			Un	Used	*Used on cover*
F1	F **1**	1d. lt blue (10.10.53)	15·00	18·00	80·00
F2	F **2**	1d. ochre (10.53)	60·00	40·00	£175
		a. *Tête-bêche* (in block of four)	£8000		
F3	F **3**	1d. pale turquoise-blue (12.53)	20·00	18·00	£140
		Wi. Watermark upright	55·00	40·00	
F4		1d. lt blue/*blue* (12.53)	40·00	25·00	£160
		Wi. Watermark upright	90·00	90·00	
F5	F **4**	1d. reddish lilac/*blue glazed paper* (25.3.55)	60·00	14·00	£110
		Wi. Watermark upright	90·00	30·00	

Only one example is known of No. F2a outside the National Postal Museum and the Royal Collection.

(b) *Wmk* F **6** (1856–57)

F6	F **4**	1d. reddish lilac (*shades*)	5·50	4·00	80·00
		Wi. Watermark inverted	90·00		
F7		1d. reddish lilac/*bluish* (*shades*) (1857)	5·50	4·00	80·00

INLAND REVENUE

(F **7**)

1860 (3 Apr). *No.* F7 *optd with Type* F **7**, *in red.*

F8	F **4**	1d. dull reddish lilac/*blue*	£400	£325	£550
		Wj. Wmk reversed			

BLUE PAPER. In the following issues we no longer distinguish between bluish and white paper. There is a range of papers from white or greyish to bluish.

F **8**

F **9**

F **10**

1860–67. *Bluish to white paper.* P $15\frac{1}{2} \times 15$. (a) *Wmk* F **6** (1860).

F 9	F **8**	1d. reddish lilac (May)	6·00	6·00	80·00
		Wi. Watermark inverted	£100		
F10	F **9**	3d. reddish lilac (June)	£250	90·00	£175
F11	F **10**	6d. reddish lilac (Oct)	£100	75·00	£200
		Wi. Watermark inverted	£150	95·00	
		Wj. Watermark reversed	£140	95·00	

(b) *W* **40**. (*Anchor 16mm high*) (1864)

F12	F **8**	1d. pale reddish lilac (Nov)	4·75	4·75	65·00
F13	F **9**	3d. pale reddish lilac	90·00	70·00	£160
F14	F **10**	6d. pale reddish lilac	90·00	70·00	£160
		Wi. Watermark inverted	£175		

(c) *W* **40** (*Anchor 18mm high*) (1867)

F15	F **8**	1d. reddish lilac	13·00	6·00	£130
F16	F **9**	3d. reddish lilac	70·00	65·00	£175
F17	F **10**	6d. reddish lilac	80·00	45·00	£170

For stamps perf 14, see Nos. F24/7.

F 11

F 12

Four Dies of Type F 12

Die 1. Corner ornaments small and either joined or broken; heavy shading under chin

Die 2. Ornaments small and always broken; clear line of shading under chin

Die 3. Ornaments larger and joined; line of shading under chin extended half way down neck

Die 4. Ornaments much larger; straight line of shading continued to bottom of neck

1867–81. *White to bluish paper. P* 14. (*a*) *W* **47** (*Small Anchor*).

F18	F **11**	1d. purple (1.9.67)	8·00	5·00	60·00
		Wi. Watermark inverted			
F19	F **12**	1d. purple (Die I) (6.68)	1·75	1·50	40·00
		Wi. Watermark inverted	50·00		
F20		1d. purple (Die 2) (6.76)	10·00	10·00	£180
F21		1d. purple (Die 3) (3.77)	4·00	4·00	75·00
F22		1d. purple (Die 4) (7.78)	3·00	2·50	65·00
		(*b*) *W* **48** (*Orb*)			
F23	F **12**	1d. purple (Die 4) (1.81)	2·00	1·50	40·00
		Wi. Watermark inverted	50·00		

1881. *White to bluish paper. P* 14.

		(*a*) *W* **40** (*Anchor 18mm high*) (Jan)			
F24	F **9**	3d. reddish lilac	£350	£225	£350
F25	F **10**	6d. reddish lilac	£190	75·00	£175
		(*b*) *W* **40** (*Anchor 20mm high*) (May)			
F26	F **9**	3d. reddish lilac	£275	70·00	£175
F27	F **10**	6d. reddish lilac	£150	90·00	£275

ISSUES EMBOSSED IN COLOUR

(Made at Somerset House)

The embossed stamps were struck from dies not appropriated to any special purpose on paper which had the words "INLAND REVENUE" previously printed, and thus became available for payment of any duties for which no special stamps had been provided.

The die letters are included in the embossed designs and holes were drilled for the insertion of plugs showing figures indicating dates of striking.

F 13

F 14

(F **15**)

(F **16**)

1860 (3 Apr)–**71**. *Types* F **13**/**14** *and similar types embossed on bluish paper. Underprint Type* F **15**. *No wmk. Imperf.*

		Un	*Used*
F28	2d. pink (Die A) (1.1.71)	£140	£140
F29	3d. pink (Die C)	£100	95·00
	a. *Tête-bêche* (vert pair)	£1200	
F30	3d. pink (Die D)	£350	
F31	6d. pink (Die T)	£700	

F32	6d. pink (Die U)	£100	90·00
	a. *Tête-bêche* (vert pair)	£1400	
F33	9d. pink (Die C) (1.1.71)	£250	
F34	1s. pink (Die E) (28.6.61)	£350	£150
F35	1s. pink (Die F) (28.6.61)	£125	£100
	a. *Tête-bêche* (vert pair)	£600	
F36	2s. pink (Die K) (6.8.61)	£275	£175
F37	2s. 6d. pink (Die N) (28.6.61)	£850	
F38	2s. 6d. pink (Die O) (28.6.61)	85·00	85·00

1861–71. *As last but perf* $12\frac{1}{2}$.

F39	2d. pink (Die A) (8.71)	£250	£130
F40	3d. pink (Die C)		
F41	3d. pink (Die D)		
F42	9d. pink (Die C) (8.71)	£275	£140
F43	1s. pink (Die E) (8.71)	£200	£130
F44	1s. pink (Die F) (8.71)	£180	£100
F45	2s. 6d. pink (Die O) (8.71)	£120	65·00

1874 (Nov). *Types as before embossed on white paper. Underprint Type* F **16**, *in green. W* **47** *(Small Anchor). P* $12\frac{1}{2}$.

F46	2d. pink (Die A)	—	£175
F47	9d. pink (Die C)		
F48	1s. pink (Die F)	£190	£100
F49	2s. 6d. pink (Die O)	—	£150

1875 (Nov)–**80**. *As last but colour changed and on white or bluish paper.*

F50	2d. vermilion (Die A) (1880)	£275	£100
F51	9d. vermilion (Die C) (1876)	£275	£150
F52	1s. vermilion (Die E)	£175	75·00
F53	1s. vermilion (Die F)	£175	75·00
F54	2s. 6d. vermilion (Die O) (1878)	£225	£100

1882 (Oct). *As last but W* **48** *(Orbs).*

F55	2d. vermilion (Die A)		
F56	9d. vermilion (Die C)		
F57	1s. vermilion (Die E)		
F58	2s. 6d. vermilion (Die O)	£500	£250

The sale of Inland Revenue stamps up to the 2s. value ceased from 30 December 1882 and stocks were called in and destroyed. The 2s. 6d. value remained on sale until 2 July 1883 when it was replaced by the 2s. 6d. "Postage & Revenue" stamps. Inland Revenue stamps still in the hands of the public continued to be accepted for revenue and postal purposes.

POSTMASTER AND U.P.U. SPECIMEN OVERPRINTS

At various times since 1847 the British Post Office, or its printers, has applied "SPECIMEN" or "CANCELLED" overprints to certain stamp issues.

Many of these overprints were purely intended for internal record purposes, but some had a wider use connected to the postal service. Between 1847 and 1873 the G.P.O. circulated examples of new stamps overprinted "SPECIMEN" to its postmasters and from 1879 similar overprints were applied to samples forwarded to the Universal Postal Union for distribution to member administrations. After 1892 such U.P.U. overprints were restricted to stamps with a face value of 1 shilling or above and they were discontinued altogether after March 1948.

In the listings below Types P **1** to P **6** are postmaster specimens and the remainder for the U.P.U.

For a complete listing of all other "SPECIMEN" overprints see the *Great Britain Specialised Catalogue*.

SPECIMEN	SPECIMEN (vertical)	SPECIMEN
P **1**	P **3**	P **4**
SPECIMEN	SPECIMEN	SPECIMEN
P **5**	P **6**	P **9**
SPECIMEN	SPECIMEN	SPECIMEN
P **16**	P **23**	P **26**
	SPECIMEN	
	P **32**	

1847–54. *Embossed issues.*

No.	*Specimen Type No.*		*Unused Price*
SP1	P **1**	1s. pale green (No. 54) (red opt)	£325
		a. Black opt	£450
SP2		10d. brown (No. 57)	£275
SP3		6d. mauve (No. 58)	£550

1855–57. *Surface-printed issues. No corner letters.*

No.	*Specimen Type No.*		*Unused Price*
SP4	P **3**	4d. carmine/*blued* (No. 62)	£160
SP5	P **4**	4d. rose/*white* (No. 65)	
SP6		6d. dp lilac/*white* (No. 69)	£100
		a. On azure paper	£140
SP7		1s. dp green (No. 71)	£100

1858–70. *Line-engraved issues.*

SP 8	P **9**	½d. rose-red (pl 10) (No. 48)	£120
SP 9		1d. rose-red (pl 146) (No. 43)	£100
SP10		1½d. rose-red (pl 3) (No. 51)	£110
SP11		2d. blue (pl 15) (No. 46)	£175

1862–64. *Surface-printed issue. Small uncoloured corner letters.*

SP12	P **5**	3d. dp carmine-rose (No. 75)	80·00
SP13		4d. brt red (No. 79)	60·00
SP14	P **6**	9d. bistre (No. 86)	£100

1867–80. *Large uncoloured corner letters. Wmk Spray of Rose.*

SP15	P **5**	10d. red-brown (No. 112)	80·00
SP16		2s. dull blue (pl 1) (No. 118)	70·00
SP17	P **9**	2s. dull blue (pl 1) (No. 118)	70·00
SP18		2s. brown (No. 121)	£600

1867–83. *Wmk Maltese Cross or Anchor* (£5).

SP19	P **6**	5s. rose (pl 1) (No. 126)	£225
SP20	P **9**	5s. pale rose (pl 2) (No. 127)	£250
SP21		10s. greenish grey (No. 128)	£625
SP22		£1 brown-lilac (No. 129)	£950
SP23		£5 orange/*blued* (No. 133)	£750

1872–73. *Uncoloured letters in corner. Wmk Spray of Rose.*

SP24	P **6**	6d. chestnut (pl 11) (No. 123)	60·00
SP25		6d. grey (pl 12) (No. 125)	70·00

1873–80. *Large coloured corner letters.*

SP26	P **9**	2½d. rosy-mauve (pl 6) (No. 141)	50·00
SP27		2½d. blue (pl 17) (No. 142)	45·00
SP28		3d. rose (pl 18) (No. 143)	60·00
SP29		4d. sage-green (pl 15) (No. 153)	70·00
SP30		4d. grey-brown (pl 17) (No. 154)	£120
SP31		6d. grey (pl 16) (No. 147)	60·00
SP32		8d. orange (pl 1) (No. 156)	60·00
SP33		1s. green (pl 12) (No. 150)	60·00
SP34		1s. orange-brown (pl 13) (No. 151)	£100

1880–83. *Wmk Imperial Crown.*

SP35	P **9**	3d. on 3d. lilac (No. 159)	£100
SP36		6d. on 6d. lilac (No. 162)	£100

1880–81. *Wmk Imperial Crown.*

SP37	P **9**	½d. dp green (No. 164)	20·00
SP38		1d. Venetian red (No. 166)	20·00
SP39		1½d. Venetian red (No. 167)	20·00
SP40		2d. pale rose (No. 168)	30·00
SP41		5d. indigo (No. 169)	30·00

1881. *Wmk Imperial Crown.*

SP42	P **9**	1d. lilac (14 dots) (No. 170)	25·00
SP43		1d. lilac (16 dots) (No. 172)	20·00

1883–84. *Wmk Anchor or Three Imperial Crowns* (£1).

SP44	P **9**	2s. 6d. lilac/*blued* (No. 175)	£175
SP45		5s. crimson (No. 181)	£175
SP46		10s. ultramarine (No. 183)	£175
SP47		£1 brown-lilac (No. 185)	£400

1883–84. *Wmk Imperial Crown.*

SP48	P **9**	½d. slate-blue (No. 187)	20·00
SP49		1½d. lilac (No. 188)	45·00
SP50		2d. lilac (No. 189)	45·00

No.	Specimen Type No.		Unused Price
SP51	P **9**	2½d. lilac (No. 190)	45·00
SP52		3d. lilac (No. 191)	45·00
SP53		4d. dull green (No. 192)	70·00
SP54		5d. dull green (No. 193)	70·00
SP55		6d. dull green (No. 194)	£140
SP56		9d. dull green (No. 195)	70·00
SP57		1s. dull green (No. 196)	70·00

1887–91. *"Jubilee" issue.*

SP58	P **9**	½d. vermilion (No. 197)	22·00
SP59		1½d. dull purple & pale green (No. 198)	35·00
SP60		2d. green & scarlet (No. 199)	35·00
SP61		2½d. purple/*blue* (No. 201)	40·00
SP62		3d. purple/*yellow* (No. 202)	30·00
SP63		4d. green & purple-brown (No. 205)	30·00
SP64		5d. dull purple & blue (Die I) (No. 207)	30·00
SP65		6d. purple/*rose-red* (No. 208)	20·00
SP66		9d. dull purple & blue (No. 209)	30·00
SP67		10d. dull purple & carmine (No. 210)	55·00
SP68		1s. dull green (No. 211)	30·00

1902–10. *King Edward VII. De La Rue printings.*

SP69	P **16**	2s. 6d. lilac (No. 260)	£120
SP70		5s. brt carmine (No. 263)	£130
SP71		10s. ultramarine (No. 265)	£200
SP72		£1 dull blue-green (No. 266)	£400

1913. *King George V. Wmk Royal Cypher.*

SP73	P **26**	1s. bistre-brown (No. 395)	£120

1913. *"Seahorse" high values. Printed by Waterlow.*

SP74	P **26**	2s. 6d. dp sepia-brown (No. 399)	£200
SP75		5s. rose-carmine (No. 401)	£175
SP76		10s. indigo-blue (No. 402)	£400
SP77		£1 green (No. 403)	£1000

1929. *Ninth U. P. U. Congress.*

SP78	P **32**	£1 black (No. 438) (opt in red)	£800

1936. *Photogravure.*

SP79	P **32**	1s. bistre-brown (No. 449)	55·00

1939. *King George VI.*

SP80	P **23**	1s. bistre-brown (No. 475)	55·00
SP81		2s. 6d. brown (No. 476)	£225
SP82		2s. 6d. yellow-green (No. 476a)	£225
SP83		5s. red (No. 477)	£225
SP84		10s. dark blue (No. 478)	£375
SP85		10s. ultramarine (No. 478a)	£325

POSTAGE DUE STAMPS

1915. *Wmk Simple Cypher.*

SP86	P **23**	1s. brt blue (No. D8)	28·00

1924. *Wmk Block Cypher.*

SP87	P **23**	2s. 6d. purple/*yellow* (No. D18)	35·00

OFFICIAL STAMPS

1887–91. *Optd "GOVT PARCELS".*

SP88	P **9**	1½d. dull purple & pale green (No. O65)	65·00
SP89		2d. grey-green & carmine (No. O70)	50·00
SP90		6d. purple/*rose-red* (No. O66)	65·00
SP91		9d. dull purple & blue (No. O67)	50·00
SP92		1s. dull green (No. O68)	65·00

POST OFFICE STAMP BOOKLETS

The following listing covers all booklets sold by post offices from 1904 until early 1995.

All major variations of contents and cover are included, but minor changes to the covers and differences on the interleaves have been ignored.

From 1913 each booklet carried an edition number, linked to an internal Post Office system of identification which divided the various booklets into series. In 1943 these edition numbers were replaced by edition dates. No attempt has been made to list separate edition numbers for booklets prior to 1943, although notes giving their extent are provided for each booklet. Edition dates from August 1943 are listed separately and exist for all £.s.d. and most Decimal Stitched booklets (except for the 1s. booklets, the 2s. booklets (N1/3), the 5s. "Philympia" booklets (No. HP34), the £1 "Stamps for Cooks" booklet (No. ZP1) and the Decimal Sponsored booklets). They are those found printed upon the booklets, either on the outer back cover or on the white leaves.

ERRORS OF MAKE-UP of booklets exist but we do not list them here. More detailed listings can be found in the 2nd, 3rd and 4th volumes of the *Great Britain Specialised Catalogue*.

ILLUSTRATIONS. The illustrations of the covers are $\frac{3}{4}$ size except where otherwise stated. Those in Queen Elizabeth II Decimal Sections C to G are $\frac{2}{3}$ size, except where otherwise stated.

PRICES quoted are for complete booklets containing stamps with "average" perforations (i.e. full perforations on two edges of the pane only). Booklets containing panes with complete perforations are worth more.

KING EDWARD VII

2s. Booklets

Type BA1

1904 (Mar). *Red cover printed in black as Type BA1. Pages of six stamps: 24 × 1d. Wmk Imperial Crown (No. 219).*
BA1 .... £160

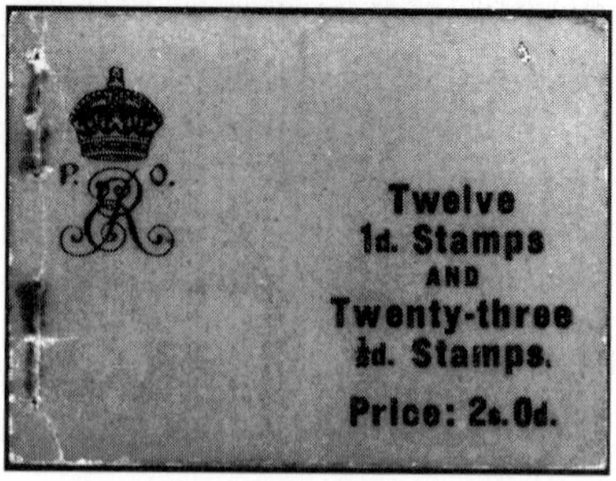

Type BA2

1906 (June). *Red cover printed in black as Type BA2. As before but make-up changed to include 12 × 1d. and 23 × $\frac{1}{2}$d. and label showing one green cross (Nos. 217 and 219).*
BA2 .... £550

1907 (Aug). *Red cover printed in black as Type BA2. Make-up changed to include 18 × 1d. and 11 × $\frac{1}{2}$d. and label showing one green cross (Nos. 217 and 219).*
BA3 .... £750

1911 (June). *Red cover printed in black as Type BA2 but showing a larger Post Office cypher on cover. As before, but containing stamps by Harrison & Sons (Nos. 267 and 272).*
BA6 .... £750

KING GEORGE V

2s. Booklets

1911 (Aug). *Red cover printed in black as Type BA2 showing King George V cypher. Pages of six stamps: 18 × 1d. and 12 × $\frac{1}{2}$d. Wmk Crown (Nos. 325, 329) Die 1B.*
BB1 .... £350

Type BB2

1912 (April). *As before, but red cover printed in black as Type BB2.*
BB2 .... £550

1912 (Sept). *As before, but wmk Simple Cypher (Nos. 334, 336) Die 1B.*
BB3 .... £500

HAVE YOU READ THE NOTES AT THE BEGINNING OF THIS CATALOGUE?
These often provide answers to the enquiries we receive.

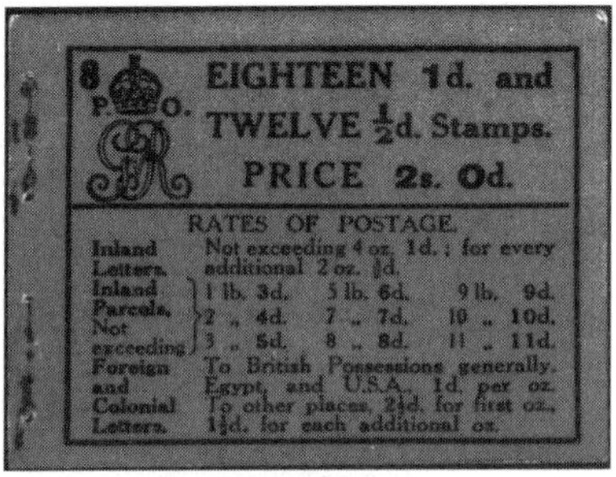

Type BB5

1913 (Jan). *As before, but red cover printed in black as Type* BB5.
BB5 No Edition number or 8 or 9 .... £550

1913 (April). *As before, but* 1912–22 *Wmk Simple Cypher* (Nos. 351, 357).
BB6 Edition numbers 10 to 45 .... £225

1916 (July). *As before, but orange cover printed in black as Type* BB5.
BB9 Edition numbers 46 to 64 .... £250

Type BB10

1917 (Sept). *As before, but orange cover printed in black as Type* BB10.
BB10 Edition numbers 65 to 81 .... £275

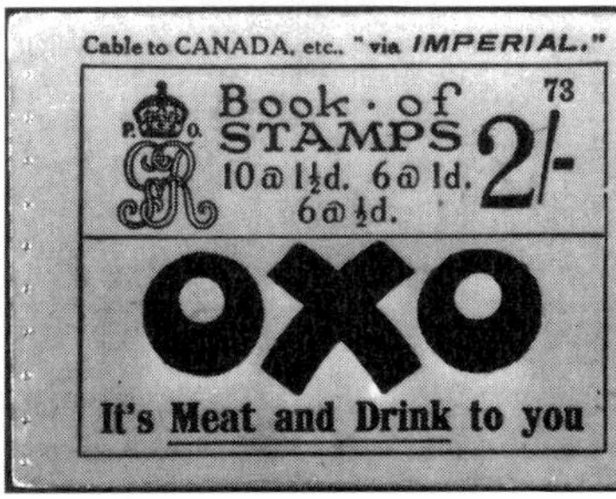

Type BB11

1924 (Feb). *Blue cover printed in black as Type* BB11. *Pages of six stamps:* $10 \times 1\frac{1}{2}$*d. (first completed by two perforated labels),* 6×1d. *and* $6 \times \frac{1}{2}$*d.* 1912–22 *Wmk Simple Cypher* (Nos. 351, 357, 362).
BB11 Edition numbers 1 or 2 .... £750

1933 (Oct). *As before, but* 1924–26 *Wmk Block Cypher* (Nos. 418/20).
BB12 Edition numbers 3 to 102 & 108 to 254 .... £225

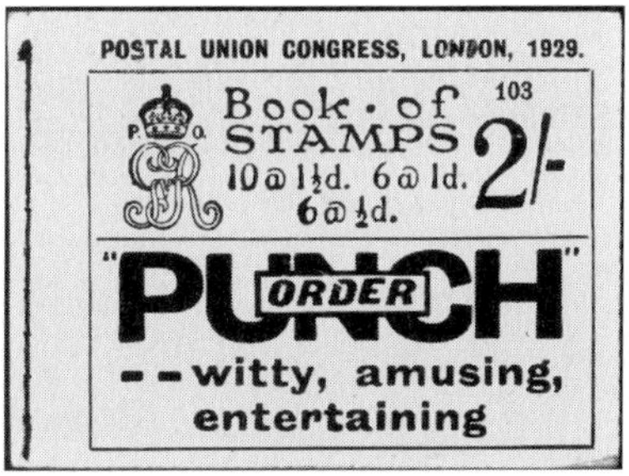

Type BB13

1929 (May). *Postal Union Congress issue. Cover of special design as Type* BB13 *printed in blue on buff as before but containing stamps of the P.U.C. issue* (Nos. 434/6).
BB13 Edition numbers 103 to 107 .... £350

1934 (Feb). *Blue cover printed in black as Type* BB11, *but containing stamps with Block Cypher wmk printed by Harrison & Sons* (Nos. 418/20).
BB14 Edition numbers 255 to 287 .... £250

1935 (Jan). *As before, but containing stamps of the photogravure issue with the se-tenant advertisments printed in brown* (Nos. 439/41).
BB15 Edition numbers 288 to 297 .... £550

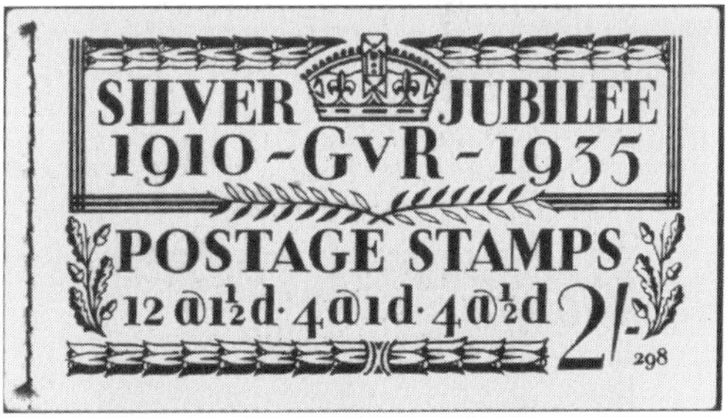

Type BB16

1935 (May). *Silver Jubilee issue. Larger size cover printed in blue on buff as Type* BB16 *and containing pages of four stamps with no se-tenant advertisments:* $12 \times 1\frac{1}{2}$*d.,* 4×1d. *and* $4 \times \frac{1}{2}$*d.* (Nos. 453/5).
BB16 Edition numbers 298 to 304 .... 45·00

1935 (July). *As No.* BB15, *but containing stamps of the photogravure issue with se-tenant advertisments printed in black* (Nos. 439/41).
BB17 Edition numbers 305 to 353 .... £125

3s. Booklets

Type BB18

1918 (Oct). *Orange cover printed in black as Type BB18. Pages of six stamps:* 12 × $1\frac{1}{2}$*d.*, 12 × 1*d. and* 12 × $\frac{1}{2}$*d.* 1912–22 *Wmk Simple Cypher* (*Nos.* 351, 357, 362).

BB18 Edition numbers 1 to 11 .... £300

1919 (July). *As before, but make-up altered to contain* 18 × $1\frac{1}{2}$*d.*, 6 × 1*d. and* 6 × $\frac{1}{2}$*d.*

BB19 Edition numbers 12 to 26 .... £300

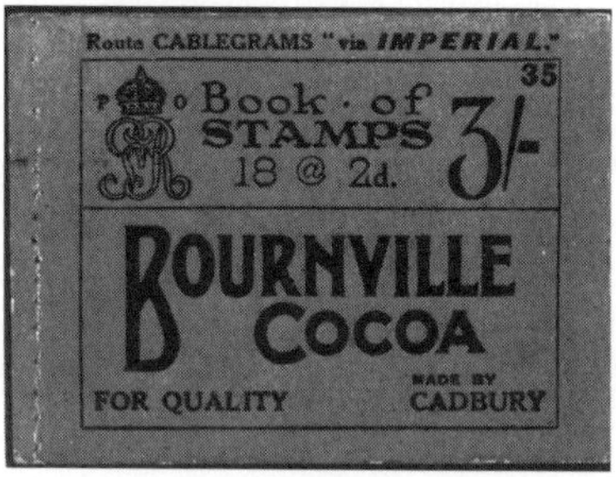

Type BB20

1921 (April). *Experimental booklet bound in blue covers as Type* BB20, *containing pages of six stamps:* 18 × 2*d.* (Die I) (*No.* 368).

BB20 Edition numbers 35 and part 37 .... £400

1921 (Dec). *As before, but containing* 2*d.* (Die II) (*No.* 370).

BB21 Edition numbers 12, 13 and part 37 .... £375

Type BB22

1922 (May). *Scarlet cover printed in black as Type* BB22. *Pages of six stamps:* 18 × $1\frac{1}{2}$*d.*, 6 × 1*d. and* 6 × $\frac{1}{2}$*d.* (*Nos.* 351, 357, 362).

BB22 Edition numbers 19, 20, 22, 23 and 25 to 54 .... £300

1922 (June). *Experimental booklet as Edition numbers* 12 *and* 13 *bound in blue covers as Type* BB22, *containing pages of six stamps:* 24 × $1\frac{1}{2}$*d.* (*No.* 362).

BB23 Edition numbers 21 or 24 .... £400

1924 (Feb). *Scarlet cover printed in black as Type* BB22, *but containing stamps with Block Cypher wmk, printed by Waterlow & Sons* (*Nos.* 418/20).

BB24 Edition numbers 55 to 167 & 173 to 273 .... £110

1929 (May). *Postal Union Congress issue. Cover of special design as Type* BB13 *printed in red on buff as before but containing stamps of the P.U.C. issue* (*Nos.* 434/6).

BB25 Edition numbers 168 to 172 .... £300

1934 (Mar). *Scarlet cover printed in black as Type* BB22, *but containing stamps with the Block Cypher wmk printed by Harrison & Sons* (*Nos.* 418/20).

BB26 Edition numbers 274 to 288 .... £175

1935 (May). *Silver Jubilee issue. Larger size cover printed in red on buff as Type* BB16 *and containing pages of four stamps:* 20 × $1\frac{1}{2}$*d.*, 4 × 1*d. and* 4 × $\frac{1}{2}$*d.* (*Nos.* 453/5).

BB28 Edition numbers 294 to 297 .... 50·00

1935 (July). *As No.* BB26, *but containing stamps of the photogravure issue* (*Nos.* 439/41).

BB29 Edition numbers 289 to 293 & 298 to 319 .... £150

3s. 6d. Booklets

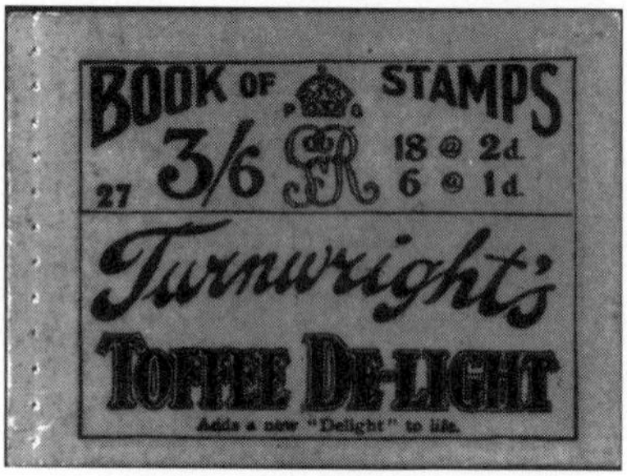

Type BB30

1920 (July). *Orange cover printed in black as Type* BB30, *containing pages of six stamps:* 18 × 2*d. and* 6 × 1*d.* (*Nos.* 357, 368).

BB30 Edition numbers 27 to 32 .... £375

Type BB31

1921 (Jan). *Orange-red cover printed in black as Type BB31, as before but make-up changed to include stamps of 1912–22 issue with the Simple Cypher wmk:* 12×2*d.,* $6 \times 1\frac{1}{2}$*d.,* 6×1*d. and* $6 \times \frac{1}{2}$*d.* (Nos. 351, 357, 362, 368 *or* 370).

BB31 Edition numbers 1 to 11, 14 to 18, 33, 34, 36 & 38 .... £375

5s. Booklets

Type BB33

1931 (Aug). *Green cover printed in black as Type BB33. Pages of six stamps:* $34 \times 1\frac{1}{2}$*d.,* 6×1*d. and* $6 \times \frac{1}{2}$*d. The first* $1\frac{1}{2}$*d. pane completed by two se-tenant advertisments. Printed by Waterlow & Sons on paper with Block Cypher wmk* (Nos. 418/20).

BB33 Edition number 1 .... £1500

1932 (June). *As before, but buff cover printed in black.*

BB34 Edition numbers 2 to 6 .... £500

1934 (July). *As before, but containing stamps with Block Cypher wmk printed by Harrison & Sons* (Nos. 418/20).

BB35 Edition numbers 7 or 8 .... £450

1935 (Feb). *As before, but containing stamps of the photogravure issue with se-tenant advertisments printed in brown* (Nos. 439/41).

BB36 Edition number 9 .... £1100

1935 (July). *As before, but containing stamps of the photogravure issue with se-tenant advertisments printed in black* (Nos. 439/41).

BB37 Edition numbers 10 to 15 .... £140

KING EDWARD VIII

6d. Booklet

1936. *Buff unglazed cover without inscription containing* $4 \times 1\frac{1}{2}$*d. stamps, in panes of two* (No. 459).

BC1 .... 35·00

2s. Booklet

1936 (Oct). *As No. BB17. except for the K.E.VIII cypher on the cover and containing Nos. 457/9.*

BC2 Edition numbers 354 to 385 .... 65·00

3s. Booklet

1936 (Nov). *As No. BB29, except for the K.E.VIII cypher on the cover but without "P" and "O" on either side of the crown, and containing Nos. 457/9.*

BC3 Edition numbers 320 to 332 .... 55·00

5s. Booklet

1937 (Mar). *As No. BB37, but with the K.E.VIII cypher on the cover and containing Nos. 457/9.*

BC4 Edition numbers 16 or 17 .... £130

KING GEORGE VI

6d. Booklets

1938 (Jan). *As No. BC1, but containing stamps in the original dark colours. Buff cover without inscription* (No. 464).

BD1 .... 35·00

1938 (Feb). *As before, but pink unprinted cover and make-up changed to contain* $2 \times 1\frac{1}{2}$*d.,* 2×1*d. and* $2 \times \frac{1}{2}$*d. in the original dark colours* (Nos. 462/4).

BD2 .... £150

1940 (June). *Pale green unprinted cover and make-up changed to include two panes of four stamps with wmk sideways. Stamps in original dark colours with binding margin either at the top or bottom of the pane:* 4×1*d.,* $4 \times \frac{1}{2}$*d.* (Nos. 462a/3a).

BD3 .... 75·00

1s. Booklets with Panes of 2

1947 (Dec). *Cream cover, unglazed and without inscription containing panes of two stamps in pale shades, all with wmk normal. Panes of two stamps:* $4 \times \frac{1}{2}$*d.,* 4×1*d. and* $4 \times 1\frac{1}{2}$*d.* (Nos. 485/7).

BD4 .... 16·00

1951 (May). *As before, but containing stamps in changed colours* (Nos. 503/5).

BD5 .... 16·00

1s. Booklets with Panes of 4

1948. *Cream cover as before, but make-up changed to contain* $4 \times 1\frac{1}{2}$*d.,* 4×1*d. and* $4 \times \frac{1}{2}$*d. in panes of four of the pale shades with wmk normal* (Nos. 485/7).

BD6 .... £3250

1951 (May). *As before, but stamps in new colours all wmk normal, margins at either top or at the bottom.* (Nos. 503/5).

BD7 .... 16·00

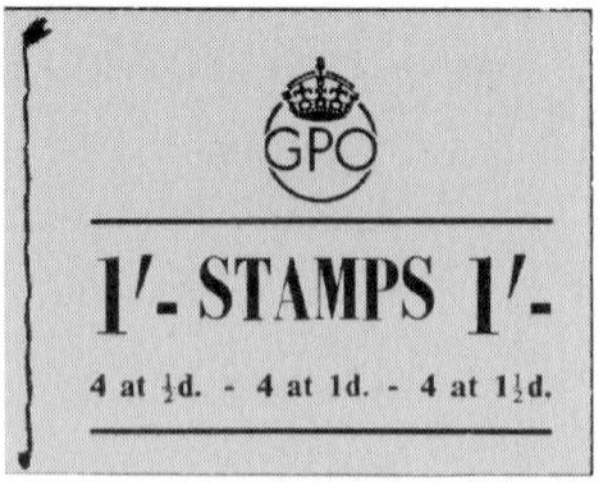

Type BD8

1952 (Dec). *Cream cover printed in black as Type BD8. Make-up as before but with wmk either upright or inverted and margins only at the top* (Nos. 503/5).
BD8 .... 12·00

Type BD10

1954. *As before but cover showing GPO emblem with St. Edward's crown and oval frame as Type BD10* (Nos. 503/5).
BD10 .... 20·00

2s. Booklets

1937 (Aug). *Blue cover printed in black as Type BB11, but with K.G.VI cypher on the cover and containing stamps in the original dark colours. Panes of six stamps:* $10 \times 1\frac{1}{2}$*d.,* $6 \times$ *1d. and* $6 \times \frac{1}{2}$*d. The first* $1\frac{1}{2}$*d. pane completed by two se-tenant advertisements.* (Nos. 462/4).
BD11 Edition numbers 386 to 412 .... £220

Type BD12

1938 (Mar). *Blue cover printed in black as Type BD12* (Nos. 462/4).
BD12 Edition numbers 413 to 508 .... £220

2s. 6d. Booklets

Type BD13

1940 (June). *Scarlet cover printed in black as Type BD13, containing panes of six stamps in original dark colours:* $6 \times 2\frac{1}{2}$*d.,* $6 \times$ *2d. and* $6 \times \frac{1}{2}$*d.* (Nos. 462, 465/6).
BD13 Edition numbers 1 to 7 .... £500

1940 (Sept). *As before, but blue cover printed in black as Type* BD13.
BD14 Edition numbers 8 to 13 .... £500

Type BD15

1940 (Oct). *As before, but with green cover printed in black as Type* BD15 (Nos. 462, 465/6).
BD15 Edition numbers 14 to 94 .... £225

1942 (Mar). *As before, but containing stamps in pale shades* (Nos. 485, 488/9).
BD16 Edition numbers 95 to 214 .... £275

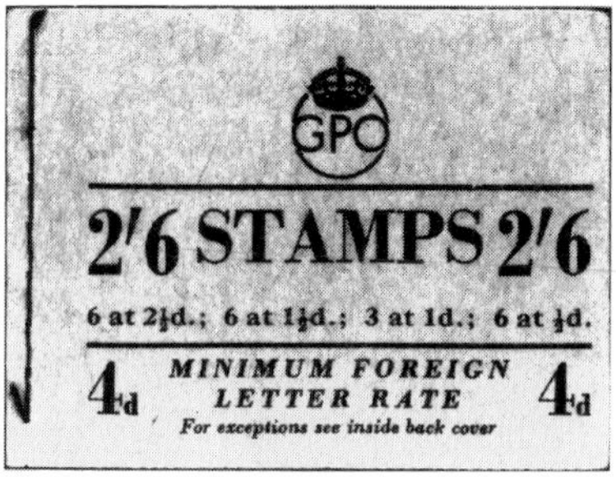

Type A
Circular GPO Cypher

1943 (Aug). *As before, but green cover printed in black as Type A, with different contents details* (Nos. 485, 488/9).

BD18 Edition dates August 1943 to February 1951 .... 30·00

(1) AUG 1943	35·00	(46) MAY 1947	50·00
(2) SEPT 1943	50·00	(47) JUNE 1947	50·00
(3) OCT 1943	50·00	(48) JULY 1947	50·00
(4) NOV 1943	50·00	(49) AUG 1947	50·00
(5) DEC 1943	50·00	(50) SEPT 1947	50·00
(6) JAN 1944	55·00	(51) OCT 1947	50·00
(7) FEB 1944	55·00	(52) NOV 1947	50·00
(8) MAR 1944	55·00	(53) DEC 1947	50·00
(9) APR 1944	55·00	(54) JAN 1948	45·00
(10) MAY 1944	55·00	(55) FEB 1948	45·00
(11) JUNE 1944	55·00	(56) MAR 1948	45·00
(12) JULY 1944	55·00	(57) APR 1948	45·00
(13) AUG 1944	55·00	(58) MAY 1948	45·00
(14) SEPT 1944	55·00	(59) JUNE 1948	45·00
(15) OCT 1944	55·00	(60) JULY 1948	45·00
(16) NOV 1944	55·00	(61) AUG 1948	45·00
(17) DEC 1944	55·00	(62) SEPT 1948	45·00
(18) JAN 1945	55·00	(63) OCT 1948	45·00
(19) FEB 1945	55·00	(64) NOV 1948	45·00
(20) MAR 1945	55·00	(65) DEC 1948	45·00
(21) APR 1945	55·00	(66) JAN 1949	45·00
(22) MAY 1945	55·00	(67) FEB 1949	45·00
(23) JUNE 1945	55·00	(68) MAR 1949	45·00
(24) JULY 1945	55·00	(69) APR 1949	45·00
(25) AUG 1945	55·00	(70) MAY 1949	45·00
(26) SEPT 1945	55·00	(71) JUNE 1949	45·00
(27) OCT 1945	55·00	(72) JULY 1949	45·00
(28) NOV 1945	55·00	(73) AUG 1949	45·00
(29) DEC 1945	55·00	(74) OCT 1949	45·00
(30) JAN 1946	50·00	(75) NOV 1949	45·00
(31) FEB 1946	50·00	(76) DEC 1949	45·00
(32) MAR 1946	50·00	(77) JAN 1950	30·00
(33) APR 1946	50·00	(78) FEB 1950	30·00
(34) MAY 1946	50·00	(79) MAR 1950	30·00
(35) JUNE 1946	50·00	(80) APR 1950	30·00
(36) JULY 1946	50·00	(81) MAY 1950	30·00
(37) AUG 1946	50·00	(82) JUNE 1950	30·00
(38) SEPT 1946	50·00	(83) JULY 1950	30·00
(39) OCT 1946	50·00	(84) AUG 1950	30·00
(40) NOV 1946	50·00	(85) SEPT 1950	30·00
(41) DEC 1946	50·00	(86) OCT 1950	30·00
(42) JAN 1947	50·00	(87) NOV 1950	30·00
(43) FEB 1947	50·00	(88) DEC 1950	30·00
(44) MAR 1947	50·00	(89) JAN 1951	30·00
(45) APR 1947	50·00	(90) FEB 1951	30·00

1951 (May). *As before, but containing stamps in the new colours* (Nos. 503, 506/7).

BD19 Edition dates May 1951 to February 1952 .... 22·00

(1) MAY 1951	22·00	(6) OCT 1951	22·00
(2) JUNE 1951	22·00	(7) NOV 1951	22·00
(3) JULY 1951	22·00	(8) DEC 1951	22·00
(4) AUG 1951	22·00	(9) JAN 1952	22·00
(5) SEPT 1951	22·00	(10) FEB 1952	22·00

1952 (March). *As before, but make-up changed to contain: 6 × 2½d., 6 × 1½d., 3 × 1d. and 6 × ½d. The 1d. pane was completed by three perforated labels in the lower row inscribed* "MINIMUM INLAND PRINTED PAPER RATE 1½d." (*Nos.* 503/5, 507).

BD20 Edition dates March 1952 to May 1953 .... 22·00

(1) MAR 1952	22·00	(9) NOV 1952	22·00
(2) APR 1952	25·00	(10) DEC 1952	22·00
(3) MAY 1952	22·00	(11) JAN 1953	22·00
(4) JUNE 1952	25·00	(12) FEB 1953	22·00
(5) JULY 1952	22·00	(13) MAR 1953	22·00
(6) AUG 1952	22·00	(14) APR 1953	22·00
(7) SEPT 1952	22·00	(15) MAY 1953	25·00
(8) OCT 1952	22·00		

3s. Booklets

1937 (Aug). *Scarlet cover printed in black as Type BB22 (without "P" and "O") except for K.G.VI cypher on the cover and containing stamps in the original dark colours* (Nos. 462/4).

BD21 Edition numbers 333 to 343 .... £400

1938 (April). *As before, but scarlet cover printed in black as Type BD12* (*Nos.* 462/4).

BD22 Edition numbers 344 to 377 .... £375

5s. Booklets

1937 (Aug). *Buff cover printed in black as Type BB33, containing stamps of the new reign in the original dark colours. Pages of six stamps: 34 × 1½d., 6 × 1d. and 6 × ½d. The first 1½d. pane completed by two se-tenant advertisements.* (*Nos.* 462/4).

BD23 Edition numbers 18 to 20 .... £450

Type BD24

1938 (May). *As before, but with redesigned front cover showing GPO emblem as Type BD24 instead of royal cypher.*

BD24 Edition numbers 21 to 29 .... £425

1940 (July). *As before, but make-up changed to contain:* 18 × $2\frac{1}{2}$*d.*, 6 × 2*d.* *and* 6 × $\frac{1}{2}$*d.* *in the original dark colours* (*Nos.* 462, 465/6).
BD25 Edition numbers 1 to 16 (part) £425

1942 (Mar). *As before, but containing stamps in pale shades* (*Nos.* 485, 488/9).
BD26 Edition numbers 16 (part) to 36 .... £425

1943 (Sept). *As before, but buff cover printed in black as Type A* (*see No.* BD18, 2*s.* 6*d.*) (*Nos.* 485, 488/9).
BD28 Edition dates September 1943 to December 1950 ..... 55·00

(1) SEPT 1943	65·00	(26) JUNE 1947	65·00
(2) OCT 1943	65·00	(27) AUG 1947	65·00
(3) NOV 1943	65·00	(28) OCT 1947	65·00
(4) DEC 1943	65·00	(29) DEC 1947	65·00
(5) FEB 1944	75·00	(30) FEB 1948	65·00
(6) MAR 1944	75·00	(31) APR 1948	65·00
(7) AUG 1944	75·00	(32) JUNE 1948	65·00
(8) OCT 1944	75·00	(33) JULY 1948	65·00
(9) NOV 1944	75·00	(34) AUG 1948	65·00
(10) JAN 1945	75·00	(35) OCT 1948	65·00
(11) FEB 1945	75·00	(36) DEC 1948	65·00
(12) APR 1945	75·00	(37) FEB 1949	65·00
(13) JUNE 1945	75·00	(38) APR 1949	65·00
(14) AUG 1945	75·00	(39) JUNE 1949	65·00
(15) OCT 1945	75·00	(40) AUG 1949	65·00
(16) DEC 1945	75·00	(41) SEPT 1949	65·00
(17) JAN 1946	65·00	(42) OCT 1949	65·00
(18) MAR 1946	65·00	(43) DEC 1949	65·00
(19) MAY 1946	65·00	(44) FEB 1950	55·00
(20) JUNE 1946	65·00	(45) APR 1950	55·00
(21) AUG 1946	65·00	(46) JUNE 1950	55·00
(22) OCT 1946	65·00	(47) AUG 1950	55·00
(23) DEC 1946	65·00	(48) OCT 1950	55·00
(24) FEB 1947	65·00	(49) DEC 1950	55·00
(25) APR 1947	65·00		

Type BD29

1944 (Apr). *As before, but buff cover printed in black as Type* BD29 (*Nos.* 485, 488/9).
BD29 Edition dates April or June 1944 .... £525

(1) APR 1944	£525	(2) JUNE 1944	£525

1951 (May). *As before, but buff cover changed back to Type A* (*see No.* BD18, 2*s.* 6*d.*) *and containing stamps in the new colours* (*Nos.* 503, 506/7).
BD30 Edition dates May 1951 to January 1952 .... 35·00

(1) MAY 1951	35·00	(4) NOV 1951	35·00
(2) JULY 1951	35·00	(5) JAN 1952	35·00
(3) SEPT 1951	35·00		

1952 (Mar). *As before, make-up changed to contain:* 18 × $2\frac{1}{2}$*d.*, 6 × $1\frac{1}{2}$*d.*, 3 × 1*d.* *and* 6 × $\frac{1}{2}$*d.* *The* 1*d.* *pane was completed by three perforated labels in the lower row inscribed* "MINIMUM INLAND PRINTED PAPER RATE $1\frac{1}{2}$d." (*Nos.* 503/5, 507).
BD31 Edition dates March to November 1952 .... 25·00

(1) MAR 1952	25·00	(4) SEPT 1952	25·00
(2) MAY 1952	25·00	(5) NOV 1952	25·00
(3) JULY 1952	25·00		

1953 (Jan). *As before, but make-up changed again to include the* 2*d.* *value and containing:* 12 × $2\frac{1}{2}$*d.*, 6 × 2*d.*, 6 × $1\frac{1}{2}$*d.*, 6 × 1*d.* *and* 6 × $\frac{1}{2}$*d.* (*Nos.* 503/7).
BD32 Edition dates January or March 1953 .... 35·00

(1) JAN 1953	35·00	(2) MAR 1953	35·00

QUEEN ELIZABETH II

I. £.s.d. Booklets, 1953–70.

TYPES OF BOOKLET COVER WITH GPO CYPHER

Type A
Circular GPO Cypher
(See illustration above No. BD18)

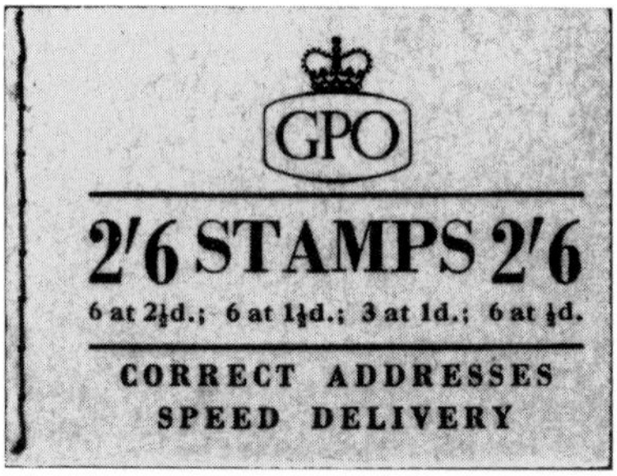

Type B
Oval Type GPO Cypher

Type C
New GPO Cypher (small)

Type D
New GPO Cypher (large)

1s. Booklets

1953 (2 Sept)–**59**. *I. White unprinted cover. Pages of two stamps: 4 × $1\frac{1}{2}$d., 4 × 1d., 4 × $\frac{1}{2}$d. For use in experimental "D" machines.*

A. Wmk Tudor Crown (Nos. 515/17)

E1	No date	3·00

B. Wmk St. Edward's Crown (Nos. 540/2)

E2	No date (11.57)	10·00

II. White printed cover as Type B. Pages of four stamps: 4 × $1\frac{1}{2}$d., 4 × 1d., 4 × $\frac{1}{2}$d. For use in "E" machines.

A. Wmk Tudor Crown (Nos. 515/17)

K1	No date (22.7.54)	4·00

B. Wmk St. Edward's Crown (Nos. 540/2)

K2	No date (5.7.56)	4·00

C. Wmk Crowns (Nos. 570/2)

K3	No date (13.8.59)	4·00

2s. Booklets

1959 (22 Apr)–**65**. *Pages of four stamps: 4 × 3d., 4 × $1\frac{1}{2}$d., 4 × 1d., 4 × $\frac{1}{2}$d.*

I. Salmon cover as Type B. Wmk. St. Edward's Crown (Nos. 540/2 and 545).

N1	No date	3·50

II. Salmon cover as Type C. Wmk Crowns (Nos. 570/2 and 575).

N2	No date (2.11.60)	8·00

III. Lemon cover as Type C. Wmk Crowns (Nos. 570/2 and 575).

N3	No date (2.61)	4·50

IV. Lemon cover as Type C. Wmk Crowns (sideways) (Nos. 570a, 571a, 572b, 575a) or phosphor (Nos. 610a, 611a, 612a, 615b).

N 4	APR 1961	15·00
	p. With phosphor bands	40·00
N 5	SEPT 1961	30·00
N 6	JAN 1962	30·00
N 7	APR 1962	30·00
N 8	JULY 1962	30·00
	p. With phosphor bands	65·00
N 9	NOV 1962	30·00
	p. With phosphor bands	50·00
N10	JAN 1963	30·00
	p. With phosphor bands	70·00
N11	MAR 1963	30·00
N12	JUNE 1963	30·00
	p. With phosphor bands	50·00
N13	AUG 1963	30·00
	p. With phosphor bands	50·00
N14	OCT 1963	30·00
	p. With phosphor bands	75·00
N15	FEB 1964	30·00
	p. With phosphor bands	48·00
N16	JUNE 1964	30·00
	p. With phosphor bands	65·00
N17	AUG 1964	30·00
	p. With phosphor bands	65·00
N18	OCT 1964	30·00
	p. With phosphor bands	48·00
N19	DEC 1964	35·00
	p. With phosphor bands	48·00
N20	APR 1965	25·00
	p. With phosphor bands	45·00

1965 (16 Aug)–**67**. *New Composition. Pages of four stamps: 4 × 4d. and pane of 2 × 1d. and 2 × 3d. arranged se-tenant horiz.*

Orange-yellow cover as Type C printed in black. Wmk Crowns (sideways) (Nos. 571a, 575a and 576ab) or phosphor (Nos. 611a, 615d (one side phosphor band) and 616ab).

N21	JULY 1965	2·00
	p. With phosphor bands	13·00
N22	OCT 1965	3·00
	p. With phosphor bands	13·00
N23	JAN 1966	3·50
	p. With phosphor bands	15·00
N24	APR 1966	3·00
	p. With phosphor bands	8·00
N25	JULY 1966	3·00
	p. With phosphor bands	40·00
N26	OCT 1966	3·00
	p. With phosphor bands	8·50
N27	JAN 1967	3·00
	p. With phosphor bands	5·00
N28p	APR 1967. With phosphor bands	6·00
N29p	JULY 1967. With phosphor bands	3·75
N30p	OCT 1967. With phosphor bands	3·75

In the *se-tenant* pane the 3d. appears at left or right to facilitate the application of phosphor bands.

The following illustration shows how the *se-tenant* stamps with one phosphor band on 3d. were printed and the arrows indicate where the guillotine fell. The result gives 1d. stamps with two bands and the 3d. stamps with one band either at left or right.

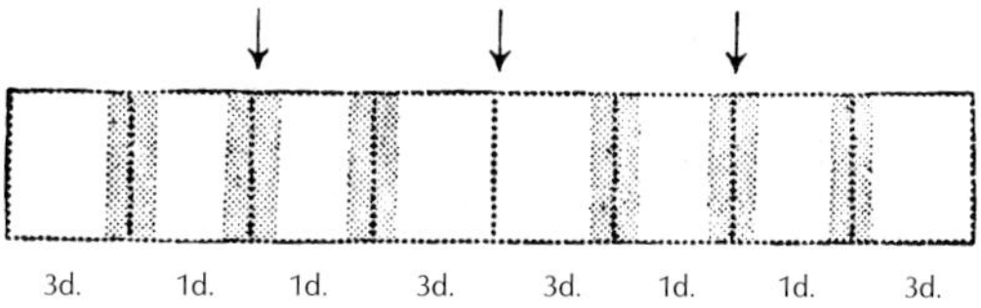

1967 (Nov)–**68**. *Composition and cover as Nos. N21/30. Wmk Crowns (sideways) (Nos. 611a, 615b (two phosphor bands) and 616ab).*

N31p	JAN 1968	2·50
N32p	MAR 1968	2·50

2s. Booklets with Machin type stamps

1968 (6 Apr–Aug). *Orange-yellow cover as Type C. Pages of four stamps: 4 × 4d. and pane of 2 × 1d. and 2 × 3d. arranged se-tenant horiz. PVA gum (Nos. 724, 730, 731Ev).*

NP27	MAY 1968	1·00
NP28	JULY 1968	1·00
NP29	AUG 1968	3·50

1968 (16 Sept)–**70**. *Grey cover as Type C. New Composition. 4d. stamps only comprising page of 4 × 4d. with two phosphor bands (No. 731Ev) and page of 2 × 4d. with one centre phosphor band (No. 732) se-tenant with two printed labels.*

NP30	SEPT 1968	1·00
NP31	JAN 1969	£125

Same composition but all six 4d. stamps have one centre phosphor band (No. 732).

NP31a	SEPT 1968	£375
NP32	NOV 1968	1·00
NP33	JAN 1969	1·00

Same composition but change to 4d. bright vermilion with one centre phosphor band (No. 733).

NP34	MAR 1969	1·50
NP35	MAY 1969	1·50
NP36	JULY 1969	1·50
NP37	SEPT 1969	1·50
NP38	NOV 1969	1·50
NP39	JAN 1970	2·00
NP40	MAR 1970	2·00
NP41	MAY 1970	2·00
NP42	JULY 1970	2·00
NP43	AUG 1970	2·00
NP44	OCT 1970	2·00
NP45	DEC 1970	2·00

2s. Booklets for Holiday Resorts

1963 (15 July)–**64**. *I. Lemon cover as Type C printed in red. New composition. Pages of four stamps: two of 4 × 2½d. and one of 3 × ½d. and 1 × 2½d. arranged se-tenant. Chalky paper. Wmk Crowns (Nos. 570k and 574k).*

NR1	No date, black stitching	2·50
	a. White stitching (3.9.63)	3·00

II. Lemon cover as Type C printed in red. Composition changed again. Pages of four stamps 2 × ½d. and 2 × 2½d. arranged sideways, vertically se-tenant. Wmk Crowns (sideways) (No. 570m × 4).

NR2	1964 (1.7.64)	1·40

2s. Booklet for Christmas Cards

1965 (6 Dec). *Orange-yellow cover as Type C printed in red. Two panes of 4 × 3d. arranged sideways. Wmk Crowns (sideways) (No. 575a).*

NX1	1965	50

2s. 6d. Booklets

Green cover. Pages of six stamps: 6 × 2½d., 6 × 1½d., 3 × 1d. (page completed by three perforated labels), 6 × ½d.

LABELS. The wording printed on the labels differs as follows:

"PPR" = "MINIMUM INLAND PRINTED PAPER RATE 1½d." Two types exist:

A. Printed in photogravure, 17 mm high.

B. Typographed, 15 mm high.

"Shorthand" = "SHORTHAND IN 1 WEEK" (covering all three labels).

"Post Early" = "PLEASE POST EARLY IN THE DAY".

"PAP" = "PACK YOUR PARCELS SECURELY" (1st label) "ADDRESS YOUR LETTERS CORRECTLY" (2nd label), "AND POST EARLY IN THE DAY" (3rd label).

1953–54. *Composite booklets containing stamps of King George VI and Queen Elizabeth II.*

A. *K.G.VI ½d. and 1d. (Nos. 503/4) and Q.E.II 1½d. and 2½d. (Nos. 517 and 519b). Cover as Type A. No interleaving pages.*

F 1	MAY 1953 (PPR 17 mm)	14·00
F 2	JUNE 1953 (PPR 17 mm)	15·00
F 3	JULY 1953 (PPR 17 mm)	18·00
F 4	AUG 1953 (PPR 17 mm)	14·00

B. *Same composition but with addition of two interleaving pages, one at each end. Cover as Type A.*

F 5	SEPT 1953 (PPR 17 mm)	£100
F 6	SEPT 1953 (PPR 15 mm)	60·00

C. *Same composition and with interleaving pages but with cover as Type B.*

F 7	OCT 1953 (PPR 17 mm)	19·00
F 8	OCT 1953 (PPR 15 mm)	50·00
F 9	NOV 1953 (PPR 17 mm)	22·00
F10	NOV 1953 (PPR 15 mm)	£100
F11	DEC 1953 (PPR 17 mm)	25·00
F12	JAN 1954 (Shorthand)	38·00
F13	FEB 1954 (Shorthand)	38·00

D. *New composition: K.G.VI 1d. (No. 504) and Q.E.II ½d., 1½d. and 2½d. (Nos. 515, 517 and 519b).*

F14	MAR 1954 (PPR 17 mm)	£375

1954–57. *Booklets containing only Queen Elizabeth II stamps. All covers as Type B.*

A. *Wmk Tudor Crown (Nos. 515/17 and 519b).*

F15	MAR 1954 (PPR 15 mm)	£200
F16	APR 1954 (Post Early)	20·00
F17	MAY 1954 (Post Early)	20·00
F18	JUNE 1954 (Post Early)	20·00
F19	JULY 1954 (Post Early)	20·00
F20	AUG 1954 (Post Early)	20·00
F21	SEPT 1954 (Post Early)	20·00
F22	OCT 1954 (Post Early)	20·00
F23	NOV 1954 (Post Early)	20·00
F24	DEC 1954 (Post Early)	20·00

B. *Same composition but with interleaving pages between each pane of stamps.*

F25	JAN 1955 (Post Early)	25·00
F26	JAN 1955 (PAP)	50·00
F27	FEB 1955 (PAP)	20·00
F28	MAR 1955 (PAP)	20·00
F29	APR 1955 (PAP)	20·00
F30	MAY 1955 (PAP)	20·00
F31	JUNE 1955 (PAP)	20·00
F32	JULY 1955 (PAP)	20·00
F33	AUG 1955 (PAP)	20·00

C. *Mixed watermarks. Wmk Tudor Crown (Nos. 515/17 and 519b) and wmk St. Edward's Crown (Nos. 540/2 and 544b) in various combinations.*

F34	SEPT 1955 (PAP)	*From* 20·00

2s. 6d. booklets dated AUGUST, OCTOBER, NOVEMBER and DECEMBER 1955, JANUARY, MAY and JUNE 1956 exist both as listed and with the two watermarks mixed. There are so many different combinations that we do not list them separately, but when in stock selections can be submitted. The SEPTEMBER 1955 booklet (No. F34) only exists in composite form.

D. *Wmk St. Edward's Crown (Nos. 540/2 and 544b).*

F35	OCT 1955 (PAP)	17·00
F36	NOV 1955 (PAP)	18·00
F37	DEC 1955 (PAP)	18·00

F38	JAN 1956 (PAP)	15·00
F39	FEB 1956 (PAP)	18·00
F40	MAR 1956 (PAP)	18·00
F41	APR 1956 (PAP)	20·00
F42	MAY 1956 (PAP)	18·00
F43	JUNE 1956 (PAP)	18·00
F44	JULY 1956 (PAP)	18·00
F45	AUG 1956 (PAP)	20·00
F46	SEPT 1956 (PAP)	20·00
F47	OCT 1956 (PAP)	18·00
F48	NOV 1956 (PAP)	17·00
F49	DEC 1956 (PAP)	17·00
F50	JAN 1957 (PAP)	19·00
F51	FEB 1957 (PAP)	16·00
F52	MAR 1957 (PAP)	13·00

E. *Same wmk but new composition. Pages of six stamps:* $6 \times 2\frac{1}{2}$*d.* (*No.* 544b), 6×2*d.* (*No.* 543*b*) *and* $6 \times \frac{1}{2}$*d.* (*No.* 540).

F53	APR 1957	16·00
F54	MAY 1957	18·00
F55	JUNE 1957	16·00
F56	JULY 1957	16·00
F57	AUG 1957	14·00
F58	SEPT 1957	15·00
F59	OCT 1957	14·00
F60	NOV 1957	13·00
F61	DEC 1957	20·00

3s. Booklets

1958–65. *Pages of six stamps:* 6×3*d.*, $6 \times 1\frac{1}{2}$*d.*, 6×1*d.*, $6 \times \frac{1}{2}$*d.*

I. Red cover as Type B.

A. *Wmk St. Edward's Crown* (*Nos.* 540/2 *and* 545).

M1	JAN 1958	12·00
M2	FEB 1958	13·00
M3	MAR 1958	13·00
M4	APR 1958	12·00
M5	MAY 1958	11·00
M6	JUNE 1958	12·00
M7	JULY 1958	12·00
M8	AUG 1958	12·00
M9	NOV 1958	11·00

The 3s. booklets dated NOVEMBER 1958, DECEMBER 1958 and JANUARY 1959 exist both as listed and with mixed St. Edward's Crown and Crowns wmks.

B. *Wmk Crowns* (*Nos.* 570/2 *and* 575) *or graphite lines* (*Nos.* 587/9 *and* 592).

M10	DEC 1958	16·00
M11	JAN 1959	14·00
M12	FEB 1959	16·00
M13	AUG 1959	16·00
	g. With graphite lines	£140
M14	SEPT 1959	15·00
	g. With graphite lines	£150

II. Brick-red cover as Type C. *Wmk Crowns* (*Nos.* 570/2 *and* 575), *graphite lines* (*Nos.* 587/9 *and* 592) *or phosphor* (*Nos.* 610/12 *and* 615).

M15	OCT 1959	17·00
	g. With graphite lines	£140
M16	NOV 1959	16·00
M17	DEC 1959	16·00
M18	JAN 1960	17·00
M19	FEB 1960	17·00
	g. With graphite lines	£150
M20	MAR 1960	16·00
	g. With graphite lines	£150
M21	APR 1960	17·00
	g. With graphite lines	£150
M22	MAY 1960	18·00
M23	JUNE 1960	18·00
M24	JULY 1960	18·00
M25	AUG 1960	18·00
	p. With phosphor bands	35·00
M26	SEPT 1960	18·00
M27	OCT 1960	18·00
M28	NOV 1960	17·00
	p. With phosphor bands	35·00

III. Brick-red cover as Type D. *Wmk Crowns* (*Nos.* 570/2 *and* 575) *or phosphor* (*Nos.* 610/12 *and* 615).

M29	DEC 1940	18·00
	p. With phosphor bands	40·00
M30	JAN 1961	18·00
M31	FEB 1961	18·00
M32	MAR 1961	17·00
M33	APR 1961	18·00
	p. With phosphor bands	30·00
M34	MAY 1961	18·00
M35	JUNE 1961	17·00
M36	JULY 1961	17·00
	p. With phosphor bands	30·00
M37	AUG 1961	18·00
	p. With phosphor bands	32·00
M38	SEPT 1961	18·00
	p. With phosphor bands	35·00
M39	OCT 1961	18·00
	p. With phosphor bands	32·00
M40	NOV 1961	18·00
M41	DEC 1961	18·00
M42	JAN 1962	18·00
M43	FEB 1962	18·00
	p. With phosphor bands	30·00
M44	MAR 1962	18·00
	p. With phosphor bands	32·00
M45	APR 1962	16·00
	p. With phosphor bands	32·00
M46	MAY 1962	18·00
	p. With phosphor bands	30·00
M47	JUNE 1962	20·00
	p. With phosphor bands	32·00
M48	JULY 1962	17·00
M49	AUG 1962	18·00
	p. With phosphor bands	32·00
M50	SEPT 1962	18·00
	p. With phosphor bands	32·00
M51	OCT 1962	21·00
	p. With phosphor bands	32·00
M52	NOV 1962	18·00
	p. With phosphor bands	32·00
M53	DEC 1962	18·00
	p. With phosphor bands	32·00
M54	JAN 1963	20·00
M55	FEB 1963	18·00
	p. With phosphor bands	32·00
M56	MAR 1963	18·00
	p. With phosphor bands	32·00
M57	APR 1963	18·00
	p. With phosphor bands	32·00
M58	MAY 1963	18·00
	p. With phosphor bands	£150
M59	JUNE 1963	18·00
	p. With phosphor bands	26·00
M60	JULY 1963	18·00
	p. With phosphor bands	32·00
M61	AUG 1963	18·00
	p. With phosphor bands	32·00
M62	SEPT 1963	18·00
M63	OCT 1963	18·00
M64	NOV 1963	18·00
	p. With phosphor bands	32·00

M65	DEC 1963	21·00
	p. With phosphor bands	50·00
M66	JAN 1964	20·00
	p. With phosphor bands	30·00
M67	MAR 1964	18·00
	p. With phosphor bands	28·00
M68	MAY 1964	17·00
	p. With phosphor bands	42·00
M69	JULY 1964	18·00
	p. With phosphor bands	32·00
M70	SEPT 1964	21·00
	p. With phosphor bands	32·00
M71	NOV 1964	18·00
	p. With phosphor bands	30·00
M72	JAN 1965	17·00
	p. With phosphor bands	24·00
M73	MAR 1965	12·00
	p. With phosphor bands	29·00
M74	MAY 1965	14·00
	p. With phosphor bands	29·00

3s. 9d. Booklets

1953–57. *Red cover as Type* B. *Pages of six stamps:* 18 × $2\frac{1}{2}$*d.*

A. *Wmk Tudor Crown* (No. 519b)

G 1	NOV 1953	18·00
G 2	JAN 1954	20·00
G 3	MAR 1954	16·00
G 4	DEC 1954	16·00
G 5	FEB 1955	18·00
G 6	APR 1955	18·00
G 7	JUNE 1955	18·00
G 8	AUG 1955	18·00
G 9	OCT 1955	15·00
G10	DEC 1955	20·00

3s. 9d. booklets dated OCTOBER and DECEMBER 1955 exist both as listed and with the two wkms mixed.

B. *Wmk St. Edward's Crown* (No. 544b). *Same composition but with interleaving pages between each pane of stamps.*

G12	FEB 1956	12·00
G13	APR 1956	12·00
G14	JUNE 1956	12·00
G15	AUG 1956	12·00
G16	OCT 1956	12·00
G17	DEC 1956	12·00
G18	FEB 1957	12·00
G19	APR 1957	10·00
G20	JUNE 1957	9·00
G21	AUG 1957	13·00

4s. 6d. Booklets

1957–65. *Pages of six stamps:* 18 × 3*d.*

I. Purple cover as Type B.

A. *Wmk St. Edward's Crown* (No. 545).

L1	OCT 1957	8·00
L2	DEC 1957	12·00
L3	FEB 1958	13·00
L4	APR 1958	13·00
L5	JUNE 1958	12·00
L6	OCT 1958	14·00
L7	DEC 1958	14·00

B. *Wmk Crowns* (No. 575).

L8	DEC 1958	45·00

II. Purple cover as Type C. *Wmk Crowns* (No. 575) *or graphite lines* (No. 592).

L 9	FEB 1959	16·00
L10	JUNE 1959	16·00
L11	AUG 1959	16·00
	g. With graphite lines	15·00
L12	OCT 1959	16·00
L13	DEC 1959	16·00

III. Violet cover as Type C. *Wmk Crowns* (No. 575), *graphite lines* (No. 592) *or phosphor* (No. 615).

L14	FEB 1959	16·00
L15	APR 1959	16·00
	g. With graphite lines	11·00
L16	JUNE 1959	15·00
	g. With graphite lines	11·00
L17	DEC 1959	16·00
L18	FEB 1960	18·00
	g. With graphite lines	16·00
L19	APR 1960	18·00
	g. With graphite lines	16·00
L20	JUNE 1960	18·00
L21	AUG 1960	19·00
	p. With phosphor bands	28·00
L22	OCT 1960	20·00

IV. Violet cover as Type D. *Wmk Crowns* (No. 575) *or phosphor* (No. 615).

L23	DEC 1960	20·00
L24	FEB 1961	21·00
	p. With phosphor bands	21·00
L25	APR 1961	19·00
	p. With phosphor bands	21·00
L26	JUNE 1961	19·00
L27	AUG 1961	19·00
	p. With phosphor bands	25·00
L28	OCT 1961	19·00
	p. With phosphor bands	25·00
L29	DEC 1961	19·00
L30	FEB 1962	19·00
	p. With phosphor bands	25·00
L31	APR 1962	20·00
	p. With phosphor bands	25·00
L32	JUNE 1962	20·00
	p. With phosphor bands	32·00
L33	AUG 1962	20·00
	p. With phosphor bands	32·00
L34	OCT 1962	20·00
	p. With phosphor bands	£100
L35	DEC 1962	20·00
	p. With phosphor bands	25·00
L36	FEB 1963	20·00
	p. With phosphor bands	25·00
L37	APR 1963	20·00
	p. With phosphor bands	25·00
L38	JUNE 1963	20·00
	p. With phosphor bands	25·00
L39	AUG 1963	20·00
	p. With phosphor bands	25·00
L40	OCT 1963	20·00
	p. With phosphor bands	25·00
L41	NOV 1963	20·00
	p. With phosphor bands	25·00
L42	DEC 1963	21·00
	p. With phosphor bands	90·00
L43	JAN 1964	20·00
L44	FEB 1964	20·00
	p. With phosphor bands	25·00
L45	MAR 1964	20·00
	p. With phosphor bands	50·00

L46	APR 1964	25·00
	p. With phosphor bands	24·00
L47	MAY 1964	20·00
	p. With phosphor bands	24·00
L48	JUNE 1964	20·00
	p. With phosphor bands	24·00
L49	JULY 1964	20·00
	p. With phosphor bands	24·00
L50	AUG 1964	25·00
	p. With phosphor bands	24·00
L51	SEPT 1964	20·00
	p. With phosphor bands	24·00
L52	OCT 1964	20·00
	p. With phosphor bands	26·00
L53	NOV 1964	20·00
	p. With phosphor bands	24·00
L54	DEC 1964	17·00
	p. With phosphor bands	24·00
L55	JAN 1965	17·00
	p. With phosphor bands	24·00
L56	FEB 1965	17·00
	p. With phosphor bands	24·00
L57	MAR 1965	17·00
	p. With phosphor bands	£200
L58	APR 1965	13·00

1965 (26 July)–**67**. *New composition. Pages of six stamps: 12 × 4d., 6 × 1d. Slate-blue cover as Type D. Wmk Crowns (Nos. 571 and 576a) or phosphor (Nos. 611 and 616a).*

L59	JULY 1965	10·00
	p. With phosphor bands	18·00
L60	SEPT 1965	10·00
	p. With phosphor bands	18·00
L61	NOV 1965	10·00
	p. With phosphor bands	18·00
L62	JAN 1966	10·00
	p. With phosphor bands	18·00
L63	MAR 1966	10·00
	p. With phosphor bands	9·00
L64	JAN 1967	10·00
	p. With phosphor bands	10·00
L65	MAR 1967	22·00
	p. With phosphor bands	12·00
L66p	MAY 1967. With phosphor bands	8·00
L67p	JULY 1967. With phosphor bands	10·00
L68p	SEPT 1967. With phosphor bands	10·00
L69p	NOV 1967. With phosphor bands	9·00
L70p	JAN 1968. With phosphor bands	9·00
L71p	MAR 1968. With phosphor bands	6·00

4s. 6d. Booklets with Machin type stamps

1968–70. *Slate-blue cover as Type D. Pages of six stamps: 12 × 4d., 6 × 1d. PVA gum (Nos 724, 731Ev).*

LP45	MAY 1968	7·00

Type LP46
Ships Series with GPO Cypher

(Des S. Rose)

Blue cover as Type LP46. Ships Series. Composition as last.

LP46	JULY 1968 (*Cutty Sark*)	1·25

Same composition but changed to 4d. with one centre phosphor band (No. 732).

LP47	SEPT 1968 (*Golden Hind*)	2·00
LP48	NOV 1968 (*Discovery*)	2·00

Same composition but changed to 4d. bright vermilion with one centre phosphor band (No. 733).

LP49	JAN 1969 (*Queen Elizabeth 2*)	3·00
LP50	MAR 1969 (*Sirius*)	2·50
LP51	MAY 1969 (*Sirius*)	2·50
LP52	JULY 1969 (*Dreadnought*)	3·00
LP53	SEPT 1969 (*Dreadnought*)	5·00
LP54	NOV 1969 (*Mauretania*)	3·50
LP55	JAN 1970 (*Mauretania*)	5·00
LP56	MAR 1970 (*Victory*)	4·00
LP57	MAY 1970 (*Victory*)	8·00

Type LP58
Ships Series with Post Office Corporation Crown Symbol

(Des S. Rose)

As last but cover changed to Type LP58.

LP58	AUG 1970 (*Sovereign of the Seas*)	3·50
LP59	OCT 1970 (*Sovereign of the Seas*)	8·00

5s. Booklets

1953–57. *Buff cover. Pages of six stamps. 12 × $2\frac{1}{2}$d., 6 × 2d., 6 × $1\frac{1}{2}$d., 6 × 1d., 6 × $\frac{1}{2}$d.*

I. Composite booklets containing stamps of King George VI and Queen Elizabeth II.

A. *K.G.VI $\frac{1}{2}$d., 1d. and 2d. (Nos 503/4 and 506) and Q.E.II $1\frac{1}{2}$d. and $2\frac{1}{2}$d. (Nos. 517 and 519b). Cover as Type A. No interleaving pages.*

H1	MAY 1953	18·00
H2	JULY 1953	17·00

B. *Same composition but with addition of two interleaving pages, one at each end. Cover as Type A.*

H3	SEPT 1953	25·00

C. Same composition and with interleaving pages but cover as Type B.

H4	NOV 1953	20·00
H5	JAN 1954	26·00

D. New composition: K.G.VI 1d. and 2d. (Nos. 504 and 506) and Q.E.II $\frac{1}{2}$d., $1\frac{1}{2}$d. and $2\frac{1}{2}$d. (Nos. 515, 517 and 519b).

H6	MAR 1954	£175

E. New composition: K.G.VI 2d. (No. 506) and Q.E.II $\frac{1}{2}$d., 1d., $1\frac{1}{2}$d. and $2\frac{1}{2}$d. (Nos. 515/17 and 519b).

H7	MAR 1954	90·00

II. Booklets containing only Queen Elizabeth II stamps. Buff cover as Type B. Two interleaving pages as before.

A. Wmk Tudor Crown (Nos. 515/18 and 519b).

H 8	MAR 1954	70·00
H 9	MAY 1954	30·00
H10	JULY 1954	40·00
H11	SEPT 1954	30·00
H12	NOV 1954	30·00

B. Same composition but with interleaving pages between each pane of stamps.

H13	JAN 1955	30·00
H14	MAR 1955	30·00
H15	MAY 1955	30·00
H16	JULY 1955	30·00

C. Wmk St. Edward's Crown (Nos. 540/3 and 544b).

H17	SEPT 1955	14·00
H18	NOV 1955	17·00
H19	JAN 1956	17·00
H20	MAR 1956	20·00
H21	MAY 1956	18·00
H22	JULY 1956	18·00
H23	SEPT 1956	17·00
H24	NOV 1956	19·00
H25	JAN 1957	22·00

5s. booklets dated SEPTEMBER and NOVEMBER 1955 and JANUARY 1956 exist both as listed and with the two watermarks mixed. There are so many different combinations that we do not list them separately, but when in stock selections can be submitted.

D. Same watermark. Introduction of 2d. light red-brown (No. 543b) in place of No. 543.

H26	JAN 1957	18·00
H27	MAR 1957	18·00
H28	MAY 1957	17·00
H29	JULY 1957	18·00
H30	SEPT 1957	16·00
H31	NOV 1957	17·00

1958–65. E. *New composition. Pages of six stamps: 12 × 3d. (No. 545), 6 × $2\frac{1}{2}$d. (No. 544b), 6 × 1d. (No. 541), 6 × $\frac{1}{2}$d. (No. 540). Wmk St. Edward's Crown.*

H32	JAN 1958	16·00
H33	MAR 1958	15·00
H34	MAY 1958	14·00
H35	JULY 1958 (11.58)	11·00
H36	NOV 1958	11·00

5s. booklets dated JULY 1958, NOVEMBER 1958 AND JANUARY 1959 exist with mixed watermarks.

F. Blue cover as Type C. Wmk Crowns (Nos. 570/1, 574/5), graphite lines (Nos. 587/8 and 591/2) or phosphor (Nos. 610/11, 614 and 615).

H37	JAN 1959	15·00
H38	MAR 1959	18·00
H39	JULY 1959	18·00
	g. With graphite lines	70·00
H40	SEPT 1959	20·00
H41	NOV 1959	18·00
H42	JAN 1960	20·00
H43	MAR 1960	20·00
	g. With graphite lines	80·00
H44	MAY 1960	18·00
H45	JULY 1960	22·00
H46	SEPT 1960	22·00
	g. With graphite lines	80·00
	p. With phosphor bands	45·00
H47	NOV 1960	22·00

G. As last but blue cover as Type D. Same composition.

I. Phosphor has two bands on $2\frac{1}{2}$d (No. 614).

H48	JAN 1961	25·00
H49	MAR 1961	25·00
	p. With phosphor bands	60·00
H50	MAY 1961	25·00
H51	JULY 1961	25·00
	p. With phosphor bands	60·00
H52	SEPT 1961	25·00
	p. With phosphor bands	60·00
H53	NOV 1961	22·00
H54	JAN 1962	22·00
	p. With phosphor bands	60·00

II. As last but phosphor has one band on $2\frac{1}{2}$d (No. 614a).

H55	MAR 1962	22·00
	p. With phosphor bands	70·00
H56	MAY 1962	22·00
	p. With phosphor bands	60·00
H57	JULY 1962	22·00
	p. With phosphor bands	60·00
H58	SEPT 1962	22·00
	p. With phosphor bands	60·00
H59	NOV 1962	22·00
	p. With phosphor bands	60·00
H60	JAN 1963	22·00
	p. With phosphor bands	£300
H61	MAR 1963	22·00
	p. With phosphor bands	70·00
H62	MAY 1963	22·00
	p. With phosphor bands	60·00
H63	JULY 1963	22·00
	p. With phosphor bands	60·00
H64	SEPT 1963	22·00
	p. With phosphor bands	70·00
H65	NOV 1963	22·00
	p. With phosphor bands	60·00
H66	JAN 1964	22·00
	p. With phosphor bands	60·00
H67	MAR 1964	22·00
	p. With phosphor bands	60·00
H68	MAY 1964	22·00
	p. With phosphor bands	70·00
H69	JULY 1964	22·00
	p. With phosphor bands	60·00
H70	SEPT 1964	22·00
	p. With phosphor bands	60·00
H71	NOV 1964	22·00
	p. With phosphor bands	60·00
H72	JAN 1965	22·00
	p. With phosphor bands	45·00
H73	MAR 1965	22·00
	p. With phosphor bands	60·00
H74	MAY 1965	22·00
	p. With phosphor bands	60·00

5s. Booklets with Machin type stamps

Type HP26
English Homes Series
with GPO Cypher

(Des S. Rose)

1968 (27 Nov)–**70**. *Cinnamon cover as Type* HP26 (*English Homes Series*). *Pages of six stamps:* 12 × 5*d*. (*No.* 735).

HP26	DEC 1968 (Ightham Mote)	1·25
HP27	FEB 1969 (Little Moreton Hall)	1·25
HP28	APR 1969 (Long Melford Hall)	2·00
HP29	JUNE 1969 (Long Melford Hall)	3·00
HP30	AUG 1969 (Long Melford Hall)	2·00

Type HP31
English Homes Series with Post
Office Corporation Crown Symbol

(Des S. Rose)

As last but cover changed to Type HP31.

HP31	OCT 1969 (Mompesson House)	2·25
HP32	DEC 1969 (Mompesson House)	2·00
HP33	FEB 1970 (Cumberland Terrace)	2·00

Type HP34

(Des P. Gauld)

As last but cover changed to Type HP34 (*special edition to advertise "Philympia" International Philatelic Exhibition, London, September 1970*).

HP34	(no date) (3.3.70)	1·00

As last but cover changed to Type HP31.

HP35	JUNE 1970 (The Vineyard, Saffron Walden)	2·00
HP36	AUG 1970 (The Vineyard, Saffron Walden)	3·00
HP37	OCT 1970 (Mereworth Castle)	2·50
HP38	DEC 1970 (Mereworth Castle)	4·00

6s. Booklets

1965 (21 June)–**67**. *Claret cover as Type* D. *Wmk Crowns* (*No.* 576a) *or phosphor* (*No.* 616a). *Pages of six stamps:* 18 × 4*d*.

Q 1	JUNE 1965	18·00
	p. With phosphor bands	18·00
Q 2	JULY 1965	18·00
	p. With phosphor bands	18·00
Q 3	AUG 1965	18·00
	p. With phosphor bands	22·00
Q 4	SEPT 1965	18·00
	p. With phosphor bands	21·00
Q 5	OCT 1965	18·00
	p. With phosphor bands	21·00
Q 6	NOV 1965	18·00
	p. With phosphor bands	22·00
Q 7	DEC 1965	18·00
	p. With phosphor bands	22·00
Q 8	JAN 1966	18·00
	p. With phosphor bands	22·00
Q 9	FEB 1966	18·00
	p. With phosphor bands	22·00
Q10	MAR 1966	18·00
	p. With phosphor bands	22·00
Q11	APR 1966	18·00
	p. With phosphor bands	40·00
Q12	MAY 1966	18·00
	p. With phosphor bands	22·00
Q13	JUNE 1966	18·00
	p. With phosphor bands	22·00
Q14	JULY 1966	18·00
	p. With phosphor bands	30·00
Q15	AUG 1966	18·00
	p. With phosphor bands	80·00
Q16	SEPT 1966	18·00
	p. With phosphor bands	18·00
Q17	OCT 1966	18·00
	p. With phosphor bands	40·00

Q18	NOV 1966	18·00
	p. With phosphor bands	18·00
Q19	DEC 1966	18·00
	p. With phosphor bands	18·00
Q20	JAN 1967	22·00
	p. With phosphor bands	22·00
Q21	FEB 1967	22·00
	p. With phosphor bands	18·00
Q22	MAR 1967	18·00
	p. With phosphor bands	18·00
Q23	APR 1967	18·00
	p. With phosphor bands	18·00
Q24p	MAY 1967. With phosphor bands	18·00
Q25p	JUNE 1967. With phosphor bands	18·00
Q26p	JULY 1967. With phosphor bands	18·00
Q27p	AUG 1967. With phosphor bands	22·00

6s. Booklets with Machin type stamps

1967–70. *Claret cover as Type D. Pages of six stamps: 18 × 4d. Two phosphor bands. Gum arabic (No. 731).*

QP28	SEPT 1967	32·00
QP29	OCT 1967	35·00
QP30	NOV 1967	35·00
QP31	DEC 1967	37·00
QP32	JAN 1968	32·00
QP33	FEB 1968 (No. 731*Ea*)	32·00
QP34	MAR 1968 (No. 731*Ea*)	30·00
QP35	APR 1968 (No. 731*Ea*)	30·00
QP36	MAY 1968 (No. 731*Ea*)	12·00

Change to PVA gum (No. 731Ev).

QP37	MAY 1968	£275

Type QP38
Birds Series with GPO Cypher

(Des S. Rose)

Orange-red cover as Type QP38 (Birds Series). Same composition. Two phosphor bands. PVA gum (No. 731Ev).

QP38	JUNE 1968 (Kingfisher) (4.6.68)	1·25
QP39	JULY 1968 (Kingfisher)	10·00
QP40	AUG 1968 (Peregrine Falcon)	1·50

Change to one centre phosphor band (No. 732).

QP41	SEPT 1968 (Peregrine Falcon) (16.9.68)	1·60
QP42	OCT 1968 (Pied Woodpecker)	1·60
QP43	NOV 1968 (Pied Woodpecker)	1·75
QP44	DEC 1968 (Great Crested Grebe)	1·75
QP45	JAN 1969 (Barn Owl)	2·00

Change to 4d. bright vermilion with one centre phosphor band (No. 733).

QP46	FEB 1969 (Barn Owl) (20.2.69)	3·50
QP47	MAR 1969 (Jay)	3·00
QP48	MAY 1969 (Jay)	3·50
QP49	JULY 1969 (Puffin)	2·50
QP50	SEPT 1969 (Puffin)	5·00

Type QP51
Birds Series with Post Office
Corporation Crown Symbol

(Des S. Rose)

As last but cover changed to Type QP51.

QP51	NOV 1969 (Cormorant)	3·50
QP52	JAN 1970 (Cormorant)	3·50
QP53	APR 1970 (Wren)	3·50
QP54	AUG 1970 (Golden Eagle)	3·50
QP55	OCT 1970 (Golden Eagle)	3·50

10s. Booklets

1961 (10 Apr–Oct). *Green cover as Type D. Pages of six stamps: 30 × 3d., 6 × 1½d., 6 × 1d., 6 × ½d. Wmk Crowns (Nos. 570/3 and 575).*

X1	No date	80·00
X2	OCT 1961	95·00

1962–64. *New Composition. Pages of six stamps: 30 × 3d., 6 × 2½d., 6 × 1½d., 6 × 1d. (Nos. 571/2 and 574/5).*

X3	APR 1962	60·00
X4	AUG 1962	80·00
X5	MAR 1963	70·00
X6	JULY 1963	70·00
X7	DEC 1963	70·00
X8	JULY 1964	60·00
X9	DEC 1964	£150

1965 (23 Aug)–**66.** *Ochre cover as Type D. Pages of six stamps: 24 × 4d., 6 × 3d., 6 × 1d. Wmk Crowns (Nos. 571, 575, 576a).*

X10	AUG 1965	16·00
X11	DEC 1965	23·00
X12	FEB 1966	23·00
X13	AUG 1966	17·00
X14	NOV 1966	16·00

1967–68. *Ochre cover as Type D. Pages of six phosphor stamps: 24 × 4d., 6 × 3d., 6 × 1d. Wmk Crowns (Nos. 611, 615c (one side phosphor band), 616a).*

X15p	FEB 1967	8·00

Composition as No. X15p. Wmk Crowns (Nos. 611, 615e (one centre phosphor band), 616a).

X16p	AUG 1967	4·00
X17p	FEB 1968	6·00

10s. Booklets with Machin type stamps

Type XP4
Explorers Series with GPO Cypher

(Des S. Rose)

1968 (25 Mar–Aug). *Bright purple cover as Type* XP4 *(Explorers Series). Pages of six stamps:* 24 × 4*d.,* 6 × 3*d.,* 6 × 1*d. PVA gum* (*Nos.* 724, 729Ev, 731Ev).

XP4	MAY 1968 (Livingstone)	3·75
XP5	AUG 1968 (Livingstone)	3·75

1968 (16 Sept)–**70**. *Yellow-green covers as Type* XP4 (*Explorers Series*) *New composition. Pages of six stamps:* 12 × 5*d.* (*with two phosphor bands*), 12 × 4*d.* (*with one centre phosphor band*) *and pane comprising* 4 × 1*d. se-tenant with vert pair of* 4*d.* (*each with one centre phosphor band*). *PVA gum* (*Nos.* 725, 732 *and* 735).

XP6	SEPT 1968 (Scott)	3·00

Change to 4*d. bright vermilion* (*one centre band*) *but se-tenant pane comprises* 1*d. with two phosphor bands and* 4*d. with one left side phosphor band* (*Nos.* 724 *and* 733/4).

XP 7	FEB 1969 (Mary Kingsley) (6.1.69)	2·25
XP 8	MAY 1969 (Mary Kingsley)	3·00
XP 9	AUG 1969 (Shackleton)	3·00
XP10	NOV 1969 (Shackleton)	6·00

Type XP11
Explorers Series with Post Office Corporation Crown Symbol

(Des S. Rose)

As last but cover change to Type XP11.

XP11	FEB 1970 (Frobisher)	6·00
XP12	NOV 1970 (Captain Cook)	6·00

£1 Booklet with Machin type stamps

Type ZP1

1969 (1 Dec). *"Stamps for Cooks". Type* ZP1 (150 × 72 *mm*) *with full colour pictorial cover showing "Baked, Stuffed Haddock". Contains* 12 *recipes on interleaving pages and on se-tenant labels attached to booklet panes. PVA gum. Stapled.*

ZP1	£1 containing panes of fifteen stamps (5 × 3): 15 × 5d. (No. 735), 30 × 4d. (No. 733) and pane comprising 6 × 4d. (three each of Nos. 734 and 734Eb) *se-tenant* with 6 × 1d. (No. 724) and 3 × 5d. (No. 735)	£140
ZP1a	As last but booklet is sewn with thread instead of being stapled	9·00

II. Decimal Booklets, 1971 onwards.

A. Stitched Booklets.

The 25p., 30p., 35p., 45p. and 50p. booklets have pictorial covers (except for the 35p. and 45p.) without the design inscription.

This was no longer necessary as the designs and background information were given on the inside of the front cover. Each series was numbered.

10p. Booklets

Type DN46
British Pillar Box Series

(Des R. Maddox)

1971 (15 Feb–1 June). *British Pillar Box Series. Orange-yellow cover as Type* DN46. *Pages of four stamps:* 2 × 2*p. se-tenant vertically with* $2 \times \frac{1}{2}$*p. and* 2 × 1*p. se-tenant vertically with* $2 \times 1\frac{1}{2}$*p.* (*Nos.* X841l *and* X844l).

DN46	FEB 1971 (No. 1 1855 type)	1·50
DN47	APR 1971 (No. 1 1855 type) (19.3.71)	1·50
DN48	JUNE 1971 (No. 2 1856 type) (1.6.71)	1·50

In No. DN47 the pillar box is slightly reduced in size.

1971 (14 July)–**74**. *British Pillar Box Series continued. Orange-yellow cover as Type* DN46. *Contents unchanged but panes are se-tenant horizontally* (*Nos.* X841l/a and X844m).

DN49	AUG 1971 (No. 2 1856 type) (14.7.71)	2·00
DN50	OCT 1971 (No. 3 1857–9 type) (27/8/71)	2·00
DN51	DEC 1971 (No. 3 1857–9 type) (6.10.71)	2·00
DN52	FEB 1972 (No. 4 1866–79 type) (8.12.71)	2·00
DN53	APR 1972 (No. 4 1866–79 type) (24.2.72)	2·00
DN54	JUNE 1972 (No. 5 1899 type) (12.4.72)	2·00
DN55	AUG 1972 (No. 5 1899 type) (8.6.72)	2·00
DN56	OCT 1972 (No. 6 1968 type) (2.8.72)	2·00
DN57	DEC 1972 (No. 6 1968 type) (30.10.72)	2·00
DN58	FEB 1973 (No. 7 1936 type) (5.1.73)	2·00
DN59	APR 1973 (No. 7 1936 type) (2.4.73)	2·75
DN60	JUNE 1973 (No. 8 1952 type) (18.4.73)	2·00
DN61	AUG 1973 (No. 8 1952 type) (4.7.73)	12·00
DN62	OCT 1973 (No. 9 1973 type) (16.8.73)	2·00
DN63	DEC 1973 (No. 9 1973 type) (12.11.73)	2·00
DN64	FEB 1974 (No. 9 1973 type) (17.12.73)	2·00
DN65	APR 1974 (No. 10 1974 type) (22.2.74)	2·00
DN66	JUNE 1974 (No. 10 1974 type) (23.4.74)	1·50

Type DN67
Postal Uniforms Series

(Des C. Abbott)

1974 (23 July)–**76**. *Postal Uniforms Series. Orange-yellow cover as Type* DN67. *Contents unchanged.*

DN67	AUG 1974 (No. 1 1793 type)	1·50
DN68	OCT 1974 (No. 1 1793 type) (27.8.74)	1·50
DN69	DEC 1974 (No. 2 1837 type) (25.10.74)	1·50
DN70	FEB 1975 (No. 2 1837 type) (12.12.74)	1·50
DN71	APR 1975 (No. 3 1855 type) (26.3.75)	1·50
DN72	JUNE 1975 (No. 3 1855 type) (21.5.75)	1·50
DN73	AUG 1975 (No. 3 1855 type) (27.6.75)	1·00
DN74	OCT 1975 (No. 3 1855 type) (3.10.75)	1·00
DN75	JAN 1976 (No. 3 1855 type) (16.3.76)	1·00

25p. Booklets

Type DH39
Veteran Transport Series

(Des D. Gentleman)

1971 (15 Feb). *Veteran Transport Series. Dull purple cover as Type* DH39. *Pages of six stamps:* $5 \times 2\frac{1}{2}$p. *with one printed label,* $4 \times 2\frac{1}{2}$p. *with two printed labels,* $5 \times \frac{1}{2}$p. *with one printed label* (*Nos.* X841m and X851l/m).

DH39	FEB 1971 (No. 1 Knife-board omnibus)	3·00

Type DH40

1971 (19 Mar). *Issued to publicise the National Postal Museum Exhibition of 80 Years of British Stamp Booklets. Dull purple cover as Type* DH40.

DH40	APR 1971	3·50

1971 (11 June)–**73**. *Dull purple cover as Type* DH39. *Veteran Transport Series continued.*

DH41	JUNE 1971 (No. 2 B-type omnibus)	4·00
DH42	AUG 1971 (No. 2 B-type omnibus) (17.9.71)	8·00
DH43	OCT 1971 (No. 3 Showman's Engine) (22.11.71)	8·00
DH44	FEB 1972 (No. 4 Mail Van) (23.12.71)	8·00
DH45	APR 1972 (No. 4 Mail Van) (13.3.72)	8·00
DH46	JUNE 1972 (No. 5 Motor Wagonette) (24.4.72)	8·00
DH47	AUG 1972 (No. 5 Motor Wagonette) (14.6.72)	8·00
DH48	OCT 1972 (No. 6 Taxi Cab) (17.7.72)	8·00
DH49	DEC 1972 (No. 6 Taxi Cab) (19.10.72)	8·00
DH50	DEC 1972 "Issues S" (No. 6 Taxi Cab) (6.11.72)	8·00
DH51	FEB 1973 (No. 7 Electric Tramcar) (26.2.73)	8·00

Nos. DH42/51 contain panes showing the perforations omitted between the label and the binding margin.

Type DH52

1973 (7 June). *Dull mauve cover as Type* DH52.

DH52	JUNE 1973	7·00

No. DH52 contains panes showing the perforations omitted between the label and the binding margin.

30p. Booklets

Type DQ56
British Birds Series

(Des H. Titcombe)

1971 (15 Feb). *British Birds Series. Bright purple cover as Type* DQ56. *Pages of six stamps: 2 panes of* 5 × 3p. *with one printed label* (*No.* X855l).

DQ56	FEB 1971 (No. 1 Curlew)	3·50

1971 (19 Mar). *Bright purple cover as Type* DH40.

DQ57	APR 1971	4·00

1971 (26 May)–**73**. *Bright purple cover as Type* DQ56. *British Birds Series continued.*

DQ58	JUNE 1971 (No. 2 Lapwing)	4·00
DQ59	AUG 1971 (No. 2 Lapwing) (23.7.71)	4·00
DQ60	OCT 1971 (No. 3 Robin) (1.10.71)	4·00
DQ61	DEC 1971 (No. 3 Robin) (10.11.71)	5·00
DQ62	FEB 1972 (No. 4 Pied Wagtail) (21.12.71)	4·00
DQ63	APR 1972 (No. 4 Pied Wagtail) (9.2.72)	4·00
DQ64	JUNE 1972 (No. 5 Kestrel) (12.4.72)	4·00
DQ65	AUG 1972 (No. 5 Kestrel) (8.6.72)	4·00
DQ66	OCT 1972 (No. 6 Black Grouse) (31.7.72)	4·50
DQ67	DEC 1972 (No. 6 Black Grouse) (30.10.72)	4·50
DQ68	DEC 1972 "Issue S" (No. 6 Black Grouse) (6.12.72)	4·50
DQ69	FEB 1973 (No. 7 Skylark) (29.1.73)	4·50
DQ70	APR 1973 (No. 7 Skylark) (2.4.73)	5·00
DQ71	JUNE 1973 (No. 8 Oyster-catcher) (8.5.73)	4·50
DQ72	AUG 1973 (No. 8 Oyster-catcher) (7.6.73)	5·00
DQ72*a*	As DQ72 but buff cover (10.8.73)*	5·00

Nos. DQ59/72*a* contain panes showing the perforations omitted between the label and the binding margin.

*No. DQ72*a* was printed with a buff cover because of a shortage of the original purple-coloured card.

1974 (30 Jan). *Red cover similar to Type* DH52. *Make-up as before but containing panes of* 5 × 3p. (1 *centre band*) (*No.* X856) *with blank label.*

DQ73	SPRING 1974	3·75

1974 (2 June). *Red cover similar to Type* DT9. *Make-up as before.*

DQ74	JUNE 1974	3·75

35p. Booklets

Type DP1
British Coins Series

(Des P Gauld)

1973 (12 Dec)–**74**. *British Coins Series. Blue cover as Type* DP1. *Pages of six stamps:* 2 *pages of* 5 × $3\frac{1}{2}$p. *with one blank label* (*No.* X858*Eb*).

DP1	AUTUMN 1973 (No. 1 Cuthred's Penny)	2·50
DP2	APR 1974 (No. 1 Cuthred's Penny) (10.4.74)	4·50
DP3	JUNE 1974 (No. 2 Silver Groat) (4.7.74)	2·50

1974 (23 Oct). *Blue cover as Type* DT9. *Make-up as before but with No.* X859.

DP4	SEPT 1974	2·50

45p. Booklets

1974 (9 Oct–26 Nov). *British Coins Series continued. Yellow-brown cover as Type* DP1. *Pages of six stamps:* 2 *pages of* 5 × $4\frac{1}{2}$p. (*No.* X865) *with one blank label.*

DS1	SEPT 1974 (No. 3 Elizabeth Gold Crown)	4·00
DS2	DEC 1974 (No. 3 Elizabeth Gold Crown) (1.11.74)	4·50
DS2*a*	As DS2 but orange-brown cover (26.11.74)*	11·00

*No. DS2*a* was printed with an orange-brown cover because of a shortage of the original yellow-brown card.

50p. Booklets

Type DT1

(Des Rosalie Southall)

1971 (15 Feb)–**72**. *British Flowers Series. Turquoise-green cover as Type* DT1. *Pages of six stamps:* 6 × 3p., 4 × 3p. *se-tenant horizontally with* 2 × $2\frac{1}{2}$p. *(side band),* 5 × $2\frac{1}{2}$p. *(centre band) with one printed label and* 5 × $\frac{1}{2}$p. *with one printed label (Nos.* X841m, X851l, X852l *and* X855 × 6).

DT1	FEB 1971 (No. 1 Large Bindweed)	7·00
DT2	MAY 1971 (No. 2 Primrose) (24.3.71)	7·00
DT3	AUG 1971 (No. 3 Honeysuckle) (28.6.71)	7·00
DT4	NOV 1971 (No. 4 Hop) (17.9.71)	8·00
DT5	FEB 1972 (No. 5 Common Violet) (23.12.71)*	8·00
DT6	MAY 1972 (No. 6 Lords-and-Ladies) (13.3.72)	7·00
DT7	AUG 1972 (No. 7 Wood Anemone) (31.5.72)	7·00
DT8	NOV 1972 (No. 8 Deadly Nightshade) (15.9.72)	7·00

Nos. DT4/8 contain panes showing the perforations omitted between the label and the binding margin.

* Although generally released on 24 December, this booklet was put on sale at the London E.C.1 Philatelic Counter and also at one other Philatelic Counter on 23 December.

Type DT9

1973 (19 Jan–June). *Turquoise-green cover as Type* DT9.

DT 9	FEB 1973	7·00
DT10	APR 1973 (26.2.73)	8·00
DT11	MAY 1973 (2.4.73)	8·50
DT12	AUG 1973 (14.6.73)	12·00

1973 (14 Nov)–**74**. *Moss-green cover similar to Type* DT9. *Pages of six stamps:* 2 *pages of* 5 × $3\frac{1}{2}$p. *with one blank label (No.* X858*Eb) and* 1 *page of* 5 × 3p. *(centre band) and one blank label (No.* X856).

DT13	AUTUMN 1973	6·00
DT14	MAR 1974 (18.2.74)	4·00

85p. Booklet

1974 (13 Nov). *Purple cover similar to Type* DT9.

DW1 Containing 3 pages of 5 × $4\frac{1}{2}$p. (No. X865) with one blank label and 1 page of 5 × $3\frac{1}{2}$p. (No. X859) with one blank label . . . . . 6·00

Sponsored Booklets

Type DX1

(Des J. Wallis)

1972 (24 May). *"The Story of Wedgwood". Full colour pictorial cover, Type* DX1 *(150 × 72 mm). Containing information and illustrations on interleaving panes and on se-tenant label attached to booklet panes.*

DX1 £1 containing 12 × 3p. (No. X855) and booklet panes X851n, X841o and X841p . . . . . 75·00

Price quoted for No. DX1 is for examples showing the $\frac{1}{2}$p. 1 side band, No. X842, (in pane No. X841p) with full perforations. Examples of the booklet with this $\frac{1}{2}$p. value showing trimmed perforations are priced at £30.

ILLUSTRATIONS. Sponsored booklet covers from No. DX2 are illustrated at one-third linear size *unless otherwise stated.*

Type DX2

(Des J. Wallis)

1980 (16 Apr). *"The Story of Wedgwood". Multicoloured cover, Type* DX2 *(163 × 97 mm) showing painting "Josiah Wedgwood and his Family" by George Stubbs. Booklet contains text and illustrations on the labels attached to panes and on interleaving pages.*

DX2 £3 containing booklet panes Nos. X849n, X849o, X888l and X895l . . . . . 8·50

No. DX2 is inscribed "January 1980".

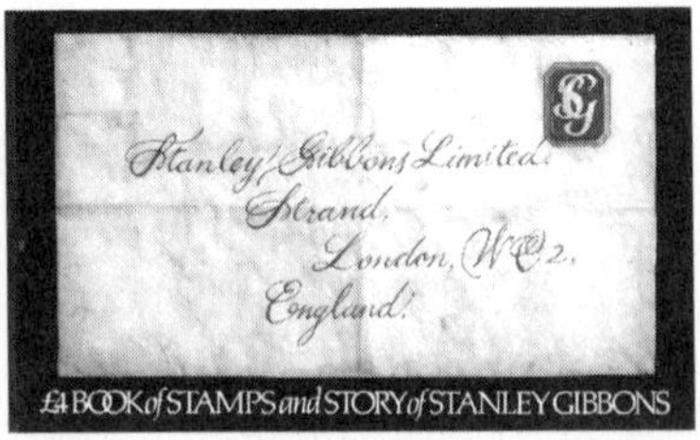

Type DX3

(Des B. Dedman)

1982 (19 May). *"Story of Stanley Gibbons". Multicoloured cover, Type* DX3 *(163 × 97 mm) showing early envelope design on front and stamp album with text on back. Booklet contains text and illustrations on labels attached to panes and on interleaving pages.*

DX3 £4 containing booklet panes Nos. X849p, X899m and X907l/m . . . . . 12·00

No. DX3 is inscribed "February 1982".

Type DX4

(Des B. West)

1983 (14 Sept). *"Story of the Royal Mint". Multicoloured cover, Type* DX4 *(163 × 97 mm) showing current coins, die and tools. Booklet contains text and illustrations on labels attached to panes and on interleaving pages.*

DX4 £4 containing booklet panes Nos. X899m × 2, X930b and X949l .... 12·00

Type DX5

(Des P. Miles)

1984 (4 Sept). *"The Story of our Christian Heritage". Multicoloured cover, Type* DX5 *(163 × 97 mm) showing mosaic of Christ from Hinton St. Mary Roman villa. Booklet contains text and illustrations on labels attached to panes and on interleaving pages.*

DX5 £4 containing booklet panes Nos. X886bl, X901m × 2 and X952l .... 32·00

Type DX6

(Des D. Driver)

1985 (8 Jan). *"Story of The Times" (newspaper). Multicoloured cover, Type* DX6 *(163 × 95 mm) showing "Waiting for The Times" (painting by Haydon). Booklet contains text and illustrations on labels attached to panes and on interleaving pages.*

DX6 £5 containing booklet panes Nos. X864l, X900l, X952l and X952m .... 22·00

Type DX7

(Des Trickett and Webb Ltd)

1986 (18 Mar). *"The Story of British Rail". Multicoloured cover, Type* DX7 *(162 × 95 mm) showing diesel locomotive. Booklet contains text and illustrations on labels attached to panes and on interleaving pages.*

DX7 £5 containing booklet panes Nos. X896l, X897m, X952l and X952m .... 25·00

Type DX8

(Des Aitken Blakeley Designers)

1987 (3 Mar). *"The Story of P & O". Multicoloured cover, Type* DX8 *(162 × 95 mm) showing the "William Fawcett". Booklet contains text and illustrations on labels attached to panes and on interleaving pages.*

DX8 £5 containing booklet panes Nos. X847m, X900l, X900m and X955l .... 22·00

Type DX9

(Des The Partners)

1988 (9 Feb). *"The Story of the Financial Times" (newspaper). Multicoloured cover, Type DX9 (162 × 97 mm). Booklet contains text and illustrations on labels attached to the panes and on interleaving pages.*

DX9 £5 containing booklet panes Nos. X1005l, X1006l, X1009l and X1009m . . . . 28·00

Type DX10

(Des Tayburn)

1989 (21 Mar). *"The Scots Connection". Multicoloured cover, Type DX10 (162 × 97 mm). Booklet contains text and illustrations on labels attached to the panes and on interleaving pages.*

DX10 £5 containing booklet panes Nos. S54l, S55l, S62l and S62m . . . . 24·00

Type DX11

(Des D. Driver)

1990 (20 Mar). *"London Life". Multicoloured cover, Type DX11 (162 × 97 mm). Booklet contains text and illustrations on labels attached to the panes and on interleaving pages.*

DX11 £5 containing booklet panes Nos. X906m, 1469n × 2 and 1493a . . . . 24·00

Type DX12

(Des Trickett and Webb Ltd)

1991 (19 Mar). *"Alias Agatha Christie". Multicoloured cover, Type DX12 (162 × 97 mm). Booklet contains text and illustrations on labels attached to the panes and on interleaving pages.*

DX12 £6 containing booklet panes Nos. X1008l × 2, X1016l and X1016m . . . . 20·00

Type DX13

(Des G. Evernden and J. Gibbs)

1992 (25 Feb). *"Cymru–Wales". Multicoloured cover, Type DX13 (162 × 97 mm). Booklet contains text and illustrations on labels attached to the panes and on interleaving pages.*

DX13 £6 Containing booklet panes Nos. 1591a, W48a, W49a and W59a. . . . . 20·00

Type DX14

(Des The Partners)

1992 (27 Oct). *Birth Centenary of J. R. R. Tolkien (author). Multicoloured cover, Type DX14 (162 × 97 mm). Booklet contains text and illustrations on labels attached to the panes and on interleaving pages.*

DX14 £6 containing booklet panes Nos. X1011l, X1012l and X1017l × 2 . . . . 19·00

Type DX15

(Des The Partners)

1993 (10 Aug). *"The Story of Beatrix Potter". Multicoloured cover, Type* DX15 (162 × 97 *mm). Booklet contains text and illustrations on labels attached to the panes and on interleaving pages.*

DX15 £5.64, containing booklet panes Nos. X1012m, 1451al, 1649a and NI48l .... 22·00

Although inscribed "£6.00" No. DX15 was sold at the face value of its contents, £5.64.

Type DX16

(Des Carroll, Dempsey and Thirkell Ltd)

1994 (26 July). *"Northern Ireland". Multicoloured cover, Type* DX16 (162 × 97 *mm). Booklet contains text and illustrations on labels attached to the panes and on interleaving pages.*

DX16 £6.04, containing booklet panes Nos. Y1748l, 1812a and NI70a/b, together with a 35p. postal stationery air card 18·00

Type DX17

(Des The Partners)

1995 (25 Apr). *Centenary of the National Trust. Multicoloured cover, Type* DX17 (162 × 97 *mm). Booklet contains text and illustrations on labels attached to the panes and on interleaving pages.*

DX17 £6 containing booklet panes Nos. Y1749l, Y1750l, 1869a and NI70d .... 18·00

Type DX18

(Des Why Not Associates)

1996 (14 May). *European Football Championship. Multicoloured cover as Type* DX18 (162 × 97 *mm). Booklet contains text and illustrations on labels attached to the panes and on interleaving pages.*

DX18 £6.48, containing booklet panes Nos. Y1752l, 1925a, 1926a and 1927a .... 14·00

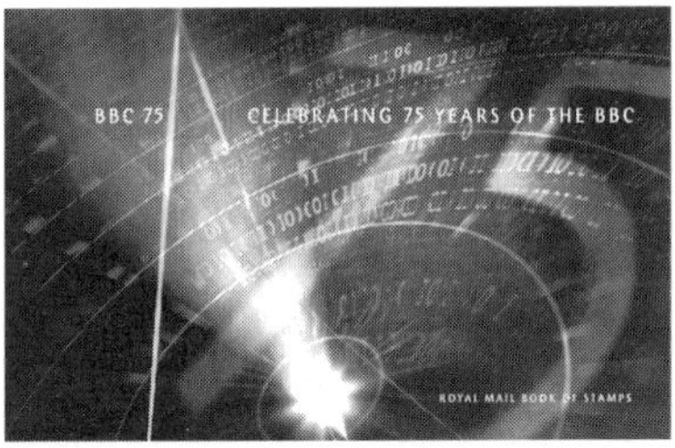

Type DX19

(Des H. Brown)

1997 (23 Sept). *75th Anniv of the B.B.C. Multicoloured cover, Type* DX19 (162 × 97 *mm). Booklet contains text and illustrations on labels attached to the panes and on interleaving pages.*

DX19 £6.15, containing booklet panes Nos. Y1675bl, 1940ab, 1978l and NI79l .... 9·25

B. Folded Booklets.

NOTE: All panes are attached to the covers by the selvedge. Inscribed dates are those shown with the printer's imprint.

Illustrations for 10p., 50p., £1 and £2 booklets are $\frac{3}{4}$ size; others are $\frac{2}{3}$ size

10p. Booklets

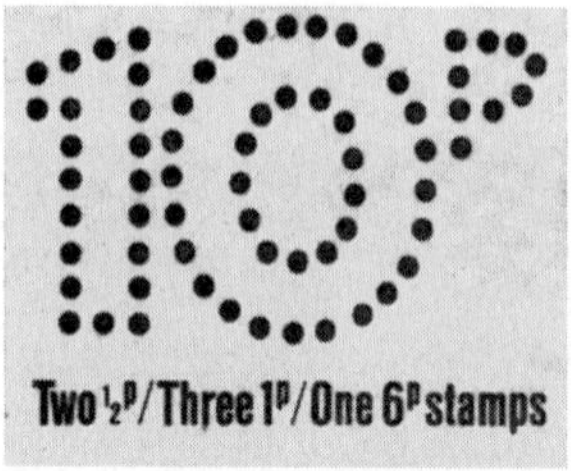

Type FA1

1976 (10 Mar)–**77**. *Cover as Type FA1 printed in dull rose on very pale lavender. Containing booklet pane No. X841r.*

FA1	NOV 1975	70
FA2	MAR 1976 (9.6.76)	80
FA3	JUNE 1977 (13.6.77)	70

Type FA4

(Des N. Battershill)

1978 (8 Feb)–**79**. *Farm Buildings Series. Bistre-brown and turquoise-blue covers as Type FA4, containing booklet pane No. X843m.*

FA4	Design No. 1, Oast Houses	75
FA5	Design No. 2, Buildings in Ulster (3.5.78)	75
FA6	Design No. 3, Buildings in Yorkshire (9.8.78)	75
FA7	Design No. 4, Buildings in Wales (25.10.78)	75
FA8	Design No. 5, Buildings in Scotland (10.1.79)	75
FA9	Design No. 6, Buildings in Sussex (4.4.79)	75

Nos. FA4/5 are inscribed "January 1978", FA6 "July 1978", FA7 "October 1978", FA8 "December 1978" and FA9 "March 1979".

Type FA10

(Des Hamper and Purssell)

1979 (17 Oct)–**80**. *"London 1980" International Stamp Exhibition. Red and blue cover as Type FA10 showing Post Office exhibition stand and containing No. X845l.*

FA10	Inscr "August 1979"	60
FA11	Inscr "January 1980" (12.1.80)	60

50p. Booklets

All booklets were sold at the cover price of 50p. although some contain stamps to a greater value.

Type FB1

1977 (26 Jan). *Cover as Type FB1 printed in maroon and pale blue.*

FB1A	Containing booklet pane X841s	2·50
FB1B	Containing booklet pane X841sa	2·50

1977 (13 June). *Cover as Type FB1. Printed in chestnut and stone.*

FB2A	Containing booklet pane X844n	4·00
FB2B	Containing booklet pane X844na	2·50

Type FB3

(Des J. Ireland)

1978 (8 Feb)–**79**. *Commercial Vehicles Series. Olive-yellow and grey covers as Type FB3. A. Containing booklet pane No. X844n. B. Containing booklet pane No. X844na.*

		A	B
FB3	Design No. 1, Clement Talbot van	4·00	3·00
FB4	Design No. 2, Austin taxi (3.5.78)	4·00	2·50
FB5	Design No. 3, Morris Royal Mail van (9.8.78)	4·50	2·50
FB6	Design No. 4, Guy Electric dustcart (25.10.78)	4·50	3·00
FB7	Design No. 5, Albion van (10.1.79)	5·00	2·50
FB8	Design No. 6, Leyland fire engine (4.4.79)	3·00	3·00

Nos. FB3/4 are inscribed "January 1978", FB5 "July 1978", FB6 "October 1978", FB7 "December 1978" and FB8 "March 1979".

1979 (28 Aug). *Contents changed. A. Containing booklet pane No. X849l. B. Containing booklet pane No. X849la.*

		A	B
FB9	Design No. 6, Leyland fire engine	2·00	2·00

Type FB10

(Des B. Smith)

1979 (3 Oct)–**81**. *Veteran Cars Series. Orange-red and reddish lilac covers as Type* FB10. *A. Containing booklet pane No.* X849l. *B. Containing booklet pane No.* X849la.

		A	B
FB10	Design No. 1, 1907 Rolls-Royce Silver Ghost	2·50	2·50

No. FB10 is inscribed "August 1979".

Contents changed. A. Containing booklet pane No. X849m. *B. Containing booklet pane No.* X849ma.

		A	B
FB11	Design No. 2, 1908 Grand Prix Austin (4.2.80) ...	2·50	2·00
FB12	Design No. 3, 1903–5 Vauxhall (25.6.80)	2·50	2·00
FB13	Design No. 4, 1897–1900 Daimler (24.9.80)	2·50	2·00

No. FB11 is inscribed "January 1980", No. FB12 "May 1980" and No. FB13 "July 1980".

Contents changed. A. Containing No. X841t. *B. Containing No.* X841ta.

		A	B
FB14	Design No. 5, 1896 Lanchester (26.1.81)	2·25	2·25
FB15	Design No. 6, 1913 Bull-nose Morris (18.3.81) ...	2·25	2·25

Nos. FB14/15 are inscribed "January 1981".

Type FB16

(Des R. Downer)

1981 (6 May)–**82**. *Follies Series. Brown and orange-brown covers as Type* FB16. *A. Containing No.* X841t. *B. Containing No.* X841ta.

		A	B
FB16	Design No. 1, Mugdock Castle, Stirlingshire	2·50	2·50

No. FB16 is inscribed "January 1981".

Contents changed. A. Containing No. X854l. *B. Containing No.* X854la.

		A	B
FB17	Design No. 1, Mugdock Castle, Stirlingshire (26.8.81)	5·00	7·00
FB18	Design No. 2, Mow Cop Castle, Cheshire-Staffs border (30.9.81)	5·00	7·00

Nos. FB17/18 are inscribed "January 1981".

Contents changed. A. Containing No. X841u. *B. Containing No.* X841ua.

		A	B
FB19	Design No. 3, Paxton's Tower, Llanarthney, Dyfed (1.2.82)	2·50	2·50
FB20	Design No. 4, Temple of the Winds, Mount Stewart, Northern Ireland (6.5.82)	2·50	2·50
FB21	Design No. 5, Temple of the Sun, Stourhead, Wilts (11.8.82)	3·00	3·00
FB22	Design No. 6, Water Garden, Cliveden, Bucks (6.10.82)	3·00	3·00

Nos. FB19/22 are inscribed "February 1982".

Type FB23

(Des H. Titcombe)

1983 (16 Feb–26 Oct). *Rare Farm Animals Series. Bright green and black covers as Type* FB23. *A. Containing booklet pane No.* X841u. *B. Containing booklet pane No.* X841ua.

		A	B
FB23	Design No. 1, Bagot Goat	3·00	3·00

Contents changed. Containing No. X845n.

FB24	Design No. 2, Gloucester Old Spot Pig (5.4.83)	5·00
	b. Corrected rate	12·00
FB25	Design No. 3, Toulouse Goose (27.7.83)	5·00
FB26	Design No. 4, Orkney Sheep (26.10.83)	5·00

No. FB23 is inscribed "February 1982" and Nos. FB24/6 "April 1983". The corrected rate reads, "36p. for 200g" instead of "37p. for 200g".

Type FB27

(Des P. Morter)

1984 (3 Sept)–**85**. *Orchids Series. Yellow-green and lilac covers as Type* FB27. *Containing booklet pane No.* X845p.

FB27	Design No. 1, *Dendrobium nobile* and *Miltonia* hybrid .	4·00
FB28	Design No. 2, *Cypripedium calceolus* and *Ophrys apifera* (15.1.85)	4·00
FB29	Design No. 3, *Bifrenaria* and *Vanda tricolor* (23.4.85)	4·00
FB30	Design No. 4, *Cymbidium* and *Arpophyllum* (23.7.85) ..	4·00

Nos. FB27/30 are inscribed "September 1984".

Type FB31

(Des M. Thierens Design)

1985 (4 Nov). *Cover as Type* FB31 *printed in black and bright scarlet. Containing booklet pane No.* X909l.

FB31 Pillar box design .... 3·00

No. FB31 is inscribed "November 1985".

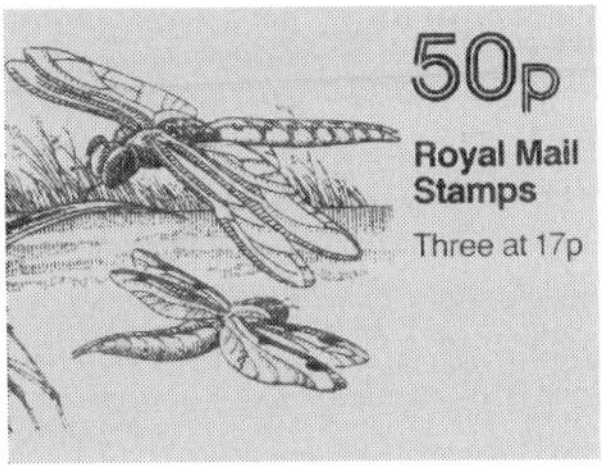

Type FB32

(Des P. Morter)

1986 (20 May–12 Aug). *Pond Life Series. Dull blue and emerald covers as Type* FB32. *Containing booklet pane No.* X909l.

FB32 Design No. 1, Emperor Dragonfly, Four-spotted Libellula and Yellow Flag .... 3·00

FB33 Design No. 2. Common Frog, Fennel-leaved Pondweed and Long-stalked Pondweed (29.7.86) .... 3·50

a. Containing booklet pane No. X909Ela (12.8.86) ... 3·75

Nos. FB32/33a are inscribed "November 1985".

Type FB34

(Des N. Battershill)

1986 (29 July). *Roman Britain Series. Brown-ochre and Indian red cover as Type* FB34. *Containing booklet pane No.* X845q.

FB34 Design No. 1, Hadrian's Wall .... 8·00

No. FB34 is inscribed "November 1985".

1986 (20 Oct)–**87**. *Pond Life Series continued. Dull blue and emerald covers as Type* FB32. *Containing booklet pane No.* X845s.

FB35 Design No. 3, Moorhen and Little Grebe .... 4·00

FB36 Design No. 4, Giant Pond and Great Ramshorn Snails (27.1.87) .... 4·00

No. FB36 is inscribed "October 1986".

1986 (20 Oct)–**87**. *Roman Britain Series continued. Brown-ochre and Indian red covers as Type* FB34. *Containing booklet pane No.* X847l.

FB37 Design No. 2, Roman Theatre of Verulamium, St. Albans 3·50

FB38 Design No. 3, Portchester Castle, Hampshire (27.1.87) .. 3·25

No. FB38 is inscribed "October 1986".

Type FB39

(Des Patricia Howes)

1987 (14 Apr)–**88**. *Bicentenary of Marylebone Cricket Club Series. Brown and dull ultramarine covers as Type* FB39. *Containing booklet pane No.* X847l.

FB39 Design No. 1, Father Time weather vane .... 3·00

FB40 Design No. 2, Ashes urn and embroidered velvet bag (14.7.87) .... 3·00

FB41 Design No. 3, Lord's Pavilion and wrought iron decoration on roof (29.9.87) .... 3·00

FB42 Design No. 4, England team badge and new stand at Lord's (26.1.88) .... 3·00

Nos. FB39/42 are inscribed "October 1986".

Type FB43

(Des G. Evernden)

1987 (14 Apr)–**88**. *Botanical Gardens Series. Covers as Type* FB43. *Containing booklet panes No.* X845s (FB43/4) *or* X845sa (FB45/6).

FB43 Design No. 1 (cover in ultramarine and rose-red), Rhododendron "Elizabeth", Bodnant .... 4·00

FB44 Design No. 2 (cover in deep ultramarine and cobalt), *Gentiana sino-ornata*, Edinburgh (14.7.87) .... 4·00

FB45 Design No. 3 (cover in dull ultramarine and orange-yellow), *Lilium auratum* and "Mount Stuart" (incorrect inscr) (29.9.87) .... 3·25

a. With corrected spelling "Mount Stewart" (30.10.87) .... 3·25

FB46 Design No. 4 (cover in dull ultramarine and yellow-orange), *Strelitzia reginae*, Kew (26.1.88) .... 3·00

Nos. FB43/6 are inscribed "October 1986".

The panes from Nos. FB45/6 have imperforate vertical sides.

Type FB47

1988 (12 Apr–5 July). *London Zoo. Children's Drawings Series. Covers as Type* FB47.

FB47 Pigs design (cover in black and rose) containing booklet pane No. X847l . . . . 3·00
FB48 Birds design (cover in black and yellow) containing booklet pane No. X845sa . . . . 3·00
FB49 Elephants design (cover in black and grey) containing booklet pane No. X847l (5.7.88) . . . . 3·00

Nos. FB47/9 are inscribed "October 1986". The pane from No. FB48 has imperforate vertical sides.

Type FB50

(Des P. Morter)

1988 (5 July). *Marine Life Series. Blue and orange-brown cover as Type* FB50. *Containing booklet pane No.* X845sa.

FB50 Design No. 1, Parasitic Anemone on Common Whelk Shell and Umbrella Jellyfish . . . . 3·00

No. FB50 is inscribed "October 1986" and has the vertical sides of the pane imperforate.

Type FB51

(Des Lynda Gray)

1988 (5 Sept)–**89**. *Gilbert and Sullivan Operas Series. Black and red covers as Type* FB51. *Containing booklet pane No.* X904l.

FB51 Design No. 1, *The Yeomen of the Guard* . . . . 4·00
FB52 Design No. 2, *The Pirates of Penzance* (24.1.89) . . . . 4·00
FB53 Design No. 3, *The Mikado* (25.4.89) . . . . 4·00

1989 (18 July). *Marine Life Series continued. Blue and orange-brown cover as Type* FB50. *Containing booklet pane No.* X904l.

FB54 Design No. 2, Common Hermit Crab, Bladder Wrack and Laver Spire Shell . . . . 4·00

For Design No. 3, see £1 Booklet No. FH17.

Type FB55

(Des P. Hutton)

1989 (2 Oct)–**90**. *Aircraft Series. Turquoise-green and light brown covers as Type* FB55. *Containing booklet pane No.* X906l.

FB55 Design No. 1, HP42, Armstrong Whitworth Atalanta and De Havilland Dragon Rapide . . . . 5·50

No. FB55 was incorrectly inscribed "Atlanta".

As before, but containing Penny Black Anniversary booklet pane No. 1468l.

FB56 Design No. 2, Vickers Viscount 806 and De Havilland Comet 4 (30.1.90) . . . . 5·50

1990 (4 Sept)–**91**. *Aircraft Series continued. Turquoise-green and light brown covers as Type* FB55. *Containing booklet pane No.* X911l.

FB57 Design No. 3, BAC 1-11 and VC10 . . . . 4·50
FB58 Design No. 4, BAe ATP, BAe 146 and Aérospatiale–BAC Concorde (25.6.91) . . . . 3·50

Type FB59

(Des A. Drummond)

1991 (10 Sept)–**92**. *Archaeology Series. Covers as Type* FB59. *Containing booklet pane No.* X925m.

FB59 Design No. 1 (cover in bright blue and lake-brown), Sir Arthur Evans at Knossos, Crete . . . . 2·50
a. Corrected rate (10.91) . . . . 3·50
FB60 Design No. 2 (cover in bright blue and yellow), Howard Carter in the Tomb of Tutankhamen (21.1.92) . . . . 2·50
FB61 Design No. 3 (cover in bright blue and yellow), Sir Austen Layard at Assyrian site (28.4.92) . . . . 2·50
FB62 Design No. 4 (cover in new blue and yellow), Sir Flinders Petrie surveying the Pyramids and temples of Giza (28.7.92) . . . . 2·50

On the inside front cover of No. FB59 the inland letter rates are shown as 1st class 24, 35, 43, 51p. and 2nd class 18, 28, 33, 39p. These were corrected on No. FB59a to read: 1st class 24, 36, 45, 54p. and 2nd class 18, 28, 34, 41p.

Type FB63

(Des J. Matthews)

1992 (22 Sept). *1000th Anniv of Appointment of Sheriffs. Dull blue and scarlet cover as Type* FB63. *Containing booklet pane No.* X925m.

FB63 Design showing Crest, with Helm and Mantling, and Badge of The Shrievalty Association .... 2·00

Type FB64

(Des M. Newton)

1993 (9 Feb–6 July). *Postal History Series. Covers as Type* FB64. *Containing booklet pane No.* X925m.

FB64 Design No. 1 (cover in grey-green and grey-black), Airmail postmarks .... 1·50

FB65 Design No. 2 (cover in dull orange and black), Ship mail postmarks (6.4.93) .... 1·50

FB66 Design No. 3 (cover in blue and grey-black), Registered mail postmarks (6.7.93) .... 1·50

1993 (1 Nov). *Postal History Series continued. Rose-red and grey-black cover as Type* FB64 *containing booklet pane No.* Y1676l.

FB67 Design No. 4, "Paid" postmarks .... 1·50

Type FB68

(Des A. Davidson)

1994 (25 Jan–6 Sept). *Coaching Inns Series. Covers as Type* FB68. *Containing booklet pane No.* Y1676l.

FB68 Design No. 1 (cover in myrtle-green and pale myrtle-green), "Swan with Two Necks" .... 1·50

FB69 Design No. 2 (cover in sepia and buff), "Bull and Mouth" (26.4.94) .... 1·50

FB70 Design No. 3 (cover in reddish brown and cinnamon), "Golden Cross" (6.6.94) .... 1·50

FB71 Design No. 4 (cover in black and slate-blue), "Pheasant Inn", Wiltshire (6.9.94) .... 1·50

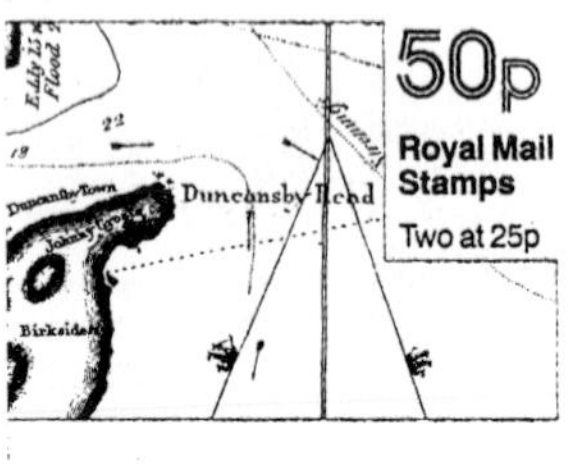

Type FB72

(Des D. Davis)

1995 (7 Feb–4 Apr). *Sea Charts Series. Rosine and black covers as Type* FB72, *containing booklet pane No.* Y1676l.

FB72 Design No. 1, John o' Groats, 1800 .... 1·50

FB73 Design No. 2, Land's End, 1808 (4.4.95) .... 1·50

1995 (6 June–4 Sept). *Sea Charts Series continued. Rosine and black covers as Type* FB72, *containing booklet pane No.* Y1677l.

FB74 Design No. 3, St. David's Head, 1812 .... 1·50

FB75 Design No. 4, Giant's Causeway, 1828 (4.9.95) .... 1·50

65p. Booklet

1976 (14 July). *Cover as Type* FB1, *but larger* (90 × 49 *mm*). *Printed in turquoise-blue and pale buff. A. Selvedge at left. B. Selvedge at right.*

		A	B
FC1	Containing ten 6½p. (No. X872)	7·00	7·00

70p. Booklets

1977 (13 June). *Cover as Type* FB1, *but larger* (90 × 49 *mm*). *Printed in purple-brown and dull rose. A. Selvedge at left. B. Selvedge at right.*

		A	B
FD1	Containing ten 7p. (No. X875)	5·00	5·00

Type FD2

(Des E. Stemp)

1978 (8 Feb)–**79**. *Country Crafts Series. Grey-green and red-brown covers as Type* FD2 (90 × 49 *mm*). *Containing ten 7p.* (No. X875). A. *Selvedge at left.* B. *Selvedge at right.*

		A	B
FD2	Design No. 1, Horse-shoeing	12·00	4·00
FD3	Design No. 2, Thatching (3.5.78)	65·00	4·00
FD4	Design No. 3, Dry-stone-walling (9.8.78)	£120	4·00
FD5	Design No. 4, Wheel-making (25.10.78)	8·00	4·50
FD6	Design No. 5, Wattle fence-making (10.1.79)	14·00	5·00

Nos. FD2/3 are inscribed "January 1978", FD4 "July 1978", FD5 "October 1978" and FD6 "December 1978".

Type FD7

(Des F. Wegner)

1979 (5 Feb). *Official opening of Derby Mechanised Letter Office. Pale yellow-green and lilac cover as Type* FD7 (90 × 49 *mm*). *Containing ten 7p.* (*No.* X875). A. *Selvedge at left.* B. *Selvedge at right.*

		A	B
FD7	Kedleston Hall	7·00	7·00

No. FD7 is inscribed "December 1978".

On sale only in the Derby Head Post Office area to promote postcode publicity and also at the Philatelic Bureau and philatelic sales counters.

1979 (4 Apr). *Country Crafts Series continued. Grey-green and red-brown covers as Type* FD2 (90 × 49 *mm*). A. *Selvedge at left.* B. *Selvedge at right.*

		A	B
FD8	Design No. 6, Basket-making	6·00	5·00

No. FD8 is inscribed "March 1979".

80p. Booklet

Type FE1

(Des P. Hutton)

1979 (3 Oct). *Military Aircraft Series. Blue and grey cover as Type* FE1 (90 × 49 *mm*). *Containing ten 8p.* (*No.* X879) *attached by the selvedge.* A. *Selvedge at left.* B. *Selvedge at right.*

		A	B
FE1	Design No. 1, BE2B, 1914, & Vickers Gun Bus, 1915	3·00	3·00

No. FE1 is inscribed "August 1979".

85p. Booklet

1976 (14 July). *Cover as Type* FB1 *but larger* (90 × 49 *mm*). *Printed in light yellow-olive and brownish grey.* A. *Selvedge at left.* B. *Selvedge at right.*

		A	B
FF1	Containing ten $8\frac{1}{2}$p. (No. X881)	7·00	7·00

90p. Booklets

1977 (13 June). *Cover as Type* FB1, *but larger* (90 × 49 *mm*). *Printed in deep grey-blue and cobalt.* A. *Selvedge at left.* B. *Selvedge at right.*

		A	B
FG1	Containing ten 9p. (No. X883)	5·00	6·00

Type FG2

(Des R. Maddox)

1978 (8 Feb)–**79**. *British Canals Series. Yellow-olive and new blue covers as Type* FG2 (90 × 49 *mm*). *Containing ten 9p.* (*No.* X883). A. *Selvedge at left.* B. *Selvedge at right.*

		A	B
FG2	Design No. 1, Grand Union	20·00	6·50
FG3	Design No. 2, Llangollen (3.5.78)	5·00	£250
FG4	Design No. 3, Kennet & Avon (9.8.78)	13·00	8·00
FG5	Design No. 4, Caledonian (25.10.78)	5·00	5·00
FG6	Design No. 5, Regents (10.1.79)	13·00	7·00

Nos. FG2/3 are inscribed "January 1978", FG4 "July 1978", FG5 "October 1978" and FG6 "December 1978".

(Des F. Wegner)

1979 (5 Feb). *Official Opening of Derby Mechanised Letter Office. Violet-blue and rose cover as Type* FD7 (90 × 49 *mm*). *Containing ten 9p.* (*No.* X883). A. *Selvedge at left.* B. *Selvedge at right.*

		A	B
FG7	Tramway Museum, Crich	8·00	8·00

No. FG7 is inscribed "December 1978".

On sale only in the Derby Head Post Office area to promote postcode publicity and also at the Philatelic Bureau and philatelic sales counters.

1979 (4 Apr). *British Canals Series continued. Yellow-olive and new blue cover as Type* FG2. A. *Selvedge at left.* B. *Selvedge at right.*

		A	B
FG8	Design No. 6, Leeds & Liverpool	4·00	4·00

No. FG8 is inscribed "March 1979".

£1 Booklets

All booklets were sold at the cover price of £1 although some contain stamps to a greater value

Type FH1

(Des N. Battershill)

1979 (3 Oct). *Industrial Archaeology Series. Red and green cover as Type* FH1 *(90 × 49 mm). Containing ten 10p. (No.* X887*). A. Selvedge at left. B. Selvedge at right.*

		A	B
FH1	Design No. 1, Ironbridge, Telford, Salop	4·50	4·00

No. FH1 is inscribed "August 1979".

1980 (4 Feb–24 Sept). *Military Aircraft Series continued. Blue and grey covers as Type* FE1 *(90 × 49 mm). Containing ten 10p. (No.* X888*). A. Selvedge at left. B. Selvedge at right.*

		A	B
FH2	Design No. 2, Sopwith Camel & Vickers Vimy	4·00	4·00
FH3	Design No. 3, Hawker Hart* & Handley Page Heyford (25.6.80)	4·00	4·50
FH4	Design No. 4, Hurricane & Wellington (24.9.80)	4·00	4·00

No FH2 is inscribed "January 1980", No. FH3 "May 1980" and No. FH4 "July 1980".

*On the booklet cover the aircraft is wrongly identified as a Hawker Fury.

Type FH5

(Des M. Newton and S. Paine)

1986 (29 July)–**87**. *Musical Instruments Series. Scarlet and black covers as Type* FH5*. Containing six 17p.* (X952).

FH5	Design No 1, Violin	5·00

No. FH5 is inscribed "November 1985".

Contents changed. Containing No. X901n.

FH6	Design No. 2, French horn (20.10.86)	5·00
FH7	Design No. 3, Bass clarinet (27.1.87)	5·00

No. FH7 is inscribed "October 1986".

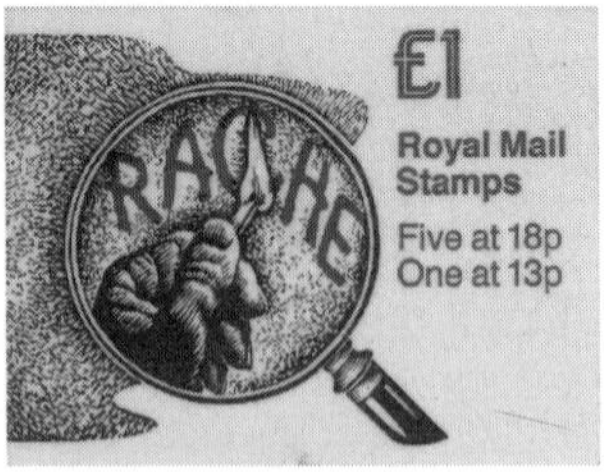

Type FH8

(Des A. Davidson)

1987 (14 Apr)–**88**. *Sherlock Holmes Series. Bright scarlet and grey-black covers as Type* FH8*. Containing booklet pane No.* X901n (FH8/9) *or* X901na (FH10/11).

FH 8	Design No. 1, *A Study in Scarlet*	5·00
FH 9	Design No. 2, *The Hound of the Baskervilles* (14.7.87)	5·00
FH10	Design No. 3, *The Adventure of the Speckled Band* (29.9.87)	5·00
FH11	Design No. 4, *The Final Problem* (26.1.88)	5·00

Nos. FH8/11 are inscribed "October 1986".

The panes from Nos. FH10/11 have imperforate vertical sides.

1988 (12 Apr). *London Zoo. Children's Drawings Series. Cover as Type* FB47 *in black and brown. Containing booklet pane No.* X901na.

FH12	Bears design	5·00

No. FH12 is inscribed "October 1986" and has the vertical sides of the pane imperforate.

Type FH13

(Des Liz Moyes)

1988 (5 July)–**89**. *Charles Dickens Series. Orange-red and maroon covers as Type* FH13.

FH13	Designs No. 1, *Oliver Twist*, containing booklet pane No. X901na	6·00
FH14	Design No. 2, *Nicholas Nickleby*, containing booklet pane No. X904m (5.9.88)	6·00
FH15	Design No. 3, *David Copperfield*, containing booklet pane No. X904m (24.1.89)	6·00
FH16	Design No. 4, *Great Expectations*, containing booklet pane No. X1051l (25.4.89)	8·00

No. FH13 is inscribed "October 1986" and No. FH16 "September 1988", Nos. FH13/16 have the vertical sides of the pane imperforate.

1989 (18 July). *Marine Life Series continued. Cover as Type* FB50 *in turquoise-green and scarlet. Containing booklet pane No.* X904m.

FH17	Design No. 3, Edible Sea Urchin, Common Starfish and Common Shore Crab	6·00

No. FH17 has the vertical edges of the pane imperforate.

Type FH18

(Des J. Sancha)

1989 (2 Oct)–**90**. *Mills Series. Grey-black and grey-green matt card cover as Type* FH18.

FH18 Design No. 1, Wicken Fen, Ely containing booklet pane No. X960l . . . . 7·00

As Type FH18 *but glossy card cover containing Penny Black Anniversary booklet pane No.* 1476l *printed in litho by Walsall.*

FH19 Design No. 1 (cover in bottle-green and pale green), Wicken Fen, Ely (30.1.90) . . . . 7·00

No. FH19 was an experimental printing to test a new cover material. This appears glossy when compared with Nos. FH18 and FH20.

As Type FH18 *but changed to matt card cover containing Penny Black Anniversary booklet pane No.* 1469l *printed in photo by Harrison.*

FH20 Design No. 2 (cover in grey-black and bright green), Click Mill, Dounby, Orkney (30.1.90) . . . . 8·50

1990 (4 Sept)–**91**. *Mills Series continued. Covers as Type* FH18. *Containing booklet pane No.* X911m.

FH21 Design No. 3, (cover printed in light blue and buff) Jack and Jill Mills, Clayton, Sussex . . . . 5·00

FH22 Design No. 4, (cover printed in dull blue and bright yellow-green). Howell Mill, Llanddeusant, Anglesey (25.6.91) . . . . 4·00

Nos. FH18/22 have the vertical edges of the pane imperforate.

Type FH23

(Des J. Gibbs)

1991 (10 Sept)–**92**. 150*th Anniv of Punch Magazine. Magenta and grey-black covers as Type* FH23 *containing booklet pane No.* X927l.

FH23 Design No. 1, Illustrations by Richard Doyle and Hoffnung . . . . 4·00

a. Corrected rate (10.91) . . . . 5·50

FH24 Design No. 2, Illustrations by Sir John Tenniel and Eric Burgin (21.1.92) . . . . 4·00

FH25 Design No. 3, Illustrations by Sir John Tenniel and Anton (28.4.92) . . . . 4·00

FH26 Design No. 4, Illustrations by Sir John Tenniel and Hewison (28.7.92) . . . . 4·00

Nos. FH23/6 have the vertical edges of the pane imperforate.
No. FH23a has corrected letter rates as No. FB59a.

(Des J. Matthews)

1992 (22 Sept). 1000*th Anniv of Appointment of Sheriffs. Scarlet and dull blue cover as Type* FB63 *containing booklet pane No.* X927l.

FH27 Design as Type FB63 but elements in reverse order . . . 4·00

No. FH27 has the vertical edges of the pane imperforate.

Type FH28

(Des J. Lawrence)

1993 (9 Feb–6 July). *Educational Institutions Series. Covers as Type* FH28 *containing booklet pane No.* X1050l *printed in litho by Walsall.*

FH28 Design No. 1 (cover in lake-brown and light blue), University of Wales . . . . 3·00

FH29 Design No. 2 (cover in deep dull green and lemon), St. Hilda's College, Oxford (6.4.93) . . . . 3·00

FH30 Design No. 3 (cover in purple-brown and flesh), Marlborough College, Wiltshire (6.7.93) . . . . 3·00

1993 (1 Nov). *Educational Institutions Series continued. Deep bluish green and lilac cover as Type* FH28 *containing four* 25*p.* (*No.* Y1752) *printed in litho by Walsall.*

FH31 Design No. 4, Free Church of Scotland College, Edinburgh . . . . 2·00

Type FH32

(Des H. Brockway)

1994 (25 Jan). 20*th-century Prime Ministers Series. Brown and pale brown cover as Type* FH32 *containing four* 25*p.* (*No.* Y1752) *printed in litho by Walsall.*

FH32 Design No. 1, Herbert Asquith . . . . 2·00

(Des H. Brockway)

1994 (26 Apr–6 Sept). 20*th-century Prime Ministers Series continued. Covers as Type* FH32. *Containing four* 25*p.* (*No.* Y1676) *printed in photo by Harrison.*

FH33 Design No. 2, (cover in sepia and buff) David Lloyd-George . . . . 2·00

FH34 Design No. 3 (cover in greenish blue and pale blue), Winston Churchill (6.6.94) . . . . 2·00

FH35 Design No. 4 (cover in black and yellow-olive), Clement Attlee (6.9.94) . . . . 2·00

Type FH36

(Des L. Thomas)

1995 (7 Feb–4 Apr). *50th Anniv of End of Second World War. Covers as Type* FH36 *containing four 25p. (No.* Y1676) *printed in photo by Harrison.*

FH36 Design No. 1 (cover in brown-olive and brownish black), Violette Szabo (S.O.E. agent) . . . . . . 2·00
FH37 Design No. 2 (cover in red-brown and black), Dame Vera Lynn (entertainer) (4.4.95) . . . . . . 2·00

1995 (16 May–4 Sept). *50th Anniv of End of Second World War Series continued. Covers as Type* FH36 *containing four 25p. (No.* Y1677) *printed in photo by Harrison.*

FH38 Design No. 3 (cover in black and steel-blue), R. J. Mitchell (designer of Spitfire) . . . . . . 2·00
FH39 Design No. 4 (cover in grey-green and black), Archibald Mcindoe (plastic surgeon) (4.9.95) . . . . . . 2·00

Type FH40

1996 (16 Jan). *Multicoloured laminated cover as Type* FH40. *Stamps printed in litho by Questa.*

FH40 Containing four 25p. stamps (No. Y1752) . . . . . . 2·00

For an initial test period No. FH40 was only available from machines at twelve post offices, five in London and seven in Scotland, in addition to philatelic outlets. Stocks were distributed nationally from May 1996.

1996 (8 July)–**97**. *Multicoloured laminated cover as Type* FH40. *Stamps printed in litho by Questa.*

FH41 Containing booklet pane of 1p. × 2, 20p., 26p. × 3 and 2 labels (No. Y1743l) . . . . . . 2·00
a. Corrected rate (4.2.97) . . . . . . 1·50

No. FH41 was reissued on 4 February 1997 showing the 200g second class rate on the inside cover altered from 47p. to 45p.

£1.15 Booklets

1981 (26 Jan–18 Mar). *Military Aircraft Series continued. Blue and grey covers as Type* FE1 *(90 × 49 mm). Containing ten* $11\frac{1}{2}$*p.* (No. X893). A. *Selvedge at left.* B. *Selvedge at right.*

		A	B
FI1	Design No. 5, Spitfire & Lancaster	4·00	4·00
FI2	Design No. 6, Lightning & Vulcan (18.3.81)	4·00	4·00

Nos. FI1/2 are inscribed "January 1981".

Type FI3

(Des R. Maddox)

1981 (6 May–30 Sept). *Museums Series. Blue and turquoise-green covers as Type* FI3 *(90 × 49 mm). Containing ten* $11\frac{1}{2}$*p.* (No. X893). A. *Selvedge at left.* B. *Selvedge at right.*

		A	B
FI3	Design No. 1, Natural History Museum (British Museum), London	4·00	4·00
FI4	Design No. 2, National Museum of Antiquities of Scotland (30.9.81)	4·00	4·00

Nos. FI3/4 are inscribed "January 1981".

£1.20 Booklets

1980 (4 Feb–24 Sept). *Industrial Archaeology Series continued. Red and green covers as Type* FH1 *(90 × 49 mm). Containing ten 12p.* (No. X943). A. *Selvedge at left.* B. *Selvedge at right.*

		A	B
FJ1	Design No. 2, Beetle Mill, Ireland	4·00	4·00
FJ2	Design No. 3, Tin Mines, Cornwall (25.6.80)	4·00	4·25
FJ3	Design No. 4, Bottle Kilns, Gladstone, Stoke-on-Trent (24.9.80)	4·00	4·25

No. FJ1 is inscribed "January 1980", No. FJ2 "May 1980" and No. FJ3 "July 1980".

1986 (14 Jan). *Pillar box "Write Now" cover as Type* FB31 *(90 × 49 mm), printed in yellow-green and pale red. Containing ten 12p.* (No. X896). A. *Selvedge at left.* B. *Selvedge at right.*

		A	B
FJ4	"Write Now" (Pillar box design) (no imprint date)	5·00	5·00

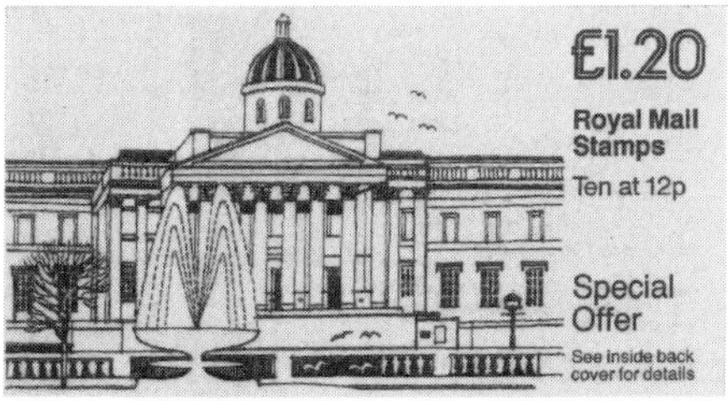

Type FJ5

(Des R. Maddox)

1986 (29 Apr). *National Gallery cover as Type* FJ5 *(90 × 49 mm), printed in magenta and blue-green. Containing ten 12p.* (No. X896). A. *Selvedge at left.* B. *Selvedge at right.*

		A	B
FJ5	National Gallery design	5·00	5·00

No. FJ5 is inscribed "November 1985".

Type FJ6

(Des Trickett and Webb Ltd)

1986 (29 July). *Handwriting cover as Type* FJ6 *(90 × 49 mm), printed in bright orange and bright blue. Containing ten 12p.* (No. X896). A. *Selvedge at left.* B. *Selvedge at right.*

		A	B
FJ6	"Maybe"	5·00	5·00

No. FJ6 is inscribed "November 1985".

£1.25 Booklets

1982 (1 Feb–6 Oct). *Museums Series continued. Blue and turquoise-green covers as Type* FJ3 *(90 × 49 mm). Containing ten* $12\frac{1}{2}$*p.* (No. X898) A. *Selvedge at left.* B. *Selvedge at right.*

		A	B
FK1	Design No. 3, Ashmolean Museum, Oxford	4·00	4·00
FK2	Design No. 4, National Museum of Wales, Cardiff (6.5.82)	4·00	4·00
FK3	Design No. 5, Ulster Museum, Belfast (11.8.82)	4·00	4·00
FK4	Design No. 6, Castle Museum, York (6.10.82)	4·00	4·00

Nos. FK1/4 are inscribed "February 1982".

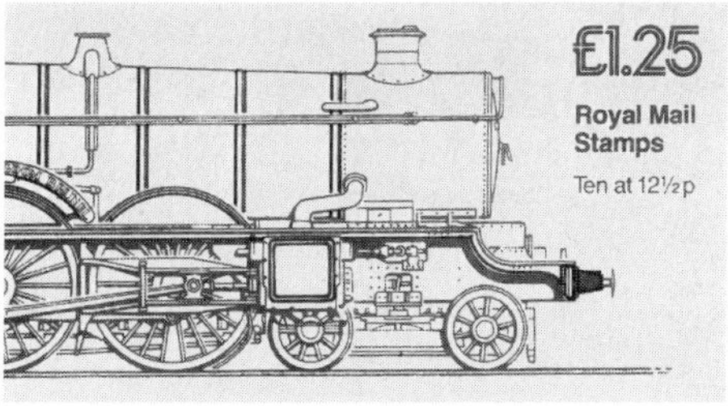

Type FK5

(Des S. Paine)

1983 (16 Feb–26 Oct). *Railway Engines Series. Red and blue-green covers as Type* FK5 *(90 × 49 mm). Containing ten* $12\frac{1}{2}$*p.* (No. X898). A. *Selvedge at left.* B. *Selvedge at right.*

		A	B
FK5	Design No. 1, GWR *Isambard Kingdom Brunel*	5·00	5·00
FK6	Design No. 2, LMS Class 4P Passenger Tank Engine (5.4.83)	5·00	5·00
	a. Corrected rate	40·00	60·00

FK7 Design No. 3, LNER *Mallard* (27.7.83) .... 5·00 5·00
FK8 Design No. 4, SR/BR *Clan Line* (26.10.83) .... 5·00 5·00

No. FK5 is inscribed "February 1982" and Nos. FK6/8 "April 1983". The corrected rate reads, "36p. for 200g" instead of "37p. for 200g".

£1.30 Booklets

Type FL1

(Des J. Gibbs)

1981 (6 May–30 Sept). *Postal History Series. Covers as Type* FL1 (90 × 49 *mm*). *Containing No.* X894l. A. *Selvedge at left.* B. *Selvedge at right.*

		A	B
FL1	Design No. 1, Penny Black (red & black cover) ...	6·00	6·00
FL2	Design No. 2, The Downey Head, 1911 (red & green cover) (20.9.81)	7·00	19·00

No. FL1 is inscribed "April 1981" and No. FL2 "September 1981".

Type FL3

(Des J. Thirsk)

1984 (3 Sept)–**85**. *Trams Series. Yellow-orange and purple covers as Type* FL3 (90 × 49 *mm*). *Containing ten* 13*p*. (*No.* X900). A. *Selvedge at left.* B. *Selvedge at right.*

		A	B
FL3	Design No. 1, Swansea/Mumbles Railway Car No. 3	4·50	4·50
FL4	Design No. 2, Glasgow Car No. 927 & Car No. 1194 (15.1.85)	4·50	4·50
FL5	Design No. 3, Car No. 717, Blackpool (23.4.85) ...	4·50	4·50
FL6	Design No. 4, Car No. 120 & "D" Class Car, London (23.7.85)	4·50	4·50

Nos. FL3/6 are inscribed "September 1984".

Type FL7

(Des Anne Morrow)

1986 (20 Oct). *Books for Children. Cover as Type* FL7 (90 × 49 *mm*) *printed in rose-red and lemon. Containing ten* 13*p*. (*No.* X900). A. *Selvedge at left.* B. *Selvedge at right.*

		A	B
FL7	Teddy bears design	4·50	4·50

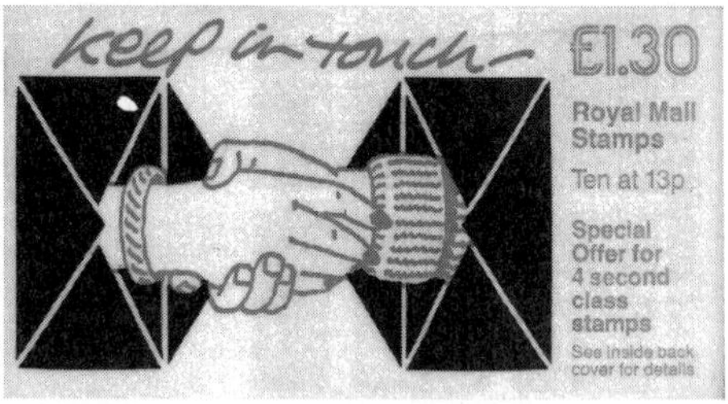

Type FL8

(Des Trickett and Webb Ltd)

1987 (27 Jan). *"Keep in Touch" cover as Type* FL8 (90 × 49 *mm*), *printed in light green and bright blue. Containing ten* 13*p*. (*No.* X900). A. *Selvedge at left.* B. *Selvedge at right.*

		A	B
FL8	Handclasp and envelope design	4·50	4·50

No. FL8 is inscribed "October 1986".

Type FL9

(Des Hannah Firmin)

1987 (14 Apr). *"Ideas for your Garden". Cover as Type* FL9 (90 × 49 *mm*) *printed in bistre and orange-brown. Containing ten* 13*p. stamps* (*No.* X900). A. *Selvedge at left.* B. *Selvedge at right.*

		A	B
FL9	Conservatory design	4·50	4·50

No. FL9 is inscribed "October 1986".

Type FL10

(Des Trickett and Webb Ltd)

1987 (4 July). *"Brighter Writer". Cover as Type* FL10 (90 × 49 *mm*) *printed in orange and bright reddish violet. Containing ten* 13*p. stamps* (No. X900). A. *Selvedge at left.* B. *Selvedge at right.*

		A	B
FL10	Flower design	4·50	4·50

No. FL10 is inscribed "October 1986".

Type FL11

(Des E. Stemp)

1987 (29 Sept). *"Jolly Postman". Cover as Type* FL11 (90 × 49 *mm*) *printed in pale blue and deep blue. Containing ten* 13*p. stamps* (No. X900). A. *Selvedge at left.* B. *Selvedge at right.*

		A	B
FL11	Boy drawing design	4·50	4·50

No. FL11 is inscribed "October 1986".

Type FL12

(Des E. Hughes)

1988 (26 Jan). *Bicentenary of Linnean Society. Cover as Type* FL12 (90 × 49 *mm*) *printed in blue and claret. Containing ten* 13*p. stamps* (No. X900). A. *Selvedge at left.* B. *Selvedge at right.*

		A	B
FL12	Mermaid, fish and insect (from "Hortus Sanibatis", 1497)	4·50	4·50

No. FL12 is inscribed "October 1986".

Type FL13

(Des Hannah Firmin)

1988 (12 Apr). *Recipe Cards. Cover as Type* FL13 (90 × 49 *mm*) *printed in brown and green. Containing ten* 13*p. stamps* (No. X900). A. *Selvedge at left.* B. *Selvedge at right.*

		A	B
FL13	Vegetables design	4·50	4·50

No. FL13 is inscribed "October 1986".

Type FL14

(Des Trickett and Webb Ltd)

1988 (5 July). *"Children's Parties". Cover as Type* FL14 (90 × 49 *mm*) *printed in blue-green and bright purple. Containing ten* 13*p. stamps* (No. X900). A. *Selvedge at left.* B. *Selvedge at right.*

		A	B
FL14	Balloons and streamers design	4·50	4·50

No. FL14 is inscribed "October 1986".

£1.40 Booklets

1981 (26 Jan–18 Mar). *Industrial Archaeology Series continued. Red and green covers as Type* FH1 (90 × 49 *mm*). *Containing ten* 14*p.* (No. X946). A. *Selvedge at left.* B. *Selvedge at right.*

		A	B
FM1	Design No. 5, Preston Mill, Scotland	5·00	5·00
FM2	Design No. 6, Talyllyn Railway, Tywyn (18.3.81)	5·00	5·00

Nos. FM1/2 are inscribed "January 1981".

Type FM3

(Des E. Stemp)

1981 (6 May–30 Sept). *19th-century Women's Costume Series. Claret and blue covers as Type* FM3 (90 × 49 *mm*). *Containing ten* 14*p*. (*No.* X946). A. *Selvedge at left.* B. *Selvedge at right.*

		A	B
FM3	Design No. 1, Costume, 1800-15	5·00	5·00
FM4	Design No. 2, Costume, 1815–30 (30.9.81)	5·00	5·00

Nos. FM3/4 are inscribed "January 1981".

Type FM5

(Des A. Drummond)

1988 (5 Sept). *"Pocket Planner". Cover as Type* FM5 (90 × 49 *mm*) *printed in grey-black and yellow. Containing ten* 14*p. stamps* (*No.* X903). A. *Selvedge at left.* B. *Selvedge at right.*

		A	B
FM5	"Legal Charge" design	5·00	5·00

Type FM6

(Des Debbie Cook)

1989 (24 Jan). *150th Anniv of Fox Talbot's Report on the Photographic Process to Royal Society. Cover as Type* FM6 (90 × 49 *mm*) *printed in reddish orange and black. Containing ten* 14*p. stamps* (*No.* X903). A. *Selvedge at left.* B. *Selvedge at right.*

		A	B
FM6	Photographs and darkroom equipment	5·00	5·00

No. FM6 is inscribed "September 1988".

£1.43 Booklets

1982 (1 Feb–6 May). *Postal History Series continued. Covers as Type* FL1 (90 × 49 *mm*). *Containing No.* X899l. A. *Selvedge at left.* B. *Selvedge at right.*

		A	B
FN1	Design No. 3, James Chalmers (postal reformer) (orange & turquoise-blue cover)	5·00	5·00
FN2	Design No. 4, Edmund Dulac (stamp designer) (brown & red cover) (6.5.82)	5·00	5·00

Type FN3

(Des J. Gardner)

1982 (12 July). *"Holiday Postcard Stamp Book". Purple and turquoise-blue cover as Type* FN3 (90 × 49 *mm*). *Containing No.* X899l. A. *Selvedge at left.* B. *Selvedge at right.*

		A	B
FN3	*Golden Hinde* on front, postcard voucher on back	5·00	5·00

1982 (21 July)–**83**. *Postal History Series continued. Covers as Type* FL1 (90 × 49 *mm*). *Containing No.* X899l. A. *Selvedge at left.* B. *Selvedge at right.*

		A	B
FN4	Design No. 5, "Forces Postal Service" (grey & violet cover)	5·00	5·00
FN5	Design No. 6, The £5 Orange (orange & black cover) (6.10.82)	5·00	5·00
FN6	Design No. 7, Postmark History (brt scarlet & dp dull blue cover) (16.2.83)	6·00	6·00

No. FN1 is inscribed "February 1982". FN2/3 "May 1982", FN4 "July 1982", FN5 "October 1982", FN6 "November 1982".

For booklet No. FS2 with cover price of £1.45, see £1.60 booklets.

£1.46 Booklets

1983 (5 Apr–26 Oct). *Postal History Series continued. Covers as Type* FL1 (90 × 49 *mm*). A. *Containing No.* X899n. B. *Containing No.* X899na.

		A	B
FO1	Design No. 8, Seahorse High Values (blue & green cover)	9·00	9·00
	a. Corrected rate	16·00	12·00
FO2	Design No. 9, Parcel Post Centenary (turquoise-blue & carmine cover) (27.7.83)	9·00	9·00
FO3	Design No. 10, Silver Jubilee of Regional Stamps (dull green & reddish violet cover) (26.10.83)	9·00	9·00

No. FO1 is inscribed "March 1983", No. FO2 "May 1983" and No. FO3 "June 1983".

The corrected rate reads, "36p. for 200g" instead of "37p. for 200g".

£1.50 Booklets

1986 (14 Jan). *Pillar box "Write Now" cover as Type* FB31 (90 × 49 *mm*), *printed in ultramarine and red.* A. *Containing No.* X897l. B. *Containing No.* X897la.

		A	B
FP1	"Write Now" (Pillar box design)	6·00	6·00

No. FP1 shows no imprint date.

1986 (29 Apr). *National Gallery cover as Type FJ5 (90 × 49 mm), printed in violet and vermilion. A. Containing No. X897l. B. Containing No. X897la.*

		A	B
FP2	National Gallery design	6·00	6·00

No. FP2 is inscribed "November 1985".

1986 (29 July). *Handwriting cover as Type FJ6 (90 × 49 mm), printed in blue-green and bright blue. A. Containing No. X897l. B. Containing No. X897la.*

		A	B
FP3	"No"	6·00	6·00

No. FP3 is inscribed "November 1985".

£1.54 Booklets

1984 (3 Sept)–**85**. *Postal History Series continued. Covers as Type FL1 (90 × 49 mm). A. Containing No. X901l. B. Containing No. X901la.*

		A	B
FQ1	Design No. 11, Old & new Postage Dues (reddish purple and pale blue cover)	6·00	6·00
FQ2	Design No. 12, Queen Victoria embossed stamps (yellow-green & blue-cover) (15.1.85)	6·00	6·00
FQ3	Design No. 13, Queen Victoria surface-printed stamps (blue-green & carmine cover) (23.4.85)	6·00	6·00
FQ4	Design No. 14, 17th-century mounted & foot messengers (dp brown & orange-red cover) (23.7.85)	6·00	6·00

No. FQ1 is inscribed "July 1984" and Nos. FQ2/4 are inscribed "September 1984".

£1.55 Booklets

1982 (1 Feb–6 Oct). *19th-century Women's Costume Series continued. Claret and blue covers as Type FM3 (90 × 49 mm). Containing ten $15\frac{1}{2}$p. (No. X948). A. Selvedge at left. B. Selvedge at right.*

		A	B
FR1	Design No. 3, Costume, 1830–50	5·00	5·00
FR2	Design No. 4, Costume, 1850–60 (6.5.82)	5·00	5·00
FR3	Design No. 5, Costume, 1860–80 (11.8.82)	6·00	6·00
FR4	Design No. 6, Costume, 1880–1900 (6.10.82)	6·00	6·00

Nos. FR1/4 are inscribed "February 1982".

£1.60 Booklets

Type FS1

(Des Carol Walklin)

1983 (5 Apr). *"Birthday Box" Design. Magenta and red-orange cover as Type FS1 (90 × 49 mm). Depicting birthday cake and associated items. A. Selvedge at left. B. Selvedge at right.*

		A	B
FS1	Containing ten 16p. stamps (No. X949) (no imprint date)	6·00	6·00
	a. Rates altered and "February 1983" imprint date	40·00	60·00

Type FS2

(Des R. Maddox)

1983 (10 Aug). *British Countryside Series. Special Discount Booklet (sold at £1.45). Greenish blue and ultramarine cover as Type FS2 (90 × 49 mm). Containing ten 16p. stamps (No. X949Eu). A. Selvedge at left. B. Selvedge at right.*

		A	B
FS2	Design No. 1, Lyme Regis, Dorset	6·00	6·00

Stamps from No. FS2 show a double-lined "D" printed in blue on the reverse over the gum.

No. FS2 is inscribed "April 1983".

1983 (21 Sept). *British Countryside Series continued. Dull green on violet cover as Type FS2 (90 × 49 mm). Containing ten 16p. stamps (No. X949). A. Selvedge at left. B. Selvedge at right.*

		A	B
FS3	Design No. 2, Arlington Row, Bibury, Gloucestershire	6·00	6·00

No. FS3 is inscribed "April 1983".

Type FS4

(Des M. Newton)

1984 (14 Feb). *"Write it" Design. Vermilion and ultramarine cover as Type FS4 (90 × 49 mm). Containing ten 16p. stamps (No. X949). A. Selvedge at left. B. Selvedge at right.*

		A	B
FS4	Fountain pen	6·00	6·00

No. FS4 is inscribed "April 1983".

£1.70 Booklets

Type FT1

(Des G. Hardie)

1984 (3 Sept). *Social Letter Writing Series. Rose and deep claret cover as Type FT1 (90 × 49 mm). Containing ten 17p. (No. X952). A. Selvedge at left. B. Selvedge at right.*

		A	B
FT1	Design No. 1, "Love Letters"	6·00	6·00

No. FT1 is inscribed "September 1984".

1985 (5 Mar). *Social Letter Writing Series continued. Special Discount Booklet (sold at £1.55). Turquoise-blue and deep claret cover as Type FT1 (90 × 49 mm). Containing ten 17p. (No. X952Eu). A. Selvedge at left. B. Selvedge at right.*

		A	B
FT2	Design No. 2, "Letters abroad"	8·00	8·00

Stamps from No. FT2 show a double-lined "D" printed in blue on the reverse over the gum.

No. FT2 is inscribed "September 1984".

1985 (9 Apr). *Social Letter Writing Series continued. Bright blue and deep claret cover as Type FT1 (90 × 49 mm). Containing ten 17p. (No. X952). A. Selvedge at left. B. Selvedge at right.*

		A	B
FT3	Design No. 3, "Fan letters"	6·00	6·00

No. FT3 is inscribed "September 1984".

Type FT4

(Des B. Smith)

1985 (30 July). *350 Years of Royal Mail Public Postal Service. Special Discount Booklet (sold at £1.53). Cover Type FS4 (90 × 60 mm), printed in rosine and bright blue. Containing ten 17p. (No. 1290Eu) with selvedge at top.*

FT4 Datapost Service design .... 6·00

The stamps from this booklet show double-lined letters "D" printed on the reverse over the gum.

No. FT4 is inscribed "September 1984".

1985 (8 Oct)–**86**. *Social Letter Writing Series continued. Black and bright scarlet cover as Type FT1 (90 × 49 mm). Containing ten 17p. (No. X952). A. Selvedge at left. B. Selvedge at right.*

		A	B
FT5	Design No. 4, "Write Now" (Pillar box)	6·00	6·00
	a. Revised rates (2nd class (60g) 12p.) (1.86)	14·00	14·00

1986 (29 Apr). *National Gallery cover as Type FJ5 (90 × 49 mm), printed in blue-green and blue. Containing ten 17p. (No. X952). A. Selvedge at left. B. Selvedge at right.*

		A	B
FT6	National Gallery design	6·00	6·00

No. FT6 is inscribed "November 1985".

1986 (29 July). *Handwriting cover as Type FJ6 (90 × 49 mm) printed in red and bright blue. Containing ten 17p. (No. X952). A. Selvedge at left. B. Selvedge at right.*

		A	B
FT7	"Yes"	6·00	6·00

No. FT7 is inscribed "November 1985".

£1.80 Booklets

1986 (20 Oct). *Books for Children. New blue and orange-brown cover as Type FL7. Containing ten 18p. (No. X955). A. Selvedge at left. B. Selvedge at right.*

		A	B
FU1	Rabbits design	6·00	6·00

1987 (27 Jan). *"Keep in Touch" cover as Type FL8 printed in magenta and bright blue. Containing ten 18p. (No. X955). A. Selvedge at left. B. Selvedge at right.*

		A	B
FU2	Handclasp and envelope design	6·00	6·00

No. FU2 is inscribed "October 1986".

1987 (14 Apr). *"Ideas for your Garden". Claret and brown-olive cover as Type FL9 (90 × 49 mm). Containing ten 18p. stamps (No. X955). A. Selvedge at left. B. Selvedge at right.*

		A	B
FU3	Garden path design	6·00	6·00

No. FU3 is inscribed "October 1986".

1987 (14 July). *"Brighter Writer". Turquoise-green and reddish orange cover as Type FL10 (90 × 49 mm). Containing ten 18p. stamps (No. X955). A. Selvedge at left. B. Selvedge at right.*

		A	B
FU4	Berries and leaves design	6·00	6·00

No. FU4 is inscribed "October 1986".

1987 (29 Sept). *"Jolly Postman". Cover as Type FL11 (90 × 49 mm) printed in deep blue and claret. Containing ten 18p. stamps (No. X955). A. Selvedge at left. B. Selvedge at right.*

		A	B
FU5	Girl drawing design	6·00	6·00

No. FU5 is inscribed "October 1986".

1988 (26 Jan). *Bicentenary of Linnean Society. Cover as Type FL12 (90 × 49 mm) printed in dull yellow-green and dull claret. Containing ten 18p. stamps (No. X955). A. Selvedge at left. B. Selvedge at right.*

		A	B
FU6	Wolf and birds (from "Hortus Sanitatis", 1497)	6·00	6·00

1988 (12 Apr). *Recipe Cards. Cover as Type FL13 (90 × 49 mm) printed in claret and Indian red. Containing ten 18p. stamps (No. X955). A. Selvedge at left. B. Selvedge at right.*

		A	B
FU7	Fruits, pudding and jam design	6·00	6·00

No. FU7 is inscribed "October 1986".

1988 (5 July). *"Children's Parties". Cover as Type FL14 (90 × 49 mm) printed in violet and rosine. Containing ten 18p. stamps (No. X955). A. Selvedge at left. B. Selvedge at right.*

		A	B
FU8	Balloons and party hats design	6·00	6·00

No. FU8 is inscribed "October 1986".

£1.90 Booklets

1988 (5 Sept). *"Pocket Planner". Cover as Type FM5 (90 × 49 mm) printed in yellow-green and magenta. Containing ten 19p. stamps (No. X956). A. Selvedge at left. B. Selvedge at right.*

		A	B
FV1	"Marriage Act" design	7·50	7·50

1989 (24 Jan). *150th Anniv of Fox Talbot's Report on the Photographic Process to Royal Society. Cover as Type FM6 (90 × 49 mm) printed in emerald and black. Containing ten 19p. stamps (No. X956). A. Selvedge at left. B. Selvedge at right.*

		A	B
FV2	Fox Talbot with camera and Lacock Abbey	7·50	7·50

No. FV2 is inscribed "September 1988".

£2 Booklets

Type FW1

(Des Debbie Cook)

1993 (1 Nov)–**94.** *Postal Vehicles Series. Covers as Type FW1. Containing eight 25p. (No. Y1676).*

FW1 Design No. 1 (cover in dull vermilion and deep blue), Motorised cycle-carrier ..... 4·00
FW2 Design No. 2 (cover in green and deep violet-blue), Experimental motor-mail van (26.4.94) ..... 4·00
FW3 Design No. 3 (cover in red and black), Experimental electric mail van, 1932 (6.9.94) ..... 4·00

Type FW3

(Des The Four Hundred)

1995 (7 Feb–4 Apr) *Birth Bicentenary of Sir Rowland Hill. Covers as Type FW3. Containing eight 25p. (No. Y1676).*

FW4 Design No. 1 (cover in purple and new blue), Rowland Hill as director of London and Brighton Railway Company ..... 4·00
FW5 Design No. 2 (cover in deep mauve and greenish blue), Rowland Hill and Hazlewood School (4.4.95) ..... 4·00

1995 (6 June–4 Sept) *Birth Bicentenary of Sir Rowland Hill Series continued. Covers as Type FW3. Containing eight 25p. (No. Y1677).*

FW6 Design No. 3 (cover in deep blue-green and dull orange), Rowland Hill as Secretary to the Post Office. ..... 4·00
FW7 Design No. 4 (cover in red-brown and orange), Uniform Penny Postage petition and Mulready envelope (4.9.95) ..... 4·00

1996 (16 Jan) *Multicoloured laminated cover as Type FH40. Stamps printed in litho by Questa.*

FW8 Containing eight 25p. stamps (No. Y1752) ..... 4·00

For an initial test period No. FW8 was only available from machines at twelve post offices, five in London and seven in Scotland, in addition to philatelic outlets. Stocks were distributed nationally from May 1996.

1996 (8 July)–**97**. *Multicoloured laminated cover as Type FH40. Stamps printed in litho by Questa.*

FW9 Containing booklet pane of 20p. and 26p. × 7 (No. Y1751l) ..... 4·00
a. Corrected rate (4.2.97) ..... 3·00

No. FW9 was reissued on 4 February 1997 showing the 200g second class rate on the inside cover altered from 47p. to 45p.

Christmas Booklets

Type FX1

(Des J. Matthews)

1978 (15 Nov). *"Christmas Greetings". Cover Type* FX1 (90 × 49 *mm*). *Printed in rose-red and sage-green.*

FX1 £1.60, containing booklet pane No. X875l .... 4·50

No. FX1 is inscribed "August 1978".

Type FX2

(Des P. Sharland)

1979 (4 Nov). *"Christmas Greetings". Red and green cover as Type* FX2 (90 × 49 *mm*), *showing Christmas cracker.*

FX2 £1.80, containing booklet pane No. X879l .... 5·00

No. FX2 is inscribed "October 1979".

Type FX3

(Des E. Fraser)

1980 (12 Nov). *Christmas. Red and blue cover as Type* FX3 (90 × 49 *mm*), *showing Nativity scene.*

FX3 £2.20, containing booklet pane No. X888m .... 5·50

No. FX3 is inscribed "September 1980".

Type FX4

(Des W. Sanderson)

1981 (11 Nov). *Christmas. Red and blue cover as Type* FX4, (90 × 49 *mm*), *showing skating scene.*

FX4 £2.55, containing booklet pane No. X893l .... 7·00

No. FX4 is inscribed "January 1981".

Type FX5

(Des A. Davidson)

1982 (10 Nov). *Christmas. Red and green cover as Type* FX5 (90 × 49 *mm*), *showing Christmas Mummers.*

FX5 £2.50, containing booklet pane No. X898l .... 7·50

No. FX5 is inscribed "February 1982" and was sold at a discount of 30p. off the face value of the stamps.

Each stamp in the pane has a blue star printed on the reverse over the gum.

Type FX6

(Des Barbara Brown)

1983 (9 Nov). *Christmas. Brown-lilac and yellow cover as Type* FX6 (90 × 49 *mm*), *showing pantomime scenes.*

FX6 £2.20, containing twenty 12½p. (No. X898Eua) .... 7·00

No. FX6 is inscribed "April 1983" and was sold at a discount of 30p. off the face value of the stamps.

Each stamp in the pane has a double-lined blue star printed on the reverse over the gum.

Type FX7

(Des Yvonne Gilbert)

1984 (20 Nov). *Christmas. Light brown and red-orange cover as Type FX7 (90 × 60 mm), showing Nativity scene.*

FX7 £2.30, containing twenty 13p. (No. 1267Eu) . . . . 7·00

No. FX7 is inscribed "September 1984" and was sold at a discount of 30p. off the face value of the stamps.

The stamps from this booklet show double-lined blue stars printed on the reverse over the gum.

Type FX8

(Des A. George)

1985 (19 Nov). *Christmas. Bright blue and rose cover as Type FX8 (90 × 60 mm), showing The Pantomime.*

FX8 £2.40, containing twenty 12p. (No. 1303Eu) . . . . 7·00

The stamps from this booklet show double-lined blue stars printed on the reverse over the gum.

Type FX9

(Des Lynda Gray)

1986 (2 Dec). *Christmas. Red and dull blue-green cover as Type FX9 (90 × 49 mm), showing Shetland Yule cakes. A. Selvedge at left. B. Selvedge at right.*

	A	B
FX9 £1.20, containing ten 13p. (No. X900Eu)	7·50	8·00

No. FX9 is inscribed "October 1986" and was sold at a discount of 10p. off the face value of the stamps.

Each stamps in the pane has a blue star printed on the reverse over the gum.

For 1990 and later Christmas stamps, see Barcode Booklets Section G.

Greetings Booklet

£1.90 Booklet

Type FX10

(Des L. Moberly)

1989 (31 Jan). *Greetings Stamps. Multicoloured cover as Type FX10 (89 × 60 mm). Containing booklet pane No. 1423a, including twelve special greetings labels in a block (3 × 4) at right, attached by the selvedge.*

FX10 Greetings design . . . . 45·00

No. FX10 is inscribed "September 1988".

The cover of No. FX10 shows an overall pattern of elements taken from the stamp designs. Due to the method of production the position of these elements varies from cover to cover.

For Greetings stamps in Barcode booklets, see Barcode Booklets Section F.

Barcode Booklets

These booklets are listed in five sections.

SECTION C. G numbers containing Machin stamps

SECTION D. H numbers containing Machin NVI stamps

SECTION E. J numbers containing Machin Penny Black Anniversary stamps

SECTION F. K numbers containing Greetings stamps

SECTION G. L numbers containing Christmas stamps

These are produced for sale in both post offices and commercial outlets.

NOTE: All panes are attached to the covers by the selvedge.

Barcode booklet covers are illustrated at two-thirds linear size *unless otherwise stated.*

C. Barcode Booklets containing Machin stamps with values shown as Type **367**.

COVERS. These are all printed in scarlet, lemon and black with the barcode on the reverse. Type GA1 has a clear "window" to view the contents. Type GB3 is shorter and has a stamp illustration printed on the cover to replace the "window". These illustrations show an oblique white line across the bottom right-hand corner of the "stamp". Unless otherwise stated all covers were printed by Harrison.

52p. Booklet

Type GA1

1987 (4 Aug). *Laminated cover Type* GA1 *(75 × 60 mm).*
GA1 Containing booklet pane No. X900n .... 2·50
No. GA1 is inscribed "20 October 1986".

56p. Booklets

1988 (23 Aug). *Laminated cover as Type* GA1 *(75 × 56 mm).*
GB1 Containing booklet pane No. X903l .... 5·00

1988 (11 Oct). *Laminated cover as Type* GA1 *(75 × 56 mm) printed by Walsall.*
GB2 Containing booklet pane No. X903l .... 5·00

Type GB3
Large Crown

1988 (11 Oct). *Laminated cover as Type* GB3 *(75 × 48 mm) with stamp printed on the cover in deep blue.*
GB3 Containing booklet pane No. X903n .... 7·00
No. GB3 is inscribed "5 September 1988" and has the horizontal edges of the pane imperforate.

1989 (24 Jan). *Laminated cover as Type* GB3 *(75 × 48 mm) with stamp printed on the cover in deep blue by Walsall.*
GB4 Containing booklet pane No. X903q .... 25·00
No. GB4 is inscribed "5 September 1988" and has the three edges of the pane imperforate.

72p. Booklet

1987 (4 Aug). *Laminated cover as Type* GA1 *(75 × 60 mm).*
GC1 Containing booklet pane No. X955m .... 3·00
No. GC1 is inscribed "20 October 1986".

76p. Booklets

1988 (23 Aug). *Laminated cover as Type* GA1 *(75 × 56 mm).*
GD1 Containing booklet pane No. X956l .... 6·00

1988 (11 Oct). *Laminated cover as Type* GA1 *(75 × 56 mm) printed by Walsall.*
GD2 Containing booklet pane No. X956l .... 6·00

1988 (11 Oct). *Laminated cover as Type* GB3 *(75 × 48 mm) with stamp printed on the cover in bright orange-red.*
GD3 Containing booklet pane No. X956n .... 7·00
No. GD3 is inscribed "5 September 1988" and has the horizontal edges of the pane imperforate.

1989 (24 Jan). *Laminated cover as Type* GB3 *(75 × 48 mm) with stamp printed on the cover in bright orange-red by Walsall.*
GD4 Containing booklet pane No. X956q .... 25·00
No. GD4 is inscribed "5 September 1988" and has the three edges of the pane imperforate.

NEW INFORMATION

The editor is always interested to correspond with people who have new information that will improve or correct the Catalogue.

78p. Booklet

GD4a (As Type GL1 but, without "4")

1992 (28 July). *Multicoloured laminated cover as Type* GD4a (75 × 49 *mm*) *with stamp printed on the cover in bright mauve by Walsall.*
GD4a Containing two 39p. stamps (No. X1058) (pane No. X1058l with right-hand vert pair removed) and pane of 4 air mail labels .... 2·00
Stamps in No. GD4a have top or bottom edge imperforate.
Booklet No. GD4a was produced in connection with a Kellogg's Bran Flakes promotion.

£1.04 Booklet

1987 (4 Aug). *Laminated cover as Type* GA1 (75 × 60 *mm*).
GE1 Containing booklet pane No. X971bl .... 16·00
No. GE1 is inscribed "20 October 1986".

£1.08 Booklets

1988 (23 Aug). *Laminated cover as Type* GA1 (75 × 56 *mm*).
GF1 Containing booklet pane No. X973l .... 10·00

1988 (11 Oct). *Laminated cover as Type* GB3 (75 × 48 *mm*) *with stamp printed on the cover in chestnut.*
GF2 Containing booklet pane No. X973m .... 25·00
No. GF2 is inscribed "5 September 1988" and has the horizontal edges of the pane imperforate.

£1.16 Booklets

Type GG1
Redrawn Crown

1989 (2 Oct). *Laminated cover as Type* GG1 (75 × 48 *mm*) *with stamp printed on the cover in deep mauve by Walsall.*
GG1 Containing booklet pane No. X1054l .... 20·00
No. GG1 has three edges of the pane imperforate.

1990 (17 Apr). *Laminated cover as Type* GG1 (75 × 48 *mm*) *with stamp printed on the cover in deep mauve by Walsall.*
GG2 Containing booklet pane No. X1055l .... 24·00
No. GG2 has three edges of the pane imperforate.

£1.24 Booklet

Type GH1
Crown on White

1990 (17 Sept). *Multicoloured laminated cover as Type* GH1 (75 × 49 *mm*) *with stamp printed on the cover in ultramarine by Walsall.*
GH1 Containing booklet pane No. X1056l .... 7·00
No. GH1 has the horizontal edges of the pane imperforate.

£1.30 Booklet

1987 (4 Aug). *Laminated cover as Type* GA1 (98 × 60 *mm*).
GI1 Containing booklet pane No. X900o .... 5·00
No. GI1 is inscribed "20 October 1986".

£1.32 Booklet

Type GJ1

1991 (16 Sept)–**92**. *Multicoloured laminated cover as Type* GJ1 (75 × 49 *mm*) *with stamp printed on the cover in light emerald by Walsall. Inscr* "For letters up to 10g" *on yellow strip at right.*
GJ1 Containing booklet pane No. X1057l and a pane of 4 air mail labels .... 5·00
a. Inscr "For Worldwide Postcards" on yellow strip (8.9.92) .... 8·00
Nos. GJ1/a have the horizontal edges of the pane imperforate.

£1.40 Booklets

1988 (23 Aug). *Laminated cover as Type* GA1 (97 × 56 *mm*).
GK1 Containing booklet pane No. X903m .... 8·00

1988 (11 Oct). *Laminated cover as Type* GA1 (97 × 56 *mm*) *printed by Questa.*
GK2 Containing ten 14p. (No. X1007) .... 14·00

1988 (11 Oct). *Laminated cover as Type* GB3 (75 × 48 *mm*) *with stamp printed on the cover in deep blue.*
GK3 Containing booklet pane No. X903p .... 9·00
No. GK3 is inscribed "5 September 1988" and has horizontal edges of the pane imperforate.

1988 (11 Oct). *Laminated cover as Type* GB3 (75 × 48 *mm*) *with stamp printed on the cover in deep blue by Questa.*
GK4 Containing ten 14p. (No. X1007) .... 14·00

1993 (1 Nov). *Laminated cover as Type GJ1 (76 × 50 mm) with stamp printed on the cover in yellow by Walsall.*

GK5 Containing four 35p. (No. Y1755) and a pane of 4 air mail labels . . . . 4·00

Type GK6 (without diagonal white line across corners of stamps)

1995 (16 May). *Multicoloured laminated cover as Type GK6 (75 × 48 mm) with stamps printed on the cover in yellow by Walsall.*

GK6 Containing four 35p. (No. Y1755) and a pane of 4 air mail labels . . . . 4·00

1996 (19 Mar). *Multicoloured laminated cover as Type GK6 (75 × 48 mm) without "International" and showing Olympic symbols on the back. Stamps printed on the cover in yellow by Walsall.*

GK7 Containing four 35p. (No. Y1755) and a pane of 4 air mail labels . . . . 4·00

£1.48 Booklets

Type GL1
("Worldwide Postcard Stamps" ranged left)
(without diagonal white lines across corner of stamps)

1996 (8 July). *Multicoloured laminated cover as Type GL1 (75 × 48 mm) showing Olympic symbols on the back. Stamps printed on the cover in bright mauve by Walsall. Inscribed "For Worldwide Postcards" on yellow tab at right.*

GL1 Containing four 37p. (No. Y1756) and a pane of 4 air mail labels . . . . 4·00

1997 (4 Feb). *Multicoloured laminated cover as Type GL1 (75 × 48 mm) without Olympic symbols on the back. Stamps printed on the cover in bright mauve by Walsall. Inscribed "For Worldwide Postcards" on yellow tab at right.*

GL2 Containing four 37p. (No. Y1756) and a pane of 4 air mail labels . . . . 4·00

No. GL2 shows a "W" on the outside back cover below the barcode.

Type GL3

1997 (26 Aug). *Multicoloured laminated cover as Type GL3 (75 × 48 mm) printed by Walsall. Inscribed "For Worldwide Postcards" on yellow tab at right.*

GL3 Containing four 37p. (photo) (No. Y1685) and a pane of 4 new design air mail labels . . . . 2·25

No. GL3 shows a "W" on the outside back cover below the barcode.

£1.56 Booklet

Type GM1

1991 (16 Sept). *Multicoloured laminated cover as Type GM1 (75 × 49 mm) with stamp printed on the cover in bright mauve by Walsall.*

GM1 Containing booklet pane No. X1058l and a pane of 4 air mail labels . . . . 7·00

No. GM1 has the horizontal edges of the pane imperforate.

£1.64 Booklets

1993 (1 Nov). *Laminated cover as Type GM1 (76 × 50 mm) with stamp printed on the cover in drab by Walsall.*

GN1 Containing four 41p. (No. Y1757) and a pane of 4 air mail labels . . . . 5·50

1995 (16 May). *Multicoloured laminated cover as Type GK6 (75 × 48 mm) with stamps printed on the cover in drab by Walsall.*

GN2 Containing four 41p. (No. Y1757) and a pane of 4 air mail labels . . . . 4·50

1996 (19 Mar). *Multicoloured laminated cover as Type GK6 (75 × 48 mm) without "International" and showing Olympic symbols on the back. Stamps printed on the cover in drab by Walsall.*

GN3 Containing four 41p. (No. Y1757) and a pane of 4 air mail labels . . . . 4·50

£1.80 Booklet

1987 (4 Aug). *Laminated cover as Type GA1 (98 × 60 mm).*

GO1 Containing booklet pane No. X955n . . . . 8·00

No. GO1 is inscribed "20 October 1986".

£1.90 Booklets

1988 (23 Aug). *Laminated cover as Type GA1 (97 × 56 mm).*
GP1 Containing booklet pane No. X956m .... 10·00

1988 (11 Oct). *Laminated cover as Type GA1 (97 × 56 mm) printed by Questa.*
GP2 Containing ten 19p. (No. X1013) .... 18·00

1988 (11 Oct). *Laminated cover as Type GB3 (75 × 48 mm) with stamp printed on the cover in bright orange-red.*
GP3 Containing booklet pane No. X956o .... 12·00
No. GP3 is inscribed "5 September 1988" and has the horizontal edges of the pane imperforate.

1988 (11 Oct). *Laminated cover as Type GB3 (75 × 48 mm) with stamp printed on the cover in bright orange-red by Questa.*
GP4 Containing ten 19p. (No. X1013) .... 18·00

£2.40 Booklets

1994 (9 Aug). *Laminated cover as Type GM1 (75 × 49 mm) with stamp printed on the cover in dull blue-grey by Walsall.*
GQ1 Containing four 60p. (No. Y1758) and a pane of 4 air mail labels .... 5·00

Type GQ2

1994 (4 Oct). *Laminated cover as Type GQ2 (75 × 49 mm) with stamp printed on the cover in dull blue-grey by Walsall.*
GQ2 Containing four 60p. (No. Y1758) and a pane of 4 air mail plus 4 "Seasons Greetings" labels .... 5·00

1995 (16 May). *Laminated cover as Type GK6 (75 × 48 mm) with stamps printed on the cover in dull blue-grey by Walsall.*
GQ3 Containing four 60p. (No. Y1758) and a pane of 4 air mail labels .... 5·00

1996 (19 Mar). *Multicoloured laminated cover as Type GK6 (75 × 48 mm) without "International" and showing Olympic symbols on the back. Stamps printed on the cover in dull grey-blue by Walsall.*
GQ4 Containing four 60p. (No. Y1758) and a pane of 4 air mail labels .... 5·00

£2.52 Booklets

1996 (8 July). *Multicoloured laminated cover as Type GL1 (75 × 48 mm) showing Olympic symbols on the back. Stamps printed on the cover in light emerald by Walsall. Inscribed "For items up to 20g" on yellow tab at right.*
GR1 Containing four 63p. (No. Y1759) and a pane of 4 air mail labels .... 5·25

1997 (4 Feb). *Multicoloured laminated cover as Type GL1 (75 × 48 mm) without Olympic symbols on the back. Stamps printed on the cover in light emerald by Walsall. Inscribed "For items up to 20g" on yellow tab at right.*
GR2 Containing four 63p. (No. Y1759) and a pane of 4 air mail labels .... 5·25
No. GR2 shows a "W" on the outside back cover below the barcode.

1997 (26 Aug). *Multicoloured laminated cover as Type GL1 (75 × 48 mm), but inscr "Worldwide Airmail Stamps". Stamps printed on the cover in light emerald by Walsall. Inscribed "For items up to 20g" on yellow tab at right.*
GR3 Containing four 63p. (photo) (No. Y1693) and a pane of 4 air mail labels .... 3·75
No. GR3 shows a "W" on the outside back cover below the barcode.

D. Barcode Booklets containing No Value Indicated stamps with barcodes on the back cover.

Panes of 4 2nd Class stamps

Type HA1
Redrawn Crown (small)

1989 (22 Aug). *Laminated cover as Type* HA1 (75 × 48 *mm*) *with stamp printed on the cover in bright blue by Walsall.*
HA1 Containing booklet pane No. 1449b .... 8·50
No. HA1 has three edges of the pane imperforate.
No. HA1 was initially sold at 56p., which was increased to 60p. from 2.10.89.

1989 (28 Nov). *Laminated cover as Type* HA1 (75 × 48 *mm*) *with stamp printed on the cover in bright blue by Walsall containing stamps printed in photo by Harrison.*
HA2 Containing booklet pane No. 1445b .... 27·00
No. HA2 has three edges of the pane imperforate and was sold at 60p.

Type HA3
Crown on white

1990 (7 Aug). *Multicoloured laminated cover as Type* HA3 (75 × 48 *mm*) *with stamp printed on the cover in deep blue by Walsall.*
HA3 Containing booklet pane No. 1515a .... 3·00
No. HA3 has the horizontal edges of the pane imperforate.
No. HA3 was initially sold at 60p., which was increased to 68p. from 17.9.90 and to 72p. from 16.9.91.

1991 (6 Aug). *Multicoloured laminated cover as Type* HA3 (75 × 48 *mm*) *with stamp printed on the cover in bright blue by Walsall.*
HA4 Containing booklet pane No. 1449c .... 3·00
No. HA4 has the horizontal edges of the pane imperforate.
No. HA4 was initially sold at 68p., which was increased to 72p. from 16.9.91.

Type HA5
Olympic Symbols

1992 (21 Jan). *Multicoloured laminated cover as Type* HA5 (75 × 48 *mm*) *with stamp printed on the cover in bright blue by Walsall.*
HA5 Containing booklet pane No. 1449b .... 3·50
No. HA5 has the horizontal edges of the pane imperforate and was sold at 72p.

PERFORATIONS. Booklets from No. HA6 show perforations on all edges of the pane.

1993 (6 Apr). *Multicoloured laminated cover as Type* HA3 (75 × 48 *mm*) *with stamp printed on the cover in bright blue by Walsall.*
HA6 Containing four 2nd Class stamps (No. 1665) .... 3·00
No. HA6 was initially sold at 72p., which was increased to 76p. from 1.11.93.
No. HA6 was re-issued on 6 December 1994 showing the inscriptions on the inside of the cover re-arranged.

1993 (7 Sept). *Multicoloured laminated cover as Type* HA3 (75 × 48 *mm*) *with stamp printed on the cover in bright blue by Harrison.*
HA7 Containing four 2nd Class stamps (No. 1663a) .... 3·00
No. HA7 was initially sold at 72p., which was increased to 76p. from 1.11.93.

Type HA8 ("Second Class Stamps" centred)
(with diagonal white line across corners of stamps)

1995 (10 Jan). *Multicoloured laminated cover as Type* HA8 (75 × 48 *mm*) *with stamps printed on the cover in bright blue by Harrison.*
HA8 Containing four 2nd Class stamps (No. 1663a) .... 3·00
No. HA8 was initially sold at 76p, which was increased to 80p. from 8.7.96.

1995 (12 Dec). *Multicoloured laminated cover as Type* HA8 (75 × 48 *mm*) *with stamps printed on the cover in bright blue by Walsall.*
HA9 Containing four 2nd Class stamps (No. 1665) .... 2·00
No. HA9 was initially sold at 76p, which was increased to 80p. from 8.7.96.

1996 (6 Feb). *Multicoloured laminated cover as Type HA8 (75 × 48 mm) showing Olympic symbols on the back. Stamps printed on the cover in bright blue by Walsall.*
HA10 Containing four 2nd Class stamps (No. 1665) .... 2·00
No. HA10 was initially sold at 76p, which was increased to 80p. from 8.7.96.

NOTE: From No. HA11 onwards, the printer of each booklet is identified by a small capital letter below the barcode on the outside back cover.

Type HA11 ("Second Class Stamps" ranged left)
(without diagonal white line across corners of stamps)

1997 (4 Feb). *Multicoloured laminated cover as Type HA11 (75 × 48 mm). Stamps printed on the cover in bright blue by Walsall.*
HA11 Containing four 2nd Class stamps (No. 1665) .... 2·00
No. HA11 was sold at 80p.

1997 (26 Aug). *Multicoloured laminated cover as Type HA11 (75 × 48 mm). Stamps printed on the cover in bright blue by Walsall.*
HA12 Containing four 2nd class stamps (photo) (No. 1663a) . 1·60
No. HA12 was sold at 80p.

Panes of 4 1st Class stamps

1989 (22 Aug). *Laminated cover as Type HA1 (75 × 48 mm) with stamp printed on the cover in brownish black by Walsall.*
HB1 Containing booklet pane No. 1450a .... 9·00
No. HB1 has three edges of the pane imperforate.
No. HB1 was initially sold at 76p., which was increased to 80p. from 2.10.89.

1989 (5 Dec). *Laminated cover as Type HA1 (75 × 48 mm) with stamp printed on the cover in brownish black by Walsall containing stamps printed in photo by Harrison.*
HB2 Containing booklet pane No. 1447b .... 27·00
No. HB2 has three edges of the pane imperforate and was sold at 80p.

1990 (7 Aug). *Multicoloured laminated cover as Type HA3 (75 × 48 mm) with stamp printed on the cover in bright orange-red by Walsall.*
HB3 Containing booklet pane No. 1516a .... 3·00
a. Containing pane No. 1516ca .... 10·00
No. HB3 has the horizontal edges of the pane imperforate.
No. HB3 was initially sold at 80p., which was increased to 88p. from 17.9.90 and to 96p. from 16.9.91.

1992 (21 Jan). *Multicoloured laminated cover as Type HA5 (75 × 48 mm) with stamp printed on the cover in bright orange-red by Walsall.*
HB4 Containing booklet pane No. 1516a .... 3·00
No. HB4 has the horizontal edges of the pane imperforate and was initially sold at 96p., which was increased to £1 from 1.11.93.

PERFORATIONS. Booklets from No. HB5 show perforations on all edges of the pane.

1993 (6 Apr). *Multicoloured laminated cover as Type HA3 (75 × 48 mm) with stamp printed on the cover in bright orange-red by Harrison*
HB5 Containing four 1st Class stamps (No. 1664) .... 2·50
No. HB5 was initially sold at 96p., which was increased to £1 from 1.11.93.

1993 (17 Aug). *Multicoloured laminated cover as Type HA3 (76 × 50 mm) with stamp printed on the cover in bright orange-red by Walsall.*
HB6 Containing four 1st Class stamps (No. 1666) .... 2·50
No. HB6 was initially sold at 96p., which was increased to £1 from 1.11.93.

1994 (27 July). *Multicoloured laminated cover as Type HA3 (76 × 50 mm) with stamp printed on the cover in bright orange-red by Questa.*
HB7 Containing booklet pane No. 1666l which includes a label commemorating the 300th anniv of the Bank of England .... 5·00
No. HB7 was sold at £1.

1995 (10 Jan). *Multicoloured laminated cover as Type HA8 (75 × 48 mm) with stamps printed on the cover in bright orange-red by Walsall.*
HB8 Containing four 1st Class stamps (No. 1666) .... 3·00
No. HB8 was initially sold at £1, which was increased to £1.04 from 8.7.96.

1995 (16 May). *Multicoloured laminated cover as Type HA8 (75 × 48 mm) with stamps printed on the cover in bright orange-red by Walsall.*
HB9 Containing booklet pane No. 1666la which includes a label commemorating the birth centenary of R. J. Mitchell (designer of Spitfire) .... 3·00
No. HB9 was sold at £1.

1996 (6 Feb–Aug). *Multicoloured laminated cover as Type* HA8 (75 × 48 *mm) showing Olympic symbols on the back. Stamps printed on the cover in bright orange-red by Walsall.*

HB10 Containing four 1st Class stamps (No. 1666) .... 3·00
a. Without diagonal white line across corners of stamps (Aug) .... 6·00

No. HB10 was initially sold at £1, which was increased to £1.04 from 8.7.96.

1996 (16 Apr). *Multicoloured laminated cover as Type* HA11 (75 × 48 *mm) with stamps printed on the cover in bright orange-red by Walsall. Inscribed* "Commemorative Label Inside" *on yellow tab at right.*

HB11 Containing booklet pane No. 1666la (includes label commemorating the 70th birthday of Queen Elizabeth II) .... 3·50

No. HB11 was initially sold at £1, which was increased to £1.04 from 8.7.96.

NOTE: From No. HB12 onwards, the printer of each booklet is identified by a small capital letter below the barcode on the outside back cover.

1997 (4 Feb). *Multicoloured laminated cover as Type* HA11 (75 × 48 *mm). Stamps printed on the cover in bright orange-red by Walsall.*

HB12 Containing four 1st Class stamps (No. 1666) .... 3·00

No. HB12 was sold at £1.04.

1997 (12 Feb). *Multicoloured laminated cover as Type* HA11 (75 × 48 *mm). Stamps printed on the cover in bright orange-red by Walsall. Inscribed* "Special Label Inside" *on yellow tab at right.*

HB13 Containing booklet pane No. 1666la (includes label commemorating "Hong Kong '97" international stamp exhibition) .... 3·00

No. HB13 was sold at £1.04.

1997 (26 Aug). *Multicoloured laminated cover as Type* HA11 (75 × 48 *mm). Stamps printed on the cover in bright orange-red by Walsall.*

HB14 Containing four 1st Class stamps (photo) (No. 1664a) .. 1·50

No. HB14 was sold at £1.04.

1997 (21 Oct). *Multicoloured laminated cover as Type* HA11 (75 × 48 *mm). Stamps printed on the cover in bright orange-red by Walsall. Inscribed* "Commemorative Label Inside" *on yellow tab at right.*

HB15 Containing booklet pane No. 1666la (litho) (includes label commemorating Commonwealth Heads of Government Meeting, Edinburgh) .... 1·50

No. HB15 was sold at £1.04.

Panes of 10 2nd Class stamps

1989 (22 Aug–2 Oct). *Laminated cover as Type* HA1 (75 × 48 *mm) with stamp printed on the cover in bright blue by Harrison.*

HC1 Containing booklet pane No. 1445a .... 6·00
a. Inside cover with new rates (2 Oct) .... 7·00

Nos. HC1/a have the horizontal edges of the pane imperforate. No. HC1 was initially sold at £1.40, which was increased to £1.50 from 2.10.89. No. HC1a was sold at £1.50.

1989 (19 Sept). *Laminated cover as Type* HA1 (75 × 48 *mm) with stamp printed on the cover in bright blue by Questa.*

HC2 Containing ten 2nd Class stamps (No. 1451) .... 6·50

No. HC2 has perforations on all edges of the pane and was initially sold at £1.40, which was increased to £1.50 from 2.10.89.

1990 (7 Aug). *Multicoloured laminated cover as Type* HA3 (75 × 48 *mm) with stamp printed on the cover in deep blue by Harrison.*

HC3 Containing booklet pane No. 1511a .... 8·50

No. HC3 has the horizontal edges of the pane imperforate.

No. HC3 was initially sold at £1.50, which was increased to £1.70 from 17.9.90.

1990 (7 Aug). *Multicoloured laminated cover as Type* HA3 (75 × 48 *mm) with stamp printed on the cover in deep blue by Questa.*

HC4 Containing ten 2nd Class stamps (No. 1513) .... 7·50

No. HC4 has perforations on all edges of the pane and was initially sold at £1.50, which was increased to £1.70 from 17.9.90.

1990 (7 Aug). *Multicoloured laminated cover as Type* HA3 (75 × 48 *mm) with stamp printed on the cover in deep blue by Walsall.*

HC5 Containing booklet pane No. 1515b .... 6·00

No. HC5 has the horizontal edges of the pane imperforate.

No. HC5 was initially sold at £1.50, which was increased to £1.70 from 17.9.90. and to £1.80 from 16.9.91.

1991 (6 Aug). *Multicoloured laminated cover as Type* HA3 (75 × 48 *mm) with stamp printed on the cover in bright blue by Questa.*

HC6 Containing ten 2nd class stamps (No. 1451) .... 4·50

No. HC6 has perforations on all edges of the pane and was initially sold at £1.70, which was increased to £1.80 from 16.9.91.

1991 (6 Aug). *Multicoloured laminated cover as Type* HA3 (75 × 48 *mm) with stamp printed on the cover in bright blue by Walsall.*

HC7 Containing booklet pane No. 1449d .... 6·00

No. HC7 has the horizontal edges of the pane imperforate.

No. HC7 was initially sold at £1.70, which was increased to £1.80 from 16.9.91.

1992 (21 Jan). *Multicoloured laminated cover as Type* HA5 (75 × 48 *mm) with stamp printed on the cover in bright blue by Walsall.*

HC8 Containing booklet pane No. 1449d .... 4·50

No HC8 has the horizontal edges of the pane imperforate and was initially sold at £1.80, which was increased to £1.84 from 1.11.93.

1992 (31 Mar). *Multicoloured laminated cover as Type* HA5 (75 × 48 *mm) with stamp printed on the cover in bright blue by Questa.*

HC9 Containing ten 2nd Class stamps (No. 1451) .... 4·50

No. HC9 has perforations on all edges of the pane and was sold at £1.80.

1992 (22 Sept). *Multicoloured laminated cover as Type* HA3 (75 × 48 *mm) with stamp printed on the cover in bright blue by Harrison.*

HC10 Containing booklet pane No. 1445a .... 4·50

No. HC10 has the horizontal edges of the pane imperforate and was sold at £1.80.

PERFORATIONS. Booklets from No. HC11 show perforations on all edges of the pane.

1993 (6 Apr). *Multicoloured laminated cover as Type HA3 (75 × 48 mm) with stamp printed on the cover in bright blue by Questa.*
HC11 Containing ten 2nd Class stamps (No. 1665) .... 4·50
No. HC11 was initially sold at £1.80, which was increased to £1.90 from 1.11.93.
No. HC11 was re-issued on 17 August 1993 showing changes to the text on the inside of the cover and again on 6 September 1994 showing further changes.

1993 (1 Nov). *Multicoloured laminated cover as Type HA3 (75 × 48 mm) with stamp printed on the cover in bright blue by Walsall.*
HC12 Containing ten 2nd Class stamps (No. 1665) .... 4·50
No. HC12 was sold at £1.90.

1995 (10 Jan). *Multicoloured laminated cover as Type HA8 (75 × 48 mm) with stamps printed on the cover in bright blue by Questa.*
HC13 Containing ten 2nd Class stamps (No. 1665) .... 4·50
No. HC13 was initially sold at £1.90, which was increased to £2 from 8.7.96.

1995 (12 Dec). *Multicoloured laminated cover as Type HA8 (75 × 48 mm) with stamps printed on cover in bright blue by Harrison.*
HC14 Containing ten 2nd Class stamps (No. 1663a) .... 4·50
No. HC14 was initially sold at £1.90, which was increased to £2 from 8.7.96.

1996 (6 Feb). *Multicoloured laminated cover as Type HA8 (75 × 48 mm) showing Olympic symbols on the back. Stamps printed on the cover in bright blue by Harrison.*
HC15 Containing ten 2nd Class stamps (No. 1663a) .... 4·50
No. HC15 was initially sold at £1.90, which was increased to £2 from 8.7.96.

1996 (6 Feb). *Multicoloured laminated cover as Type HA8 (75 × 48 mm) showing Olympic symbols on the back. Stamps printed on the cover in bright blue by Questa.*
HC16 Containing ten 2nd Class stamps (No. 1665) .... 4·50
No. HC16 was initially sold at £1.90, which was increased to £2 from 8.7.96.

NOTE: From No. HC17 onwards, the printer of each booklet is identified by a small capital letter below the barcode on the outside back cover.

1996 (6 Aug). *Multicoloured laminated cover as Type HA11 (75 × 48 mm) but with diagonal white lines across corners of stamps, showing Olympic symbols and "H" on the back. Stamps printed on the cover in bright blue by Harrison.*
HC17 Containing ten 2nd Class stamps (No. 1663a) .... 4·50
No. HC17 was sold at £2.

1996 (6 Aug). *Multicoloured laminated cover as Type HA11 (75 × 48 mm) showing Olympic symbols and "Q" on the back. Stamps printed on the cover in bright blue by Questa.*
HC18 Containing ten 2nd Class stamps (No. 1665) .... 4·50
No. HC18 was sold at £2.

1997 (4 Feb). *Multicoloured laminated cover as Type HA11 (75 × 48 mm). Stamps printed on the cover in bright blue by Harrison.*
HC19 Containing ten 2nd Class stamps (No. 1663a) .... 3·00
No. HC19 was sold at £2.

1997 (4 Feb). *Multicoloured laminated cover as Type HA11 (75 × 48 mm). Stamps printed on the cover in bright blue by Questa.*
HC20 Containing ten 2nd Class stamps (No. 1665) .... 4·50
No. HC20 was sold at £2.

Panes of 10 1st Class stamps

1989 (22 Aug–2 Oct). *Laminated cover as Type HA1 (75 × 48 mm) with stamp printed on the cover in brownish black by Harrison.*
HD1 Containing booklet pane No. 1447a .... 8·00
a. Inside cover with new rates (2 Oct) .... 10·00
Nos. HD1/a have the horizontal edges of the pane imperforate.
No. HD1 was initially sold at £1.90 which was increased to £2 from 2.10.89. No. HD1a was sold at £2.

1989 (19 Sept). *Laminated cover as Type HA1 (75 × 48 mm) with stamp printed on the cover in brownish black by Questa.*
HD2 Containing ten 1st Class stamps (No. 1452) .... 11·00
No. HD2 has perforations on all edges of the pane and was initially sold at £1.90, which was increased to £2 from 2.10.89.

1990 (7 Aug). *Multicoloured laminated cover as Type HA3 (75 × 48 mm) with stamp printed on the cover in bright orange-red by Harrison.*
HD3 Containing booklet pane No. 1512a .... 6·00
No. HD3 has the horizontal edges of the pane imperforate.
No. HD3 was initially sold at £2, which was increased to £2.20 from 17.9.90 and to £2.40 from 16.9.91.

1990 (7 Aug). *Multicoloured laminated cover as Type HA3 (75 × 48 mm) with stamp printed on the cover in bright orange-red by Questa.*
HD4 Containing ten 1st Class stamps (No. 1514) .... 6·00
No. HD4 has perforations on all edges of the pane and was initially sold at £2, which was increased to £2.20 from 17.9.90 and to £2.40 from 16.9.91.

1990 (7 Aug). *Multicoloured laminated cover as Type HA3 (75 × 48 mm) with stamp printed on the cover in bright orange-red by Walsall.*
HD5 Containing booklet pane No. 1516b .... 6·00
No. HD5 has the horizontal edges of the pane imperforate and was intially sold at £2, which was increased to £2.20 from 17.9.90 and to £2.40 from 16.9.91.

1992 (21 Jan). *Multicoloured laminated cover as Type HA5 (75 × 48 mm) with stamp printed on the cover in bright orange-red by Harrison.*
HD6 Containing booklet pane No. 1512a. .... 6·00
No. HD6 has the horizontal edges of the pane imperforate and was sold at £2.40.

1992 (21 Jan). *Multicoloured laminated cover as Type HA5 (75 × 48 mm) with stamp printed on the cover in bright orange-red by Walsall.*
HD7 Containing booklet pane No. 1516b. .... 6·00
No. HD7 has the horizontal edges of the pane imperforate and was sold at £2.40.

1993 (9 Feb). *Multicoloured laminated cover as Type HA3 (77 × 44 mm) with advertisment for Greetings Booklet on reverse showing Rupert Bear as in Type KX5. Stamp printed on the cover in bright orange-red by Walsall.*
HD8 Containing booklet pane No. 1516b .... 6·00
No. HD8 has the horiziontal edges of the pane imperforate and was sold at £2.40.

PERFORATIONS. Booklets from No. HD9 show perforations on all edges of the pane.

1993 (6 Apr). *Multicoloured laminated cover as Type HA3 (75 × 48 mm) with stamp printed on the cover in bright orange-red by Harrison.*
HD9 Containing ten 1st Class stamps (No. 1664) .... 5·50
No. HD9 was initially sold at £2.40., which was increased to £2.50 from 1.11.93.
No. HD9 was re-issued on 17 August 1993 showing changes to the text on the inside of the covers.

1993 (6 Apr). *Multicoloured laminated cover as Type HA3 (75 × 48 mm) with stamp printed on the cover in bright orange-red by Walsall.*
HD10 Containing ten 1st Class stamps (No. 1666) .... 6·00

No. HD10 was initially sold at £2.40., which was increased to £2.50 from 1.11.93.

No. HD10 was re-issued on 17 August 1993 showing changes to the text on the inside of the covers.

1993 (1 Nov). *Laminated cover as Type HA3 (75 × 50 mm) with stamp printed on the cover in bright orange-red by Questa.*

HD11 Containing ten 1st Class stamps (No. 1666) .... 5·50

No. HD11 was sold at £2.50.

No. HD11 was re-issued on 6 September 1994 showing changes to the text on the inside of the cover.

1993 (1 Nov). *Laminated cover as Type HA3 (75 × 50 mm) with advertisement for Greetings Booklet on reverse showing Rupert Bear as in Type KX5. Stamp printed on the cover in bright orange-red by Walsall.*

HD12 Containing ten 1st Class stamps (No. 1666) .... 6·00

1994 (22 Feb). *Multicoloured laminated cover as Type HA3 (75 × 48 mm) with stamp printed on the cover in bright orange-red by Walsall. Inscribed "FREE POSTCARDS" on yellow tab at right.*

HD13 Containing ten 1st Class stamps (No. 1666) and additional page giving details of Greetings Stamps postcard offer .... 6·00

No. HD13 was sold at £2.50.

1994 (1 July). *Multicoloured laminated covers as Type HA3 (76 × 50 mm) with advertisement for Greetings Booklet on reverse showing Rupert Bear as in Type KX5. Stamp printed on the cover in bright orange-red by Walsall. Inscribed "OPEN NOW Chance to win a kite" on yellow tab at right.*

HD14 Containing ten 1st Class stamps (No. 1666) with "Better luck next time." etc on inside back cover .... 6·00

HD15 Containing ten 1st Class stamps (No. 1666) with "You've Won!" etc on inside back cover .... 6·00

Nos. HD14/15 sold at £2.50 each and were initially only available from branches of W.H. Smith and Son. They were issued in connection with a competition in which the prizes were Paddington Bear kites. The booklets were not available from Royal Mail philatelic outlets until 4 October 1994.

Type HD16

1994 (20 Sept). *Multicoloured laminated covers as Type HD16 (76 × 50 mm) printed by Walsall. Inscribed "ORDER YOURS INSIDE" on yellow tab at right.*

HD16 Containing ten 1st Class stamps (No. 1666) with "DO NOT OPEN UNTIL....." on front cover .... 6·00

HD17 Containing ten 1st Class stamps (No. 1666) with "KEEP IN TOUCH" on front cover .... 6·00

HD18 Containing ten 1st Class stamps (No. 1666) with "HAPPY BIRTHDAY" on front cover .... 6·00

HD19 Containing ten 1st Class stamps (No. 1666) with "What's Happenin'?" on front cover .... 6·00

Nos. HD16/19 were sold at £2.50 each.

1995 (10 Jan). *Multicoloured laminated cover as Type HA8 (75 × 48 mm) with stamps printed on the cover in bright orange-red by Harrison.*

HD20 Containing ten 1st Class stamps (No. 1664) .... 6·00

1995 (10 Jan). *Multicoloured laminated cover as Type HA8 (75 × 48 mm) with stamps printed on the cover in bright orange-red by Questa.*

HD21 Containing ten 1st Class stamps (No. 1666) .... 6·00

1995 (10 Jan). *Multicoloured laminated cover as Type HA8 (75 × 48 mm) with stamps printed on the cover in bright orange-red by Walsall.*

HD22 Containing ten 1st Class stamps (No. 1666) .... 6·00

Nos. HD20/2 were initially sold at £2.50 each, which was increased to £2.60 from 8.7.96.

Type HD23

1995 (14 Feb). *Multicoloured laminated cover as Type HD23 (76 × 50 mm) showing card, Thorntons chocolates and box, printed by Walsall. Inscribed "DETAILS INSIDE" on yellow tab at right.*

HD23 Containing ten 1st Class stamps (No. 1666) .... 6·00

No. HD23 was sold at £2.50.

1995 (4 Apr). *Multicoloured laminated cover as Type HA8 (76 × 48 mm) with stamps printed on cover in bright orange-red by Harrison.*

HD24 Containing ten 1st Class stamps (No. 1664a) .... 5·50

No. HD24 was sold at £2.50.

1995 (24 Apr). *Multicoloured laminated cover as Type HA8 (75 × 48 mm) with stamps printed on cover in bright orange-red by Walsall. Inscribed "W H Smith Special Offer" on yellow tab at right.*

HD25 Containing ten 1st Class stamps (No. 1666) .... 5·50

No. HD25 was sold at £2.50 and was initially only available from W. H. Smith branches and offered 50p. off the purchase of own brand stationery. The booklet was not placed on philatelic sale until 3 October 1995. Its price was increased to £2.60 on 8.7.96.

1995 (26 June). *Multicoloured laminated cover as Type HA8 (76 × 48 mm) with stamps printed on cover in bright orange-red by Questa. Inscribed "Sainsbury's Promotion" on yellow tab at right.*

HD26 Containing ten 1st Class stamps (No. 1666) .... 5·50

No. HD26 was sold at £2.50 and was initially only available from Sainsbury's branches and offered the chance to win a year's free shopping. The booklet was not placed on philatelic sale until 5 September 1995. Its price was increased to £2.60 on 8.7.96

1995 (4 Sept). *Multicoloured laminated cover as Type HD23 (76 × 48 mm) showing ceramic figures of Benjy Bear and Harry Hedgehog, printed by Harrison.*

HD27 Containing ten 1st Class stamps (No. 1664a) .... 5·50

No. HD27 was initially sold at £2.50, which was increased to £2.60 from 8.7.96.

1996 (6 Feb). *Multicoloured laminated cover as Type HA8 (76 × 48 mm) showing Olympic symbols on the back. Stamps printed on the cover in bright orange-red by Walsall.*
HD28 Containing ten 1st Class stamps (No. 1666) . . . . 5·50
No. HD28 was initially sold at £2.50, which was increased to £2.60 from 8.7.96.

1996 (19 Feb). *Multicoloured laminated cover as Type HD23 (76 × 48 mm) showing Walt Disney World, printed by Harrison.*
HD29 Containing ten 1st Class stamps (No. 1664a) . . . . 5·50
No. HD29 was initially sold at £2.50, which was increased to £2.60 from 8.7.96.

1996 (19 Mar). *Multicoloured laminated cover as Type HA8 (76 × 48 mm) showing Olympic symbols on the back, printed by Harrison.*
HD30 Containing ten 1st Class stamps (No. 1664a) . . . . 5·50
No. HD30 was initially sold at £2.50, which was increased to £2.60 from 8.7.96.

Type HD31

1996 (13 May). *Multicoloured laminated covers as Type HD31 (76 × 48 mm) showing woman lighting Olympic torch, printed by Harrison, with each booklet showing a scratchcard on the reverse based on different Olympic events.*
HD31 Containing ten 1st Class stamps (No. 1664a) (Shot Put) . 5·50
HD32 Containing ten 1st Class stamps (No. 1664a) (Hurdles) . . 5·50
HD33 Containing ten 1st Class stamps (No. 1664a) (Archery) . 5·50
Nos. HD31/3 were initially each sold at £2.50, which was increased to £2.60 from 8.7.96.

NOTE: From No. HD34 onwards, the printer of each booklet is identified by a small capital letter below the barcode on the outside back cover.

1996 (15 July). *Multicoloured laminated cover as Type HA11 (76 × 48 mm) showing Olympic symbols and "W" on the back. Stamps printed on the cover in bright orange-red by Walsall. Inscribed "WH Smith Offer Inside" on yellow tab at right.*
HD34 Containing ten 1st Class stamps (No. 1666) . . . . 5·50
No. HD34 was sold at £2.60 and was initially only available from branches of W. H. Smith and Sons. It was issued in connection with a special offer of AA/OS Leisure Guides. The booklets were not available from Royal Mail philatelic outlets until 17 September 1996.

1996 (16 Aug). *Multicoloured laminated cover as Type HA11 (76 × 48 mm), but with diagonal white line across corners of stamps and showing Olympic symbols and "H" on the back. Stamps printed on the cover in bright orange-red by Harrison.*
HD35 Containing ten 1st Class stamps (No. 1664a) . . . . 5·50
No. HD35 was sold at £2.60.

1996 (16 Aug). *Multicoloured laminated cover as Type HA11 (76 × 48 mm) showing Olympic symbols and "W" on the back. Stamps printed on the cover in bright orange-red by Walsall.*
HD36 Containing ten 1st Class stamps (No. 1666) . . . . 5·50
No. HD36 was sold at £2.60.

1996 (9 Sept). *Multicoloured laminated cover as Type HD31 (76 × 48 mm) showing iced cakes on front and back, printed by Walsall. Inscribed "OPEN FOR DETAILS" on yellow tab at right.*
HD37 Containing ten 1st Class stamps (No. 1666) . . . . 5·50
No. HD37 was sold at £2.60.

1996 (7 Oct). *Multicoloured laminated cover as Type HA11 (76 × 48 mm) showing Olympic symbols and "W" on the back. Stamps printed on cover in bright orange-red by Walsall. Inscribed "Offer Inside" on yellow tab at right.*
HD38 Containing ten 1st Class stamps (No. 1666) . . . . 5·50
No. HD38 was sold at £2.60 and was initially only available from ASDA stores and offered £1 off greetings cards. The booklet was not placed on philatelic sale until 13 January 1997.

1997 (4 Feb). *Multicoloured laminated cover as Type HA11 (76 × 48 mm). Stamps printed on the cover in bright orange-red by Harrison.*
HD39 Containing ten 1st Class stamps (No. 1664a) . . . . 4·00
No. HD39 was sold at £2.60.

1997 (4 Feb). *Multicoloured laminated cover as Type HA11 (76 × 48 mm). Stamps printed on the cover in bright orange-red by Walsall.*
HD40 Containing ten 1st Class stamps (No. 1666) . . . . 5·50
No. HD40 was sold at £2.60.

1997 (21 Apr). *Royal Golden Wedding. Multicoloured laminated cover as Type HA11 (76 × 48 mm). Stamps printed on the cover in gold by Harrison.*
HD41 Containing ten 1st Class stamps (No. 1979) . . . . 4·00
No. HD41 was sold at £2.60.

1997 (21 Apr). *Royal Golden Wedding. Multicoloured laminated cover as Type HA11 (76 × 48 mm). Stamps printed on the cover in gold by Walsall.*
HD42 Containing ten 1st Class stamps (No. 1980) . . . . 4·00
No. HD42 was sold at £2.60.

1997 (15 Sept). *Multicoloured laminated cover as Type HD31 (76 × 48 mm) showing a tropical beach scene printed by Harrison. Inscr "FIRST CLASS TRAVEL" on front, "OPEN FOR DETAILS" on yellow tab at right and "H" on reverse.*
HD43 Containing ten 1st Class stamps (No. 1979) . . . . 4·00
No. HD43 was sold at £2.60.

1997 (18 Nov). *Multicoloured laminated cover as Type HA11 (76 × 48 mm). Stamps printed on the cover in bright orange-red by Walsall.*
HD44 Containing ten 1st Class stamps (photo) (No. 1666) . . . . 4·00
No. HD44 was sold at £2.60.

Type HD45

1998 (2 Feb). *Multicoloured laminated cover as Type HD45 (76 × 48 mm) showing Disney illustration printed by De la Rue, with a scratch card on the reverse. Inscr "See reverse for Scratch and Win" on yellow tab at right.*
HD45 Containing ten 1st Class stamps (photo) (No. 1664a) . . . 4·00
No. HD45 was sold at £2.60.

Panes of 20 1st Class Stamps

Type HE1

1993 (19 Oct). *Multicoloured cover as Type* HE1 (91 × 77 *mm*).
HE1 Containing booklet pane No. 1789a .... 15·00
No. HE1 contains self-adhesive stamps and was initially sold at £4.80 which was increased to £5 from 1.11.93.

E. Barcode Booklets containing Penny Black Anniversary stamps with barcodes on back cover.

60p. Booklet

Type JA1

1990 (30 Jan). *Laminated cover as Type* JA1 (75 × 48 *mm*) *showing Penny Black Anniversary stamp in bright blue. Containing booklet pane. No.* 1475l, *printed in litho by Walsall.*
JA1 Containing booklet pane No. 1475l .... 7·50
No. JA1 has three edges of the pane imperforate.

80p. Booklets

1990 (30 Jan). *Laminated cover as Type* JA1 (75 × 48 *mm*) *showing Penny Black Anniversary stamp in brownish black and cream. Containing booklet pane No.* 1476m, *printed in litho by Walsall.*
JB1 Containing booklet pane No. 1476m .... 7·50
No. JB1 has three edges of the pane imperforate.

1990 (17 Apr). *Laminated cover as Type* JA1 (75 × 48 *mm*) *showing Penny Black Anniversary stamp printed on the cover in brownish black by Walsall containing stamps printed in photo by Harrison.*
JB2 Containing booklet pane No. 1469r .... 6·00
No. JB2 has three edges of the pane imperforate.

£1.50 Booklets

1990 (30 Jan). *Laminated cover as Type* JA1 (75 × 48 *mm*) *showing Penny Black Anniversary stamp in bright blue. Containing booklet pane No.* 1467l *printed by photo by Harrison.*
JC1 Containing booklet pane No. 1467l .... 7·50
No. JC1 hs the horizontal edges of the pane imperforate.

1990 (17 Apr). *Laminated cover as Type* JA1 (75 × 48 *mm*) *showing Penny Black Anniversary stamp printed on the cover in bright blue by Questa.*
JC2 Containing ten 15p. (No. 1477) .... 18·00

1990 (12 June). *Laminated cover as Type* JA1 (75 × 48 *mm*) *showing Penny Black Anniversary stamp in bright blue. Containing booklet pane No.* 1475m, *printed in litho by Walsall.*
JC3 Containing booklet pane No. 1475m .... 8·00
No. JC3 has three edges of the pane imperforate.

£2 Booklets

1990 (30 Jan). *Laminated cover as Type* JA1 (75 × 48 *mm*) *showing Penny Black Anniversary stamp in brownish black and cream. Containing booklet pane. No.* 1469m, *printed in photo by Harrison.*
JD1 Containing booklet pane No. 1469m .... 9·00
No. JD1 has the horizontal edges of the pane imperforate.

1990 (17 Apr). *Laminated cover as Type* JA1 (75 × 48 *mm*) *showing Penny Black Anniversary stamp printed on the cover in brownish black by Questa.*
JD2 Containing ten 20p. (No. 1478) .... 16·00

1990 (12 June). *Laminated cover as Type JA1 (75 × 48 mm) showing Penny Black Anniversary stamp in brownish black and cream. Containing booklet pane No. 1476n, printed in litho by Walsall.*

JD3 Containing booklet pane No. 1476n .... 10·00

No. JD3 has three edges of the pane imperforate.

F. Barcode Booklets containing Greetings stamps with barcodes on the back cover.

£2 Greetings Booklet

Type KX1

(Illustration reduced. Actual size 135 × 85 mm)

(Des Michael Peters and Partners)

1990 (6 Feb). *Greetings Stamps. Cover printed in scarlet, lemon and black as Type KX1 (135 × 85 mm). Containing booklet pane No. 1483a, and a separate sheet of 12 greetings labels.*

KX1 "Smile" design cut-out showing stamps inside .... 28·00

Greetings Booklets containing No Value Indicated stamps

Type KX2

(Des T. Meeuwissen)

1991 (5 Feb). *Greetings Stamps. Multicoloured laminated cover as Type KX2 (95 × 69 mm). Containing booklet pane No. 1536a, including twelve special greetings labels in a block (3 × 4) at right, attached by the selvedge.*

KX2 "Good Luck" charms design .... 12·50

No. KX2 was initially sold at £2.20, which was increased to £2.40 from 16.9.91.

Type KX3

(Des Michael Peters and Partners)

1991 (26 Mar). *Greetings Stamps. Multicoloured laminated cover as Type KX3 (95 × 69 mm). Containing booklet pane No. 1550a, including twelve special greetings labels in a block (3 × 4) at right, attached by the selvedge.*

KX3 Laughing pillar box design .... 8·00

No. KX3 was initially sold at £2.20, which was increased to £2.40 from 16.9.91 and to £2.50 from 1.11.93.

Type KX4

(Des Trickett and Webb)

1992 (28 Jan). *Greetings Stamps. Multicoloured laminated cover as Type KX4 (95 × 69 mm). Containing booklet pane No. 1592a, including twelve special greetings labels in a block (3 × 4) at right, attached by selvedge.*

KX4 Pressed Flowers design .... 7·00

No. KX4 was initially sold at £2.40, which was increased to £2.50 from 1.11.93 and to £2.60 from 8.7.96.

Type KX5

(Des Newell and Sorrell)

1993 (2 Feb). *Greetings Stamps. Multicoloured laminated cover as Type KX5 (96 × 60 mm). Containing booklet pane No. 1644a and pane of twenty special greetings labels in a block (5 × 4), both panes attached by a common gutter margin.*

KX5 Children's Characters design .... 7·50

No. KX5 was initially sold at £2.40, which was increased to £2.50 from 1.11.93.

Type KX6

(Des Newell and Sorrell)

1994 (1 Feb). *Greetings Stamps. Multicoloured cover as Type KX6 (96 × 60 mm). Containing booklet pane No. 1800a and pane of twenty special greetings labels in a block (5 × 4), both panes attached by a common gutter margin.*

KX6 Children's Characters design .... 4·00

No. KX6 was initially sold at £2.50, which was increased to £2.60 from 8.7.96.

Type KX7

(Des Newell and Sorrell)

1995 (21 Mar)–**96**. *Greetings Stamps. Multicoloured cover as Type KX7 (96 × 60 mm). Containing booklet pane No. 1858a and pane of twenty special greetings labels in a block (5 × 4), both panes attached by a common gutter margin. Inscr "Pull Open" on yellow strip at right.*

KX7 Clown design .... 4·00

a. No inscr on yellow strip (13.2.96) .... 4·00

Nos. KX7/a were initially sold at £2.50, which was increased to £2.60 from 8.7.96.

Type KX8

(Des M. Wolf)

1996 (26 Feb–11 Nov). *Greetings Stamps. Multicoloured cover as Type KX8 (96 × 60 mm). Containing booklet pane No. 1905a and pane of twenty special greetings labels in a block (5 × 4), both panes attached by a common gutter margin.*

KX8 "MORE! LOVE" design .... 4·00

a. Containing pane No. 1905pa (11 Nov) .... 4·00

No. KX8 was initially sold at £2.50, which was increased to £2.60 from 8.7.96.

No. KX8a shows a redesigned inside front cover which omits references to 1996 dates.

Type KX9

(Des Tutssels)

1997 (6 Jan). *Greetings Stamps. 19th-century Flower Paintings. Multicoloured cover as Type KX9 (96 × 61 mm). Containing booklet pane No. 1955a and pane of twenty special greetings labels in a block (5 × 4), both panes attached by a common gutter margin.*

KX9 *Gentiana acaulis* design .... 4·00

No. KX9 was sold at £2.60.

1997 (3 Feb). *Greetings Stamps. 19th-century Flower Paintings. Multicoloured cover as Type* KX9 *(96 × 61 mm) but with box inscribed* "WIN A BEAUTIFUL BOUQUET INSTANTLY?" *printed in yellow on red over the flower on the front and with a scratch card on the inside back cover. Inscribed* "Open now – See if you've won" *on yellow tab at right. Containing booklet pane No.* 1955a *and pane of twenty special greetings labels in a block (5 × 4), both panes attached by a common gutter margin.*

KX10 *Gentiana acaulis* design . . . . 4·00

No. KX10 was sold at £2.60.

Type KX11

1998 (5 Jan). *Greetings Stamps. 19th-century Flower Paintings. Multicoloured cover as Type* KX11 *(96 × 61 mm). Inscribed* "See reverse for special offer" *on yellow tab at right. Containing booklet pane No.* 1955a *and pane of twenty special greetings labels in a block (5 × 4), both attached by a common gutter margin.*

KX11 Chocolate design . . . . 4·00

No. KX11 was sold at £2.60.

G. Barcode Booklets containing Christmas stamps with barcode on the back cover.

Type LX1

(Des A. Davidson)

1990 (13 Nov). *Christmas. Multicoloured laminated cover as Type* LX1 *(95 × 60 mm). Containing booklet pane No.* 1526a, *attached by the selvedge.*

LX1 £3.40, Snowman design . . . . 9·00

1991 (12 Nov). *Multicoloured laminated cover as Type* LX1, *but 95 × 70 mm. Containing booklet pane No.* 1582b *attached by the selvedge.*

LX2 £3.60, Holly design . . . . 8·25

Type LX3

(Des Karen Murray)

1992 (10 Nov). *Multicoloured laminated cover as Type* LX3 *(95 × 70 mm). Containing booklet pane No.* 1634a *attached by the selvedge.*

LX3 £3.60, Santa Claus and Reindeer design . . . . 7·50

1993 (9 Nov). *Multicoloured laminated covers as Type* LX3, *but 95 × 60 mm, each showing Santa Claus and Reindeer. Panes attached by selvedge.*

LX4 £2.50, containing ten 25p. stamps (No. 1791) . . . . 5·00

LX5 £3.80, containing twenty 19p. stamps (No. 1790) . . . . 7·50

No. LX4 was only available from Post Offices in the Central T.V. area and from philatelic outlets.

Type LX6

(Des Yvonne Gilbert)

1994 (1 Nov). *Multicoloured laminated covers as Type* LX6 *(95 × 60 mm), showing different Nativity Play props. Panes attached by selvedge.*

LX6 £2.50, containing ten 25p. stamps (No. 1844) . . . . 5·00

LX7 £3.80, containing twenty 19p. stamps (No. 1843) . . . . 8·00

Type LX8

(Des K. Lilly)

1995 (30 Oct). *Multicoloured laminated covers as Type LX8 (95 × 60 mm), showing Robins as depicted on the contents. Panes attached by selvedge.*

LX8	£2.40, containing four 60p. stamps (No. 1900) plus 4 air mail labels	5·00
LX9	£2.50, containing ten 25p. stamps (No. 1897)	5·00
LX10	£3.80, containing twenty 19p. stamps (No. 1896)	8·00

Type LX11

1996 (28 Oct). *Multicoloured laminated covers as Type LX11 (89 × 60 mm), showing scenes from the Nativity as depicted on the contents. Panes attached by selvedge.*

LX11	Containing ten 1st class stamps (No. 1951)	4·00
LX12	Containing twenty 2nd class stamps (No. 1950)	6·00

No. LX11 was sold at £2.60 and No. LX12 at £4.

Type LX13

1997 (27 Oct). *Multicoloured laminated covers as Type LX13 (89 × 60 mm), showing Father Christmas and crackers as depicted on the contents. Panes attached by selvedge.*

LX13	Containing ten 1st class stamps (No. 2006)	4·00
LX14	Containing twenty 2nd class stamps (No. 2007)	6·00

No. LX13 was sold at £2.60 and No. LX14 at £4.